YALE UNIVERSITY PRESS
PELICAN HISTORY OF ART

Founding Editor: Nikolaus Pevsner

A. W. Lawrence

GREEK ARCHITECTURE

Revised with additions by R. A. Tomlinson

A. W. Lawrence was educated at the City of Oxford School and New College, Oxford. He then became a student of the British Schools at Athens and Rome, and in 1923 took part in the Ur excavations. In 1930 he became Reader in Classical Archaeology at Cambridge University, and from 1944 to 1951 was Professor there. In 1951 he travelled, upon a Leverhulme Research Fellowship, to study ancient and medieval fortification in classical lands, and was (1951–7) the first Professor of Archaeology at the University College of the Gold Coast (now the University of Ghana); one outcome of this stay is his *Trade Castles and Forts of West Africa* (1963). He has also published books on classical sculpture and revised and annotated Rawlinson's translation of Herodotus. His most recent work is *Greek Aims in Fortification* (1980).

R. A. Tomlinson was educated at King Edward's School, Birmingham, and St John's College, Cambridge. He became a student of the British School at Athens in 1954. After a year as Assistant in the Department of Greek at the University of Edinburgh he became Lecturer and, subsequently, Senior Lecturer in the Department of Ancient History and Archaeology at the University of Birmingham. He was appointed Professor of Ancient History and Archaeology in 1971. He directed supplementary excavations at Perachora for the British School at Athens in 1964–6, and again in 1972. He has published books on Argos and the Argolid and on Greek sanctuaries. He is editor of the Annual of the British School at Athens.

A. W. Lawrence

GREEK ARCHITECTURE

Revised with additions by R. A. Tomlinson

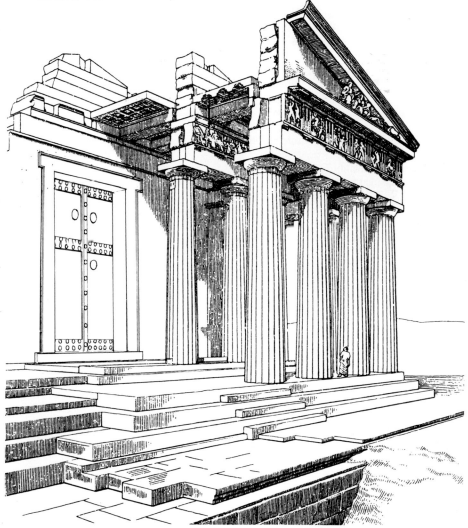

Yale University Press · New Haven and London

First published 1957 by Penguin Books Ltd
Fourth edition, revised by R.A. Tomlinson 1983
20 19 18 17 16 15 14 13 12 11 10 9 8 7 6 5 4

Copyright © A.W. Lawrence 1957, 1962, 1967, 1973, 1983
New material copyright © R.A. Tomlinson 1983

Set in Monophoto Ehrhardt, and printed in Hong Kong through World Print Ltd

Maps, drawings and adaptations made by Donald Bell-Scott and Reginald Piggott

Series designed by Gerald Cinamon
This volume designed by Judith Gordon

ISBN 0-300-05289-8
Library of Congress catalog card number 82-21397

CONTENTS

FOREWORD TO THE
FIRST EDITION

My treatment of the subject calls, I feel, for some explanation, especially as regards the proportions in which I have allotted space to the various topics.

A volume of the Pelican History of Art should be both somewhat more and somewhat less than a text-book, and in the present instance the editor and the author gave due weight to the fact that there are two masterly text-books in print, neither of which is seriously out of date. The scope of each is considerably wider than mine; W. B. Dinsmoor's Architecture of Ancient Greece *continues its encyclopaedic description of buildings in Greek lands through the three additional centuries in the Roman Empire, while all the classical styles are correlated in D. S. Robertson's more selective* Handbook of Greek and Roman Architecture. *But pre-classic remains were scarcely relevant to the purpose of these books, which also deal summarily with the less distinguished periods of later architecture and with its humbler types of buildings; the inadequate consideration given to such topics obscures historical connexions, to some of which I ascribe great importance.*

I should, ideally, have preferred to devote less space to pre-classic building, but no other writer has collated the whole body of information now available. If the degree of relationship to Hellenic architecture is to be shown, the facts must be presented as a whole; selection would falsify the picture. Admittedly I could have compressed the material further, and thereby have brought my Part One into closer conformity with Part Two, but at the cost of leaving a gap in the literature still unfilled; the average reader would then have had no means of checking my conclusions by comparison with the evidence.

On the other hand I have considered myself free in Part Two to supply only as much factual detail as was requisite to the argument. The greater erudition of Dinsmoor and Robertson will serve any who require more information upon individual temples, decorative conventions, and technical matters, as well as those who demand comprehensive glossaries and bibliographies.

Moreover I have almost ignored architectural sculpture, though I have taken care to illustrate some of the finest examples. Other volumes in the series are planned to cover Greek Sculpture, and in any case I could have done little better than repeat passages I wrote nearly thirty years ago in a book on that subject.

Because I am concerned exclusively with architecture before the time of Christ, dates throughout are printed without the customary addition of 'B.C.'. On the contrary, the few dates mentioned which fall within the Christian era are distinguished by an 'A.D.'.

All dimensions stated in terms of feet and inches are approximations: dimensions cited in the metric system are intended to be accurate measurements.

For the convenience of students, the modern Greek names of sites are normally transliterated either in the form adopted by an excavator or by the old-fashioned method of giving for each letter the nearest equivalent in our alphabet, regardless of pronunciation.

The production of a much-illustrated book is inevitably a long process, and about three years will have elapsed between the completion of the manuscript and the day of publication. The publishers, however, have approved the addition of new information in the proofs, so that results of excavations and investigations should have been included up to September 1955. I fear, though, that lack of access to specialist libraries at the time is bound to have curtailed the benefits of this generous privilege.

I owe to a Leverhulme Research Fellowship, awarded for the study of ancient and medieval fortification, most of my first-hand knowledge of the defences mentioned. Unfortunately preoccupation with other work has so far restricted deductive use of that knowledge, and my account of Greek fortification represents only provisional views. My travels with this objective enabled me also to examine buildings of other types and to take many of the photographs reproduced (the negatives of which now belong to the Courtauld Institute of Art, London University).

For help in the field and in the study, and in obtaining illustrations, I am indebted to many friends and chance associates, too many to thank individually by name, in England, Cyprus, Greece, Egypt, Turkey, the United States, and West Africa. To those among them who may read these words I gratefully acknowledge their kindness.   A.W.L.

FOREWORD TO THE

SECOND EDITION

For the present edition, the book has been revised to take account of discoveries and changes of opinion during the past twelve years (as known from publications available in London up to the end of 1966). The fact that this alone has entailed hundreds of alterations or additions in the text and notes (together with corresponding changes in the bibliography, chronological table, etc.) shows the rate at which field-work and study are advancing. I have also introduced other (as I thought) improvements, and have included some new views of my own. I should have liked to make more drastic changes in the few pages devoted to fortification, but any attempt to justify them by argument would involve detailed comparison of a sort appropriate only to a book on the subject, and I am engaged in writing one.

Several drawings and plans that appeared in the first edition are now known to be inaccurate or incomplete. The fact has merely been stated in one case, because a corrected version is not yet available; for the rest, new blocks have been substituted. Illustration 34 is reproduced by permission of the École Française d' Athènes. For illustration 79 the Greek Archaeological Society and Mme. Threp-

siades have allowed the use of a revised plan in which the late J. Threpsiades embodied the corrections due to his excavations. The two plans of illustration 122 are from originals by Professor Friedrich Krauss; the upper is based on a print which he generously supplied in advance of his own publication. Illustration 153 is used by permission of the Deutsches Archäologisches Institut, Abteilung Athen.   A.W.L.

FOREWORD TO THE

THIRD EDITION

Revision, with the aim of bringing the book up to date (as at New Year, 1973), has entailed substantial alterations to almost a hundred pages of text and many of the Notes, the addition of new Notes, the replacement of one Plate and five Figures, the inclusion of an additional drawing, and a large number of minor changes.

I am greatly indebted to Professor J. Walter Graham for advice and for permission to reproduce one of his restorations (illustration 33), likewise to Dr R. A. Higgins for advice and for the photograph of a restoration drawn to his instructions (illustration 59). My thanks are also due, for information, to Mr Gerald Cadogan, Professor J. N. Coldstream, Professor J. D. Evans, Mr D. E. L. Haynes, and Dr G. B. Waywell; for permission to reproduce illustration 229 to the American School of Classical Studies, Athens.
                                            A.W.L.

FOREWORD TO THE

FOURTH EDITION

In this fourth edition I have taken advantage of the complete resetting of the text to include in it material which Professor Lawrence had, perforce, to add to the second and third editions in the form of notes. The text also takes into account new discoveries and discussion published before February

1981 (but also the exceptionally important excavation at Lefkandi in Euboea, carried out in April 1981). Otherwise, of course, the text remains very much that of Professor Lawrence, except that I have in places modified his emphasis on the direct link between 'Pre-hellenic' and 'Hellenic' architecture to take into account the comparative emptiness (in architectural matters) of the years between the late twelfth and the eighth centuries B.C. *(though, thanks to Lefkandi, these years are less empty than they were). The original illustrations have been retained wherever possible; only where they were unobtainable have I included alternatives. Additions have also been made.*

For the fourth edition I would like to add my own thanks to Professor Peter Warren, Dr Kenneth Wardle (who wrote the entry on prehistoric Macedonia, and the redrafted comments on Temple B at Thermum), and to Peter Callaghan. This revision was made in the library of the British School of Archaeology at Athens; it owes more than I can express to its comprehensive – and immediately accessible – resources, and to the unfailing help and efficiency of its officers, particularly the Assistant Director, Tony Spawforth, and the Deputy Librarian, Mrs Babette Young.

R.A.T.

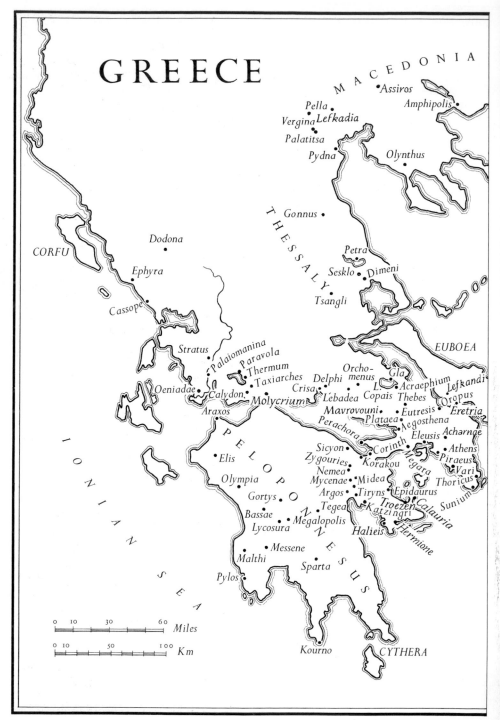

GREECE

MACEDONIA

Assiros

Pella
Vergina Lefkadia
Palatitsa
Pydna

Amphipolis

Olynthus

Gonnus •

THESSALY

CORFU

Dodona

Ephyra

Cassope

Petra
Sesklo • Dimeni
Tsangli

EUBOEA

Stratus

Palaiomanina
Paravola
Thermum
Taxiarches
Oeniadae
Calydon
Molycrium
Araxos

Orcho-
menus
Delphi
Crisa
Lebadea Copais Thebes
Mavrovouni
Plataea
Perachora
Aegosthena

Gla
Acraephium Lefkandi
L.
Oropus
Eretria
Eutresis
Acharnae
Eleusis

PELOPO

Elis

Olympia

Gortys

Bassae
Lycosura
Megalopolis
Malthi
Messene
Sparta

Sicyon
Zygouries
Nemea
Mycenae Midea
Argos Tiryns
Tegea
Katzingri
Halieis

Corinth
Korakou
Megara
Epidaurus
Troezen Calauria
Hermione

Athens
Piraeus
Vari
Thoricus
Sunium

N
E
S
U
S

IONIAN SEA

Pylos

Kourno

CYTHERA

0   10   30   60   Miles
0 10   50   100 Km

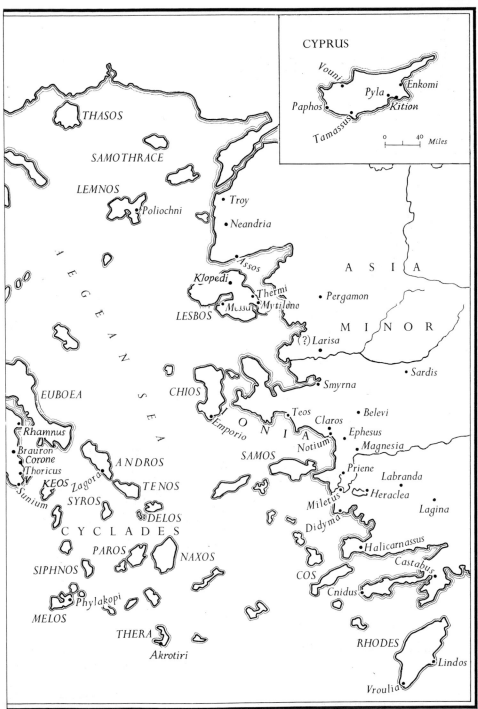

THASOS

SAMOTHRACE

LEMNOS

• Poliochni

• Troy

• Neandria

A E G E A N   S E A

Assos

Klopedi •

Thermi

Messa • Mytilene

LESBOS

(?) • Larisa

CHIOS

EUBOEA

• Pergamon

A S I A

M I N O R

• Sardis

• Smyrna

Emporio

• Teos

Claros

Notium

Ephesus

• Belevi

I O N I A

SAMOS

Magnesia

Rhamnus

Braurion

Corone

Thoricus

Sunium

KEOS

Zagora

ANDROS

TENOS

SYROS

DELOS

C Y C L A D E S

PAROS

NAXOS

SIPHNOS

Phylakopi

MELOS

THERA

Akrotiri

Priene

Labranda

Miletus

Heraclea

Didyma

Lagina

Halicarnassus

COS

Castabus

Cnidus

RHODES

Lindos

Vroulia

CYPRUS

Vouni

Paphos

Tamassus

Pyla

Kition

Enkomi

0   40 Miles

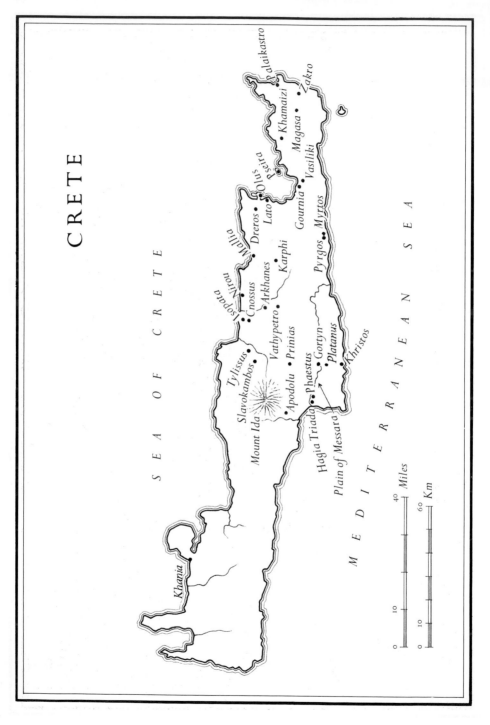

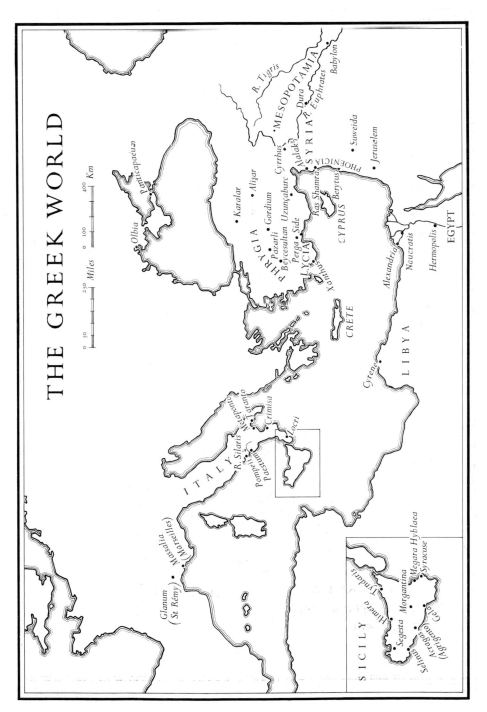

THE GREEK WORLD

Km
400
100
0
Miles
250
0
50

R. Tigris
MESOPOTAMIA
Dura
R. Euphrates
Babylon
SYRIA
Cyrrhus
PHOENICIA
Malak?
Suweida
Ras Shamra
Jeruselem
Berytus
Panticapaeum
CYPRUS
Olbia
Karalar
Alişar
Gordium
Uzuncaburc
Pazarli
PHRYGIA
Beycesultan
Side
Perga
LYCIA
Xanthus
Naucratis
Alexandria
Hermopolis
EGYPT
CRETE
LIBYA
Cyrene
Metaponto
Taranto
Crimisa
R. Silaris
Locri
Pompeii
Paestum
ITALY
Glanum
(St. Rémy)
Massalia
(Marseilles)

SICILY
Tyndaris
Megara Hyblaea
Syracuse
Morgantina
Segesta
Himera
Selinus
Acragas
(Agrigento)
Gela

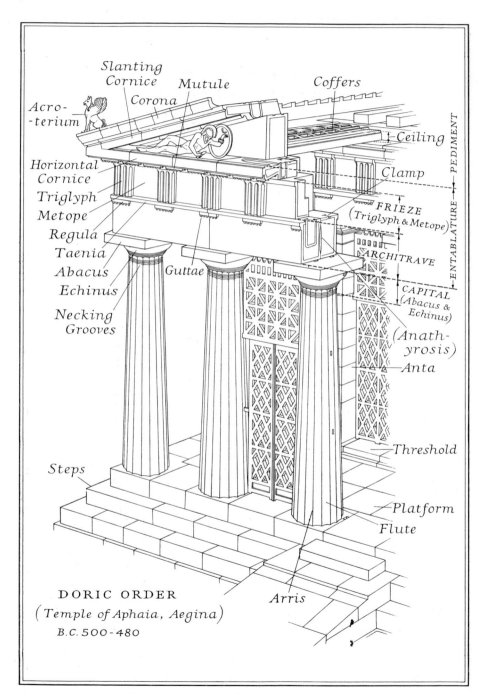

Acro-terium

Slanting Cornice

Corona

Mutule

Coffers

Ceiling

Clamp

PEDIMENT

Horizontal Cornice

Triglyph

Metope

Regula

Taenia

Abacus

Echinus

Necking

Grooves

Guttae

FRIEZE
(Triglyph & Metope)

ARCHITRAVE

CAPITAL
(Abacus & Echinus)

ENTABLATURE

(Anath-yrosis)

Anta

Threshold

Steps

Platform

Flute

Arris

DORIC ORDER
(Temple of Aphaia, Aegina)
B.C. 500-480

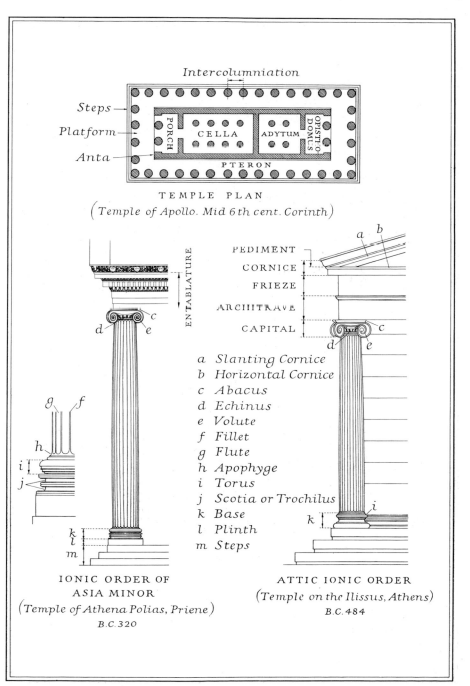

Intercolumniation

Steps —

Platform —

Anta —

PORCH · CELLA · ADYTUM · OPISTO-DOMUS

PTERON

TEMPLE PLAN

(Temple of Apollo. Mid 6th cent. Corinth)

ENTABLATURE

PEDIMENT

CORNICE

FRIEZE

ARCHITRAVE

CAPITAL

a Slanting Cornice
b Horizontal Cornice
c Abacus
d Echinus
e Volute
f Fillet
g Flute
h Apophyge
i Torus
j Scotia or Trochilus
k Base
l Plinth
m Steps

IONIC ORDER OF
ASIA MINOR
(Temple of Athena Polias, Priene)
B.C. 320

ATTIC IONIC ORDER
(Temple on the Ilissus, Athens)
B.C. 484

CHRONOLOGICAL TABLE

This table shows the comparative chronology of Greek prehistory. There are no fixed and precise dates: these are approximate only (particularly for the earlier periods). All dates are B.C.

	CRETE	MAINLAND	CYCLADES	
3000				
2900				
2800	Early Minoan I	Early Helladic I	Grotta–Pelos	
2700				
2600				2600
2500				
2400	Early Minoan II	Early Helladic II (Early Bronze II in Thessaly)	Keros–Syros (and Grotta–Pelos overlap?)	
2300				
2200				2200
2100	Early Minoan III (mainly in Eastern part)	Early Helladic III (Early Bronze III in Thessaly) Lefkandi 1 and 2	Phylakopi 1 (and Keros-Syros survival)	
2000	Middle Minoan IA			2000
1900				
1800	Middle Minoan IB – Middle Minoan II	Middle Helladic	Middle Cycladic	
1700				
1600	Middle Minoan III A–B			
1500	Late Minoan IA	Late Helladic I	Late Cycladic I	1500
	Late Minoan I B	Late Helladic II A	Late Cycladic II	
1400	Late Minoan II	Late Helladic II B		1400
	Late Minoan III A1	Late Helladic III A1		
1300	Late Minoan III A2	Late Helladic III A2	Late Cycladic III early	
	Late Minoan III B	Late Helladic III B1		
1200		Late Helladic III B2	Late Cycladic III middle	1200
	Late Minoan III C	Late Helladic III C		
1100		Sub-Mycenaean and later Late Helladic III C	Late Cycladic III late	
	Sub-Minoan			
1000		Protogeometric		
	Protogeometric after 1000			

PART ONE

PRE-HELLENIC BUILDING

CHAPTER I

INTRODUCTORY SUMMARY

Remains of prehistoric buildings in the Aegean lands cover, with a few short gaps, every period from the latter part of the Stone Age, before 3000 B.C.,[1] to the formation of the Hellenic civilization of Classical Greece. From the beginning distinctive types of houses are among the factors which differentiate the peasant cultures of the Greek mainland, the small islands (particularly the Cyclades), and Crete, as well as a higher, bronze-using culture centred in the interior of Asia Minor, which reached the coast at Troy and occupied adjacent islands. Buildings of some architectural merit were constructed in the Early Bronze Age – the palace at Troy with its great hall, the House of the Tiles at Lerna near Argos, a large round building at Tiryns – while in Crete substantial buildings apparently of a communal nature were produced, for tombs and dwellings. The Trojan type of palace with a great hall is the oldest achievement of architectural merit. In the other regions, all the buildings known are of poor quality till the last centuries of the Early Bronze Age, which ended about 2000 B.C. That is the approximate date of the first attempt at aesthetic architecture in Greece itself, a façade of burnt brick (at Tiryns) which seems to have been indirectly inspired by Mesopotamian practice. Crete, however, had begun, some generations before, to produce huge rambling buildings of a communal nature for tombs and dwellings, and another type of tomb, the walls of which were circular and which may have curved inwards till they met in the shape of an egg, in which case it must have been impressive.

In the Middle Bronze Age, 2000-1600, the Cretans exploited their geographical advantage by trading with Syria and Egypt, and through the stimulus of contact with advanced peoples they developed the first European civilization. The palaces they built and rebuilt during these centuries were profoundly influenced by oriental architecture – at first mainly Asiatic, though the Egyptian element eventually became dominant. The surviving plans show an abhorrence of symmetry and look the more chaotic because of the multiplicity of rooms, none very large and many very small; the structure tended to be shoddy, the decoration ill-formed, but vivid and sprightly. As time passed, however, sophistication imposed a little discipline, making the plans more rational and the decoration comparatively formal in the Late Bronze Age, till the second half of the fifteenth century B.C., when destruction came upon Crete, apparently at the hands of invaders from southern Greece.

These people, the Myceneans (a modern conventional naming, which acknowledges the importance of Mycenae, but does not necessarily imply either that the people concerned came from Mycenae, or that, throughout the Late Bronze Age, Greece was ruled from there), had only recently been affected by the glamour of Cretan art, and their own taste had been very different. In the mainland, custom had always dictated that a house, whether rectangular or rounded, should contain at ground level a large hall and if possible a storeroom behind it. When standards improved, as they did in the south at the Middle Bronze Age, a porch was often added, making a straightforward oblong plan, divided by cross-walls into three compartments. But the walls were often crooked and the work unsightly. An appreciation of rigidly symmetrical design, such as had been applied at Troy to comparable plans, might have developed in due course with civilization, but must have been accelerated by the introduction in the Middle Bronze Age of an apsidal type of house with a high thatched roof, the structure of which demanded a symmetrical plan. As a natural result, simplicity of form, axial planning, and symmetry characterize the Mycenean architecture of the Late Bronze Age. The first new type to appear, late in the sixteenth century, was the tholos tomb – a circular chamber roofed in the manner postulated for the early Cretan tomb, but buried in a hill-side, through which a level passage was cut to the doorway. The latest examples of the fourteenth century are admirably built in very large blocks of well-cut stone, and show a sensibility to the material such as the Cretans cannot have felt. This care for appearances is, however, a sign of late date in megalithic construction, which actually began in the fifteenth century with the use of enormous untrimmed boulders to build defences around the residences of kings. The whole idea was probably derived from Asia Minor, where the Mycenean royal families may have originated. In the fourteenth century the greater citadels were rebuilt and their old palaces replaced. The new accommodation invariably included an oblong suite with a porch and a great hall – or megaron, as Homer calls it – in accordance with mainland requirements. The design was excellent and shows Cretan influence; moreover, the megaron suite stood among an extensive system of lesser rooms which closely imitated various portions of a Cretan palace. In both structure and decoration the influence of Crete is so overwhelming, although the island had already begun to decline, that its Mycenean conquerors would seem to have transported shiploads of artisans to the mainland. The style, once established, changed but little. The scale and magnificence of buildings increased in the course of the fourteenth century, and in the thirteenth a megalithic form of vaulting, used in Asia Minor, was adopted in the fortifications and engineering works. If the evidence of Homer can be trusted, there must have been progress too in the provision of many separate bedrooms at the sides of the palace courtyard, but the actual ruins contain only a few doubtful instances of any such arrangement. In other respects the Homeric data agree fully with the remains although the poems themselves must have taken their final shape several hundred years later. By that time Mycenean palaces were fast dissolving into the clay of which they had been built; all alike perished by fire before 1100, and the Bronze Age civilization then dwindled away in the protracted warfare and migration that accompanied the introduction of iron. Only the simplest structural methods and basic types of plan endured, crudely executed (though perhaps a more direct tradition was preserved by Aegean settlers in the island of Cyprus), to be inherited by the classical Greeks.

CHAPTER 2

NEOLITHIC AND EARLY BRONZE AGE

The remains of early structures in the Aegean lands deserve attention because they reveal the forms from which the subsequent architecture evolved. These forms, although simple, were remarkably varied almost from the beginning; the nature of the country encouraged diversity. Each year includes long periods of great heat and biting cold, droughts and torrential rains, and in such a climate primitive man could not follow his normal custom of building only in the easiest materials. In summer he could live in a hut of sticks covered with thatch, but he required a solid house for winter, both for his own protection and to preserve his stores of food until the next harvest. This basic need was complicated by various types of social organization; for it appears that the system was by no means uniform among the prehistoric inhabitants of the area. The types of building created to meet their requirements were, of course, structurally akin because they utilized the same materials.

MATERIALS AND METHODS OF BUILDING

Greece suffers from a poverty of natural resources, and primitive man had therefore to exert ingenuity in building. With only crude implements of stone or soft metal at his disposal, the use of durable materials presented difficulties that could be surmounted in several ways, each involving its own advantages and drawbacks. As a result, few communities restricted themselves to a single manner of building, and there were also local differences, either because of the divergent needs of the various races that made up the population, or because a solution favoured in one district did not suit the physical conditions of another – for which reason there are also distinct local types of building in modern Greece.

Subsidence in pre-human times had put most of the original Aegean land-mass beneath the sea, leaving only the former highlands exposed. They consist very largely of barren mountains of hard rock, separated by deep but narrow valleys, if not by stretches of sea. Few of the valleys expand to a width of half a dozen miles before their submergence, and every stream that falls from the surrounding hill-sides has spread countless layers of gravel across their floors. The soil is the least productive in Europe, and the total area now under cultivation in what corresponds to ancient Hellas might be contained in three or four English counties. With primitive farming a shortage of land must have developed after a few centuries of occupation, though erosion in historic times has certainly enhanced the denudation of the mountains and the stoniness of the valley soil.

One result of the land shortage has been an inadequate supply of timber, and that of poor quality. Flat ground is too precious for many trees to be allowed there, pasturage on the nearer slopes discourages the growth of anything except scrub within a convenient distance from habitations, while the transport of large beams across the mountains involves immense labour (and there were no horses around the Aegean till the Middle Bronze Age). Consequently, builders have always used wood sparingly, and very often have made do with shorter pieces than they would have liked. This handicap must have been especially severe on the primitive carpenter, who did not possess tools adequate for proper joinery.

The usual building material was sun-dried brick (adobe), which is easily prepared in the heat and drought of summer. All that is necessary is to wet the soil, mould it into the shape of bricks, and spread them about till they have hardened; they can then be laid in courses, with mud for mortar. The whole surface of the wall must be smoothed with mud and plastered with clay or lime to prevent the rain from percolating into the joints, and the top must be water-proofed by eaves projecting forward from the wall; if kept so protected, it will last for several generations or even centuries, provided the base stands dry. A single course of stone was gener-ally enough for this purpose, and very often supplies the only remaining indication that a building has existed, though at some places the stone-work normally ran up to a height of several feet or even formed the entire wall. Stone-cutting was rarely attempted in the Early Bronze Age. As a rule, the builders relied on finding suitable pieces of rock lying ready to hand; there was usually an abundance. And, as it happens, the limestone formations in many parts of Greece tend to split into more or less rectangular blocks when exposed to the weather; the wall could generally be given a fairly straight face on either side, though its core was filled with irregular stones. The interstices were packed with mud, or preferably clay, and by that means the top of the rubble was levelled as a plinth for the brick superstructure, which was usually a few inches narrower than the stone-work. There are instances of herringbone masonry. The walls of some buildings slant in-wards as they rise, each course overlapping the one below, in order to reduce the span of the roof. Where the whole structure consisted of stone, this corbelling sometimes continued till the gap could be bridged with a slab.

Kiln-burnt bricks occur very occasionally towards the end of the Early Bronze Age, and never came into regular use. The soil over most of the country was too dry and pebbly for even the sun-dried bricks to be of good quality. Straw or grass was usually added to the mud to give them cohesion – 'no bricks without straw' was said of sun-dried brick – but even so they tended to crumble under pressure. The walls of large buildings were therefore reinforced with a timber frame, consisting of both upright and horizontal beams, between which panels of brick were inserted. Sometimes projecting spurs of wall bore a wooden sheathing. Such precautions were the more necessary because of the great weight of the most favoured type of roof. This was flat – actually not quite flat but gently inclined in one or more directions; a con-siderable thickness of mud, or preferably clay, was required to make it waterproof, and the beams which carried it had to be correspond-ingly heavy.[1] The customary method was to bed the clay upon a layer of reeds or small branches, placed crosswise either directly on the beams or over another intervening crosswise layer of thin logs [1]. Occasionally stone slabs were used for roofing; also, in only one known instance, terracotta slabs.

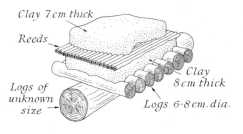

1. Eutresis, structure of the ceiling of a Middle Helladic house

The floors consisted of beaten earth or clay if available; often they were strewn with rushes or covered with rush-matting. Stone slabs were occasionally laid as 'crazy-paving' in streets or courts, but seldom occur in houses except in small patches, such as the threshold of a door-way. For intermediate support, tree-trunks were used as columns and set on stone bases, to prevent subsidence, and to keep the wood dry.

Domestic fittings tend to be stone-paved or coated with clay; they normally include a hearth, and pits for the storage of food or for slow cooking, frequently also a domed oven, one or more platforms for beds, a bench, and smaller stands. Huge storage jars kept the stocks of grain comparatively safe from vermin.

The extent to which the more perishable

materials were used cannot be ascertained, and must have varied in accordance with local conditions. As a substitute for sun-dried brick, builders on occasion adopted the cob or pisé method of compressing mud inside a wooden shuttering, which they transferred as each layer of the wall dried.[2] Mud partitions occur on Cretan sites. Remains have been found, too, of both walls and roofs made of intertwined reeds fastened to a wooden framework and plastered with clay; a stuffing of seaweed filled the gaps between the reeds. Besides this true wattle-and-daub, huts appear to have been covered with brushwood, rushes, or straw, with or without the impervious coating of clay. These short-lived buildings took a variety of forms – rectangular, circular, oval – and so did their roofs: some were conical, or like pointed domes; others may have been either gabled or hipped, like a boat upside down, with a tall arch at one end and sloping down to the other. The influence of such hut-shapes may be seen in tombs, for which purpose they were translated into permanent materials, and so led to new methods of building.

THE REGIONAL CULTURES

Regional differentiations in the Aegean area indicate local traditions within the broader framework of cultural sequences. Causes of this are obscure, particularly in the earlier period, and though there is some information relating to the second millennium on linguistic differences which presumably also existed in earlier times, we know nothing of their nature or distribution. Clearly there was movement within the Aegean area even in the Neolithic period – Mainland Greece was obtaining obsidian from the island of Melos before 7000 B.C. – and migration of populations is a factor which must be reckoned with.

Troy

The communities of the eastern coasts of the Aegean cannot strictly be called pre-Hellenic,

because they owed their more advanced condition to familiarity with the interior of Asia Minor. The best-known culture is the Trojan, which did not extend westward of the neighbouring islands; related shapes of pottery and other objects, however, are widespread throughout the archipelago and even in the Greek mainland, so that the population may have been similar in part. Most houses of the Trojan culture consist of a long, more or less rectangular hall, often preceded by a porch [2].

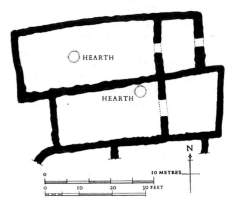

2. Thermi I,
houses of beginning of Trojan culture, plan

Occasional instances are found of a shorter form, and this may have been the older, for it was habitually used in the Cyclades, while at Thermi (in Lesbos) it appears only in the three lowest strata, which were roughly contemporary with the First Settlement at Troy.[3]

The earlier excavators of Troy distinguished seven main periods of prehistoric habitation, which they called 'Cities', an ill-chosen term because at all times the whole of the solidly built-up area consisted merely of a fortified palace enclosure – a citadel, in fact. The latest excavations have made it possible to subdivide the 'Cities' or 'Settlements' into a large number of phases; no fewer than ten compose the First Settlement. The earliest house [3] of which the

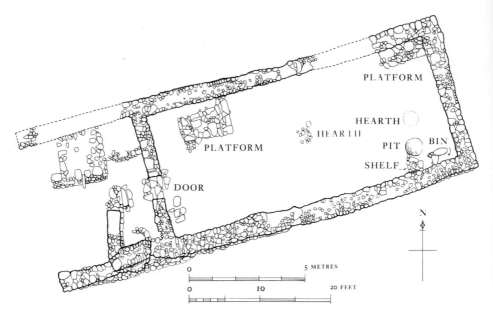

3. Troy Ib, house, plan

complete plan has been preserved is that which the excavators have numbered 102; it dates from the second phase of the First Settlement (Ib). It is 61 feet long and 23 feet wide (18·75 by 7 m.); one end was left open as a porch, 15 feet long, and the remainder was occupied by a single room which measures 41 by 18 feet internally (12·50 by 5·50 m.). Originally it must have been 6 feet longer, for there are remains of a previous cross-wall and threshold buried beneath the floor. This older wall had run obliquely, and in the acute angle formed on the inner side of its junction with the external wall is a seepage pit, which served as a domestic sink and latrine. The room contains raised platforms at the sides for beds, a hearth (with a stone paving) in the centre of the floor, a smaller cooking-hearth against the back wall, and beside it a pit for setting the dough of bread. Rush-matting was used to cover parts of the floor; the occupants threw the refuse of their fires and meals upon the rest of it. At intervals of a few years they spread another layer

of clay over the accumulation of bones, shells, and carbonized matter; consequently the threshold had to be repeatedly repaved at a higher level. The door swung on a pivot stone. The walls were built (2½ by 3 ft thick; 75 by 90 cm.) of stone up to a height of a couple of feet, but of sun-dried brick above; the inner face would have been plastered with clay, to judge from a house of Id. The roof appears to have had no internal support, though the span is several feet wider than usual; presumably it was flat in the normal Trojan manner. Fragments of roofing in other houses of the First Settlement prove that small boughs or reeds supported the overlying clay. Evidence has been found in southwest Anatolia for ridged roofs.

This house is like a crude predecessor of the type which Homer calls the megaron, in which the Myceneans lived at the close of the Late Bronze Age, perhaps 1,500 years later. There are many similar houses of later periods at Troy, the culture of which developed without radical change throughout the Early Bronze Age. Increasing prosperity is shown by successive enlargements of the citadel, each time with fortifications of more skilful design, in the course of the First and Second Settlements [4]. Even the oldest well-preserved piece, dating from a latish Middle Stage of Troy I, is a work superior in scale and quality to anything produced in the Greek mainland or islands during the Early Bronze Age. The wall ran up to an unknown height in sun-dried brick upon a massive rubble substructure, which stands over 11 feet high (3·35 m.); the face has a pronounced batter. A gate-passage leads inwards between two huge towers of apparently solid masonry, which project far beyond the adjoining curtain-wall. The citadel at this period occupied only the summit of the hill, and the subsequent walls were built progressively farther down the slopes. In Troy IIa, the earliest phase of the seven which compose the Second Settlement, the perimeter was increased to some 200 yards; in IIb it was made slightly longer, in IIc twice as long.[4]

The citadel of Troy IIc had now become extensive enough to allow of the creation of an inner enclosure to contain the courtyard and buildings of the palace, while still leaving space for a number of large buildings between that and the wall-circuit. One of these (known as IIF) exemplifies a modification, found only in IIc, of the long type of house which had persisted from Troy I and normally comprised one room and a porch formed by prolongations of the side walls. In this and a few other buildings of IIc, the walls are also prolonged behind the room, making a shallower back-porch – in this instance less than 3 feet deep. In no case does there appear to have been a doorway through the back wall, and the chief benefit gained by providing a false porch is likely to have been the ability to extend the flat roof well beyond the wall-face, and so protect the sun-dried bricks from rain. The ends of the side walls were given a wooden facing, also protective; the custom in IIc was to set it on a block of stone, the border of which projected beyond the wood and was

sunk a couple of inches lower for better drainage.

The experimental first excavation at Troy, a trench cut in 1871, destroyed the western part of the palace without record, and there are minor gaps elsewhere. As, however, the buildings were orientated to face south-east, the main outlines of the plan are fairly clear [5]. The design is a work of considerable architectural merit. The enclosure was practically rectangular, at any rate at its south-east end. Its wall is buttressed externally, at somewhat irregular intervals. The entrance is situated not at the centre of the south-east end but nearer the southern corner; it actually overlies the citadel gate of the First Settlement. The doorway through the wall lies between an outer and an inner porch, together forming a propylon. In plan this is like a smaller and simpler version of the defensive gateways of the IIc citadel, which contain an inner room or court between two doorways, each with a two-leaved door, while the side walls are prolonged to form deep porches on both the outward and the inward side; in these and in the central space (if unroofed) an enemy could be exposed to missiles from above from virtually all directions. The propylon evidently did not need to be defensible, and therefore had no court, but only one double door separating its outer and inner porches, which presumably were roofed to shelter attendants and persons awaiting audience.

The propylon led into a court, which was lined with a veranda built against the inner side of the enclosing wall. Spurs of masonry, placed opposite the external buttresses, project from the wall for a distance of 6 feet into the court, and midway in each of the gaps between their ends stood a wooden column on a stone base. The column rested on a circular portion of the slab, 1½ feet in diameter (46 cm.), which is a couple of inches higher than the remainder of its surface. The spur-walls must have carried most of the weight of the roof and partitioned the veranda into a series of rooms open towards the court; when seen from the court the front was composed of alternate posts and masonry.

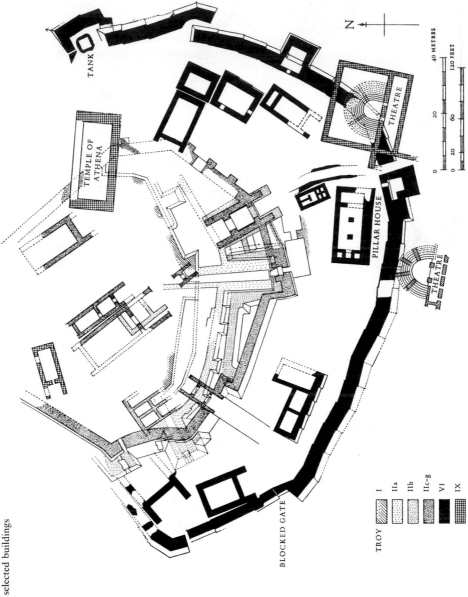

4. Troy, plan of selected buildings

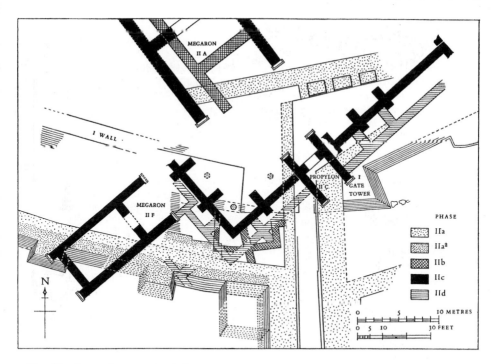

5. Troy II, palace enclosure, restored plan

Across the court from the propylon, 30 feet away, lies the porch of an exceptionally large building (called IIA) of the long type, obviously the main structure of the IIc palace.[5] The porch is 33 feet square internally (10·20 m.) and communicated by a central doorway with a hall, which has largely perished, but probably its length equalled twice the width; a hearth occupied a fairly central position in its floor. With such a width to span, the roof, especially if flat (as it almost certainly was), would have needed intermediate supports, both inside the hall and at the front of the porch, but no trace of columns has been found; probably they were removed for use in some later building. A building (known as IIB) existed parallel with and almost adjoining the north-east side; though not much shorter it is less than half as wide, but designed in such a way as to minimize that fact. Its porch is set 20 feet behind the other and is deeper than it is wide; the central doorway at the back leads to an anteroom of slightly more elongated proportions, at the end of which a doorway, placed next the side wall, gives on a hall nearly twice as long as it is wide. An exceptionally deep false porch seems to have brought the back roughly into line with that of the larger building alongside. In a corresponding position beyond the opposite side of the main building a wood-clad spur meets another fragment of wall at right angles, as though a third long building had existed, balancing IIB.

Outside the palace enclosure [4] another building (known as IID) of phase IIc, and its successor of IIg on the same site (miscalled the 'House of the City King'), seem to have had three or four parallel sets of rooms, partly above the west wall of IIa. Some carelessly built structures of IIf and IIg contain squarish rooms, and corridors led to apartments at the back. Other buildings of the Second Settlement are irregular in shape, but most conform, like those of the palace at its various stages, with the type represented in Troy Ib by the great house with a porch and a long hall. In the case of the palace, the optional addition of an intervening ante-room only enhances the resemblance to the Mycenean type of megaron palace with its porch, optional anteroom, and hall. But even more striking is the resemblance of the double-porch variant to the Hellenic temple, in which the walls are often prolonged at either end to make both a porch and a false porch. A wooden facing was similarly applied to the brick ends of the porch walls in both Mycenean and primitive Hellenic building; the classical Greeks retained the shape of it in stone construction, calling it an 'anta'. The veranda that lined the court is comparable with the porticoes in the courts of Minoan palaces, nearly a thousand years later, in that its front rested on alternate cross-walls and wooden columns, and theirs on alternate pillars of masonry and wooden columns. And the entrance to the palace enclosure could be the prototype of both the Mycenean and the Hellenic form of propylon, though all these are separated by great intervals of time, and examples to form the intervening sequences would be necessary to demonstrate a direct link; more likely we have the separate re-invention, perhaps from a continuing basic form, the 'megaron'.

At present there is no firm evidence that the Trojan culture had any direct effect on the architectural evolution of Greece, either pre-Hellenic or Hellenic, although the megaron plan, in straight-ended and apsidal form, is found over a wide area, from Thrace and Thessaly to south-west Anatolia. But the parallels go deeper than mere customary plans and technique. The sense for form, expressed in symmetrical plans and simple arithmetical proportions, and the appreciation of axial layout, clearly anticipate the classical Greek spirit. In this respect (as in most others) the Trojans of the Bronze Age present an almost complete contrast with the Cretans. But their architectural mentality differed in quality rather than in kind from that of the less advanced peoples in the Cyclades and on the mainland of Greece, whose undistinguished buildings gave little opportunity for self-expression. The local pre-eminence of Troy is attested by its cultural subjugation of a much older town, Poliochni, situated less than 40 miles away but on the island of Lemnos.[6] This remained a slum by comparison. Winding alleys divided blocks of contiguous misshapen houses, each with a porch and hall in Trojan style and sometimes no other rooms. The fortifications, of rustic crudity, are, in part, earlier than Troy I.

The Cyclades and Related Islands

In general the oldest remains yet found on the smaller islands belonged to the Early Bronze Age, but settlement in the Cyclades can be traced back to the later part, at least, of the middle neolithic. A neolithic settlement at Saliagos [6],[7] an islet off Paros, was inhabited about 4000 according to a radio-carbon analysis. Several little cottages and a more substantial house have been identified from scatters of stones, while a paved circular structure, 13 feet (4 m.) in diameter, may have been a granary.

Few buildings have been recovered belonging to the Grotta Pelos culture which begins in the Early Bronze Age, though traces of both rectangular and curved structures were found at Pyrgos on Paros. Of the succeeding Keros-Syros culture, the most impressive evidence comes from Kastri near Khalandriani on Syros [7], a fortified site less than 160 feet (50 m.) in width.[8] The surrounding wall has a series of projecting semicircular bastions at intervals of roughly 20 feet. Within, the buildings comprise agglomerations of small rooms, rarely more than 9 feet in diameter, with paths or narrow streets between them. They are irregular in shape.

Phylakopi on Melos in its earliest phase (Phylakopi I) belongs to the last two centuries of the Early Bronze Age. The settlement of this period is covered by the 'Second City' and 'Third City' (which belongs to the Late Bronze

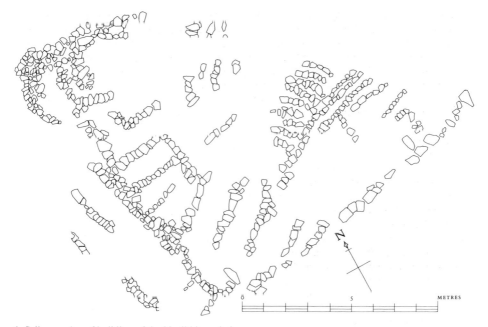

6. Saliagos, plan of building of the Neolithic period

7. Khalandriani, plan of Early Cycladic town

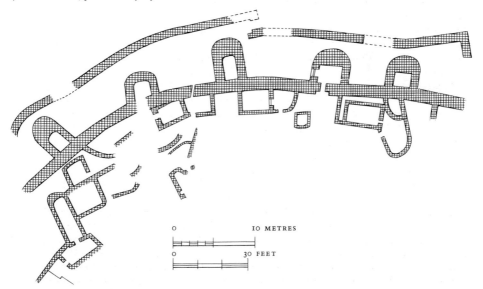

Age) which it equalled in size. It covers a size-able area, about 600 feet (over 180 m.) long, and is the only Early Cycladic site which constitutes a recognizable town. Unlike Khalandriani, the houses have straight walls, right-angle corners, and consistent orientation. They are run together in blocks, with narrow streets dividing them. Most important are the signs of planning and rational organization in the layout.

The Mainland of Greece

On the Greek mainland, too, all the very early buildings, apart from a few crude fortifications, are houses, careless as a rule of appearance but sometimes interesting as prototypes of later architectural forms. At Tsangli in Thessaly, all the houses are square or nearly square, frequently measuring 25–30 feet (7·50–9 m.) a side, and comprising only a single room; buttress-like spurs project inwards from the walls to reduce the span of the roof-beams, and in one case a row of four posts across the floor gave additional support [8]. In the succeeding cultural phase, for which datings of about 3700 and 3550 have been given by radio-carbon analyses, Dimeni became the one solidly-built

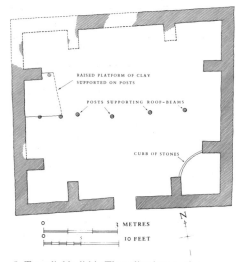

8. Tsangli, Neolithic Thessalian house, plan

Neolithic town yet discovered in Thessaly. There [9] and near by, at Sesklo, the practice was to build a roughly square room of compar-able size (usually a trifle smaller), but as the

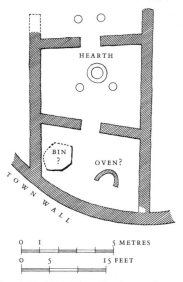

9. Dimeni, Neolithic Thessalian house, plan

central apartment of three; a doorway in its back wall opens into a room about half as large, while outside the front doorway a shallow porch is formed by prolongation of the side walls. In a few porches two wooden columns stood be-tween the ends of the walls, in front of the jambs of the doorway. Other posts in the main room supported the roof-timbers, perhaps in relation to a smoke-hole, for there is invariably a hearth there, whether in the centre or elsewhere. The markedly rectilinear planning characteristic of all three Thessalian sites may have resulted from a habitual use of sun-dried bricks, as is suggested by the thickness of the stone wall base (often as much as 2 feet). But the same people also built both circular – or oval – and rect-angular huts of intertwined reeds, daubed with clay, on a wooden framework; some fragments of the latter seem to indicate that their roofs sloped considerably and may have been gabled. The modern population constructs similar huts with the same indifference as to shape. The alternation of the seasons has always obliged men to migrate with their animals between the mountains and the plains, and a temporary home is still made with a frame of poles and a covering of brushwood, reeds, or rushes; with some renewal the hut may remain in service year after year, to be occupied for several months in each.[9]

In the more southerly parts of the mainland the use of both rounded and rectangular habitations persisted from the neolithic far into the Bronze Age. At Orchomenus in Boeotia a settlement of round houses has been excavated[10] which includes some in more durable materials. They probably date not long after the beginning of the Bronze Age, otherwise the earth which the builders deposited to raise the floors would have contained sherds of other pottery besides neolithic. The internal diameters range up to some 20 feet (6 m.). The walls stood on a stone base, a few feet high, and either thin or thick depending on whether the upper part consisted of brushwood or sun-dried brick. The stonework slopes steadily inwards as it rises, so that the complete house should have formed a tall pointed dome, in height approximately equal to the lower diameter. Such houses are still built, of sun-dried brick, in north Syria.[11] They have the advantage of requiring no wood except for the lintel of the doorway, and are exceptionally pleasant in summer; heated air rises from the floor-level to the peak, cools there, and descends to refresh the occupants.

The prevalent shape of Early Helladic houses is more or less rectangular, and the walls are usually as straight as could be expected with the low standards of construction, in sun-dried brick on a base of stones, especially considering that the use of flat roofs allowed any degree of irregularity. The main room is squarish; the entrance to the house opens directly into it, often in the side wall, while another door in the back wall leads to an inner room which is seldom more than half as long. The normal arrangement of rooms, in fact, is the same as the Thessalian, and precisely the opposite of the Trojan scheme in which the anteroom (if any) precedes the hall. Sometimes an Early Helladic house contains more rooms than the regular two, but perhaps only to meet the peculiar needs of the occupants, not for luxury's sake. The two alone were provided in an exceptionally large, but only roughly rectangular, house ('H') of the last phase, Early Helladic III, at Eutresis in Boeotia [10]. The main room, entered from the village street by a doorway in the end-wall, measured internally about 20 feet wide by no less than 33 feet long, while the back room scarcely exceeded 7 feet in length with the same width. The exceptional proportions of the main room must be ascribed to the wish to obtain an unusually large floor-area in spite of indifferent roof-timbers. The actual span is wider than was customary, and in the centre of the room stood a column about 2 feet in diameter, made of a core of sun-dried bricks rounded off in clay. There is a pit of ashes beside it, and another hearth against the side wall – allowing respectively of slow and quick cookery; one huge jar (*pithos*) for storing dry foodstuff stood next the hearth with a small pot alongside, another against the opposite wall.

At Lerna, a site occupied during the neolithic was abandoned and reoccupied in the Early Bronze Age. The principal building, called by its excavator the House of the Tiles [11], is dated to Early Helladic II.[12] There are traces of a comparable monumental building which seems to have been a forerunner and prototype. The House of the Tiles is about 80 feet long and 40 feet wide (25 by 12 m.). A porch on the east side leads to the main hall measuring 21 by 26 feet (6·43 by 8·05 m.). West of it lie three rooms in turn, 19 feet wide, between corridors along both north and south, where wooden staircases rose from clay steps at floor level.[13] The roof consisted of well-fired terracotta tiles, about 1 cm. thick, laid overlapping in clay supported by wooden beams and smaller timbers. Floors were of thick layers of yellow clay, walls were coated with lime plaster, with some rooms unfinished. It was destroyed in a violent conflagration, before completion. To the south is a

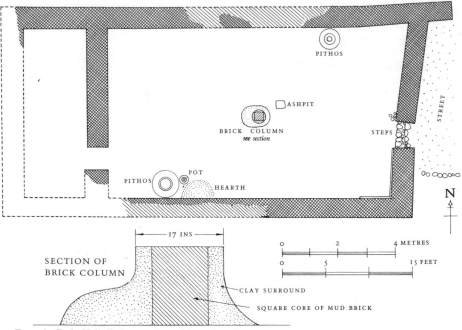

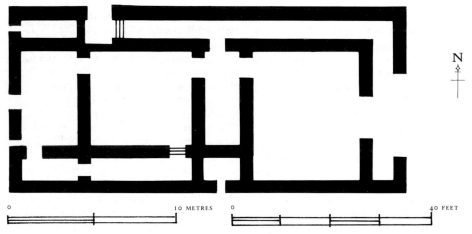

10. Eutresis, Early Helladic house, plan, with section of column

11. Lerna, House of the Tiles, Early Helladic II, plan

double line of walls, divided into compartments, and with a projecting buttress, which may represent the fortification. They seem to have been dismantled before the House of the Tiles was built; if so, the conflagration may have been the work of an enemy, to whose attack it was exposed. Subsequently, in the final phase of the Early Bronze Age (when the material from the occupation is very different from that of its earlier phases), the ruins of the House of the Tiles were partly covered by a substantial tumulus.

Only the base remains, and that fragmentary [12], of an enormous and extraordinary structure at Tiryns which the Myceneans demolished; it underlies the smaller megaron of

some others which are unquestionably Early Helladic.

Crete

When it became sharply differentiated from the rest of the pre-Hellenic world during the Bronze Age by developing a complex urban civilization,

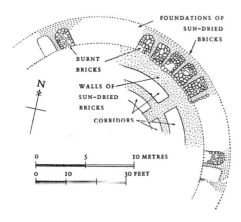

12. Tiryns, Early Helladic round building, plan

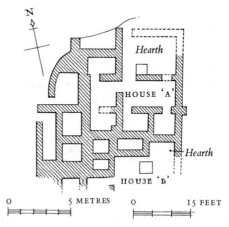

13. Cnossus, Late Neolithic houses, plan

their palace, and itself overlays an earlier, oval building. Finds of pottery prove that the date cannot be long before the close of the Early Helladic period. The plan was circular, at least in the main; scraps of more than half the circle are preserved, and determine the diameter as about 91 feet at the outer edge of the plinth. In the interior there remain only stretches of concentric walls and of narrow corridors between them; obviously all this was substructure to carry a raised floor. The outer wall is 6 feet thick, of sun-dried brick. It is encircled by a stone plinth, 10 feet wide, upon which, backed against the wall, stood a series of tongue-shaped piers of burnt brick, which stop short within 3 feet of the edge of the plinth, so that each measures nearly 8 feet long, with a width of 4 feet, while it is separated from the next by a gap of 1 foot. Burnt bricks make their first appearance in Europe with this building and

Crete still based its peculiar architectural habits on those of its neolithic inhabitants. At Cnossus their houses (of pisé on a base of stones) had been consistently small-roomed from, roughly, 6000 to 3000, though the plans grew more complex. A grouping of about twenty little apartments [13] seems to represent the major part of at least two residences, for it contained two relatively spacious rooms each with a hearth; the better-preserved measures only about 10 feet square (3 m.). A room beside it necessarily had the same length but a width of 7 feet, and that is approximately the larger dimension in the other rooms – excluding some tiny storage chambers, which were made accessible only from above in order to exclude mice and rats. A house at Magasa appears at first sight to have gone to the other extreme in the size of rooms [14]. It would seem to have been entered through a room about 10 feet wide and 23 feet

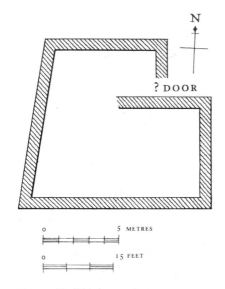

N

? DOOR

0   5 METRES

0   15 FEET

14. Magasa, Neolithic house, plan

long, and to have contained only one other of 20 by 33–36 feet. All that remains, however, is a single course of large stones, the base for walls which may have been of sun-dried brick; even so they would scarcely have been strong enough to carry even the lightest roof unless several equally solid partitions or piers had divided the interior. The main interest of the house is its use of the 'but-and-ben' (Scots for 'out-and-in') method of planning, which involves passing through the entire length of one room to enter another parallel with it. This habit persists in Crete throughout the Bronze Age – when the culture of the island is called Minoan (after the legendary king Minos of Cnossus).

The but-and-ben scheme was also applied in Early Minoan II to family tombs which can be regarded as reproducing a type of cottage, not necessarily of the latest fashion; the walls consisted entirely of roughly squared stones, to last out the eternal tenancy of occupants who in life would have been content with sun-dried brick. Larger buildings, of several rectangular rooms combined as artlessly as in neolithic Cnossus, served at this period for communal ossuaries in

which the bones of the dead were deposited after the flesh had decayed in a temporary grave; the custom persists in modern Greece, because soft ground is too scarce to waste on large cemeteries. Residences of the living, too, were sometimes communal. The two such discovered, at Vasiliki and Myrtos, are basically similar; the latter is the more informative, especially in its southern portion, which was inhabited from about 2400 to 2200 with only minor alterations [15]. Like Vasiliki, Myrtos formed a cluster of nearly a hundred rooms in seemingly haphazard aggregation. Although passages threaded devious ways through it, expanding here and there into a little open yard, the whole straggle of buildings was unified. The straggle was by no means limited to a horizontal plane, because the slope of the ground encouraged diversity in the levels of the flat roofs (which were clay-topped over a bed of reeds laid on timbers). Some rooms were accessible only by ladder from an adjoining roof, some only through an outer room; in neither case could much light have penetrated. The walls consisted of mud brick and unworked stones, held by a facing of plaster, which sometimes was coloured red. The roof-spans were usually much shorter than the maximum found, 2·60 metres (8½ feet); even with the support of an angular pillar, no room was appreciably larger than 5 metres (16 feet) square, and the majority very small.

No other huge complexes of buildings are known that antedate the oldest remnants of palaces, though under the west court of the Palace at Cnossus are remains of storerooms which must have belonged to some extensive building of Early Minoan II:[14] otherwise it seems that the top of the mound at Cnossus, with probable Early Minoan structures, and even Late Neolithic, was removed when levelling work was undertaken for the subsequent palace construction. Myrtos and Vasiliki are villages, and differ in character from the later palaces such as Cnossus.

Ossuaries of circular plan[15] were built at many places in central Crete, particularly around the Mesara plain, during Early Minoan

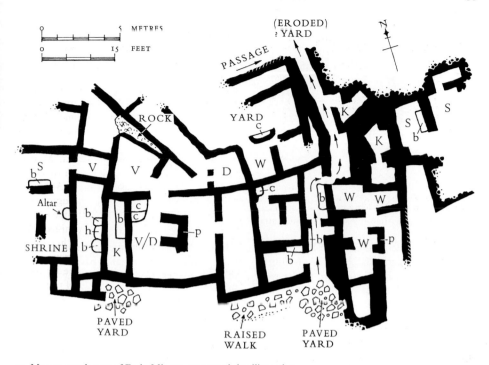

15. Myrtos, south part of Early Minoan communal dwelling, plan

Probable uses: D – dining room, K – kitchen, S – store, V – vintner, W – workshop, B – bench or stand (solid), C – 'cupboard' or bin (enclosed by upright slabs), H – hearth (enclosed by kerb of stones), P – pillar (built like a wall).

times, and a few still in Middle Minoan [16]. The internal diameters vary between 14 and 43 feet. The walls slope inwards as they rise, like the bases of the round houses at Orchomenus, but the stone-work was carried up past the level of the doorway, which is of megalithic construction and therefore needed to be held firmly in place. Each jamb is a single block only about 3 feet high, while the lintel is a far larger block – 7 or 8 feet long and very thick in the middle; the top rises in a hump over the door opening but is trimmed down at the sides where the walls would give support. Most ossuaries stood isolated (generally within a paved area), but in approximately seven instances a few low rooms adjoined either the little entrance chamber or a

part (eastward as a rule) of the circular wall. A conjunction of a large ossuary with a smaller, both entered through the same group of little rooms, probably resulted from the need to receive more bones than the original space could hold; rooms were never put to that use. A Middle Minoan ossuary at Arkhanes is unique in that the whole circle was enclosed by an externally square complex of rooms, through which a passage cut obliquely to the entrance.

The question of the roofing has given rise to much dispute. There is insufficient debris in the ruins to demonstrate a stone roof, and recent studies in the engineering and mechanical problems of the Mycenean tholos demonstrate that a stone roof in the Minoan structure would

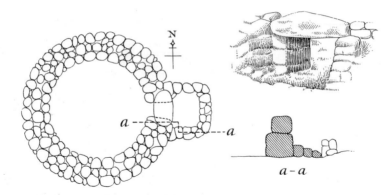

16. Kumasa, Early Minoan ossuary, plan and entrance

have been completely unstable.[16] Possibly timber and thatch were used, but if so it is difficult to explain the massive structure of the stone walls. The problem is essentially unresolved. It has been suggested that these ossuaries are the origin of the Mycenean tholos. The relative chronology, the lack of any clear overlap in time between the two groups of structures, renders this inherently improbable. In addition, there are fundamental differences between them. The Cretan ossuaries are normally above ground (some are cut into hillsides): the tholos tombs, on the other hand, were completely subterranean, and entered through a passage. In some of the ossuaries, it is true, the floor was sunk below the level of the ground outside, in which a shallow pit had to be made to expose the door, but that awkward method of approach seems involuntary; it resulted from the necessity of setting the whole wall, and especially the jambs, directly on a foundation of native rock. The largest, Tomb A at Platanus, with an internal diameter of 47 feet (13·10 m.) is obviously too large to have been vaulted like a tholos.

CHAPTER 3

THE BEGINNINGS OF THE CRETAN PALACES:

THE PROTO-PALATIAL PERIOD

(MIDDLE MINOAN I–II)

After many generations of slow progress, Crete developed the first civilization of the Aegean, with towns, palaces, art, and a system of writing. It began in a modest way with Middle Minoan I, around the turn of the second millennium, and advanced constantly and with increasing impetus till the catastrophic end of Late Minoan I, shortly after the middle of the fifteenth century. Throughout these six centuries there is abundant archaeological evidence for close relations with Egypt and Western Asia; moreover the ships that maintained the traffic seem to have been Cretan – the Cyclades now came under overwhelming Minoan influence, whereas it had previously been negligible. Direct contact with the civilized nations of the East may have provided the impulse to the initial spurt from semi-barbarism, and certainly dictated much of the form afterwards taken by Minoan civilization. In architecture particularly, both Egyptian and Asiatic influences are prominent, and may have inspired the very notion of making a building a work of art, together with the ambition to use well-cut masonry; the Early Minoans left the stone rough. But, whatever importance we may attach to the overseas contributions in architecture[1] and decoration, there appears to have been far more adaptation than actual copying involved, and the native element is perhaps fundamental in the great architectural expression of Minoan civilization, the palaces, which were continuously inhabited from Middle Minoan I to the final disaster.

In the Early Bronze Age, two distinct traditions in architectural habit may be observed: that in which families lived in separate houses, the best of which consisted of little more than one large hall, symmetrically planned; and that of which the Early Minoan settlement at Myrtos is an excellent example (and which is also attested in Anatolia) where there is an agglomeration of rooms which show a complete disregard for symmetry. This latter type persists into Middle Minoan, and in the palaces. Whether an actual transition led from tenement to palace, inspired and guided by the new familiarity with the East, cannot be decided, since practically nothing is known about building during the intervening period, Early Minoan III, and very little about the oldest palaces. The later occupants destroyed them in the course of successive reconstructions, and at Phaestus alone have the buried foundations been uncovered in coherent groupings, at Mallia, however, the layout is ascribed to 2000.[2]

The first palaces at Cnossus, Phaestus, and Mallia – that is, those which Doro Levi terms proto-palatial – date back towards the beginning of Middle Minoan I, after 2000 B.C. There are also remains of an early palace at Zakro. At Phaestus the proto-palatial work has been divided into three phases (the earliest subdivided into two). All these palaces [23, 30, 35] were laid out on an intelligible unified plan, of which the basic feature is a central courtyard – an idea novel in Crete, but traditional in both Egypt and Asia. Contrary, however, to the practice in those countries, the court is invariably twice as long or more from north to south as its east-west breadth, averaging some 170 by 80 feet; the motive, no doubt, was to obtain as much warmth as possible from the lower winter sun, especially since the normal method of heating was by charcoal braziers. The court is of crucial importance in understanding the architecture of the Cretan palaces, for although, as we shall see, the exteriors were not disregarded, the palaces were undoubtedly turned in on themselves: it was the arrangement in relation to the court, rather than the world outside, which was of importance. (The contrast between buildings which are essentially free-standing and viewed externally, set in space, as it were, and those which are viewed from within, enclosing space, remains important in Hellenic architecture, distinguishing, for example, the temple from buildings consisting of rooms arranged round a peristyle court.) Long stretches of wall were avoided, probably because the builders distrusted their stability, but an architectural sense is also shown by the manner in which a long façade was diversified by placing some sections back or forward as much as several feet or even yards, while the individual sections were broken by recessing the central part only a foot or less; examples can still be seen on the western frontages of all three palaces. Both schemes were habitually used in Mesopotamia and occasionally in Syria; Egyptian parallels are neither precise nor numerous. An appreciation of craftsmanship – hitherto lacking in Crete – is shown by the builders' technique. The walls consisted, as before, of rubble or small roughly-dressed stones, or else of sun-dried brick, but were now lined at the base with a row of facing-slabs (orthostats) to a height of some 3 feet, and the entire face was stuccoed or plastered. Orthostats were used too in northern Mesopotamia and Syria, where they were attached by the same means of wooden bars mortised into the wall. The whole wall with its orthostats stood on a plinth a couple of feet high, which along an important frontage was allowed to project some 18 inches. The slight recessing of the middle of a façade accordingly involved similar re-entrants in the edge of the plinth, and gained emphasis thereby. This likewise was a common practice in Mesopotamia. The system of drainage, using earthenware pipes, could also have been derived from Mesopotamia –

indirectly, no doubt, through contact with the coast of Syria or Asia Minor. Altogether there can be no doubt that Middle Minoan I architecture owed much to Asia, and there is little evidence of borrowing from Egypt till considerably later. The strict formality and symmetry of Egyptian design must have been very alien to Cretan minds at first.

In the case of Cnossus, the site chosen was a hillock low by nature but considerably raised by the debris of early habitation; much of this was cleared away, and the top levelled into a great terrace to form the eventual core of the palace. This was arranged round a courtyard, but it is doubtful whether the buildings were originally divided into separate or semi-independent buildings, as was once believed.[3] Rooms on the north and west sides stretched back to two other courts, each connected by passages with the central court. In a part of the west court stood detached buildings, with basements deeply sunk into the made ground behind the retaining wall. The eastern slope, which descends steeply to a stream-bed, was made into several narrow terraces, occupied by further buildings, down to the limit marked by another great retaining wall. At their south end, east of the south end of the central court, a basement room is preserved together with two rectangular monolithic pillars to support the floor above.[4] The Egyptians had long used such pillars, and they also occur in Syria; no previous instance in the Aegean is known.

At Phaestus the palace stood on the very brow of a hill, the remainder of which was too abrupt for use, and a compact plan would have involved an excessive amount of terracing. Instead, the buildings straggled along a plateau, west, north, and north-east from the central court, which extended southward to the edge of a steep drop, the natural boundary of the palace. That end (now eroded) must have been more or less open; the rest was lined with buildings. The court measured about 168 by 73 feet (51 by 22 m.). The buildings on the west side backed on another court, to the north of which lay a third, on higher ground. All three courts are paved with irregular slabs ('crazy pavement'), such as had already been used at Cnossus. The west court at both Phaestus and Cnossus is crossed by raised pathways which led to main entrances. But one of those at Cnossus, which ran straight through a passage to the central court, was blocked before the end of Middle Minoan I, when the western façade was reshaped, using the same orthostats.

Of these palaces Mallia alone gives any appearance of having been defensive, and that merely by chance. At Cnossus and Phaestus in this period, and in all subsequent Minoan palaces, the planning shows clearly that no thought of defensibility entered the minds of those responsible for the layout. Furthermore, the Minoan towns were absolutely indefensible, and even in the countryside, well adapted to brigandage as it is, no vestige of Minoan fortification has been identified.[5] It would seem that the Minoans anticipated, if not actually enjoyed, unbroken peace, though we cannot hope to recover any understanding of the political means by which this was achieved. The concentration of important palace sites in a small area of central Crete (albeit one divided into distinct regions by mountains) is in part at least to be attributed to the chances of survival and archaeological discovery.

Even so, the architecture of the palaces must reflect their function. In the ancient oriental countries a palace was equivalent to the government offices as well as forming a residence for the ruler, his family, his officials and servants with their families, together with guards and artisans. (The Fourth Gospel reflects the system: 'In my Father's house are many mansions', says the Son of the King of Heaven.) A provincial governor needed a palace similar to a king's, though smaller, while a king with an extensive realm might move regularly from one district to another, maintaining a somewhat comparable palace in each for the temporary accommodation of the same staff. In Crete the obviously intentional similarity in plan between the four large palaces is so emphatic that their functions must have been almost identical; but there is no

real reason to suppose that this implies anything other than that they were seats of administration for separate states organized in an identical manner. It is impossible to tell how much they differed in scale even at their final stages, because the average height of buildings probably varied considerably between one palace and another while we can only guess how many storeys existed in any section of each. Sir Arthur Evans thought that in parts of the Residential Quarter at Cnossus 'there were at least three storeys'. It is usually accepted that Cnossus ran up higher than the others, but J. W. Graham doubts this, preferring to argue that the upper flight of stairs led to a flat roof.[6] Both it and Phaestus cover between 3 and 4 acres ($1\frac{1}{2}$ hectares), and within a mile or two of each are lesser though very extensive buildings of a palatial character which may have been subsidiary. At Mallia, the palace was only half as large, and that at Zakro may have provided a comparable number of rooms. The site at Zakro is waterlogged and the palace in bad condition; built shortly after 1600, it was extensively repaired about 1500 and finally destroyed half a century later. The excavator, Platon, believes that the rooms along the west side of the central court should be associated with the tiny shrine amid them; the kitchen and storage appertaining to it were clearly located farther north, while the main living-quarters seem to have extended eastward from the central court to another (or perhaps it was a hall) which is roughly 45 feet (14 m.) square and contains a circular spring-fed basin, originally surrounded by columns. A precisely similar division by functions can be envisaged at the other palaces. Two other so-called palaces are relatively insignificant; at Gournia, in the east of Crete, the compound embraces half an acre, while at Apodulu, one of the few Minoan sites yet noticed in the west, the actual ruins are a mere 100 feet long. These perhaps represent the seats of local governors or magnates, if they do not belong to small independent states.

The original palace at Cnossus was not grandiose. A suspicion that it may have been almost as slum-like as the great tenements of Early Minoan II can be based only on the miserable planning of the few rooms that are certainly of Middle Minoan I and on the whole-sale reconstruction which later generations thought necessary. Most of Cnossus was in fact demolished and laid out afresh as early as Middle Minoan II, though again the details of the plan cannot be distinguished. An earth-quake at the end of that period may have given cause for the further rebuilding which preserved only the general lines of the Middle Minoan II plan, and a description ought therefore to be postponed. The same earthquake may have occasioned extensive rebuilding at Phaestus. Both sites retain a little of the Middle Minoan II work unaltered,[7] but it reveals few significant pieces of architectural design. The west porch of each palace was very similar (that at Cnossus was reconstructed in Late Minoan I), consisting of a wide room open at the front where a central column of exceptional girth supported the ceiling. At Phaestus three doorways in the back wall led respectively to a corridor (in which a stair rose to the floor above), a porter's lodge, and another parallel set of small rooms, while a doorway on the north side gave access to a wing mainly devoted to a jumble of storerooms of various shapes. At Cnossus only two doorways led from the porch, both through the back wall, to a corridor and to a porter's lodge. There too the north-west wing was given up to storage, but on a methodical plan; a corridor ran past the entrances to a long row of magazines, each so narrow as to leave barely space for a man to walk beside the line of huge jars (*pithoi*) or boxes placed against one or both of its side walls. At Mallia the similar row of magazines is quite likely to date from Middle Minoan I. There are Asiatic parallels to the arrangement.

At Phaestus there was a shrine (room 2 on illustration 30), buried when the level of the west court was raised. It measures only 12 by 8½ feet (3·62 by 2·57 m.), and its area is reduced by low benches along three walls; analogies of later date suggest that they supported sacred objects. A clay 'table of offerings' is set into the floor and helps to prove the religious dedication of the room. Two even smaller rooms were soon added. They project into the north-east corner of the west court, and the shrine proper was now entered through them instead of from the east. A terracotta model, found at Cnossus in a stratum of Late Middle Minoan II, apparently represents such a shrine. In every palace the shrine was architecturally insignificant, a 'holy of holies' for severely restricted access; near-by rooms may have been sacred, though not to the same degree, on account of ceremonial uses. Some caves and mountain-tops also were sacred, and there are larger buildings at them, of Middle Minoan and Late Minoan I date, but these may have been intended to accommodate priests or pilgrims. The best known, on a hill at Khristos in central Crete, consists of a room measuring 28 by 13 feet with a square projection in the middle of the east side; a chasm in the floor may have been the mouth of a cave but is now choked. Subsequent Minoan shrines and a 'temple-tomb' are described in the next chapter. A building outside the palace at Mallia also deserves mention because its three fair-sized rooms may together have formed a sanctuary.[8]

Like all subsequent Minoan columns, those of Middle Minoan II were of wood and set on stone bases. At this period the bases were generally drum-shaped, the height being usually equal to more than half the diameter; often they are made of attractive coloured rocks, mostly of igneous formation and very hard. A little terracotta model of three columns from a stratum of Middle Minoan II at Cnossus may give a rough idea of the contemporary form in wood. The bases are circular, quite low, and much wider than the cylindrical shafts, which carry square capitals slightly taller than the bases and of roughly the same width; upon each of these two logs are shown, with birds seated on them. The presence of the birds ought to imply that the logs were mere tie-beams and that the ceiling came higher up, on the assumption that the model can be trusted, but it seems to have been a cult-object and perhaps reproduces a symbolic rather than a structural architectural shape. Where a more sturdy prop than a wooden column was required, we find rectangular pillars of masonry; superimposed blocks take the place of the earlier monoliths. The two kinds of support were often used together, preferably in alternation. That convention was at any rate established early in Middle Minoan III, and an example at Phaestus [17] seems likely to date from Middle Minoan II in spite of low column-bases such as are typical of Middle Minoan III;

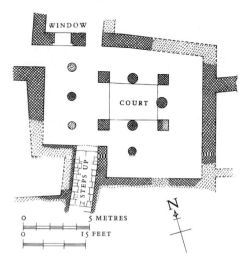

17. Phaestus, Middle Minoan II hall with court, plan

at any rate sufficient time elapsed for a partial substitution of solid walls (ignored on the plan) to have become desirable before its destruction in Middle Minoan III. The apartment in question (numbered by the excavators 103 or XLII) stood on a terrace near the north-east extremity of the palace. In the middle, but off-centre, was a small court (11¾ by 9¾ feet; 3·60 by 2·70 m.) with square pillars at the corners and intervening columns on three sides. This open space was paved with limestone slabs, the rest with gypsum, a stone which disintegrates when wet. To the west there was no column at the edge of the court, but a row of three halfway to the wall. These are differently spaced. An alcove on the

south was given only one column, set opposite that of the court. This absence of symmetry characterizes Minoan planning at all times, but at later periods it is rare to find a pretentious room with walls that do not meet approximately at right angles.

The construction of theatral areas just outside the palaces was probably an innovation of Middle Minoan II. At Phaestus the rock slope which made the north border of the west court was cut back and revetted by a wall [30]. Against its base a flight of steps was built for a length of some 80 feet; originally there were nine steps, 2 feet (65 cm.) wide and averaging 9 inches (23 cm.) in height, and a wider platform above the top step; this was subsequently enlarged by building a new wall 6 feet farther back at the same time as the lowest four steps were covered by a higher pavement of the court. A raised pathway cuts across the court obliquely from the west porch to meet the lowest step about midway, where a narrow stair rises through the steps at a slant intermediate between the angles of the path and of the steps; since it starts 4 inches (10 cm.) higher, its treads come level with the middle of the second and following steps. There is space on the steps for 500 people, and the only plausible explanation of them is that they were intended as a grandstand for the spectators of events that took place in the court. One fresco may depict a dance in a theatral area; otherwise the nature of these events is unknown. Minoan paintings frequently show youths somersaulting over the horns of a charging bull, but no such performances can have been given here, for lack of a barrier to separate the steps from the court. Moreover the open space is too small. At Phaestus it may eventually have stretched over 150 feet in both directions, but at Cnossus it was hopelessly inadequate [23, *left*]. There the theatral area occupied part of the north court, enclosed for the purpose by a wall; the five steps on the south side may be still older, but another flight of seventeen was added in Middle Minoan III on the east side, together with a higher platform set behind the junction of the two flights as though to form a 'royal box'.

The open space was then restricted to 42 by 33 feet (12·94 by 10·16 m.). A wider platform runs above the top steps, as at Phaestus, but in the case of the older flight it is abbreviated by a pathway which cuts aslant from the back of the 'royal box' to the far end of the third step; the lowest step also was shortened for the insertion of the later flight. Such arrangements again exhibit the Minoan dislike of regularity and symmetry.

No ruin of Middle Minoan II is sufficiently preserved to restore the whole elevation, in contrast to the Late Cycladic remains at Thera (see below), but the appearance may well have been similar, and this is supported by models. A collection of faience plaques, obviously meant to join up and compose a scene of a whole town (they seem to represent individual houses), was found at Cnossus in a deposit of early Middle

Minoan III and cannot be appreciably older; most of them were partially destroyed and the restorations may not always be correct [18]. The makers too are certain to have been guilty of inaccuracies because of the scale – each plaque is only an inch or so wide. Façades alone are represented. Some are shown as though composed of large blocks of stone, probably to imitate an effect produced in stucco on actual buildings. Some models are striped horizontally, as though by bands of timber; we know that Minoan buildings were half-timbered, but the beams can scarcely have been laid at such close intervals. Or the horizontal stripes alternate with a row of disks, suggesting the protruding ends of logs that carried the ceilings, but as many as half a dozen disks are shown on models no taller than others which are represented with windows indicating two storeys. It would ap-

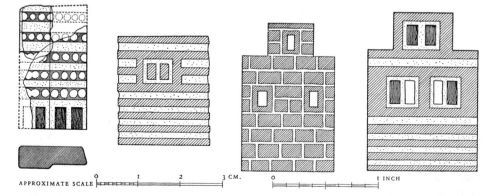
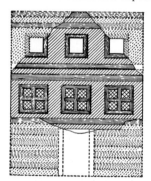
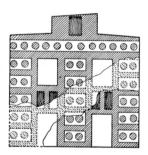
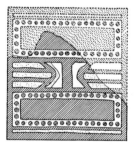

APPROXIMATE SCALE

0   1   2   3 CM.   0   1 INCH

18. Restored Minoan models of buildings. *Heraklion Museum*

pear, therefore, that Minoan builders must have drawn patterns on the plastered façades of houses. These models are all coloured; the walls have a pale cream or greyish ground, the sham timber is usually brown, but shades into crimson or green. A few models have blank façades, but generally they have a few windows, with rectangular frames; some windows are left plain, others divided vertically by a mullion or into four panes by mullion and transom. Occasionally the panes are scarlet, and it has been suggested that the Minoans used parchment in the place of glass and sometimes dyed it red, but the red is more likely to represent the painted boards of solid shutters, which are still used in peasant houses; besides, the effect of red panes is distressing, as may be observed in Victorian lavatories. The roofs are flat or nearly so, except that some have what look like attics built upon them, each with a window; probably these were not rooms but enclosed and covered stairheads, the larger examples of which would be combined with a well for light and ventilation.

A terracotta model of a two-storeyed house has been found at Arkhanes among pots datable shortly before 1600 [19].[9] It has a projecting porch, with a door in its side and a large window (divided in two by a column) at the front. The column supports a beam circular in section which crosses the window, and another which divides the porch ceiling in two. From the porch a corridor leads to a room in the next corner: by the side of the corridor a staircase (made in simplified form, as a ramp) ascends to the upper floor. On the ground floor the corner room gives access to a small veranda, half roofed, half open on two sides. A central column supports another circular sectioned beam. The remainder of the ground floor is occupied by a large room, entered from the corner room, with two small windows in the side, and a single central column. The upper floor is open-plan – a single space, unwalled, except for a section by the stairhead, the roof being supported by piers and columns. It follows the ground plan, except for a most interesting projecting balcony, supported on two sets of circular beams. The roof is missing – it is suggested that it was made of

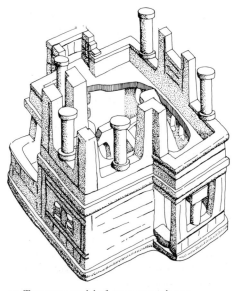

19. Terracotta model of a two-storey house from Arkhanes, c. 1600

perishable material. The upper floor would have constituted a cool, airy place if it were a real building – a true summer room. The model was coloured: orange for bases and capitals, beams, etc. The rest was black or white, not sufficiently well preserved for their application to be interpreted.

Burial in ossuaries continued during this period, but they were gradually replaced by large communal burial pits, and built complexes. A good example is the building at Khrysolakkos near Mallia, 130 by 100 feet (39 by 30 m.) divided internally by cross walls to form small compartments, perhaps each allotted to a family. A veranda outside provided shelter for visitors, and there is also a room which seems to have served as a chapel.

Another tomb, built above ground at Apesokari, might be considered a link between the Early Minoan ossuaries and later, mainly underground, structures. It contained pottery of Middle Minoan I and II. A whole cemetery of tombs, with rectangular and circular rooms, extending into Late Minoan times, has been excavated at Arkhanes.

CHAPTER 4

THE PALACE AGE IN CRETE: THE NEO-PALATIAL PERIOD

(MIDDLE MINOAN III—LATE MINOAN)

After the earthquake which destroyed the old palaces, a wholesale redevelopment took place. Not only were the old palaces at Cnossus, Phaestus, and Mallia rebuilt, but other new palaces and country houses were created. The island seems to have entered a most prosperous period. Trade increased with Egypt and Syria, particularly in the fifteenth century. It was at this most flourishing epoch that the palaces were destroyed, at the middle of the century. Two causes have been suggested, and they may well be connected: the first is the catastrophic eruption, perhaps after the middle of the fifteenth century, of the volcano that is the island of Thera, which covered and preserved the houses of this period at Akrotiri (architecturally, at least, a second-millennium Pompeii) but which also seems to have deposited a thick covering of volcanic ash over Crete, ruining the agriculture; the second cause suggested is the aggressive development of the Myceneans of the mainland, who may have taken advantage of the catastrophe. All the known palaces of Crete were destroyed about 1450, except Cnossus; and from the clay tablets found there by Sir Arthur Evans with writing in the script he called Linear B, and generally believed to belong to the year of destruction, about 1375, it is clear that Cnossus was now controlled by a Mycenean Greek dynasty from the mainland.[1] Another palace centre at Khania in western Crete may also have continued (and, indeed, could well have endured after 1375 as the main political centre of Crete); excavations have revealed floors of the Late Minoan IIB period, which were destroyed by fire.

By the end of Late Minoan IB, the moment of destruction around 1450 B.C., their own taste had reached a higher pitch of magnificence and refinement but remained essentially similar to that at the beginning of this neo-palatial age. So far as architecture is concerned, the forms were those already employed in the proto-palatial phase; the new palaces retained their original form, essentially, throughout the period: the few drastic changes that were made in them, and the new buildings at hitherto unused sites, employ methods of structure and decoration scarcely distinguishable from those of Middle Minoan III, except for a more sparing use of wood and an increase in the size of frescoes. A strictly chronological treatment has therefore ceased to be necessary; only the few buildings subsequent to the catastrophe, of Late Minoan III, need be segregated, and these are mentioned at the end of the chapter.

In Middle Minoan III the standards of building were generally higher than before. An entire wall was now sometimes composed of well-shaped blocks. The door-jambs were wooden, but stood on bases of gypsum, obtained from local quarries; in Late Minoan I the whole jamb might consist of gypsum. The softness of this stone, which enabled it to be cut with a bronze saw, accounts for its popularity; being merely plaster of Paris in a natural form, it has the drawback that it dissolves on prolonged contact with water. Consequently a flooring of gypsum slabs was often used indoors; most of the floors constantly exposed to rain consist of limestone slabs. The better rooms were lined with a dado of gypsum slabs, placed either flush or alternately forward and recessed a trifle. The column-bases too were more often made at these periods of gypsum or limestone than of harder stones. They are lower in proportion, but from representations in frescoes it appears that the bottom of the wooden shaft was sometimes painted to simulate the colouring of the old-fashioned tall bases of breccia or other ornamental rock. Occasionally column-bases were cut into two square steps below the round pedestal on which the shaft rested, and sometimes the shaft was set directly into a hole in the pavement. Although shafts were occasionally composed of several pieces of wood (and half-columns of stuccoed limestone have also come to light), the normal procedure was to use a single tree-trunk, rounded and plastered, and more often than not with the original tapering preserved. The frescoes and other representations [20] suggest that most columns tapered downwards as the result of the tree-trunk being stood upside down. The columns attracted attention. The motive of downward tapering was presumably to gain a trifle more floor-space; only in rare conditions can there have been reason to set the trunk on its head as a precaution against its sprouting new shoots, while the angle of taper would not have sufficed to shed rain-drops off the shaft and so prevent them from running down it and rotting the bottom. That sort of explanation is weakened too by the fact that a few columns are represented[2] as tapering upwards or as having straight shafts.

Possibly the normal procedure may have been to leave the shaft smooth, but when the buildings were destroyed, some columns fell into a mass of clay which has retained impressions of fluting. In accordance with Egyptian

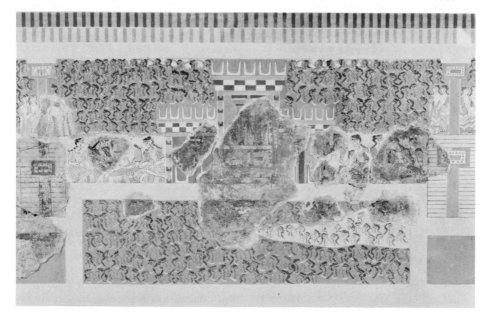

20. Minoan miniature fresco of shrine, etc., restored from fragments, c. 1600. *Heraklion Museum*

used in some rooms that were 6–10 feet high must have had shafts only about five times as tall as their lower diameter, and as a rule the height of a shaft must have been so little in proportion to its girth that the tapering can scarcely have precedent, the flutes in Crete took two forms, concave (as in the Doric of a thousand years later) and convex, or in other words corrugated and cannellated. Examples of each type apparently bore twenty-eight flutes, running perpendicularly up and down the shaft. Occasionally the fluting may have twined around in a spiral, but this method of decoration is preserved only in Minoan small objects and on Mycenean half-columns of stone.[3] It was too sophisticated for everyday building. Straight fluting, on the contrary, must have resulted involuntarily from the process of trimming the log (p. 126).

On the evidence of frescoes [20], the usual type of capital for a column of downward taper involved a low cushion, separated by mouldings both from the shaft below and from the square abacus above. A black capital crowns a red shaft, a red capital a black shaft; the mouldings are white or yellow. Columns or pillars of upward taper carry an oblong block as a capital; the block over a red shaft has a blue centre and edge and an intervening stretch of yellow decorated with alternate red disks and black spots.

The wall surface too is shown covered with rows of gaily coloured disks, stripes, and denticulations, and a woman appears standing behind the bars of a large window or balcony. Windows, doors, and sometimes fanlights over the doors were formed by the timber framework of the walls; there are instances of a coping-block of limestone having been laid over the sill of a window to preserve the wood. Cornices seem to have risen in overlapping strips and to have carried a pseudo-battlemented coping made up of a row of the U-shaped 'horns of consecration', probably in clay.

The fresco decoration is of two kinds. In one, which is characteristic of Middle Minoan III, the medium dried instantaneously, enforcing hasty work and on a miniature scale [20]; its vogue seems to have been brief, and with reason, because the vitality of the figures – the scenes involved a considerable number of human figures – does not compensate for their crudity.[4] Most paintings in the other technique appear to be somewhat late, and the large compositions of Middle Minoan III were generally in relief, modelled in plaster and coloured. Some of these included human figures of life-size or more, and at the northern entrance of

Cnossus a colossal bull was represented charging human figures against a background of trees and rocks. Among the earliest frescoed ornament of Middle Minoan III are pieces of imitation marbling and of an elaborate spiral pattern; to its latest stage belongs a picture of blue dolphins swimming amid fish of all colours. At Middle Minoan III the field for wall-painting was broken into panels by exposing the timber frame, which presumably had an aesthetic appeal. That may explain why the practice of timbering persisted after the introduction of good masonry, whereby it lost all structural advantage except for defence against earthquakes. In Late Minoan I, however, builders commonly dispensed with vertical ties and reduced the thickness of the horizontal beams, which alone would have been almost equally serviceable in earthquakes; it then became customary to plaster the entire surface of the wall, and paint continuous friezes round the room. Frescoes of Late Minoan Ia rarely introduce human figures; typical subjects are partridges and hoopoes, a cat stalking a bird, monkeys, a leaping deer, all in a setting of rocks, plants, and flowers [26]. It must soon, however, have been realized that the work in painted relief could not compete with the easier technique of pure fresco; in Late Minoan Ib, processions of human figures are represented life-size in paint alone.

A ceiling of Late Minoan Ia has been found, moulded and painted like a wall-relief [21]. The pattern consists of linked spirals in white on a blue ground, with red and yellow rosettes outlined in black on the centres of the spirals and at intervals imposed on blue escutcheons. Another such Minoan ceiling in plaster may have inspired the stone ceiling inside a Mycenean tomb at Orchomenus which is carved with a more elaborate but related design [61], such as appears at that time on Egyptian painted ceilings – probably also through Minoan influence.

A pattern of two half-rosettes separated by an upright band [22],[5] which first occurs in Middle Minoan III, was used repetitively in architecture to form the ornament of painted or carved

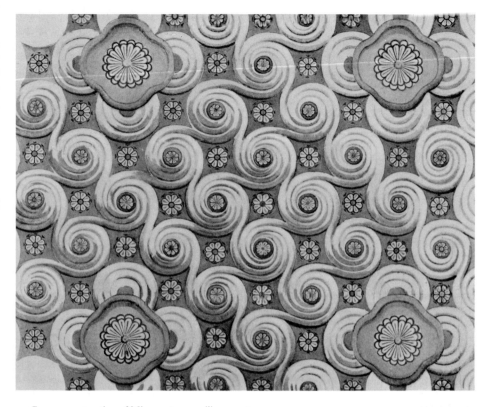

21. Cnossus, restoration of Minoan stucco ceiling, *c.* 1500

strips along the walls, often as a dado near the base. The miniature fresco which presumably represents a shrine [20] shows a single large example covering the central mass of the façade.

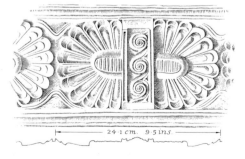

22. Carved band from Cnossus. *Heraklion Museum*

The pattern, which also appears as a decorative element on pottery, remained so long in favour that it was transmitted to Mycenean architecture [68]. And the division, in some instances only, of the central band into three upright strips has even inspired a theory which regards the pattern as a forerunner of the Doric frieze of triglyphs and metopes. A simpler form of decoration found in the country house at Pyrgos (below, Note 8), with long flat rectangular panels recessed between upright rectangles with vertical grooving, seems even closer to the triglyph and metope pattern. Direct influence is unlikely; but the possibility will be considered (below, p. 125) that the pattern was transmitted indirectly through the Dark Ages, probably outside Greece.

The remainder of this chapter is occupied by descriptions of individual buildings, or rather of their more important recognizable features. No brief account can deal adequately with the horrifying complexity of what remains, and it is in fact impossible to write a complete description of any Minoan palace because of the destruction of their upper storeys.

Greek legends, it appears, refer to the palace at Cnossus as the Labyrinth which, they say, was built by Daedalus for King Minos, and no term could be more apt. The complexity resulted partly from the use of flat roofs, which enable a building to straggle horizontally and vertically, partly from alterations during six centuries of continuous habitation, including repairs after earthquakes at the close of Middle Minoan II, IIIa, and IIIb. In the process of change the palaces did not expand laterally to any appreciable extent, but perhaps they gradually became taller in accordance with the need for more accommodation and of a better quality; the building of an extra storey would have involved putting more support below, and this may have been effected as a rule by partitioning the earlier rooms with additional cross-walls. But in parts where the palace was originally tall, frequent cross-walls may have been thought essential from the first.

The intricacy of the ground-plan must be due largely to this structural necessity and did not correspond in all parts with the arrangement above; in some instances a single upper room extended over the area of several below, though elsewhere the same plan was repeated almost unchanged in spite of its awkward turns and corners – perhaps in order to carry yet another storey. The Minoans obviously saw no advantage in symmetry at all costs, but this is not to say that symmetry is entirely lacking from their designs; it is, for some reason, much more noticeable at Phaestus than at Cnossus. But the planning was very largely dictated by an obligation to segregate groups or suites of rooms; bearing that principle in mind, the apparent confusion is generally seen to be logical and due to meticulous ingenuity. Certain features are

characteristic. The love of the unexpected: splendid staircases (as at Phaestus) lead to apparently blank walls, with small openings, perhaps to the side, into shaded passages. The contrast between shaded and illuminated areas, roofed room and light-well, with only screens of columns or piers separating them. Windows, both to the court and exterior, deliberately arranged to give views towards the mountains, the spectacular scenery of Crete. All these seem essentially different to the architecture of classical Greece (though it might be remarked that some – particularly the alternation between lit and shaded interiors – are revived in the palatial and wealthy domestic architecture of Imperial Rome). Actually a contemporary Egyptian house was planned in the same way, with bent corridors, small rooms opening out of each other or forming boxes one within the other, and a few larger apartments; these contained columns to support either the ceiling or a lantern with clerestory sides. Only one element in this system, the arrangement of intercommunicating small rooms, occurs in Early Minoan buildings; for the remainder we cannot tell whether any practice adopted in Crete had evolved there independently or was introduced from Egypt. The use of some at least of these elements must go back to Middle Minoan II, if not to Middle Minoan I, but they do not appear clearly till Middle Minoan III, if only because the ruins of that period are better preserved. By that time the Mesopotamian influence which had so much effect in Middle Minoan I and II is no longer perceptible as an active force; perhaps Egypt had taken the place of Asia in supplying ideas to Crete.

The Palace at Cnossus in its Final Form

The main approach to the palace was from the south, by a paved road, which crossed the ravine outside the palace over a massive viaduct, pierced to allow the passage of water; the sides of the culverts rise perpendicularly till near the top, and are then corbelled inwards at a slant till the gap became narrow enough to be covered by slabs or boards. This viaduct is of Middle Minoan origin, but was reconstructed in Late Minoan Ia, when a stepped portico seems to have led from the termination up to the south-west corner of the palace [23]. A visitor who continued straight ahead along the exterior of the west wall would have passed around the back of a tall projection and found on reaching its open front on the north side that this was the west porch (already described as an example of Middle Minoan II design, though rebuilt at the end of Middle Minoan III). Here a raised path, a typical Minoan feature, branches off west-wards across the paved court to the retaining wall which bounded the palace enclosure, and descended the slope on a ramp – part of the original layout of Middle Minoan I. Another raised path runs northwards along the exterior of the magazines beside the buried face of the original outer wall. The wall built a few yards east of its course dates from the latter part of Middle Minoan I, though the magazines behind it were replanned in Middle Minoan II; it runs in jags, each diversified by the recessing typical of the period. The north-west corner is broken by very bold jags, and in the first of these a stair ascended to an entrance on top of the maga-zines. The path drops northward by means of steps to the lip of the theatral area, where it meets another paved road (the so-called Royal Road) that comes in from the west. A corridor led southward from the west porch and then turned and ran across the south of the palace, behind a portico with masonry pillars along the façade. The middle of the south-west quarter was occupied by a stately approach to the upper floor. Off the north side of the corridor opened a propylaeum, which was built early in Middle Minoan III and rebuilt on a slightly different plan at the end of that period. In the first design [24a] the side walls projected southwards into the corridor, forming an anteroom 48 feet wide in front of a line of five double doors, of which the central doorway was wider than the others. Two columns stood 3 feet within, a foot farther apart from each other ($14\frac{3}{4}$ feet; 4·50 m.) than from the walls; if the spacing had been equal

they would have projected very little to the side of the central door-posts, but as it was, they partially obstructed each of the intermediate doorways. At a distance of 16 feet behind the columns spurs of wall ran out 16 feet from either side, leaving a gap equal to the space between the columns, and 11 feet farther back two more columns were placed opposite the first pair, marking the end of this propylaeum. The area comprised between the four columns was prob-ably treated in a different manner from the rest of the room; perhaps its ceiling stood higher in order that light might be admitted through clerestory openings in the sides.

The south propylaeum as rebuilt at the end of Middle Minoan III [24b] was given similar proportions through being made narrower by 11 feet (3·3 m.) as well as shortened owing to the replacement of the integrated anteroom by a light-well. The outer doorways were blocked, the width of the intermediate doorways reduced, and new columns placed straight behind them. Otherwise the arrangement remained much as before. A frieze of men carry-ing cups, etc., was painted on the west wall. Beyond the far end rose a wide staircase of a dozen steps to a landing and vestibule on the floor above. The excavator has reconstructed this upper south propylaeum with flanking colonnades, the evidence for which is weak; in fact almost every detail above ground level is conjectural.[6]

The exceptional grandeur of this approach matched spacious planning and ornate treat-ment on the floor to which it led, in the block between the central and the western courts. Only a few of the densely crowded underlying walls are likely to have continued above. Some unquestionably did not; wherever these expand to form a pier it surely passed through the upper storey as a free-standing pillar of the type occasionally used at ground level [29, 38, 45]. Since also any part of a wall could bear a column, the weight of the roof might be spread over very large rooms.

A corridor at the side of the south pro-pylaeum led northwards past the magazines,

23. Cnossus, palace, restored plan

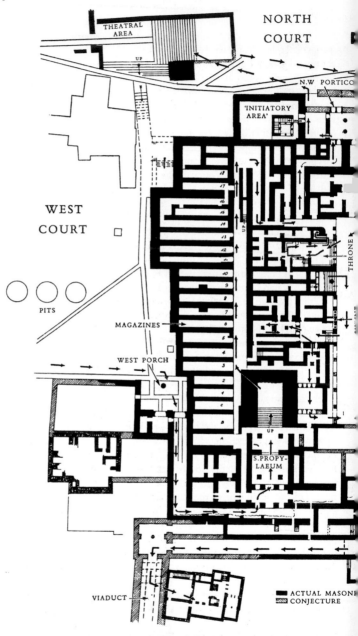

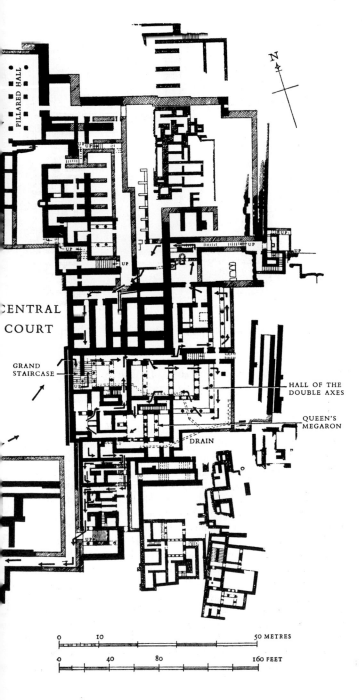

PILLARED HALL

N

CENTRAL
COURT

GRAND
STAIRCASE

HALL OF THE
DOUBLE AXES

QUEEN'S
MEGARON

DRAIN

UP

0   10   50 METRES

0   40   80   160 FEET

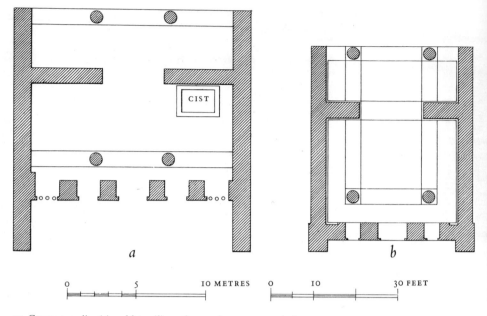

CIST

a

b

0   5   10 METRES   0   10   30 FEET

24. Cnossus, earlier (*a*) and later (*b*) south propylaeum, restored plans

and continued, with two abrupt turns, to the central court, or else, with further turns, to the north-western salient of the palace. There had been an entrance here in Middle Minoan III, but it was abandoned in Late Minoan I. Beside this north-west portico lay an open space, called the initiatory area because it contains a 'lustral basin', of Middle Minoan II. The basin itself is a square tank, sunk in the ground, and is approached by a stair which descends along two sides; a balustrade with columns stood on the intervening parapet, and continued on the other sides at ground level. Consequently the columns must have been of diverse height. Several such basins, all apparently of Middle Minoan date, existed in the palace; their original floors consisted of gypsum slabs, which would have dissolved if water had been allowed to stand upon them, but some were afterwards lined with cement and converted to water storage. For lack of any better explanation, the original use is assumed to have been religious, in connexion with some ritual of anointing, but there would have been no drawback to using the basin as a shower-bath provided the water were mopped up quickly.[7]

Outside this part of the palace lies the north court, which extends westwards to the theatral area. On the other side a porch opened westward in the side of a long salient, the greater part of which constituted a pillared hall. It was actually divided internally by two rows of supports, all in the form of square pillars, except for a pair of columns at the north end. This hall was built in Middle Minoan III outside the old north entrance, which had previously sloped as a broad passage down to a narrower opening on to the central court, but was then contracted uniformly to that width. The sides of the passage then consisted of walls upon which stood colonnades, accessible from the upper floor of the pillared hall. The back wall inside each of the colonnades, above the old wall, was lined with a huge relief in painted stucco (that

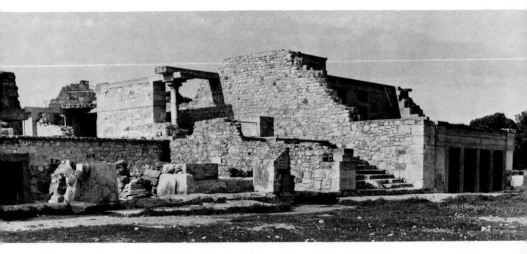

25. Cnossus, reconstructed throne room (to right of staircase) from court, *c.* 1600, altered late fifteenth century

on the west including the group with a charging bull).

The central court had been slightly reduced in area by setting forward the surrounding buildings during Middle Minoan III. In the north-west corner were entrances to a jumble of small rooms and to the corridor which eventually led past the magazines. The whole northeast quarter was also given up to storage and craftsmen's activities, at any rate on the ground floor; the planning looks quite haphazard, involving but-and-ben means of communication even more often than elsewhere.

Only one ground-floor suite of reasonable plan existed on the west side of the court; it contains the throne room [25, 26]. An anteroom was entered from the court by a line of four double doors and led to a small room lined with

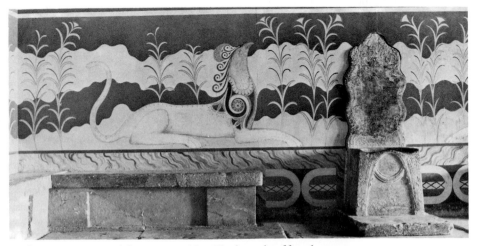

26. Cnossus, reconstructed throne room with griffin fresco, late fifteenth century

benches among which stood a tall chair of gypsum. The walls were frescoed with a great frieze of griffins (now restored on the insufficient evidence of fragments) and a blotch pattern above. A recess opposite the throne is occupied by a sunken 'lustral basin', entered by steps at the side, and closed off by a parapet which carried a column; the roof probably ran up higher than that of the throne-room, forming a lantern. This should date from Middle Minoan III, by analogy. The throne-room suite, however, was redecorated, if not partly rebuilt, in Late Minoan II.

A tiny shrine stood a few yards to the south; the façade on the court comprised pairs of columns on either side of a block of masonry which supported a central column. A building of similar tripartite design is represented on a fresco of Middle Minoan III [20] and probably the decorative treatment was much the same. This is a regular form for the Minoan shrine; an entire building, identifiable as a shrine by the presence of 'horns of consecration', in the central court of a small palace or large house at Vathypetro, consisted of a central room and two shorter side rooms. A similar shrine is depicted on a rhyton from Zakro. The other rooms along the west side of the court must be regarded as substructures for the more spacious apartments on the upper floor. The same may apply at the south end of the court, where the ruins are too scanty for plausible interpretation.

The south-east quarter was suited to domestic occupation. Its buildings, which date as a whole from Middle Minoan III, stood in a deep cutting made in the original slope during Middle Minoan II. Their third floor came slightly below the level of the central court, and some parts rose at least one floor higher. Midway along the east side of the court an oblong space was occupied by a grand staircase, lit by windows at various levels, some opening on to an adjoining light-well. The stairs mounted from landing to landing in alternate east and west flights of wide shallow treads, divided by a parapet which rose in a series of taller steps,

each with a column on the end to support the flight above [27].[8] Superimposed corridors ran eastward from three of the landings, passing the north side of the light-well, and communicating with the two or more floors of, first, an open-fronted 'Hall of the Colonnades' on its far side, and then of the suite beyond, called the Hall of the Double Axes (from the sacred mark of a two-bladed axe carved repeatedly on the walls). This suite [28] was probably the finest on the entire ground floor of the palace. It was apparently duplicated above. It was open at both ends; two columns separated it from a light-well at the west, and a colonnade bordered another light-area at the east end and its extension along the adjoining part of the south side. Behind this colonnade there was no solid wall within but only a series of wooden piers fitted with double doors on either side of the corner pillar. The hall itself could be divided into two rooms by a line of four double doors. With all doors open, the entire apartment must have been admirably adapted to hot weather, and when they were closed the eastern half ought to have been tolerable in winter with braziers to warm it. The twin rooms measure 18 by 26 feet internally (5·5 by 8 m.). The walls were sheathed with a dado of gypsum slabs beneath a frescoed strip; its pattern of running spirals is repeated in a fresco of the 'Hall of the Colonnades', where, however, great shields, dappled in the manner of ox-skin, are painted as though fastened to the strip.[9]

A corridor, which turned twice at right angles to avoid an intervening small staircase, led from the Hall of the Double Axes to another suite on the south, the 'Queen's Megaron'. The name is totally unjustifiable. There is, in fact, no indication that these were specifically women's quarters; they were little more secluded than the others. The notion of associating them with a queen occurred to the excavator, who distinguished here and elsewhere (especially the throne room) between low seats, which he regarded as designed for women, and higher seats for the men: low wooden seats were provided along the central pillared stylobate of

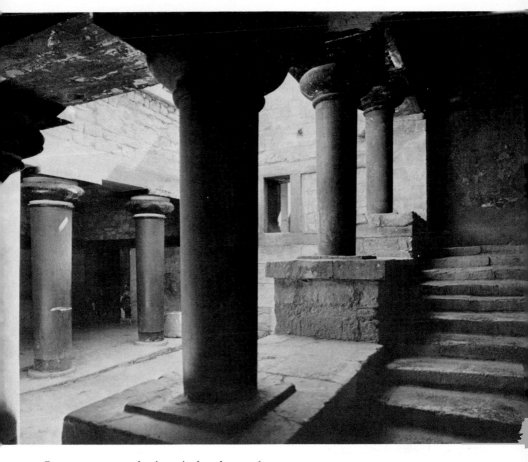

27. Cnossus, reconstructed staircase in the palace, c. 1600

this room. More importantly, these apartments have scarcely anything in common with the Mycenean type of great hall to which the term megaron should strictly be confined, still less with its prototypes in the Second City of Troy. The living-room here measures only 14 by 20 feet (4·3 by 6·1 m.), which alone makes the comparison ridiculous. But a specious similarity to Mycenean porches has been seen in the arrangements at the east [29]. The main room had a semi-open front here, consisting of a doorway and a space crossed by a stylobate-bench out of which rose two piers; beyond lay a five-foot anteroom with two columns separating it from a light-well. One might suppose the purpose of the anteroom to have been to interpose a gap between the bench and the light-well, from which some rain would occasionally have splashed past the columns even if a lantern covered its top. But another bench which ran along the south side of the main room actually formed the division between it and a second light-well. The west side also was largely open, with a window and doorway to a bathroom,

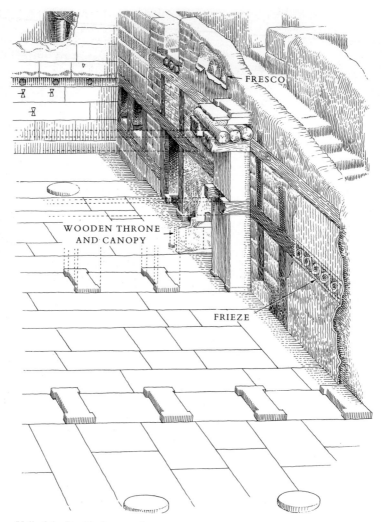

28. Cnossus, Hall of the Double Axes, c. 1600

which contains a terracotta tub of Late Minoan II, and another doorway into a corridor. Through this, after turning several corners as usual, a latrine could be reached; there are fittings for a wooden seat. The pit beneath discharged into one of the palace drains, so that this may be termed a water-closet, but the water supply in summer is unlikely to have provided adequate flushing. The provision of bathrooms and latrine-seats may be due to Minoan contacts either with Egypt, where they are found in every respectable house at the best-known period (which, however, is two hundred years later), or with Western Asia; already the Mesopotamian drainage systems were even more advanced.

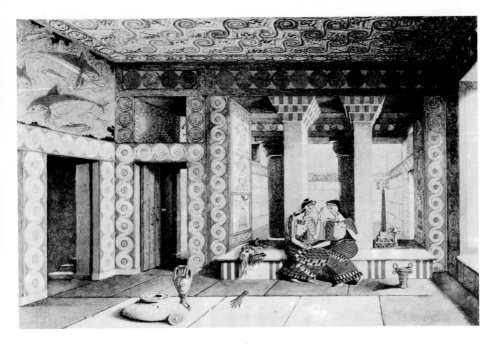

29. Cnossus, 'Queen's Megaron', *c.* 1500, reconstruction

The Final Palace at Phaestus

An almost complete rebuilding was begun after an earthquake in Middle Minoan III; the remains of the first palace were mainly cleared away or levelled to allow its successor to take a different plan [30]. A fine entrance was made from the west court, parallel with the steps of the theatral area (which were remodelled at the same time). The passage (67) began with a great staircase [31] and continued, maintaining a width of some 45 feet, through a propylaeum (68), at the front of which was one central column between short spurs of wall. Two doorways opened through a cross-wall close behind, and three columns stood at the back on the edge of a light-well (69). This projects into a peristyle court but at a lower level. The court could be reached only by devious routes. A passage on the north led up a few steps to the west, and then bent around north and east to arrive at a corner of the court. Or one could go through the lightwell and turn north up a narrow stair into a wider passage, which ended with a thick central column on the south side of the peristyle. Each side of the peristyle was composed of four slimmer columns (counting those at the corners in each case); they stood along the edges of an open court, 27 feet square, and supported verandas of different widths on every side of it – 5 and 6 feet on the west and east, 9 feet on the south, while the north wall was placed 15 feet from the colonnade, and in between ran a line of six double doors. But for this feature and the lack of symmetry the plan might have been copied from some Egyptian building. Particularly interesting is the close parallel with the main feature of Hellenic houses more than a thousand years later, a court to which the term peristyle, i.e. 'columned around', was then applied.

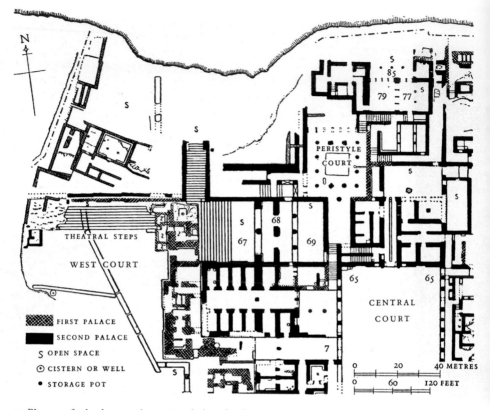

30. Phaestus, final palace, c. 1600, restored plan of main part

A staircase that encroached upon the northeast corner of the peristyle court descended, after a right-angled turn, between two suites reminiscent of the domestic quarter at Cnossus. The larger suite to the north was, in fact, like a smaller, simpler version of the Hall of the Double Axes. The inner room (79), which is nearly square (18 by 21 feet), was separated only by lines of four double doors from a colonnade on the north (85) and from the shallower anteroom on the east (77), which led past two columns into a light-well on the east, while two double doors on the north gave on the colonnade. A bathroom and latrine were provided west of the inner room. The smaller suite on the south side of the staircase was also trebly divided, but by means of two pairs of columns,

into inner room, anteroom, and light-well. Only one other feature in the palace need be mentioned, the new façade of the central court. On the east side it consisted of a portico (65) with alternate square pillars of masonry and columns on smaller bases. The arrangement on the west side may have been similar in parts; at one place a column served instead of a pillar, at the entrance hall to some magazines, in order perhaps to match other columns behind it which divided the hall longitudinally. The north façade was emphatically symmetrical, with a corridor opening at the centre, and, to each side of it, a half-column and then a recessed doorway [32], though it should be noted that the symmetry is restricted to the façade, not the rooms, corridors, and staircases that lay behind it; so it

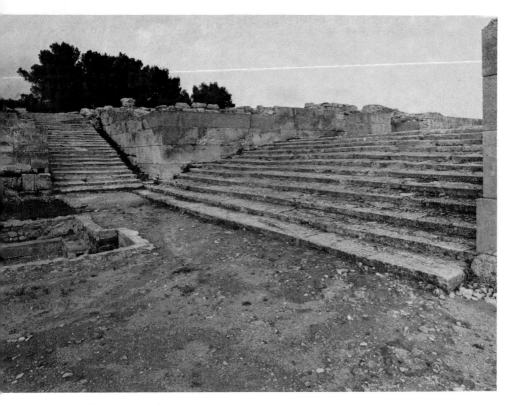

31. Phaestus, final palace, *c.* 1600, entrance

is symmetry imposed for appearance on a structure which is still basically asymmetrical. Graham's very plausible restoration[10] [33] in an earlier version is accompanied by dimensions in terms of a hypothetical 'Minoan foot', a module he has found to obtain in the central court and main rooms at Phaestus and other palaces with only a negligible margin of error; its calculated length of 30·36 cm. would make it almost identical with the English standard foot, but is, of course, unlikely to have agreed precisely with every Minoan mason's rule.

Hagia Triada

This minor palace or large 'villa', a mile and a half from Phaestus, stood on a hill-side. The ground did not suit the usual method of building around a central court, and as a compromise an L-shaped plan was adopted, the court occupying the re-entrant [34]. The longer portion stretches across the slope; the wing projects uphill but it is very thin and composed of small, poor rooms, with floors only of beaten earth, so that it may be regarded as a mere annex. On closer inspection the plan of the main rectangle is seen to divide into semi-independent blocks of fairly compact arrangement, in which the partition walls run with as much regularity as was compatible with the Minoan temperament. The domestic quarter at the junction with the wing repeats the normal scheme; the large room (20 feet wide) had two solid walls and communicated by lines of double doors on the east with an anteroom, which leads to a light-well, and on the north with a portico that contained a little square court.

The Palace at Mallia

Practically none of the original Middle Minoan I structure remains, and in general the palace [35] seems a work of Middle Minoan III. As at Phaestus, the façade of the central court had no uniform design. A portico with alternate columns and square pillars occupied the centre of its east side. Along the north end stretched a colonnade 10 feet deep; between the columns lie blocks bearing emplacements for some kind of barrier which apparently blocked every inter-

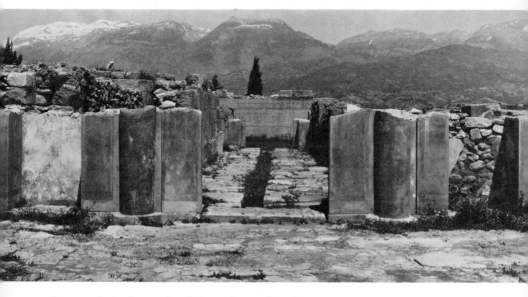

32. Phaestus, final palace, north end of central court, fifteenth century

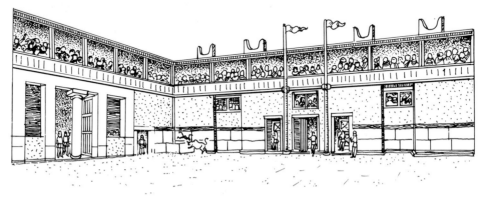

33. Phaestus, final palace, north end of central court, fifteenth century, new restoration by Giuliana Bianco for J. W. Graham

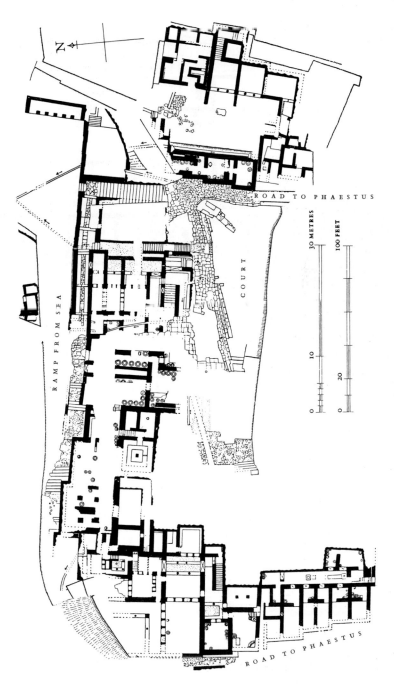

ROAD TO PHAESTUS

COURT

RAMP FROM SEA

ROAD TO PHAESTUS

30 METRES

100 FEET

34. Hagia Triada, 'villa', plan

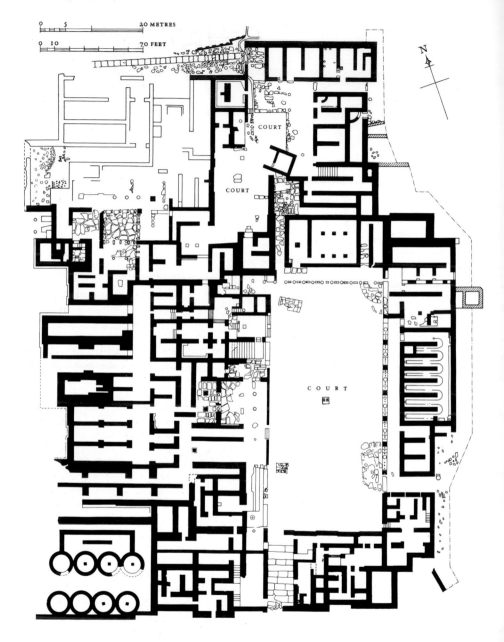

35. Mallia, palace, *c*. 1600, plan of main part

columniation except one where a door was fitted. At the back of this colonnade lay an isolated couple of rooms planned in a strangely primitive fashion. The entrance doorway, at the western extremity of the colonnade, occupied most of the extremely short end of a long anteroom, and immediately on the right another doorway led into the very corner of a practically square hall (30 by 31 feet; 9·10 by 9·45 m.). Two rows of three pillars, carelessly shaped and irregularly spaced, divided the hall into sections of unequal width, the central being the largest – a plan that might have been imitated from a common Egyptian scheme. But the avoidance of symmetry, and the siting of a door off the axis of a room, are characteristically Minoan. None of the other rooms at Mallia approaches this one in size. They compose suites extremely complex in their arrangement of rooms that differ so much in size as to suggest that the use of each had been predetermined and could scarcely be changed thereafter without inconvenience or waste of space. Again, though, the purpose of a jigsaw layout must have been largely to enable an upper storey to contain huge rooms, particularly over the magazines beside the west edge of the palace; every sudden thickening in their party-walls marks, no doubt, the position of a masonry pillar above (cf. p. 47).

The 'Little Palace' at Cnossus

The site of this town-house or 'villa', a couple of hundred yards west of the theatral area, sloped towards the south, where a terrace of basement rooms containing pillars was built to bring the whole area to a more or less uniform level. Most of the ground floor so formed [36] was occupied by small rooms, but there was a remarkable suite of rooms leading one into the other along the eastern (right) edge. They are so badly eroded that the plan cannot be wholly restored, except at the north-east corner. Here a room, with a latrine off its west side, opened through four double doors on another room southwards, and that by similar means on a peristyle court, south of which there were ap-

parently several more rooms on the same axis. Three columns composed the inner side of the peristyle, and probably there were three, more widely spaced, on its north and south sides. A colonnade started at the north-east corner of the building and ran along the exterior of at least the first two rooms, from which it was separated only by double doors; probably it continued along the entire suite. The width of the colonnade was 5 feet, of the rooms 20 feet. Ashlar masonry was used, but of gypsum, a stone easily cut. A bridge led to a much smaller annexe, which is still called 'The Unexplored Mansion' although it has now been excavated. Largely of Late Minoan Ia, it was not completed till Late Minoan II.[11]

The 'Royal Villa' at Cnossus

This building near the palace probably dates from an advanced stage of Late Minoan Ia. Though by no means symmetrical, it is exceptionally regular in plan, mainly perhaps because of its small scale; the masonry is ashlar, of gypsum. It was built on a hill-side in a cutting, so that on the west the upper floor must have stood approximately at ground level. The arrangements on the two floors seem to have been very similar [37]. Across the centre, from side to side, ran a suite comprising an outer and an inner room, divided by a row of three double doors, with a light-well on either side behind a pair of columns. The inner room is the larger, but measures only 13 by 14 feet (4 by 4·5 m.). The wings of the building differ somewhat in extent and shape. Each contained a staircase; in addition, the south wing held four or five small rooms, while the remainder of the north wing on the ground floor was occupied by a single room roughly 13 feet square (4 by 4·15 m.). A massive square pillar stood in the centre of this room [38]. Gypsum slabs both lined the walls and paved the floor. A gutter ran in a square, half-way between the pillar and the walls, and incorporated a drainage cist on either side. The walls of this pillar crypt are preserved to a sufficient height to retain sockets for the ceiling timber.

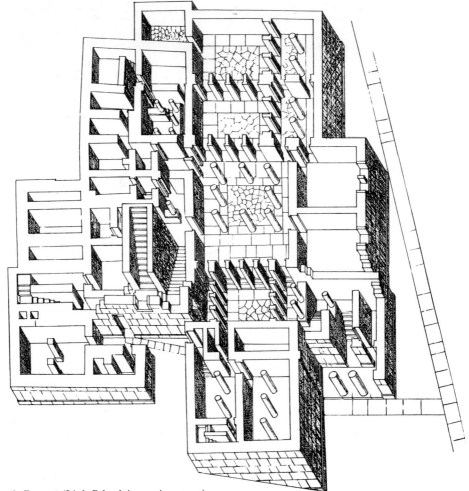

36. Cnossus, 'Little Palace', isometric restoration

The central beam apparently consisted of a split tree-trunk, and the two semicircular holes for its reception suggest that it tapered as much as a foot from side to side of the room (from $2\frac{1}{2}$ to $1\frac{1}{2}$ feet; 80 to 50 cm.). Thin logs, round in section, were placed across it as rafters.

'Villas' at Sklavokambos and Tylissus

A large 'villa' at Sklavokambos, built and destroyed during the sixteenth century, has a most confused ground plan (but the upper floor may have been divided less strangely); it is remarkable for the extensive use of masonry pillars. A stretch of the north façade adjoining

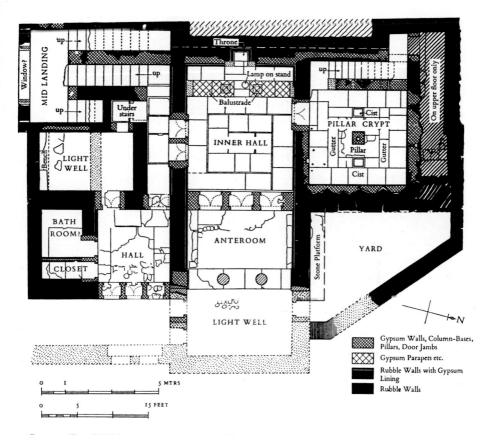

37. Cnossus, 'Royal Villa', *c.* 1500, plan of ground floor

the west wall was left open as a veranda for a distance of 26 feet, with three pillars standing along the frontage. A curious feature is that at the centre of the largest room three pillars are set to form a square with the corner of an encroaching room. The space so enclosed, 7 feet square, might have been a court, but no drain was provided; moreover Sklavokambos is a very cold place, situated high on the side of Mount Ida, so that an unroofed aperture of such dimensions would have made the room intolerable for most of the year. Scarcely any light, however, could have been obtained from a window, since the room touches the outside wall

only at one corner, which is 40 feet away from the opposite corner. Surely, therefore, there must have been a light-well covered by a lantern with clerestory sides.

A group of large buildings at Tylissus, dating roughly from Late Minoan I, illustrates even better the late tendency towards orderly planning. The exterior of the south-western house forms a rectangle, an extremely rare occurrence in Minoan building, and the internal divisions were also comparatively regular; it is, in fact, a reconstruction of Late Minoan III. In conformity, however, with ancient Cretan tradition, many of the rooms were entered on

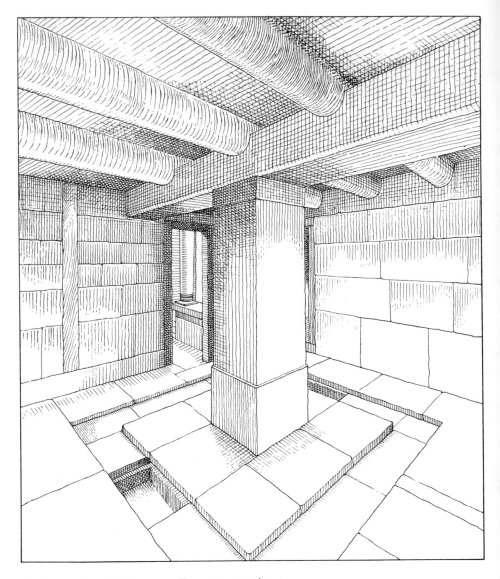

38. Cnossus, 'Royal Villa', c. 1500, pillar crypt, restoration

the but-and-ben system, and none of the doorways came at the centre of a wall. The south-
eastern house [39] is connected northwards with
a smaller building which was mainly, if not

wholly, devoted to storage. The house itself is
most excellently built, with very high quality
ashlar work. A large number of its windows are
preserved. In these two buildings, masonry

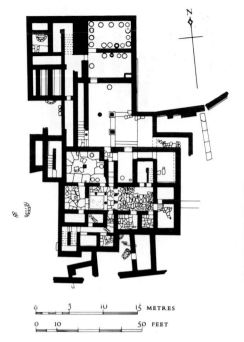

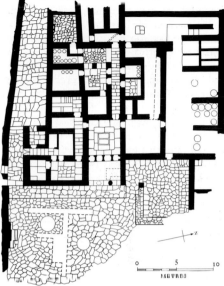

40. Nirou, Minoan villa, plan

39. Tylissus, Minoan house, *c.* 1550–1450, plan

pillars stood inside several of the rooms, as well as beside courts or light-wells where their weather-resistant character made them preferable to wooden columns. The first excavator's plan was found imperfect on subsequent investigation, especially where the original structures had undergone alterations; a revised plan is displayed in the museum at Iraklion.

Nirou

Another fine house, with features derived from the palaces, is at Nirou Khani [40]. A porch with two columns leads through a set of doorways separated by three piers with a hall, from which doors lead into three separate parts of the house. That to the north contained storerooms; that to the south has been interpreted as the private quarters of the owner; the central part, imposing rooms decorated with frescoes, may have been for more public use.

Towns

The remains of several Cretan towns have been excavated, wholly or in part, though of course none are in the same marvellous state of preservation as the town at Akrotiri on Thera, buried intact by the erupting volcano. Generally, they are adjacent to the palaces, whose functioning has to be interpreted in relation to the settlement round them: an apparent exception is Palaikastro, where no palace has been found, though this is not to say that one did not exist.

At Mallia the houses line streets leading to the palace. Particularly important here is the large open square, 100 by 160 feet (29·10 by 39·80 m.), close to the north-west corner of the palace, which has been identified as a market place or agora; storerooms line its southern side. The square was laid out in the proto-palatial period. The recently excavated area to the west, towards the sea, includes workshops.

Two small towns of Late Minoan I, at Gournia and Pseira, have been completely excavated, and a considerable part of a larger town at Palaikastro has also been cleared. (There are remains at Gournia of a Middle Minoan town, too.) Most of the streets are only a few feet wide, and very winding; in steep places they become staircases. Clearly no wheeled traffic was anticipated. The ground floor of the house seems to have frequently consisted merely of storage places except for one living room entered through a light-well; usually there was an upper floor also. In a two-storey house at Palaikastro the intervening floor was made of pebbling and plaster on a base of clay and wattle. In the poorer houses the plans are extremely irregular, with walls at any angle, and even quite large houses show little or no regard for appearances in this or other respects; the most confused parts of any palace appear straightforward in comparison. The nucleus around which Gournia had formed seems a provincial imitation of a palace on a diminutive scale; a few steps rising above part of the court provided a theatral area.

Another small town (or rather village) at Pyrgos on the south coast of Crete has a long history, from Early to Late Minoan. In the neo-palatial period a particularly fine country house was built at the top of the hill on which the village was situated [41]. The whole arrangement recalls, on a much smaller scale, that of palace to town; but it must be remembered that the village already had a long history before the country house was built.

Tombs

An interesting series of built tombs has been discovered at the cemetery of Arkhanes, extending from the pre-palatial period into Late Minoan. They vary considerably in form, though most are rectangular, subdivided into small rooms with the irregularity of planning and arrangement that characterizes Minoan architecture. They do, however, include cir-

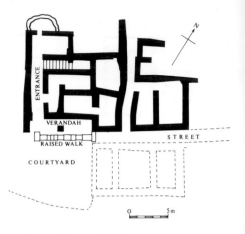

41. Pyrgos, Minoan villa, plan

cular elements (tholoi) either contained within the rectangular structure or free-standing. One smaller tomb, rectangular outside, has an apsidal chamber within [42]. Otherwise the general practice was to make rock-cut chambers of no architectural interest. But two great tombs of masonry are worth describing; both date approximately from Late Minoan I. The 'Temple Tomb' at Cnossus was only partly subterranean [43]. A court, of crazy paving, was bordered on one side by an open-fronted pavilion, while on the other [44] a pylon led into the first of a chain of rooms opening one into the other. An additional room on top, probably intended for a chapel, was divided longitudinally by two columns; they were supported by pillars underneath [45]. The burial chamber [46], at the far end, is rock-cut but panelled with socketed slabs of gypsum. The whole scheme was obviously adapted from a Minoan residential plan – compare the eastern suite of the 'Little Palace' [36] – but the idea of such a tomb may have been inspired by Egypt. The masonry too seems to imitate Egyptian: the blocks are exceptionally large for Minoan work.

The 'Royal Tomb' at Isopata was sunk more

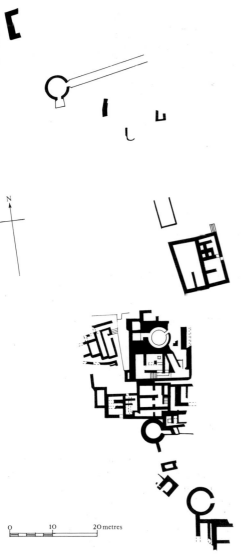

feet wide. The upper parts of the side-walls were probably corbelled inwards at a slant till they either met or approached so near that the gap could be spanned by slabs laid flat. The doorways at either side of the anteroom and several niches in the walls were certainly closed above by one or other of those methods. Chambertombs, with similar roofs which are still complete, were built in the fourteenth and thirteenth centuries at Ras Shamra on the Syrian coast, where the type is quite likely to have been introduced from Crete; great quantities of imports, ranging from Middle Minoan to Mycenean, prove that Aegean traders went there regularly.

The Decline: Late Minoan III

Apparently Cnossus endured unscathed for a lifetime or two under the control of Myceneans (in which case the simplicity of their mainland taste may have encouraged designers to the restraint shown in the throne room). But probably other Mycenean invaders either caused or completed the general collapse of Minoan civilization about 1450, and then settled as conquerors. At any rate the burning of practically every residence of any consequence throughout Crete initiated an inglorious final period of the Bronze Age, Late Minoan III. None of the palaces was ever rebuilt; at most, a part was made poorly habitable or a group of inferior new rooms imposed on the ruins. No new buildings comparable in size or architectural form to the Minoan palaces are known. But a small palace added at Gournia virtually duplicates the plan of the Mycenean one at Phylakopi [77], and a megaron was also built at Hagia Triada. On the other hand, the lesser houses of Late Minoan III resembled their predecessors, the type of shrine remained unchanged, and a new portico at Hagia Triada [47], if it is to be dated to Late Minoan III, rather than Late Minoan I, as has been suggested, was faced, like some of the palace courts, with alternate columns and pillars, though at the

0   10   20 metres

42. Arkhanes, tombs, plan

deeply into the ground and had to be approached by a sloping passage which ends at an anteroom on the same axis. The burial chamber, set askew behind it, is oblong, and nearly 20

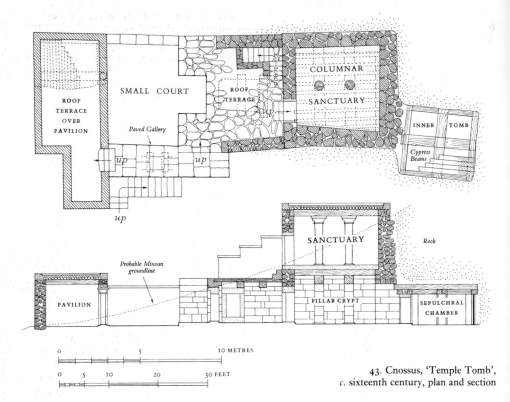

SMALL COURT

ROOF TERRACE OVER PAVILION

Paved Gallery

ROOF TERRACE

COLUMNAR

SANCTUARY

INNER   TOMB

Cypress Beams

up   *up*

up

SANCTUARY

Rock

Probable Minoan groundline

PAVILION

PILLAR CRYPT

SEPULCHRAL CHAMBER

0 ——————— 5 ——————— 10 METRES

0 — 5 — 10 — 20 — 30 FEET

43. Cnossus, 'Temple Tomb',
c. sixteenth century, plan and section

back of it lay a row of stores or shops, a scheme to which no parallel is known except at the Mycenean fortress of Tiryns [63, south-east corner]. The indigenous culture remained strong enough to absorb that of the conquerors; early Greek buildings in Crete reflect the Minoan tradition, even at 600 B.C.

44 and 45. Cnossus, 'Temple Tomb',
court and pylon and restored pillar
crypt, *c.* sixteenth century

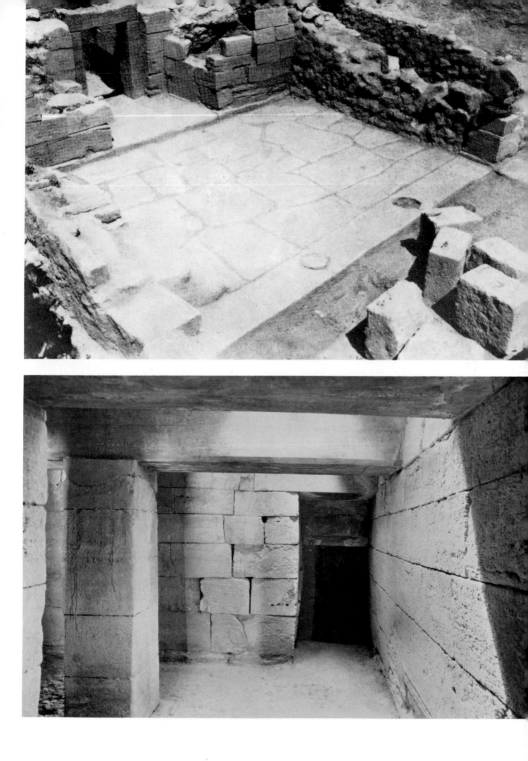

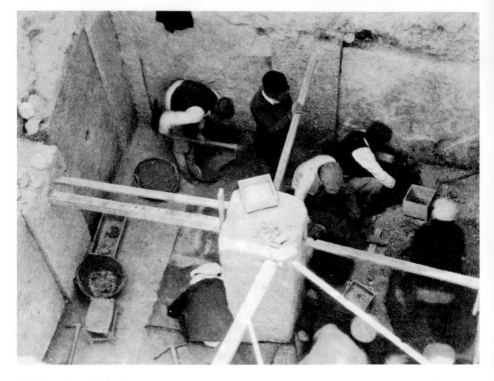

46. Cnossus, 'Temple Tomb',
burial chamber during excavations,
c. sixteenth century

47. Hagia Triada,
Late Minoan III portico, plan

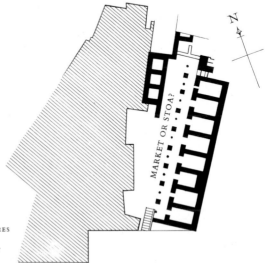

MARKET OR STOA?

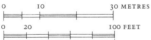

0   10   30 METRES

0   20   100 FEET

CHAPTER 5

CYCLADIC AND MAINLAND SETTLEMENTS

CONTEMPORARY WITH CRETAN PALACES

(MIDDLE AND LATE BRONZE AGE TO 1400 B.C.)

Whereas in Crete the transition from the Early to the Middle Bronze Age, soon after 2000, means the rise of a true civilization, in other Aegean regions it signifies the introduction of extraneous cultures and may be dated slightly later. In the Middle Bronze Age Cretan influence permeated the Cyclades so thoroughly that eventually they ceased to have an independent culture, but Troy and the southern part of the Greek mainland both appear to have been conquered by some alien people, who introduced in Greece a class of pottery (called Minyan) extraordinarily similar in both fabric and shapes to one which now appeared at Troy. In the Middle Helladic culture an apsidal type of building is also added to the previous types, another fact suggesting that groups of intruders had gained control over native settlements. The extension of Cretan influence to this region marks the beginning of the Late Bronze Age, shortly after 1600. In its first hundred years, the period Late Helladic I, the ruling caste indulged a taste for Minoan luxury goods, preferably of gold or silver, and encouraged local imitations, but the bulk of mainland products can fairly be described as still barbaric. In Late Helladic II, which corresponds roughly with the fifteenth century or the latter half of Late Minoan I, imitation turned to rivalry; the royal families of Mycenae and a number of other principalities were developing a civilization of their own, by imposing a veneer of Minoan refinement on their semi-feudal, warlike society. Their influence over the Cycladic islands (never entirely absent, despite the Cretans) extended considerably.

The exact political relationship between Crete and the Cyclades from Middle Minoan onwards is uncertain, given that we are dealing with prehistoric societies; it is perhaps better not to speak of a Minoan empire, or even Minoan colonies, though both may have existed. What is clear is that the adjacent Cycladic islands were culturally subjected, and in most of their arts the Minoan influence became overwhelming. Elsewhere buildings conserved the regional character to a remarkable extent. Nowhere is this clearer than at Akrotiri on Thera.[1] Though many of the houses are relatively small, they reproduce the architectural features of the Cretan buildings: irregularity of shape, internal screens of piers, angled stairways leading to the upper storeys (which here, of course, are excellently preserved), large windows, looking out over relatively narrow, twisting streets. They are tall, for their area, some with three storeys. Ashlar masonry is used, of true Cretan quality; otherwise the walls are of timber-laced rubble, or mud brick. Windows may be stone or timber-framed, and ashlar blocks as quoining may reinforce the corners. Rooms included storerooms, of Cnossian type, as well as those corresponding to Cretan domestic quarters. Another internal feature to be found of clear Cretan origin is lack of correspondence between ground and upper floors; upper floors are often more luxurious than the ground floors or basements. Particularly interesting is the well-built West House, the House of the Admiral [48]. This was, probably, only two storeys high. A wide door, with a window at its side, leads to a vestibule with two corridors

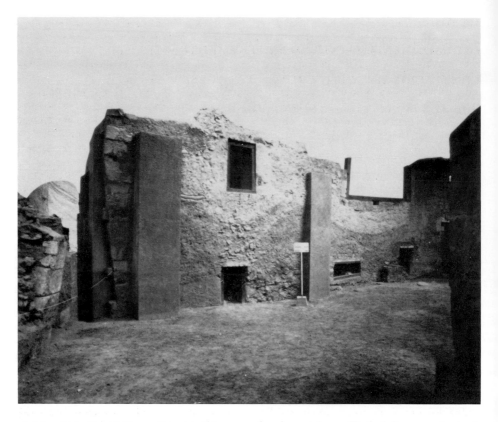

48 (A) and (B). Akrotiri, House of the Admiral, Middle Cycladic, façade and plan

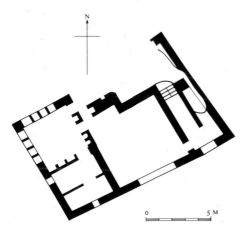

forming a staircase. To the left, an opening leads to the central room, in which a large window, wider than it is high, faces the street. On the west side are three rooms. The north-west room had on both exterior walls four adjacent windows: on its eastern wall were cupboards and shelving. The other rooms, to the south of this, were luxuriously appointed; Room 4, probably a bedroom, had at its side an *en-suite* bathroom. Room 5 contained miniature frescoes depicting an expedition by sea, together with vivid representations of towns, showing clearly the irregular appearance and flat roofs of Minoan architecture.

Few other house-plans of the Middle Bronze Age in the Cyclades could be mistaken for Cretan; they are usually based on the Early Cycladic oblong combination of two wide rooms, but the inner room now tended to be considerably longer. And the Middle Cycladic builders occasionally duplicated this scheme as though to make two semi-detached cottages, or added to it in various ways; sometimes a corridor led from the frontage to an extra room or two at the back [49]. It is exceptional to find a

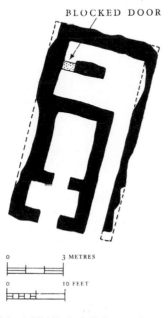

BLOCKED DOOR

0   3 METRES

0   10 FEET

49. Phylakopi, Middle Cycladic house, plan

room that was not rectangular, and the various rooms of a house still did not differ in size as much as in Crete; consequently its whole plan tended to be more regular. The exterior formed an oblong rectangle whenever possible. But it was difficult to realize that ideal in the towns, where the streets were narrow and winding, and the houses crowded together to occupy the entire area. That applies especially to the fortified settlements, of which three have been examined. An older village at Phylakopi, in Melos, became a walled town in the Middle Cycladic period; a short stretch of the original defences has survived, incorporated in a reconstruction of the early fourteenth century. The

wall was built in a series of straight lengths which met by being more or less alternately set forward and recessed by several feet. A smaller site, at Hagios Andreas in Siphnos, seems to be Late rather than Middle Cycladic, though there are houses of the earlier occupation. The main walls are, for the most part, Mycenean, repaired in Late Geometric times. The houses found within the fortification, with one minor exception, were Geometric. At Phylakopi the stability of the walls was increased by the interruptions to the outward face of the masonry. Rectangular towers were built at a town on Keos before and after the end of Middle Cycladic; a round-ended tower there belongs to a previous Middle Cycladic wall. The successive walls on Keos barred off the promontory of Hagia (or Ayia) Irini, the whole of which was presumably occupied by the town. Half of the area behind the fortifications has been excavated. The buildings include a shrine, as well as houses.[2]

In the southern mainland, too, the standard of housing improved during the Middle and Late Bronze Age. The circular type may have persisted only for temporary habitation, the oval became less common, and the rectangular houses still conformed with Early Helladic practice in providing one fairly large hall and a store behind it, but more often contained additional accommodation. Sometimes small rooms were attached to both the side and the back of the hall, making the whole plan approximately square, but generally it was elongated and that seems the older method. Occasionally part of a house was partitioned lengthwise, and another room occupied the full width, but as a rule the old Helladic basic scheme was merely extended by the addition of a porch (as in the case of the older of two houses [50]); often the porch was formed by simply prolonging the side walls as antae. The addition of the porch perhaps resulted from contamination with the new apsidal type which may have been introduced by foreign overlords; it was especially favoured for larger houses [50, 51]. The plan was U-shaped, and the curved end was normally partitioned off to make a back

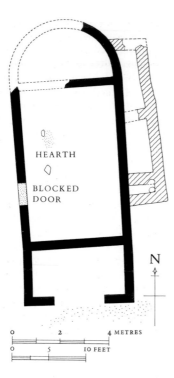

HEARTH

BLOCKED
DOOR

N

0   2   4 METRES

0   5   IO FEET

50. Korakou, superimposed Middle Helladic
houses, plan

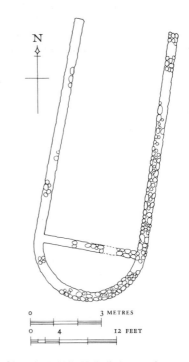

N

0   3 METRES

0   4   12 FEET

51. Olympia, Middle Helladic house, plan

room; the straight end may usually have been left open as a porch, and another cross-wall separated it from the main room, which invariably occupied the greater part of the house and contained a hearth, often slightly to one side. The plan was then identical with that of the long rectangular houses except for the rounded back wall. But the roofs, at least in some cases, do not seem to have been flat, as in rectangular houses, but ridged. The stone lower parts of the walls slant inwards as they rise and so presumably did the superstructure of sun-dried bricks and its timber frame, but the wall-base is too thin to have supported a corbelled vault; it appears that the roof consisted of reed thatch [1], probably fastened to horizontal logs which stiffened a hooped or triangular framework.[3] The curvature of the end provided an easy method of

weather-proofing what would otherwise have formed a gap; the thatch could merely be brought down in the shape of a truncated cone, whereas the straight end may have been left open right up to the gable. Some models of early Greek temples imitate such houses [80]. The same method of roofing may have been used for the apsidal houses of the Early Cycladic culture, which seems to have originated in Asia Minor.

With a ridged roof internal supports would have needed to be tall – perhaps taller than the available timber; that may explain why columns were not used, although in default of them the only means of achieving a large floor-area was by elongation. The width in fact was usually much the same, about 13 feet, though the length varied considerably; often it reached some 35 feet, so that the larger apsidal houses are generally termed 'hairpin shaped'. An extreme instance (probably Late Helladic) is the gigantic house or small palace at Thermum which is called 'Megaron A';[4] the width ($19\frac{1}{2}$ feet; 6 m.), although half as large again as was normal, equalled little more than a quarter of the length (72 feet; 22 m.). The straight, south end was left open towards its west side to make a porch; the length of this was 8 feet, of the main room nearly 40 feet, and of the back room, which occupied the whole of the curved end, 16 feet. The doorways through the cross-walls must have been centrally placed; of course the method of roofing is best suited to a building of which the left and right sides correspond exactly, and a taste for the symmetry of axial planning would naturally have developed.

The majority of the population continued to live in defenceless villages, in which houses of the several types were placed near one another at any angle. But small fortified towns of Middle Helladic date are also known, the defences consisting of a ring of wall lined with the continuous backs of houses; in two instances a similar inner ring surrounded the centre of the town. At Malthi (in south-west Greece) a previously unwalled settlement was enclosed in that manner late in the period, when a hundred new rooms were built, and almost as many of Early Helladic origin remained in use [52]; the town was continuously inhabited till the end of the Bronze Age and was then consumed by fire. It appears that the Middle Helladic builders there relied far less on sun-dried brick than their predecessors had done, and gradually abandoned the use of curved structures. The houses normally comprised one or two rooms, but as many as five in exceptional cases. The rooms often contained a single column, so that the almost flat roof may have sloped four ways; gutters conveyed the rain water into cisterns. A row of square rooms for storage was built against the west wall. A third of the total area was an open space. Most of the gateways into the town were formed by mere gaps in the walls, which usually projected as a salient on the right

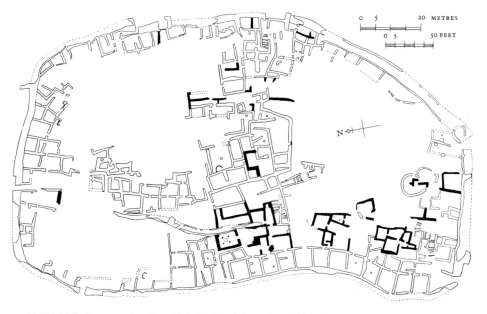

52. Malthi, Helladic town, plan. Late Helladic III additions in solid black

of the entrance. The west gate, however, lay in a straight piece of the wall and its passage was therefore prolonged straight inwards for greater security, while at one of the narrow posterns the passage continued sideways along the back of the wall. That method was also used at Aegina, in successive stages of Early Helladic defences and again in a Middle Helladic extension, behind a salient stretch of wall which formed one side of the gate. The face of the Middle Helladic wall was alternately set forward and recessed in the Cycladic manner, as is not surprising since the island had long been culturally associated with the Cyclades; indeed its Early Helladic fortifications, which inspired the whole of this scheme, appear Cycladic in design. A Late Helladic wall of 1500 at the same site seems to have had a tortuous entrance through a re-entrant, involving at least one gateway only 3 feet wide. The first defences at Tiryns, though

Late Helladic II in date, exemplify a different style characteristic of Late Helladic III and are included in the description of that period.

Tombs, as a rule, were rock-cut chambers, very roughly shaped.[5] But excavators at Mycenae have found Middle Helladic shaft graves roofed with wooden beams overlaid with stone slabs, and a chamber-tomb with a roof built of large blocks corbelled to meet in saddle form. Pottery found within is datable to about 1450, and the closest architectural parallel may be found in contemporary Crete, the 'Royal Tomb' at Isopata, for example. The comparison again illustrates the prevalent difference between mainland and island standards. Only in the tholos tombs was equality on the verge of attainment when this period ended; the slow progress from crude beginnings, in their respect, is described in the next chapter, though chronologically appropriate here.

CHAPTER 6

THOLOS TOMBS

A new architectural form, the tholos tomb, makes a sudden appearance in the Peloponnese about 1600, early in Late Helladic I, and persists through Late Helladic II and Late Helladic IIIa, becoming obsolete by the thirteenth century. It is likely that on the mainland they first developed in Messenia. An important (but ruined) early tholos has been excavated recently at the so-called 'Tomb of Thrasymedes' at Voïdokilia, near Pylos, dating from early in the Late Helladic period.[1] The novelty lay in the combination of a monumental approach with the circular chamber corbelled upwards into a conical roof. In the case of the best Cretan tholos, at Cnossus [53], the few sherds found in and behind the walls are all Middle Minoan, except for two which might be Late Minoan Ia, so that the excavator was reluctant to date it appreciably later than 1550. In general tholos tombs were restricted to the mainland, and most examples are found in the Peloponnese, though a few occur as far north as Thessaly. None of the neighbouring countries built anything resembling such tombs. (Indeed, the closest analogies

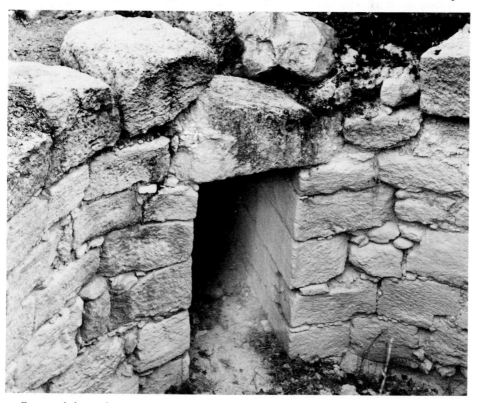

53. Cnossus, tholos tomb, c. 1500

are to be seen in the megalithic tombs of western Europe, particularly one at New Grange in Ireland, and these belong to a much earlier period.) A tholos tomb [53–8] has an underground circular chamber of stone which rises, by corbelled courses, in the shape of an old-fashioned beehive, so that the height of the pointed dome is more or less equal to the diameter at the base, and the approach is formed by a level passage cut through sloping ground to the doorway of the chamber, like a railway cutting ending at the mouth of a tunnel. The Helladic circular huts and the Early Minoan circular ossuaries had probably taken the same form as the chamber itself, though in sun-dried brick on a stone base, but they were built above ground, whereas the Mycenean tholoi were completely subterranean. The method of procedure was to start by cutting the open passage (conventionally termed a 'dromos') horizontally into a sloping hill-side till the ground rose high enough above it; a round hole was then made and a slightly smaller chamber built inside it. This intervening gap between the masonry and the rock was eventually filled in, and soil replaced over the exterior of the dome; after the last burial the dromos too was filled in, to a retaining wall at its outer end. The very best tombs seem to have been surrounded by a low wall which formed the revetment of the tumulus. Otherwise only a mound of earth remained visible, so long as the dome could withstand the percolation of water between the joints; in most cases the washing-away of the clay mortar has caused its collapse, especially if the builders' technique was poor. At any rate in the case of the finest tombs, buttress walls encircled the vault to support the weight of earth above, and also took the lateral thrust of the façade and provided a firm backing for the upper courses of the dromos walls.

Investigations of the tholoi have shown that though the technique of the masonry was improved in the course of time, the fundamental design and procedure for construction remained unaltered, and the size was not appreciably increased.[2] The tombs at Mycenae can be divided chronologically into three groups, and those elsewhere fit approximately into this sequence, allowing for local variations in materials, etc. The following account applies particularly to Mycenae and its surroundings. The earliest group ranges approximately from 1510 to 1460; the first examples belong to the close of Late Helladic I and the latest to the middle of Late Helladic II. The building material is a hard limestone used in the form of rubble, with rather larger blocks at the exterior of the doorway and a series of much bigger roughly-dressed blocks laid across the doorway as lintels; these, however, are little wider than the gap they span and therefore cannot have been overlaid by a relieving triangular gap as in later tombs. The wall rises directly from the top of the lintels; the inward face of the innermost lintel is cut straight and therefore stands out from the curve like a shelf. The dromos is merely a rock-cutting. The chambers vary in diameter between 26 and 43 feet (8 and 13 m.).

The second group [54, 55] is well-constructed. The sides of the dromos are lined with a rubble of hard limestone or with ashlar blocks of soft limestone – in some cases with both in combination. The jambs and the sides of the doorway-passage behind them are built of large blocks of conglomerate, roughly dressed and sometimes faced with ashlar masonry of soft limestone; in one tomb a door was fitted at the exterior. The lintel blocks extend farther sideways into the walls, and the inward face of the innermost curves in conformity with the masonry. The tholos itself is built, as before, of limestone rubble, but the stones tend to be better shaped; in two instances, moreover, the lowest course consists of ashlar blocks of conglomerate as a basis for the rubble. The great length of the lintel blocks throughout the group implies that the masonry above them was habitually laid in much the same arrangement as in the Panagia tomb [55], where alone it has been preserved; the builders stopped the first overlying course in line with the jambs, leaving an empty space over the doorway, then corbelled out each successive course till the gap was

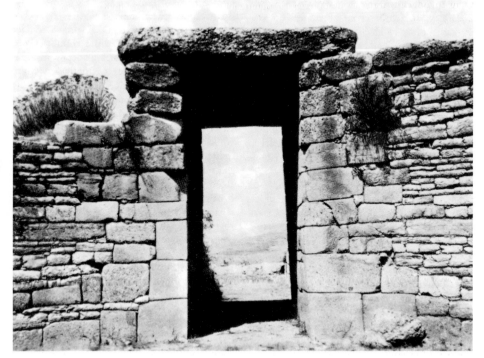

54. Mycenae, Kato Phournos tholos tomb, *c.* 1400

55. Mycenae, Panagia tholos tomb, *c.* fourteenth century

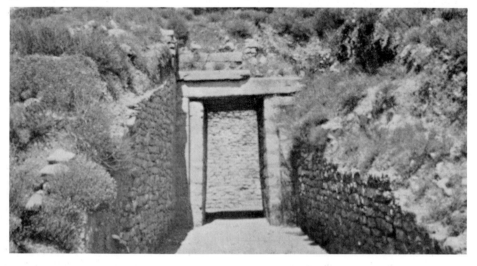

completed in the form of a triangle, which they closed with a thin screen of stone. But the Panagia tomb is more advanced than other members of the second group; the outward face of its lintel is elegantly dressed in steps, and rectangular pilasters frame the doorway. This care for architectural seemliness presages the luxury of the third group, and the interval of time would have been fairly brief if we assume that much of the pottery found in the collapsed tholos had accompanied the original burial, because sherds of Late Helladic III vastly outnumber those of Late Helladic II.

In the third group [57, 58, 60], solely of Late Helladic III, good masonry is used throughout dromos and tholos alike. Large blocks of conglomerate compose the threshold, jambs and sides of the doorway passage; the exposed surfaces are often smooth, having been cut with a saw. Two tombs at Mycenae (the 'Treasuries' of 'Atreus' and 'Clytemnestra') had an ornamental façade carved in coloured stones, and a door was fitted on a threshold block midway through the passage. The lintels are uniformly longer, overlapping the sides of the dromos; they are also individually wider and taller, so that their number was often reduced to two. A relieving triangle is always found. The tholos itself consists of blocks of conglomerate, very neatly dressed on the exposed curved face, at which they meet exactly. Each course overlaps and counterweighs the one below, on the cantilever system. In the higher part of the pointed dome the curvature is so great vertically as well as horizontally that the blocks run back at widely divergent angles; the blocks are wedge-shaped but not so carefully trimmed as to fit together except at the inner face, and the interstices are filled with pieces of stone packed with clay. The exterior of the dome was coated all over with clay to make it watertight under the earth covering. Drains were provided to remove any seepage from the floor, which is of rock, levelled with cement where required. The diameters of the tholoi vary from $27\frac{1}{2}$ to $47\frac{1}{2}$ feet in the case of 'Atreus'. A rectangular side-chamber opens off the tholos of both this tomb and the one at Orchomenus. The grandest of all tholos tombs is the

'Treasury of Atreus' at Mycenae [56-60]. Its date, along with that of the tomb of Clytemnestra, is a vexed point. It must be later than the end of Late Helladic IIIA1 (c. 1350 B.C.) for its dromos cuts through deposits of that date. On the other hand, it is unlikely to have been erected nearly a century later, for the sherds of that period found under its threshold must result from later re-use. The tomb of Clytemnestra is slightly later than 'Atreus',[3] whose dromos is nearly 20 feet wide and 120 feet long (6 by 36 m.). Its side walls rise in steps to the inner end where they meet the top of the façade; they are composed of large blocks of dark grey conglomerate, well-shaped and with a hammer-dressed surface, laid in more or less regular courses. The floor of the dromos is cemented. The façade[4] stands over 34 feet high and has in its centre a doorway nearly 18 feet high (5·40 m.) and half as wide at the bottom as it is tall; the sides slant towards one another as they rise (contracting to 8 feet from $8\frac{1}{2}$ feet; 2·45 m. from 2·70 m.), and the whole doorway is inclined inwards, in imitation of the Egyptian pylon. Two flat rebates, sunk into the façade, frame the doorway, and their sides slant parallel therewith. At the top the inner rebate is narrower than at the side, and both are cut into the lintel. This block extends right across the façade into the walls of the dromos; a second block lies behind it. Above, the relieving triangle, which reaches to the cornice, is now empty but originally was faced with carved slabs.

The space between each of the outer rebates of the doorway and the dromos wall was occupied by a half-column, which stood straight upright and reached well up the lintel. The bases of the columns (still in place) are rectangular, of yellow conglomerate, sawn at the edge into three steps. The half-columns[5] were of green limestone; large portions are preserved in the British Museum. The shafts tapered downwards, reducing the diameter $1\frac{1}{2}$ inches (from $22\frac{1}{2}$ inches at the top to 21 inches at the bottom; 58 cm. to 54 cm.) in a height of nearly 19 feet (5·70 m.). The proportion of height to width is very slender; in the Minoan wooden

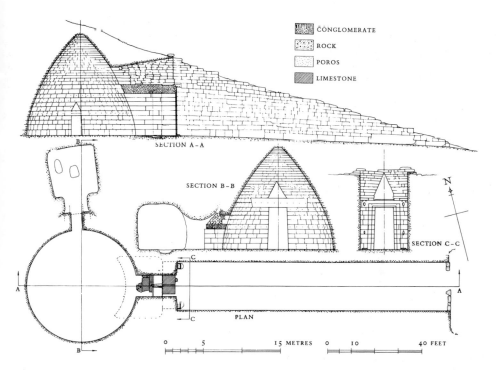

CONGLOMERATE

ROCK

POROS

LIMESTONE

SECTION A-A

SECTION B-B

SECTION C-C

N

PLAN

0   5   15 METRES   0   10   40 FEET

56 and 57. Mycenae, 'Treasury of Atreus', c. 1300–1250, section and plan, and exterior

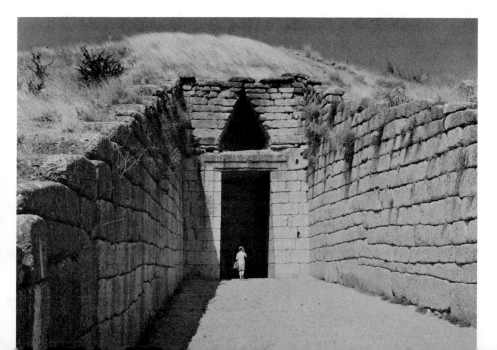

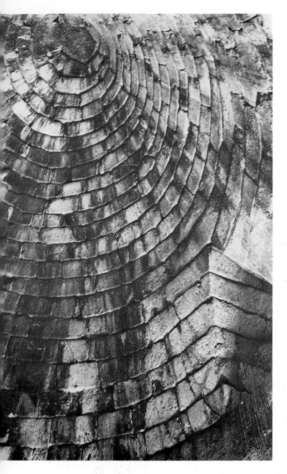

which is divided into rows of superimposed tongues, pointing upwards, as in the water-lily capitals of Egypt. Next came a thick concave moulding, like a Minoan echinus, which bears the same pattern as the shafts but with the points of the zigzags placed sideways instead of up and down. A low cavetto, undecorated, separated the echinus from the highest member of the capital, a rectangular abacus such as the Minoans used, which was left plain except for a slight set-back along the lower edge. The top of the abacus stood level with the apparent upper edge of the lintel – the block actually rises somewhat higher behind the face of the wall.

Above the capitals larger square plinths of conglomerate are built into the façade, and upon them probably stood smaller half-columns of the same green stone, engaged in the walls. The fragments show that they bore similar decoration but twined round the shaft (following Minoan precedent) instead of zigzagged, and that this faded out nearly 2 feet above the base. It is not known whether the decoration on the upper parts of the shafts was continuous or interrupted by other plain stretches, as the restoration assumes. On top of the shafts were set beaded collars and capitals like those of the larger half-columns beneath. Probably the abacus reached to the cornice of the façade, a row of projecting slabs of conglomerate.

Along the upper edge of the lintel, between the plinths that separated each couple of half-columns, ran a strip of green stone[6] carved with a row of disks, such as Minoan frescoes habitually place on façades, probably in simulation of log rafters. A pattern of connected spirals ran immediately above. The next layer probably bore a frieze of half-rosettes, the Minoan 'triglyph' pattern [cf. 22]; this would have run across the base of the relieving triangle to the undecorated lower portions of the smaller half-columns. The triangle itself contained slabs of a deep red colour[7] carved with sets of three horizontal bands of connected spirals separated by mouldings, in alternation perhaps with plain horizontal bands of the same stone or of a pinkish variegated stone, and bands of spiral

58. Mycenae, 'Treasury of Atreus', c. 1300–1250, vault from cap-stone to lintel

columns a ratio of 5:1 may have been normal, yet this is almost certainly a case of copying a Minoan form [cf. 33], possibly also of copying the carving or painting on Minoan columns. The shafts are ornamented in zigzags, with narrow strips of beading separating wider bands which are alternately plain and carved with a Minoan pattern of connected spirals against a sunken background; the plain bands are fluted. At the top of the shaft there was probably a beaded collar, beneath a cavetto moulding

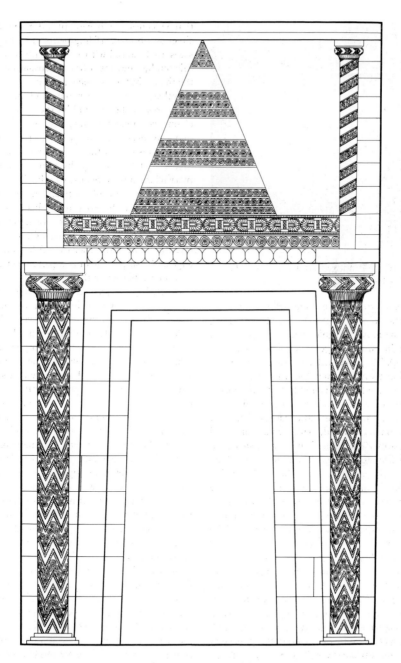

59. Mycenae, 'Treasury of Atreus', *c.* 1300–1250, restoration of façade

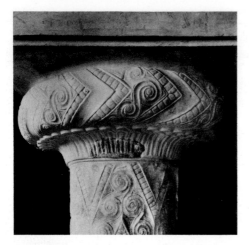

60. Mycenae, 'Treasury of Atreus', c. 1300–1250, restored capital from façade

patterns in green stone fitted somewhere. The restoration drawn for the British Museum [59], as yet the most plausible, cannot be definitive.

The doorway passage runs inward for 18 feet (5·40 m.). It is paved with limestone slabs, interrupted midway by a four-foot threshold of two conglomerate slabs, wedged tight by the insertion of pieces of softer rock cut to fit. The remains of bronze nails show that the threshold was originally covered, with bronze or wood presumably. The door frame was also nailed into the stone; it held a double door which folded back against the walls, the handles fitting into slots in the masonry. Comparatively little weight rested upon the passage walls because of the great length of the lintels. The inner lintel, which took the downward lateral thrust of the vault, is a block some 26 feet long, 16 feet wide, and 4 feet high, and must weigh about 100 tons. The tholos chamber measures 47½ feet (14·50 m.) in diameter and 43 feet (13·20 m.) in height, and is still intact except that the floor has been broken up and decoration plundered from the walls; here and in other parts of the tomb bronze nails show that a considerable amount of decoration was once attached, but the only indication of its nature is the Homeric tradition

that Mycenean walls were plated with gold and silver and bronze. If fragments of two gypsum slabs, each carved with a bull, really came from this tomb,[8] they must have been placed, not in the tholos, but off to one side of it, in a rock-cut chamber, some 20 feet square and high, which in its present state resembles the contemporary chamber-tombs; the rough walls and ceilings may, however, have been lined. The doorway which leads to it, although no more than 8 feet high and 5 feet wide (2·50 by 1·50 m.), is covered by two long lintels, beneath a relieving triangle.

The 'Treasury of Minyas', a magnificent tomb (though the roof has fallen) at Orchomenus in Boeotia, also has a rectangular side chamber, where a flat ceiling of carved stone slabs hides the native rock [61]. A beading at the edge and a single line of complete rosettes next to it form a border to the main pattern of interconnected spirals packed with conventionalized water-lilies - Egyptian by derivation, whereas the rosettes and the spirals are purely Minoan. A Minoan ceiling [21], modelled in plaster and painted, supplies a general prototype, and no doubt colour was applied to the stone in a comparable manner. All the ingredients of the pattern were used in contemporary Egyptian painted ceilings through Aegean influence.

The ruined tomb of 'Clytemnestra' at Mycenae is one of the latest tholoi, probably the last of the 'luxury' group. Comparison with 'Atreus' shows a tendency towards less ponderous, more refined design. The chamber differed much less in diameter and height (44 and 42½ feet; 13·40 and 12·95 m.) and so was slightly narrower but taller; the upper part of the vault[9] climbs more steeply, as has been discovered when reconstructing it. The doorway is a couple of feet narrower though the height is the same as in 'Atreus' (6½ by 17½ feet; 2 by 5·40 m.). The dromos is practically identical in size. Its outer end was blocked, as usual, by a retaining wall for the earth fill, but an extension at either end, not bonded in, runs out some 13 feet farther as though to finish the sides of the dromos by returns. The façade still retains pieces of decoration and some loose fragments are also

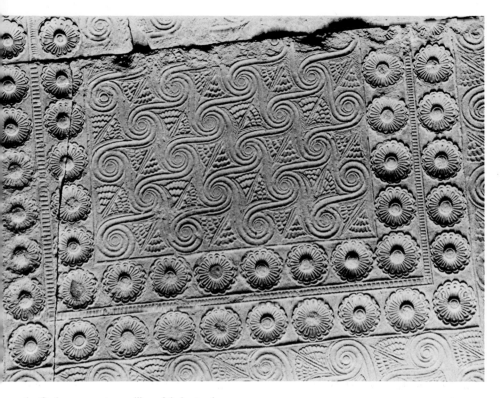

61. Orchomenus, stone ceiling of tholos tomb, *c.* 1300

preserved; in general they resemble the remains from 'Atreus'. A pair of upright half-columns, tapering downwards, flanked the slanting doorway in the same manner, but the shafts are of gypsum and extraordinarily slender – fifteen times as high as the lower diameter – and they bear no ornament other than thirteen shallow concave flutes.[10] Semicircular bases of polished conglomerate are cut in two steps. The capitals are lost except for the abaci, which still project from the wall. A frieze of disks runs between them across the top of the lintel, and a spiral pattern in a pale greenish stone probably came from the course above. Instead of an upper pair of half-columns a low rectangular pilaster runs from this level to just below the cornice. Fragments of red slabs, some plain, others with the half-rosette pattern, represent the intervening decoration. An interesting technical detail, paralleled at another late tholos at Mycenae, is the shaping of the two threshold slabs to meet in an oblique joint at the middle of the passage.

On the average, not more than one tholos tomb can have been built in one generation at the same town, almost certainly for the burial of a king and his family; in the case of the one tholos found with its original contents intact, the treasure deposited with the dead is of such value that no other explanation can plausibly be maintained. For the rest of the population tombs of various types were merely cut in the rock. The chamber-tombs, which begin in Late Helladic I before the tholoi, may have contributed to their evolution. The method was to drive a tunnel into the hill-side and dig a cave at the end of it, as soon as the rock stood high enough to form a roof with safety. Early tholos tombs follow the precedent set in the chamber-tombs of having a short wide dromos, whereas in the later examples of either type the dromos is long and relatively narrow.

Whether a knowledge of the Cretan ossuaries had any direct part in inspiring the Mycenean innovation of the tholos tomb is questionable. Chronologically the evidence speaks neither for nor against the supposition (p. 34). Mere chance would account for the fact that the earliest tholos tombs yet discovered are in the south-west corner of the Peloponnese, a district less accessible than the east coast to voyagers from Crete, or even from the long-established Minoan base on Cythera. A strong argument against derivation from ossuaries is their lack of an entrance passage, except in one instance where there is no real analogy to a dromos (p. 33). As regards technique, the sight of con-temporary Minoan tombs would more effec-tively have taught the Myceneans how to build inward-slanting courses and massive doorways, but apparently they learnt to do both indepen-dently of Crete. They were extraordinarily slow to realize the structural value of humping the upward surface of lintels, as had been usual in ossuaries and in later Minoan tombs; the ex-pedient reappears in precisely the same form over the thirteenth-century gateways of the Mycenae citadel (but also, rather earlier, in Hit-tite gateways), whereas the nearest equivalent in tholos tombs – not in many – is a less pronoun-ced, comparatively seemly curve on a thinner block. Actually, though, the blocks employed as lintels were allowed to retain their natural shape to a great extent; they were dressed no more than could be helped, for fear of weakening them. Inequalities were mostly hidden by the overlying masonry, and additional weight scarcely mattered since lintels did not need to be lifted; they could be dragged into position across the hill-side.

The expedient of the relieving triangle is not known to have been used by the Minoans. The Myceneans could have learnt it from Egypt, and the extent of their obvious borrowings of Egyp-tian ornament justifies an assumption that they did so. A less effective Egyptian device with the same purpose was adopted in a fourteenth-century tholos at Acharnae (Menidi) in Attica [62]; a taller gap was left above the lintel and

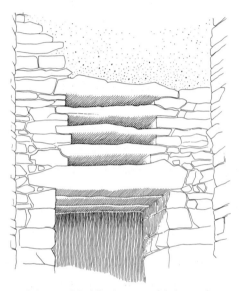

62. Acharnae (Menidi), doorway of tholos tomb, fourteenth century

spanned horizontally by a series of blocks, laid like bars one above the other with intervening gaps, only the ends being embedded in the masonry at either side. The admirable masonry of the late tholoi may also have been inspired by the example of Egypt. But no round buildings existed in that country, and all those in western Asia seem to have been crude structures above ground, such as huts or kilns. The tholos tomb was almost certainly a Mycenean innovation.

CHAPTER 7

MYCENEAN CITADELS AND HOUSING

(LATE HELLADIC III, 1400–1100)

Probably it was an invasion from the Helladic area which effected the Minoan collapse before 1400, after which the leadership of the whole Aegean centred there – with Mycenae predominating, it would seem. In the remainder of the Bronze Age, the three centuries of Late Helladic III, an almost uniform Mycenean civilization overlaid its predecessors in Crete and the smaller islands; colonists then introduced it to coastal Asia Minor and Cyprus. The legends of the Trojan war preserve a description of its characteristics. Troy had hitherto had little contact with the peoples of the western and southern Aegean but Mycenean imports were numerous for several generations before a catastrophe which broke the prosperity of the Seventh City about 1260. In the traditions of that event Agamemnon of Mycenae stands out, like Charlemagne in the romances of chivalry, the acknowledged superior of all other kings and nobles. Mycenae itself, in spite of having suffered unusually severe damage, remains equally superior in grandeur to the other seats of power. That the owners were, as a rule, war-lords of predatory habit is manifest from the strong fortifications within which they lived – an innovation in mainland Greece, possibly traceable in crude form back into the Middle Helladic period. The megalithic structure of the fortifications was another innovation; nowhere in the world except in Hittite Asia Minor had any been built with such enormous blocks. The hall around which each palace centred was a larger apartment than previous social conditions in Greece had demanded; it, no less definitely than the fortifications, bears witness to a baronial style of life, possibly introduced by groups of invaders whose subjects continued to build in the manner

of the past. The original country of the presumed conquerors (Achaeans, they seem to have called themselves) is, as yet, unidentifiable. The striking resemblance of their type of hall, the megaron, to that found at Troy (and at one site in the centre of Asia Minor), many centuries earlier, could be due merely to similarity of requirements. Information on Hittite methods of building might have been obtained on voyages from Greece.

As a seafaring people the Myceneans far excelled the Minoans, whose trade they took over, and must have had greater opportunities of learning foreign ways through their dealings on the eastern shores of the Mediterranean and in Egypt, where their art became fashionable at court. An incidental result of the frequent interchange of products with Egypt is to enable a more precise chronology to be established for the last centuries of the Bronze Age.

The Mycenean royal architecture of the last three centuries of the Bronze Age presents an extraordinary contrast with all previous building on the mainland.[1] Such houses of Late Helladic I and II as have been excavated were built on the same principles as their Middle Helladic predecessors, and that may have been the case with the contemporary palaces, which obviously failed to satisfy the more exacting standards of Late Helladic III; for they were completely demolished to give place to better palaces. But the process of improving the royal residences started just before the close of Late Helladic II with the fortifications that surrounded them. In the Peloponnese, the naturally defensible positions chosen were large enough to contain various houses as well as an enormous palace, and the main purpose of any extension to the original enclosure was apparently to build more houses within the fortified area; this, how-ever, did not include the whole town (anyway at Mycenae and Tiryns) and must therefore be termed a citadel. The shortest enceinte known was built at Pylos in the sixteenth century, and demolished when or before the thirteenth-century palace spread across the entire top of the little hill; perhaps there was then no further need for a defensive wall, or there might have been some aversion to retaining a fortification that could no longer protect anything except a palace. The perimeter of Mycenae eventually measured about 1000 yards (900 m.) and that of Tiryns 750 yards (700 m.) The extremely im-posing wall at Midea, on a hill between Mycenae and Tiryns, enclosed an area smaller than either of these citadels; it has been planned but not excavated. A less extensive hill in the north-west Peloponnese, near Araxos, retains stretches of Mycenean wall, interrupted or overlaid by later work; under the name 'Wall of the Dymeans', the fortress was conspicuous in Hellenistic warfare.

In central Greece the practice was to enclose the whole town with a wall, and in two instances the area was so large that the surrounding popu-lation and their animals could not have filled it; at Gla, no lesser extent would have suited the terrain, but the perimeter of Crisa could have been halved to military benefit. The perimeter of Gla is estimated at 2 miles (3 km.). The wall at Crisa runs for 1500 yards (1400 m.), more or less straight, enclosing uneven ground along the top of a cliff; a depression midway cuts across the enclosure, and there are traces of a possible cross-wall or terracing along one side of it, but not for military purposes. The palace relied on the town wall for its protection at both Gla and Crisa, and could easily have been captured from the town. At Eutresis, discontinuous remains, mostly of no more than a few blocks here and there, are thought to represent the wall of an enclosure approximating to a square of 550 yards (500 m.), of which only a small proportion was occupied by the houses; the ground offered not the slightest military advantage. Presum-ably the wall consisted of sun-dried brick except

for the stone base, as was almost certainly the case also at Crisa, where, however, the solid base is faced with great orthostats. The Acropolis of Athens is more likely to have contained the town than a palace alone, and two definite town walls, of short perimeter, have been found in Attica, at Hagios Kosmas and Rafina. Several town walls in Thessaly may be Mycenean rather than Greek. The construction of every fortification is megalithic, but ranges from mere piling of boulders (notably on the Acropolis of Athens) to precise fitting of gigantic smoothed blocks – a style seemingly introduced from Asia Minor and found at its stupendous best in the Peloponnese. Some details of the design, too, are paral-leled at cities of the Hittite empire, and in every case the work in Asia Minor seems to be the older.

But the internal transformation at the great Mycenean centres resulted from Minoan in-fluence. This had steadily increased during Late Helladic I and II and did not reach its height till after the collapse of Minoan civilization, a process which was completed before the begin-ning of Late Helladic III about 1400. Artisans must have been fetched from impoverished Crete to help build and decorate the palaces all through the following century; for the technique was almost purely Minoan, although the planning deferred to local taste by invariably providing a great hall, a feature alien to Crete. The structure usually consisted of sun-dried brick upon a base of rubble set in clay. Base-ments were built entirely in rubble. A frame of upright horizontal beams reinforced both faces of each brick wall and incorporated the lintel, jambs, and threshold of the doorways. If a base-ment existed underneath, the timber rose from the top of its rubble wall, where horizontal beams were sunk into chases in each face and tied together by transverse beams running through the masonry. In the most opulent sec-tions of a palace the exposed base of a wall might be faced with ashlar blocks, held by wooden clamps which passed through the rubble core, precisely as Middle Minoan orthostats had been tied back. The surface of the walls was mud-plastered in the case of basements and other unimportant rooms but otherwise stuccoed with lime-plaster, and sometimes frescoed with patterns or scenes; the timber seems to have generally been left exposed. The floors consisted of beaten earth or cement and were sometimes plastered and painted like the walls. Windows, to judge from the little that is known, were small. The doors, often two-leaved, were made of wood. Wooden columns (often fluted)[2] and pillars of masonry were used to support the roofs, which were flat; a row of timbers carried a layer of brushwood or reeds as a bed for the clay or earth, which was compressed so as to resist the weather, if not coated with cement.[3] Drains are so frequent that they may be assumed to have been used to carry off domestic waste as well as rain-water. Bathrooms were provided with pottery tubs. The furnishings included low plastered benches in the porches and anterooms, lamps on stands, and charcoal braziers; in addition a large fixed hearth invariably occupied the centre of the great hall. The hall and hearth form the only unmistakably mainland features among this whole list; several elements could have been derived from either mainland or Cretan practice, but everything else is Minoan by origin. One other feature, however, was probably derived from Syria or Asia Minor – the use in the main doorways of massive stone thresholds into which were sunk bronze-shod pivots of wood on which the doors turned. Bronze pivot caps, however, have been found at Mallia, Phaestus and Hagia Triada.[4]

A considerable amount is also known about the private houses of Late Helladic III. The poor continued to live in huts of one or two rooms, built of sun-dried brick or vegetable material daubed with clay, flat-roofed, and floored with beaten earth. And many larger houses have been excavated; as a rule the structure was not much better, but in some instances it approximated to that of the worse rooms in a palace. The Middle Helladic types of plan persisted, with modifications; the apsidal houses tend to be shorter, and almost all small houses may now have been approximately rectangular.

The larger rectangular houses consist, in their entirety or in great part, of what Homer calls a megaron, a type of hall which in its pure form was restricted to palaces and to a few mansions in their vicinity which may have belonged to junior members of the royal families. For an exceptionally simple example we may take the megaron of a crude little palace at Malthi [52, in solid black]; it is a room $14\frac{1}{2}$ feet wide and $18\frac{1}{4}$ feet long (4·40 by 5·60 m.), entered by a doorway in the centre of one short wall, and containing bases for four wooden columns, arranged in a rectangle around a hearth so as to stand equidistant from the other walls. In a room of this width so many columns cannot have been required merely to support the roof; probably they ran up above it and formed the open sides of a lantern with an impervious top to shelter the hearth [cf. 66]. But in a large megaron at Pylos there was also a gallery cantilevered from every wall, and its front rested on the columns around the hearth. Huge pipes (found there and in a house at Mycenae) drew up the smoke – in one case, through an upper room.

It is questionable whether earlier rectangular houses had been provided with any aperture to emit the smoke, other than the doorway; in the apsidal vaulted houses there may well have been a gap at the straight end, and in any case the greater height would have had the effect of keeping the floor-level reasonably clear of smoke. But a megaron with a chimney-pipe hung above the hearth, and a lantern to let out stray smoke and admit light, could have been comfortable as well as almost fireproof and weatherproof. (The efficiency of the hearth would be greater than one might expect; even a few centuries ago, a lantern above an open hearth was still considered preferable to a chimney for heating a large hall, such as those of the Oxford and Cambridge colleges.) In addition the grouped columns enabled a large room to take more convenient proportions. It may therefore appear that the 'hair-pin' type of house should have been superseded; but the difficulty of obtaining timber to bear the weight of a large flat roof probably made the building of a megaron impracticable for anyone who did not command a considerable labour force. In any case we do not know how long the 'hair-pin' houses continued to be built after the first appearance of the megaron, of which all securely dated examples belong to Late Helladic III. The type itself may not be appreciably older.

The influence of the megaron can plausibly be traced in the lesser rectangular houses during Late Helladic III. A very frequent plan is derived from the previous long type (of Middle Helladic to Late Helladic II), but normally contains an anteroom as well as a porch. In the palaces the same long form persists; the megaron was always entered from the south, through a porch,[5] and sometimes also through an anteroom, of the same width as itself. The houses were narrow enough to dispense with the columns that were required in palaces to support the open front of the porch, and instead of four columns around the central hearth they normally had two, placed on either side of it along the middle of the room in line with the door, so that presumably the smoke-hole took the form of a slit. A storcroom too was added in private houses behind the pseudo-megaron, while in the palaces the stores were more often kept in a separate wing or upstairs.

Comparison with the Middle Helladic scheme of porch, main room and store [50, 51] must allow for the fact that in the palaces, as well as in contemporary houses at some localities, the anteroom was an optional feature. Consequently the houses and palaces of Late Helladic III show only this essential difference in plan, that the hearth now occupied a central position and that columns stood in a significant relation to it – not necessarily in a square; a megaron below the citadel at Tiryns contained a row of three columns along its centre as well as a hearth. But in elevation and ornament the palaces differed enormously from all that we know of Middle Helladic building, and almost entirely through Cretan influence; they wore a Minoan dress over their mainland form. In this combination may be found, I suggest, the origin of the innovation which distinguishes the megaron from

the Middle Helladic hall. The hearth is a characteristically mainland feature, very rarely found in Crete, and its central position also accords with the Helladic mentality and not with the Minoan, however much weight should be attached to practical considerations; still, the cluster of columns might have been adapted from Minoan usage in, say, peristyle courts. On this theory the invention of the megaron could be ascribed to a Minoan architect working for one of the mainland kings. The most likely date would be the beginning of Late Helladic III, or at earliest some time during Late Helladic II, the period at which the fusion of Minoan and Helladic art began in earnest, and the effect on the design of private houses might not have become widespread for a generation or two.

An obvious prototype for the megaron suite, with the important exception of the columns, can be seen in the palace buildings of Troy II, which must be roughly a thousand years earlier [5].[6] In these, too, a porch, and sometimes also an anteroom, preceded a great hall with an approximately central hearth, while the roofs likewise seem to have been flat (whether monopitch or imperceptibly ridged). And the small houses of the same culture at Thermi consisted of one room like a small version of the palace halls, in many cases with the addition of an anteroom [2]. It might seem therefore that the Late Helladic III houses, with their porch, anteroom, large room, and small back room, could represent a combination of the old Trojan scheme with the Early Helladic, which normally comprised only one large room and a small back room. But the porch had been added to this basic minimum in the Middle Helladic period, and the anteroom does not appear till centuries later, in Late Helladic III. Moreover, in Troy VI, which was contemporary with Middle Helladic and Late Helladic I–IIIA, the buildings contain no anteroom between the porch and the large room. If, in fact, it was not independently invented at that time, the anteroom must be an idea derived either from Crete, where the Minoans had long been addicted to it, or from Asia Minor. And the obvious choice is

Crete. At any rate if the source did lie in Asia Minor, it cannot be localized at the Troy of the relevant date. Excavation has revealed a number of houses of Troy VI, a settlement contemporaneous with the entire Middle Helladic period and with Late Helladic I–IIIA [4]. The basic feature of these houses is one large room, in addition to which is found sometimes a porch, sometimes a back room, but never an anteroom. Still less has any indication of a megaron been detected, although the Trojans of the later phases imported quantities of Mycenean goods, and on occasion even visited Greece if we may believe the legend of Helen's abduction.

Actually a similarity in architecture between Troy VI and Greece can be seen only in the fortifications. An imposing new circuit of walls was begun about 1425 – the last improvements seem to have been added not long before 1300 – and remained in service till the destruction of Troy VIIA, about 1260 (the destruction is assumed to be the result of the attack which became the basis for the Greek stories of the Trojan War). The work is contemporary with the less ambitious, early stages at Tiryns, with which it is comparable in general though not in detail.[7] It offers no ground for thinking that the Myceneans were influenced by Troy or *vice versa*. Instead, both peoples seem to have been inspired by a style which had already become widespread in Asia Minor, where, however, it was soon to be abandoned in favour of a Mesopotamian system (introduced by the Hittites) which involved a double line of walls with towers at regular intervals.

Tiryns

This citadel [63] eventually occupied the whole of a ridge which emerges near the sea from the alluvial plain of Argos; the total area is 4 acres (1·6 hectares). The top of the rock forms three terraces, rising from the north to a height of 80 feet at the south. Reoccupied in the Middle Helladic period after destruction, a long sequence of buildings has been found below the Late Helladic III palace. Some of these have been identified as fortifications, but without certainty. The upper citadel was probably first fortified in Late Helladic IIIA2 (second half of the fourteenth century) with its approach and entrance on the east side. The earliest wall is rougher than later work. It consists of enormous blocks (weighing several tons) of most irregular shapes, scarcely trimmed at all, and fitted together with the insertion of smaller pieces and clay packing; the wall averages 20 feet in thickness and was at least as high. This monstrous barbaric masonry seemed superhuman to the classical Greeks, who ascribed it to the mythical Cyclopes; hence it is termed Cyclopean. The same method is found contemporaneously in Asia Minor, and its sudden appearance in Greece on such a scale implies its introduction by the Achaean rulers of the Mycenean states. The first wall kept near the crest of the rock and was built throughout in straight stretches, joined by recessing with short right-angled turns except where the ground required bolder corners. The main gateway (on the east side beneath the subsequent outer propylon) opened straight on to the undefended slope, between a pair of towers, the fronts of which were parallel; the door stood between their backs. The approach and entrance were progressively elaborated; the chronology of these improvements and other additions is uncertain. The gate towers were doubled in thickness by extension within, which made the passage continue 22 feet (6·70 m.) inward of the door; it maintained a uniform width of $9\frac{1}{4}$ feet (2.84 m.).

Additional walls enlarged the citadel. These enclosed a strip on the south, the slightly lower terrace to the north across the middle of the ridge, and a shelf below the main gateway, which was now approached thereby from the north instead of the east; two gates in quick succession were placed at the entrance to the shelf, between the original wall on the inward side and a tower at the end of the new outwork. Subsequently the outwork was prolonged northward, terminating in a spur 26 feet (8 m.) thick which projected 56 feet forward from a

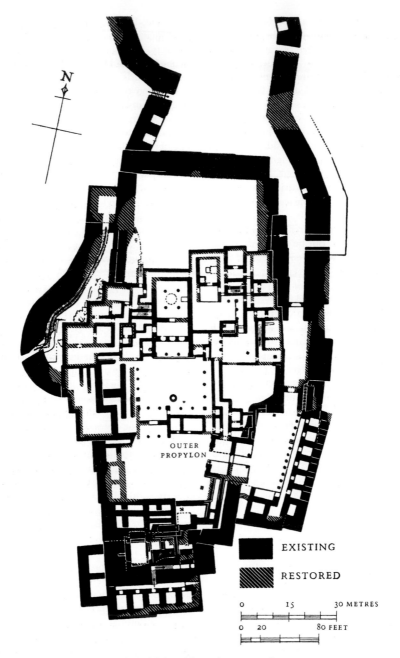

N

OUTER
PROPYLON

EXISTING

RESTORED

0   15   30 METRES

0   20   80 FEET

63. Tiryns, palace and south part of citadel, late thirteenth century, plan

new outer gate, placed between it and a correspondingly thickened part of the inner wall. An enemy who tried to attack the gate had first to get through the corridor between these two immense bastions, on the tops of which dozens of men could have been stationed with missiles. A minor entrance was also formed near the (then) north end of the west side, by building out a huge tower with a doorway through its south side adjoining a similar thickening of the main wall. Along the 10-foot frontage of this bastion a pit was dug and a drawbridge installed across it. Later, probably towards the end of the thirteenth century, a convex outwork was built southwards from the outer corner of the tower along the slope and finally bent inwards to join the main wall. A narrow door led through it at the bulge to the foot of a staircase, which rose over a distance of 150 feet to the drawbridge and was exposed all the way to missiles from every direction.

Late in the thirteenth century the area of the citadel was doubled, mainly by enclosing the north end of the ridge. On the east side the new wall ran straight southward towards the spur by the outer gate, but stopped short of it, leaving a gap of 15½ feet (4·70 m.). The end was built thick to match the spur and must have been 30 feet high. Outside the gap a ramp of the same width descended northwards along the face of the new wall. An enemy trying to reach the outer gate from the plain had to expose his unshielded right side for the whole length of the ramp and then make two right-angled turns under fire from all directions. (A prototype for this system has been found at Alişar in Asia Minor; it is a much older work retained in use under the Hittite empire.) The remains of extensive occupation in this area are in the course of excavation;[8] they have revealed that the earlier arrangements of Late Helladic IIIB2 differ considerably from those of the subsequent phase (Late Helladic IIIc). In both, buildings consist of rectangular rooms, rather irregularly arranged. Among them was a shrine building. In addition to this there was extensive building outside the fortified area, on the flat ground.

With these improvements to the fortification, it was thought safe to demilitarize the inner part of the entrance system. The south end of the shelf was widened into a forecourt by a new outer wall, and a colonnade built in front of it. A row of magazines [64][9] is contained in the thickness of the new wall. The enormous size of the roughly trimmed blocks facilitated roofing; the highest course on each side merely leans inwards against the other. A similar row was built 24 feet below the inner ground-level in the wall of another extension at the south end of the citadel; the purpose of these pitch-dark cells must have been to economize in stone and labour rather than to obtain storage space.

Although the fortifications were megalithic, the palace inside them was built of sun-dried brick, with wooden columns; this contrast is typical of Mycenean sites. At Tiryns, the earliest elements of the palace may well date from Late Helladic IIIA2 (late fourteenth century): but the main building is (as at Mycenae) of the thirteenth century [65, 66]. The old main gateway was then replaced by a flimsy, imitation-Minoan, propylon in the form of a duplicated porch. The building was almost square, 43¾ by 45¾ feet (13·34 by 13·64 m.); two columns supported the front and two the back; in the middle spur-walls ran out from either side leaving a wide central doorway. The base of the walls was faced with a wooden wainscot. A narrow side-door led northward into a corridor of the palace, but the inward porch opened westward on a corner of the great court. All this court was lined with buildings. On its north side a rather smaller propylon opened on the corner of an inner court, which was surrounded by a colonnade aligned with its inward porch, except on the opposite side, the north, where the megaron stood. This court, like the outer court, is longer west and east than north and south (66½ by 51½ feet; 20·25 by 15·75 m.), contrary to Minoan practice with the central courts of palaces; in fact these were not central courts but means of approach northwards. The megaron at the centre of the north side was advanced a trifle by the stone-based antae in which the walls

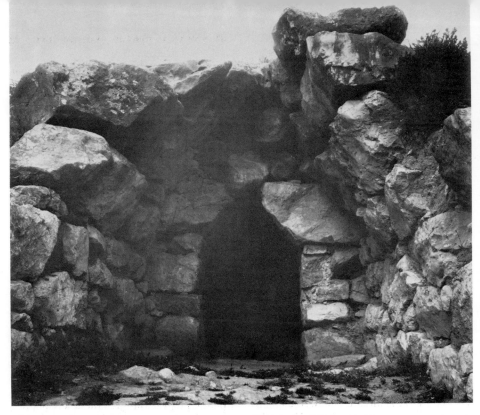

64. Tiryns, citadel, late thirteenth century, chamber in the thickness of the east wall

65. Tiryns, lower citadel, Late Helladic III, recent excavations

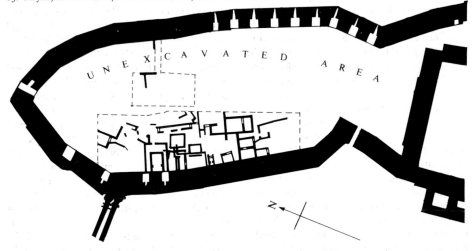

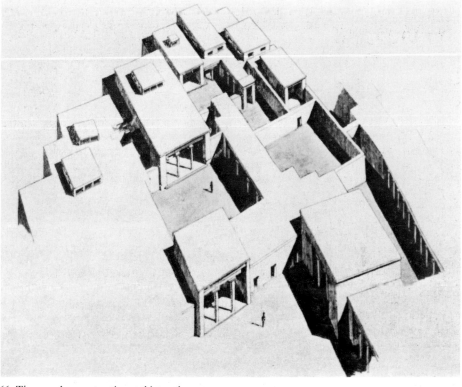

66. Tiryns, palace, restoration at thirteenth century

terminated and the two steps between them; but the two columns which carried the roof of the porch were recessed into line with the wings of the façade. The porch faced south and was 41 feet (12·50 m.) wide. Some 11 feet (3·80 m.) inwards a row of three double doorways separated it, in Minoan style, from an anteroom. At the back of the anteroom a central doorway formed the only entrance to the hall; this, one of the largest Mycenean rooms, measured internally 32 feet wide and 38½ feet long (9·80 by 11·80 m.). In its centre was the circular hearth, amid the four columns, which stood slightly nearer the side- than the end-walls. The plastered floor [67] was painted in alternate squares with a net pattern, an octopus, and a pair of dolphins, except for a space against the east wall, marked out by three bands of rosettes, where the king's throne must have been; the creatures of the sea face submissively towards it. The floors of the outer rooms were divided merely into blank squares. The walls of the porch, however, were lined at the base with an alabaster frieze [68] carved into an elaborate version of the Minoan split-rosette pattern, inset with blue glass; above it were frescoes. No doubt the inner rooms were frescoed too, and probably an extensive hunting-scene, of which many scraps remain, came from the fallen walls of the hall. The style of all the paintings at Tiryns is a clear-cut and unimaginative, directly representational version of the Minoan idiom.

A doorway through the west wall of the anteroom led to a confusion of small rooms

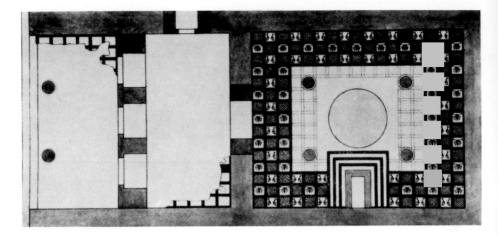

67-9. Tiryns, palace, restoration of floor
of great megaron (*above*),
restoration of ornamental dado (*right*),
and detail of floor of small megaron (*below*),
late thirteenth century

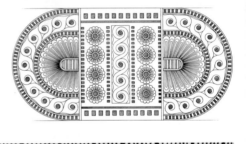

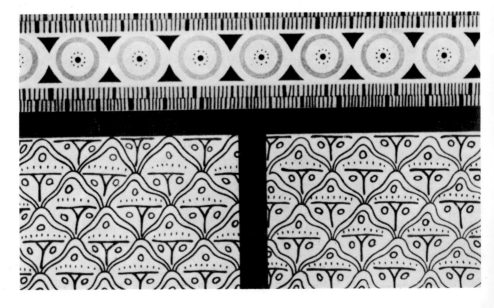

reminiscent of a Minoan palace, including a bathroom which was no doubt equipped with a terracotta tub such as the Minoans used. But its floor consists of a single twenty-ton block of limestone, such as no Minoan would have thought of obtaining, and its walls were panelled with boards, at any rate near the base; in this respect too the Mycenean taste for good materials had enforced a deviation from Minoan practice. A passage continued, with many abrupt turns in the Minoan fashion, past the back of the great hall to a court adjoining its east wall. Here stood two smaller megaron suites, each of porch and hall with no anteroom. On old plans the more westerly is described as the Women's Megaron, although all the available information on Mycenean life indicates that both sexes ate and conversed together freely in the same hall; only one or two secluded rooms were given up to feminine use. And it is now certain that these buildings were actually earlier than the great megaron suite, though all dated from Late Helladic III and utilized the same architectural forms; the decoration too was similar [69]. The late rooms west of the great megaron, and the early rooms east of its predecessors represent the domestic offices of each; the private apartments must have been placed above these rooms, and approached by staircases of the Minoan sort.

Mycenae

The citadel and palace of Mycenae overlook the inland end of the plain of Argos. The earliest fortifications to survive date from Late Helladic IIIA2 (after 1350). It was destroyed about 1200; after partial rebuilding came a final destruction about 1120. The work must be roughly contemporary with the first fortification of Tiryns, and the earliest work on the palace there; the similarity between the two indicates that the same artisans were employed. The wall surrounded a larger and less regular hill, not at its crest but along the slopes; an extension westward, about 1250, curved around a lower shelf, with a new main gate on the north beside the old west wall. The masonry is generally Cyclopean, of limestone boulders roughly shaped or left untouched, but for appearance's sake some ashlar conglomerate was used around the gates; the blocks are even more gigantic, but hammer-dressed into polygonal shapes and laid in more or less regular mortised courses. A sprinkling of pebbles upon the bed made it comparatively easy to align them, although an average block weighed 5 or 6 tons. The wall is normally 20 feet thick – in places 25 feet. 'Well-built Mycenae', Homer's stock phrase, is a masterpiece of understatement. But the upper part of the walls seems to have consisted of sun-dried bricks.

The road from the plain ascended a long foothill, in which the tholos tombs are sunk, and after passing close to the curve of the late wall, turned sharply inwards to the main gate, which lies in a re-entrant [70, 71]. On the downhill side a spur more than 20 feet wide projects 31 feet from the wall but 46 feet (14 m.) from the gate; opposite, on a shelf of rock, the only stretch of the original west wall still used runs out much farther (137$\frac{3}{4}$ feet; 42 m.) to a corner (rounded off in classical times), where the north wall begins. The intervening space is 20 feet wide at ground-level. The gate at its inner end is composed of two long blocks, making the lintel and threshold, and two shorter jambs. The doorway is 10 feet (3·10 m.) high and almost as wide at the bottom but narrows upwards as the jambs incline inwards (10–9 feet; 3·00–2·74 m.). The two wooden leaves of the door opened inwards, swinging on pivots sunk into the lintel and threshold, and folded back against the wall, in which slots were cut to receive the handles. A beam to bolt the two leaves horizontally could be slid out of a deep hole in one jamb till it locked into a shallower hole in the other. The lintel must weigh about 20 tons, for it is nearly 15 feet long and 7 feet wide (4·50 by 2·10 m.) and about 3 feet tall; the top rises in a hump above the doorway,[10] just as in Early Minoan ossuaries. The presence of a relieving triangle above it [71] is masked externally by a carved slab 2 feet thick, equal in height to the doorway and rather wider at the base (11$\frac{3}{4}$ feet; 3·60 m.).

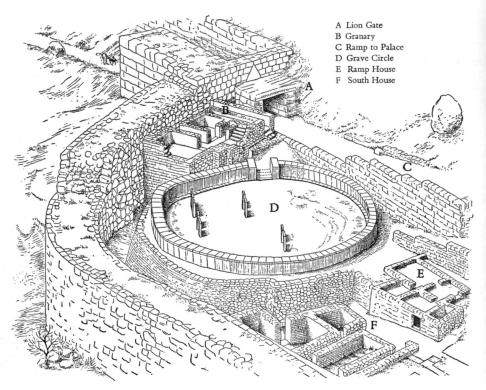

A Lion Gate
B Granary
C Ramp to Palace
D Grave Circle
E Ramp House
F South House

70. Mycenae, citadel, restoration of entrance from within

The relief of two lions on either side of a column has lost some of its effect with the heads, which were carved on separate blocks and dowelled into place; they must have faced outwards, whereas the bodies are cut in profile.[11] The paws rest on a plinth, represented as composed of four courses of masonry in which the blocks are alternately set forward and recessed. The column above it tapers downwards slightly – the degree is exaggerated to the eye by weathering – and stands on a low base which is only a trifle wider than the bottom of the shaft. The capital consists (going upwards) of a low collar edged at top and bottom with mouldings, a spreading cavetto, a thick cushion or echinus, another cavetto, and a square abacus equal in thickness to the echinus. On the top, a row of four disks and another plain block presumably simulate

respectively logs and the clay ceiling which rested upon them, but Minoan representations of buildings and the façade of the 'Treasury of Atreus' give warning that such interpretations must not be expected to correspond exactly to any actual structure. The column was probably meant to symbolize a deity of the royal household, whose attendant lions guarded the enclosure; the lions and monsters at the gates of Asiatic palaces are known to have had that function.

On the inner side of the Lion Gate [70], flanking walls run back 13 feet to form a porch, off which is a minute shelter for a porter or sentry, largely cut into the cliff that rises on the east. To the west a building called the Granary, which is backed against the citadel wall, appears most suitable for storage; perhaps dues paid to

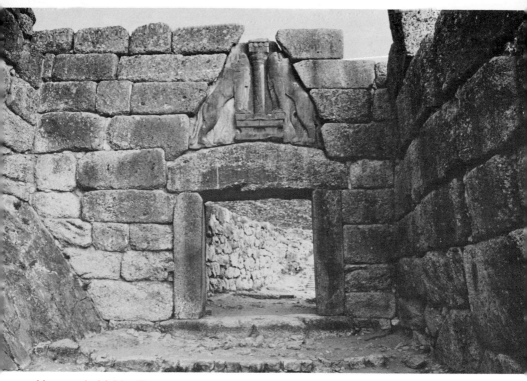

71. Mycenae, citadel, Lion Gate, c. 1250

the king were deposited here. The space beyond, around which the citadel wall was made to curve, is occupied by the Grave Circle and the shaft graves within it. They contained very rich, obviously royal burials older than the tholos tombs, in ground banked up by a Middle Helladic wall. When the venerated site came to be included in the citadel, about 1250, a space 85 feet in diameter was delimited, on top of this old retaining-wall, by a hollow double barrier (actually with two entrances; in illustration 70 one is omitted). Two rows of slabs were set upright in the soil and a continuous series of other slabs fixed across them, forming a flat top 4 feet (1·25 m.) wide; the height as exposed must have slightly exceeded 3 feet. The method of construction is unique in Greece, but a crude predecessor for the layout has been found in a

Middle Helladic double ring of stones that surrounded yet older graves at Malthi, just within the town gate.

South of the Grave Circle lay a number of buildings which excavators have long been gradually uncovering. The 'Ramp House' and 'South House' seem middle-class residences of Late Helladic III, and so probably were 'Tsountas' House' and another found more recently, although in each of these a room with many cult objects may have been a public shrine. The plans were compact, as befitted the situation; each building was quartered by cross-walls in both directions, not far from the middle. An open-fronted porch occupied nearly half the frontage of each. In the case of 'Tsountas' House', a doorway in its back wall opened into a pseudo-megaron, a longer room with a

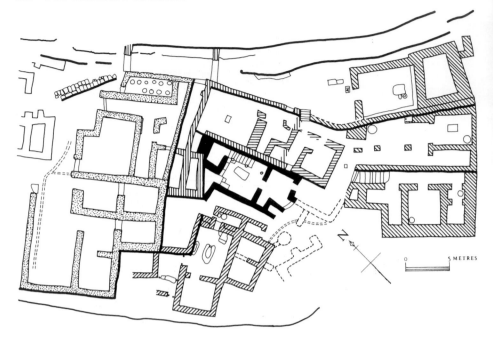

72. (A) (*above*) Mycenae, shrine building and adjacent houses, plan; (B) (*right*) Mycenae, 'House of Columns', thirteenth century, restored plan

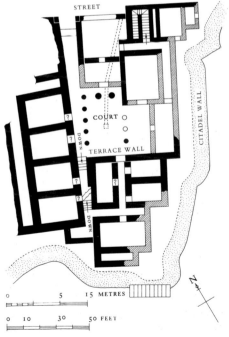

square hearth in the centre, while a side door-way led from the porch into a narrower front room, from which alone a room behind could be entered; this side was wholly basement. In the Ramp House and South House there were again doorways at both the back and the side of the porch, but the room at the back had no importance and the larger half of the frontage formed an anteroom to a pseudo-megaron behind. These plans have more in common with Cycladic than with Helladic predecessors of the Middle Bronze Age – presumably because they owe something to Crete, the influence of which had extended at that period to the Cyclades but not the mainland. In the 'House with the Idols' a full shrine was discovered [72A], irregularly planned, like that at Tiryns, and recognized by the fresco painting and terracotta figures it contained.[12] It is noticeable that shrines of this

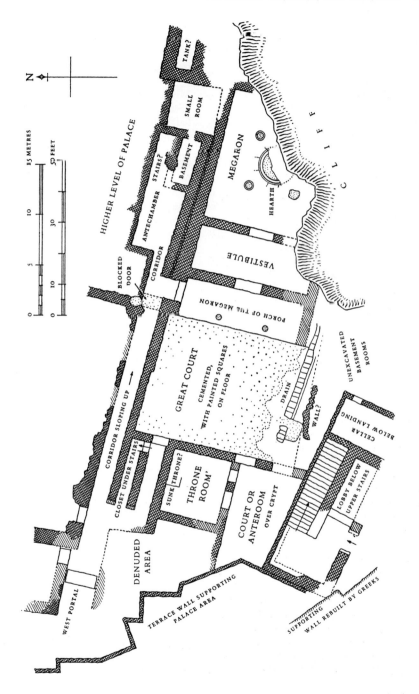

73. Mycenae, palace, plan

sort, series of rooms without any resemblance to the megaron arrangement, are normally found close to the fortifications of Mycenean citadels, as though their purpose was to protect them.

The chariot road to the palace climbed the slope behind the Lion Gate on a ramp, last rebuilt about 1200 across the original west wall. It must next have zigzagged to reach the western extremity of the terrace occupied by the buildings [73]; a short cut for foot-passengers ended with a two-flight staircase of Minoan inspiration, which was apparently added shortly before 1200. The area between the top landing and the head of the road overlies an older basement filled up at that date, where the Minoan device of supporting the upper floor by a single pillar had been adopted. Adjoining this on the north was the most westerly room of the new palace; a throne is presumed to have been set against the back wall in a sunken part of the floor. To the east lay the great court,[13] some 50 feet wide and 40 feet across, where the stuccoed surface of the floor [74] and the surrounding wall bore paintings, and a split-rosette frieze ran as a dado along the base of the walls, immediately below the first horizontal beam of the half-timbering. The buildings on the west and north sides contained two storeys, and the megaron suite on the east probably reached a comparable height. The two columns that supported the front of the porch stood on conglomerate bases less than 2 feet (57 cm.) in diameter, which on Minoan analogies should imply columns of barely 10 feet, but if the proportions of the stone half-columns at the tombs can be trusted their height may have considerably exceeded 20 feet; otherwise there may have been a loggia above. The porch was paved with gypsum slabs. In the centre of its back wall is a doorway 6 feet (1·80 m.) wide, with no sockets for a door; this opened on an anteroom behind which a similar doorway formed the entrance to the megaron. Half of the megaron has fallen into a precipitous ravine which bounded the citadel, but apparently the room measured about 40 feet (13 by 12 m.) each way. Its plastered floor and that of the anteroom were painted in brightly coloured patterns, except for a gypsum surround. The frescoes on its walls included groups of warriors and squires with horses and chariots, and of women standing in front of a palace; its timber frame is exposed, as indeed the ruins indicate to have been customary. The hearth was shaped like a shallow basin with a raised flat rim, the

74. Mycenae, palace, restoration of floor of court, late thirteenth century

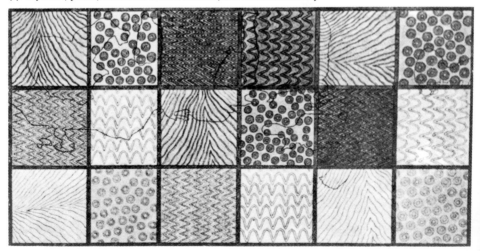

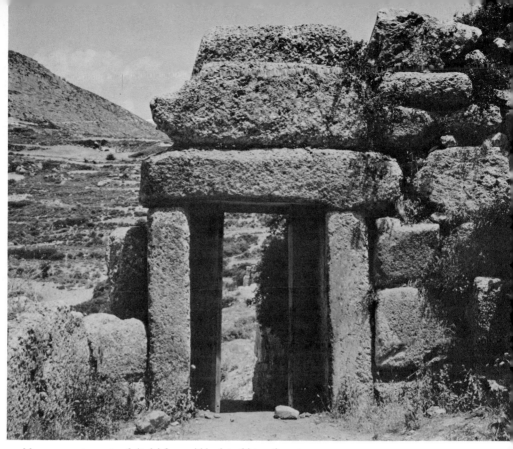

75. Mycenae, postern gate of citadel from within, late thirteenth century

edge of which has been painted at least ten times in successive patterns. Three bases of the four surrounding columns remain; they match those in the porch and are placed at a greater distance apart than from the walls. Along the north side of the megaron suite and the preceding court and rooms ran an earlier, straight corridor and beyond it the remainder of the palace occupied a higher terrace, which extends to the north edge of the hill; all this, however, has been reduced to insignificant scraps of foundation, except for one room which seems identifiable as a bathroom because of a sunken floor, plastered red inside a raised surround. The straight corridor on the lower terrace must have been duplicated at this level; a staircase rose from one to the other, beside the megaron.

Eastward of the palace proper, though linked with it, was the House of Columns [72B], which in plan anticipates the houses with colonnaded courts built for well-off Greeks a thousand years later. It was entered from the north by a cement-floored corridor, the mouth of which formed a little covered porch, because the doorway was set a few feet within. A double door was fitted to swing inwards. The corridor proceeded along the western wall of the megaron and of its anteroom, but the wall then stopped and a row of five columns prolonged its line along the side of the porch and onwards through a court. The eastern wall of the megaron continued till it turned a corner opposite the second column on the west, but three columns traversed the court in prolongation of its previous course. The façade of the porch apparently ran between the anta block at the wall corner and the second column of the west row, although a pair of thicker columns gave intermediate support to the roof opposite the first column. No other Mycenean instance is known either of an open-sided porch or of a court with colonnades aligned with the walls of the megaron suite. Presumably the space enclosed by the colonnades was left open, and the sides formed verandas – of unequal width, as a matter of fact. At the south end of the court, opposite the porch, ran a terrace wall, beyond which only basement rooms are preserved; there were probably two storeys above them. West of the corridor, along the edge of the house, was a row of four rooms, almost identical in plan; the two at the south overlay basement rooms. The worst of this accommodation was probably devoted to stores and the remainder mainly to bedrooms.

Late in the thirteenth century, well after the completion of the Lion Gate, an entrance was made through the north wall of the citadel, below the upper terrace of the palace. This minor gate is derogatively called the 'Postern' although it took a double door [75]. It opens at right angles to the face of the wall in a re-entrant formed by an overlapping spur. The doorway, over 6 feet in height and width, is incorporated in a tall cross-wall, and the lintel had to be safeguarded from the weight; the large block which lies immediately above is slightly concave on the under side where it spans the doorway, so that only its ends made contact with the lintel. This means of substitution for a relieving triangle is otherwise found only in the tholos tomb at Acharnae, where it is used repeatedly and conspicuously [62]; at the 'Postern Gate' it scarcely shows.

Practically the entire hill of the citadel was crowded with buildings. There even were two of quite large size in an eastward extension which was incorporated not long before 1200. Its purpose was probably to contain an underground passage to a 'Secret Cistern', so cut in the rock as to tap a spring outside the new piece of north wall; a roof like an inverted V was formed by leaning the highest courses of great blocks against one another, and in some places a flat ceiling of slabs was laid beneath, presumably to catch any earth that might fall through the rough joints. A sallyport, which pierces the wall close by, and another, inconspicuously placed by the south corner of the extension,[14] are roofed in the same form, which at Tiryns likewise appears only in the latest work; it is found there in two smaller tunnels to springs,[15] and in posterns and niches of the northern extension as well as in the magazines. Tunnels of similar form, on a much larger scale, were habitually constructed for posterns under the walls of Hittite and earlier cities in central Asia Minor, so that the expedient could have been introduced from that direction; it has been found nowhere else except in Assyria (at Asshur, approximately at the fifteenth century). As at Tiryns, there are other houses outside the citadel. Near the Tomb of Clytemnestra are the House of the Oil Merchant and the House of the Wine Merchant, so called from the large number of stirrup jars found in them which apparently contained these liquids. The jars are largely of Cretan origin, and indicate a lively trade with the western part of that island, well after the destruction of Cnossus and the other palaces.

Pylos

Greek tradition asserts that Nestor's father came from Thessaly and built a palace at Pylos: the original palace on a hill in that neighbourhood is of the requisite time, about 1300. This has a courtyard, on the north-west side of which is a porch with two columns in the opening and another single column below. Surprisingly, this does not lead to a conventional megaron-type hall. The hall is there, complete with four internal columns, but it is set to the side, more perhaps in the manner of Minoan architecture. Below these two rooms are storerooms, and a stairway leading, presumably, to the domestic quarters. Not long after[16] a second section was built, which was situated immediately to the

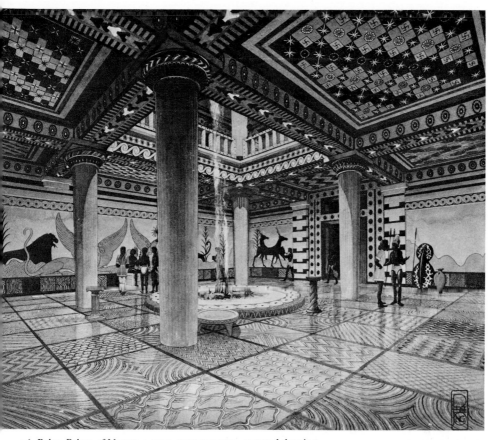

76. Pylos, Palace of Nestor, *c.* 1300, great megaron, restored drawing

east. This is clearly more important than the original building, which, however, remained in use.

The new section is entered from a formal propylon. Front and back porches each have a single column between the side walls; the cross-wall separating them has a single door. Across a small inner court, and directly facing the porch, there is now a regular megaron, with a two-column porch, a chamber, and a magnificent main room [76], 42 feet long and 37 feet wide (12·90 by 11·20 m.). At the centre is the great hearth where four columns supported a balcony which ran round all four sides; above

this came a lantern, to let out the smoke, and to admit light and air. The megaron has corridors to either side, flanked by suites of lesser rooms, again for storage purposes. Again, also, there are stairs to the upper-floor domestic quarters. The main megaron room was sumptuously paved, its walls lavishly decorated with frescoes; a restoration in colour gives a superb impression of its appearance. There was a formal throne placed against the east wall.

Two other separate parts of the palace are plainly built and equipped: the north-east building, which was a workshop, and the wine magazine.

Phylakopi

The layout of the public and private apartments at Mycenae may have been comparable in principle with that of a rather small palace of Late Helladic III at Phylakopi in Melos [77]. Here

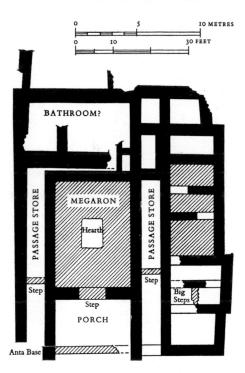

77. Phylakopi, palace,
Late Helladic III, plan

the megaron suite comprised a deep porch, no less than 15 feet by 20½ feet wide (4·60 by 6 m.), and a hall with a rectangular hearth of clay in the middle of the concrete floor; no traces of columns remain. On either side ran a corridor, 5 feet wide, which may have been used partly for storage. The one on the west turned along the back wall of the hall, narrowing to less than 2 feet, and led to a partitioned room which stretched to the full width of both hall and corridor. The corridor along the east side of the

megaron suite apparently ends abruptly, but perhaps a stair rose in prolongation to a corresponding corridor above. On the far side of it is a suite of interconnected rooms, averaging roughly 12 feet wide by 7 feet, most of which we may tentatively identify as bedrooms. The excavators thought the north room might have been a bathroom. Recent excavations have revealed a shrine; like those at Mycenae and Tiryns, it has no architectural pretensions. It has two parts: a simple rectangular room (the East Shrine, of Late Helladic IIIB date) and a larger West Shrine which appears to be older (Late Helladic IIIA). A blocking wall was built in the West Shrine in Late Helladic IIIc. The West Shrine contained a splendid wheel-made terracotta figure of a woman or goddess, a mainland piece dating to the second part of the fourteenth century (Late Helladic IIIA2).[17]

Gla (more properly Goulas)

A steep-edged plateau, which then formed an island in Lake Copais, was fortified all round and partially built over towards the end of the Mycenean period; the comparatively brief occupation endured long enough for some walls to need re-plastering twice. Each of the main gates on the perimeter was set in a thin inner wall forming the back of a rectangular court which was entered between towers of slight projection – a scheme used in the Hittite empire, the influence of which appears at Mycenae only in the last additions. There was a double enclosure [78] within the fortified area, approached from the principal gate, which was on the south side. The southern enclosure wall had a gate flanked by towers; within there were long ranges of buildings to east and west, with a large, apparently open space between them. The ranges were not identical, but had pairs of large rooms placed at their southern ends. At the north was the inner enclosure, which included the summit of the hill. This seems to have been the palace compound. The building occupied a corner of it and consisted of two wings joined at right angles and facing inwards, approximately to the

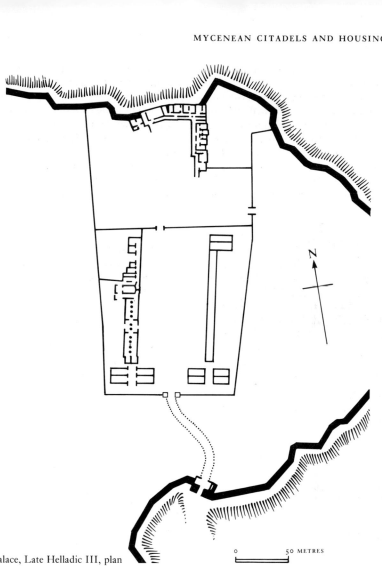

78. Gla, palace, Late Helladic III, plan

0   50 METRES

south and west; the total length comes to almost 500 feet (80·20 by 72·65 m.), and the width is usually 40 to 50 feet. The walls must have consisted of sun-dried brick above the stone base. A corridor ran the entire length of the façade except for the end of each wing; the inner wall is 3 feet thick, but the outer 4 feet thick, which suggests that it possessed greater structural importance, but it might have been largely opened by means of pillars or windows, recessed to ob-

tain protection from the rain. A megaron suite occupied most of the north wing. The remainder of the building consisted of suites of interconnected rooms, separated from the façade corridor by subsidiary corridors running parallel to it, which may in parts have been used for storage. The arrangement seems comparable to that along the sides of the 'House of Columns' at Mycenae and the palace at Phylakopi, but most of the rooms were larger in both dimensions; to judge from Homeric evidence they should have included married quarters for the king's family and dormitories for slaves.

Gla is a puzzling site.[18] It is definitely to be connected with the elaborate drainage system which in the Late Bronze Age made the area of Lake Copais available for agriculture. It has been suggested that it was, in some way, an artificially created city (it could not have existed as such until the lake was properly drained) which was never completed.

Macedonia

The rolling landscape of Central Macedonia is dotted with small steep-sided mounds which were occupied for long periods during the Bronze Age. At Assiros [79],[19] where excavation has demonstrated the existence of mud-brick fortifications and terrace walls, the summit of the mound may have contained nearly a hundred small rooms and open spaces grouped

in an orderly fashion and divided by roughly parallel streets or alleys. The framework of the buildings and the principal roof supports were provided by timber uprights set in the line of the walls, which were solidly built of sun-dried mud bricks. The defensible nature of the site, the organized plan, and the large provision for storage are all reminiscent of contemporary Mycenean settlements, contact with which is proved by imports and imitation of pottery.

Homeric Evidence

The great Mycenean strongholds and many of the lesser settlements perished by fire around the turn of the twelfth-eleventh century, and there was further destruction later in the eleventh century, causing movements of people[20] which gave rise to the Greek national states. In the buildings of the ensuing Iron Age, however, the Mycenean heritage remained for some centuries the predominant element and

79. Assiros, plan of buildings

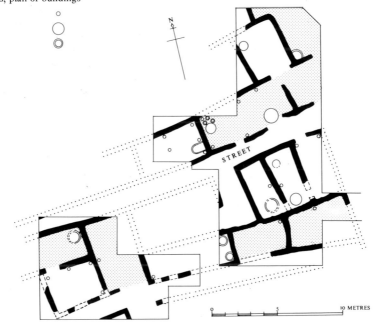

its effects endured, to a large extent it dictated the forms taken in classical architecture. The Homeric poems too preserved a distorted record of Mycenean life which yet seems strangely accurate if they date from as late as the eighth century; their architectural descriptions at any rate cannot have applied as closely to the buildings of that period as to those which had actually been inhabited by the heroes of the poems, in the thirteenth century.

Probably we should assume that Homer incorporated such material from ballads, composed at the transition from the Bronze to the Iron Age, when the old pattern of life survived, although its splendours were known to memory rather than in actuality. In the palace court 'dung of mules and cattle lay deep in heaps before the doors', horses are being kept in the colonnades and pigs are turned out from the sties there to graze in 'the fair courts' (*Odyssey* XVII. 296; IV. 40; XX. 164) (though pigsties have been identified at the palace of Cnossus[21]); that can scarcely have applied to the most important royal households. Thanks, no doubt, to the propylon, the court's 'double gates are well fenced' (*Od.* XVII. 267). The occupants of the palace, both men and women, spend most of their indoor time in 'the shadowy megaron' (*Od.* I. 365). Here 'they set up three braziers to give them light and place dry faggots round about and kindle the flame' (*Od.* XVIII. 307). The serving-maids come out 'from the megaron, beginning to take away the abundant food, the tables and the cups from which the lordly men had been drinking, and they threw the embers from the braziers on to the floor and piled fresh logs on the braziers to give light and warmth'

(*Od.* XIX. 60). 'Pass quickly through the megaron', directs the princess, 'till thou comest to my mother who sits by the hearth in the firelight, spinning the purple yarn, leaning against a column; her handmaids sit behind her. There too, propped against the same column is set the throne of my father' (*Od.* VI. 303). The smoke bedims the weapons hanging in the *oikos* – another word for the megaron, it seems (*Od.* XIX. 18). Bedsteads are placed in the porch or in the colonnade around the court for guests (*Od.* IV. 297, 302; VII. 336, 345; *Iliad* XXIV. 643). Male and female slaves sleep in rooms surrounding the court (*Il.* IX. 478). But the king's fifty sons and their wives also sleep in as many adjoining rooms off one side of the colonnades, and his daughters and their husbands opposite in 'twelve roofed chambers of polished stone, built close together' (*Il.* VI. 241); perhaps a wall of smooth plaster counted as stone. Polished wood too is mentioned. The king's bedroom was built high up in the fair court in a place with a wide view' (*Od.* I. 425). The bathroom always lies on the ground floor; the women's private apartments are upstairs as a rule, and have their own fireplace. The flat roof is used as a sleeping-place, and to dry foodstuffs. The Homeric data on ornamental features likewise both correspond with the archaeological evidence of Mycenean practice and amplify it. A precious 'blue' material must be the glass paste used to brighten a carved frieze; thresholds are described as of oak, stone, or bronze, the walls as covered with gold, silver, and bronze. The 'gleam as of the sun and moon through the lofty halls of renowned Menelaus' may not have been vastly exaggerated (*Od.* IV. 45).

PART TWO

HELLENIC ARCHITECTURE

CHAPTER 8

INTRODUCTORY SUMMARY

The Bronze Age ended in wholesale destruction, before 1100 B.C., after which four centuries of poverty ensued.[1] When eventually the Hellenic civilization took shape, its architectural requirements differed from those of its already legendary predecessor. Temples for the gods were now of first importance, whereas in the Bronze Age there had been none; if palaces were still built they have left no traces, and tombs ceased to be monumental and impressive. Only the cheapest methods of construction persisted through the Dark Age; houses and huts were of the simpler types, retaining forms which had prevailed in the Bronze Age. With the revival of prosperity these served as prototypes of more ambitious Hellenic designs, for religious as well as secular buildings. The aesthetic possibilities of each type were gradually explored, with the result that one or two were discarded as unsatisfactory and the remainder transformed almost beyond recognition.

This process required many generations, stimulated by the developing prosperity of the more progressive Greek communities, and marked by distinct improvements in the technical quality of their construction, most noticeably in the seventh and sixth centuries B.C. From this time the aim was always to perfect a type of building, and in the case of each the speed of development slackened as they approached success. In general the types reached that stage in the late fifth and early fourth centuries, after which they were changed comparatively little. A great increase in the population of certain cities gave rise to new problems, especially as regards municipal buildings, but solutions were found which preserved the types without drastic alteration, a more ornate treatment compensating for larger scale. Indeed, the architects of later times devoted most of their creativeness to the enrichment of decoration, for which they applied functional elements, such as columns, in an unfunctional manner. A few buildings of striking originality do, in fact, date from the later centuries, but it is significant that these were evoked by unusual requirements, which could not readily be fulfilled by adherence to one or other of the defined types. Although the habit of restricting average building to a narrow range of types eventually resulted in stultifying architectural genius, the effect till as late as the fourth century remained beneficial. Acceptance of limitations naturally directed effort towards attaining perfection in each class of design, as would scarcely have been the case if the architects had allowed themselves wider scope for originality and experiment; instead, their constant aim was to achieve ideal proportions in every detail. In that they succeeded to a degree which no other race has emulated. The Parthenon came as near perfection as is humanly possible, both in design and in meticulous execution. But historically its significance lies chiefly in the fact that the most ambitious of the art-forms, the Doric temple, had reached its zenith; a decline inevitably followed, and because of the supremacy of the Doric temple over all other types of building they too became aesthetically impoverished. Most other types reached their culmination within the next two or three generations, when taste was already less sure. It would be anachronistic to say less correct, because that priggish word represents a Renaissance, not a classical, mentality.

Adherence to types characterizes Greek art as a whole; this must have aided Plato to formulate his doctrine of Ideas, which strikes a modern reader as far-fetched, but no doubt seemed obvious in his own surroundings. In architecture the types were closely related to one another and utilized the same few structural methods and decorative elements. All alike retained to the end clear signs of having originated from the adaptation in stone of domestic buildings constructed largely of timber and unbaked brick.

The Greek temple, the purpose of which was to house a deity, not to accommodate worshippers, originated in imitation of the Dark Age house, and in primitive times took the same variety of form. The room, or rooms, and the porch, where one existed, likewise followed precedent in the manner of arrangement and design. But of all the prototypes, that which contributed most to the eventual temple-type was the megaron, though whether this represents a memory of the Mycenean palace or imitation of the homes of the petty rulers of Dark Age Greece is debatable. Its adoption may have been only indirectly due to its manifest architectural superiority; the anthropomorphic beliefs of the Greeks would in any case have inspired a preference for the palace type as the most suitable home for their deities, to whom, moreover, legends ascribed a practice of visiting palaces. There is also a possibility of influence, particularly in the eighth century B.C., from areas outside the narrow limits of Aegean Greece, such as Cyprus, where Phoenician builders at Kition had re-used and re-formed late Bronze Age buildings whose constructional details uncannily anticipate those of stone construction in classical Greece.[2] The form of temple which became canonical retained the traditional plan in that the entrance consisted of

a porch, usually with two columns to support the roof, and a large hall, called the cella. A smaller room might be placed behind the cella, in accordance with older or plebeian Bronze Age practice (which, perhaps more significantly, is also found in later structures in Syria), but the back room is rare in temples built after 500; an alternative, which then became dominant, duplicated the form of the porch at the opposite end, against a blank wall, the back of the cella. The purpose can only have been embellishment, in conformity with the Greek passion for symmetry.

Technically the primitive temple was much inferior to the average megaron in the Bronze Age palaces. The walls consisted of the same material, sun-dried brick raised upon a rubble base and strengthened with a timber frame, but were thinner, and so could not have supported the flat mud roof of Mycenean times. The earliest temples must have been thatched and consequently ridge-roofed. Another divergence from Bronze Age precedent, found only in a very few of these temples, was the addition of a veranda around the cella, which was thereby protected from the rain. It is most unlikely that this was done before the eighth century B.C. No Bronze Age building is known to have been completely surrounded in that manner, though the courtyards of many palaces had been lined in part with verandas. When, in the course of time, stone was adopted as the usual material for temples, a surrounding colonnade of stone became fashionable, although walls, being of stone, no longer needed shelter. But the expense was greater than could usually be afforded; most temples therefore continued to be built without columns except in the porch (and in the false porch, wherever that existed).

The notion of building in cut stone developed in the seventh century B.C. External influences from the Near East or Egypt may have been the cause. But a compelling reason for the use of stone was provided by the invention of roofing tiles, the weight of which far exceeded that of modern tiles. Another result of the invention was the prevalence of rectangular plans, since a rectangular roof is most easily tiled, and a gable at either end became inevitable. But the pediment, created by placing an unnecessary ledge across the gable, was a purely arbitrary innovation, perhaps of slightly less antiquity. With this doubtful exception, the entire structural and ornamental system of the stone temple seems to have been devised simultaneously, by copying predecessors built of wood and mud. At first stonework was restricted to the walls, and the earliest examples retain the pattern formed by mud brick laced with timber, while retaining wooden columns. Later these and their superstructure were made of stone. No doubt some features were transposed or otherwise modified, but every detail of the whole system from the foot of the columns to the gutter is an apparent translation from carpentry. This is particularly true of Doric, which from its very beginning formed an Order, in this sense, that the position and shape of every portion never varied. In the case of Ionic the translation from wood or metal seems to have been less pedantic, perhaps because of the later date of the event; the Order allowed of considerable variation until more than a century after its first appearance, and never became so rigid.

While the Orders took their names from the two main variant forms of Greek spoken in their respective areas of origin, their geographical distribution never altogether conformed with that of dialect. Broadly, Doric began as and remained the style of the Greek mainland and (by extension) of the western colonies, Ionic that of some Aegean islands and the coast of Asia Minor, though it was also introduced to Athens barely a generation after it took shape and became an alternative to Doric there; the Athenians might have justified themselves by their claim to be Ionians who had not migrated.

In the oldest columns and other members the proportions followed the traditional measurements of wooden architecture, but soon it was realized that, when building in stone, the greater weight and the lack of tensile strength demanded thicker proportions. When more experience had been gained and confidence returned, the tendency was reversed; henceforth the proportions in general became ever more slender, and gradually the proportionate relations of the various members were also improved aesthetically in the two Orders. After several generations of constant progress, marble came into use, and whenever financially possible took the place of softer and less reliable stone. Greater liberties could therefore be taken with the structure, and now the best proportions were ascertained.

With this mastery, the architects of the late fifth century exploited the capacity of marble for sharp definition and polished surface, to a degree which has never been equalled. In Doric, perspective and foreshortening were countered or simulated by means of scarcely perceptible distortions. Ionic offered less scope for such 'refinements', but a comparable subtlety was lavished on elaborating the capitals, bases, and ornament; yet the treatment was utterly formal in spite of the incomparable richness. At the same time the invention of the Corinthian capital gave opportunities, not fully realized till the middle of the fourth century, for developing carved foliage to the opposite extreme of naturalism. Corinthian, however, never became an Order in the same sense as the two older forms; only the capital distinguished Corinthian from Ionic construction, and the effect of the capital was too undignified to be suitable for repetition on a large scale along the exterior of a religious building.

Now that so much success had been achieved, a loss of vitality began to appear. This was mitigated to some extent by a loosening of conventions, especially when Greek civilization spread among Hellenized orientals, a process which became more rapid after Alexander's conquests, in the period therefore called the Hellenistic Age (330 onwards). To some extent too the decline was postponed by the need to solve problems that arose from the progressive lightening of the Orders. Columns became continually slimmer and were spaced further apart, while the size of the capitals diminished relatively to the shaft. But the nature of the structure set limits to this process and these were reached during the second century. The only other way of advance had been to increase the opulence of decoration, which passed the bounds of decency contemporaneously or soon after. Accordingly Greek temple-forms came to the end of their development before the time of Christ.

At great sanctuaries the various states sometimes built treasuries to hold objects dedicated by their citizens, especially when the temple, which should have contained everyone's votive offerings, was in a ruined or unfinished condition. A treasury, being really a satellite temple, always took the general shape of a temple but on a miniature scale, which gave opportunity for more elaborate decoration than could be afforded in the case of a large building. Moreover the decorative scheme tended to a playfulness which would have been thought unseemly in a temple. This applies especially to the sixth century; few later examples showed originality.

The other types of Greek architecture may have been ultimately derived, at several removes, from Mycenean forms, though the immediate influence was rather that of the Hellenic temple and of the contemporary house. Streets in a Greek city ran as straight as the ground permitted, though unless the town was deliberately planned the exact line was determined by natural features, contour forms, and obstacles. In planned cities streets were straight, and crossed at right angles. Whatever the alignment the streets enclose either an individual building or a continuous block of houses. The middle of each house was occupied by a courtyard, with a veranda or colonnade along at least one side; the rooms, which lay between the court and the outer wall, remained comparatively small, even as late as the fourth century. In the course of time, the size of the rooms increased and the quality of the building materials improved, while the mosaic floors and mural decorations became more elaborate. The plan, however, remained essentially unchanged, though the court more often was colonnaded on all sides. Because of this concentration on the court, the external appearance of houses can have had little or no architectural interest, unless they were palatial in scale.

The type of the public hall was apparently derived in the first place from the veranda attached to the Mycenean palace, though any direct derivation is impossible.[3] It was more immediately influenced by the design of the temple. Early examples of the hall consisted simply of a long stoa – an open-fronted shed, the roof of which sloped from the back wall to a row of posts along the front. By the fifth century stone columns were normally used instead of wooden posts. Later stoas were often immense, running to two storeys, each with a colonnade of a different Order, and so wide as to require a ridged roof, carried on internal colonnades, while a row of shops or offices lined the back wall. In every large city the market-place became more or less surrounded by such stoas. A similar scheme was adopted on a smaller scale for the principal structures of the gymnasium, which consisted of a court enclosed on all four sides by a colonnade, with rooms behind. Halls for holding formal meetings often took the form of an abbreviated stoa, with the front more or less closed by a wall. Sometimes tiers of benches were provided inside, in which case the shape necessarily approximated to a square, though the benches themselves in late examples were curved in imitation of the seating in a theatre.

Natural hollows were used for semi-religious spectacles, and the growth of an architectural form for the theatre and stadium was consequently slow. Not till the fourth century was it thought essential to excavate and bank up the auditorium into a regular shape. Then the benches invariably described a curve of more than a semicircle, enclosing most of the dancing place (orchestra) on which much of the interest of the play was concentrated. Behind this, however, stood a low building which served as a background, supporting the scenery. The later innovation of a stage was easily effected by adding an upper storey to the scene-building. Now the action of the play lay too far back to be visible from the outer arms of the auditorium, but the Greeks were unaccountably slow to adopt the Roman expedient of restricting the auditorium to a semicircle (see below p. 373), though the Romans believed that their first permanent theatre, that built by Pompey, was derived from the Greek theatre at Mytilene. The developed Roman theatre, of which examples were built in Greece, made extensive use of vaulting to support the auditorium, whereas the Greeks had made only occasional use of vaults to cover entrance passages to theatre and stadium. The boldness of Roman vaulting also contrasted with Greek practice; the Greeks had been backward in their very limited use of the arch. This fact accounts to some extent for their adherence to long-established types of design, many of which were transformed or superseded under the Roman Empire, when the principle of vaulting was fully applied. But the excessive conservatism of Greek architecture had been justified by its perfection, and because of the infinite variety of treatment possible within each type. A contributory factor to this variety was the elevation of masonry into a fine art, thus allowing it to become an important element in design.

CHAPTER 9

PRIMITIVE TEMPLES

The Bronze Age in Greece was followed by a period of confusion and poverty, the Dark Age. A wholesale movement of peoples is recorded, involving Greek colonization of the Aegean coast of Asia Minor, and may be attributed to distressed conditions more than to displacement by the influx of kindred, though barbarous, tribes from the northern fringe of the Helladic area. To the eyes of archaeologists the standard of the material remains drops catastrophically in the eleventh century and begins a slow, somewhat erratic and variable recovery in the tenth; perhaps the truth is that a process of levelling reduced disparities, bringing the whole population to a fairly uniform state of poverty, without the outstanding wealth attributed to the rulers of the Mycenean world. The kingdoms had broken up, and of the towns some had perished and the others dwindled: the new aristocracy of village squires had greater possessions than their cottagers, yet not much better as regards quality.

The culture of the eleventh century was pre-Hellenic in a degenerate and degenerating form, and this heritage continued to suffer a gradual attenuation till the eighth century, when it had almost ceased to exist; the Hellenic civilization was then beginning to evolve – out of virtual nullity, to judge by material evidence. The literature confirms this view. Hesiod, writing in the eighth or seventh century, stresses the poverty and misery of his times, compared with the Golden and Silver Ages of the past, but his topics are up to date and his literary forms largely fresh invention, whereas Homer, perhaps a hundred years earlier, ignores the present; he is concerned purely with legends of Mycenean glories, and transmits as faithfully as possible all the details of that ancient life. To some extent his architectural data must have agreed with the circumstances of his own day, but not

necessarily in entirety; the ballad-singers in the United States have preserved all the obsolete architectural data transmitted from Britain. In any event Homer's aristocratic patrons are likely to have been worse housed than any village princeling of the poems; the fall in architectural standards had been catastrophic. The surviving buildings of the Dark Age are few in number and of deplorable quality; they can excite interest only because they show the genesis of the Greek temple.

In the Bronze Age there had been no temples. The Minoans regarded certain caves and mountain tops as sacred, but otherwise the only places they set aside for worship were small shrines, occupying at most a couple of rooms and sometimes only part of a room, in a palace or over a tomb; they can be identified as shrines by the presence on a bench of sacred images or symbols. On the mainland several shrines or places of cult have now been discovered. Architecturally these are not impressive, and their recognition depends rather on the objects discovered in them, or the decoration of their walls. Significantly, they do not make use of the megaron plan employed for the principal room of the palace, and are invariably found away from the palace structure, often by or close to the perimeter fortification. Homer, however, represents the gods as constantly visiting their royal relations in the palaces. But in the early Hellenic period almost every building that has left a trace was a temple.

This completely different state of affairs illustrates the extent of the changes that took place in Greece in the early Iron Age. When the Hellenic civilization began, about 800, the shape it took was new in practically every way. Artistically it retained very little from the Bronze Age except the technique of essential handicrafts, such as the making of utilitarian pottery, simple metal-working, and rough methods of building. Actually continuity is more apparent in building than in any other class of remains. The same materials were used: timber for columns and doorways, sun-dried brick for the upper part of the walls, stone for their base – but very little of the stone was dressed, and for most purposes rough blocks picked off the fields were considered adequate. The methods of roofing were similar, but thatch may have gained the ascendancy over the heavier flat roof; the acceptance of the pitched roof as the proper covering for temples must go back to the Dark Age, and probably began with thatch, as a means of saving material and labour. A prevalence of thatch may be deduced too from the frequency of curved walls in the early temples. The sites chosen for these are frequently those with Bronze Age associations; some, indeed, are actually placed on the ruins of Mycenean palaces, though whether any memory survived of the precise function these ruined buildings had when they were intact is doubtful; possibly the choice was due to a more vague association of appropriate antiquity.[1] In general, the building of a temple was not undertaken before the eighth or seventh century; many a sanctuary began as an open enclosure containing nothing but an altar.

The dating of early Greek remains is extremely difficult. The ancient historians supply no reliable chronological data for events prior to the sixth century, and the exchange of goods with oriental countries probably cannot be traced further back than the eighth century and gives little firm evidence for that period. A complete sequence of pottery from the Mycenean age onwards has been established for Athens and other centres of production, such as Argos; these, with all the limitations and approximation involved, form the general basis for chronology. All datings appreciably before 600 must be liable to a wide margin of error, even in the case of the few buildings which were clearly associated with a particular kind of pottery. But fragments of pottery and other material which might determine the relative date of a structure

have seldom been found in such quantities, or so well recorded, as to leave no doubt either of their relevance or of their character. The discoveries at Lefkandi are an exception to this.

A largely open-air sanctuary at Karphi, in Crete, is a survival of Minoan practice. The earliest monumental building of the Iron Age in Greece is undoubtedly that recently excavated at Lefkandi in Euboea. Dated securely to Late Protogeometric times (the tenth century B.C.), it was apsidal in plan, measuring 30 feet by at least 150 feet (10 by 45 m.). Its similarity to the later temples is emphasized by a surrounding colonnade, of wooden posts. In all appearances, this marks the beginning of the temple form, later repeated at the Heraeum of Samos and Argos. Yet it was not a temple, for it covers, in a precise arrangement, a grave, containing in one shaft a warrior and his wife, in another shaft his horses. The exact relationship between this surprising structure and the later temples which are so similar in form requires further analysis, and, one hopes, fresh discoveries. This building had a short life, being deliberately filled in, perhaps as a result of partial collapse, in the same period – Late Protogeometric – as its construction. Thus this particular structure can itself have had no influence on the architecture of the eighth century; but its discovery means that we cannot be sure that other examples did not exist. What was once thought to be the oldest Greek building, a fragment of wall underlying the Oikos of the Naxians at Delos, has now been demonstrated to be part of a Mycenean structure.[2] The Oikos itself (in all probability the first temple of Apollo on Delos) was not built until the seventh century.

A curved wall found at Perachora, near Corinth, formed the back of a temple of Hera, which must have resembled the apsidal houses introduced in Middle Helladic times. The foundations of the wall were associated with pottery ascribed to the ninth century, but this was possibly already lying on the ground when the temple was built. The temple may belong rather to the following century, when at least four pottery models of the building were

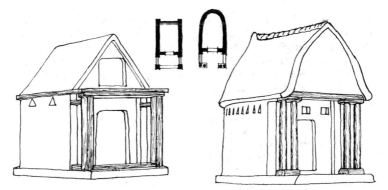

80. Restoration of model temples from the Argive Heraeum and Perachora

dedicated there, though too much of each has been lost for a complete restoration to be feasible [80]. The roof seems to have been shown as a tall pointed vault of convex curvature, like a boat upside down, with a keel ridge and wide eaves – manifestly a reproduction of thatch. The temple consisted of a single room, slightly longer than it was wide, curved at the back and separated in front from the porch by a straight wall with a central doorway. The front of the porch was carried by pairs of square posts, set close together, which stood prostyle (i.e. forward from the side walls) at each corner. This arrangement occurs in the 'House of Columns' at Mycenae, but no other pre-Hellenic instance is known; the normal practice of the Bronze Age had been to place the columns *in antis* (between the ends of the side-walls).

The other rounded plans of pre-Hellenic huts were also used for temples. In some cases the walls curved throughout in the form of an ellipse, or it may be better to call it an elongated horse-shoe since one end was cut across by the doorway. A good example is the eighth-century temple in the sanctuary of Apollo Daphnephoros at Eretria [81]. This was simply a hut, whose curving walls were stabilized with posts resting on stone bases, placed in contact with the wall both inside and out, and supporting the roof structure. There was a porch in front of the door, which was at the southern end. There is another example at Gonnus in Thessaly, a back-

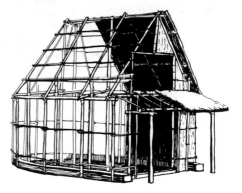

81. Eretria, sanctuary of Apollo Daphnephoros, wooden-framed temple, eighth century

ward district; it may therefore be later than the apparent date, the seventh century. It was rebuilt on the same lines about 300 B.C. The greatest width (some 26 feet) came midway along the length (33 feet); the doorway was at the south end. The original walls consisted of sun-dried brick on a base of dressed stone and bore features made of terracotta, including decorative antefixes, a cornice, and plain metopes (p. 130). Chips from a stone column suggest that there may have been a prostyle porch. Probably this was by no means the only early building in which the Doric order was applied to curved walls, but no other example has been discovered older than the mid-sixth-century tholos at Delphi. The method of roofing a temple of a horse-shoe plan is likely to have resembled that of Greek tholoi; they bore a conical roof on the wigwam principle, supported by poles which met in the centre so that their ends crossed.

The later Greeks built very few temples with curved walls and as a rule those definitely later than the sixth century conform to another type, in which the sides are straight and only the central stretch of the back wall is rounded into an apse, leaving the corners rectangular. The oldest example, a little temple of Earth at Delphi, was destroyed about 500 B.C. and can scarcely have been built as early as 600. Probably the shape originated from a compromise with the rectangular types of plan which were then becoming almost universal.

On the evidence of pottery models, some rectangular temples of the Dark Age were flat-roofed, while others had steep roofs with a pronounced ridge. The Heraeum of Argos is represented [80][3] with a combination of both methods. A pitched roof covered a flat ceiling, from which eaves projected beyond the side walls, and a hood also extended forwards from a cross-wall so as to cover a porch, at the front of which it was supported by a round post on either side, standing prostyle; each of the side walls ended in a pilaster of slight projection, from the top of which a beam seems to have run across to the column. A large window (or door) occupied most of the gable above the cross-wall. The pitched roof apparently did not overlap the flat ceiling at the sides but rose from behind the eaves, and at the front it did not overlap the ends of the side walls; its outline is straight or slightly sagging. If the model is really trustworthy in that respect, it ought to represent some thinner material than ordinary thatch – possibly wattle-and-daub. The walls were presumably of sun-dried brick; patterns are represented upon them, as is usually the case with such models. In the single instance of a model from Ithaca the roof is painted to represent tiles.

The first of the successive temples of Hera at Samos is ascribed to 800 B.C. because of the pottery found under and above it; this can only be a quite tentative dating, for it assumes that the development of eastern Greek wares kept pace with Attic; a date later in the eighth century is preferable. Undoubtedly this Heraeum [82] is the oldest peripteral temple (i.e. one surrounded by an external colonnade, or pteron); its pteron, however, seems to have been

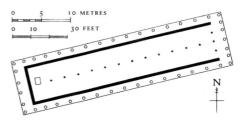

82. Samos, first Heraeum, eighth century, restored plan

added later, though not more than fifty years after the construction of the cella, the inner portion. Very little of this temple actually survived, and its restoration therefore is not completely certain. The original plan, when the cella comprised the entire temple, would have been monstrously ill-proportioned; the length (32·86 m.) was a trifle more than five times the width (21½ feet; 6·50 m.). The entrance, as in the vast majority of later temples, was at the east end, which was left open, with three columns in antis. There was no separate porch, and the central column of these three was the first of a row of thirteen which divided the interior into two aisles, each only 8 feet wide. The image of the goddess, at the far end, had to be placed a little to one side of the centre, in order that the colonnade should not block the view of it. The columns must have been wooden; as at Eretria flat slabs served as bases. The roof was probably flat.

The addition of the pteron brought the overall ratio of length to width below 4:1 (121 by 31 feet; 36·86 by 9·50 m.), measured at the edge of the platform. At the front end, three columns were placed opposite those of the entrance, and two others in line with the cella walls, making, with the angle columns of the long sides, a total of seven. At the back only six columns were used, so that the distance from axis to axis amounted to 5 feet. On each of the long sides there were seventeen, spaced over 7 feet apart. The shafts were wooden and stood on plain cylindrical bases of stone, such as the Minoans had used for the same purpose of raising the timber above the damp.

This temple was replaced by another on the same site, perhaps early in the seventh century [83]. The new cella was the same length but a foot wider (22¼ feet; 6·80 m.); with a pteron nearly twice as wide as its predecessor, the total width exceeded 38 feet (11·70 m.) The overall ratio of length to width came to less than 3½:1, in spite of a second row of columns at the front – a feature characteristic of later temples in the eastern Greek area. The pteron contained six

83. Samos, sanctuary with second Heraeum, perhaps early seventh century, restored plan

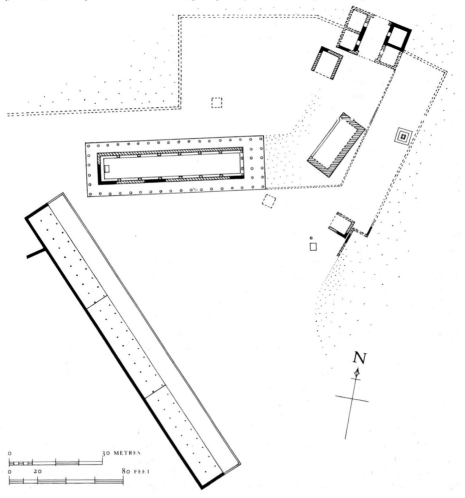

N

| 0 | | | | 30 METRES |
| 0 | 20 | | | 80 FEET |

columns on the ends and eighteen on the sides (counting those at the corners each time); they were evenly spaced at an interaxial distance of 7 feet (2·14 m.). The internal arrangement marks a great improvement: the cella was left clear except for a row of six columns close beside each wall, opposite every alternate column of the pteron, and the image occupied the centre of the back wall – the normal position in later temples. Two additional columns, evenly spaced, stood in the entrance, between those beside the antae. The bases are plain square slabs. All the columns were made of wood, and the antae were strengthened with wooden beams and panelled in wood. No use whatever was made of terracotta. In the absence of tiles the manner of roofing cannot be proved, but the internal columns would surely have been placed farther from the walls if they had carried the great weight of a flat roof; probably timbers laid between them and across to the pteron formed the base of the framework for a double-pitched roof, which covered the whole building at an even slope. The placing of the inner and outer columns to correspond must imply that they were connected above.

This second Heraeum may therefore have resembled the subsequent classical temples in elevation as well as in plan. The origins of the type remain obscure. The absurdly elongated cella of the first Heraeum recalls the 'hair-pin' plan of Middle and Late Helladic houses, which, however, required no internal supports because of the lightness of the roof; the Greeks may have wished to give their temples a more durable kind of roof, whether of mud or with heavier timbers, and a greater depth of thatch. The pteron seems to have been a Greek innovation. No pre-Hellenic building is known to have been completely surrounded by a colonnade, though in a few instances a colonnade ran along one side of the exterior, or a part of it; perhaps the Greeks may have consciously adapted the Mycenean scheme to an isolated structure, comparable in function to a megaron.

Another building, at the remote and possibly backward sanctuary of Thermum, has received more attention than it deserves, both because of a mistake in dating which ascribed it to the tenth century and because of a misunderstanding of the relationship between the earlier Bronze Age structures and the first signs of religious construction. The earliest houses on the site date from the early Mycenean period and include elliptical and rectangular types as well as one example of the 'hair-pin' form (Megaron A). Later, perhaps c. 1250, a rectangular house was constructed at a higher level and used for an indefinable period (Megaron B).[4] Level with the top of the ruined walls of this building was a widespread ash layer containing votive bronzes dating to the eighth and early seventh century. At the same level, and presumably to be related to the burnt debris, were eighteen stone column supports surviving from a series which formed a hair-pin shape. It is impossible to discover whether the apparent arrangement of these around the earlier Megaron B is more than fortuitous, for this must have been long out of use and perhaps hardly visible. This alleged 'pteron' is more probably the surviving trace of a largely timber-built sanctuary building which happened, as at many sites, to be over a Bronze Age settlement, and was later replaced by a peripteral temple (see below, p. 124).

As a rule, however, the primitive temples had no pteron. Stone sockets for posts, which fulfilled a different function from those at Thermum, occur in the first temple of Artemis Orthia at Sparta, only a corner of which survived the construction of a sixth-century temple; it probably dates from soon after 700.[5] An inner row of columns stood at intervals of only 4 feet on flat slabs, opposite each of which lies a similar slab with a socket built upon it, to hold a post upright in the external wall. This may well have needed such reinforcement, for it was very thin and consisted of sun-dried brick with a base of slabs set on edge, bedded on round pebbles. No doubt the half-timbering included horizontal beams at a higher level, in the Bronze Age manner, together with cross-pieces linking the wall frame with the colonnade. Assuming that only one row of columns existed along the

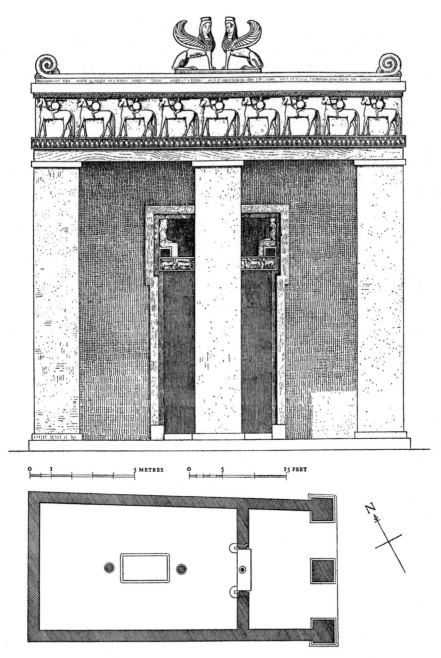

84. Prinias, Temple 'A', c. 630–580, restored front elevation and plan

centre of the temple, the total width would have been scarcely 15 feet (*c.* 4·50 m.). The wooden framework might have enabled the structure to withstand a mud roof, perhaps of double pitch; it received a tiled roof, presumably of this form, during the latter half of the seventh century.

Several non-peripteral temples have been found in Crete. Most are wider than the length from front to back, probably owing to a survival of Minoan usage for living rooms. (Greeks elsewhere avoided such a plan, though they built square temples occasionally at any period.) A seventh-century example, the temple of Apollo at Gortyn, measured 16·70 metres from doorway to back but 19 metres from side to side (54¾ by 62¼ feet). This great space cannot have been roofed without more internal support than efficient builders gave, many centuries later, by inserting eight marble columns; there are faint indications that it was originally partitioned midway and the rear half divided into narrow compartments, while the other half must also have contained props of some kind, whether continuously in that fashion or at short intervals. The exterior of the early temple was surrounded by two wide steps and a smaller projecting sill below them; the walls consist of large slabs of limestone, carefully dressed, and the interior seems to have been sheathed, at least in parts, with bronze plates. Another early Greek instance of such sheathing is recorded – the 'Bronze House' of Athena at Sparta. Precedents may be found in the metal facings sometimes used by the oriental peoples, as well as in the traces of attachments at the 'Treasury of Atreus', and in the Homeric descriptions of walls plated with gold, silver, and bronze.

But some Cretan temples were entered from the end. Two such buildings at Prinias stood side by side. The better preserved, known as Temple 'A' [84], is twice as long as it is wide. The porch, at the east end, contained a square pillar in the centre, between antae. The doorway in the cross-wall dividing the porch and the cella was also centrally placed; on its inner side two stone bases of semicircular form may have received the pivots of the door, or else supported wooden half-columns which flanked the door, as at the tholos tombs of Mycenae. On the central axis of the cella stood a slender column on a stone base beside a sacrificial pit or hearth, and another ought perhaps to be assumed on the far side of the pit; Mycenean houses often had the same arrangement, probably with a smoke-hole above. In another temple in Crete, at Dreros, a column base was similarly placed at the side of the pit nearer the door. Bronze images found inside the temple at Dreros must belong to the middle of the seventh century, while Prinias 'A' can be vaguely dated around 630–580 by its sculpture. A pair of seated statues of a goddess, about half life-size, seem to have been placed confronting one another over the doorway to the cella, immediately above a frieze of animals which decorated the side of the lintel; a figure carved in relief on the under side of the block would have been visible to those who passed through the door. Somewhere in the temple there was a frieze of cavalry, less than 3 feet high and not long enough as preserved to extend half the width of the building; if it did not belong to the internal decoration (of the porch wall, probably), it may have formed a parapet along the front of the roof, between stone volutes which seem to have occupied the angles. Probably the roof was flat.

CHAPTER 10

THE DORIC ORDER

On the mainland, roofing tiles were in common use by the middle of the seventh century. The innovation had tremendous architectural consequences. It caused a preference for ridged roofs, of lower pitch than thatch required, and for buildings of strictly rectangular plan: above all it stimulated an improvement in the structure of walls, and a changeover from wooden to stone columns, because the tiles were several times as thick as those manufactured today, and correspondingly heavy, necessitating in turn more massive roof timbers to support them. Few temples of the Dark Age can have been solid enough to receive a tiled roof, and the fact that nearly all of them had to be replaced during the hundred years which followed the introduction of tiles may be attributed as much to their structural as to their aesthetic failings.

The new methods of construction evolved during the seventh century, a leading part being played by Corinth. Before the end of the first half of that century Corinth possessed at least two developed temples, a forerunner of the surviving temple of Apollo, and another, of Poseidon at his sanctuary by the Isthmus which was replaced early in the fifth century, but which fortunately has left remains sufficient for its understanding [85]. Here the walls were built

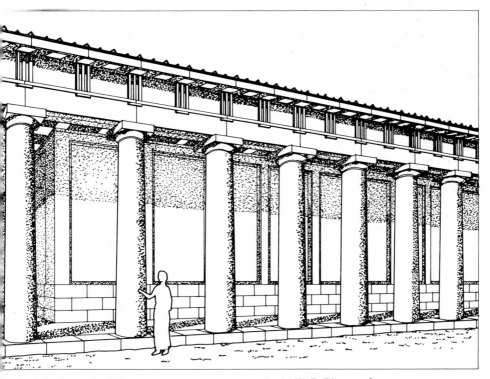

85. Isthmia, temple of Poseidon, seventh century, restoration by W. B. Dinsmoor Jr

entirely of cut stone. They were decorated with a series of recessed panels, the raised sections between them giving the effect of the timber framework which was presumably employed in the better quality mud-brick structures. The columns, though apparently substantial and with the spacing that is familiar from later temples, were of wood and supported a wooden entablature (that is to say, the superstructure above the columns). Unlike later temples, this building had a hipped roof, rather than one terminating in pediments, attested by the form of the tiles used at the junction of the roof sections. The contemporary early temple of Apollo at Delphi had a hipped roof, and there is another example of a similar roof in a later, but still early temple at Foce del Sele near Paestum. In the same period, probably, a similar substantial temple was built at the Argive Heraeum, presumably replacing a simpler structure of the type represented by the temple model described above.

Slightly later – from the second half of the century – is the peripteral temple of Apollo at Thermum (Temple C) [86]. Here the upper parts of the wall were apparently built of sun-dried brick. The original columns were probably of wood, later replaced by stone. This temple is important because its wooden entablature was embellished with painted terracotta panels, which have survived, and which undoubtedly constituted a set of metopes: that is, the temple had the regular frieze of the Doric order. Quite likely the other, earlier temples at Corinth and Argos had the same arrangement – the clay of the Thermum panels proves that they were made in Corinth and exported to Thermum. Though much is uncertain, it seems clear that the improvement of building technique on the mainland took place at the same time as the development of decorative forms which led to the classical Doric order. Moreover, the use of these decorative forms implies a lively appreciation of the aesthetic possibilities of temple construction. Modern attempts to reconstruct these early forms on the evidence of stone-work reach diverse conclusions, an indication that there had been free adaptation as well as copying, and ancient illustrations of wooden buildings prove that their designs varied widely [87, 301].

By the sixth century, Greek architects on the mainland were beginning to construct entirely of stone, up to the wooden beams and rafters and terracotta tiles. These stone temples essentially reproduced the forms employed in the previous wooden and mud-brick structures. In the walls, the panelling system of Poseidon at Isthmia was discarded (if, indeed, it was ever repeated), but the distinction between footing and superstructure was always retained, though in an elaborate form which recalls the Late Bronze Age buildings at Kition in Cyprus, of

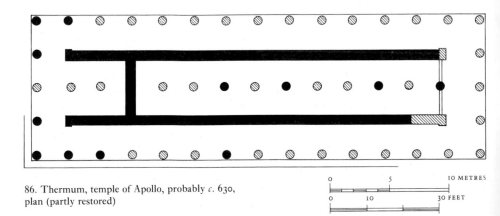

86. Thermum, temple of Apollo, probably c. 630, plan (partly restored)

0   5   10 METRES

0   10   30 FEET

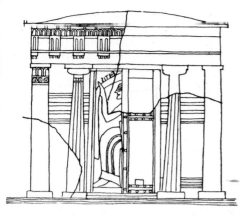

87. Drawing of a temple on the François Vase

dado surmounted by upright slab (orthostats) and (in classical buildings) a string course above which came the main structure of the wall, now ashlars where previously mud bricks were used In colonnades and, above all, the entablature, the forms of developed seventh-century wooden architecture were retained to the end; but it must be emphasized that these were in their original seventh-century form as much decorative as structural, and their retention was due to their aesthetic purpose. Particularly important here is the frieze, described below, its origin to be sought in decorative schemes found on eighth-century pottery (and certain Near Eastern ivories). It may derive from the Near East, which in turn may have taken the motif from Mycenean Greece; the inspired borrowing of this concept for the decoration of buildings is almost certainly to be attributed to a Corinthian architect. Thus the form and essential appearance was the work of the seventh century. At the end of the century it was translated into stone, and structural details modified accordingly: once this was done, in the first part of the sixth century, the essential Doric temple was formed, and though much modification and refinement, both in niceties and methods of design, was to follow, there were no major alterations of concept. This system, with its multifarious rules for correct proportion, was then accepted by Roman architects as constituting an 'Order' (superior to their local variant of Doric, which was independently derived from wooden prototypes). In fact Greek practice had always tended to admit only minor deviations from the forms accepted at each stage of evolution (though startling departures from the norm do occur now and then), and considering how unfunctional are the decorative elements when applied to stone, Doric may justifiably be termed an Order from its very start. But at the early stages the word does not connote more than a set of conventions as to what elements could properly be combined to make up a Doric building; the proportions depended on the evolution of regular methods of procedure in construction (rather than design in the drawing-board sense), which vary from region to region and century to century.

The foundations of a temple were constructed from roughly dressed masonry which contrasted with the smooth surfaces above, in so far as it was not concealed below the ground. Foundations were laid only below the essential elements of the superstructure: the outer colonnade, the walls, and any inner colonnades which might exist. The top course made a level base for a platform which raised the temple well above its surroundings. The edge of the platform usually retreated in three steps, often too tall to be ascended with comfort, and in that event a staircase or ramp was provided at the entrance and sometimes elsewhere too. From the late sixth century onwards the upper surface of the platform is rarely flat, but slopes downwards to the edges; originally an expedient for draining off rain-water, this practice was found to have aesthetic advantages. In the fifth century especially, the floor often curves as an elongated dome from a summit at the centre of the building, and dips lowest at the four corners. The walls and columns on a sloping platform would have leant outwards if they had stood perpendicular, and adjustments were made, causing them to lean inwards, if at all [197]. The inward slant may have been originally adopted in association with a level floor in order to counteract the outward thrust of the roof, but it soon acquired great aesthetic value.

Several peculiarities in the methods of building the walls were obviously inherited from the technique of the Dark Age. Even after 500, a wall might taper upwards, as had naturally been the case in sun-dried brick, and, as mentioned above, it remained customary, for appearance's sake, to place taller slabs as orthostats to form the lowest course of a wall, long after the use of good masonry throughout the entire structure had abolished the need for differentiating the base by building it alone in cut stone. Spurs of wall terminate in a wider anta, which preserves the aspect of the rectangular wooden sheathing that had enclosed the sun-dried brick; sometimes, however, a half-column is substituted for an ordinary anta. In general, the masons broke with the past. The entire wall was uniformly composed of smooth rectangular blocks, but the height of the courses often varied, whereas bricks presumably had been uniform, being shaped in moulds. There would, of course, have been no practical advantage in standardizing the height of blocks in the case of a wall with an inclined face, but variation occurs also in many perpendicular walls, for aesthetic effect; whenever the face was not concealed by stucco, the jointing of masonry formed a valuable element in the design. The courses often correspond, for example, with the horizontal divisions in the columns and capitals. The jointing of the paving slabs was systematic and often varies according to the position in the building [169, 203].

In Doric columns the shaft almost invariably stands directly upon the floor; a base is quite exceptional. Early columns (that is, those of the sixth century) are usually monolithic, but later the shaft is composed of superimposed drums, which were generally rounded by turning on a lathe, an invention traditionally ascribed to the mid sixth century. The drums were dowelled together by spikes of wood or sometimes bronze (or iron), enclosed in square blocks of the same material, within which the metal could expand and contract without splitting the stone; a hole for their reception is sunk into the top and bottom of the drums at the centre. In temples the columns were invariably fluted (unless unfinished); in a few temples and many secular buildings of late date the lower portion of the shaft was left plain, as a precaution against injury, but only in exceptional cases was a Doric column intended to remain smooth for its entire height. The fluting was executed after the erection of the column, because exact correspondence of the lines could not be guaranteed if they were carved while the drums were still separate. Unfinished buildings demonstrate that the beginnings of the flutes were always indicated before the bottom drum was put in position, to ensure that it was correctly placed. The flutes are almost always concave, broad and shallow, and meet to form sharp edges (arrises) so that an added advantage of not carving them until the temple was structurally complete was that the risk of accidental damage was reduced. The earliest shafts are mostly very slim, in imitation of wood, and often bear sixteen flutes. A change to heavier shafts ensued before the middle of the sixth century, and may have aided the final acceptance of twenty as the proper number of flutes; only very rarely were they thereafter reduced or increased by two or four, regardless of the scale or proportions of the column. Fluting of the same concave type (which the Egyptians had been the first to use in stone) had been applied by the Minoans and Myceneans to wooden columns, though perhaps less frequently than the convex type which the Greeks very rarely adopted. In fact, the easiest and quickest way to shape a tree-trunk, by chopping off the rough exterior with an adze, would have resulted in concave fluting provided that the blade were rounded[1] – and a straight blade would have been too liable to catch in the wood. In stone, fluting had the valuable effects of distinguishing the shaft from masonry in the background and of emphasizing the function of lifting.

The capital might also have been developed from pre-Hellenic wooden forms. It consists of two members. That which fits on to the top of the shaft is the cushion or echinus (so called after the sea-urchin), and spreads outwards as it rises, in order to effect a gradual transition to the overlying flat slab, the abacus. In wood, both members would have distributed the super-imposed weight, and so have safeguarded the post from splitting. The echinus was presumably a slice off the foot of a large tree-trunk, and the abacus a taller portion, squared and placed on its side so that the grain ran at right angles. But the stone capital is normally carved in a single block, which also extends a few inches down the shaft. Its junction with the top drum is normally bevelled, making a clearly defined ring, and in many buildings, from the mid sixth century on-wards, additional necking-rings are carved close to it [88]. Their function was purely aesthetic,

beginning of the curve, and so mask an awkward transition; they usually number three or four, but in the Parthenon there are as many as five.

All the proportions of the column were trans-formed in the course of time, but the shapes of its parts remained much the same, except for the profile of the echinus. At every period the maximum circumference of the echinus equals the full width of the abacus; as that was gradu-ally reduced, so the side descended more evenly to effect a more obvious transition between column shaft and abacus [88–94]. In the oldest examples, which date roughly from the late seventh and early sixth centuries, the abacus

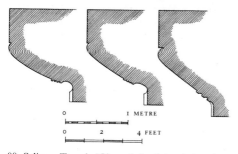

88. Selinus, Temple 'G', capitals of the sixth and early fifth centuries

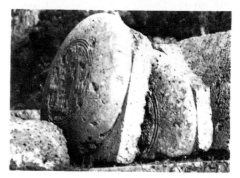

89. Delphi, first temple of Athena Pronaia, capitals, probably late seventh century

90. Argos, Heraeum, upper stoa, capital, probably late seventh century

to repeat the horizontal direction of lines higher up, and they were substituted for an earlier practice of contracting the top of the shaft into a neck, as the Minoans had done; the tops of the flutes in such a column bend inwards into the hollow. An alternative early method dispensed with the hollow, and became almost universal after the adoption of necking-rings. In this, the tops of the flutes curl outwards, and terminate by widening into round-ended scallops like the stylized palm-leaves that occur in a similar position on the 'Treasury of Atreus'; their upper edges stand out as a continuous shelf around the echinus. This lowest part of the echinus is almost always flattened. Some flat projecting annulets, separated by troughs, are carved on the

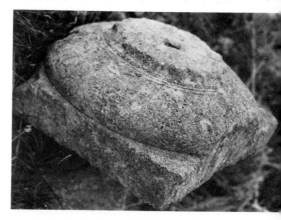

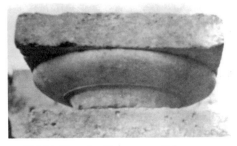

91. Delphi, Sicyonian Treasury, capital, mid sixth century

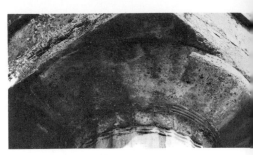

93. Paestum, temple of 'Neptune', capital, early or mid fifth century

92. Delphi, second temple of Athena Pronaia, capital, end of the sixth century

94. Nemea, temple of Zeus, capital and triglyph, late fourth century

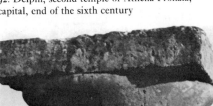

and echinus are about equal in height, and the echinus is flat beneath for almost its entire width, and almost perpendicular at the side. The spreading shape of these very early capitals is due largely to their being much wider than the top drum of the shaft. An extreme case, from the first temple of Athena Pronaia at Delphi [89, 95], is aggravated by the pronounced tapering of the shafts, which are extremely slender even at the foot; their outline, no doubt, imitates that of a tree-trunk. The total height of these columns (including the capital) equals $6\frac{1}{2}$ times the diameter at the foot, which is almost double the diameter at the top; the abacus is $2\frac{1}{2}$ times as wide as the top of the shaft. The height of the shaft (11 feet) is almost 14 times that of the capital. Some monolithic columns [108] of the early and mid sixth century, which are twice as tall and therefore had by convention to be thicker, are little more than 4 times as high as their lower diameter, while they taper only to two-thirds of it; the abacus is now twice as wide as the top of the shaft. The height of sixth-century columns, if built up of several drums [115, 121], varies around $4\frac{1}{2}$ or 5 times the lower diameter. The shafts are about 8 times as high as the capitals at this period. At the middle of the fifth century [149, 151, 152, 162, 164, 170] the ratio of a column's total height to its lower diameter ranges about $5\frac{1}{2}$ or $5\frac{3}{4}$:1; the shaft now tapers less, and may be 11 or 12 times as high as the capital. The capital had in fact become both lower and narrower although it still remained wider than any part of the shaft. The reduction of the tapering, which widened the top of the shaft, and the narrowing of the capital, would in any case have enabled the side of the echinus to curve more gradually, but another means of

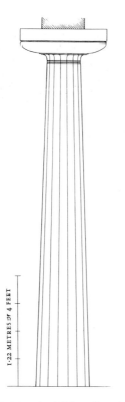

1·22 METRES or 4 FEET

95. Delphi, first temple of Athena Pronaia, probably late seventh century, restoration of column

achieving that improvement had come into use, which was to make the echinus taller than the abacus [88]. At the beginning of the fifth century its height is greater by one-third and soon afterwards by nearly one-half.

Columns of the late fifth century are perfect to the eye, but the proportions are thicker than the structure requires; they involve not merely an unnecessarily large quantity of stone but unnecessarily large blocks, the transport of which was extremely costly. The trend to slighter proportions therefore continued, although the aesthetic results never equalled those of the late fifth century. In the fourth century, the ratio of a column's height to its lower diameter frequently exceeds 6:1, and by 330 (in the tem-

ple at Nemea) has returned to the 6½:1 of the small primitive columns at Delphi, though with a shaft 21 times as high as the capital [230, 231]. Again, too, the side of the echinus has scarcely room to curve, but for the opposite reason; the width of the fourth-century capitals is so restricted that the side could only slant [94]. Some redress was found by making the echinus again equal in height with the abacus, but the continual shrinkage of the whole capital in relation to the shaft continued to make straight slanting sides almost inevitable. From the third century onwards, the columns of temples sometimes have rather heavier proportions, and the capitals are narrower than all but the highest part of the shaft [241, 259, 264, 317]. In some temples, however, the columns are even slimmer, with the ratio of height to lower diameter exceeding 7:1. In secular buildings, the design of which was less subject to tradition, the process of diminution went to the utmost limits that the structure permitted, even to the extent of reducing the echinus to nothing but a moulding around the base of the abacus.

The primitive columns at Delphi may have been spanned by wooden beams, but a stone substitute, the architrave, soon became almost invariable in temples. If large, it usually consists not of one stone beam but of two or even, in very large temples such as the Parthenon, three, laid in contact, one behind the other, between one capital and the next. The outline of an architrave is normally marked on the blank walls of non-peripteral buildings in a more or less vestigial manner. The early builders never ventured to make the architrave overlap the shafts of the columns, and preferred it somewhat narrower, so that it often covers little more than half of the very wide abacus of the time, but from the fifth century onwards, the face of the architrave projects beyond the shaft, almost as far as the edge of the abacus. The junctions between the blocks of an architrave invariably stood above the centre of columns, and the joint played an important part in the design of the temple. For this reason the face of the architrave was habitually left smooth; sometimes it was decorated with paintings, but only in two instances, both on the east side of the Aegean [111], is it carved with a continuous frieze in imitation of a local Ionic fashion.

In Doric the term frieze should properly be applied to the course which overlies the architrave, and is composed of a succession of alternate triglyphs and metopes. Such a frieze regularly occurs above a colonnade, whether of porch or pteron; it completely surrounds a peripteral building and often a non-peripteral, forming in the latter case the sole alleviation of the blank walls except for the line of the architrave. Each triglyph [87, 96, 303] consists

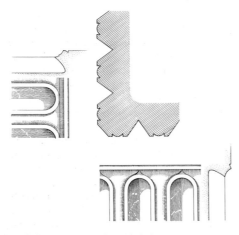

96. Selinus, Temple 'C', mid sixth century, triglyphs from the corner

of one block, which is plain at the back, but in front is carved to simulate three contiguous upright bars, chamfered on the sides so that each presents three facets: this faceted section usually extends to either side beyond the block section. These triglyphs correspond to the sections of upright lines separating the 'metopes' in the decorative schemes found on eighth-century pottery; they originate in an attempt to turn this element into a plastic form suitable for a building, and at the same time serving to retain in position the terracotta slabs of the metopes. In stone temples, metopes are usually thin slabs,

recessed behind the triglyphs, and either plain or decorated with painting and sculpture (in more mundane buildings such as stoas, pairs of triglyphs and metopes are often carved as a single block). The original function of the metopes was believed in Roman times to have been that of screening gaps, which would otherwise have formed windows between the triglyphs. The derivation of the word[2] and the whole system of the frieze both appear to agree with that supposition, but in stone temples metopes are always given a substantial stone backer, and it is hard to believe that this was not also the case with the earlier, terracotta metopes. The rhythm of this decorative scheme may have been suggested by the sequence of beam ends inspiring the triglyph,[3] but there are difficulties with this interpretation: beams in Greek architecture are normally square, not rectangular in section. Principal beams run from side to side, even in non-peripteral buildings where triglyphs and metopes may well be restricted to the porch end, while in stone buildings the beams usually come well above the level of the architrave (by the fifth century they are normally above the top of the frieze itself). It is hard to see how the firm rule that both sides of the corners must be formed by triglyphs could have originated if the triglyphs really were beam ends. Nor do the metopes seem to have served any useful – or enduring – purpose as openings for light or ventilation. Such openings seem to have existed (they are represented as triangles in the wall of the temple models from Perachora), but not in a position or shape in which they could have become prototypes for the metope system.

Some of the earliest triglyphs – those at the Heraeum of Foce del Sele near Paestum – taper upwards and the metopes were correspondingly widened. The reason for this is not clear. But towards the middle of the sixth century the convention became firmly established that the sides must be upright.

The frieze is separated from the architrave beneath by a thin shelf which projects beyond the face of either course and should correspond to a board in the wooden prototype. Below this is a series of plain bands (regulae), which likewise project and are placed one beneath each triglyph, extending to its full width; the under side is carved to reproduce a row of cylindrical pegs (guttae). The regulae and guttae would have served to secure the triglyph face, particularly if this were made of separate strips attached in front of a main block of wood. The arrangement indicates that the prototypes of triglyphs took the weight of the overlying structure, and that is confirmed by the position; triglyphs stand above columns, metopes never do. In very early times, when builders underestimated the strength of stone columns and placed them absurdly close together, the frieze contained a triglyph above each column and one oblong metope occupying the whole of the intervening stretch. Such a system has been restored, without supporting evidence, however, for the Temple of Poseidon at Isthmia. But the original decorative pattern demands square metopes (as already at Thermum) and it is usual to find an additional triglyph over the centre of each intercolumniation, with a metope on either side. This arrangement is therefore preferable for seventh-century temples with their wider spaced wooden columns. In stone temples with the additional triglyph, the metopes could thus be shortened, and this tendency continued during most of the sixth century; on occasion metopes are actually of greater height than width, so that they are little wider than the triglyphs, but an approximately square form eventually proved most satisfactory. The triglyphs vary in width too, though in a lesser degree; the bars could be extended by widening the outward facet and flattening the angle of those which recede. In extreme cases [96] their great width is broken by mouldings; these are linked by means of ogival arches across the tops of the recesses but this is most unusual. The junctions of the recesses with the flat upper border of the triglyph are otherwise simply bevelled, horizontally or (more often) in a low ogival arch.

Theoretically each triglyph above a column should be placed with its centre precisely over

the middle of that column, but the rule could seldom be enforced at the corners of the building, where two triglyphs met at right angles, flush with the architrave corner, over the same column.[4] Even in the sixth century, when the architrave corner might not project so far as to overlap the foot of the column, the normal width of a triglyph was often considerably less than the column's, and the half of it could not reach from the centre of the column to the corner of the architrave. The simplest solution, to make the angle triglyphs wider than the others, could rarely prove adequate, because their height could not be altered in proportion; quite a small increase in width would wreck the appearance. As a rule, therefore, the centres of the angle triglyphs had to be displaced outwards from the centre of their column. But the nearest metope would then need to be widened in compensation, and that was only slightly more feasible. The Greeks of Sicily and south Italy used these two methods alone, throughout the sixth century, a good example of a particular region of the Greek world retaining its own local and traditional method of design. But in Greece itself it was then already customary to reduce the distance between the angle column and its neighbours till extension of the metopes became either insignificant or altogether superfluous. The problem became more difficult in the fifth century, when the introduction of marble roofing-tiles led to the use of thicker architraves, to support the increased weight. The triglyphs and the architrave continued to be set flush in the same vertical plane, with the architrave now wider than the shafts of the columns.[5] At each corner of the building the two triglyphs above either side of the angle column had accordingly to reach still farther outwards from the centre of the column. They could not be correspondingly widened in the opposite direction, because of the additional weight which a taller frieze would have imposed on the columns; on the contrary, the height of all the masonry carried by the columns is reduced. The old devices of widening the nearest metopes and contracting the angle intercolumniations are therefore

supplemented by displacing additional triglyphs so that their centres come nearer to the
corner, and extending more distant metopes,
and sometimes by contracting the next intercolumniations – a favourite device in Sicily.
Architects exercised their ingenuity in finding
new and subtler ways of designing the corners
of the frieze. Never (a fresco from Pompeii is
hardly reliable evidence) did they evade the
issue by leaving the angle triglyphs centred over
the column and placing short metopes at the
corners. That, however, is the solution which
Vitruvius recommends; by the time of Christ,
when he wrote his handbook, Doric had ceased
to be a medium for progressive building, and he
attributes the fact to the hopeless irregularity of
angle triglyphs as the Greeks had treated them.
The true explanation of the obsolescence of
Doric would seem to be that the possibilities of
development had been exhausted.

But the latest type of frieze known to
Vitruvius was indeed intractable, and boring.
The trend towards lightening the structure had
led inevitably to this final great innovation
in Doric. For the whole entablature (i.e.
architrave, frieze, and horizontal cornice) had
become gradually lower; in the sixth century it
is half as high as the columns, in the late fifth
century one-third, in the fourth century one-
quarter as high [264, 317]. The individual
triglyphs and metopes had then become

disproportionately low for their width, and in
many, though by no means all, later buildings
the number of these units is increased above
each intercolumniation, and the height of the
frieze drastically reduced to allow for the
presence, no longer of one intermediate triglyph, but of two or three, always separated
by metopes. This device of multiplying the
units had been used in the fifth century to cover
a span of exceptional width (e.g. in the Propylaea and in less substantial buildings, particularly stoas, such as the Stoa of Zeus at
Athens); in conjunction with a lower frieze it
seems to date from the third century and
becomes common only in the second.[6]

Upon the upper border of the triglyph rests
a strip in the same vertical plane, the bed-mould
for the horizontal cornice. The cornice literally
overhangs it, slanting downwards as well as
projecting outwards, in eaves form. The
projecting face (corona) is vertical, but recessed
along the lower edge in order to shed rain-water
more effectively [97]. This cornice surrounds
the entire temple; on the short ends of the
building it projects as an edge to the floor of
the pediment, the recessed triangular space
described by the gable. A second cornice slants
up the gable from the corners of the horizontal
cornice. The top of the slanting cornice and,
along the sides of the building only, that of the
horizontal cornice also, swing farther outward

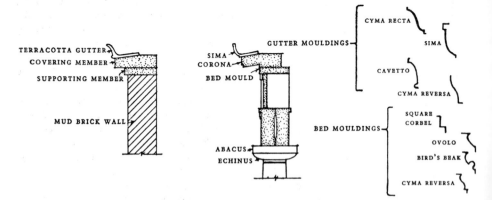

97. Adaptations in stone building of wooden functional mouldings

in an undercut moulding, which usually takes the shape of a hawk's beak. And the under side of these cornices is carved to represent fittings which in wooden buildings had secured the bedding of the roof. They simulate a board set with three rows of cylindrical pegs (guttae); one such (a mutule) projects from the overhang above each triglyph and another above each metope, but until fairly late in the sixth century, those above the metopes are narrower – generally only half as wide.

The pitch of roofs must have been changed on the adoption of tiles; thatch, even if surfaced with clay, would have required a steeper pitch, while a roof of clay alone would have been almost flat. There is some evidence of the seventh century for a method of laying the tiles on a clay bedding; otherwise the practice was to attach them directly to rafters or stone equivalents; a stone framework to carry the roof was occasionally built in the sixth and later centuries. From the rare stone examples which have survived and from the beam-holes in wooden-roofed temples it is easy to visualize the normal system of support [143]. Horizontal crossbeams spanned the room, aisle, porch, or pteron, smaller horizontal beams overlay them in the opposite direction, and others again were placed across on top of these, till the gaps could be ceiled with panels of coffering [175–7]. Often the main beams were placed so close together that the gaps could be filled with coffering only, the smaller beam not being required. The reproductions in stone of this carpentry were necessarily megalithic and therefore extremely costly; hence wood always remained the normal material for ceilings, in spite of the risk of fire, which caused the destruction of many a temple. Internal ceilings were invariably of wood, though in the better temples the ceilings over the pteron would be of stone. Occasionally a pitched ceiling was constructed below the roof, enabling fewer and shorter timbers to be used. In a Cypriot tomb[7] of the sixth century a ceiling of this kind is reproduced in stone [98]. The curved portions must represent the outward surfaces of split logs, and the flat strips superimposed upon the intervals may be interpreted as the split surface of another layer. An ostentatiously crude ceiling of this type, Hellenistic in date, survives at Delos, covering an artificial cave, and one or two otherwise conventional temples at Delos seem to have had pitched ceilings. Inclined ceilings, formed by the rafters rather than horizontal beams, were quite usual in stoas of the fourth and subsequent centuries

Above the ceiling [143] rose a framework of props which held up the immediate supports of the rafters, that is to say, the ridge-beam and other beams which ran parallel to it at various levels as purlins; holes for their reception occur at intervals in the back of the gables. The upright props themselves must have been held rigid by other beams. The whole system apparently relied purely on its solidity, the weight being entirely dead load; it is doubtful whether the Greeks ever thought of the truss-roof. (A truss roof maintains itself owing to the tension of its cross beams, which tie together the lower ends of principal rafters that slant from the ridge in compression, while the king-post and any slanting timber are not props but prevent buckling.) Some Sicilian temples may have had more complex roofs, and something akin to a truss-roof has been suggested (perhaps wrongly) in the fourth-century temple of Athena at Delphi. On the other hand the very large rooms in the palace at Vergina, if they indeed had clear spans of over 50 feet (16 m.), must have had a most unusual roof; here a truss is reasonable, though we would expect more examples if it were in fact used here.[8] The normal Greek method was merely to impose a ridge roof upon a framework adapted from the system of a wooden doorway, which has a flat lintel across two upright posts. If greater height were needed, they repeated the procedure higher up. The columns in the cellas of large temples often carried other columns [143, 151], which generally supported a ceiling close below the ridge of the roof; the aisles of such temples had lower ceilings, with lofts above.

The exterior of the roof must now be considered. Early tiles [99] are of the 'Laconian'

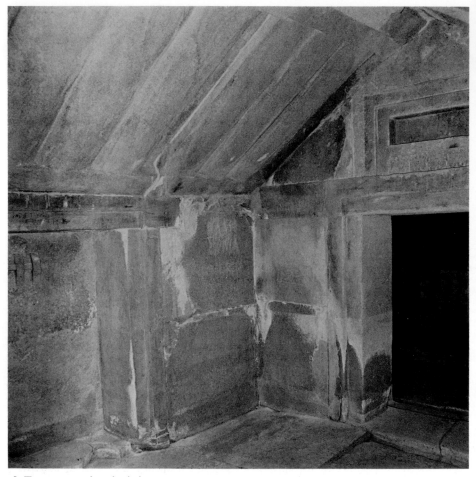

98. Tamassus, royal tomb, sixth century

99. Systems of tiling: 'Laconian', Sicilian, 'Corinthian'

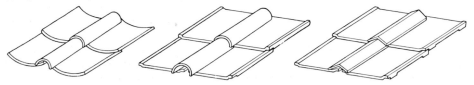

type, approximately semicircular in section; one layer was placed with the concave side upwards and another was then laid, convex side up, to cover the joints. Alternatively, the lower layer might consist of flat tiles and the joints were then covered by ridged tiles which shed the rain sideways; this, the 'Corinthian' method, was copied in the marble tiles of the fifth and late fourth centuries. (A combination of flat tiles with semicircular covers is found in Sicily and Aeolis.) A gutter was provided on the ends of the building, and frequently also along the side; this was formed, when using pottery tiles, by turning their edges upwards. When there was a gutter along the sides, it was pierced by spouts – preferably in the shape of lion heads with open mouths. In the absence of a gutter, the side was lined with upright antefixes, ornamental attachments which concealed the ends of the covering tiles; antefixes of terracotta often took the form of human heads, but when carved in stone the decoration is usually restricted to a palmette [100]. The row of covering tiles on the ridge of the roof was generally ornamented with palmettes, facing both sides. Ventilating tiles are sometimes found, pierced with holes beneath a projecting lip which kept out the rain. Upon the four corners of the roof and on top of each gable [111] stood acroteria in the form either of large ornaments or, in later times, often statues; those above the gables began as terracotta disks [106], covering the ends of the wooden ridge beam.

In general the decoration of temples seems to have originated in terracotta, which was used to face the portions most liable to damage if surfaces of wood or sun-dried brick were exposed. The adoption of stone did not result in the immediate abandonment of terracotta, particularly in lesser buildings such as stoas. Largely, one may suppose, for the sake of the permanence of the kiln-baked colouring, facings of terracotta were made all through the sixth century [103, 116, 117]; and terracotta antefixes continued to persist, because they had the advantage that they could be mass-produced from moulds. Statues of terracotta were also used in early pediments, because of the lightness of the material. Sculpture in pediments was customary (though never obligatory) in Doric from at least the early part of the sixth century, and the pediment itself may have been intentionally created to receive the figures. A cryptic statement of Pindar's apparently claims it to have

been a Corinthian invention, and it certainly seems an artificial combination of structural incongruities. In structures resembling the primitive Heraeum of Argos [80], the gable behind the low porch may sometimes have been blocked instead of open, and a pediment would thus have been formed, with the roof of the porch as its floor; moreover the front of the porch would have required a drip-stone cornice. But when the porch rose to the full height, the beams of its ceiling would merely have been embedded in the wall, an upward continuation of which could just as well have blocked the gable flush with the frieze, without a horizontal cornice. Only aesthetically was there need for a pediment; a sculptured group within it can counteract the tendency for the eye to be drawn upwards. Figures on the metopes have the same effect. The higher the position of the sculpture, the more pronounced it requires to be; metopes are generally in fairly high relief, pedimental figures almost or completely in the round, acroteria in the round and thickened by excrescent drapery or pierced ornament. The sculptures thereby serve to blur the building's directional lines, which would otherwise point too insistently, especially at the top. On the other hand some pediment groups have static figures with a strong vertical emphasis (the sixth-century Temple of Apollo at Delphi, and the east pediment of the Temple of Zeus at Olympia). In any case, the sculpture is never merely decorative. At times it seems to have the purpose of protecting the building, frightening away potential sources of evil. Other examples depict stories connected, directly or allegorically, with the particular cult. The complicated patterns of the early terracotta decoration also had the effect of distracting attention from the strict geometry of the building; the colours, being fired, were necessarily sombre, ranging from purples, browns, and reds to buff. An alternative method of decoration, by painting on the stone, supplanted terracotta before the end of the sixth century. The colours were applied after the designs had been incised upon the stone, which, if rough or absorbent, was given

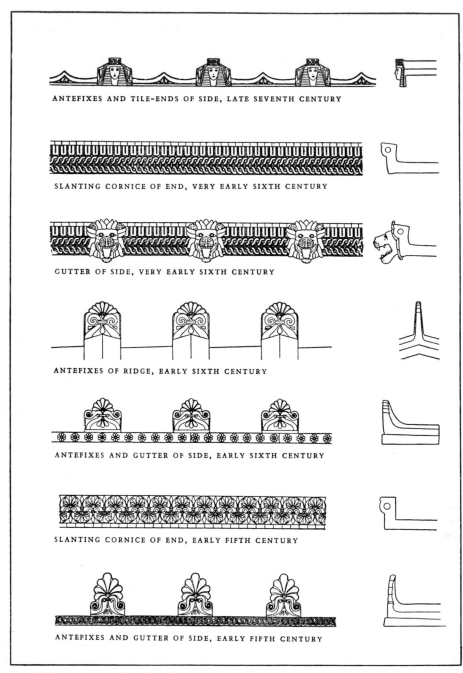

ANTEFIXES AND TILE-ENDS OF SIDE, LATE SEVENTH CENTURY

SLANTING CORNICE OF END, VERY EARLY SIXTH CENTURY

GUTTER OF SIDE, VERY EARLY SIXTH CENTURY

ANTEFIXES OF RIDGE, EARLY SIXTH CENTURY

ANTEFIXES AND GUTTER OF SIDE, EARLY SIXTH CENTURY

SLANTING CORNICE OF END, EARLY FIFTH CENTURY

ANTEFIXES AND GUTTER OF SIDE, EARLY FIFTH CENTURY

100. Calydon, terracotta decoration of temple roofs

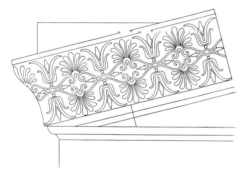

101. Sunium, temple of Poseidon, mid fifth century, pattern incised on slanting cornice

a coating of limewash or marble-dust stucco, and very bright colours were then obtainable; the detail, however, had to be on a larger scale [101, 163, 167, 168]. That mattered little, because it was soon realized that the old finicky patterns were less effective than a combination of flat washes in general with a few bold designs at specially important parts. As a rule such major features as the cornice face, the architrave, and the columns were left pale (either uncoloured or slightly toned down to reduce glare); the rhythm of the frieze was emphasized by black or dark blue triglyphs, regulae, and mutules, against the red that was applied to the plain surfaces of metopes, the bed-mould and the underside of the cornice. Evidence for the painted decoration rarely survives: traces of it, the colours faded and distorted, were noted by F. C. Penrose on the Parthenon in the nineteenth century. Recent discoveries of underground built tombs in Macedonia with Doric and Ionic façades have however produced examples of architectural painted decoration in pristine state. It is particularly noticeable that in Doric façades the red bands on the bedding of the cornice are embellished with a delicate yellow-gold maeander pattern.[9] The broken lines of the sculptured figures on metopes and pediments were still more broken by the application of various colours to drapery and other accessories; on the other hand, the carved ornament of such parts

as the gutter and capitals received the utmost possible clarification, its detail being picked out in contrasting paints, sometimes with the addition of gilt.

The colours in general were crude and appear too vivid in restorations, but when toned down by strong sunlight they must have fulfilled their purpose admirably. The whole design of a temple is a matter of contrapuntal relationships; it depends ultimately on the clear demarcation of its parts, which must be so shaped as to keep the spectator's eye continually on the move. Every part must be rightly proportioned in itself as well as in relation to the rest, but none may attract more attention than another. Each line points towards one which turns at a different angle and obliges the eye to follow it; some lines, moreover, ought to be so constructed as to lead in either direction simultaneously. The Egyptians had long contrived to get that effect with columns, designing them against exclusively upward movement by making the shaft bulge as it rises and contract again before it meets the heavy capital; the Doric column needed to be more subtly designed, though on the same principle [121]. The columns in Egypt were almost invariably in the interior of a building, either bordering the sides of a court or supporting the ceiling of a hall, and their relation to what came above and below them offered a far less difficult problem. The tapering shafts of a Doric pteron have to link the peaked superstructure with the platform in such a manner that the eye will travel both up and down them, and eventually that requirement was fulfilled by an almost imperceptible convex curvature of the side in conjunction with an inward slant of the whole column, gently anticipatory of the gable [197, 201].

Actually the Greek temple is the oldest type of building designed to be seen externally more than internally, and that from all round the compass. The pyramids of Egypt and the stepped towers of Mesopotamia were solid hills of masonry and the temples which they accompanied presented impressive but comparatively uninteresting façades, barely hinting at the magnificence of the courts within. And, fanciful as the idea may seem, the interior of the temples in each country is congruous with the dominant character of the surrounding landscape. The Nile valley is a corridor between cliffs, and the Egyptian temple was given a processional plan, with a central path that led between the massed, heavy columns of court after court. The court of a Mesopotamian temple was spacious and unobstructed; outside was an interminable empty plain. The Greeks lived in flat-bottomed valleys enclosed by mountains, and the interior of their temples held a constricted patch of floor surrounded by disconcertingly lofty walls.

In general conception, therefore, the Doric temple had nothing in common with contemporary design in the older civilized countries. Absolutely self-sufficient, equally satisfactory from any outside viewpoint, and internally imposing, it began a new sort of architecture. Naturally its development was slow, because of the novelty of the problems as well as their complexity, and still slower because of Greek inexperience in stone construction. The history of

Doric therefore consists of perpetual attempts to discover the right proportions and to adjust them to economic structural requirements; in particular, to do this in conformity with traditionally established procedures for design and construction, which avoid the need for detailed drawings (impossible without scaled rulers).[10] Two hundred years of experiment (640 or 620–440) resulted in the Parthenon, which has the best proportions, enhanced by meticulous, and therefore very expensive, workmanship; after three hundred more years, the structure was as light as possible, and the proportions correct in every respect, but their total effect was aesthetically poor beyond redemption [259, 264]. The Greeks therefore lost interest in Doric in the second century B.C. and almost ceased to use it; taste changed, particularly with the widened horizons of the Hellenistic age, and a better knowledge of more flamboyant architectural forms in Egypt and the Near East. The Romans, who had inherited a variant of Doric, continued to experiment for a while by disregarding the rules of the Greek Order, but with little success.

CHAPTER 11

EARLY DORIC TEMPLES AND SIMILAR BUILDINGS

No temple of the sixth century remains standing to its full height. Only rarely is part of the external colonnade preserved with the architrave; a few temples are represented by one or more complete columns, and many are known only from fragments. Sometimes, however, these supply data for a more or less trustworthy restoration of the whole building. The restoration can seldom be entirely reliable, because a gap in the remains cannot safely be complemented at this period from analogies in contemporary usage. On the one hand, dating is problematical; except for a few cases in which excavation has found evidence, a margin of error of not less than thirty years must be allowed, and in some instances the experts still differ in their estimates by fifty years or even more. There were also distinct regional variations in design, within which there might be established procedures, but which seem to have allowed scope for variation. Until the proportions in Doric became fairly satisfactory – and that stage was not reached till the next century – its conventions were few and often broken. Even in the mainland of Greece, where the Order was formulated, local variants persisted for several generations, and individual buildings tended to depart considerably from the local norm. The Greek colonies in Sicily developed other habits affecting both the plan and the elevation; here again fairly consistent divergences can be ascribed to local schools, and the individual discrepancies are wider than in Greece. The Greek cities in south Italy adhered to the general characteristics of Sicilian Doric, but their practice was to allow incomparably greater latitude in experiment; most elements in the elevation are subject to all manner of variation, so much so as to suggest that Doric was not envisaged as a coherent system there.

In reality, only one native form of architecture existed in any one area: Doric in the mainland of Greece and in the west, Ionic in the Aegean islands and on the coast of Asia Minor. Except for one Doric temple in Asia Minor, and the very occasional use of Ionic at Athens and in Italy, intrusions of the one Order into the territory of the other are virtually limited to buildings in the national style erected at overseas sanctuaries. But in Sicily and Italy, owing to connexions with the eastern Aegean, Doric incorporated some Ionic features. The isolation of the Greek cities in Italy, strung out along the coast amid an alien population, caused the development of a stone architecture to take an uncertain, rather nondescript, course; this is affected also by the limitations of building stone available. And both there and in Sicily it was able to proceed semi-independently of Greece, because the great colonial cities could afford to build more lavishly. But the designs show less aesthetic perception.

GREECE

The oldest peripteral temple of stone in mainland style[1] is probably that of Artemis at Corfu.[2] Though demolished, the scattered blocks prove that it consisted entirely of limestone, at any rate externally. The width was about 77 feet, the length only a trifle more than double, proportions which are found in other sixth-century temples of the mainland, at Athens and in the adjacent area, though not at Corinth which colonized Corfu; and there seem to have been two rows of columns inside the cella. One pediment has been pieced together [102]. It is carved in high relief, with a central heraldic group of an enormous Gorgon flanked by her two children and two leopards. Much

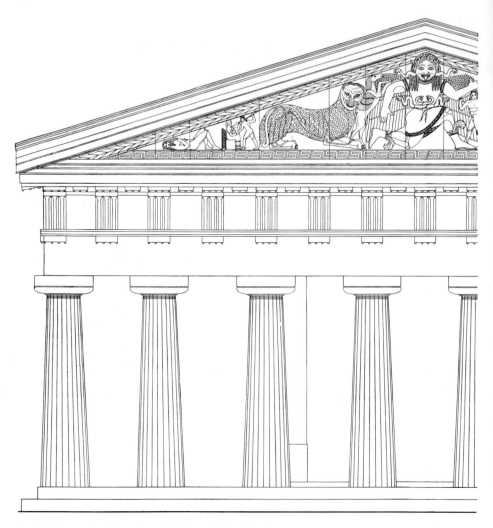

102. Corfu, temple of Artemis, c. 580, restored front elevation

smaller figures at the sides represent the battle between the gods and the giants. Consequently, the composition fails as an illustration of mythology and is too uneven in scale to balance; it looks as though it had been one of the first attempts at pedimental sculpture, though it is possible that pedimental groups of opposed animals at Athens may be earlier. From the style of the sculpture, which is Corinthian,

the date should be about 580. The cornices were sheathed with terracotta; some parts of the stone-work were painted with patterns, and others merely tinted [103].

The temple of Hera at Olympia was built at the same time (recent investigations have demonstrated that there was unlikely to have been a predecessor on the same site).[3] In technique and material it recalls the seventh-

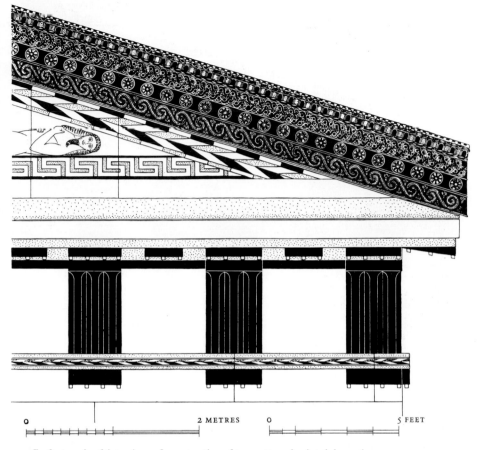

103. Corfu, temple of Artemis, c. 580, restoration of terracotta and painted decoration

century temples, but excavation has proved an early-sixth-century date, although it was slightly smaller and stood in an international sanctuary [153, 154]. The cella walls are built of good limestone masonry to a height of little more than 3 feet and were continued in sun-dried brick. All the rest of the structure must originally have consisted of wood, apart from the tiled roof. The columns were replaced in stone [104, 105] at times which ranged, to judge by the capitals, from the mid sixth century to the Christian era; shafts that stand next to each other vary nearly a foot in diameter, and one bears sixteen flutes

instead of twenty. One wooden column is recorded to have still existed in A.D. 173, in the opisthodomus; the entrance to the porch as well as to this false porch was supported by two columns, between wooden antae. The cella was divided by two rows of columns into a nave perhaps as much as 12 feet wide, and aisles of little more than 3 feet, but originally the place of every alternate column was taken by a spur-wall which projected thus far into the cella. This arrangement, which made a series of bays, each with a column at its middle, is strangely similar to one adopted long before at Troy (p. 23). The

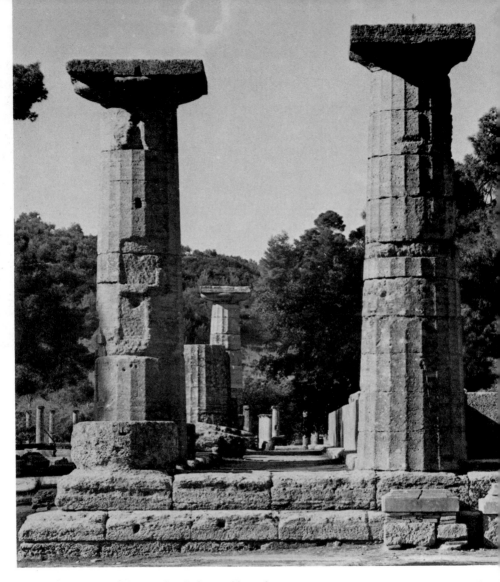

104. Olympia, temple of Hera, *c.* 580, platform and late columns

internal columns supported a flat ceiling; their alignment opposite those of the pteron, which were presumably taller (17 feet), implies that the props for the roof were held rigid by lateral beams which passed through the walls to the pteron. The overall dimensions are 61 by 164 feet (18·75 by 50 m.). Six columns stood at either end, and sixteen on the sides; the spacing is closer on the sides, where the normal distance from the axis of one to that of the next averages 1 foot less than on the ends (3·26 compared with 3·56 m.). The purpose, no doubt, was to increase the rigidity of the long colonnade. The angle intercolumniations form exceptions; they

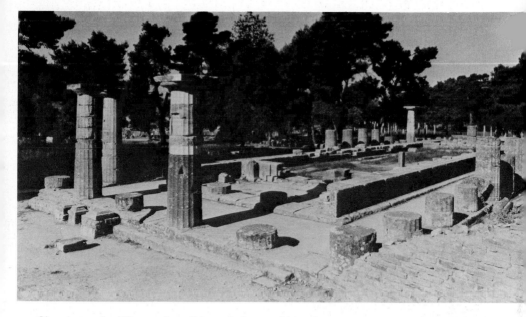

105. Olympia, temple of Hera, *c.* 580, wall-base, platform, and late columns

are narrower, so that the last interaxial spacing on the ends equals the normal side spacing, and the last side spacing is still smaller (by 5½ inches). This inconsistency enabled the metopes nearest the corner to match the rest in length, although the pair of triglyphs over the angle column could not be centred upon its axis but had to be placed nearer the corner. The trick does not appear in the western colonies till a hundred years later. Likewise the porch design of two columns *in antis*, which was immediately recognized in Greece as the best possible solution, gained favour in the west only very slowly. In fact the planning of the temple is quite advanced, but for the excessive length of the cella, and the backwardness of the structure was probably due not so much to conservatism as to lack of money.

The Heraeum may have been influenced by Spartan architecture, on the doubtful evidence of the style of its image and a certain accordance of its roof terracottas with practice at Sparta. Especially characteristic are the disk acroteria painted in concentric circles; one stood on each gable, and it measured over 7 feet in diameter. Only fragments survive; illustration 106 shows the latest restoration of it, by N. Yalouris. Similar (but much smaller) disk acroteria have been found at the sanctuary of Helen and Menelaus (the Menelaeum) near Sparta. If the pediments ever contained sculpture it must have been made of terracotta. A contemporary pedimental design at Sparta itself is known, if only vaguely, from crude representations on votive offerings discovered there, at the sanctuary of Artemis Orthia: in the pediments of a new temple, which replaced the primitive shanty, a pair of lions confronted one another, apparently in relief. A fragment of the original sculpture shows that they were gaily painted.

Only one pteron of the sixth century remains standing in Greece, to the extent of seven columns; they belong to the temple of Apollo at Corinth, which can be dated about 540 by pottery found among the masons' chippings [107–9]. Each shaft is a monolith, nearly 21 feet

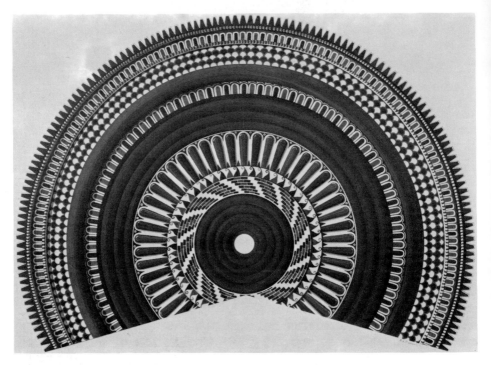

106. Olympia, temple of Hera, terracotta disk acroterium, early sixth century.
Restoration drawn from fragments in Olympia Museum

107–9. Corinth, temple of Apollo, mid sixth century, view (*below*), columns (*right*),
and restored plan (*below, right*)

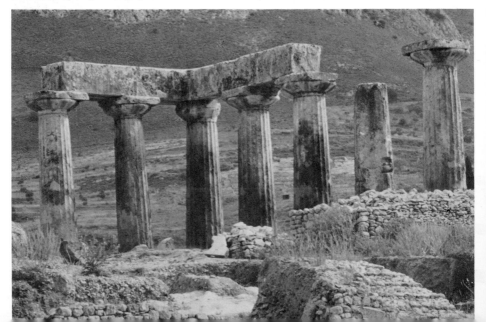

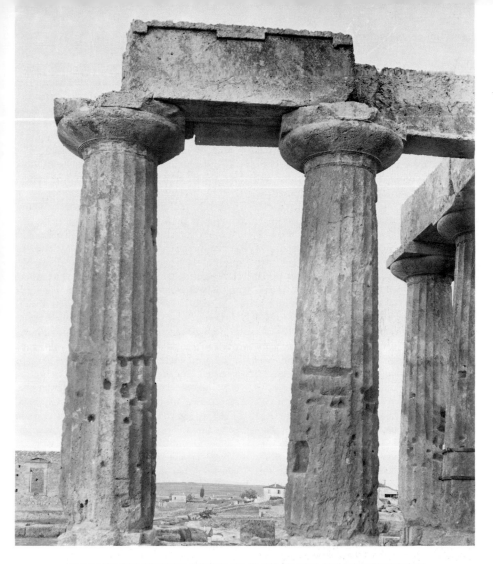

high, with rectilinear tapering; the capital is carved in a separate block. The rough limestone was surfaced with a white stucco composed of marble dust. There were six columns on the ends and fifteen on the sides; the latter are spaced 11 inches closer, and are also thinner by nearly 4 inches, making the height equal to 4·40 times the lower diameter instead of 4·15 times. The intercolumniations at the corners are narrowed but not quite to the same extent, so that the nearest metopes had to be 2 inches wider than the rest in order to reach the angle triglyphs. The floor beneath each colonnade rises in a convex curve – the earliest instance of this refinement. The inner building held two cellas, back to back, each entered by a porch with the usual two columns *in antis*, and containing two rows of smaller columns. With this abnormal amount of accommodation the overall length equalled $2\frac{1}{2}$ times the width.

Some twenty years later, perhaps, the Temple of Athena on the Acropolis at Athens was rebuilt on the foundations of its predecessor.[4] This was the principal Athenian temple, in which was housed the venerable wooden cult statue (the 'old image') soon to be evacuated with the Athenians to Salamis when the Persians invaded and sacked the temple along with the other buildings of the Acropolis. Minor deities were associated with Athena at this building (marked by dotted lines in illustration 156) which, like Corinth, had two cellas, the western being divided into two side-by-side adyta with an anteroom. Despite this, the temple conforms to the proportions of other near-contemporary temples in the Saronic Gulf area, being only twice as long as it was wide, with six columns on the ends and twelve on the sides. They were differentiated as at Corinth. The main portions of the structure were built in limestone, but marble, brought from the Aegean islands, was used for the metopes, pedimental groups, gutter, slanting cornice, and tiles.

The gigantic temple of Olympian Zeus at Athens[5] was a Pisistratid venture, begun about 520 and left so unfinished that only the platform was kept for the much later building, which followed the same plan but used the Corinthian Order (invented a century after Pisistratus). The platform measures 135 by $353\frac{1}{2}$ feet (41·10 by 107·75 m.) and the pteron would have comprised, as its successor did, two rows of columns along the sides, and three on the ends. The intention may have been to use the Doric Order, but the scheme was clearly inspired by emulation of the Ionic temples of comparable size at Ephesus and Samos [cf. 130]; the columns, though, seem to have been of poros.

An exiled Athenian family, the Alcmaeonids, set an important precedent in 513 by covering most of the front of a large temple with marble. This was the temple of Apollo at Delphi, where the island state of Siphnos had built a little Ionic treasury entirely of marble, a dozen years earlier.

Treasuries, small temple-like buildings dedicated as offerings (as much as to hold offerings), were built on special occasions – perhaps victories over enemies which needed celebration – by individual Greek cities in the international sanctuaries of Delos, Delphi, and Olympia. They belong chiefly to the sixth century, when some fine and ornate specimens were constructed at Olympia. The Megarian Treasury at Olympia, built at the end of the sixth century, consisted, like most treasuries, of a cella and a porch with two columns *in antis*. The front was as ornate as the Doric Order permitted, with sculpture in the pediment and a frieze. A short regula was also placed just past each corner on the otherwise blank side wall, where another metope might be expected to stand above. Treasuries were still being constructed in the fifth century B.C.

Few experimental buildings of the sixth century have been found in Greece. The old round-ended types were losing favour (though some were still being built with as many as three or four columns *in antis*), and the vast majority of temples must have been rectangular. If peripteral, the front almost always had six columns, though, as we have seen, the number along the flank varied, along with the relative proportions of length to width. Eventually the ratio of length to width settled at about 2½:1, giving in a temple with a façade of six columns a length sufficient for thirteen. The inner building was normally given two columns *in antis* at either end (though the Old Temple at Athens had four columns in front of the antae) and that was also the general rule with non-peripteral temples.[6]

A strange departure from convention occurs late in the century. A small non-peripteral temple at Taxiarches in the relatively backward region of Aetolia consists of a square cella and a porch; the width is two-thirds of the length (24½ by 37 feet; 7·50 by 11·25 m.). The entrance

width of the blank wall which stretches to the corner of the building. A horizontal dripstone projected at a somewhat higher level than the architrave along the front alone.

The abnormalities of some other structures are due to the influence of Ionic. The great throne of Apollo at Amyclae,[7] a village south of Sparta, is known to have been designed by an architect from Asia Minor, Bathycles of Magnesia, and he extended the bearing surface of its Doric capitals by bracketing to one side of each a console which resembles half of an Ionic capital; mouldings round the neck of the column curve up sideways into a volute, solidified in the

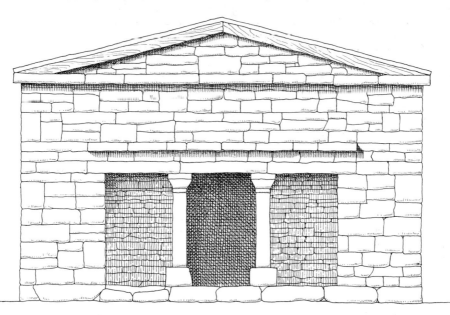

110. Taxiarches, larger temple, late sixth century, restoration

[110] was 7 feet high and 14 feet wide, with two intermediate pillars instead of columns; each is less than a foot wide but extends inwards for nearly three times its width, and broadens at the front into a capital and base of no recognized Order. The central span, measured from axis to axis, is equal to the width of each lateral passage plus the base of the nearest pillar, and also to the

usual Ionic manner by water-lily ornament in the re-entrants. This was an altar with an enclosure and a colossal cult statue standing in the open, rather than a temple. The peculiarities of the temple at Assos in Asia Minor, the only notable Doric building of the eastern Aegean, also resulted from imitation of Ionic habits [111]. The columns, for this reason, are very

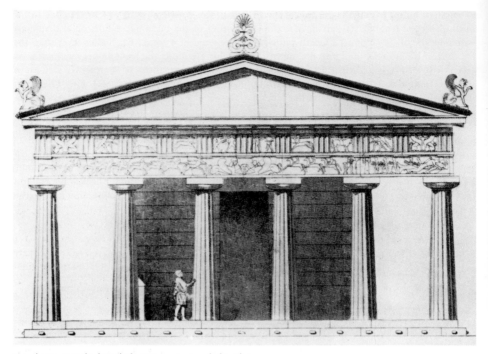

111. Assos, temple, late sixth century, restored elevation

slender, only 3 feet in lower diameter and nearly $5\frac{1}{4}$ times as high; they are, of course, placed closer together than usual. And there was precedent in the Ionic of Asia Minor for carving the architrave with a continuous frieze. It ran along the ends of the temple but apparently did not extend the entire length of the sides. Above it[8] came the normal frieze of triglyphs and metopes, which likewise are sculptured; the pediments seem to have been left empty, as is customary in Ionic, especially in Asia Minor. The material of the entire building is andesite, a volcanic stone, the hardness of which may be largely responsible for the archaic aspect of the reliefs; opinions differ widely as to their date, some placing it before 550. A much lower date, towards the end of the century, is preferable. That supposition accords with the fully-developed pteron scheme, of six by thirteen columns. The cella, though 26 feet (7·97 m.) wide, contained no columns; its porch, however,

was given the usual pair between spurs that terminate, in Ionic fashion, without overlapping antae. These porch columns stand opposite the third column of the pteron, but the back wall of the cella is aligned with the penultimate column – a differentiation frequent in western Doric.

SICILY

There are no marble deposits in Sicily, and all buildings there consist of local stone. The early temples have been so much destroyed and so badly excavated that their elevations remain doubtful and their dating is pure guess-work; the plans, however, are generally certain. Two non-peripteral buildings at Selinus are extreme-ly primitive in aspect. The so-called Megaron on the acropolis [112] dates from about 600. A doorway in the end wall leads directly into the cella, a room 16 feet (4·80 m.) wide, with bases for two wooden columns; the adytum is practic-

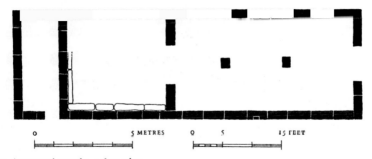

112. Selinus, 'megaron' temple, c. 600, plan

ally square. The other is in the sanctuary of Demeter at the site called Gaggera just outside the city (which is believed to have been founded in 628). The latter temple was 31 feet wide by 67 feet long (9·52 by 20·41 m.) and divided into a short anteroom, a long cella, and a short adytum. No traces of columns have been found, although the supposed cella could not have been roofed without intermediate supports; perhaps it was really a court, as in another temple of Demeter: that at Delos, which dates from the early fifth century (p. 168). The exterior lacked both architrave and frieze but had a pediment of abnormal width [113]. It reached almost to the

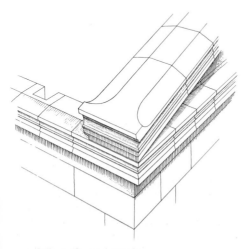

113. Selinus, Gaggera temple, restoration of pediment

corners of the front, because the slanting cornice was not cut below to merge with the horizontal cornice but retained its full depth practically to the corners, where its edge directly overlay that of the horizontal cornice. The cornices are concave-faced in the upper part, have a projecting moulding along the centre, and recede in two steps below. There was no gutter, or rather it is incorporated in the cornice.

The earliest of the peripteral temples seems to be that of Apollo at Syracuse; it is obviously a pioneer building, characterized by an extraordinary heaviness which amounts to a misuse of stone. The pteron comprised six columns on the ends and seventeen on the sides [114].[9] They are monoliths, 26 feet high (7·98 m.), sharply tapered, and very irregular in size; those of the opposite corners of one end differ by as much as a foot in lower diameter. Along the sides, the average diameter is 6 feet and the spacing so close as to leave a gap of only 1½ feet between the capitals, which spread to a much greater width than does the shaft even at its foot. The columns on the ends are still thicker, making their height barely four diameters, but are placed farther apart, and the central intercolumniation is especially wide, in accordance with the Ionic practice of the eastern Aegean; the angle intercolumniations are not contracted. Nothing is preserved above the architrave except scraps of the terracotta sheathing of both cornices and their gutters – a second gutter is regularly applied to the pediment floor in Sicilian Doric. But evidently the frieze could have contained

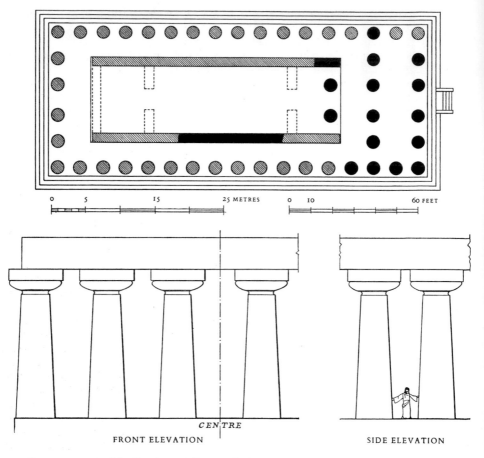

FRONT ELEVATION   CENTRE   SIDE ELEVATION

114. Syracuse, temple of Apollo, plan and diagram of columns

nothing but a metope over each intercolumniation, except perhaps at the central span of the ends, where there may have been space for a triglyph and two metopes; wider metopes were no doubt used along the rest of the end. The great length of the pteron is due to an inner colonnade behind the front; it runs from the third column of each side, and is spaced like the pteron. This duplication again suggests Ionic influence, though there is nothing exactly like it in Ionia itself; it becomes a quite regular feature in Sicilian temples of the sixth century. Also Ionic is the termination of the cella walls in a spur with no anta facing. The entrance to the cella is aligned with the fifth column of the side; two columns stand between the spurs, in line with the two middle columns of the double front. The outer face of each wall of the cella is aligned with the axis of the penultimate columns. The plan of the interior cannot be ascertained, but may be guessed from analogies: a shallow porch and an adytum are almost invariable in Sicily, and not till the fifth century does the opisthodomus appear.

Three other Sicilian temples – the Olympieum at Syracuse[10] and 'C' and 'F' at Selinus

– have a second colonnade at the same interval of two intercolumniations from the front [118]. But only the Olympieum cella corresponded with that of the temple of Apollo in that it is entered through a porch with two columns, which naturally are aligned with those on the front, and that the side walls of the cella are aligned with pteron columns. In fact the Sicilians were gradually finding means to dispense with porch columns and thereby avoid the obligation to align the cella with the pteron (indeed, many temples give the impression of an independent cella around which an unrelated pteron has been constructed, though it is quite clear that both parts belong to the same construction and it would be normal for the pteron to be laid out first); whereas in Greece the pteron along the side always had to be given the precise depth of one front intercolumniation, or two if it were doubled, in Sicily its depth became a matter of free choice, and for the remainder of the sixth century is always greater than one intercolumniation. The cella could therefore be built so narrow as to require no internal columns, without affecting the overall proportions, while its own proportions were kept reasonable by its triple division into an open-fronted porch, a long room which is the cella proper, and an adytum.

The Sicilians now abandoned the rule that a pteron should be more closely spaced along the sides than on the ends; in Greece the differentiation remains emphatic till the beginning of the fifth century, and afterwards persists to a scarcely noticeable degree. The latest Sicilian instance of it (apart from one or two fifth-century cases in which the difference is negligible) is Selinus 'C', which may be the oldest temple with a pteron deeper on the side than the front intercolumniation [118]. The distance between its columns axis to axis is less on the sides than on the ends by about one-eighth; this is an average figure, ignoring considerable irregularities. With a narrow cella (34 feet wide out of the total $78\frac{1}{2}$ feet), a disproportionate amount of light must have been visible through the corner of the pteron, and so have broken the uniformity of the design. In order, no doubt, to avoid that defect the spacings in the Olympieum at Syracuse were made all alike, and three later temples of the sixth century at Selinus were even given a closer spacing on the ends than on the sides, though the reduction in the interaxial distance is trifling – between one-thirtieth and one-fortieth in temples 'D' and 'F', barely one-ninetieth in the later temple 'G'.

The temples at Selinus are all ruined – though part of 'C' has now been rebuilt [115] – and the attempted restorations[11] are hypothetical in important respects. The construction of 'C' must have been spread over several decades, in the course of which the original columns became old-fashioned. Some of them bear twenty flutes, the rest sixteen. Some were modernized at the junction with the capital by carving away a moulding, incising necking-rings in its place, and continuing the flutes in stucco. The entablature was exceptionally tall (from architrave to horizontal cornice), more than half as high as the columns. The frieze[12] was so tall that the width of the metopes (which are sculptured) had to be less than their height and scarcely exceeds that of the triglyphs; the mutule that overhung each metope was accordingly less than half as wide as that above each triglyph. The cornices too were very high, and partially sheathed in terracotta, pinned to the stone [116]; the manner of their junction at the corners is disputable.[13] The gutters were made of terracotta, and a gorgon's head of terracotta, 9 feet high, occupied the centre of the pediments.

A treasury built at Olympia by the city of Gela was similarly provided with terracotta facings to its limestone cornices, and terracotta gutters [117]. The Sicilian habit of placing a duplicate gutter along the pediment floor caused the designer some trouble at the corners, where the slanting cornice cuts diagonally across its rectangular upper border and the concave face below. The border of the gutter is bent downwards from the point at which it meets the cornice, though not at such a pronounced slant, and tapers as it slopes; its 'Greek key' pattern

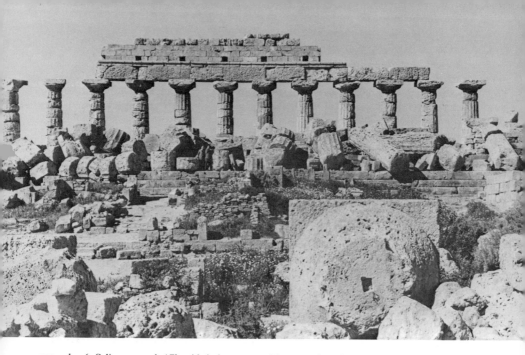

115 and 116. Selinus, temple 'C', mid sixth century, with restoration of terracotta cornice sheathings and gorgon's head from the pediment

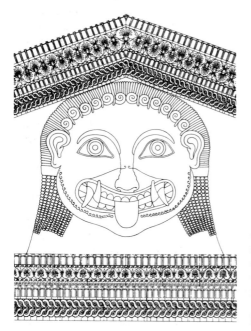

diminishes in scale to match. All the slabs bear elaborate ornament in red, black, and buff.

In temple 'D' at Selinus [118], the porch of the cella is designed to compensate for the lack of a second colonnade. It is built at the appropriate distance of two intercolumniations behind the front, and its façade consists of a row of four small columns, the outer two being engaged in the ends of the cella walls. Apparently by afterthought,[14] the pteron of temple 'F' [118] was blocked, in Egyptian fashion, by placing stone screens across the intercolumniations up to half the height of the columns (which is 30 feet). On the sides and back of the temple a lintel ran across each screen and from it pilasters descended to a projecting course immediately above the floor, and so outlined a false doorway and threshold. A real doorway opened through each of the screens placed between the columns of the front. The porch colonnade was left completely unobstructed.

Temple 'G' was one of the largest of antiquity [118]. It was laid out before the end of the sixth

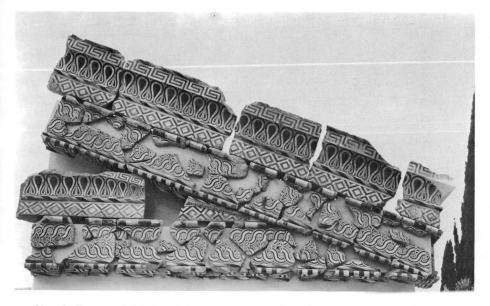

117. Olympia, Treasury of Gela, late sixth century, terracotta decoration

century but much of the structure is later; it was still incomplete in 409 when the Carthaginians destroyed Selinus. The pteron measures 164 by 361 feet (50·07 by 110·12 m.) with eight by seventeen columns, and its depth is precisely equal to two intercolumniations; the ceiling beams had to cover a gap of 38 feet. As the work proceeded, from the front of the temple westwards, the builders seem to have become apprehensive that the original design of the columns (which appear to have been about 50 feet high) might prove inadequate to bear the weight imposed upon them. Partly for this reason, but also in conformity with changing fashion, the shafts tapered less and less the farther they were placed from the east front. In the back colonnade, which is the latest part, the lower diameters also were greater. So, contrary to general practice, the fifth-century columns in this temple are thicker than those of the sixth. The shape of the capitals changed even more noticeably during the construction [88]. In the earliest capitals, the echinus is separated from the shaft by a deep hollow and extends almost horizontally to the same width as the abacus. In the latest capitals, which can be dated about 470, no hollow intervenes between the echinus and the shaft, and the echinus climbs rapidly to the abacus. Other capitals are intermediate between the two extremes, both in date and in shape.

The cella of temple 'G' was entered through a prostyle porch with a façade of four columns, aligned on those of the front, and placed two intercolumniations behind. Between each angle column of the porch façade and the cella wall stood another column. The area contained within the porch columns was too wide to be roofed and must have formed a court, which extended as far back as a line of three great doorways. This number was chosen, not merely for the sake of alignment with the porch and pteron columns, but also because the great width of the cella, 59 feet, was most conveniently spanned by two rows of very small columns; each column apparently supported two others,

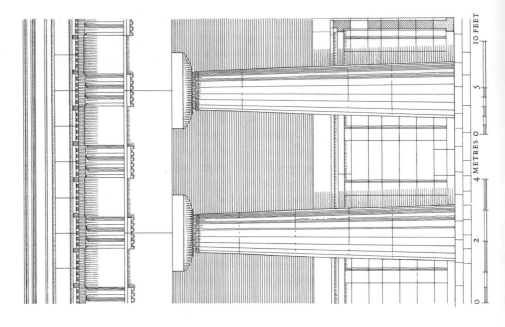

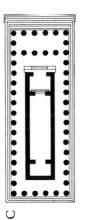

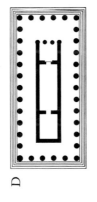

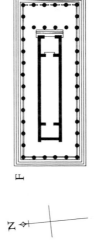

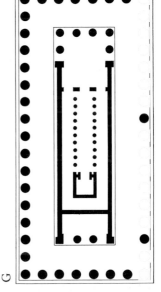

118. Selinus,
plans of temples 'C',
'D', 'F', 'G'
(scale 10 mm = 46½ feet),
and restored order of 'F'

C

D

F

G

10 FEET

5

4 METRES 0

2

0

superimposed. The nave between the colonnades led to a cult-room, but this seems to have been built during the fifth century in substitution for an adytum, which according to the original intention would have occupied the site behind it eventually given to an opisthodomus.

SOUTH ITALY

No connected account can be written of early architectural development in south Italy. Dating is almost entirely conjectural and is hampered by extraordinary differences in the Doric of one city compared with another's; there was nothing approaching a standard pattern. Sicilian influence is dominant, but that of Greece is also apparent, and Ionic features too are utilized, to a degree which varies in each locality. The average result is a more or less discordant compromise; many buildings are frankly experimental. Only rarely does it appear that an experiment proved successful enough to establish a new convention, and then only within the territory of one or two cities. All the work is in local stone, often of a friable nature.

Some examples of the architectural oddities ought first to be described. The most remarkable of all is the temple of Apollo Alaeus at Crimisa (Punta Alice), presumably of exceptionally early date. It consisted merely of a cella

and an adytum. A central row of wooden supports began at the very front, as in the temple of Apollo at Thermum, but four in the adytum were arranged in a square. Terracotta facings were attached to the wooden cornices, and in the case of the slanting cornice they take an unparalleled form [119]: two plain bands stand above a recessed strip from which regulae with moulded knobs project at intervals, and below this the same scheme is repeated, but the lower regulae are placed under the gaps between those above. The terracotta gutter is an obvious imitation of the Egyptian concave cornice together with its pattern of upright leaves. Antefixes stood all round the roof, instead of along the sides alone, and their bases too are shaped like regulae. The antefixes on the ends leant in conformity with the slope.

A sanctuary of Hera at the mouth of the river Silaris (Sele) contained a temple which probably dates from the middle of the sixth century. Its triglyphs taper upwards to such an abnormal degree that the width diminishes by one-fifteenth, and the metopes (which are sculptured) expand upwards correspondingly. A pair of anta capitals[15] must be of oriental inspiration, perhaps transmitted through some Ionic intermediary. The sides of the lower member curve outwards, as though to form a volute, which is only vestigially represented by a rosette-faced

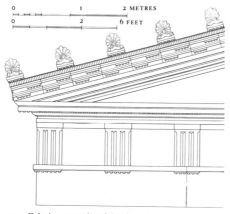

119. Crimisa, temple of Apollo Alaeus,
early sixth century,
restored pediment and entablature

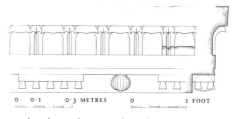

120. Locri, temple, restored cornice

cylinder under the corner of the abacus. In one capital the abacus is carved with rosettes, in the other with alternate palmettes and water-lilies, linked by curling petals. The frieze of a latish temple at Locri contained five-bar equivalents of triglyphs, and was overhung [120] by short mutules alternating with pomegranates sus-

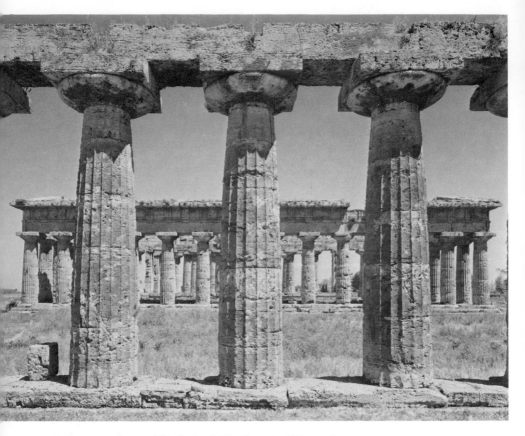

121. Paestum, columns of 'Basilica' and side of temple of 'Neptune',
mid sixth and early or mid fifth century

pended beneath the cornice, which bore a leaf-pattern.

Most of the temples in south Italy are ill-preserved. There is a single complete column at Taranto, and two long stretches of pteron remain standing, with architraves, at Metaponto. Nowhere else is anything intact above the floor except at Poseidonia, or Paestum as the Romans renamed it. Here two temples of the sixth century and one of the fifth are still in fair condition. The oldest, of the mid sixth century, is the so-called 'Basilica', recently identified as a temple of Hera. The entire pteron remains standing, with the architrave, but no walling

[121, 122]. There are nine columns on the ends and eighteen on the sides, a strange ratio for a temple which measures 80 by 178 feet (24·51 by 54·27 m.). Because the pteron is very broad, almost as wide as two intercolumniations, the spacing on the ends needed to be closer, according to the Sicilian principle, but the difference is about twice as large as it should have been by Sicilian standards, averaging 9 inches (23 cm.), or proportionately one-fourteenth. If an additional column had been placed on each side, the spacing on the ends would still have been closer by one forty-fifth, and that amount of differentiation would have conformed to

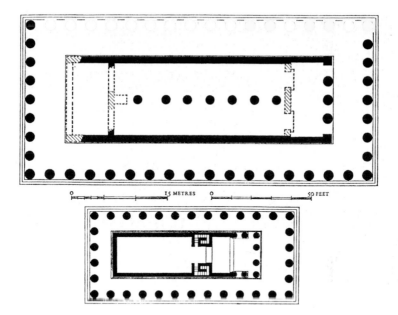

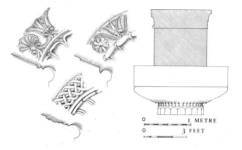

122. Paestum, 'Basilica', mid sixth century, and temple of Ceres, late sixth century, plans (partly restored)

Sicilian practice. It therefore seems as though the architect had been determined to give his pteron exactly double the number of columns on the sides. In the present condition of the building, in which the cella has been demolished to floor level, the aesthetic effect of the differentiation cannot be fairly judged; it makes no conscious impression on the spectator, but the pteron's appearance of placid solidity must be largely due to it.

The sides of the cella are set almost two intercolumniations from the pteron; so too were the porch and the adytum (on foundations for an opisthodomus). The junction of porch and cella is marked by a change in the thickness of the side-walls; a rise in the floor implies a step. The cella contained a central row of columns, which were, abnormally, of the same diameter and height as in the pteron. There the shafts taper by as much as one-third of the lower diameter (4¼ feet; 1·45 m.) and their sides curve convexly – thus adding to their apparent height and strength – to a greater degree than in any other

building. The capitals are very wide and are ornamented in a manner peculiar to Paestum [123]. The flutes terminate in semicircles as in Ionic, beneath a projecting moulding; a deep necking above it is decorated with narrower leaves, which curl over at the top. The base of the echinus bears mouldings instead of flat annulets, and at the back of the temple (facing the main street of the city) these are decorated with patterns, which differ in each column.

123. Paestum, 'Basilica', mid sixth century, ornamented capitals

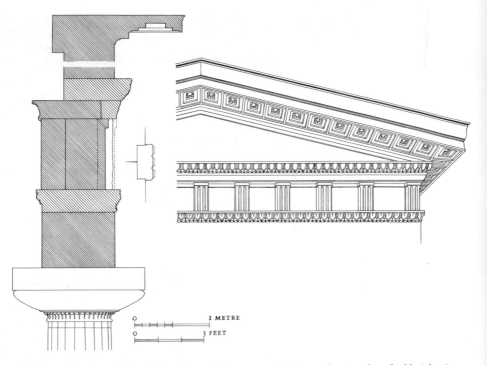

I METRE

3 FEET

124 and 125. Paestum, temple of 'Ceres', late sixth century, entablature and restoration of gable (*above*) and view (*opposite*)

The only other building with ornamented capitals[16] is the so-called Temple of 'Ceres' – though really of Athena – at Paestum, which looks as though it might be twenty or thirty years later [124]. The pteron of six by thirteen columns, uniformly spaced, is one intercolumniation wide [122, 125]. The cella is entered through a prostyle porch, with a row of four Ionic columns in front and one other on each side between them and a three-quarters column engaged in the anta, on a raised piece of the floor. Two stairs preceded the cella. There was neither an inner colonnade nor an adytum. But this fairly conventional plan was accompanied by a most original entablature. Along the top of the architrave runs an Ionic moulding, carved with egg-and-dart pattern; other temples in south Italy had comparable substitutes for the canonical band and regulae. The structure of

the frieze, however, is unique. The triglyphs are set into the wall, the face of which is exposed as metopes between them. Another moulding of two carved strips ran along the top of the frieze. On the ends of the temple there was only smooth masonry between this and the gable, for there was no horizontal cornice, and consequently no pediment. The slanting cornice was exceptionally wide, and it continued along the sides at the same inclination, forming eaves.[17] Its under side is coffered, in imitation of a wooden ceiling, and a carving of a star was leaded into the centre of each coffer. (Likewise in the Hall of Votive Gifts at Samothrace, datable about 540, the raking cornice merged with the horizontal, but mouldings of slighter projection outlined the base of pediments.)

Freedom either to discard or modify a feature in a Doric elevation, or to substitute an Ionic

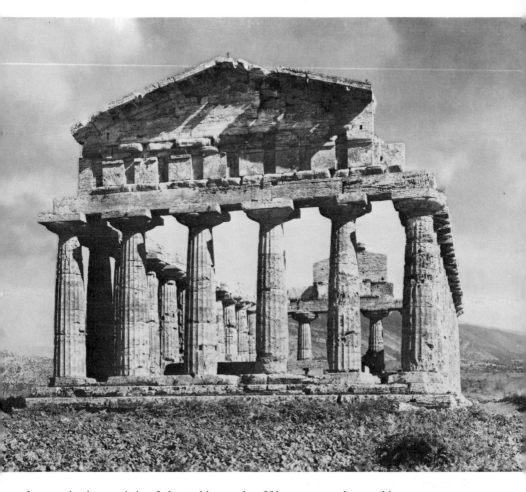

element, is characteristic of the architectural outlook among the Greeks of south Italy; Sicily was conservative, and Greece itself hidebound in comparison. But this inventiveness was accompanied by a lack of delicacy. In Greece there was nothing to distract architects from the study of proportions, and they were in fact doing the preparatory work for the perfectionists of the fifth century, whose achievements were so plainly superior that the western schools abandoned their originality, together with their crudity. The distinctiveness of western Doric thus came to a dead end, so far as the Greeks were concerned, but it was to leave behind it an abiding legacy in the architecture of Roman temples.

CHAPTER 12

THE FORMATION OF THE IONIC TEMPLE

This chapter treats of eastern Greek building from about 600 to 450; only towards the close of this period did the Ionic Order take its final shape. Very few of its constituent parts can have evolved as early as those of Doric, and the stage at which a coherent set of conventions was adopted, as an Order, occurred two or three generations later, and then in a less definite form; moreover local variations persisted longer, and many of them eventually became universally accepted as alternatives. Features in use by the middle of the sixth century include the capital, two types of column base – Asiatic-Greek and Samian – and two of architrave, the frieze, which was characteristic of the Aegean Islands, and the dentils that formed a substitute for it in Asia Minor, but the peculiar Ionic method of fluting does not appear till about 500, and yet another type of base developed at Athens towards the middle of the fifth century, when the Samian was on the verge of extinction.

No capital yet found in the eastern Aegean is likely to be much earlier than 600 B.C.[1] and the oldest examples are not strictly Ionic, though clearly related; they are often called 'Aeolic'. (Part of one was found at Old Smyrna, belonging to a temple which was being built when that city was destroyed by Alyattes King of Lydia shortly before 600.) It is questionable whether they can be accepted as prototypes, for the decorative elements, though similar, are very differently arranged; but the basic principle is the same, in that the bearing surface is extended upwards far to either side, making the top oblong. That is the essential factor which distinguishes the early Ionic from the Doric capital. Translated into terms of carpentry, it should mean that greater care had been taken to distribute the weight that rested on a wooden column. Apparently the wooden echinus was a knob comparable to the Doric type, but carried a taller block than the Doric abacus, laid flat in the same manner, so that the grain ran horizontally. But the Greeks never gave a clear representation in stone of the functional shapes, and sometimes omitted the echinus.

Even the earliest 'Aeolic' capitals, almost all of which have been found in Aeolis (north-west Asia Minor and Lesbos), are highly ornamental carvings [126]. The abacus is transformed into

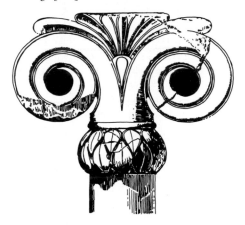

126. Neandria, temple, restored capital

two volutes, of a vaguely floral aspect, and a palmette which fills the gap between them; this is flattened on top to fit the architrave, but in some capitals the volutes rose to the same level and supplied the major part of the supporting surface. The echinus, if present at all, is disguised as the bud of a water-lily, the sepals of which either enclose the knob tightly or droop to form a second and wider echinus immediately below. The entire scheme was borrowed from the Near East.[2] Architectural examples have been found dating back to the tenth century B.C.[3] and they are also used to decorate Phoenician and Syrian ivory and metal work, which would have served as examples for the Greek archi tects. The temple at Neandria was built in local stone, about the middle of the sixth century. It consists of a rectangular foundation measuring 42 by 84 feet (12·87 by 25·71 m.), with inner and outer sections, the space between being filled with variable material. There was a single, central row of seven stone columns (the only internal division of the foundation) in line with a doorway at the centre of one short end, here, because of the unusual orientation, facing north-west. It is disputed whether or not there was an external colonnade as well. Three different parts to the capital survive; a block with the volutes, small leaf drums, with leaves in low relief, and larger leaf drums. Koldewey combined all three to form capitals with the large leaf drum under the smaller. Recent studies prefer to assign the smaller drums to inner columns (perhaps as bases), the larger to an external colonnade without volutes above: but there is still much uncertainty about this.[4]

All the known 'Aeolic' capitals seem to date from the end of the seventh until the end of the sixth century (the splendid, well-built peripteral second temple at Klopedi on Lesbos), while the oldest Ionic capitals cannot be appreciably earlier than 550. The difference is largely a matter of decoration. Whereas in the 'Aeolic' type the volutes spring upwards from separate stalks and then curl outwards, in Ionic they curl downwards and inwards like the ends of a scroll, in continuation of a band which outlines the top of a cushion laid horizontally across the echinus. In fact, an Ionic echinus is often carved as part of the highest drum of the shaft, and inserted into the cushion, the base of which is cut away to receive it. The top of the cushion block rises as a low abacus, which extends outwards to the droop of the volutes; in the earliest capitals its length considerably exceeds its width, but a gradual reduction ended by making it square. That is its normal shape from the beginning of the fifth century, and a perfectly logical one for stone. The entire scheme of the decoration might have originated in metal work.

Assyrian reliefs prove that capitals with a generic resemblance to Ionic had already been used farther east, apparently by the Greek colonists in Cilicia, and there is no evidence to support the theory that the Greeks developed Ionic from 'Aeolic'. There are, as it happens, some capitals[5] of an intermediate character, but these need not represent a transitional stage; they may have resulted from deliberate attempts at compromise. Moreover, they belong to solitary columns which supported votive offerings (mainly at Athens), and for that reason are likely to have been fanciful in design, just as the 'Aeolic' and Doric capitals of other votive columns do not reproduce the exact form used in buildings.

The stalkless volutes on some of these intermediate capitals are actually painted or incised on a flat block, and in such cases no importance can be attached to whether they curl upwards or downwards, as two separate entities or as the ends of a scroll. Nor, perhaps, is the divergence between the genuine 'Aeolic' and Ionic types of much greater significance, although the general outline of the block differs somewhat, being more compact in Ionic, because the capital is lower in relation to its height. Consequently, it has a more efficient shape; the 'Aeolic' capitals from Neandria are particularly enfeebled by contraction into a neck; but at the best, 'Aeolic' was more suitable for pilaster capitals – the purpose for which the orientals had devised it.

While 'Aeolic' columns rarely stood on bases, and then always of simple form, an elaborate base was invariably used for Ionic columns. This departure from Greek custom – for it must be remembered that Doric columns required no base either – might have been inspired from the usage in Cilicia and other parts of the Turkish-Syrian border lands, where the base was often composed of several stages, cylindrical or convex. But of the two characteristic decorative motives of those countries, the notched edges and cable mouldings, the first never occurs in Ionic, and the second rarely.

Definitely Ionic features appear first in two temples, of Hera at Samos (which replaced the second Heraeum) and Artemis at Ephesus, which resembled one another very closely, and seem to have been undertaken almost simultaneously at the middle of the sixth century. King Croesus of Lydia, to whom Ephesus was more or less subject, paid for most of the columns of the Artemisium about 560 or soon afterwards; there is no external evidence by which to date the Heraeum, but the bases of its columns are obviously less advanced in type. This might conceivably have been due merely to an enforced economy in carving, but the temple is also rather smaller, and in view of the rivalry that prevailed between Greek cities, the probability is that it was begun slightly earlier. A Samian of engineering genius, Theodorus, is recorded to have worked at both temples, in conjunction with other architects – at the Heraeum with Rhoecus, another Samian, and at Ephesus with a Cretan, Chersiphron of Cnossus, whose son Metagenes completed the building.

The Heraeum and the Artemisium were the first really large Greek temples. They are of a scale rarely surpassed in later times, and they were the first to be surrounded by a double pteron. Both temples perished by fire, and their ruins were almost completely demolished to make place for successors, so that the plans[6] and elevations can only be partly ascertained. In each case the edge of the platform dropped in two steps, instead of three, as is customary in Doric. At Samos the outer colonnade was set back from it, like the walls at Neandria, to leave a bare space of 10 feet, and a similar arrangement is alleged for Ephesus. The Heraeum faced east, like most Greek temples, but the Artemisium west, in accordance apparently with earlier practice in Asia Minor. At the front of each temple stood two rows of eight columns – an unprecedented number, though soon to be surpassed [cf. 130]. Their spacing was graduated to emphasize the entrance by a wider intercolumniation; the Egyptians habitually designed the halls of temples in that manner, and the idea of massing great numbers of columns may also have been inspired by knowledge of Egypt. At the front of the Heraeum, the

two columns nearest the centre were spaced about 28 feet apart, axis to axis, but the next pair on either side 24 feet, and the outer two pairs 17½ feet; the diameters of the columns also diminished. In the Artemisium the spacings seem to have decreased from 28 feet (8·62 m.) at the centre, to nearly 24 feet at the nearest intercolumniations, and 20 feet (6·12 m.) at the outer pairs; the diameters of the columns exceeded 6 feet (1·725 m.) in the case of the central pair, but appear to have been steadily reduced to either side, by 5 inches, 6 inches, and 1 inch in turn. The gaps between the columns would therefore have measured roughly 22 feet at the central intercolumniation, 18 feet at the next, and then 14½ feet, but widened again to nearly 15 feet between the two side colonnades. The number of columns along the sides is uncertain in both temples, but approximated to twenty-one in each row. At the back of the Artemisium there seem to have been nine, where the Heraeum may have had either nine or ten. In neither temple can the pteron have comprised less than a hundred columns in all.

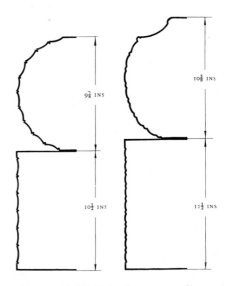

9⅞ INS

10⅝ INS

10½ INS

11½ INS

127. Samos, third Heraeum, begun c. 570 (?), column bases (the two parts of each may not belong together)

The cella of each temple was entered through a deep porch, in which stood two more rows of columns; the entire forest of columns must have been extremely impressive. At the Heraeum the cella also contained two rows of columns with ten apiece. Its length equalled three-quarters of the building's, measured along the pteron, where the length, some 290 feet, was practically double the width, some 150 feet. The Artemisium was wider, and also much longer owing to an opisthodomus; if its pteron stood on the edge of the platform, it could have measured 171 by 358 feet (55·10 by 109·20 m.). The cella may perhaps have formed an open court, around a reconstruction of an early shrine which had also been surrounded, in all probability, by a similar cella-like court. The entrance to this seems to have always faced west, which accounts for the peculiar orientation of the temple.

Not a single capital of the Heraeum has survived. Drums of columns and their bases remain, and clearly had been turned on a lathe, an invention ascribed to Theodorus; the material is a soft limestone. The bases [127] consist of a convex upper member, called the torus, and a taller spira, which is really cylindrical, though mouldings cut into its outline. The bases were carved on the lathe with shallow horizontal flutes, six or seven on a torus, six to fifteen on a spira; these are often separated by pairs of narrower convex pipings, and sometimes wide shallow pipings serve instead of the concave flutes. The shafts of some columns were carved with forty shallow flutes which meet in sharp edges, precisely as in Doric. But many shafts and bases were left smooth, probably only because they were never finished; the temple seems to have been burnt within thirty or forty years of its commencement. Part, at least, must have been roofed, for there remain scraps of flat tiles and ridged cover tiles, on the Corinthian system, and of palmette antefixes, likewise in terracotta.

Later builders at Ephesus utilized blocks from Croesus's Artemisium in their own foundations, with the result that many details of it are preserved, though disarranged. The walls consisted of limestone, but were faced with marble, and the columns were entirely of marble [128]. Their bases,[7] at least in some cases, stood on tall square plinths, and in a few shafts the lowest drum was carved with figures in high relief; these peculiarities seldom recur later, and then only locally. A convex moulding, the apophyge, surrounds the foot of the shaft, and makes a transition to the base. The base consists of a torus and spira, carved more elaborately than at the third Heraeum of Samos, and so as to break up the profile. An occasional torus has a triple curve, resembling that of the contemporary Doric echinus, upon which is carved a 'heart-and-dart' pattern of drooping leaves, alternately broad and narrow, like a more refined version of the sepals on 'Aeolic' capitals. But generally the torus keeps the regular convex shape, and is fluted horizontally in the manner which later became characteristic of the Ionic shaft, the flutes are narrow, and separated by fillets which preserve the preliminary convex outline of the whole member. This type of fluting is not suited to carpentry and obviously originated in stone; in fact, when carving a Doric shaft, masons began by cutting a narrow trough to the required depth up the middle of each flute before they shaped the edges to meet, and at that stage the work only needed smoothing to produce the appearance of Ionic fluting. The spira too was novel; it is the earliest instance of the Asiatic type which comprises three superimposed concave parts, together equivalent in height to the single cylindrical or slightly hollowed member of the Samian type. The Asiatic spira retains vestiges of that shape only in the pairs of convex pipings at its top, mid-height, and bottom, between which the profile recedes deeply; the middle pipings do not project so far as the others, which extend to a greater breadth than even the centre of the torus.

The mouldings of the Artemisium may have set types for the Order. Special attention is due to the triple curve mentioned in relation to the torus, because this moulding [97] remained permanently in favour and was applied to various

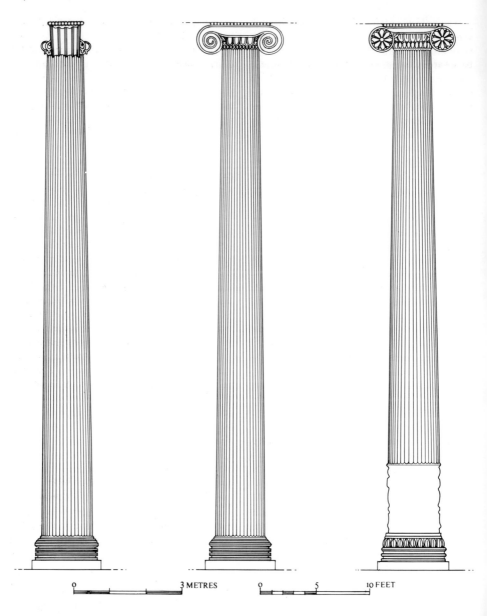

128. Ephesus, temple of Artemis, *c.* 560,
restoration of columns

portions of later Ionic buildings. One of its conventional names, cyma reversa, combines the Greek for 'wave' with the Latin for 'turned backwards'; the other, Lesbian cymatium, was certainly used in antiquity but perhaps with a different sense. The opposite form, the cyma recta, seems of Doric inspiration. The most frequent ornament on a cyma reversa at all periods was leaf-and-dart, but on a cyma recta water-lilies and palmettes, or scrolls of foliage.

Vitruvius tells us that the total height of the Artemisium columns (which, of course, had been destroyed three centuries before he wrote) equalled eight times their lower diameter; accordingly they must have been little more than half as thick as contemporary Doric columns. Studies of other Ionic columns suggest that even this is too thick, and that the height was more likely to have been closer to ten times the lower diameter.[8] This contrast between the Orders persists, and was anticipated in the 'Aeolic' buildings. The Artemisium shafts bear Doric-style flutes, varying in number from forty to forty-four, or even forty-eight, in which case they are cut alternately wide and narrow.

The capitals [129],[9] though finely shaped, are extraordinarily long, and equally undeveloped in several details. The spiral bands of the volutes project as single pipings, whereas in later times they would be channelled in multiple shelves, and they terminate in a hook instead of an eye. Large, though cramped, palmettes fill the re-entrants at their junction with the echinus, which curves inwards at the top, in reminiscence of the 'Aeolic' form; later architects preferred to make the echinus bulge towards the overlying scroll, and so needed less filling at the sides. The abacus is very low, and almost twice as long as it is wide, owing to the great spread of the volutes; its profile is convex. Both abacus and echinus are richly ornamented with various patterns, and in a few capitals the volutes were carved with rosettes instead of the usual spirals: it has been suggested that these capitals came over the columns whose lower drum was carved with figures in relief. The decoration on the upper portions of the building seems to have been limited to a tall moulding with egg-and-dart pattern, which ran at some level between the architrave and the cornice, and a gutter-parapet, carved with a procession of figures in low relief, from between which there projected spouts in the form of lion heads. Similar parapet gutters (but in terracotta) have

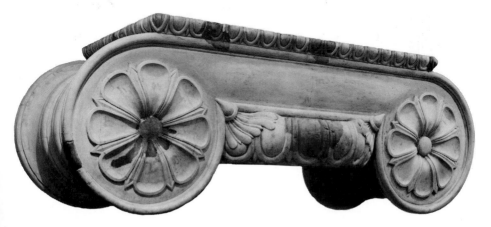

129. Ephesus, temple of Artemis, *c.* 560, restored capital. *London, British Museum*

been found elsewhere in Asia Minor.[10] The roof was tiled with marble along the edges, but otherwise with terracotta.

The third major Ionic temple of the sixth century was that of Apollo at Didyma, in the territory of Miletus, ascribed to 540–520, and destroyed by the Persians in 494. There was a predecessor going back to *c.* 700, which was improved towards the end of the seventh century. It seems to have been influenced by the Heraeum, and particularly the Artemisium; one can see in these buildings the architectural expression of political rivalries. The plan as restored[11] comprises a double pteron of eight by twenty-one columns with nine across the back on a base (125 by 280 feet; 38.39 by 85.156 m.) calculated on the axis of the columns. There were human figures carved to surround several column bases. A sculptured sphinx masked each corner of the architrave, which took the true Ionic form of three fasciae, overlapping strips which simulate weatherboarding. A deep porch had two rows of columns, beyond which steps

led to the interior, which was unroofed, and contained an inner shrine in the form of a small but complete temple building, probably with two columns *in antis*. The whole arrangement was recreated, with additional features, in the Hellenistic period when the temple was at last rebuilt (below, p. 261). As in this successor, the inner sides of the interior walls were reinforced with projecting piers. The remains of other Ionic temples of the late sixth century[12] may give an idea of some missing features, upon which they are not likely to have improved. At Naxos and Paros are marble doorways, providing a clear passage roughly 20 feet high and 12 feet wide. The architrave at Paros also has three fasciae. The temple of Paros has been tentatively restored as being either six by twelve or six by thirteen columns, with dipteral ends and a consequently short cella building, with an opisthodomus.

After the burning of the third Heraeum at Samos, about 530, a fourth[13] was laid out, which is the largest of all Greek temples [130].

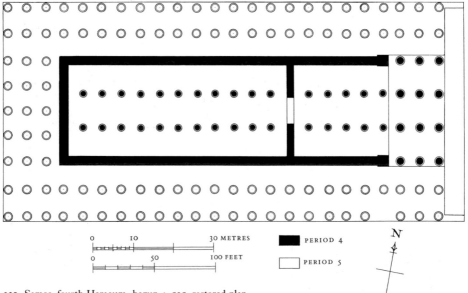

0   10   30 METRES
0   50   100 FEET

■ PERIOD 4
□ PERIOD 5

N

130. Samos, fourth Heraeum, begun *c.* 525, restored plan (late additions outlined; position of extant column left blank)

It measures 179 by 365 feet and was never completed. The platform rises unusually high above the ground, without steps – a flight of ten steps across the front dates from the second century A.D. The outer colonnade followed the edge. But in most other respects the plan is based on the precedents of the Artemisium and third Heraeum. The pteron was meant to be double along the sides, with twenty-four columns in each row, and triple along both ends, with nine columns at the back and eight at the front; most of its foundations seem to date from between 525 and early in the fifth century, but the columns themselves are mainly very late. The cella was entered through a deep porch, in which stood two rows of five columns apiece, and only these portions of the building can have been completed in the sixth century, together with the pteron columns aligned with the porch colonnades and walls, i.e. four in each of the three rows. An extreme differentiation in the eventual spacing of the pteron must correspond with the original scheme.[14] Only one column remains standing, and its low capital and base are obviously late; however, it proves the height, 63 feet (18·96 m.). The original columns have limestone shafts, but capitals and bases of marble. The capitals resemble those of Croesus's Artemisium, except that the volutes spread even wider, so that they are completely detached from the echinus; the amount of ornament is less. The bases retain the old Samian feature of a single spira, but compromise with the Asiatic type by making it extremely concave; at top and bottom it extends to precisely the same width as the centre of the torus. Both members are horizontally banded with alternate single fillets and concave mouldings; the latter are not strictly flutes, because the curvature varies from one to another in keeping with the general outline. Some of the column shafts always remained smooth, but others are fluted in the Ionic manner, with narrow, deep flutes separated by almost imperceptibly convex fillets. Their number, twenty-four, is that which became canonical in the Order, and they may have been carved long after the erection of the columns. A

somewhat later temple of Artemis in Asia Minor, at Magnesia, seems to represent an experimental stage in the development of Ionic fluting [131]. The shaft bears as many as thirty-two flutes, an excessive number in view of the width of the intervening fillets. The bases at Magnesia naturally belong to the Asiatic type, but stood on much lower square plinths than at the Artemisium; such plinths are an optional feature in the Ionic of later times.

At no early temple in the eastern Aegean is the exterior preserved between the architrave and the cornice. In later times the Greeks of Asia Minor placed a row of small square blocks at intervals immediately below the cornice, and these dentils ('little teeth') reproduce the shape of beam-ends, as though the joists of the ceiling had previously been allowed to protrude from the wall and support the cornice.[15] The Ionic of the western Aegean substitutes for dentils a band of either plain or sculptured stone, which is called the frieze. In a temple of the late sixth century at Paros, the frieze was carved with

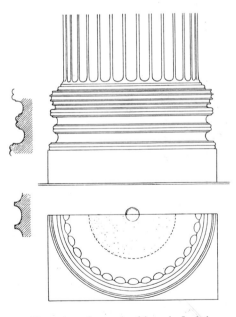

131. Magnesia, early temple of Artemis, Ionic base

three superimposed strips of egg-and-dart pattern, except where brackets rose to the cornice in the curly form of consoles ornamented with volutes.

The only example of western Ionic known in its virtual entirety is the marble treasury built at Delphi by the island state of Siphnos, at approximately 525; the date is historically attested. The building measures only 20 feet wide and 28 feet long (6·13 by 8·55 m.) and consisted of a cella and a porch with two statues of women instead of columns in antis [132]. (Female figures had been used for the same purpose in a Cnidian treasury of the previous generation, also at Delphi.)[16] They stood on square pedestals and wore tall hats carved with figures, upon which rested the capitals. The echinus takes the form of an inverted bell, sculptured with a scene of two lions killing a bull, and immediately above it lies a plain square abacus; there are no volutes. The architrave was smooth, perhaps because a division into two or three fasciae would have appeared fussy at such a small scale; along the sides its height was less. Above its upper border ran the bands of ornament normal in later Ionic, a low bead-and-reel beneath a taller egg-and-tongue pattern. Next comes the frieze, carved in this instance with figures in high relief. The pediment too contained sculptured figures, a rarity in the Ionic Order, which was too ornate in itself to require such additional embellishment. Both the under side of the horizontal cornice and the gutter upon the slanting cornice are richly carved with a pattern of palmettes and water-lilies. For acroteria, a sphinx sat on each corner and a flying Victory was placed over the ridge of the pediment. The doorway to the cella was framed all round with three fasciae and bands of carved patterns (wrongly omitted across the threshold in the plaster reconstruction), and surmounted by an elaborately ornamented cornice, which was bracketed to the lintel by voluted consoles. A huge bead-and-reel was carried along the base of the walls, both externally and in the porch; the plaster reconstruction wrongly puts it only upon the antae – which were actually broader

and taller by a few inches. This statement applies to the whole spur-wall and not merely to its termination, which in Ionic is not thickened like a Doric anta.

All the sculptured ornament and figures in this treasury were gaily painted, as seems to have been the invariable practice. The ornament of this period is carved rather flat, and must have depended for its effect upon colour almost as much as upon the elegance of the patterns, which are less austere than in later work, and sometimes quite naturalistic [133]. Two other treasuries of roughly similar date are surrounded at the base [134] by a large fluted torus, upon which rests a small bead-and-reel, and their ornament is almost equally abundant and quite as delicate [133]. Considerable fragments remain in the case only of the treasury ascribed to the Massalians, whose city is now named Marseilles [135, 136]. The bases belonged to the Asiatic type, and the shafts had the Doric-style fluting invariable at the time, but the design of the capitals is an obvious adaptation from the palm capitals of Egypt, probably through a Phoenician rather than Mycenean intermediary. The echinus[17] is shaped like an inverted bell and formed by leaves which curl outwards and downwards at the top. From the shaping of the block it seems as though two such bells must have been placed, one above the other, between the plain square abacus and the shaft; if so, the duplication is paralleled only in non-structural work, whereas capitals with a single round member of this sort were very occasionally used in buildings at any period.

The Ionic remains of the early fifth century are scanty, only vaguely datable, and in the main of little interest.[18] The most remarkable building is the Thesmophorium at Delos, a sanctuary of Demeter and Persephone (measuring 48½ by 123½ feet; 14·75 by 37·65 m.) [137]. The building was partitioned into three to provide for the separate worship of the two deities and for the Mysteries celebrated in their joint honour; twin cellas occupied the north and south ends, on either side of a square peristyle court such as

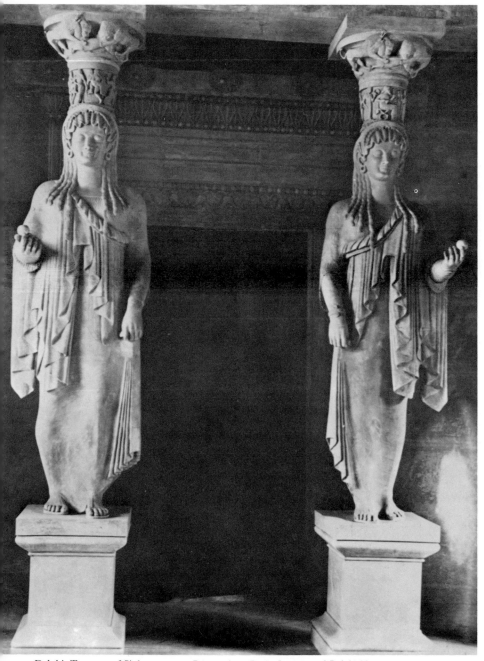

132. Delphi, Treasury of Siphnos, *c.* 525. Restoration. *Paris, Louvre, and Delphi Museum*

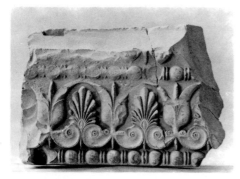

133. Ornament from an Ionic treasury, late sixth century. *Delphi Museum*

134. Delphi, Treasury of Massalia, late sixth century, base

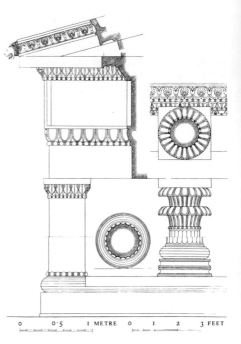

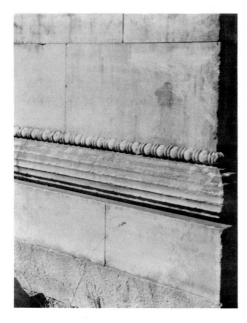

0   0·5   1 METRE   0   1   2   3 FEET

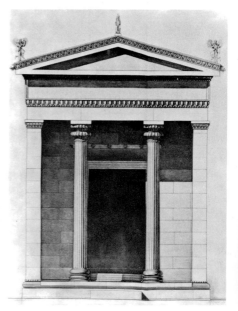

135 and 136. Delphi, Treasury of Massalia, late sixth century, detailed restorations (front, column base seen from above, capitals and entablature seen from below) (*above, right*) and restored elevation (*right*)

might be found in a house. Its central space, 20 feet square, was open to the sky, and bordered by a colonnade, comprising four Doric columns on each side. Each cella is slightly wider than it is long, and contained four columns, with extremely simple Ionic capitals but ornate bases of contemporary Persian type. The Persian kings are known to have employed their Greek subjects as sculptors, and presumably one of these artists had returned to his city in Asia Minor and was responsible for the design.

Fragments of a temple at Locri in Italy, and old drawings of one at Athens which was

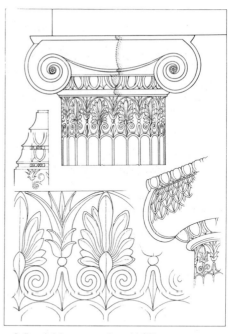

138. Locri, Maraza temple, mid fifth century, columns

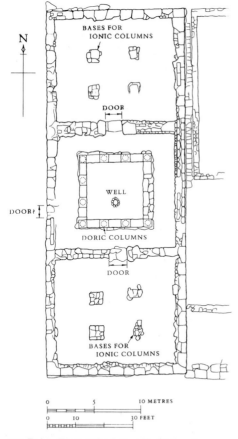

137. Delos, Thesmophorium, early fifth century, plan

destroyed in 1778, illustrate the transition, apparently at the middle of the century, to the Order as it is treated on the Acropolis during the last quarter. The dainty luxuriance of the ornament at Locri [138], and its impeccable carving (though in limestone), express a refined taste such as was to govern the Erechtheum. But owing to the virtual abolition of the abacus, the capitals are disagreeably squat, and in this respect had no successors, except perhaps at Bassae. Their spiral bands are single pipings in the old-fashioned manner, but terminate in an eye instead of a mere hook. The bases are among the latest examples of the Samian type, with a horizontally fluted torus placed upon a simple moulding, from which the side of the spira dropped in a smooth concave curve like an enormous horizontal flute; the lower end of this was sharply undercut, to demarcate it from the floor. A close prototype for the decoration on the column shaft has been found in Samos.[19] The

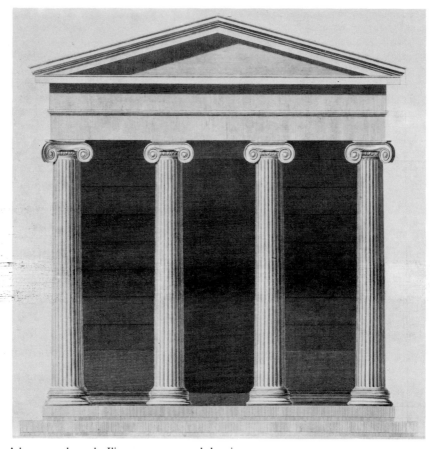

139. Athens, temple on the Ilissus, c. 450, restored elevation

use of dentils instead of a frieze also points to the eastern Aegean.

An extraordinary contrast is seen on comparing this Eastern style with the Ionic evolved at Athens about 450. The lost marble temple on the Ilissus, which had been converted into a chapel, was carefully drawn and measured, and restorations published in 1762 seem reliable [139, 140]. The foundations have been restudied recently,[20] and though little of the temple survives, the general arrangements were confirmed. It was very small, 19 feet wide and 41½ feet long, and consisted of a cella and porch and a row of four columns placed prostyle at either

end. At the front the antae projected 9 feet from the cross-wall and the columns stood 4 feet beyond, while at the back the columns were 5 feet distant from the blank wall. The columns were nearly 15 feet high, equivalent to eight-and-one-quarter times the lower diameter. They had none of that fanciful detail which makes the Locri fragments so attractive; instead the work had a formal, perhaps frigid, elegance such as might only too easily have resulted from an Athenian architect trained exclusively in Doric. The capitals were narrow compared with those of the sixth century, the spirals of the volutes were double and ended in an eye, the

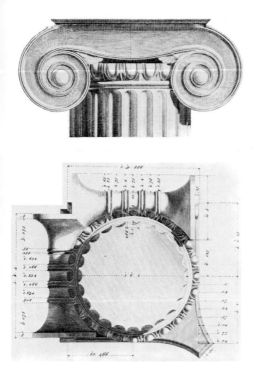

abacus was very low. The bases [141] represent a new Attic type, composed of a torus above, a single concave moulding of the kind used in triplicate in the Asiatic type, and an additional torus below. Bases of this type have been recognized in a depot of ancient architectural fragments by the Tower of the Winds at Athens. They probably come from the columns which stood between the antae of the porch, removed when the building was converted into a chapel.[21] The three steps of the building were undercut. A severe moulding separated the smooth architrave from a sculptured frieze, and the cornice was plain except for another moulding at the top. The whole scheme of the building with its detail is reflected twenty or thirty years later in the temple of Victory on the Acropolis.

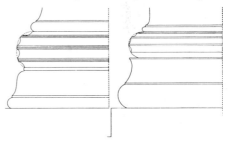

140. Athens, temple on the Ilissus, *c.* 450, capital, and plan of angle capital

141. Delphi, Athenian Stoa, and Athens, Temple on the Ilissus, column bases

CHAPTER 13

EARLY-FIFTH-CENTURY DORIC TEMPLES AND TREASURIES

The Doric Order was brought to perfection shortly after the middle of the fifth century, and most of the necessary preparatory work was completed when the century began.

The ideal relation between the columns on the ends of a temple and those on the sides, six to thirteen, was already known to the architect of a temple at Sunium which was destroyed long before completion, probably by a Persian raid in 490. Remains of it have been found around its successor, the existing temple of Poseidon, and prove that differentiation in the width of spacing of columns had been abandoned, except at the corners; the columns all had practically the same diameter; and the normal intercolumniations, alike on ends and sides, was almost $2\frac{1}{2}$ times that diameter. The side of the building could have been given virtually the same ratio to the end by the addition of an extra column, but the comparative lack of interest on the side would have made such a length tedious, and so out of balance with the gabled end; the design therefore allowed about $2\frac{1}{3}$: 1 by providing only one column more than double the number on the end. This is an important precedent. Many subsequent temples, especially the most successful, were given thirteen columns on the sides; six had always been the commonest number on the ends, and afterwards became habitual.

Marble was still little used in temples of the first half of the century, although previous instances at Delphi must have demonstrated that the extreme clarity of line which both Orders required could not be achieved in softer stone. Delphi again is the site of the first known Doric building to consist entirely of marble, the Athenian Treasury, and this may even date from a few years before 500, though ancient tradition put it after 490; scholars have argued the matter on a variety of grounds, inconclusive-ly but on balance in favour of the later dating.[1]

Like most other treasuries, it resembled a miniature temple [142A] comprising only a porch with two columns *in antis* and a very short cella. In fact the width is more than two-thirds of the total length (22 by 32 feet; 6·68 by 9·75 m.). The front faced the Sacred Way, and the rest of the building cannot have been conspicuous, but the frieze, all the metopes of which are sculptured, is continued along the three blank walls, and the courses of masonry alternate in height to diversify them.[2] The walls grow thinner as they rise, following an early convention which must have arisen in imitation of work in sun-dried brick and has the effect of increasing the apparent height. Another primitive feature is that the metopes are half as long again as the triglyphs. The roof is pitched very low, giving a squat effect; but the pedimental figures and an acroterium on the gable, representing an amazon on horseback, may have partially corrected this failing. In the interior of the cella, strips of incised and painted ornament ran along the top of the walls [142B].

In structural details the Athenian Treasury is closely related to the fine temple in Aegina, the third built in the sanctuary of a local goddess, Aphaia [143–6]. It occupies a magnificent position on a ridge commanding views out to sea on either side, replacing a temple of about 570, now known also to have been peripteral. The architecture probably followed closely that of the Temple of Apollo completed in Aegina town just before, though this is so badly preserved that its details have to be restored on the analogy of the later temple.[3] In Aphaia's temple most of the pteron[4] has survived up to the level of the architrave, and there are enough fragments to confirm the restoration of everything except the wooden roof-supports and ceiling. The material throughout is limestone (originally stuccoed),

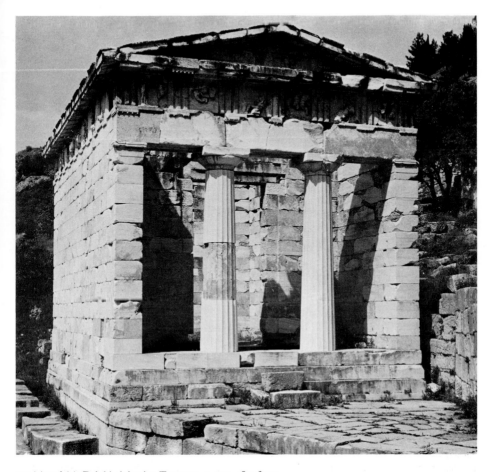

142 (A) and (B). Delphi, Athenian Treasury, *c.* 500–485, front
and patterns incised on inner cornice (*below*)

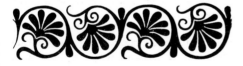

except for the tiles and the sculptures of pediments and acroteria – the metopes are plain slabs of limestone. Fragments of three sets of marble pedimental statues, all representing battle scenes, have been excavated on the site; the third apparently stood on a pedestal close to the temple, and there was even a third acroterium like those placed on top of the two gables. The sculptures from the east pediment must be distinctly later than 490 – the likely date is about 475 – whereas those of the west pediment display more archaic characteristics,

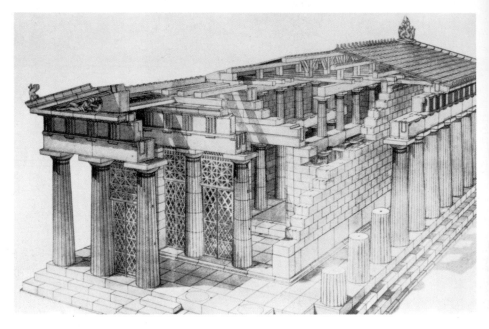

143 and 144. Aegina, temple of Aphaia, early fifth century, sectional restoration and interior columns (restored)

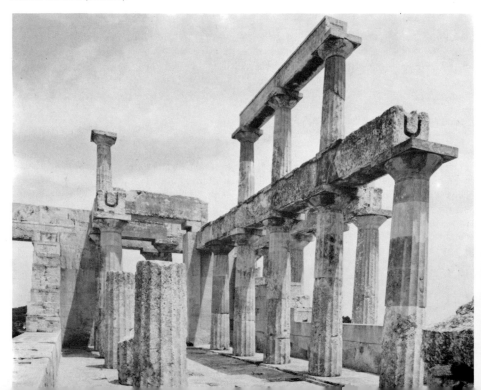

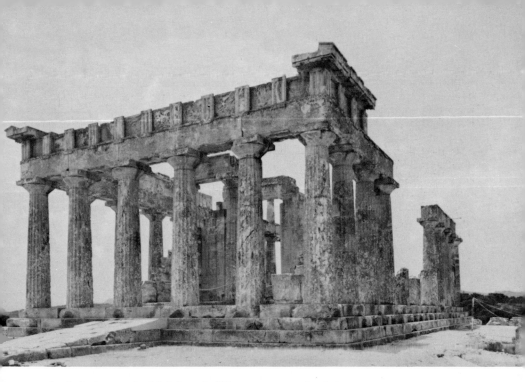

145 and 146. Aegina, temple of Aphaia, early fifth century, east end and plan

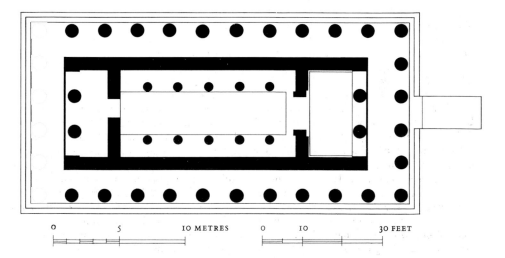

0   5   10 METRES   0   10   30 FEET

which to some experts suggest the end of the sixth century rather than the beginning of the fifth. The spare figures are of both these styles and may therefore include remnants of an older east pediment as well as some replacements afterwards removed from it.

A ramp led up to the entrance of the Aphaia Temple [146]. The pteron, of 45 by 94½ feet (13·77 by 28·82 m.), comprised six by twelve columns, nearly all of them monolithic; the proportions and number of columns place this temple securely in the local group of the late sixth century, which includes the Old Temple at Athens, Apollo at Aegina, Poseidon at Calauria, and another of Poseidon at Hermione.[5] They slope sharply inwards, which gives an appearance of great strength. The height of the columns exceeds 17 feet (5·272 m.); their diameter and spacing are almost uniform on the sides and ends, except at the corners. The architrave projects outwards beyond the column shafts; this is among the earliest instances of such thickening, which permitted the superstructure to be made higher, so that the temple escaped the squatness of archaic buildings. The tiles along the edge of the roof were marble, and carved with lions' heads for waterspouts; the other tiles were of terracotta. A row of coloured antefixes shaped like palmettes ran along the eaves, and the upstanding tiles that coped the ridge were modelled on either side in the form of palmettes, and painted red and black on a cream ground. These colours predominated in the stone-work; the triglyphs and their footing with the guttae were dark blue, but separated by the red horizontal band of the taenia, red and black strips alternated above them, and red rings surrounded the junctions of capital and column shaft. The plain surfaces were covered with cream stucco. The lions' heads, pedimental sculptures, and acroteria were all picked out in colours. The acroteria, moreover, were designed to have very irregular outlines and many interstices through which the light passed; upon each corner of the roof stood a griffin with curved wings, uplifted paw, and curly tail, and each gable was crowned by an elaborate fret palmette, flanked on either side by a statuette with drapery that hung clear of the figure. The interior was first laid out with a porch and an opisthodomus, each with two columns *in antis*, but during the construction a doorway was provided through the back wall of the cella, slightly off centre, to convert the opisthodomus into an adytum, and a metal grille blocked the back entrance. Similar grilles, but fitted with doors, closed the porch. The cella was spanned with the aid of two rows of small columns, the architraves of which carried yet smaller columns, since the tapering of the lower shafts was continued at the same inclination above the interval formed by the architrave. This two-storeyed colonnade must have conformed well with the scale of the cella and of the cult image, and at some later date it was also put to practical use by the insertion of wooden floors across the aisles at the level of the architraves.

The colonies in Sicily were still building larger temples than the cities of Greece itself, and in greater numbers, till near the end of the century. To some extent they continued to progress independently. The influence of Greece, however, can be seen at Selinus, in the decision to finish Temple 'G' with an opisthodomus instead of an adytum [118], and in the provision of both an adytum and an opisthodomus in three smaller temples[6] – 'A', 'E', and 'O'. And in each case the opisthodomus was fronted with two columns *in antis*, as also was the porch at the three latter temples, in contrast to the porch of 'G', which, being a relic of the sixth-century local style, was supported by a row of four columns standing two intercolumniations before the antae. But these temples are distinguished from those of Greece by their greater proportionate length, due to the additional accommodation they contained, so that with six columns on the ends they required fourteen or even fifteen on the sides. Similarly in the Syracusan temple of Victory at Himera, begun after 480, and that of Athena at Syracuse[7] (which is incorporated in the Cathedral, with the result that its partitions cannot be traced), the pteron comprised six by fourteen columns, likewise with two columns *in antis* at either end. The temple at Syracuse was famous for its doors covered with ivory and gold. These two are the first buildings in which the penultimate as well as the last intercolumniation is narrowed on the sides and the front alike, in order to make less noticeable the displacement of the corner metopes; the device was no doubt inspired by the old temple of Apollo at Syracuse. The temple at Himera is also the earliest equipped with stone staircases beside the doorway of the cella, to facilitate maintenance of the roof and ceiling; the stairs at Paestum [122] seem to have been wooden.

The most remarkable Sicilian building is the temple of Olympian Zeus at Agrigento, or Acragas as the Greek city was called [147]. This was the largest of all Doric temples (173 by 361 feet; 52·74 by 110·09 m.) – possibly the intention was a peripteral measurement of 1000 feet [8] It was left unfinished because of the sack of Acragas in 406, at least eighty or possibly a hundred years after the work began. The temple was raised by five steps above a platform nowhere less than 15 feet above ground. Plan, elevation, and structure were all revolutionary,

and perhaps more from choice than necessity, for the Heraeum at Samos and the Artemisium at Ephesus had already demonstrated that it was feasible to build on a huge scale in the traditional manner, though handicapped by the less sturdy proportions of Ionic columns; on the other hand, the vastly greater weight of a Doric entablature may have appeared to involve even worse hazards. At any rate the solution adopted at Acragas was to build a pseudo-pteron. It consisted of half-columns engaged in a continuous wall and backed on its inner side by rectangular pilasters, each extending the full width of the half-column; at the corners of the temple, however, the columns were three-quarters round, with no backing other than the wall. A series of mouldings, 4 feet high, surrounded the foot of the wall, both outside and inside, curving around the columns in the manner of an Ionic base [148]. And instead of building up the columns in drums, each comprising one layer, and spanning each intercolumniation, from axis to axis, with a single architrave block, the entire construction was achieved with comparatively small blocks; the stucco coating would have concealed the joints. This expedient must have

147. Agrigento, Olympieum, begun *c.* 500, plan (partly restored)

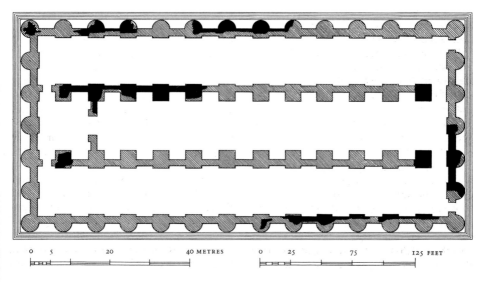

| 0 | 5 | | 20 | | 40 METRES |

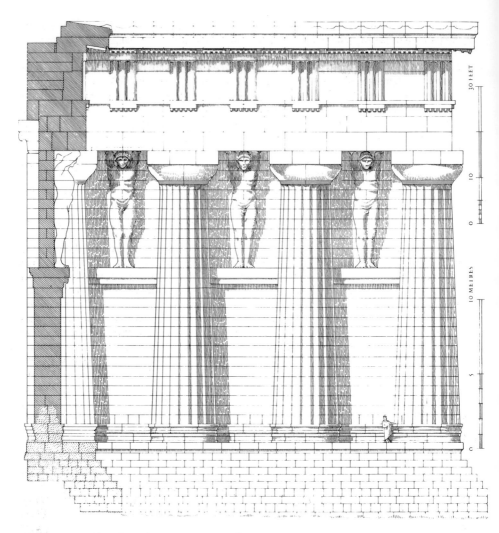

148 Agrigento, Olympieum, begun c. 500, restoration

enormously reduced the cost of transport (usually the heaviest item in the construction of a
temple) and of labour, seeing that the diameter
of each half-column exceeded 13 feet.

Seven half-columns were engaged along the
end and fourteen along the side of the temple,
and the length of each intervening stretch of
wall was roughly equal to the combined width

of a half-column and its backing, although the
spacing from axis to axis was the longest ever
built in Doric almost 27 feet for the side intercolumniations, 6 inches less on the ends. In the
Artemisium the entire intercolumniation over
the doorway had been spanned with a single
block over 28 feet long, but the builders of the
Olympieum did not even use single blocks to

span the actual gap between the capitals, a distance of barely 11 feet. The break with tradition was whole-hearted. The capitals were built in two courses, the lower of two blocks forming half each of the echinus and necking, and the abacus was divided into three, so as to avoid placing one joint immediately above another. The architrave consisted of three superimposed courses of larger blocks, arranged likewise with alternating joints, and was three blocks thick. In its lowest course one of the exposed blocks was set upon the axis of the column. The next on either side overlapped most of the outer abacus block and extended to the centre of the gap. The face projected nearly 7 feet above the wall; because the weight of masonry above might have proved insufficient to prevent these cantilevered blocks from subsiding into the gap, they seem to have been reinforced with iron bars, as well as dowelled together, and direct support too appears to have been given. When the stone of the temple was plundered in the eighteenth century as material for harbour works, some sculptured blocks of the size used in the wall-courses were left on the ground outside, and these have been reassembled and compose male figures, over 25 feet high (7·65 m.), with lowered heads and raised arms bent at the elbows in the attitude of carrying. Alternately bearded and beardless, they probably stood between the columns about midway between the mouldings along the foot of the wall and the architrave, and projected farther in each course from the feet upwards as the wall receded. (The restoration shows the feet close together but, at least in one instance, they were wide apart and a slightly recessed supporting pier ran up between the legs.) The style dates these Atlas figures to approximately 470–460; the Olympieum was allegedly built by the labour of Carthaginians taken prisoner in 480 at the battle of Himera, as Diodorus records.

Diodorus, who visited the temple in the first century B.C., refers to battle-scenes in the pediments. To these some surviving fragments of carving in relief can be assigned. The metopes were plain; an equal lengthening of the last two

on either side of the corners masked the displacement of the angle triglyphs. The interior according to Diodorus had not been roofed (archaeological evidence supports this), as would not be surprising, since its three spans average about 40 feet, but quantities of tiles have been found in the aisles, and the provision of lions' head water-spouts in the horizontal cornice is evidence of at least an intention to roof them. The cella walls were only thin screens, linking two rows of twelve great square pillars which projected from its outer side as pilasters, set opposite those on the back of the pseudo-pteron, while most of their bulk projected into the cella, presumably to diminish its span with a view to roofing that also. The last two bays at the west end of the cella were separated by a cross-wall to form an adytum. The spaces between the last pair of pillars at the east and the back of the pseudo-pteron were left open, for there was no doorway in this stretch of the outer wall; to reach the cella from the external platform one had first to enter one or other aisle and then pass through the gap here.

The one notable Italian temple is that of 'Neptune' – really of Hera – at Paestum [149–51], the best preserved of all temples (79½ by 196¾ feet; 24·26 by 59·98 m.). It was obviously built under the influence of Greece, for it consists of a pteron with six by fourteen columns, a porch and an opisthodomos, each with two columns in antis, and a cella with two rows of seven smaller columns and on the architraves others yet smaller, the tapering being continued, as at Aegina. Two recesses, one fitted with a staircase, lie between the porch and the cella. Of the freedom from convention which had characterized the sixth-century architecture of the region there is scarcely a trace, except in the fluting; the number of flutes on the external columns is twenty-four, in the lower columns of the cella twenty, and in the upper sixteen. The external columns, 29 feet (8·88 m.) high, taper from a lower diameter of nearly 7 feet by about 2 feet in the case of those on the ends – less on the sides. The 4¼:1 proportion of height to lower diameter is abnormally low for

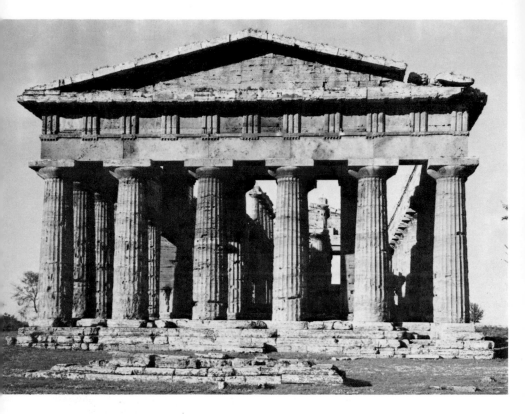

149–51. Paestum, temple of 'Neptune', early or mid fifth century, east end (*above*), restored plan (*below*), and interior (*opposite*)

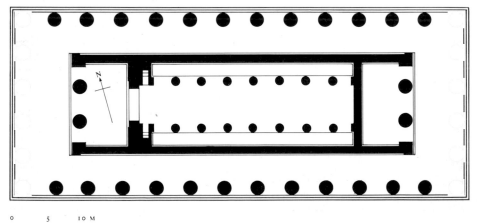

0   5   10 M

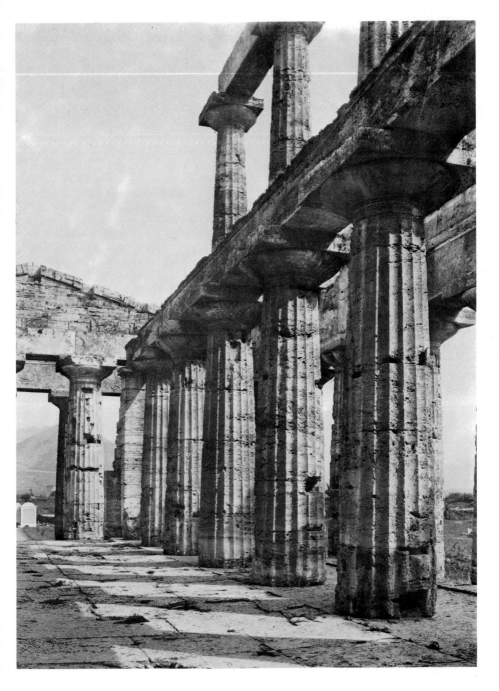

the fifth century, even allowing for the fact that such tall columns would have been given more than the average thickness at the time. The date of the temple would therefore seem not later than about 460; in fact it is likely to have been started before 474, when the prosperity of the city began to decline.[9] If the device of narrowing the last two intercolumniations on the sides was borrowed from Sicily, where it appears soon after 480, the thickness of the columns would still be anomalous and presumably anachronistic.

The contemporary Doric of Greece is best known from the temple of Zeus at Olympia (91 by 210½ feet; 27·68 by 64·12 m.). The work of a local architect, Libon of Elis, its construction seems to have begun about 470, and it may have been externally complete, or practically so, when the Spartans presented a golden shield to be hung on top of one of the gables in commemoration of a victory they won in 457. Pausanias describes the temple in great detail, and the ruins have been excavated with unusual care; consequently it has been possible to restore the plan[10] and elevation reliably, although nothing above the lowest drums of the columns

remains standing [152–4]. The material is local limestone, covered with stucco, apart from marble tiles and gutter and sculptures. Libon's main interest seems to have been proportions, which he designed with the simplest ratios. That becomes apparent by measurements in terms of the foot he used, which was 7 per cent longer than ours (326 mm.): total length, 200; height of external columns, 32; normal intercolumniation – those at the corners were narrower – 16; width of abacus, 8; distance between triglyph centres, 8, between mutules and lions' head waterspouts, 4; tiles, 2. The forms of the Order[11] are as conventional as the plan, with its pteron of six columns by thirteen, a porch and an opisthodomus, each with two smaller columns in antis, and a cella containing staircases either side of the doorway and divided by two rows of yet smaller columns with others superimposed. The cult statue was made by Phidias during his exile from Athens, which began in 432. It is unlikely that the cella was not built until then; presumably an earlier cult statue was replaced when the authorities at Olympia were given the opportunity to rival the new gold and ivory Athena by Phidias in the Parthenon. His Zeus

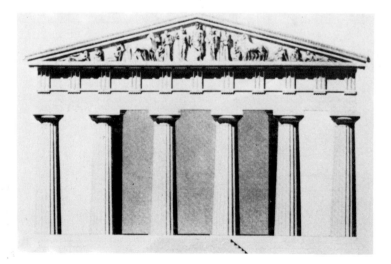

152(A). Olympia, temple of Zeus, c. 460, restored elevation of east front

was seated, and (to increase its mystery) out of scale with the building;[12] it was remarked that if the god had risen from his seat, his head would have gone through the ceiling. The statue was 40 feet high, and placed at the end of the cella on a sunken pavement of Eleusis limestone, which was kept black and shiny by the oil used to preserve the ivory. Access was restricted by a stone screen, with folding gates, placed across the cella at the second pair of columns, from which similar screens ran to the far end of the colonnades. Floors were inserted over the aisles at the level of the lower architrave and visitors were admitted to these galleries by means of the winding stairs, one of which (says Pausanias) continued to the roof. The entrance to the porch was guarded by three double doors of bronze.

The statues from the pediments are exceptionally well preserved. They are among the finest of Greek sculptures, and admirably designed to fit the triangular shape of the gable; moreover the resemblance of some folds in the drapery to Doric fluting may have been intentional. For acroteria, there were gilt tripods at the corners and a gilt statue of Victory upon each gable; beneath the feet of the one on the front hung the Spartan gold shield. The external metopes remained as plain slabs for three centuries, till a Roman general commemorated his capture of Corinth by hanging gilt shields upon twenty-one out of the total thirty-six. But a frieze of triglyphs and sculptured metopes stood above the architrave of the porch and opisthodomus columns; the cornice on top of it continued around the entire cella. The precedent of these sculptured panels may have influenced the architects of Athens to embellish the temples of the next generation with friezes of continuous sculpture behind the pteron. Limiting the sculptured metopes to inner friezes over the porch is repeated elsewhere in the Peloponnese (for example, in the late-fifth-century Temple of Hera in the Argolid); it may have been anticipated at Aegina, in the Temple of Apollo.

With no other innovation but its scheme of proportions, the uninspired temple of Zeus yet marks the culmination in soft stone of the Doric Order in its academic form. The building may have lacked life; it certainly lacked the subtlety to which is due the intense vitality of marble Doric in the second half of the century.

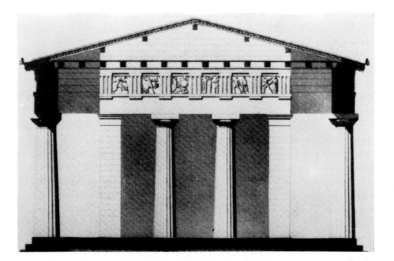

152(B). Olympia, temple of Zeus, *c*. 460, section through porch

CHAPTER 14

EARLY SANCTUARIES AND THE ACROPOLIS OF ATHENS

The primitive Greek idea of a sanctuary may be defined as an open space dotted with altars or other small shrines and enclosed by a wall; sometimes a sacred grove was planted. The earliest instance of an architectural layout dates from about 600 [83], when a monumental entrance was inserted in the wall enclosing the Heraeum of Samos, and a long shelter for pilgrims built on the far side of the temple. The entrance was situated near the east end of the north wall, and so gave a corner view of the temple's front and side – the best of all views, considering the nature of the building. The actual gateway apparently consisted of a long passage between side wings of similar dimensions, each containing an outer and an inner room with doors opening on to the passage. No doubt the whole structure was roofed as a unit, with a gabled porch at each end of the passage, forming a propylon such as led into many later sanctuaries. The shelter too was an example of a type of open-fronted building which the Greeks usually provided in later sanctuaries and called a stoa (a word the Romans translated as *porticus*). It measured 228½ feet in length (69·70 m.), and was walled only along the back and sides; the open front, supported by a wooden colonnade, faced north towards the temple. An inner row of posts, placed opposite those along the front, gave intermediate support to the roof, which could have been built either with a ridge above them or with a single pitch from back to front, as is more likely considering the small girth of the posts.

The sanctuary of Aphaia in Aegina was given a comparable entrance early in the sixth century. The propylon seems to have been fitted with a double door across the centre; each end formed a porch with two columns *in antis*. Again the opening faced a corner of the front of the temple, this time the south-east corner. The frontage of the inward porch was prolonged to the east by the colonnaded side of a larger room which extended back to the same depth as the propylon; it resembled a short stoa. Opposite its east end, and facing the temple, stood a long altar; at many later temples such an altar runs parallel to the entire length of the front.

At many sanctuaries, from the third Heraeum of Samos onwards, the main temple was accompanied by some half-dozen heterogeneous buildings in no coherent grouping; rarely, even on sloping sites, was a grand or even formal staircase incorporated. Stairs were used to the best architectural effect to enter the acropolis at Lindos. There appears to be a monumental staircase (dangerously narrowed at the top) at the Argive Heraeum. This has been interpreted as a stepped wall, though it is no steeper than the steps at Lindos; probably there was also a road which passes its foot. The stepped section leads directly to the front of the late-fifth-century temple. Perhaps this is a place on which spectators could stand to watch the athletic contests of Hera, or religious processions.[1]

In the main precinct at Delphi,[2] dedicated to Apollo (there was also a separate precinct of Athena Pronaia), the layout dates from the sixth century, though with many subsequent changes and additions. It was complicated by the steep slope of the ground. A Sacred Way – paved in Roman times – enters the enclosure at the lowest (south-east) corner, and slants up westward between the sites of two crowded rows of early treasuries and many lesser dedications of all periods, chiefly statues. Turning back along the side of the Athenian Treasury (below a pedestal which exhibited the Persian armour captured at Marathon), the road converges upon a magnificent supporting-wall in polygonal masonry, against which the Athenians built a stoa, probably in 477 and certainly before the middle of the fifth century [268]. The slender Ionic columns, though of marble, are so widely spaced that the entablature and roof can only have been wooden. The paved way turns again beneath the south-east corner of the supporting wall, then rises between it and various dedications to a terrace outside the front (the east end) of the temple of Apollo. All but the last few yards of the wall support a slightly lower terrace which runs more than the full length of the temple, along the south side, but separated from the building by a narrow strip of this upper terrace, where statues were placed. The temple's own terrace was cut into the hill-side on the north. There the ground rises far more steeply and was not included within the precinct till shortly before 500. With stairs to make them accessible, buildings and statues were dotted about the slope there too. The west end of this extension is occupied by the theatre, fitted into a largely natural hollow, and high above it lies the stadium on a shelf which had been artificially widened. Larger stoas were built in Hellenistic times on ground added to the precinct, eastward and westward from the temple terrace.

The sanctuary of Apollo at Delos contained an extraordinary number of buildings in a very confined area, even during the sixth century. But there is evidence of attempts to make axial relations with the strictly sacred buildings at the centre when adding stoas, treasuries, dining-halls, etc., in their vicinity.

In the extensive sanctuary of Zeus at Olympia buildings were sited without concern for any niceties of relation, among an outrageous multiplicity of statues of all periods. Yet the layout dates more from the fifth than the sixth century and the site is flat, two circumstances which should have encouraged a better ordering. In the fifth century the enclosure, called the Altis [153, 154], was very roughly square, except for a prong at the north-west corner. In this lay the Prytaneum (a civic building containing a dining-hall), slewed at a strange angle behind the temple of Hera, which faced east towards a row of a dozen treasuries. These little buildings were packed close together with their backs to

the north boundary, as far as the opposite corner; their fronts are not aligned, their length and breadth differ, the axis is always much the same, but not identical. In front of them a row of bronze statues of Zeus was gradually erected from the fines levied upon competitors who fouled in the Games. Near the centre of the enclosure was the altar of Zeus, a great heap of ashes formed by countless sacrifices: the whole sanctuary was dotted with lesser altars, of which Pausanias mentions no less than sixty-nine. The south-west area was occupied by the temple of Zeus, which extended considerably eastward of the Heraeum but was overlapped by it on the west, and did not have quite the same axis. Across the south wall of the enclosure, and opposite the centre, lay the Bouleuterion (council house), overlapping the east end of the temple of Zeus and again on a slightly different axis (to which the Hellenistic South Stoa behind it more or less conformed). The Echo or Painted Stoa lined most of the inner side of the east wall; it was rebuilt in the fourth century slightly inwards of the previous site. Outside, at the back of this stoa, was the stadium, a mere hollow in the ground; a passage in front of the most easterly treasury leads to it, under an arch. A small fourth-century temple, the Metroum, was built between some of the other treasuries and the Altar of Zeus on an axis unlike any other, which gave the effect of cutting off the corner of the precinct. A fourth-century circular building, the Philippeum, was placed between the Heraeum and the boundary. Outside, in a row close to the west wall, were fourth-century and Hellenistic buildings – the stoas of the gymnasium, the palaestra, a Priests' House, the hostel called the Leonidaeum, etc.; also the workshop of Phidias.

The sanctuaries so far described seem to prove that the Greeks gave very little thought to planning in the modern sense and contented themselves with grouping their buildings intelligibly but quite roughly. The same applies to their arrangement of temples in cities. At Selinus, those on the acropolis were arranged on the same axis in a staggered line, with the later

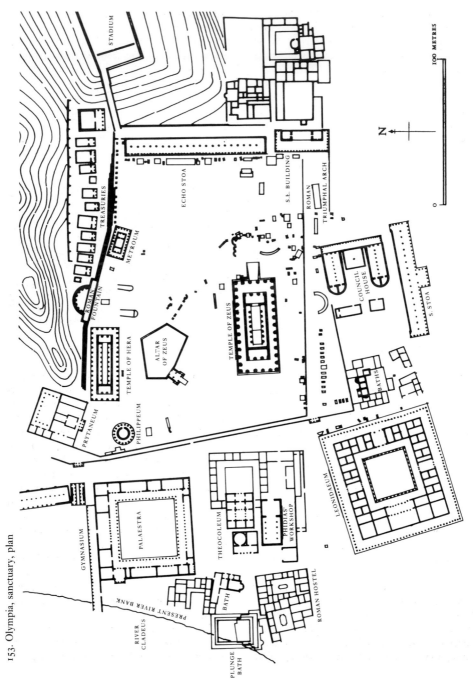

153. Olympia, sanctuary, plan

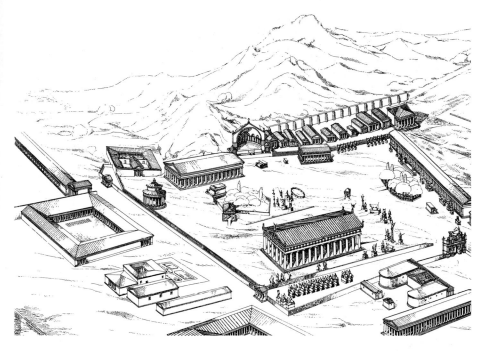

154. Olympia, sanctuary, restoration

buildings towards the south overlapping at the east end; of the three on the eastern plateau, however, the earliest ('G') likewise stood at the north, while the smaller temples were built closer together, on the same axis, and practically opposite the centre of the side. At Acragas, a ridge overlooking the city was nobly crowned by a line of half a dozen temples of the sixth and fifth century.

A new kind of sacred precinct was introduced by the fifth-century transformation of the Acropolis of Athens. Because of the constant warfare in ancient Greece, almost every city was divided into a lower town and an acropolis, a word which literally meant a 'city (i.e. fortified town) on the height', but was applied to whatever was the most defensible area, whether a densely inhabited quarter or a mere fortress which could form a last refuge in a siege. In early times the Acropolis of Athens formed no exception. Nature had left it as a great isolated slab of limestone, tilted towards the west, where alone it could be approached without rock-climbing. The circuit of Mycenean walls long remained the sole fortification of the State; late in the fifth century, when the Acropolis had lost all military importance, the citizens continued to speak of it as *Polis*, 'The City', just as Londoners so refer to the area formerly enclosed by walls. But the Acropolis still remained the spiritual centre of Athens owing to its sacred places which testified to the divine guardianship of the State. On the Acropolis was the altar of Athena, and her temple, the Old Temple whose complex building history certainly extends back to the seventh century and which may well have had an earlier predecessor (see Note 4 to Chapter 11). The entrance, like the fortifications, was still Mycenean.

The first architectural signs of major redevelopment belong to the 480s: they include a new temple, intended perhaps to

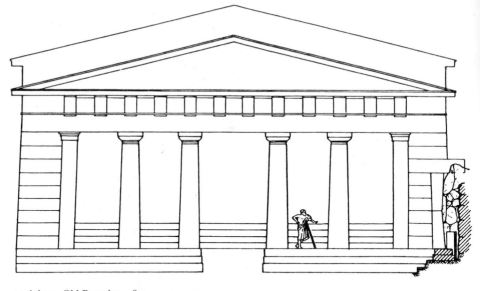

155. Athens, Old Propylon, 480s,
restoration of exterior

commemorate the victory of Marathon, and a
monumental propylon [155].[3] In this propylon
marble porches, probably with a façade of four
Doric columns between antae which terminate
returns from the side walls, projected back to
back. The front porch was deeper than that at
the rear, and probably required two rows of
three columns running from front to back to
support the roof. The rear porch was shallow,
and at a higher level, approached up a flight of
stairs. Both the new temple (not yet completed)
and the propylon were destroyed by the Persians. The propylon seems to have been refur-
bished, perhaps in the 460s. About the same
time long stretches of the walls themselves were
being straightened by rebuilding lower down
the slopes of the rock in handsome masonry,
such as was fitting to enclose a sanctuary. But
the individual buildings which have made the
Acropolis the wonder of Greece all date from
the second half of the century, when Athens,
mainly under the leadership of Pericles, diver-
ted to that purpose the annual subventions her

allies had agreed to contribute for mutual
defence against Persia [156, 157].

What Pericles did was to revive the concept
of the 480s, a large marble temple to Athena and
a related propylon; the substantial foundations
already created for the temple of the 480s were
re-used for the southern side, but the new
building was to be wider, extending nearer to
the centre of the Acropolis. The old temple,
badly damaged and patched up to serve as a
storehouse, was to be removed, creating an open
axis for the Acropolis; and the alignment of the
new propylon changed to that of this axis.

Pericles first undertook the building of the
Parthenon, a Doric temple, entirely in marble,
dedicated to the city's patron goddess, Athena
[158–68]. The Persians, in their invasion of 480,

156. Restored plan
of the Acropolis of
Athens at 400 B.C.

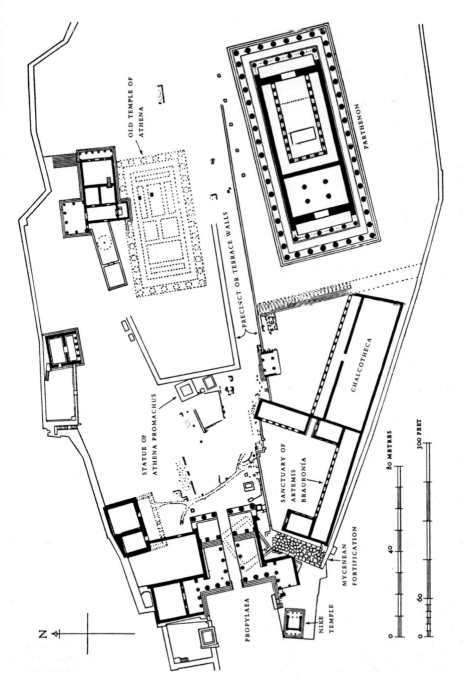

OLD TEMPLE OF ATHENA

PARTHENON

PRECINCT OR TERRACE WALLS

STATUE OF ATHENA PROMACHUS

CHALCOTHECA

SANCTUARY OF ARTEMIS BRAURONIA

MYCENEAN FORTIFICATION

PROPYLAEA

NIKE TEMPLE

80 METRES

300 FEET

40

60

N

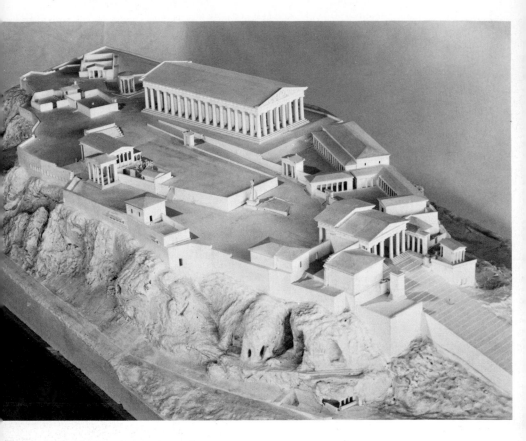

had burnt the scaffolding of the uncompleted predecessor, the substructure of which remained fit for use. This provided an unusually tall platform on the highest part of the Acropolis, close to the south wall, and only needed extension along the north to accommodate a building wide enough to be visible from the town below on that side too. The architect of the new temple was Ictinus, in some sort of partnership with Callicrates, who is named in an inscription, probably to be dated to the middle of the fifth century, as architect for a project at the precinct of Nike, by the entrance to the Acropolis; Phidias, in addition to being certainly the sculptor of the cult image, was probably responsible for designing the sculp-

157 (*above*). Model of the Acropolis of Athens under the early Roman empire.
Athens, Agora Museum

158 (*right*). Athens, Parthenon, 447-432, from behind east front of Propylaea

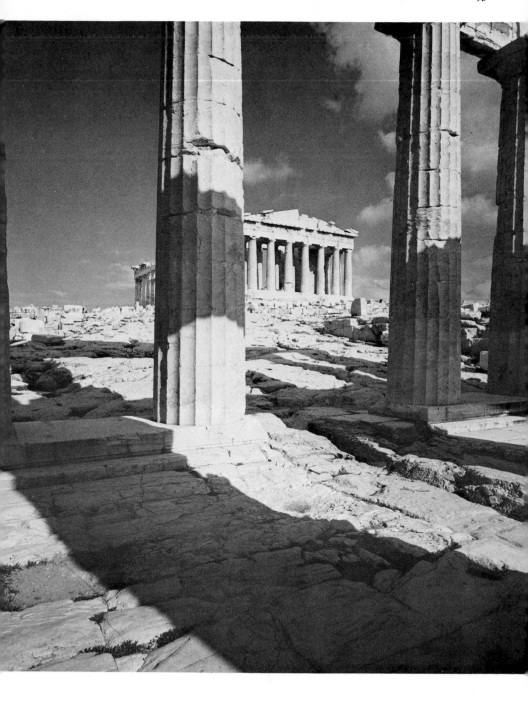

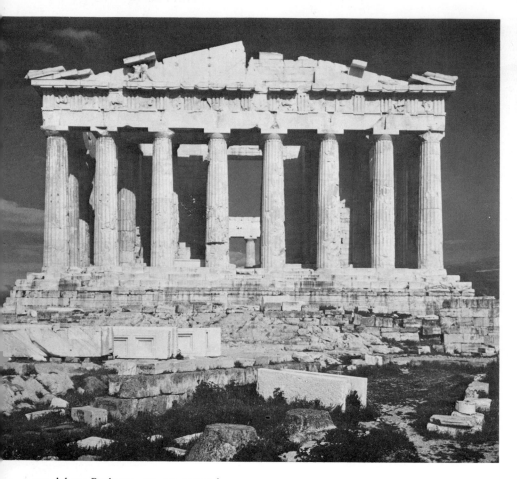

159. Athens, Parthenon, 447–432, west end

ture on the building, and tradition credited him with an indefinite general supervision over all Pericles' works. In accordance with custom, because treasurers then had no other lasting methods of publishing their accounts, the dates of the temple are recorded in inscriptions of State expenditure;[4] it was begun in 447 and dedicated in 438, complete except for the sculptures, which were not finished till 432. The interior was restored under the Roman Empire (probably at the time of the Emperor Julian's brief revival of official Paganism) and alterations were made when the building became in turn a Byzantine church, a Catholic cathedral, and a mosque; but it remained in good condition till in 1687 the centre blew out from the explosion of gunpowder stored in the cella. The ruins then deteriorated rapidly. Lord Elgin removed some of the sculptures in 1801–3 and ceded them to the British Museum.[5] In recent

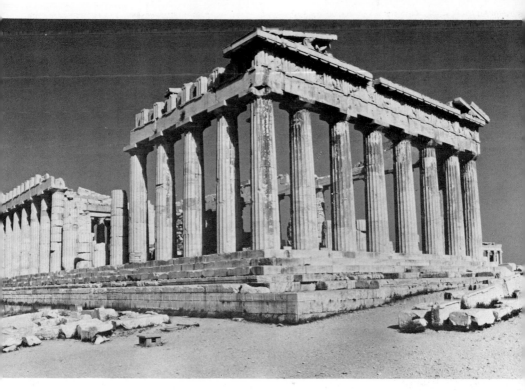

160. Athens, Parthenon, 447-432, south side and east end

years the northern colonnade has been rebuilt, improving its appearance, but unfortunately reinforcing the broken columns and other fragments with steel, whose deterioration threatens the stability of the restored structure, and the marble itself.

The plan[6] of the Parthenon was evidently dictated partly by the wish to obtain an extraordinarily wide cella in which to frame the image, partly by the fact that hundreds of ready-made marble column-drums from the burnt temple were available on the site in good condition, though others had been damaged. A lower diameter of $6\frac{1}{4}$ feet (1·91 m.) had therefore to be accepted for the pteron columns, and they were spaced 14 feet from axis to axis, so as to make the ratio of intercolumniation to diameter 9:4. The same ratio was applied to the width and length of the building, $101\frac{1}{2}$ by 228 feet (30·88 by 69·51 m.). Hence the pteron comprises eight by

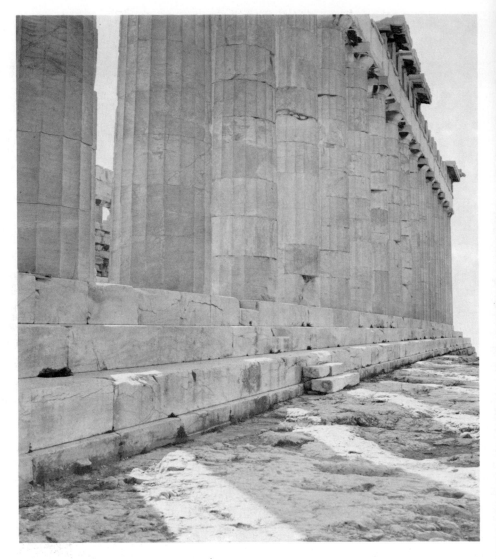

161. Athens, Parthenon, 447–432, curvature in steps

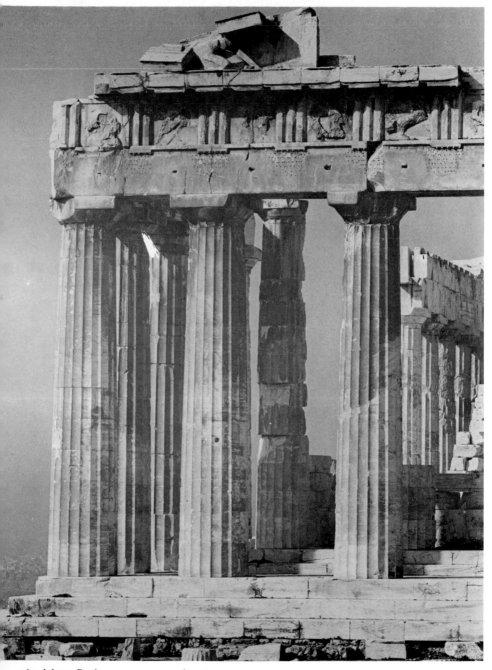

162. Athens, Parthenon, 447-432, south-east corner

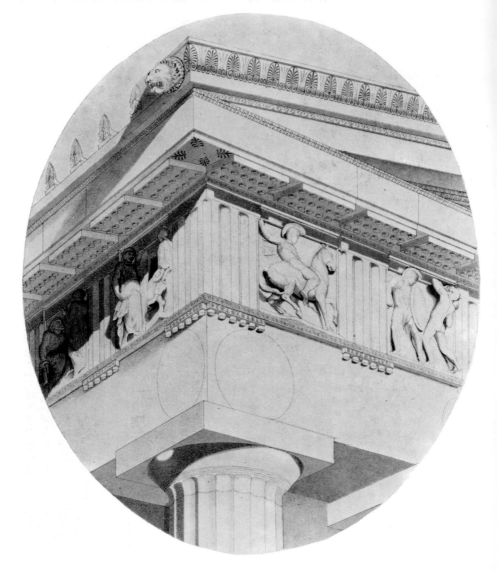

163. Athens, Parthenon, 447–432, restoration of north-west corner with painted decoration

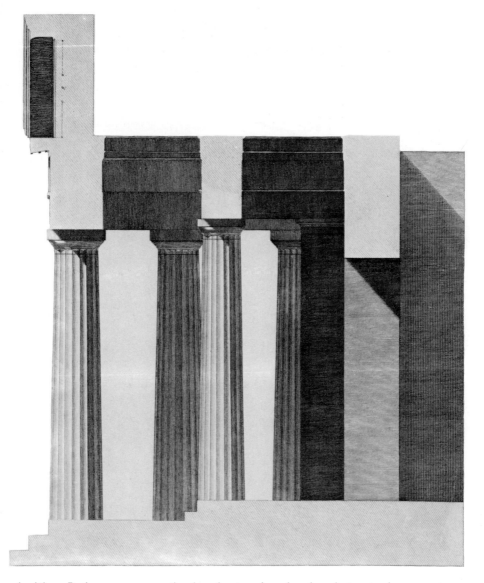

164. Athens, Parthenon, 447-432, section through outer colonnade and porch at west end

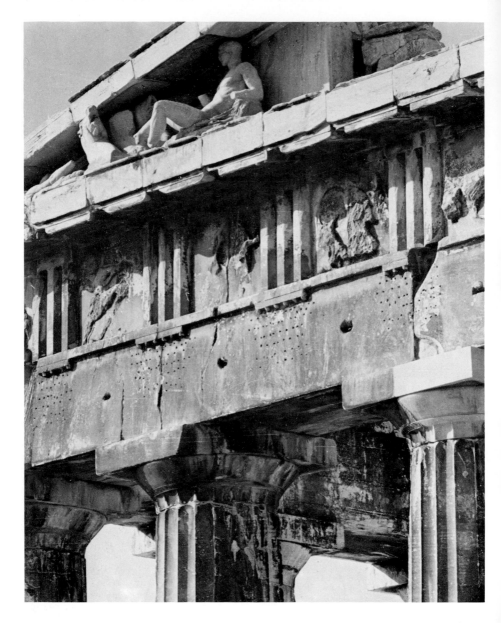

165. Athens, Parthenon, 447–432, east pediment, metopes, and frieze

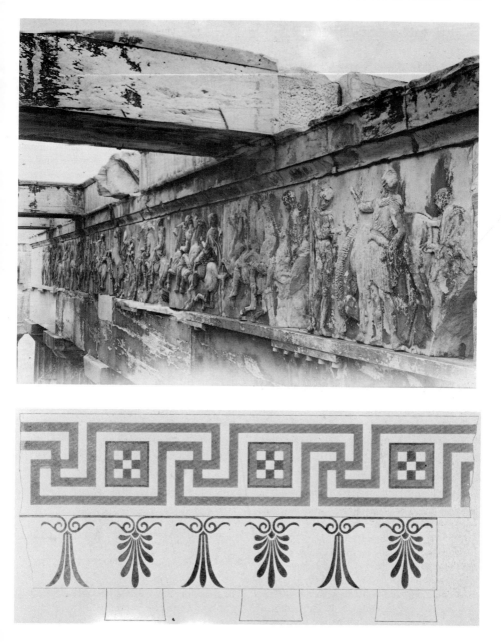

166 and 167. Athens, Parthenon, 447–432, frieze on the west end (*above*) and ornament painted along top of architrave (*below*)

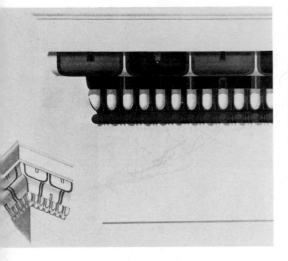

168. Athens, Parthenon, 447–432,
ornament painted on anta capital

seventeen columns, in accordance with the rule that the number on the sides should be one more than double that on the ends; the 4:9 relation was exactly obtained because the corner intercolumniations are shorter by as much as 2 feet. The height of the columns equals 5·48 times the diameter (a figure which reflects the times of the original temple: by the mid fifth century the normal proportion at Athens seems to have been 5.6:1, that is $5\frac{2}{3}$, instead of $5\frac{1}{2}$, though that figure is retained for the inner porch of the new Propylaea, facing the Parthenon). Column height amounts to $34\frac{1}{4}$ feet (10·433 m.) and that of the entablature $10\frac{3}{4}$ feet (3·295 m.). The two heights combined equalled $3\frac{1}{5}$ intercolumniations and stood in the same ratio of 4:9 to the width of the building.

Most exceptionally for fifth-century temples, all the metopes were sculptured in high relief, and the pediments were filled with groups of figures in the round. At each corner a lion's head was carved on the cornice of the pediment, facing outwards but slightly turned towards the end of the building; although such heads customarily served as water-spouts, they could have no function in this position except decora-

tion. Along each side of the temple was placed a row of marble antefixes, carved in low relief with a palmette between two spiral volutes. Four antefixes were allocated to each intercolumniation, to which also correspond six marble tiles; alternate antefixes therefore did not perform their traditional duty of masking the joints. But the cover tiles behind them were considerably higher and wider than the intermediate pairs, and the entire row was composed of such up to the ridge, so that the roof was striped with prominent bands. The acroteria on the corners stood 9 feet high, and consisted of floral open-work, following the precedent set at Aegina. From a central leaf at the base rose acanthus stems, one near each edge and two up the centre, from all of which grew curling tendrils, and a large palmette crowned the top.

The façade of porch and opisthodomus alike consisted of six Doric columns prostyle, raised on two steps [169]; they are all 33 feet high, but those in the porch (at the east) are a few inches thinner, making the height equal to more than

169 and 170. Athens, Parthenon, 447–432, paving on side and front and (*opposite*) sectional view of front

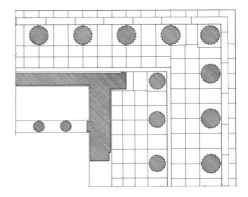

six times the lower diameter – an exceptionally slim proportion for the period. The architrave in either case was equipped according to Doric rules with pegged regulae, but above it runs a frieze of continuous sculpture after the Ionic manner [170]. Such friezes are also found above

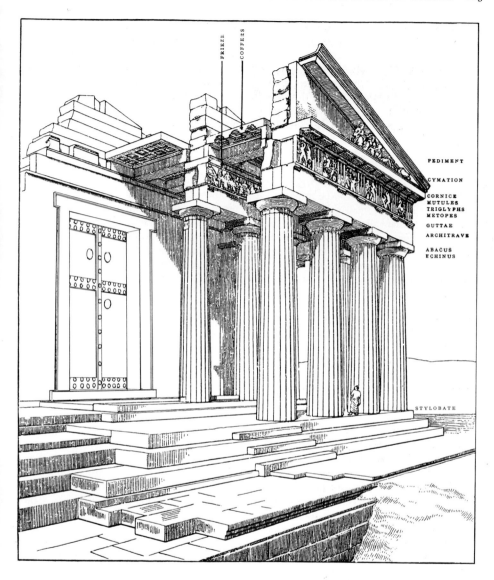

the porch and opisthodomus in the temple of Hephaestus beneath the Acropolis; this temple was probably started before the Parthenon, but work seems to have been interrupted, and the use of friezes here may well be influenced by the Parthenon, rather than the reverse; but the frieze of the Parthenon ran also along the sides of the cella, completely surrounding it, and for that there was no precedent. The frieze, nearly 524 feet long, meticulously designed, and carved in greater elaboration than any previous relief, was, however, so placed that it could scarcely be seen. It has been suggested[7] that the subject of the sculpture, which recalls but surely does not represent the procession which took place at the festival of Athena, the Great Panathenaia, alludes to the 192 Athenians who met a hero's death at Marathon. If this is so, it emphasizes the link in purpose between this building and its predecessor of the 480s. In the comparatively small temple of Hephaestus the frieze was not uncomfortably above eye-level; in the Parthenon even the base stands nearly 40 feet above the pteron floor, which is only 15 feet wide, and no human eyes can be turned up at such an angle longer than a few seconds. A slightly more distant view from still lower could be obtained from the ground outside, which in antiquity reached up to the bottom step of the temple – it has now been cleared away, so that the rock is exposed all round the foot of the tall platform beneath the steps. If one walked along outside, however, the columns interrupted the continuity of the sculpture, and at a little distance the architrave of the pteron masked the frieze altogether.

From any standpoint the angle of vision must therefore have been awkward, and if the frieze had been carved in the normal way, to uniform depth, the legs of the figures would have masked their heads. The solution adopted was to retain a perpendicular outward surface but to cut the background deeper towards the top; the feet are carved in extraordinarily shallow relief, while the heads project a couple of inches. But no trick could mitigate another most serious disadvantage involved by the position of the frieze; it was very ill-lit. Being placed close under the ceiling of the pteron, with only an elegant cornice intervening, no direct light could reach any part of it unless the sun stood low in the sky. Reflections from the polished marble surfaces of ceiling and wall and floor and columns must have helped, but the method of ceiling was unfortunate in that respect. Marble beams stretched from the cella wall to the pteron, behind the cornice, and the gaps between the beams were covered by slabs laid upon them, carved into the shape of the receding coffers of a wooden ceiling. It was inevitable that the beams would cast shadows on the ceiling, but the depth of the coffering greatly extended the shadowed area; of course the recessing improved the appearance of the ceiling. However, the obscurity which always veiled most of the length of the frieze at any one time had itself a certain value, in that it prevented anybody from seeing at one visit all that the Parthenon had to offer. With other Greek temples the exterior held no secrets, but could be fully appreciated in a few minutes. That, in any case, would have been untrue of the Parthenon, because of the 'refinements' and other niceties described in the next chapter.

The prostyle porch and the opisthodomus are both remarkably shallow in proportion to their width, and so space was obtained for a room behind each. The shorter, reached from the opisthodomus, was officially termed the Parthenon (the room of Athena 'the Virgin') before that name came to be applied to the whole temple. The ceiling rested upon four columns, which probably were Ionic. The cella is nearly 100 feet long and 34 feet wide and contained colonnades of small columns upon which still smaller columns were superimposed, in accordance with the usual Doric scheme. But in this instance a cross row behind the image linked the two rows parallel with the side walls. The latter were attached to the entrance wall by antae, and if the gaps were of uniform length throughout the colonnades, there must have been a thicker support at each turn, in the form of a pillar with similar antae in either direction. The whole of the area enclosed by the colonnades is slightly lower than the rest of the floor, like the sunken pavement in the temple at Olympia, where Phidias's image of Zeus was placed. The image of Athena was another statue in ivory and gold by the same master, a standing figure which reached to a height of 40 feet, including the pedestal. It seems to have been lit only from the doorway, which is suitably colossal, 32 feet high.

The second of the buildings commissioned under Pericles is the Propylaea, which replaced the earlier entrance to the Acropolis. The architect was Mnesicles. Work began in 437, the

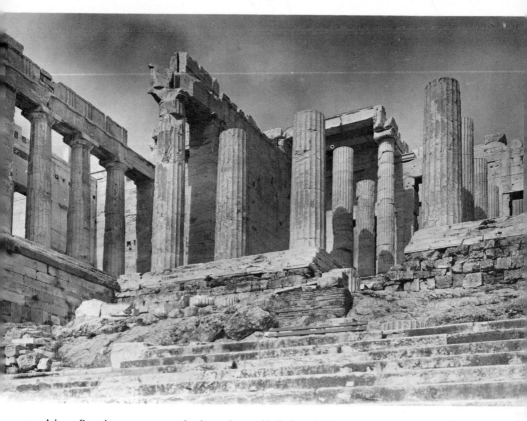

171. Athens, Propylaea, 437–432, north wing and central hall, from the west

year after the structure of the Parthenon had been completed, and continued till 432, after which the remainder of the project had to be abandoned because of the Peloponnesian War. The building was extravagantly costly, being entirely of marble. The design is an enlarged and complex adaptation of the usual propylon block [171–8]. So far as it was completed, it consists of a very wide central passage with porches outward and inward of a line of five doorways, and an outer wing on either side at right angles with a colonnade facing the approach; preparations had been made on the inward side of the wings for a pair of large rooms that would have flanked the passage.[8] But the plan was complicated by the steepness of the

site; the building stands across the top of the western slope of the Acropolis. The roadway from the town[9] ended in a straight, steep ramp which led directly to the centre of the outward porch. It then runs straight through the building, still slanting upwards, till it emerges from the inward porch. Though 12 feet wide, the road occupies less than a quarter of the passage width and to either side is a higher terrace for pedestrians, continuous with the floor of each wing. The steps that lead up to them begin at the outer extremity of each wing and turn along the façade of the outward porch, stopping abruptly at the verge of the sunken roadway. The marble ceiling of the porch involved beams with a clear span of 18 feet and weighing over 11

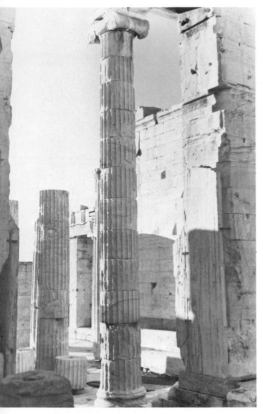

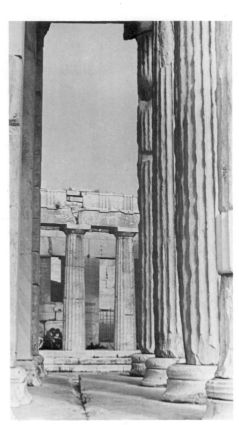

172. Athens, Propylaea, 437-432, central passage seen through the main doorway, with the north wing in the background

173. Athens, Propylaea, 437–432, north wing seen through the porch of the temple of Athena Nike, c. 425

174. Athens, Propylaea, 437-432, inner porch and back wall of north wing

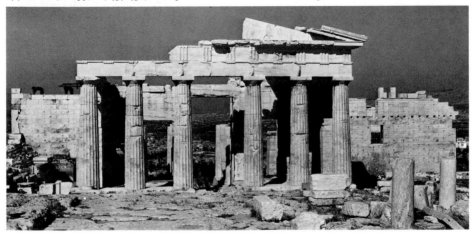

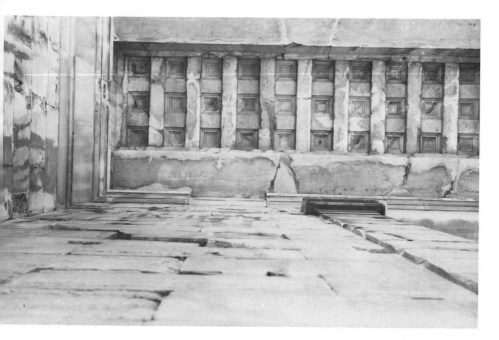

175. Athens, Propylaea, 437-432, inner porch, pilasters and ceiling

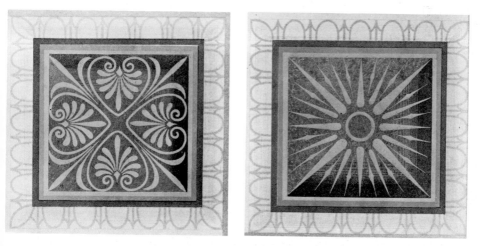

176 and 177. Athens, Propylaea, 437-432, painted ornament on ceiling coffers

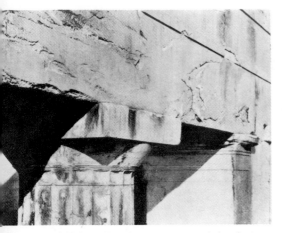

178. Athens, Propylaea, 437–432, capital and anta
in the south wing

tons. It rested upon two lines of three Ionic
columns apiece, placed along the verge of the
road behind two of the façade columns; the
latter are Doric and six in number, set prostyle
in front of the antae of the passage walls. The
Ionic columns,[10] though nearly 5 feet taller (33¾
feet), required only two-thirds of the diameter;
they carried an Ionic architrave of three fasciae,
reinforced by iron bars.[11] Steps lead up from
each terrace to the two side doorways, a very
small one beside the wall, a larger extending
from the dividing pillar to a larger pillar aligned
behind the Ionic columns; the doorway across
the road is still wider and taller. The thresholds
of the side doorways are level with the floor of
the inward porch; the façade of that too contains
six Doric columns prostyle. (They have been
reconstructed in the present century, together
with most of the frieze and one corner of the
pediment.) The central intercolumniation,
which spans the road, is half as wide again as the
others, and here (as, of course, over the outer
porch also) the frieze contained two intermediate metopes instead of one. The ceiling of
this porch remains in fair condition, with its
three tiers of marble beams, and above them the
coffers, which were ornamented with painted
patterns and a gilt star in the centre. The vast

expense of the Propylaea must have been largely
due to its ceilings, though the general excellence
of the masonry and the abundance of 'refinements' added greatly to the cost. Both porches
had pediments. There is a third pediment over
the dividing wall, quite invisible from ground
level, but fully constructed where it comes clear
of the lower roof to the outer porch (the first
triglyphs of the frieze which would have run
beneath it are also fully executed).

The side wings of the Propylaea could not be
made symmetrical because the wall of the
Acropolis more or less followed the irregular
outline of the cliffs it encased, but they are
intended to give the effect of symmetry when
their façades are seen from the approach ramp.
The wall comes to an end on the north by forming a projecting platform under the wing to the
left of the approach. Upon this blank wall stands
the outward wall of the wing, equally blank except for a Doric frieze. This continues past the
corner, above a façade with three columns *in
antis* which makes a porch to the wing, running
inwards behind the taller façade of the passage.
The room inside the wing is called by Pausanias
the Pinakotheke, or picture gallery. It has been
suggested recently[12] that it is a formal dining
room, as perhaps was an earlier room which
contained famous paintings, the Lesche or
'club' of the Cnidians at Delphi. In the
Pinakotheke, light was supplied by a door and
two windows in the partition wall [179]. These
openings are unsymmetrically arranged; this is
made necessary by the classical Greek custom of
reclining at banquets on couches placed along
the walls. One wall had to accommodate the foot
of the couch from the adjacent wall, as well as
its own couch or couches, and hence the door
could not be placed centrally. The opposite
wing required different treatment. The
Acropolis wall projects much farther westwards, and its outward end was soon to be
shaped into a narrow bastion, upon which
stands the miniature temple of Athena Nike
(Victory) built a few years later. The outward
face of the bastion and the end of the temple
itself slant backwards towards the north wing,

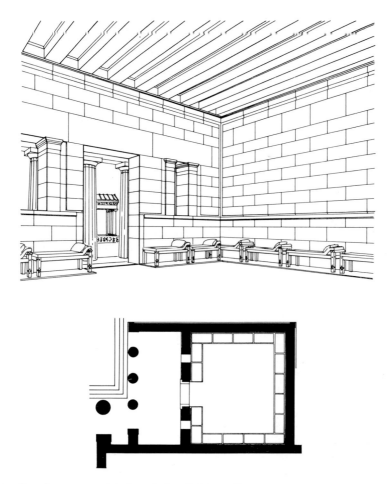

179. Athens, Propylaea, 437-432, interior and plan of picture gallery
(restored as dining room)

and when seen from the west this difference in axis goes some way to concealing the actual distance between the wings. The slant also puts the north-west corner of the temple into line with the façade of the south wing and makes the sides of the temple point towards the Parthenon, thereby bringing the whole entrance of the Acropolis into relation with the main building upon its surface. But access to the projected temple of Nike had to be provided by leaving some empty space in a position corresponding to the back of the north wing, and the temple would have been too cramped if the south wing had been allowed to project equally far outwards. On the other hand, the façades of the two wings were unquestionably required to match. The problem was solved by a trick [157]; the colonnade extends the same distance but terminates against an otherwise useless pillar opposite the corner of the north wing, while the outward side of the south wing is aligned with the next column of the north and is not a solid wall, but only an architrave and entablature. And since the wing had to be truncated at the back, the architrave is supported by only one intermediate pillar before it meets the outward corner of the back wall. This wall is aligned upon the south-east corner of the Nike temple. When seen from the west, the huge plain mass of the north wing and its supporting wall is aesthetically balanced by the narrower but very elaborate complex formed by the little temple on its tall bastion in front of the shadowy mouth of the south wing.

The construction of the temple of Nike does not seem to have been undertaken till at least five or six years after 432, when the work on the Propylaea ceased;[13] the design may have been that of Callicrates executed in accordance with the decree of some twenty-five years earlier. (It would be interesting to know how the design was preserved, and whether it was modified as

a result of the building of the Propylaea.) The building was extricated more than a century ago from a Turkish fortification and has since been reconstructed a second time [173, 180−3]. It closely resembled the temple on the Ilissus, but is shorter (17$\frac{3}{4}$ by 26$\frac{3}{4}$ feet; 5·39 by 8·16 m.) and less tall. The four prostyle columns at each end, with monolithic shafts 13 feet high, are 7·82 times as high as the lower diameter, a very heavy proportion for Ionic, and the entablature also is heavy. The motive was presumably to avoid too pronounced a contrast with the Propylaea, where the height of the various Doric columns which are visible in conjunction with the temple of Nike equals about 5$\frac{2}{3}$ times the lower diameter (main porch) and 5$\frac{1}{2}$ times (north and south wings), compared with nearly 10 for the Ionic within. The architrave is carved in three fasciae. The frieze is sculptured; there are attachments for figures in the pediments, and

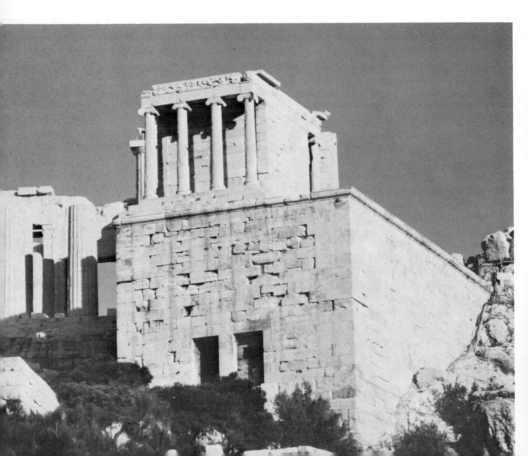

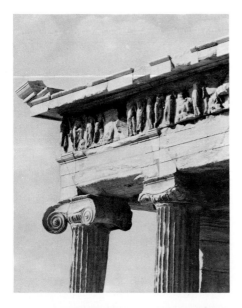

180-2 (*opposite, left, and below*). Athens,
temple of Athena Nike, *c.* 425

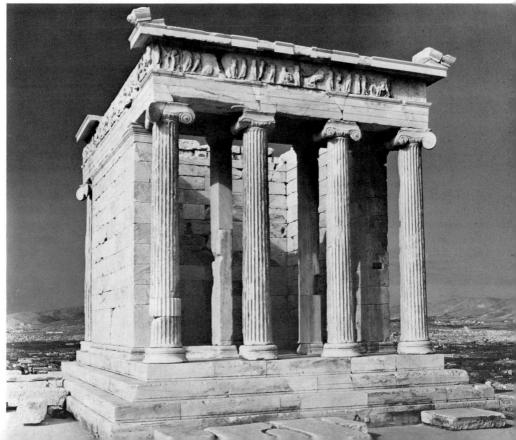

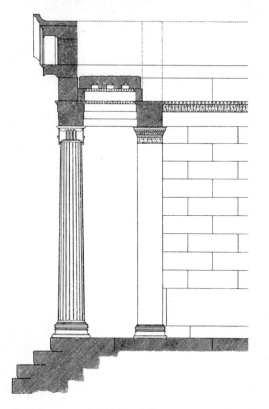
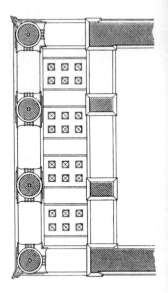

183. Athens, temple of Athena Nike, *c.* 425, restored section and ceiling of porch

corner acroteria are known to have existed. The cella is an almost square room, entered by a doorway between two monolithic pillars, from which bronze lattices stretched to the antae, a feature not found in the Ilissus temple, but employed in a temple built by the Athenians on Delos, when they 'purified' the island in 426. It was this that made it possible to reduce the length of the temple of Nike, compared with the Ilissus temple, to accommodate it to the restricted space of the bastion. An anta also covered each corner of the exterior. The three little steps to the platform are undercut, an embellishment now normally found on Ionic buildings, and not unknown on Doric. A balustrade, or rather parapet, was erected some years later along the

edge of the Acropolis wall around the sides and back of the temple; the outward face is richly carved with figures of Victory, etc.

Visitors to the Acropolis at the period were confronted [157] as they left the Propylaea by a colossal bronze statue of Athena Promachus ('the Warrior Champion'), slightly to their left, and behind it was the retaining wall of a terrace which formed a sort of separate precinct for the Parthenon.

Another Ionic temple on the Acropolis, the Erechtheum, was begun in 421 and finished in 405 opposite the north side of the Parthenon. It was intended to replace the old temple, to house the old image, and to unite in an organized building several shrines and places of religious

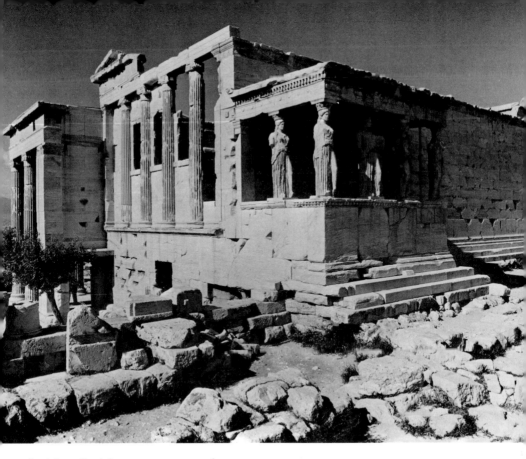

184. Athens, Erechtheum, 421-405, west end

significance. It is less than half as long or (excluding projections) as wide as the Parthenon, and was sited on the lowest ground available, where it could not compete [157]. Both plan and elevation are unique, and can only be explained on the supposition that it was intended as an unobtrusive counterweight to the Parthenon, the existence of which then made the centre of the Acropolis unbalanced; some complications were also forced on it by the location of the various sacred places it covered. A porch projects from either side of the Erechtheum, to north and south, at the west end of a central block which corresponds in shape with the whole of a normal temple [184–95].[14] These porches differ tremendously in all three dimen-

sions and rise from very different levels. Seen from the west, they double the width of the building. The north porch is the larger in every respect; it projects two intercolumniations northwards and is so high that its roof came almost level with the eaves of the central block, which stands on equally low ground. The south porch is actually less than half as high, but is raised upon a terrace, so that its flat roof appeared roughly level with the capitals of the other porch. Instead of columns, it is supported by statues of women in heavy drapery, the folds of which resemble the fluting seen opposite on the columns of the Parthenon. They stand close together on a solid parapet as tall as themselves (stopped short to leave an entrance). The effect

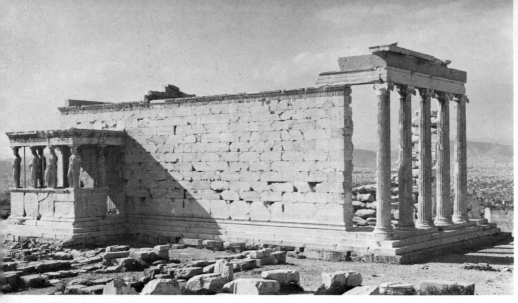

185. Athens, Erechtheum, 421-405, south side

186. Athens, Erechtheum, 421-405, west end and north porch, from within

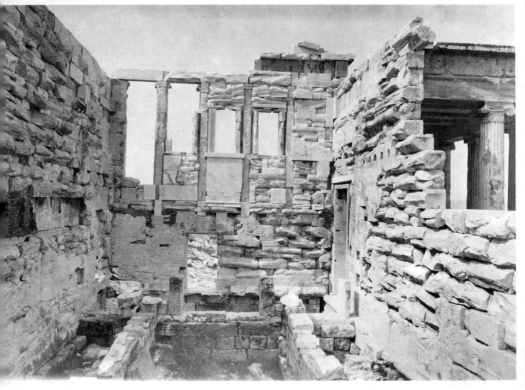

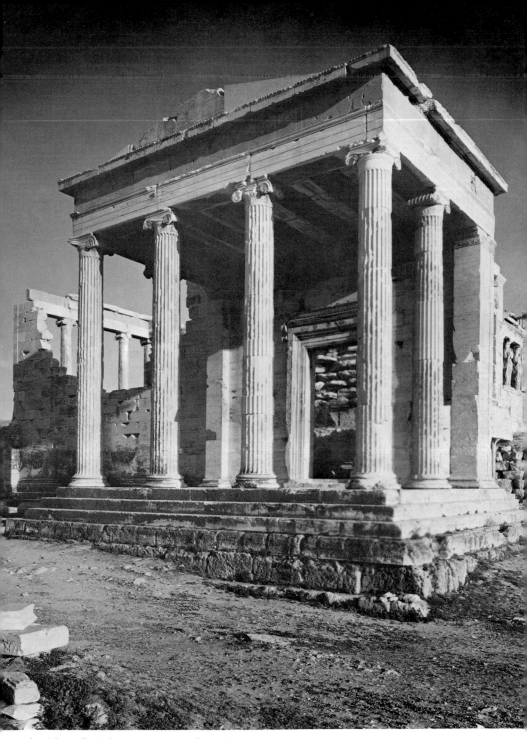

187. Athens, Erechtheum, 421-405, north porch

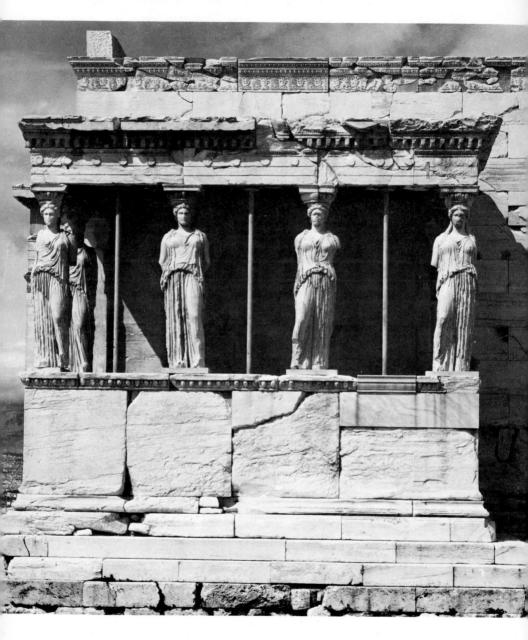

188. Athens, Erechtheum, 421-405, caryatids of south porch

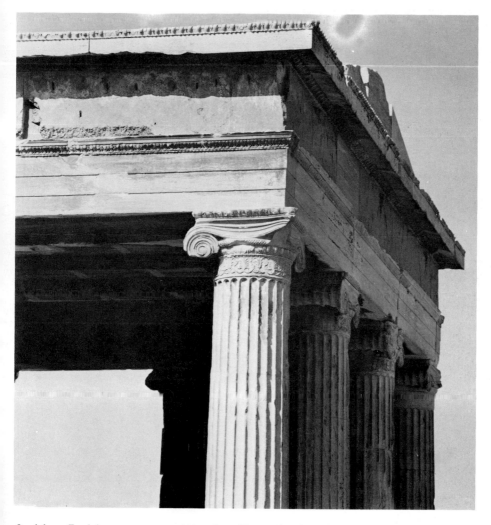

189. Athens, Erechtheum, 421–405, capitals and entablature of north porch

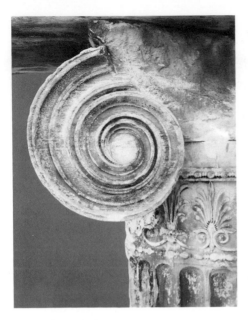

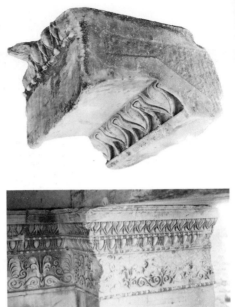

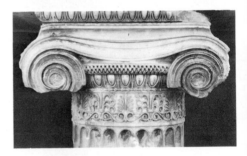

190–4. Athens, Erechtheum, 421–405,
part of capital of east porch (*above*),
and cornice, anta capital, capital,
and angle capital of north porch (*right*)

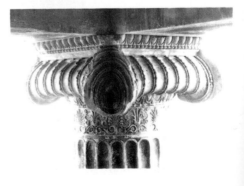

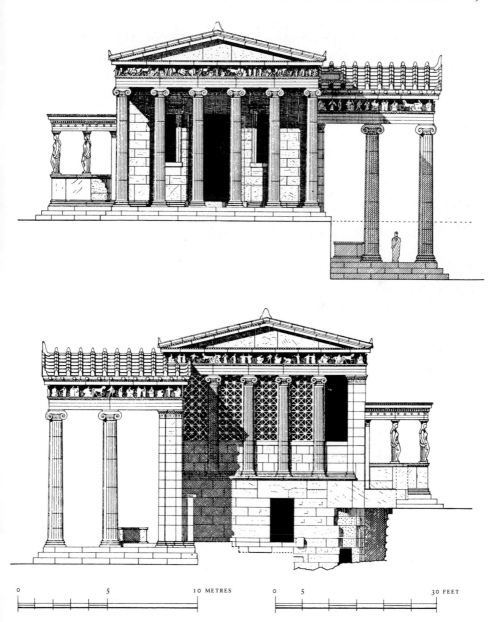

195. Athens, Erechtheum, 421-405, restored east and west elevations

of this porch is therefore extremely massive, whereas the other has very thin columns extremely widely spaced. Seen from the west the two porches subtly balance one another. Moreover, their conjunction with the central block causes the Erechtheum to make a unified composition with the Parthenon, seven-tenths as wide and to all appearance about seven-tenths as high. The small south porch, attached at mid-height, points like a blunt finger at the Parthenon, while the north porch acts as a counterpart to the sturdy pteron by providing a flimsy, airy cluster of columns – four along the north façade, and one more on each side between them and the antae. The value of the porch is emphasized by its westward projection from the central block; only the east anta is attached to the north wall of the central block, the other to a spur which prolongs the wall more than 9 feet beyond the west end of the block. The extent of this overlap was increased during construction; the original intention[15] had been to build the west end of the block 2 feet outward of its actual position.

The central block stands upon lower ground at its west than at its east end. Three doors lead into it; the great door of the north porch, a plain opening at the bottom of the west wall slightly south of centre, and a small door on the south side, to which a staircase leads down from the interior of the Caryatid porch. At the west end, above the plain opening, at half the height of both the column shafts in the north porch and the parapet of the south porch, is a ledge upon which stands a row of four columns. The wall continues upwards only a few courses, in which the backs of the columns are engaged, but above that level there are windows between the columns – originally all the way up to the architrave it seems, though a reconstruction in the Roman period has left them shorter. Bronze lattices filled the windows, at any rate in their final form. The height of the columns above the window-sills equals the vertical distance between the ledge and the floor of the north porch; the height of the engaged portions of the columns equals the vertical distance between the window-sills and the flat roof of the south porch, and, moreover, between that roof and the moulding on top of the architrave above the windows. Some order was thus introduced into the strangely heterogeneous composition. The roof of the south porch too is actually level with the moulding on top of the north porch architrave, but the fact is scarcely perceptible owing to foreshortening. Above each of these mouldings ran a frieze of grey Eleusis stone to which figures of white marble were attached. The two friezes – one on the three faces of the north porch, the other surrounding the central block – differ slightly in height. The south porch bears dentils instead of a frieze, but the highest fascia of the architrave is taller than the other two and embossed with a line of rosettes; the dentils themselves are ridiculously small by the standards of Asia Minor, and abnormally close together. Each porch contains an elaborate coffered ceiling; bronze rosettes hung from the coffers in the north porch. The most ornate doorway behind the north porch [196] gives a clearance 16 feet high (4·882 m.) and 8 feet wide at the floor (2·427 m.) compared with 7¾ feet (2·34 m.) at the top; the carving, however, was left unfinished except on the lintel and the consoled cornice. The capitals and bases of this porch are the most elaborate ever designed. The ornament of the Erechtheum is all extremely formal and meticulously carved, at a cost which, as the inscribed accounts reveal, exceeded that of figure sculpture.

The front of the Erechtheum was, as usual, at the east, where the ground is level with the south porch. Six columns stand prostyle; in the wall behind them is a tall doorway between a pair of windows. The interior of the temple has been destroyed by its conversion into a church and afterwards into the harem of the Turkish governor of Athens. But there seem to have been two cross-walls and a lengthwise partition in the space between them, making a total of four rooms; the eastern room would have been the largest, and its floor stood higher than the others. The temple is known to have been dedicated to other deities and semi-deities

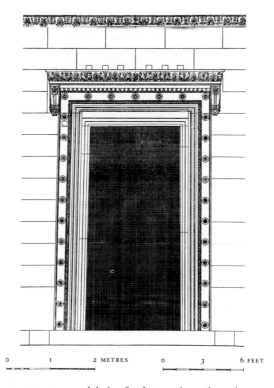

196. Athens, Erechtheum, 421–405, restored design for doorway in north porch

besides Athena, a circumstance which may have helped the architect (probably Mnesicles again) to justify the anomalies of its external as well as its internal design.[16]

It should be added that the south porch of the Erechtheum overlies part of the pteron of the old temple of Athena. Only the cella had been repaired after the Persian invasion, and that may have been preserved for several more generations. There are no other considerable remains of Greek buildings on the Acropolis. The space west of the Parthenon terrace, along the south wall, was occupied by a depository for weapons (Chalcotheca), which extended to the precinct of Brauronian Artemis at the back of the Propylaea, but only a few broken foundations remain in all that area.

The diminutive round building, shown in the restoration [157] beyond the Parthenon, was a temple of Rome and Augustus, and so does not come within the scope of this book, though its architectural details are based on the Erechtheum: it was presumably built at the time when the Erechtheum underwent considerable repair.

CHAPTER 15

NICETIES OF DORIC DESIGN

Greek architecture began to decline towards the end of the fifth century, because nothing new or better could be achieved in the same line and no really adequate alternative was found. The buildings on the Acropolis are the most ambitious the Greeks ever attempted, and come very near perfection – which is equivalent to saying that the architects' ambitions were strictly limited. Different regions seem to have worked out their own standard rules of procedure. Athenian architecture in the fifth century had evolved its own particular method. Compared with this, differences might have been introduced, but these would hardly have been improvements. In essentials, the design of a Doric temple was becoming standardized, at any rate as regards the exterior, though Ionic, far less standardized, offered greater possibilities of variation. At Athens, the rules of procedure and proportion were not only satisfactorily determined in respect of every detail, but were applied with meticulous workmanship.

Architects habitually wrote books about their work – it is particularly tantalizing to know of two on the Parthenon, one of them by Ictinus himself – and it must have been feasible for a man of no aesthetic gifts to design quite a tolerable building by following published instructions (as often happened in England during the eighteenth century). Vitruvius, writing just before the time of Christ, has recorded a most elaborate set of rules taken from Greek authors, who must have compiled them gradually in the course of the preceding centuries. Anyone who reads this section of Vitruvius (Book IV) would suppose the designing of a temple to have been purely mechanical, demanding no artistic judgement, and in fact the rules and the accompanying diagrams provided an answer to every factual question that might arise.[1] But in the fifth century, at any rate, the rules were not yet applied with mechanical precision, but altered in accordance with the particular requirements of the site, the cult, and the image inside the building.

At no period, however, were the rules enforced with such rigidity as to involve identical measurements for all units of the same type. The Greeks habitually allowed some variety in repetition, for example in the thickness and spacing of columns. In early times this may have been due mainly to incompetence, as in the case of the temple of Apollo at Syracuse, where the columns at either corner of the front differ to the extent of a foot in diameter. But there is ample evidence that Sicilian builders later in the sixth century, when their standards of workmanship had vastly improved, still permitted variations of several inches. In the Parthenon the errors in laying out the building total only a quarter of an inch, and the masons had obviously trained their faculties to almost machine-like precision, but they made no attempt to secure identity of measurements in some respects. For instance, the capitals on the front and on the south side differ by an average of $2\frac{1}{4}$ inches, although both sets could be seen together. Among other inequalities it will suffice to mention that the intercolumniations vary up to $1\frac{3}{4}$ inches in length, and the blocks of the architrave do not always meet over the centre of a column. The Greeks never ceased to tolerate such irregularities: it was an easy way of avoiding monotony, and harmless when the differences were too small to be consciously apprehended.

The practice of departing from true geometric shapes was also established long before the Parthenon. Theoretically the elevations of a temple form geometric figures and apparently they were often drawn as such in the architect's sketches, but in the completed building some of the lines were deliberately bent out of true. Among the earliest of these intentional distortions, which are termed 'refinements', is entasis, the outward curvature of the column shaft.[2] To some extent this device may be regarded as corrective to an optical illusion, because a column with perfectly straight sides, if seen against a background of light, appears thinner about half-way up than at the top and bottom.[3] But in the sixth century the entasis much exceeded the degree of curvature needed for mere correction, and even when it had been reduced to approximately that curvature its function was not only to obviate the appearance of weakness that straight sides would have entailed. The entasis gave the column vitality and elasticity, and diminished any tendency for the eye to be carried exclusively upward along the shaft.[4] The eye, in fact, travels both up and down a Greek column, in spite of the tapering of the shaft towards the top

The degree of tapering increased with the height of the column but also varied from one period to another. Vitruvius prescribes that the diameters at the top and bottom should be given the ratio 5:6 in columns not more than 15 feet high; $5\frac{1}{2}$:$6\frac{1}{2}$ in 15–20 feet; 6:7 in 20–30 feet; $6\frac{1}{2}$:$7\frac{1}{2}$ in 30–40 feet; 7:8 in 40–50 feet. Tapering originated, no doubt, from the natural diminution of the tree-trunks that were used as columns, and was perpetuated in stone for its aesthetic benefits. One effect is to increase the apparent height, because we are so accustomed to objects becoming smaller at a distance that the eye attributes the diminution to the wrong cause. A greater advantage is to reduce the feeling of strain which a perpendicular shaft imparts. Entasis also helps in this respect, and so does the inward slant of columns – a normal Greek practice. When all three devices were used in conjunction, the pteron on the end of a temple acquired a somewhat pyramidal outline, and with it a share of that sense of repose and power in which the pyramid excels all other shapes.

On the topic of entasis Vitruvius refers his readers to a diagram which the copyists of the manuscript have omitted, and modern research has been hampered by the difficulty of obtaining exact measurements from the weathered and often broken remains of columns. The effect can be judged only when the entire shaft remains standing. The most notable early case is the 'Basilica' at Paestum, where the shafts taper obtrusively at the top and their sides curve very noticeably, diverging $2\frac{1}{8}$ inches from the straight. In no Greek instance, however, does entasis involve a greater diameter above than at the foot of the shaft. The curve [201] usually reaches its maximum about one-third or (as in the Parthenon) two-fifths of the way up the shaft. In the Parthenon the curve entails, at its maximum, a divergence from the perpendicular of barely more than two-thirds of an inch, and anybody might think, at a casual glance, that the shafts tapered regularly upwards with straight sides. The lower diameter is actually 110 times as large as the maximum divergence of the entasis, and the height of the column 552 times as large. In the Hephaesteum, which was built immediately before the Parthenon, the entasis is still less, the diameter being 140 times as large, but the discrepancy is usually attributed to the fact that the columns are little more than half as high. In the Propylaea, with Doric Orders of different heights, each with a more pronounced entasis, there is again a differentiation according to size. In its taller columns, which are not much lower than those of the Parthenon though distinctly thinner, the diameter equals 80 times the divergence, compared with 100 times in the case of others that are similar to the Hephaesteum's. But another clue to the principle of entasis may be obtained by comparison with Ionic usage. In the north porch of the Erechtheum (where the shafts are intermediate in height) the divergence is negligible, amounting to less than a quarter of an inch, and other Ionic columns of the fifth century are straight-sided. Since the fundamental difference between Doric and Ionic columns is the greater thickness of Doric, the degree of entasis should have increased with the thickness of the column, not its height. But the general increase in the entasis of the Propylaea compared with the Parthenon and Hephaesteum must be due to a reaction towards more perceptible swellings. In later times the entasis again became emphatic. It is remarkable that the columns of the Temple of Poseidon at Sunium, under construction at the same time as the Parthenon and Propylaea, have no entasis at all.

This exaggeration of entasis after the fifth century is typical of the universal coarsening which proceeded in Greek architecture. The great Attic buildings of the mid and late fifth century display unequalled subtlety in all details, but especially in 'refinements', several of which appear to have been invented specifically for them; some never recur again. This exceptionally lavish use of 'refinements' was made feasible by the tribute Athens extorted from its allies; the expense of carving the precise curves was, of course, enormous. But the impulse came at that period more than any other, and to Athens in particular, because marble had only just been adopted there, and there alone, as the sole material for large buildings. No other stone gave equal opportunities for 'refinements', and its potentialities were immediately exploited to the full. A significant fact is that the limestone temple at Bassae, although allegedly another work by the architect of the Parthenon, is devoid of 'refinements', except for entasis.

At the end of the sixth century, when the first marble buildings were put up at Delphi, they were distinguished by the delicacy of their workmanship, the slightness of their proportions, and the liveliness of the surface compared with the matt effect of stuccoed stone. The temple of Apollo exemplified the structural efficiency of the new material; the columns on the front, built in 513–505 of marble, were slighter than the older, limestone columns at the back. Architects evidently felt safe in using thinner blocks and wider spans than had been the custom when dealing with softer loose-grained rock. Consequently they could take liberties with the shapes, working now as artists rather than engineers. And they learnt to utilize their powers of obtaining greater definition,

with sharper angles and a polished surface, till the design could be bound together where desirable by means only of incised lines. In the buildings of the Acropolis a column and the neighbouring anta are associated by horizontal lines incised at the same height [178], while other lines emphasized the greater height of the architrave. The pattern formed by the jointing of slabs is intensified in marble by their reflecting surface, and the pavement accordingly supplies a decorative base to the cella wall. The contrasts between smooth expanses of polished masonry and crisp ornament are accompanied by contrasts between brilliant highlights and shadows. These, however, were toned down here and there by colour; the incised beds for polychrome patterns on plain surfaces or mouldings can still be seen [101, 163, 167, 168, 177]. The sculptures were polychrome against a coloured background (usually red in a metope, blue in a pediment and continuous frieze), while capitals and architrave and ceiling beams might be red all over and the triglyphs blue. Now that all colour has faded and most of the sculpture has gone, almost the entire design of the Parthenon is composed of different types of shadow, thin or thick, grey or black, single or repetitive, but never identical in the repetition. The comparatively blurred transitions in stuccoed stone had possessed no such value, and the early marble buildings were too small to do more than suggest the aesthetic possibilities of the material.

Above all, distortion was still a field for experiment just after the middle of the fifth century. So was perspective, the study of which inspired the architects. This subject apparently came into prominence when the painter Agatharchus designed the background for a tragedy and wrote a book on scene-painting based upon his experience. The theory was then investigated from the mathematical standpoint by Democritus and Anaxagoras. The influence of these discoveries upon architects seems immediately to have been overwhelming, and in an attenuated form it lasted for centuries. Heliodorus of Larisa, the author of a much later book on perspective (probably of the first century A.D.), expresses a view which Ictinus and Mnesicles would have considered absurdly elementary: 'The aim of the architect is to give his work a semblance of being well-proportioned and to devise means of protection against optical illusions so far as possible, with the objective, not of factual, but of apparent equality of measurements and proportion.' Vitruvius too explains that if someone stands in front of a perpendicular building and if two lines are drawn from his eyes, one to the lowest part of the structure and the other to the highest, the line of vision to the upper part is longer and gives it the appearance of leaning backwards, whereas if the façade actually leans forwards the whole of it will appear perpendicular.

The 'refinements' in the Hephaesteum, Parthenon, and Propylaea extend far beyond the mere optical corrections which these late authors recommend: very few portions of the buildings are actually straight, perpendicular or horizontal. Broadly speaking, the lines which should be horizontal are curved upwards convexly while those which should be perpendicular slope inwards. All the distortions are too small dimensionally to be easily noticed.

It will be simpler to take the Parthenon [197] by stages, noting only the main variants found in the other buildings. The treads of the steps and the platform rise from each corner to the middle of the frontage [161]; on the ends of the temple the gradient of the curve is 1 in 450, on the sides 1 in 750 – a matter of 4 inches. But there is also an inward slant, and so the whole floor is very slightly domed, with its highest point at the centre of the building and lowest points at the corners of the platform (which, no doubt, were meant to be level but actually differ by nearly 2 inches in elevation). The inward slant also applies in the steps, although the inclination is at the rate of only 1 in 250. All four rows of pteron columns slant inwards 2⅜ inches, or 1 in 150; the side colonnades would actually meet if prolonged to a height of rather more than a mile [201]. The columns at the corners

have a diagonal slant in order to conform with both rows; incidentally these columns are a couple of inches thicker than the rest, to allow for the diminution in their apparent girth when seen in isolation. An additional 'refinement' in the Hephaesteum makes all the individual columns on the ends slant not only inwards but towards the longitudinal axis of the temple, so that the tilt increases with each column to a maximum at the corner. The architrave and frieze slant inwards at 1 in 80, and so do the walls of the cella. The architrave and entablature also rise at a gradient of 1 in 600 to the centre of each frontage. Consequently the domed shape of the floor is carried to the entire height of the temple.

Some very small portions of the exterior slant downwards and outwards, whether to counteract foreshortening, or to reflect the light, or to gain emphasis by contrast with the adjoining larger members which slant in the opposite direction. The last reason seems plausible in the case of the anta capitals which slant outwards though the anta itself slants inwards. The projecting face (corona) of the horizontal cornice has an outward inclination of 1 in 100, and the antefixes and acroteria of 1 in 20, presumably to catch the light better as well as to counteract foreshortening. A really extraordinary instance is that the abacus face in the Parthenon leans outward 1 in 140, which amounts only to one-sixteenth of an inch. There was certainly some advantage to be obtained from not leaning such a thin slab inwards, though one would think that a perpendicular surface would have done as well. Perhaps an inaccurate set-square was used. However, this trifling refinement has been observed elsewhere, in the temple of 'Concord' at Acragas and at Segesta; it does not exist in the Hephaesteum.

A number of other tiny irregularities must surely be accidental, if that is the right word for variations which the architect may have deliberately encouraged. It would seem that he must actually have given definite instructions against carving any straight lines or flat surfaces in some portions of the Parthenon – notably the

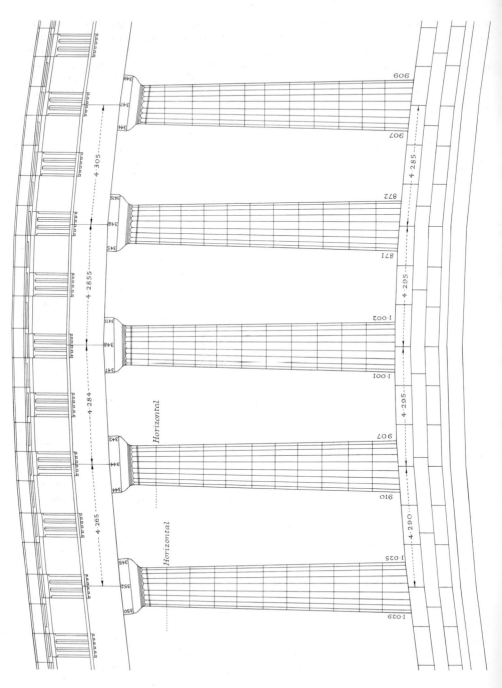

197 (*opposite*). Athens, Parthenon, 447-432, exaggerated diagram of distortions in north colonnade

gables, where everything bends one way or another, while incised lines make false shadows that mislead the eye. At that height such details can scarcely have been perceptible, and many of the obviously intentional 'refinements' lower down involve such slight distortions that it has often been doubted whether they can really affect the appearance of the building. On this question Ruskin commented: 'Let it not be said, as it was of the late discoveries of subtle curvature in the Parthenon, that what is not to be demonstrated without laborious measurement, cannot have influence on the beauty of the design. The eye is continually influenced by what it cannot detect; nay, it is not going too far to say, that it is most influenced by what it detects least.'[5]

One point should be remembered in this connexion, that 'refinements' would not have been undertaken light-heartedly, because they introduced terrifying complications into the masons' work. To bed a slanting column on a sloping floor involved grinding the lowest drum till it stood at the required angle, or alternatively adjusting a higher drum instead. The rise of the architrave gave less trouble than might be expected, because of the adoption of an irregular broken curve for the whole façade: the top and bottom of each block were always straight, and the bends occurred at joints. The ends of the blocks had therefore to be cut obliquely in order to meet, and the top of the abacus beneath them had to slope away to each side of the joint. The rise of the steps likewise proceeds by a series of bends so rounded away as to approximate to the regular curvature of a parabola. And in fact no curves in the Parthenon are arcs of a circle. The echinus of the capital is a rectangular hyperbola, and the under side of the sloping cornice above the pediment is a hyperbolic surface. Even the flutes on the columns were given a 'refinement':

they become deeper towards the top of the shaft.

Much of this subtlety in curvature is certainly wasted on modern visitors who expect a building to be strictly rectangular. It ought to have been appreciated with comparative ease by contemporaries because of the prevalence of sun-dried brick in their domestic building; with eyes habituated to gentle curves they would have resented mechanical accuracy and repetition. And if (as is conceivable) precautions were sometimes taken in domestic building against the sagging of wooden architraves, these would have been propped so that they rose convexly, producing the effect of a horizontal 'refinement', while settlement of foundations would make the supporting posts lean inwards. The introduction to stone building of the inward inclination did actually provide some practical benefit, by buttressing the structure, and the slope of the floor enabled rain-water to drain away. But most other 'refinements' seem purely aesthetic. And although the suggestion that they were inspired by the various curvatures to be seen in popular building is reasonable up to a point, some were so aesthetically desirable that they would certainly have been invented even had there been no precedent. That may be said of the inward inclination of columns. The taper of the shafts causes the intervening gaps to widen upwards, and the effect becomes cumulative towards the corners of a temple, with the result that perpendicular columns there must seem to lean outwards. (This can be seen perhaps at Bassae although some of its columns are no longer quite upright.) The solution of inclining all the columns in the opposite direction was therefore a most persistent 'refinement', used long after the majority of those invented in the fifth century had been discarded. It became such a matter of course that Cicero could repeat, without a word of explanation even to a Roman audience, the story of how the Governor of Sicily swindled a contractor over the repairs to a temple by testing the columns with a plumb-line and condemning them as crooked.

CHAPTER 16

LATE-FIFTH-CENTURY TEMPLES EXCEPT ON THE ACROPOLIS

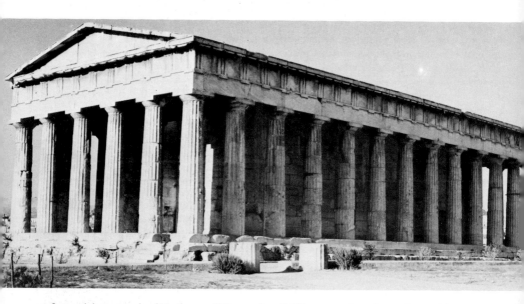

198-201. Athens, temple of Hephaestus ('Theseum'), mid fifth century, from the south-west (*above*), west end, north-east corner, and interior of southern colonnade (*right*)

The most sensitive, Attic, form of Doric, in which all the potentialities of marble were exploited with more lavish use of 'refinements', first appears immediately after 450 and endured only some thirty years. In the course of this one generation Doric was carried to perfection, with the aid of elements borrowed from Ionic, and the juxtaposition of two or three Orders in a single building became habitual. The third Order, the Corinthian, was actually an Athenian invention of rather late in the same generation; only the capital was novel, and in every other respect the Corinthian Order is always indistinguishable from Ionic.[1]

The oldest of the distinctively Attic buildings is the temple of Hephaestus at Athens, the

'Theseum' as it is popularly called,[2] the foundations of which were probably laid in 449 [198–201, 330]. This is the oldest temple built entirely of marble (except for the lowest step, of limestone, a wooden ceiling over the cella, and terracotta tiles), and it incorporates 'refinements' to excess; in the slightly later buildings of the school, the Parthenon and Propylaea, the subtlety is controlled by a keener aesthetic sense. With all the ingenuity of its unknown architect[3] and in spite of its excellent condition, the Hephaesteum lacks vitality when seen from any direction except below, from the agora (the civic meeting place) of ancient Athens, to the steep verge of which the east front of the temple extends. But there is clear evidence that this

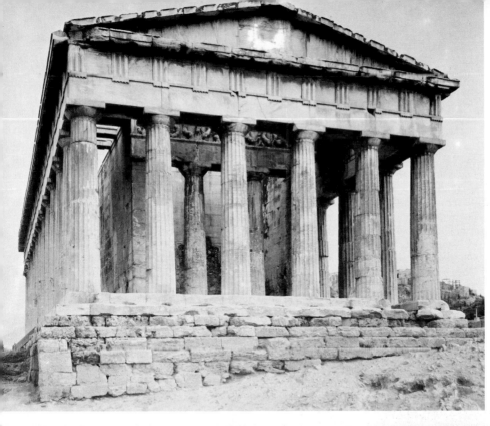

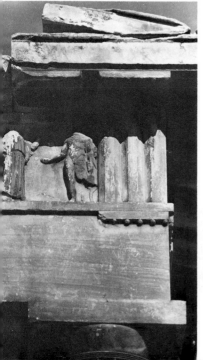

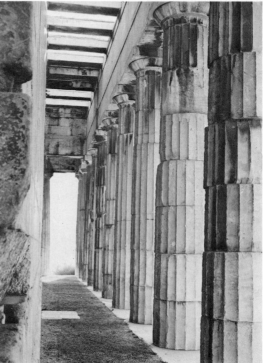

viewpoint was regarded as the most important, in the circumstance that all the sculptured metopes of the temple are concentrated on the front or just around its corners over the two most easterly intercolumniations of each side; elsewhere the metopes are plain. Furthermore, the worst fault of which the architect is accused is his unprecedented combination of a relatively high entablature (6½ feet high) with unduly slim columns (18¾ feet high, equal to 5·6 times their lower diameter), though these proportions are in fact more normal for this period than those employed in the Parthenon. The superiority of the upward view results, of course, from the shortening of vertical lines while the width of horizontals remains unaffected. Since the study of perspective formed one of the intellectual and artistic preoccupations of contemporary Athens, and this particular building abounds with minor optical corrections, it may have been designed specifically to be seen from the agora. Perhaps the expectation was that no other general view would be obtainable owing to the planting of trees and bushes on the little plateau of rock which formed the sanctuary, but there are reasons for believing that the pits in which these grew may not have been hewn till the third century B.C.

In plan [330],[4] the Hephaesteum is comparable with the temple of Zeus at Olympia [153], though on half the scale (45 by 104 feet; 13·708 by 31·77 m.). But the porch is set farther inwards than the opisthodomus, in perfect alignment with the third columns of the sides instead of slightly forward of them, as both were at Olympia. Moreover, the columns of the porch and opisthodomus are made uniform in height and thickness with those of the pteron (disregarding a step in the pavement). The effect, especially at the porch, is to knit the external and internal design together more closely than could have been achieved with smaller columns. The greater distance between pteron and porch is an anomaly that requires explanation, since the motive can scarcely have been only to increase the accommodation of the covered area. Again, perhaps the view from the agora was

taken into consideration; seen from below, the roof is in shadow and the floor beneath eye-level, so that the columns of the porch and pteron come closer together, and with their uniformity of size might have appeared jumbled if not actually separated by a considerable distance. But the different siting of the porch and opisthodomus gave occasion for variation in their decorative treatment, more ornate at the front and justifiably economical at the back of the temple. The façade of the porch is joined to the pteron architrave by another of the same height which carries a continuous sculptured frieze, framed above and below with Ionic mouldings; as the opisthodomus is isolated from the pteron, a similar architrave and frieze run only across its façade, starting from the corner above each anta.

All the existing sculpture of the Hephaesteum would seem from the style to date within a dozen years of its foundation, though some scholars have proposed dates in the late 420s for the frieze. Besides the friezes and metopes, which remain in their original position, fragments have been excavated of pedimental statues, including one of the finest nude male figures extant, and of a gable-top acroterium, a group of one girl carrying another. But inscriptions prove that the lost cult images, a pair of bronze statues of Hephaestus and Athena, dated between 421 and 415; expenditure upon them may have been postponed because of other commitments even before the outbreak of the Peloponnesian War in 432. And the greater expense of fitting up the cella with its two-storeyed colonnades and the ceiling may also have been postponed; in fact, the internal design seems to have been inspired by the Parthenon, and the foundations indicate that the cella was originally intended to be both longer and narrower. The inner colonnades were entirely destroyed when the temple became a church, but apparently they not only ran parallel with the side walls but also met behind the images, as in the Parthenon. The gap between each column and the side wall is much narrower than in the Parthenon, only about a foot wide, and

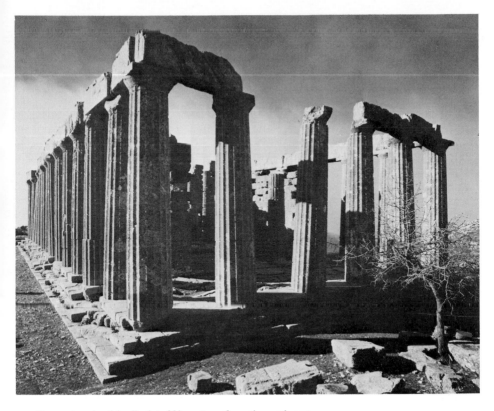

202. Bassae, temple of Apollo, late fifth century, from the north-east

the cella itself is so narrow (26 feet externally) that it could easily have been spanned without props; the main function of the colonnades was evidently to alter the scale of the cella in keeping with the god and goddess. Perhaps they were altogether an afterthought, and prevented the fulfilment of an intention to fresco the walls, the surface of which is roughened to receive plaster. The joints are made watertight by lead fillings.

Two stages of work, begun at roughly the same dates but probably of longer duration, and the first restricted to merely the pteron and walls, may be recognized in the temple of Apollo at Bassae [202].[5] Situated high in the mountains of Arcadia, it was built by the little state of Phigalia in fulfilment of a vow taken for deliverance from plague, so Pausanias records, and

he names as its architect Ictinus, the designer of the Parthenon. An analysis of the Doric capitals suggests that the two Orders are not the same; and it is clear that there are three different groups at Bassae, those of the front (which, exceptionally, faces north), the remainder of the external colonnade, and the porch columns. There are also signs of alteration in the interior, though the exact nature of this is disputed. There seem to be two distinct phases of construction, the earlier dating to the middle of the fifth century, the later to 420; but decidedly lower dates have been suggested. The involvement of Ictinus is also a matter of dispute; some scholars suggest it is a mistake, or misinformation, on the part of Pausanias. Others suggest the first phase is the work of the young Ictinus,

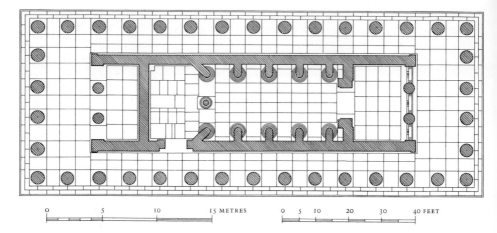

203-5. Bassae, temple of Apollo, late fifth century, plan (*above*), interior looking towards adytum (*below*), and restoration of interior looking towards adytum (*opposite*)

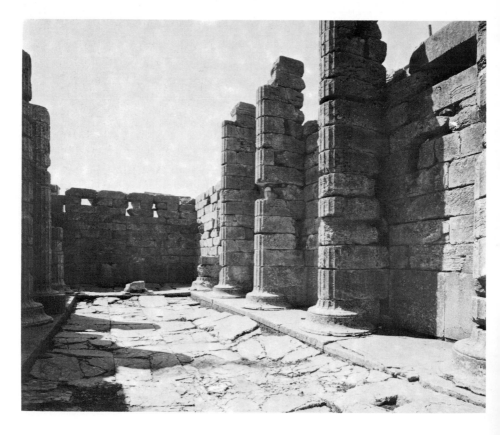

before he made his reputation in Athens; others again that it is the second phase which saw Ictinus, or his workshop, taking over and improving the uncompleted temple. The temple seems old-fashioned in its proportions, six by fifteen columns; but this was because an adytum, entered most unusually by a door in the side wall, had to be added behind the main section of the cella [203]. Perhaps the adytum was imitated from Apollo's temple at Delphi. The north alignment, and probably the existence of an adytum, were already to be found in the temple's predecessor, and are clearly deliberate features. The temple was quite small ($47\frac{1}{2}$ by $125\frac{1}{2}$ feet; 14·48 by 38·24 m.) and built as far as possible of the brittle grey limestone of the hillside, with none of the subtle distortions which

added so much to the cost of the Parthenon, except that the column-shafts curve convexly in elevation; the columns stand bolt-upright, and the floor is quite level. The gutters, with an Ionic pattern of water-lilies and palmettes, and the palmette antefixes, could not easily have been carved in the local stone and were of marble; from their style, they should not be earlier than about 420 and could, perhaps, belong to the turn of the century.

The earliest plausible dating is, again, 420 for a marble frieze of continuous sculpture which unprecedentedly surrounded the *interior* of the cella [204, 205]. The position must have been chosen in order to display the whole frieze at once, instead of only short stretches as was the case at the Parthenon. But very little light can

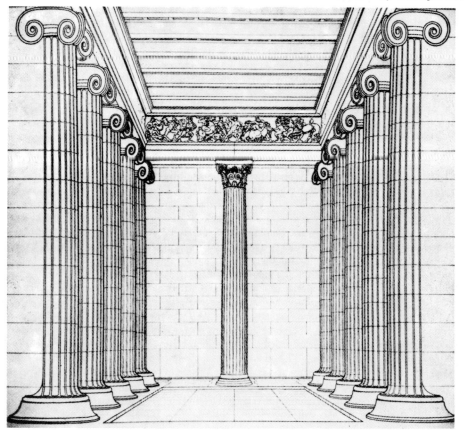

have reached the top of the walls. The ceiling was probably inclined, to improve the view of the frieze, and this may account for the massive masonry flanking the main, north doorway. The frieze (which has clear indications of not being in the precise arrangement or positioning for which it was designed) rested upon Ionic half-columns[6] joined to the walls by buttress-like spurs of masonry – which might well have been a rational improvement on the Hephaesteum scheme but was actually a much older method, used in the Heraeum of Olympia. The bases projected abnormally far, owing mainly to an exaggerated outward flare (apophyge) of the bottom of the shaft, which thereby met them in a very shallow curve; the mouldings of the base could therefore be taken farther back, and in fact they describe more than three-quarters of a circle before they touch the spur. Marble half-capitals were engaged along what would have been the centre of a complete capital; the front and sides of each curved concavely, so that each corner with its back-to-back volutes was bent outwards in the same manner as the one corner of a normal angle capital. In a capital carved as a provisional model for the sculptures and eventually buried near the temple, the band linking the tops of the volutes runs horizontally, but in the design finally adopted this band curved boldly upwards, so high that no abacus was required, as had been the case with the rejected model.

No wall divided the cella from the adytum. Instead, the frieze was carried across from half-columns on the ends of spurs which project diagonally from each side-wall, and midway a slender free-standing column gave it support. This bore the oldest known Corinthian capital,[7] and perhaps the half-columns on either side were also topped with Corinthian capitals – necessarily three-quarters capitals, since the diagonal projection would have revealed two complete sides and two halves. The proven capital has now perished, but the excavators of 1811–12 preserved drawings of the fragments discovered. The original motive for the invention of the Corinthian capital had probably been

to obtain a better substitute for Ionic at corners; Corinthian was more suitable in such positions because the abacus has four concave sides of equal length while the body of the capital is round, shaped like an inverted bell. Two rows of tiny acanthus leaves, one above the other, rose from the base of the bell; pairs of tall leaves sprang from them to the corners of the abacus, under which their tips curled downwards and outwards in spiral form; in between a pair of spirals, surmounted by a central palmette, spread in low relief over the bell beneath each side of the abacus.

A marble temple of Poseidon at Sunium in Attica [101, 206, 207] appears slightly later than the older parts of the Hephaesteum and Bassae, though still contemporary with the Parthenon. The most likely date is about 440 or a little later. As Dinsmoor has pointed out, the similarities between Sunium and the Hephaesteum are so great that they must be ascribed to the same architect,[8] along with the Temple of Ares moved by the Romans from Acharnae to the Athenian agora, and the smaller temple of Nemesis at Rhamnus, left unfinished at the outbreak of the Peloponnesian War in 431. At Sunium he developed an additional method of relating the outer and inner portions of the design. The cella walls are exactly aligned with the penultimate columns on the ends, while in the Hephaesteum the outer face is placed opposite the centre of the columns. The interior of the cella has perished, but no comparable delay in completing it need be assumed, because the building of the temple was accelerated by using the substructures of its predecessor. This to some extent determined the plan; for instance, the existence of a ready-made foundation accounts for the siting of the opisthodomus façade, with the ends of the antae opposite the centre of the third column on the sides, whereas the porch façade is exactly aligned with the corresponding columns, as in the Hephaesteum.

A frieze of continuous sculpture, likewise enframed by Ionic mouldings, not only ran across the façade of the porch but continued along the back of the external colonnade, surrounding all

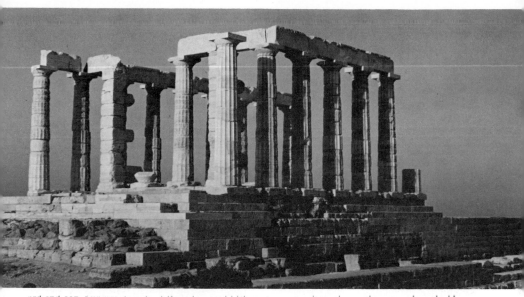

266 and 267. Sunium, temple of Poseidon, mid fifth century, view from the north-east, and south side

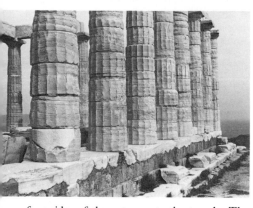

four sides of the entrance to the temple. The pediments contained sculptured figures, but the metopes were plain and the acroteria consisted of palmettes and spirals. In general, the dimensions throughout were almost identical with those of the Hephaesteum. A notable exception is the increase of the height of the columns by a foot (making them 5·78 times as high as their lower diameters), while the entablature was not perceptibly taller. Nothing remains in position above the architrave by which to judge the effect. Theoretically, however, the nature of the site again justifies the architect. The temple occupies the entire top of an isolated promontory overlooking a cliff which drops hundreds of feet into the sea. The promontory is a turning-point on one of the busiest shipping-lanes of Greece, and the views from the sea (to the god of which it was dedicated) ought to have dictated the shape of the building; foreshortening had also to be countered on the steep approach by land. From such angles the entablature should therefore have looked high enough for the columns, assuming that the lines of the temple were intended to make it spring upwards as the situation required. Each column is carved with sixteen very shallow flutes instead of the usual twenty; they were therefore more conspicuous from a distance and made the shafts appear even thinner.[9]

The later temples of the fifth century are of less artistic or historic interest. That of 'Concord'[10] at Agrigento (built of local stone) illustrates another stage in the Sicilian attempt to solve the problem of angle triglyphs by means of an irregular ground-plan. Here all the columns are uniform, but each in turn of the last two intercolumniations is shorter on the back as well as on the front, and likewise on the sides, where the spacings are slightly longer in each case. The two sets of three different lengths of intercolumniation involve diverse arrangements of the jointing far down into the foundations; the metopes too are of three different lengths. The height of the columns equals 4·61 times their lower diameter, following Sicilian practice of early in the century. The cella remains standing to its full height [208]; even its cornice is still

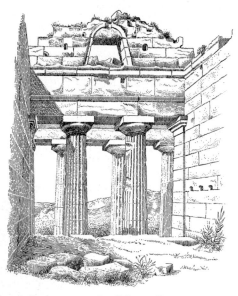

208. Agrigento, temple of 'Concord', late fifth century, interior

in place and contains a rebate to receive the timbers that covered the room. Inner gables too are almost intact over the walls which separate the cella from the porch and opisthodomus. Each of these gables is pierced at the centre by a doorway with a narrow lintel, slanting sides, and a wide threshold, and framed with an ogival arch which rises above the lintel. The purpose may have been to reduce the weight of masonry

as well as to facilitate maintenance of the roof-timbers. Two staircases led up for this purpose, beside the doorway to the cella. Markings on the inward sides of the gables indicate that a pitched roof formerly existed over the cella, though perhaps not till after its conversion into a church.[11]

Certainly, however, in a temple of Apollo which the Athenians built at Delos[12] between 425 and 417, the cella had no ceiling, only a ridged roof, with pediments on the inward side of its gables. But in this case the roof covered the whole temple, which occupied such a cramped site as to allow no space for colonnades along its sides. Six Doric columns stood prostyle at front and back. The porch rested on four thin pillars, as in the Nike Temple, and pilasters to match projected from the back wall opposite the rear external columns. The doorway to the cella opened between two windows, following the precedent set in the Picture Gallery of the Propylaea, the possible reason being that the cella contained a wide semicircular statue base, on which a group of seven statues (one of them the Apollo) was placed, rather than the normal single cult statue. The female statues which stood as acroteria on the gable and corners of the roof are well preserved. The material for building and sculptures alike is marble.

The unfinished Doric temple at Segesta in Sicily must also date from the last quarter of the century [209]. It comprises six by fourteen columns, uniform in size and placed about the corners with graduated intercolumniations as in the temple of 'Concord'. The scale is considerably larger ($75\frac{3}{4}$ by $190\frac{1}{2}$ feet; 23·12 by 58·04 m.). There is no inner building, though foundations had been made ready for the walls of a cella, porch, and opisthodomus or adytum.[13] The pteron is complete only in rough state; the shafts of the columns were left smoothed in readiness for fluting, and the blocks of the steps retain the bosses around which the rope had been secured when they were hoisted into place. But the upper surfaces of the steps had already been trimmed into a rising curve. A convex curvature may also be observed up above, for example along the top of abaci, and their outward faces

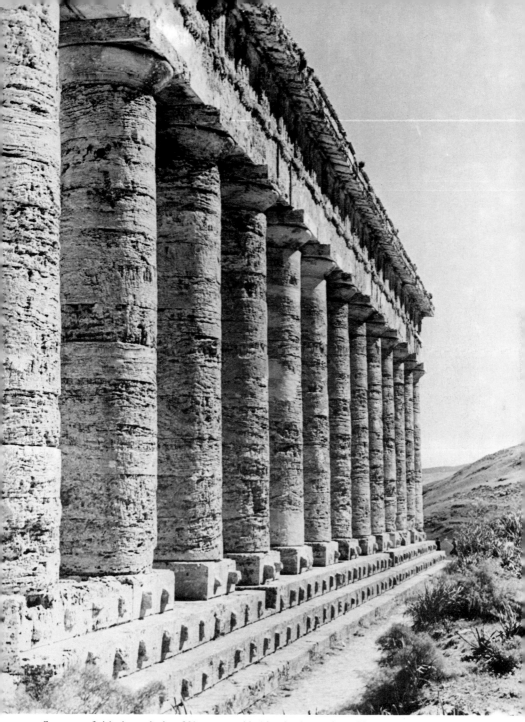

209. Segesta, unfinished temple, late fifth century, side (showing bosses for tackle)

project further at the top than at the bottom. The metopes are longer than they are tall, as had not been permissible for over a hundred years. This peculiarity is the more striking because the upper structure is abnormally tall, so that narrower rather than wider metopes might be expected. In fact the entablature, from architrave to cornice, stands $11\frac{3}{4}$ feet high, the columns $30\frac{3}{4}$ feet, giving a ratio of 1:2·6, while in Greece during the late fifth century the average comes to about 1:3. But the elongation of the metopes reduces the visual disparity by increasing the horizontal as opposed to the perpendicular direction in the frieze. And, paradoxically, the great height of the entablature makes the building appear less tall; the heaviness of the top adds emphasis to the horizontal elements in the design. These are stressed too by the unusual solidity of the columns, which are only 4·79 times as high as

their lower diameter, compared with an average of more than $5\frac{1}{2}$ in contemporary Greece. This cannot be entirely explained as a precautionary measure, although the local stone of which they are built was not as trustworthy as marble. The architect must have intended to give a squat effect to the building in keeping with its situation in a wide valley. The temple has been considered the work of an Athenian architect; the inhabitants of Segesta were not Greeks but native Sicilians, who entered into an alliance with Athens in 426 and may well have sent there for an architect when they became sufficiently Hellenized to require a temple. Though in some details of design the temple approaches mainland types, it still has the Sicilian characteristics; it is not simply a matter of Athenian design transported to Sicily. Work must have stopped in 398 when the Syracusans massacred some of the population and introduced new settlers.

CHAPTER 17

CIRCULAR BUILDINGS

From the earliest times to the present day the inhabitants of Greece have built round huts for temporary occupation. Circular tombs, the tholoi, were built in the Late Bronze Age; some of these were known and accessible at later times, and may have exerted some influence, although very few Greek tombs followed the type with any exactitude; these belong to all periods from sub-Mycenean onwards. But the oldest common type of Greek tomb, the tumulus, was possibly inspired by the Mycenean tholos which, though largely constructed underground, was usually topped by a small mound. In Asia Minor, the tumulus was often revetted by a perpendicular or sloping wall round the base, above which rose a conical mound of earth topped with an upright stone, more or less carefully worked. In general such tombs date from the sixth century, but some are older. The largest example, nearly a quarter of a mile in diameter and 900 feet high, was the tomb of Alyattes, near Sardis, which Herodotus describes (I. 93); the exterior has lost its shape, but there remains a barrel-vaulted passage and a flat-roofed burial-chamber at its end. Alyattes reigned about 600. A considerably later date is plausible for the 'Tomb of Tantalus' outside Smyrna, which measured about 100 feet both in diameter and in height; the corbelled vault of the rectangular burial-chamber recalls the Minoan tomb at Isopata.

The first imposing round building above ground dates from the middle of the sixth century, and was a limestone structure of the Doric Order, some 20 feet in diameter. Its precise site at Delphi has not been identified, and the material (notably triglyphs and metopes) was found re-used in a treasury of the late fifth century.[1] A very plain building of three times that diameter, erected in the agora at Athens about 470, served as the meeting place for the

prytaneis, and was known simply as the tholos, a term which implies not merely a round plan but also a conical roof. Outwardly the building looked like a revetted tumulus; for the conical roof rose from a circular upright wall. The roof

210. Delphi, tholos, c. 375, from the east

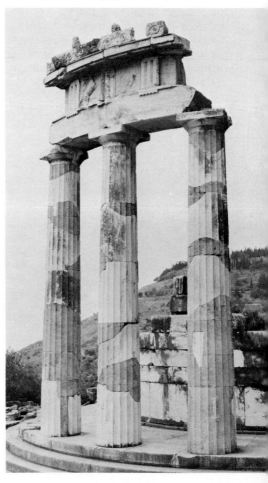

was supported also by six internal columns, arranged in an ellipse, three on the west and three on the east; each set of three described a greater arc than the curve of the wall, so that a wider intercolumniation was left at both north and south for doorways. The columns were not fluted.

Theodorus of Phocaea is recorded to have written a book about a tholos at Delphi, and may fairly safely be identified as the architect of the marble tholos which was built there early in the fourth century, around 375 to judge from the style of the carved metopes; it has been partially reconstructed in recent years [210–12]. The floor is raised 3 feet above the ground and upon it stood successively an external ring or pteron of twenty Doric columns,[2] the circular wall of the cella, and a ring of ten Corinthian columns,

adjoining the inner face of the wall but not engaged in it; the Corinthian columns stood in their inner circle each on the same radius as every alternate Doric column, except for the necessary gap outside the doorway. Since the diameter of the whole building is less than 49 feet (13·5 m.) and that of the cella 28 feet (8·41 m.), the spacing of both sets of columns is much closer than in contemporary rectangular buildings, but a close spacing of the pteron was most desirable in order to carry the eye smoothly round the curve. In the interior, the nuisance which the multiplicity of columns would otherwise have caused was avoided by placing them off the floor; they rose from a bench of black limestone, which lined the cella wall. The cella itself was paved with slabs of the same stone, except for a circle of white marble in the centre.

211 and 212. Delphi, tholos, *c.* 375, from the west (*below*), and restored section with capital (*opposite*)

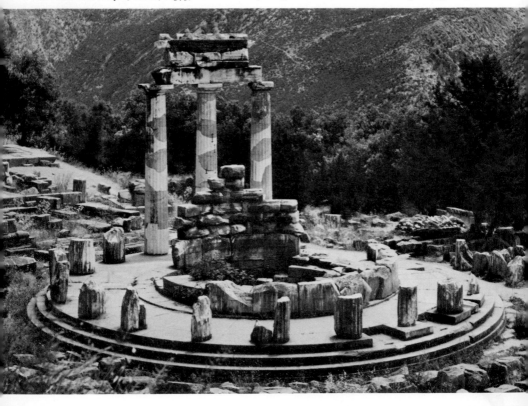

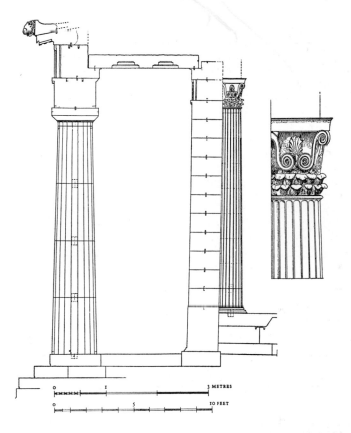

On the outside, too, the base of the wall was black. There was, apparently, a conical roof over the cella and a separate roof over the pteron, sloping down from a lower level of the wall; the cella may have been lit by windows in the upper part of the wall. The gutter of the Doric entablature was richly ornamented and bore lion-head spouts. The Corinthian capitals are very formal in treatment compared with late examples; their design is like that of the Bassae capital except that the inner and outer spirals join to form a scroll.[3]

Theodorus set the pattern for tholoi, both in that he utilized the conventions of temple architecture so far as they could be adapted to the round form, and that he gave his building a more decorative treatment than would then have been permissible in a temple. In the next generation the finest of all tholoi, according to ancient opinion, was begun in the sanctuary near Epidaurus [213–16]. The architect, so Pausanias states, was Polycleitus, presumably one of the sculptors of that name (unless Pausanias' statement is completely erroneous).[4] An inscription records the accounts of moneys received and spent on the building under a series of piecemeal contracts spread over nearly thirty years, as funds permitted; progress depended on gifts. The design may be dated about 360. Presumably for cheapness' sake, the building consisted of limestone, except where precision of carving was so important as to demand the use of marble. The tholos was somewhat larger than Theodorus's, with a diameter of 66 feet (21·82 m.). It was surrounded by three steps, interrupted by a sloping

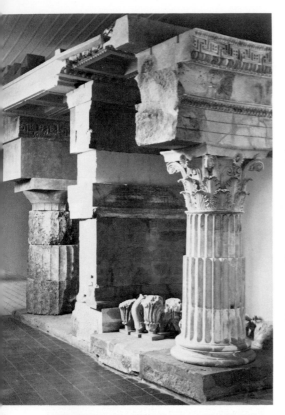

213-16. Epidaurus, tholos, mid fourth century, truncated reconstruction from within (*left*), coffer from ceiling (*below*), external entablature (*bottom*), and plan (*opposite*)

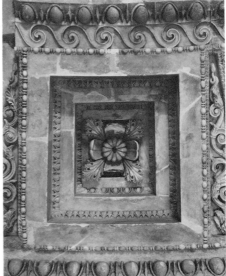

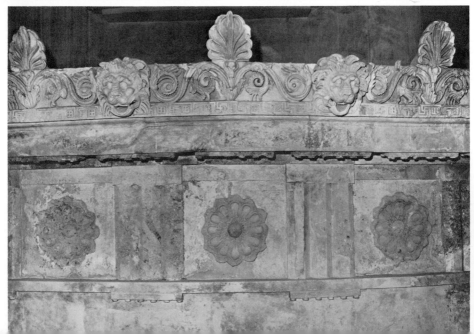

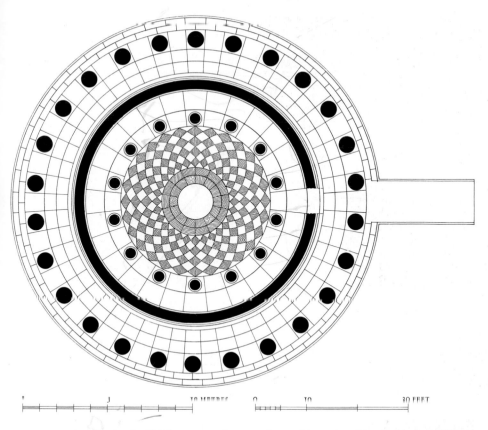

causeway at the entrance [216]. The twenty-six columns of the pteron were not quite so closely spaced, an economy made possible only by the flatter arc. The frieze contained metopes carved with a large rosette in the middle. The marble gutter was lavishly adorned with ornament based upon the foliage of the acanthus; the plant which had inspired the decoration of the Corinthian capital was still a subject for study, as is confirmed by the introduction of the cauliculus in capitals designed contemporaneously for the temple at Tegea. The antefixes, which edged the tiled roof behind the gutter, are shaped like palmettes, but their foliage is curly instead of stiff as in earlier examples; this too was due to the influence of acanthus ornament. The cella wall was stuccoed white except for a black base

on the outside, and a white marble top and base on the inside; the artist Pausias is recorded to have painted frescoes on the stucco. Fourteen Corinthian columns of marble stood within the cella, 3 feet away from the wall. Their capitals[5] are extraordinarily dainty but otherwise have more in common with those of later times than have any others of the fourth century. To a large extent the bell is left exposed, and the foliage, naturalistically carved, therefore looks as though it were growing against a background of the bare stone. A flower at the centre of each side touches the abacus, a precedent generally followed in later Corinthian; the petals are carefully separated. The stems of the spirals are cut entirely free from the upper half of the bell, and the bent tops of the leaves are very thin. This delicate sort of ornament was too fragile to survive the ultimate collapse of the building, but a capital of the same design, found outside, remains in perfect condition; probably it was a copy, made long afterwards for some unknown reason. The frieze of the Corinthian Order is curved into a wave-moulding, a common feature in subsequent buildings. Most of the cella was paved with black and white slabs of rhomboidal shape, alternating in an elaborate pattern, but at the centre a pit in the floor gave access to a labyrinthine crypt.[6]

A pair of windows on either side of the doorway allowed some indirect light to enter the cella. The roof was a single cone, rising from the outer entablature, rather than in two stages, a main roof over the cella, and a lower roof from pteron to cella wall. It culminated in an elaborate acroterion of floral form. The coffers of the ceiling slabs retain traces of paintings, and in one row [214] the centre of each was carved into a flower; the geometrical reproduction in stone of carpentry, which had satisfied the Greeks for so long, was not enough for the increasing vulgarity of the age, though the ceiling panels of the tholos took more complex and interesting shapes than in a rectangular building.

A smaller tholos, the Philippeum at Olympia, was built about 335 B.C. to house the statues of the Macedonian royal family [153, 154]. Its pteron was Ionic, and gives further evidence of the breaking-down of the old conventions, in that a row of dentils was placed above the frieze.[7] This seems to be the earliest instance of combination of the two originally incompatible elements in the structure. Corinthian half-columns[8] were engaged in the inner face of the cella wall, and can have performed no structural duty, whereas those in the tholos of Theodorus and at Epidaurus may conceivably have supported a division between open and ceilinged parts of the building. In the Philippeum the roof – again a single overall cone – terminated in a bronze poppy-head which masked the ends of the beams, as Pausanias states.

The Choragic Monument of Lysicrates at Athens may conveniently be included here because it offers a contemporary representation of a tholos, though adapted to a small scale and fantastically treated, and because it shows a

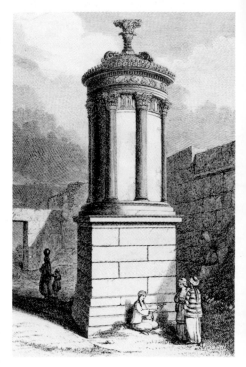

217 (*above*) and 218 (*opposite*). Athens, Choragic Monument of Lysicrates, late fourth century, with elevation of part of the monument

further development of the Corinthian Order [217, 218]. The lower part consists of a square base of limestone, faced in the highest course with bluish marble from Hymettus; and upon this stands a cylindrical structure of white marble, like a miniature tholos; six Corinthian columns are engaged beneath an architrave, a sculptured frieze, a row of miniature dentils, and a wide cornice. The roof is slightly convex, and a mass of acanthus foliage rises from the centre; upon the spreading top of this foliage

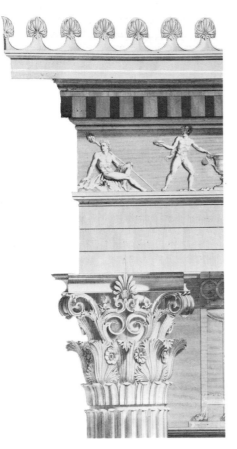

foliage and the heavy scrolls which pointed upward towards the feet of the tripod, 54 feet above the ground.

This is probably the oldest building in which Corinthian columns are used externally, and it may have set the pattern for the Order; at any rate the conjunction of frieze and small dentils became normal in Corinthian façades. The design of the capitals[11] is unusually elongated, in keeping with the whole monument. Flowers like poppies are carved between the upper row of leaves, which alone imitate the acanthus. The lower leaves are rush-like, long and slender, and curve over at the tip; such leaves often occur in late Greek ornament, in which they are placed alternating with acanthus.

The Monument of Lysicrates is, of course, a folly, and no building intended for practical use can have been so whimsical – it may, in fact, be legitimately described as baroque. But the growth of a tendency towards the baroque can be detected in the architecture of the fourth century, especially in the tholoi, because their more or less secular functions gave partial exemption from the austere conventions that governed the design of temples. Lysicrates's Monument is the extreme instance of the tendency, mainly owing to the complete freedom from convention given by the personal nature of the dedication, its lack of function, and an unsanctified site (the road to the theatre precinct). But the wholesale divergence between the apparent and the true structure was inspired by the minor divergences which had been introduced by the past two generations into real buildings, such as the tholoi and the temple at Tegea.

The remains of a poorly preserved circular building of late-fourth-century date have been found at Samothrace, c. $13\frac{1}{2}$ feet (4.10 m.) in diameter. As restored, it has a lower section with doorway, capped by a simple moulded crown leading to an upper section decorated with engaged Doric half-columns (a form found later at the Bouleuterium of Miletus) and surmounted by a conical roof. A better known tholos of novel design, called the Arsinoeum, was built at

stood the bronze tripod, a cauldron on a tall triple stand, which was the prize won by Lysicrates in 334 when he provided a chorus in the theatre. The circular part of the monument is hollow: the latest study has suggested that there was originally a door to the east; there are traces of a former step in the adjacent columns; the diameter is barely 7 feet. The columns[9] conceal the joints between the various slabs of the cylindrical wall; and each panel between them consists of one slab, including the top portion with the carvings of tripods. The roof,[10] which is carved to simulate bay-leaf thatching, is made of a single block, together with the acanthus

Samothrace shortly before 270 [219]. The foundation exceeds 20 m. in diameter. On the upper part of the circumference stood pillars, between marble screens, among which some windows may have been interspersed; the exterior was given a Doric treatment, but Corinthian half-columns were engaged in the inner face of the pillars. The lower parts of the screens were filled by parapets carved with saucers and bulls' skulls, differently arranged on the exterior and interior. The roof[12] was covered with terracotta tiles of scale shape, like the leaves represented on Lysicrates's Monument; it terminated in a pierced finial which acted as a ventilator. Scale-shaped tiles were also used on a recently discovered tholos at Argos, the finial of which consisted of acanthus foliage. This building contained a well and was accordingly termed a nymphaeum, as is known from an inscription upon the frieze. The excavators provisionally suggest a date in the second century. There is a small circular building at Paros, whose walls were subsequently moved and re-erected. 12¼ feet (3·752 m.) in diameter, it had no surrounding colonnade, but was decorated with a Doric triglyph frieze.

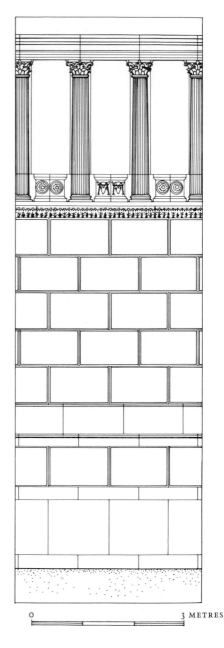

219. Samothrace, Arsinoeum, shortly before 270, restoration of interior

0   3 METRES

CHAPTER 18

TEMPLES AND TOMBS OF 400–330

In the previous chapter, two of the achievements of the fourth century are described, the perfecting of the tholos and of the Corinthian capital; two others were the perfecting of the Ionic temple and the adaptation of the temple form to tombs. This last event occurred in Asia Minor and the idea may not have been entirely Greek. In Athens the most sumptuous type of funerary monument at 400 consisted merely of a niche filled with sculpture, and framed by pilasters and a pediment. These were normally placed with other types of monument or marker, on a raised walled enclosure, a peribolos, generally rectangular in plan. In other cities, where suitable cliffs existed, the wealthier Greeks had long favoured tombs cut in the rock, with façades resembling the porch of a house or of a temple. There are splendid and idiosyncratic examples at Cyrene, from the sixth century to the Hellenistic age. The Lycians, a people who spoke an altogether different language but to some extent adopted Greek ways, had habitually cut tombs in the form of their own peculiar wooden-framed houses (though later examples use the concept of the Greek porch, with Ionic columns). The new temple tomb is used by them, particularly for their ruling dynasts. The inspiration may have come from the Persian Empire, of which they were nominal subjects, and in particular the tomb of Cyrus the Great; there are early tombs in the form of pillars, and sarcophagi mounted on high podia, but now the superstructure over the high podium employs the regular forms of Greek architecture. The supreme example of the type, the Mausoleum at Halicarnassus, was built by a whole team of Greeks for the king of another foreign race, the Carians, and it is questionable whether such tombs would have evolved in Greece. But the splendour of the Mausoleum ensured their adoption throughout the classical world.

An early example of the new form is the Nereid Monument.[1] This has been dated by its architectural details to around 400. It stood on a cliff overlooking the Lycian town of Xanthus, and took the form of an Ionic temple measuring 22 by 33 feet (6·80 by 10·17 m.), raised upon a solid base, whose greatest height was $26\frac{1}{2}$ feet (8·107 m.). The base is still standing in part, but the building upon it was destroyed by earthquakes; the ornamental portions were collected and shipped to the British Museum in 1842, and a complete reconstruction of the front is now exhibited. This is almost certainly correct in placing together two long bands of continuous sculpture, one above the other, immediately below the cornice that edged the top of the base. The cornice is decorated with two rows of egg-and-tongue moulding; the upward surfaces of the same blocks bear marks where columns and statues were embedded in alternation along all four sides of a platform. The statues – female figures in wind-blown drapery, with sea-creatures at their feet – must represent Nereids or Aurae (Breezes); the intercolumniations were made unusually wide to allow space for them. The pteron, of four columns on the shorter and six on the longer sides, bears an architrave carved with a third sculptured frieze, on which rest dentils; the pediments are filled with sculpture, figures stood as acroteria above the peak and corners of each gable, while the gutter is enriched by lion-head water-spouts. Some statues of lions, found lying about the site, had obviously fallen off either the platform or the roof. The cella, with its shallow porch and opisthodomus, raised upon a solid base which contained the burial chamber, was surrounded at the top by a fourth frieze. There was a doorway at either end; inside were couches of stone. There are consoles beside the cella doorways. The upper surface of the broad antae is carved with rosettes, beneath a bead-and-reel moulding and a series of three wave-mouldings. A coffered ceiling, between the colonnade and the walls, was painted with bead-and-reel and egg-and-tongue patterns, while the central panel of one coffer still bears traces of a painting of a female head. (Some metopes from Cyrene, belonging to a later tomb of the fourth century, are painted with groups of figures.)

So far as Doric temples were concerned, the perfection which the architects of the fifth century had attained left their successors very little scope for originality if similar proportions were retained. The first to be changed were the proportions of the plan, by the expedient of truncating or omitting the opisthodomus. Among the pioneers in this respect was Theodotus, who designed the temple of Asclepius at Epidaurus about 370. He placed the entrance of the porch opposite the third column on the side and ended the cella with a blank wall, opposite the penultimate column. The interior of the cella contained a colonnade which can only have been for decoration; the small size of the temple makes it unnecessary for structural reasons. Other, later and even smaller temples at Epidaurus similarly possess decorative interior colonnades, in the Corinthian order. That in the temple of Asclepius has not survived, but it is reasonable to assume that it set the pattern by employing the Corinthian order. Externally, there were only eleven columns on the side, accompanying the usual number of six on the ends, and the temple must therefore have looked thick-set, since no attempt was made to compensate for its shortness by tricks.[2] The pteron in a temple of Apollo at Thebes, with six by twelve columns, must have looked more satisfactory at a distance, but the greater length of side was due to a vestigial opisthodomus which may have appeared ridiculous at close quarters, for the columns in antis stood just beside the back wall of the cella.

Perhaps as a result of disappointment at such experiments, the temple of Artemis at Calydon was built about 360 on the fifth-century type of plan, with a pteron of six by thirteen columns

and a full-sized opisthodomus (and a temple of similar plan, perhaps by the same architect, at Molycrium, in the same part of Greece). But a decadence in architectural sense is clearly shown in the temple of Apollo at Delphi, which reproduced the elongated plan (with six by fifteen columns) of its predecessor, destroyed in 373, and incorporated much of the old material, repaired where necessary with patches of stucco. At both Calydon and Delphi, innovations were restricted to minor features. The gutter at Delphi was perpendicular instead of convex, and above the intervals between the lion-head spouts stood antefixes; previously antefixes and gutters had not been used in conjunction, but the taste of the age demanded more abundant decoration and in greater variety. Heads of hounds instead of lions formed the water-spouts at Calydon, and set a precedent for later temples of Artemis the huntress.

The temple of Athena at Tegea [220], which Scopas, the famous sculptor, built after 350,[3] ranked among the best in Greece; Pausanias thought it the finest and largest in the Peloponnese.[4] Its reputation seems to have been due largely to such incidentals as the pedimental sculpture and the ornate treatment of the cella, in which Corinthian half-columns were engaged along both side walls, but the basic factor of success must have been the excellent proportions. The opisthodomus was almost as deep as the porch, while the cella was unusually long, with the result that the pteron comprised six by fourteen columns. The choice of an even number for the side was presumably dictated by the provision of a doorway into the cella at the centre of the north side; ramps crossed the steps here and at the main entrance on the east end. The columns were more slender than in any previous temple, over six times as high as the lower diameter, and carried a relatively low entablature. If the restoration is correct, the Corinthian colonnades in the cella, like those at Epidaurus, can have had no function other than decoration; the wall is drawn wider above the architrave, making the face stand flush with the capitals. Comparison with the engaged Ionic

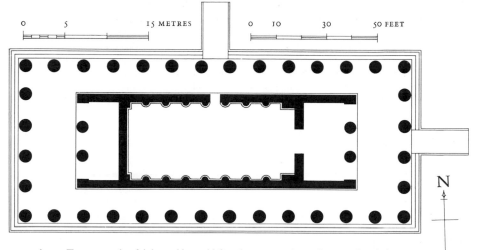

220 and 221. Tegea, temple of Athena Alea, mid fourth century, plan and restored capital

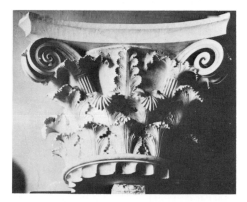

colonnades at Bassae, which narrowed the span of the cella, illustrates the tendency towards the separation of form from structure, so apparent in the round buildings of the time. The capitals at Tegea [221][5] are exceptionally squat, and their design is correspondingly peculiar. There would scarcely have been height enough for the usual pair of spirals in the centre of each side; instead a single acanthus leaf stands upright in their place, and the vacant space beside them was reduced by making the angle spirals spring from a fluted sheath, the cauliculus. This new feature (borrowed from the natural form of the plant) became an almost indispensable element in the Corinthian capitals of later times.

Very occasionally the Greeks built temples on a roughly square plan, without a pteron, and two such at Delos can be dated close to 350. Like others of this type, they consisted of a porch and a cella of greater width than depth. The façade of the smaller held four columns *in antis*, and that of the larger ten columns prostyle, of the Ionic Order.

Ionic reached its highest development in several large temples begun about 350. The best-known (chiefly because some of the remains were brought to the British Museum and to Berlin) is that of Athena Polias at Priene. It was dedicated by Alexander the Great.[6] Pythius, its architect, who also designed the Mausoleum at Halicarnassus, wrote a book on this temple, the proportions of which were exceptionally systematic. The plan [222] was traditional, comprising a pteron of six by eleven columns, a deep porch and shallow opisthodomus (as in the archaic temple at Naxos), each with two columns *in antis*, and a cella reached by steps from the porch. The opisthodomus may result from a later completion of

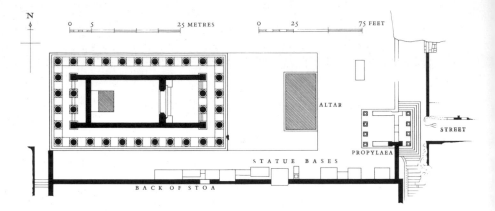

222. Priene, sanctuary of Athena Polias, dedicated 334 or subsequently, restored plan

the temple. A pedestal at the far end of the cella, on which stood the cult image, was not added before the middle of the second century, and its surroundings, too, may have been left unfinished till then. The building was clearly designed in multiples of a foot equal to 294 mm., nearly half an inch shorter than the English foot. In the following, I quote all dimensions in terms of the ancient measure. The larger proportions work out in simple ratios. The width: length ratio was as near 1 : 2 as was compatible with equal intercolumniations. The desired relationship was obtained along a line drawn through the axes of the pteron columns, with 60 by 120 feet. The axial spacing of the columns was 12 feet; their bases stood on square plinths, 6 feet wide and 6 feet apart, and so the overall dimensions of the platform came to 66 by 126 feet (19·53 by 37·17 m.), making the ratio of end to side 11 : 21. The antae of the porch and opisthodomus stood opposite the penultimate columns of the ends and sides, and were each 4 feet square; consequently the rectangle they enclosed within them measured 40 by 100 feet. The interior of the cella was 50 feet long. An unusual alternation of courses, two tall followed by two low, varied the construction of the walls. The roof was covered with terracotta tiles.[7]

The Order of the temple is an example of Ionic at its most classic [223-5]; although some elements, notably the use of plinths below the column bases, remained optional in later times, this may be regarded as the nearest equivalent to a canonical form in an Order which never attained complete definition. The column bases belong to the Asiatic type, placed on square plinths (square plinths had been used at Ephesus, circular ones for the Ionic columns of the Propylaea at Athens). The spira (the lower part of the base) consists of two concave mouldings between three pairs of convex pipings, a scheme adapted from the sixth-century Artemisium at Ephesus. The torus (which overlies the spira) is fluted horizontally on the under surface of the curve, but the top is left smooth, either from intent or because the carving was never completed. The spreading foot of the shaft does not curve evenly like a normal apophyge, but is broken into three parts – a convex moulding at the bottom, a low fillet with a perpendicular face, and a small apophyge which curves steeply upwards to the flutes. There are the usual twenty-four deep flutes separated by fillets which keep the general curve of the shaft. The flutes fade out at the top below a smaller apophyge crowned with another perpendicular fillet, upon which rests a convex moulding carved with bead-and-reel pattern. The capital is carved with the already traditional ornament – egg-and-dart on the echinus, a

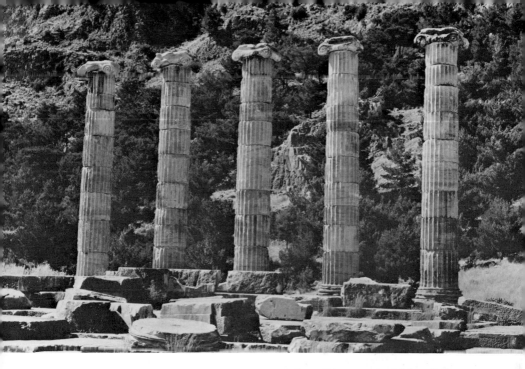

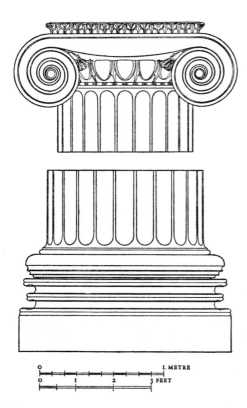

223 and 224. Priene, temple of Athena Polias, dedicated 334 or subsequently, re-erected columns, and capital and base

palmette masking the junction of echinus and volute, and a leaf-pattern on the 'Lesbian' (convex) moulding of the abacus. The cushion between the volutes sags over the echinus, whereas in later times the line is tautened, and the eye of the volute is placed only a trifle further out than the edge of the shaft, a position transitional between the extreme out-thrust in the Artemisium and the flush setting of Hellenistic Ionic. Capitals from the inner corners of the colonnades are supplied with complete though abbreviated volutes instead of the usual intersecting volutes, but at the cost of some distortion.

From the lowest fascia of the architrave to the cornice,[8] every step upward involves farther projection outwards. Above the third fascia run in turn an astragal, a row of egg-and-dart, the dentils, another astragal and another row of egg-and-dart; then comes the cornice, a plain band crowned by a small convex moulding and a flat fillet. The total height of the entablature is only seven Ionic feet, owing to the lack of a frieze, a

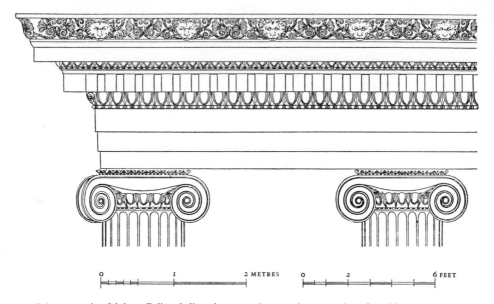

225. Priene, temple of Athena Polias, dedicated 334 or subsequently, restoration of entablature

feature which had not yet become admissible in temples among the eastern Greeks, although they had already built tombs with a frieze. At Priene the lowness of the entablature has been criticized as incompatible with the great height of the columns, 38½ Ionic feet; this is almost nine times as high as the width of the lower diameter (not excessive for Ionic), but Pythius may have decided that a heavier entablature would have seemed to overload the columns. Certainly an architect so occupied with the theory of design would have given adequate attention to a proportion of such consequence.

His thoughtfulness is evident throughout the building. The disposition of the waterspouts may serve for an example. Amid the luxuriant ornament of the gutter, where palmettes alternate with a foliated pattern derived from the acanthus plant, the lion-head spouts cannot have been as conspicuous as on a Doric temple, but they took an important part in binding the design together. Three were allotted to each intercolumniation, one over the centre, the

other two over the eyes of the volutes; moreover the column shaft tapered in such a manner that at half its height the side passed under the eye of the volute. Three points, therefore, stood in a perpendicular line on either side of the perpendicular centre of each column. The arrangement of the spouts in threes accords with the division of the architrave into three fasciae, and the repetition above it of two more triple schemes, the first consisting of astragal, egg-and-dart and dentils, the second of astragal, egg-and-dart and cornice; moreover the cornice itself is tripartite.

Another and more famous work by Pythius, the Mausoleum at Halicarnassus, was built in collaboration with an architect called Satyrus. A book which they wrote jointly must have been the ultimate source of the summary descriptions by Vitruvius and Pliny. (Pythius's name as the architect of the Mausoleum is restored from the manuscript reading in Vitruvius.) The construction of the tomb is known to have been far advanced before Mausolus' death in 353 and completed four or more years later. The entire structure was demolished many centuries ago, for the purpose of re-using the material, but thousands of carved fragments were collected in the 1850s and taken to the British Museum.[9] With the aid of those most readily fitted together, as well as the ancient descriptions, it became evident that the building had consisted of three parts, of which the lower two together recall the entire 'Nereid Monument'. On a very tall base stood thirty-six Ionic columns in temple-like arrangement. Upon all this was imposed a pyramidal formation of twenty-four steps, ending 140 feet above ground in a platform occupied by a sculptured group of a chariot and four horses. Three carved friezes and a large number of individual statues, of

human figures, horsemen, and lions, were distributed around the base and the central portion; four of the most distinguished sculptors of Greece are recorded to have been employed – Bryaxis, Leochares, Timotheus, and Scopas (or, according to Vitruvius, Praxiteles). Many scholars have attempted to envisage the manner in which all these components of the monuments were disposed but their solutions differed radically and in some cases involved structural improbabilities. The evidence was, in fact, hopelessly inadequate till 1972, when Jeppesen's re-excavation of the site enabled him to supply an accurate ground-plan to his collaborator, Waywell, who thereupon arrived at a satisfactory restoration (in, of course, broad outline) [226] deduced from his own study of

226. Halicarnassus, Mausoleum, completed *c.* 349

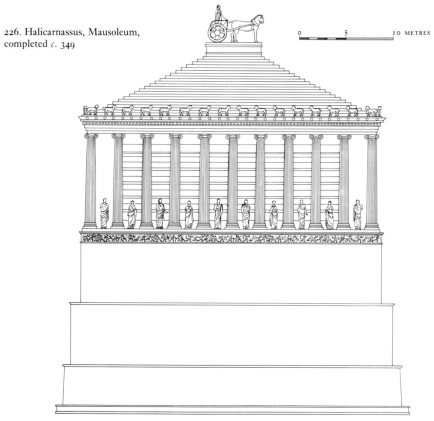

0 ___ 5 ___ 10 METRES

the sculptural fragments.[10] The monument was rectangular rather than square. It had eleven by nine columns, giving a stylobate dimension of 105 by 85 feet (32 by 26 m.). The base, however, was 126 by 105 feet (38·4 by 32 m.), so that the podium must have contracted between base and summit. Waywell suggests that was achieved in three 'steps', and that it was on these steps that the series of free-standing statues were placed: there were also free-standing statues, interpreted by Waywell as representations of Mausolus' ancestors, male and female, between the columns, in the manner of the 'Nereid Monument'. There was also a series of lions over the entablature, at the foot of the crowning pyramid.

The Lion Tomb, built on a steep promontory in Cnidian territory, not far from Halicarnassus, seems to have been an imitation of the Mausoleum [227]. The lower portion was square, plain at the foot but ornamented higher up with engaged columns of the Doric Order; above rose a stepped pyramid, which culminated in a platform occupied by a colossal statue of a lion, now in the British Museum. The total height came to at least 40 feet. The lower portion was mainly hollow; it contained a circular room and eleven small burial chambers radiating therefrom. The walls of the room were corbelled inwards till the gap could be closed by a flat ceiling of blocks cut with tapered sides. The date could be contemporary with the Mausoleum or as much as – some would say more than – a hundred years later.[11] The choice of a lion, the conventional symbol for valour, and of a remote position overlooking the sea, suggests that the monument commemorated a naval battle.[12] The Mausoleum (and particularly its burial chamber) may have influenced the series of Macedonian tombs described in the next chapter, which appears to begin around the middle of the fourth century.

The ornamental part of a tomb built with engaged Ionic columns seems to be represented on a sarcophagus found in the royal burial-cave at Sidon [228]. In the position of the carved frieze underneath, the sculptor followed a precedent set, in all likelihood, by both the 'Nereid Monument' and the Mausoleum, of which it is a near contemporary. The figures of mourning women between the columns, moreover, occupy a position corresponding to that of the 'Nereid' statues. The frieze that runs along the top of the sarcophagus recalls the sculptured gutter-parapet used in the sixth-century Artemisium at Ephesus, and may well conform to contemporary practice in Asia Minor. For in a few temples of the Roman Empire a carved attic remains in place, and continuity of usage may be presumed. But on an actual building the attic would be relatively much lower than the sculptor has made it.

Fire destroyed the Artemisium in 356, and the Ephesians quickly began to build a new Ionic temple on the same spot; Paeonius of Ephesus, and a slave of the temple, Demetrius, seem to have been the original architects, with the possibly later addition of Deinocrates. Pliny's statement that completion was delayed 120 years may refer to the previous building, but applies better to the later, so far as the almost equally scanty remains go to show; these are mostly in the British Museum. In order to utilize the old work as foundations, the floor level was raised and the plan repeated[13] without perceptible alteration except for the replacement of the opisthodomus by a closed adytum, the addition of a third row of columns at the front, and the unavoidable increase in the number of steps. The elevation[14] conformed to the practice of the time, except for imitating a peculiarity of the old design, the sculptured bases of certain columns. In the later Artemisium groups of figures, well over life-size, were carved not only on cylindrical bases[15] but also on square pedestals; the two shapes were probably used in different parts of the building as alternatives, and not in conjunction under the same column. Pliny states the number of sculptured columns as thirty-six, with reference probably to this temple rather than to its predecessor. He quotes for the height of the columns 60 feet, equivalent to 58 English feet (17·65 m.), a figure which presumably refers to

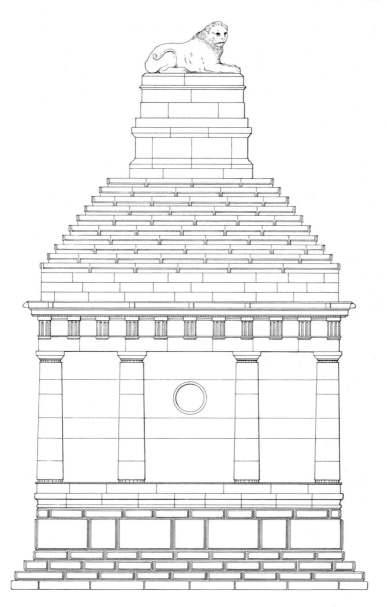

227. Cnidus, Lion Tomb, probably Hellenistic, restored elevation (height 63 feet overall)

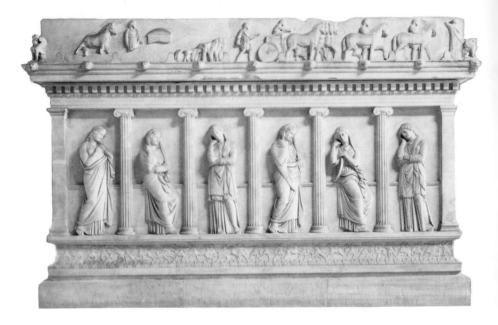

228 (A) and (B). Sarcophagus of mourners
from Sidon, mid fourth century. *Istanbul Museum*

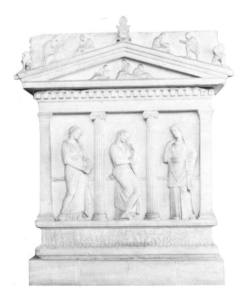

the later temple. One novel feature of the temple
is known from representations on late coins of
Ephesus; three apertures are shown in the back
wall of the pediment, comparable to the single
window in the inner gables of the temple of
'Concord' [208]. The purpose must have been
to reduce the weight in view of the enormous
central span. It is not clear whether or not there
was pediment sculpture in front of these. It has
been suggested that this temple, as well as its
predecessor, had an unroofed cella.

In Greece,[16] a great temple, that of Zeus at
Nemea, was completed about 330 or soon after
(if we may trust the dating of pottery found in
a near-by kiln where the tiles for the roof were
baked). The unknown architect improved on
the precedent of Bassae by making a free-
standing internal colonnade return across the
cella by means of two widely-spaced columns
instead of one at the centre, so as again to mark
off the semblance of an adytum – with good
reason, because at Nemea the space at the back
contains a pit and a flight of steps leading into
it (presumably in order that offerings might still

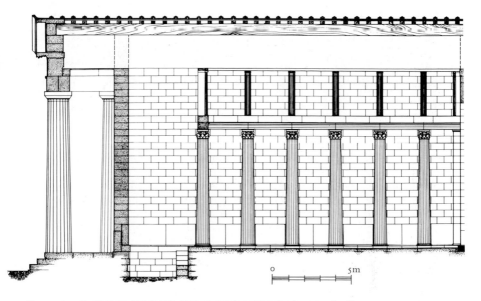

229. Nemea, temple of Zeus, late fourth century, section through adytum and cella

be placed on an especially hallowed spot which had, in fact, been level with the floor of the older temple he replaced). Whether remembrance of Bassae also accounts for the use of two Orders in the cella is questionable, since they were mingled in a different way [229]; on all three sides an upper Ionic colonnade stood upon one that was Corinthian, in detail imitative of the half-columns which ran up the full height at Tegea. It has been suggested that this arrangement might be due to Macedonian prototypes.[17] The Nemea temple was otherwise Doric throughout and singularly austere, with none of the ornament lavished on Tegea, though the design clearly owed much to Scopas' work there (already almost, if not quite, completed). The width chosen for Nemea was a trifle greater, but the lack of an opisthodomus enabled the length to be reduced; the Doric pteron therefore comprised six by twelve columns instead of six by fourteen as at Tegea. The Doric columns of the pteron [230, 231], a little more slender than those at Tegea, are $6\frac{1}{3}$ times as high as their lower diameter; compared

with the columns of the Parthenon, the height (34 feet) is almost identical, the width one foot less, the spacing from axis to axis two feet closer. The reduction in thickness, which is technically the more remarkable since the material is a limestone, lightens the appearance very noticeably. In the capital the echinus is so low that the side had scarcely room to curve [94]. In this temple, therefore, the transition to Hellenistic Doric is clearly perceptible; the columns were already so slim that a smaller frieze of the Hellenistic type would probably have been advantageous.

An extraordinary and fatuous essay in the application of mathematics to architecture has been revealed by investigating fragmentary remains at Delphi which have proved to belong to the Doric Treasury of Cyrene; the base, at least, seems to have been completed before 334 (though the mathematical complexities should not be regarded as certain, and much of the detail is in fact normal practice at Cyrene). It is suggested that the architect apparently worked out his design in units of two distinct measures,

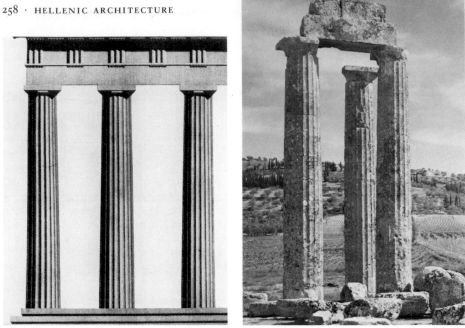

230 and 231. Nemea, Temple of Zeus, late fourth century, order at front, and columns

the foot and the dactyl (finger). He gave his columns a lower diameter of 30 and a height of 208 dactyls, figures equal respectively to ten times the square root of nine and one hundred times its cube root. (The number nine was receiving much attention from contemporary mathematicians.) The lower and upper diameters of the shaft, moreover, were related as the square roots of three and two, while the heights of architrave and frieze were related as the diagonals of a square and of its cube. To what extent aesthetic demands were sacrificed to these intellectual sports can hardly be decided, since the building can be seen only on paper. These suggestions run counter, in many ways, to the established practices of Greek architects. Features which are part of the architectural tradition of Cyrene include the following. Beneath the echinus of the capitals came a moulding like the apophyge whereby an Ionic shaft spreads towards its base. Across the top of each metope ran a cavetto (concave) moulding, painted with leaves. The cornice rose from an elaborate Ionic moulding, richly ornamented. A half-column was attached at either end of the façade to an anta which would otherwise have been only half as long in front as on the side, but the capital was continuous over both shaft and anta in spite of their partial separation. There are many instances of these peculiarities in the fourth century and Hellenistic tombs at Cyrene, which often have elaborate architectural façades.

In general, though, architects seem to have concentrated their attention on Ionic when Pythius had revitalized that Order by devising a more harmonious synthesis of its constituent parts. He must have been still active when the successor of Mausolus, Idrieus, made extensive improvements to the sanctuary of Zeus at Labranda (since this happened before the building of the temple at Priene), including a delightful but rather eccentric temple (its eccentricities have been explained as the result of adding a pteron to an older in antis temple, which, if it existed, must have been demolished to foundation level);[18] it was given eight Ionic columns on the sides and six on the ends. An Ionic Order resembling that of Priene has been found at the temple of Hemithea at Castabus,[19] where the pteron comprised twelve columns by six. The porch was square, and the cella precisely twice as long; a shrine stood within, towards the back. Behind the steep edge of the sanctuary ran a screen, diversified by rectangular panels framed with mouldings, and interrupted at the corner by a building like a diminutive temple. This work, at least, might well be Hellenistic; on the other hand, the niches at Messene [294] offer a partial analogy, for which, indeed, a Hellenistic dating has been proposed, though in my opinion wrongly.

In Greece, Ionic seems to have been considered only one degree less frivolous than Corinthian, so that it could not be used on the exteriors of temples, but it became popular for lesser buildings, even in sanctuaries. The influence of Bassae can be discerned in some experimental capitals and bases, but soon the Attic type of base was generally accepted; capitals tend to be squat, and shafts bear twenty flutes instead of the canonical twenty-four. Practical advantages may account for these characteristics of 'Peloponnesian Ionic' (examples are mainly concentrated in the Argolid or Corinthia); since the material was normally limestone or even poros, only relatively coarse detail would stay sharp when exposed to the weather.

CHAPTER 19

HELLENISTIC TEMPLES AND RELATED MONUMENTS

The conquest of Egypt and Western Asia, which Alexander completed in 330, quickly affected the design of temples. The old Greek cities of Asia Minor became prosperous again, and new cities arose with a mixed population of Greeks and Hellenized orientals. Consequently Greek architecture spread throughout the civilized world, but the traditional conventions of the art lost some of their hold; in the East, quite early in the diffusion, architectural progress allowed liberties which did not conform with the taste of contemporary Greece. But the division between the pure Hellenic style and the forms to which it was adapted for Hellenized communities can never have corresponded to any geographical boundaries, so that freedom of design became universal in this Hellenistic Age. Even in its later stages, however, some purist architect might build a temple in close adherence to the ancient principles.

The development of the Hellenistic temple and of related architectural concepts is by no means clear. The problem is complicated in the first place by divergences of taste, whether the architect's or the client's, because of which it may happen that two buildings of the same date, one of them conservative and the other not, appear to belong to different periods. There was also the possibility of variable influence (perhaps unconscious rather than deliberate) from the non-Greek architecture which now became even more familiar to the Greeks. It must be remembered that in Hellenistic Egypt buildings in the Egyptian style were being built, and used by Greeks as well as Egyptians. If a great many of these buildings had survived, there might be no serious difficulty in establishing the sequence, but actually more temples of each of the three preceding centuries are extant than of the entire Hellenistic Age, from 330 to the time of Christ. Such remains as exist are often in poor condition, and only in rare instances have they been adequately studied. This neglect is consistent with the usual attitude of scholars; by normal classical standards, such buildings tend to lack interest and may even seem repulsive.

On average, the Hellenistic temples follow early precedent only superficially, as a result of the continual evolution of the Orders, a process which did not approach finality till late in the second century. In Doric particularly the Hellenistic changes (summarized in Chapter 10) transformed the proportional balance of the temple. The column shafts became so thin and the entablature so low as to give the building a sense of upward movement, and the precise shape of all features above the shafts mattered comparatively little, especially considering the smaller scale of capitals, frieze, etc. Changes in Ionic and Corinthian had less drastic effects, since the columns had always been slighter than in Doric, but involved a similar reduction in the scale of capitals; the height of the entablature, however, became greater, owing to acceptance of the frieze as a customary feature instead of dentils alone. All the Orders, in fact, now gave much the same effect in elevation. And in all three a greater range of variation was allowed in decoration. As for the plans of temples, religious conservatism preserved the traditional scheme of arrangement, except in comparatively few cases. Originality was freer in other types of building more or less imitative of temples, such as propylons, altars, honorific monuments, and tombs.

The influence of the Mausoleum is very clear in the case of a tomb at Belevi, which may date from the fourth century or may have been built for Antiochus II, who died near by at Smyrna in 246. The lower part, a podium nearly 100 feet square, contained a burial-chamber covered with a barrel-vault, and externally was plain except for a Doric entablature. Corinthian columns stood above, eight along each side, and colossal statues occupied the intercolumniations; the coffers of the ceiling bear sculpture in relief. The cornices were lined with statues – of men and horses at the corners, and along the remainder of each side were three pairs of griffins, heraldically confronted with vases in between them. These seem to have been placed against a background of masonry which tapered in some form to the top of the tomb.

The prevailing uncertainty of dating obscures the formative period of Hellenistic temples. One which used to be placed in this period, the Metroum at Olympia [153, 154], is better dated to the beginning of the fourth century.[1] The unfinished temple of Zeus at Stratus can be placed at approximately 320. The pteron was Doric, and an inner colonnade, Ionic or Corinthian, stood close beside the cella walls; probably with an inclined ceiling.[2] A small temple of

Earth-Demeter at Acraephia, near the Ptoion, is not so closely datable, but was probably built late in the fourth century. It stood upon a platform wider than the building, as though a pteron had existed; but no traces of any such feature remain, and perhaps the surround served as an open terrace. Internally a row of pillars, 2 feet square, ran along the centre of the cella, in line with the doorway. No doubt this is an instance of provincial, not to say bucolic, work. A choicer example of a small temple, the Dodekatheon at Delos, built at the very end of the century in honour of the Twelve Gods, was a simplified version of the fifth-century Athenian temple of Apollo in the same sanctuary. A row of probably six Doric columns stood prostyle at either end. The angle triglyphs are wider than the others and seem to have projected farther forward from the metopes.

Like its archaic predecessor, the new temple of Apollo at Didyma, outside Miletus [232–7],

232. Didyma, temple of Apollo, fourth century and later, front and north side

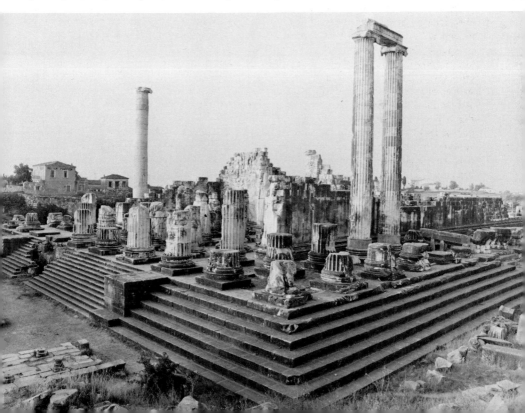

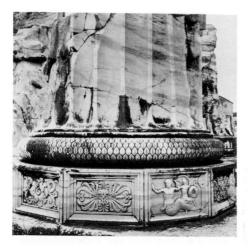

233. Didyma, temple of Apollo, fourth century and later, decorated column base from front

234. Didyma, temple of Apollo, fourth century and later, interior of cella with entrances and inner staircase

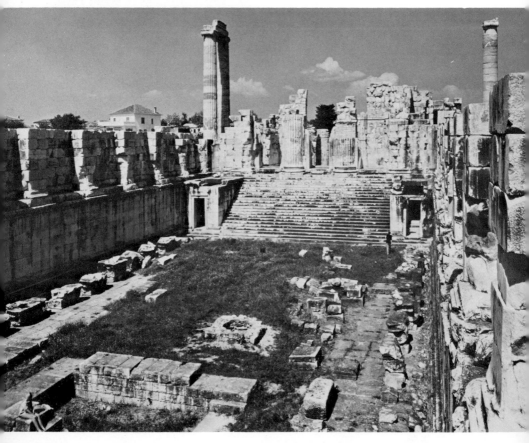

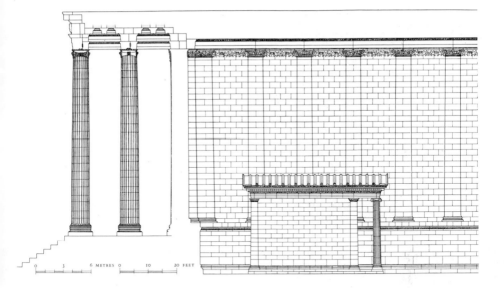

235 and 236. Didyma, temple of Apollo, fourth century and later, restored section through porch and part of court with side of shrine, and restored plan

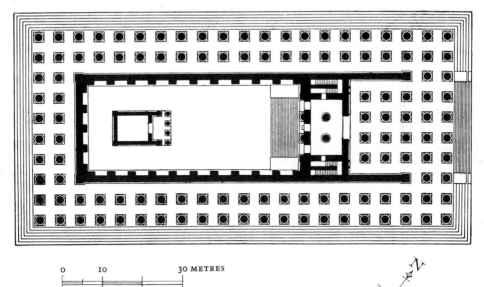

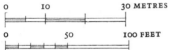

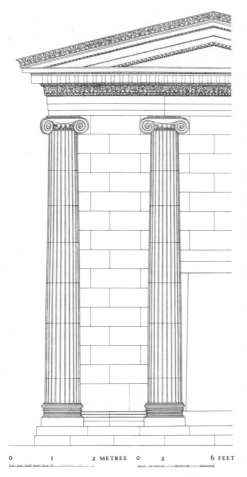

0   I   2 METRES   0   2   6 FEET

237. Didyma, temple of Apollo, fourth century and later, restored elevation of front of shrine

contained an open court, originally planted with bay trees, in which stood a shrine like a fair-sized Ionic temple, with both frieze and dentils; this building seems to date from the late fourth century, while most other parts of the temple are very much later. The architects are said to have been Paeonius of Ephesus, who is also recorded to have worked on the Artemisium there, and Daphnis of Miletus. Much of the plan may have been their work, though its

execution took well over 300 years, and was eventually abandoned during the Christian era. The Ionic double pteron stood on a platform raised seven huge steps above the ground, and 13 feet higher than the court within. The dimensions, 167 by 358 feet (51·13 by 109·34 m.), were exceeded only by the Heraeum of Samos, the two successive temples at Ephesus, and the Olympieum at Agrigento; the columns were the tallest in any Greek temple, with a height of over 64 feet (19·70 m.), and very slim, the height being equal to $9\frac{3}{4}$ times the lower diameter; they are evenly spaced at a distance exceeding 17 feet (5·30 m.), axis to axis.

On the front, instead of differentiation by spacing, different types of base are found; every column between the corner and the centre rests on an elaborately carved base,[3] to which a pair exists only in the corresponding positions beyond the centre. These bases, however, look extremely late. The frieze,[4] with Medusa heads among acanthus foliage, can scarcely be older than the Roman Empire, nor can the angle capitals,[5] which are carved with busts of deities upon the volutes, a bull's head at the centre, and winged monsters projecting instead of corner volutes. The columns in the rest of the pteron and in the deep porch stand on orthodox bases of the old type of Asia Minor. The back wall of the porch is set back behind a dado topped with a series of mouldings, including two richly carved convex pipings, which again seem Hellenistic. The doorway[6] in this wall opens nearly 5 feet above the porch, level with the floor of a room behind; perhaps the oracles for which Didyma had long been renowned were delivered from the threshold. A small doorway on either side allowed access from the porch to the court through a sloping tunnel, covered by a barrel-vault. Each vault supports a staircase which leads upwards from the supposed oracle room; the flat ceiling over the stairs is carved with a large-scale fret pattern, painted blue, and is edged with a red moulding. A magnificent flight of steps, 50 feet wide, led down from the room to the court. The walls of the court were plain to a height of $17\frac{1}{2}$ feet, at which level stood a row of pilasters, continued all round, except at the head of the steps, where two Corinthian half-columns[7] instead are engaged between the doorways. The capitals of the pilasters[8] are richly carved on the face with a variety of designs, above a moulding which connects the small volutes at either end. A strip carved with foliage and griffins ran between the pilaster capitals [238]. This work should probably be ascribed to late in the Hellenistic Age, together with the approaches to the court.

The temple of Artemis at Epidaurus,[9] built about 300, is small – only 27 feet (8·20 m.) wide – but received lavish treatment more suited to a larger building. Interest is concentrated on the front, where the altar is linked to the temple by a short paved walk and exterior ramp (the back is left plain). Six Doric columns are crammed into the restricted width; there were statuettes of Victory on the peak and corners of the roof, while the cella had a Corinthian internal colonnade. The large temple of Artemis-Cybele at Sardis, founded about 300, seems to have contained no walls before the middle of the second century and remained incomplete till three hundred years later. Among temples of the early third century,[10] a conventional Ionic building

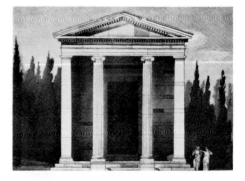

239. Cos, temple 'B', early third century, restoration

at Cos is worthy of mention only because enough remains to justify a restoration [239], and temple 'L' at Epidaurus for its conjunction of an Ionic pteron with a Corinthian internal colonnade.

At Samothrace a long propylon, built by Ptolemy II of Egypt (285–246), was entered at either end by a porch with six prostyle columns, Corinthian on the west, Ionic on the east [240], where gay capitals conformed with a Hellenistic tendency to bring the eye of the volute ever closer to the edge of the shaft and level with the

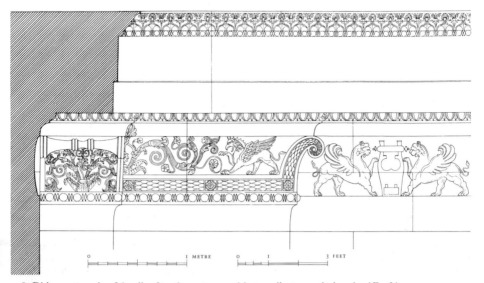

238. Didyma, temple of Apollo, fourth century and later, pilaster capital and griffin frieze

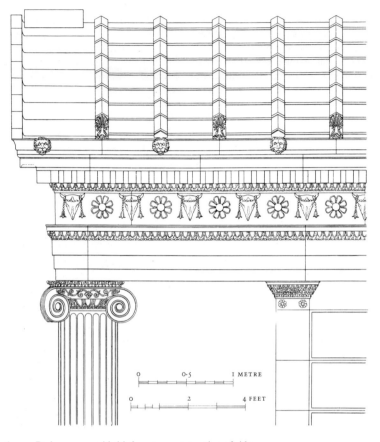

240. Samothrace, Ptolemaeum, mid third century, restoration of side

top of it. The substructure was built over a stream, which flowed through in an oblique barrel-vaulted culvert. This same Ptolemy built a small temple on Delos to Agathe Tyche (Good Fortune), with whom his wife, Arsinoe, was identified. The temple proper consisted of a prostyle porch with four Doric columns and a cella, but stood at the east end of a court, between other rooms, and from these ran colonnades to the west end of the court, which was therefore very narrow for its length. The prostyle columns were actually enframed by the ends of the colonnades, across a narrow passage which gave access to the rooms; the doorways

were slightly west of the wall that divided the porch and cella of the temple itself.

Another little Doric temple to Arsinoe, identified this time with Aphrodite, was built on Point Zephyrium, near Alexandria. This has been destroyed, and no full record exists. There was a pair of columns in front and a row of three columns on the side, separated by a pillar shaped into a half-column on each lateral face, but squared externally; the maximum dimension of the pillar was one metre in either direction to the centre of the half-column. The shafts were fluted only in the upper portion. In traditional Egyptian buildings, whether Ptolemaic or of the old native dynasties, it was customary to terminate a colonnade by square piers, without antae, and there is a possibility that the architect of the temple had that practice in mind.[11] But a scheme more comparable to the Egyptian occurred in a temple at Kourno, in the extreme south of Greece; a half-column was engaged only in the back of each pier, with which the side columns were aligned. The pteron comprised six by seven columns, making an exceptionally short plan. Although Doric, the shafts stood upon bases. Two metopes were placed above the interval between each pair of columns.[12]

The same allowance of two complete metopes and two halves to each intercolumniation appears in a fair-sized Doric temple at Pergamon, dedicated to Athena Polias Nicephorus ('Bringer of Victory'). In other respects the design is old-fashioned, and a date rather early in the third century seems most likely; scholars began

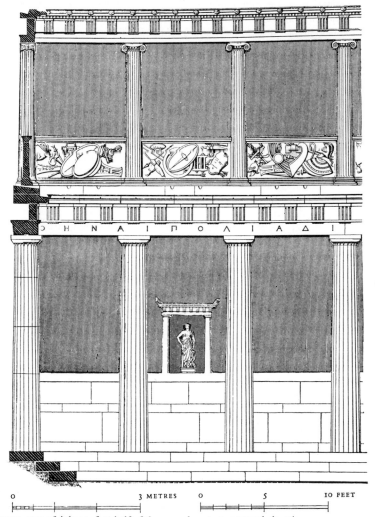

241. Pergamon, stoa of Athena, first half of the second century, restored elevation

by proposing the fourth century, in conformity with the lettering of some inscriptions, but in fact any period in the third century may prove correct. The columns (six by ten) were fluted only immediately below the capital, a fact explicable if the work had been abandoned. But it is strange that no attempt was made to complete the fluting when, during the first half of the second century, the court around the temple was lined with colonnades of two storeys, like a stoa [241]. A balustrade on the upper floor is carved with a frieze of weapons, in allusion to the deity's function of Nicephorus. This scheme of surrounding a temple court by colonnades immediately became popular in Roman architecture, but few Hellenistic examples are known;[13] the most spectacular was the Serapeum of Alexandria, to be mentioned later.

From the sixth century onwards, statues had normally been set on rectangular pedestals, but occasionally upon columns. By the third century both methods were used on a scale large enough to qualify as architecture. Statues of Ptolemy II and Arsinoe at Olympia stood each on top of a tall Ionic column. The monument of Aristaeneta [242], also of about 270, exemplifies a new type of support composed of two columns joined by an architrave. No less than ten of these extravaganzas existed at Delphi, and all were Ionic [243]. In some cases a frieze or dentils or both overlay the architrave, and the frieze might be cut either perpendicular or in a wave moulding to make the profile less abrupt. Usually a group of statues or an equestrian figure stood on top, some 30 feet above ground. A single column of that height, also at Delphi, carried a group of three dancing female figures, which evidently stood beneath the legs of a tripod.[14] The shaft is carved like an acanthus stalk, and surrounded by leaves at the foot of each drum [244]. The excavators believed that the monument had been thrown down by the earthquake of 373, and the generally accepted date is just before that event, but in the course of ten days at Delphi in 1952 I became convinced on stylistic grounds that the third century is the earliest conceivable period for the statues.

The Serapeum at Alexandria has almost completely perished, but some information has been obtained about the surrounding court by excavations, which also revealed foundation deposits at two corners of the precinct. In each of these a gold tablet gave the name of Ptolemy III (246–221) as the builder of the sanctuary, though by ancient tradition it is ascribed to his predecessor, Ptolemy II. Possibly the actual temple of Serapis was built before the rest of the precinct, but the tablets certainly decide the question as regards the colonnades which surrounded the court. In all, the precinct measured roughly 580 by 250 feet (173 by 77 m.). A comparatively small sanctuary at Hermopolis, the modern Ashmunein, in Egypt, was also built during the reign of Ptolemy III, by ex-cavalrymen whom he had settled there. It contained a Doric temple and other buildings, all of limestone covered with a hard fine stucco and gaily painted. In some Corinthian capitals (probably from a stoa), the acanthus leaves were yellow, the inner curling stems blue with brown tips, the stems that rose to the corner volutes brown, the thin wavy stems at the top blue-green, all against a purplish pink ground. The frieze of this Corinthian building bore a red design on a blue ground.

Even the remotest of Hellenistic new cities, at a site called Ai Khanum on the Afghan bank of the Oxus, made some architectural effort. A heroum, the Temenos of Kineas, consisted in its original state of a cella and a wider porch where two small rectangular bases in antis carried wooden supports for the roof. A sarcophagus was found buried under the floor of the cella. In subsequent reconstruction, the podium on which it stood was buried behind an enlarged terrace, and the porch reduced to the same width as the cella. The original construction probably belongs to final quarter of the fourth century. An inscription gives us the name of the original occupant of the tomb, Kineas: since he has the signal honour of burial within the city limits, and is given a cult, he must have been the founder of the city. The modest dimensions of the heroum, 33 feet (10·20 m.) wide in its origin-

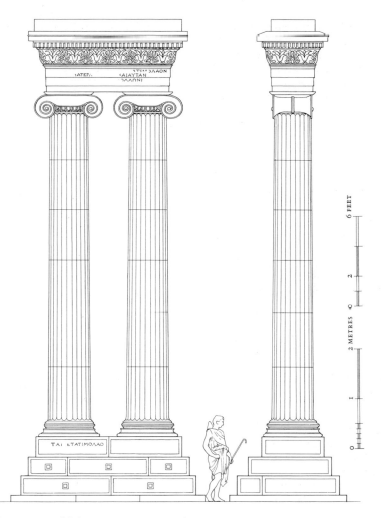

242. Delphi, monument of Aristaeneta, *c.* 270, restoration

al state, 50 feet (15·30 m.) long, are characteristically Greek. The administrative quarter, on
the other hand, has a grandiose layout which to
its excavators suggested rather the influence of
Achaemenid Persian architecture. An enclosure
of 450 by 355 feet (136·80 by 108·10 m.) was
then lined with colonnades surrounding an apparently empty courtyard, the function of which
is unknown; since access was restricted to

passages on two opposite sides, Bernard thinks
it cannot have been an agora. (But would not the
maximum of control be essential if wild tribes-
men of the district came to market?) There must
have been a hundred and sixteen Corinthian
columns, now represented by a few lathe-turned
bases of Attic-Asiatic type, unfluted drums, and
scraps of capitals with abnormally simplified,
labour-saving, ornament. The columns on the

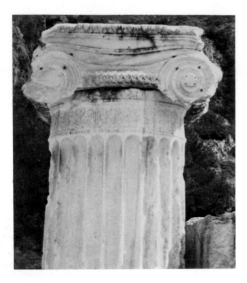

243. Delphi, capital of two-columned monument, third century

244. Delphi, reconstructed shaft of acanthus column, probably third century. *Delphi Museum*

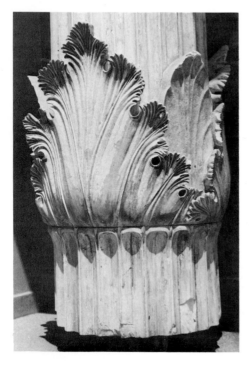

southern (or rather south-western) side were a trifle over half as thick again as those elsewhere; Bernard assumes that they were taller and made a Rhodian peristyle. (Since, however, the roof-span of this colonnade was more than correspondingly deeper, these columns must have taken nearly twice the strain imposed on any others and may on that account alone have needed all the extra thickness.) A later hall, opening off this colonnade, contained three rows of six Corinthian columns apiece; their capitals are comparable to those of the Temple of Olympian Zeus at Athens and the Council House at Miletus except that the stem of each leaf is jointed and looks like a string of large beads – an anomaly shared by the Parthian realm in Central Asia. In a still later phase of attenuated Greek heritage a vast complex of rooms, halls, and corridors was built in brick with stone detail. A contemporary temple is of purely Mesopotamian style, but when the interior was reconstructed after a fire the builders inserted an Ionic capital that, although of wood, is well preserved; it conforms with the best standards of the late second century.[15]

There is an important series of tombs from Macedon of the fourth century and later [245–9].[16] These seem to develop out of an earlier, simpler form of grave, in which a burial pit was given a rough timber roof before being buried under a low tumulus. During the course of the fourth century, as Macedon became more involved with the Greek city states, these tombs became larger and were given stone-built chambers with true vaults. The earliest in the great cemetery at Vergina are undoubtedly the tombs of the fourth-century Macedonian kings. The earliest, dated by the rich collection of silver objects it contained, has been tentatively identified as the burial place of Amyntas III, killed in battle in 359. The next in the sequence, whose lavish furnishings of gold and silver and bronze, arms and armour, and the decayed remains of fabric and finishings constitute one of the most spectacular archaeological discoveries in Greece, is most likely to be that of Philip II [248]. Other adjacent tombs were

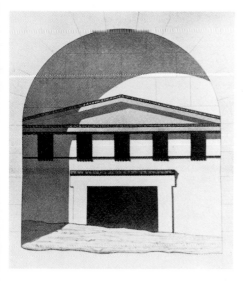

245. Pydna, façade of tomb inside tumulus, late third–early second century

246. Vergina, Ionic tomb, mid third century (?), interior (with marble throne and sarcophagus)

247. Vergina, Ionic tomb, mid third century (?), façade

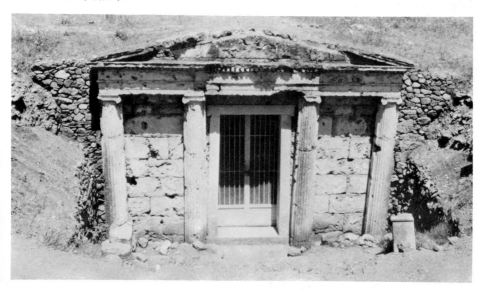

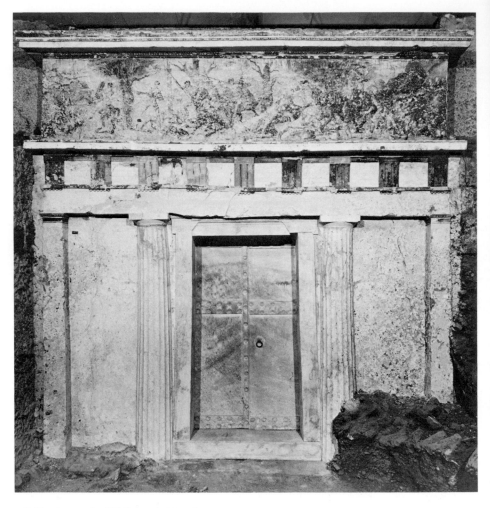

248. Vergina, tomb of Philip, probably 336

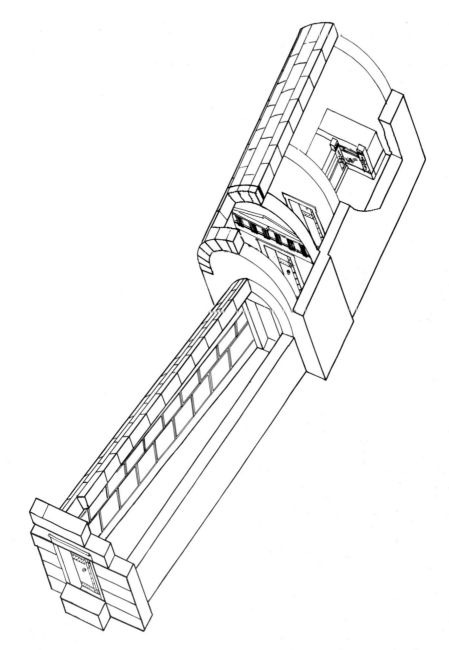

249. Pydna, Macedonian vaulted tomb, late third or early second century, axonometric view

found plundered, and this particular complex was concealed under an enormous tumulus, almost certainly put there later by the Hellenistic king of Macedon, Antigonus Gonatas, after the royal cemetery had been plundered by Gallic soldiers employed by Pyrrhus of Epirus. Tombs of similar type are found in several parts of Macedon – quite clearly the type was used by nobles as well as members of the royal family [249]. Most are totally robbed, but preserve intact their structure and decorated façades; particularly important here is the way in which the colours with which they were painted are unfaded.

The plans vary considerably, but in the important examples include at least an antechamber as well as the main burial chamber. Both are entered through doorways, treated in the same manner as those of temples. The doors, however, had to be more durable and were carved in two leaf forms on slabs of marble. (There is usually a rougher blocking of stonework in front of the outer door.) These are decorated to resemble wooden doors, each leaf of two panels between the framing, with large circular 'nail heads' and other fittings exactly recalling the actual metal examples which have been found in the houses of Delos and Priene, and elsewhere. It is clear that this is the regular pattern for wooden doors. The façade was decorated architecturally as a porch, usually with a pediment. The more important tombs have columns, or rather, giving the effect of free-standing columns, half-columns placed against the front wall of the antechamber, between antae. Both Doric and Ionic examples occur. The tomb of Philip is Doric: another at Vergina, some distance from the earlier tombs, and not concealed under the great tumulus, copies the distinctive Ionic order of the Philippeum at Olympia. One further to the north, near the modern village of Lefkadia (Petsas' tomb), has two storeys, a Doric ground floor surmounted by an Ionic upper storey whose columns are not (in distinction to the invariable practice in 'real' architecture) necessarily aligned to come over one of the lower columns.

To the owners of the tombs the façades may have recalled the courtyard fronts of great mansions or palaces, and therefore have seemed fit for their eternal homes. To us, ignorant as we are of domestic columns and entablatures (which seem to have been mainly constructed of wood), the only possible comparison is with temples, and it is equally likely that the owners and their architects consciously aimed at imitation of temples, so close was the relation of the dead to minor divinities. Foundations near the tomb of Philip have been identified as belonging to the heroum erected in his honour by his son Alexander the Great. Many of the details must correspond to the ornamental treatment of temples, notably the marble doors fitted in many of the tombs [250]. These obviously

250. Langaza, marble door of tomb, third century. *Istanbul Museum*

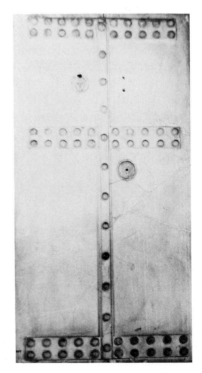

represent real doors, strengthened with battens which were secured by bolts, and equipped with metal handles to pull. The number of bolts would be preposterous for a plain wooden door, but might be needed to hold leather or bronze sheathing taut across the wood. All the mock-metal work on some tombs is covered by gold leaf, which no doubt was also applied to a few of the originals; such doors suggest emulation of a temple rather than even the wealthiest of residences.

Some allowance should be made for changes required in translating the façade of an ordinary building to rock-cutting, which allowed of little projection. The whole design may often have been flattened, and in particular engaged columns may have taken the place of free-standing. That, however, need not have been invariably the case; when an anteroom was added to the temple of Apollo at Gortyn, about the beginning of the second century, the new front was ornamented with Doric half-columns. Between the half-columns stood tapering pedestals, which were used for inscriptions. The frieze contained the now common additional triglyph in each intercolumniation. The cornice was very tall, and formed by elaborate mouldings.

Freedom from convention characterized a roughly contemporary small temple of Dionysus at Pergamon. Although Doric, the columns stood on bases and were fluted in the Ionic manner; mouldings took the place of the echinus and the regulae. At Lycosura, the temple of Despoena ('The Mistress'), where Damophon's group of colossal cult-images must have been installed before 150, was old-fashioned except for the proportions of its Doric Order, in which the frieze was nearly half as high again as the architrave. There is an additional door in one side of the temple, recalling Bassae and Tegea (which are both in the same region, Arcadia); steps placed on the slope which runs up from this side of the temple may have provided accommodation for spectators watching some sacred procession or other ritual. At Delos, a temple of Artemis (temple 'D') was built about 179 with half-a-dozen Ionic columns at either end, standing prostyle in front of prolonged antae, and the cella was wider than it was long. A cella of relatively even greater width, behind a porch with four columns in antis, was built at the same time in a sanctuary of the Cabeiri at Delos. Elsewhere the mystery-cult of these deities gave occasion for unusual plans, sometimes involving an apse in the centre of the back wall; presumably this projection was roofed in a half-cone. An internal apse, backed against the rectangular end of the building in order to frame the image, is mentioned among the specifications for a temple of Zeus at Lebadea, undertaken by Antiochus IV of Syria.

Another project of the same king, begun in 174 and completed 305 years later by the Emperor Hadrian, was the building of the temple of Olympian Zeus at Athens, on a platform which had been made ready about 520. The plan[17] followed the original Pisistratid scheme (evidently influenced by the Heraeum of Samos and the Artemisium at Ephesus); the pteron was double, with eight by twenty columns in each row, and a third row ran across either end. A Corinthian Order, however, was substituted in the new design. The architect, curiously enough, was a Roman citizen, Cossutius, but may have been of Greek ancestry. No trace of Roman influence shows in his work of 174–165, which is distinguishable from the more plentiful Hadrianic additions by the crisp carving of the foliage. His capitals [251, 252][18] might in fact have been inspired by those on the tholos at Epidaurus [213]. The main difference is that the central spirals, on either side of each corner, rise from the same cauliculus as the corner volute, the junction being masked by a third row of leaves, more widely spaced than those below. The flower, too, is differently placed, on the centre of each side of the abacus, instead of against the lower edge; a stalk descends to give apparent support. The columns [251, 252] are over 55 feet high, and unusually thickly proportioned, the height being equal to $8\frac{3}{4}$ times the lower diameter. The temple, which itself measured 135 by 354 feet (41·110 by 107·89 m.),

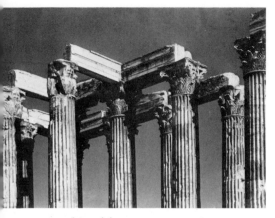

251 and 252. Athens,
temple of Olympian Zeus, c. 170

stood within a precinct of 424 by 680 feet; the extraordinary discrepancy in the proportions would be reasonable if the intention had been to place subsidiary buildings beside the temple.

Antiochus IV during his brief reign made a determined effort to revive the declining fortunes of the Seleucid empire: religion was used for political purposes, and the gifts of temples served this. There was, therefore, something of an architectural revival, and in this the Corinthian Order (which seems to have suited the tastes of a kingdom subjected to distinct oriental influence) may have been particularly developed. It seems best to attribute to Antiochus IV and his revival the best-preserved Greek Corinthian temple, that of Zeus Olbius at Uzunçaburc high in the Taurus mountains of

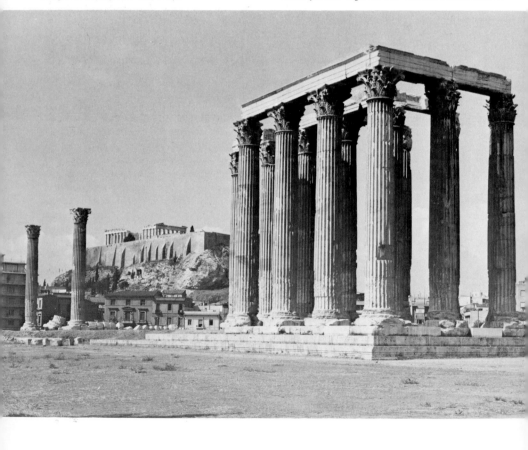

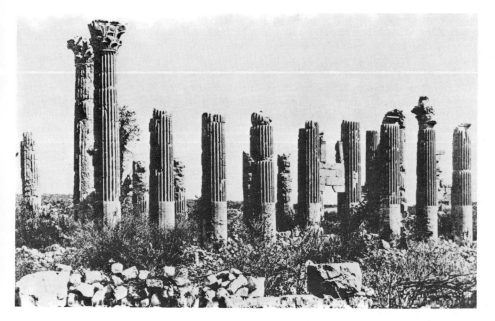

253. Uzunçaburc, temple of Zeus Olbius, second century

Cilicia [253].[19] Antiochus' religious propaganda centred round the cult of Zeus, and the details of the Corinthian capitals suit this period. Their upper part is very formal and wide spaced; the design includes inner spirals, but above them, instead of a central flower, is a mere knob – perhaps originally painted. The fluting of the columns is barely indicated up to one-third of their height; that precaution was commonly adopted in stoas where fluting would have been likely to suffer casual damage.

The sanctuary of Asclepius at Cos deserves attention because of the effective terraced layout [254]. The temple, a conventional Doric build-

254. Cos, sanctuary of Asclepius, second century, restoration

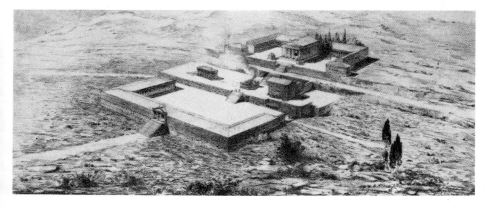

ing, and the adjoining stoas, were built mainly before the middle of the second century; an imposing altar may be somewhat later than the enormous one at Pergamon which was begun, if not finished, by Eumenes II (197–159).

Greek altars had usually taken the form of a narrow pedestal, placed opposite the front of a temple, and often of the same length. From the sixth century onwards a Doric frieze might be applied all round, a type which seems restricted to the area where the Doric order originated, Corinthia and the Argolid, or to Corinthian colonies. Ionic builders placed mouldings beneath the cornice or even a pair of volutes at the corners, in adaptation of an angle capital[20] (at Cape Monodendri, near Miletus). But the enormous Hellenistic altars set an altogether different standard. For mere size none surpasses that built at Syracuse by Hiero II (269–215), on which hundreds of cattle could be sacrificed at a time; the traditional narrow shape was retained over a length of nearly 650 feet, and the height of some 35 feet was relieved only by a Doric entablature at the top. The stairs were placed on the ends.

At Pergamon, though, the altar stood within a court of its own, following a precedent set, about 330, at Samothrace,[21] in turn following the 'Altar of the Twelve Gods' in the agora at Athens, where the altar was in a square enclosure surrounded by a stone fence (rather than a wall) with two entrances in opposite sides, probably flanked by slabs bearing relief sculpture. At Samothrace the court was enclosed on three sides by walls 26 feet high, and their blankness was relieved merely by an entablature, which was continued externally from the Doric colonnade of the fourth side. At Pergamon the actual altar was architecturally insignificant in comparison with the enclosing structure, the shape (and sculpture) of which suggested 'Satan's Throne' to an early Christian (Revelation ii, 13); a full-scale reconstruction[22] of this surround enables the Berlin Museum to display all the sculpture and a few other remains. The altar itself was placed in a court raised 17½ feet above the ground [255, 256]. The platform seems to have measured 112 feet from

front to back and 120 feet across, except where a flight of steps cut the centre of the front, to a width apparently of 68 feet. The exterior, up to the level of the court, was treated as a podium, with a plain base, beneath mouldings upon which stood a frieze 7½ feet high, sculptured with a horrific Gigantomachy (battle of the gods and giants). This was carried all round the outside, ending where the steps rose against it. Above the frieze dentils supported a projecting cornice, upon which stood an Ionic colonnade that formed the front of a portico. A coffered ceiling of marble was provided over the portico, of which the back consisted of a solid wall, rising only from the court. The colonnade returned beside the steps, parallel with which a short piece of wall, joined at right angles to that along the side, again supplied a background for the beginning of a continuation across the head of the steps. There was, however, no wall behind the presumed central stretch, which would have occupied most of the width of the steps; here a pillar on the inward side seems to have corresponded with every column. An Ionic three-quarter column was engaged on both the inward and the outward face of each pillar.

Similar pillars were almost unquestionably disposed parallel to the walls of the court, and joined by architraves, but this attempt to line the court with a portico was never finished. A smaller frieze, representing the adventures of Telephus, the mythical founder of Pergamon, was obviously intended to be seen no more than a few feet away, and most likely was placed in the court, along the foot of the walls. This frieze is clearly of later style than the Gigantomachy and may be dated, together with its unfinished portico, after the death of Eumenes in 159, though necessarily before the Roman annexation of Pergamon in 133. The beginning of work upon the altar should probably be dated about 165.

A very minor but intact Pergamene work of about 175 is the Monument of Agrippa outside the Propylaea at Athens. This tall pedestal supported the chariot group of some member of the royal house, but was re-used to honour the Minister of Augustus. Such pedestals became

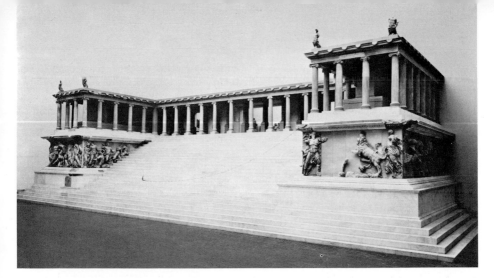

255 and 256. Pergamon, altar of Zeus, *c.* 165, restoration and restored plan

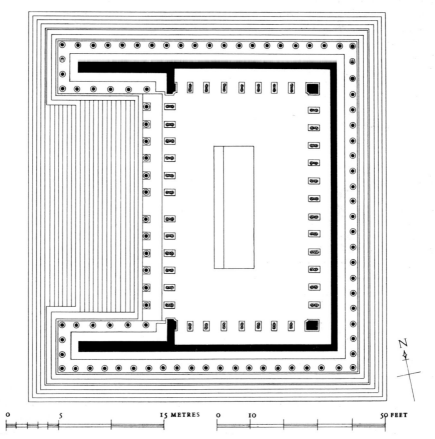

0   5   15 METRES   0   10   50 FEET

257 (*below*). Delphi, pedestal of Prusias, *c.* 180

258 (*below, right*). Delphi, pedestal of Aemilius Paulus, *c.* 168, restoration

fairly numerous during the second century, and the elaborate cornices are of some interest. At Delphi can be seen a rather crude example built to hold the equestrian statue of Prusias of Bithynia, about 180 [257]. There are also enough remains at Delphi to restore other pedestals, notably that [258] of Aemilius Paulus, whose conquest of Macedonia in 168 was commemorated by reliefs on the sides.

A temple of Hera Basileia at Pergamon bore a dedicatory inscription of Attalus II (159–138) on the architrave. The position chosen was a steep slope, into which the back was sunk; at the front four Doric columns stood prostyle at the head of a flight of steps. The columns were so slim as to make their height equal to $7\frac{1}{2}$ times the lower diameter, and instead of being fluted the shaft was cut into a polygon of twenty facets. The columns of some other Pergamene buildings were similarly treated, at least near the foot; the upper drums were fluted as a rule. The frieze was low, even allowing for the additional triglyph in every intercolumniation, but was

nearly half as high again as the architrave. The mouldings reveal Ionic influence. On the under side of the slanting cornice were placed mutules, complete with guttae, a device abhorrent to purist architects – Vitruvius condemns it; but in fact the maximum of detail must have been requisite in order that the top of the building might not appear ridiculously light. The effect may be judged from the little temple of Isis at Delos, to which the Athenians after 166 added a marble front, with two Doric columns *in antis*. The proportionate relation between the tall columns and the low entablature and gable shows more clearly if seen from within, free from distracting detail [259]. But externally the shortness of the cella also emphasizes the height,

259. Delos, temple of Isis, second century

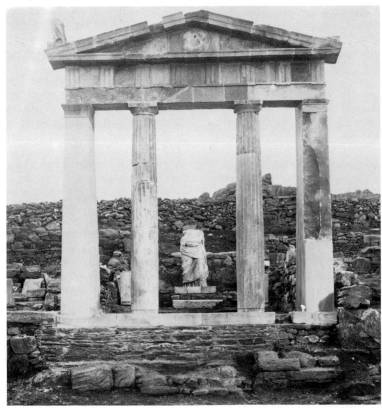

especially when seen cornerwise. The whole building measures about 17 by 40 feet.

The tendency to concentrate attention on the front appears in an Ionic temple of Zeus and Tyche, at Magnesia,[23] wherein four prostyle columns at the front corresponded to two columns *in antis* at the back. And in the extreme case of an undatable temple at Messene, the porch, with two Doric columns *in antis*, extends to a considerably greater width than the cella.

A peculiar arrangement at Olus in Crete may be provincial. When the ancient temple of Aphrodite was rebuilt, probably in the latter half of the second century, twin cellas, dedicated to Aphrodite and Ares, were placed side by side behind a porch of their joint width. From the existing remains the porch would seem to have been enclosed by solid walls, broken only by the doors, but an inscription refers to it as a veranda (*pastas*) covered by a separate roof. Presumably the front wall was only a parapet, of a few courses high, upon which posts stood. Perhaps other instances of this kind have escaped recognition.

Like Antiochus IV, the Kings of Pergamon used architecture for propaganda purposes. One architect they employed in the second century was Hermogenes, who acquired a considerable reputation (Vitruvius probably made extensive use of his writings for the Greek parts of his 'De architectura'). He proclaimed that Doric was unsuitable for temples – a reasonable opinion considering the contemporary state of the Order – and invented a new system of ideal proportions for Ionic. One element in this was a scale which related the diameter and height of columns to the distance between them (Vitruvius III. 3.6). In the scheme which Hermogenes called pycnostyle ('densely columned'), he decided that the gap between one column and the next should equal $1\frac{1}{2}$ times the lower diameter (or in terms of interaxial spacing 2 times); in systyle, the figure should be 2(3), in diastyle 3(4), in his own favourite eustyle $2\frac{1}{4}(3\frac{1}{4})$, etc. The closer the spacing, the slighter, of course, was the column to be. A height of ten diameters was prescribed for the pycnostyle, $9\frac{1}{2}$ for systyle, $8\frac{1}{2}$ for diastyle, but for eustyle the

figure was the same as for systyle (unless a copyist's error be assumed).

Hermogenes chose a pseudodipteral plan, of eight by fifteen Ionic columns, for the temple of Artemis Leukophryene at Magnesia [260]. It measured 103 by 190 feet, and was raised upon stone steps. The column spacing was slightly narrower than systyle, except for the central gap at each end which was one-third wider than the rest, about ten feet instead of six; the square plinths beneath the column-bases equalled the normal gap between them. Internally the planning was pedantically regular; the porch (towards the west) and the cella were equal in size, the opisthodomus half as long, while the partitions and the inner columns were needlessly aligned on the pteron. All ceilings were of wood.

The elevation can be judged only in detail since the height of the columns[24] is uncertain [261]. There is evidence, however, that the wall of each pediment was interrupted, to relieve the weight, by a large doorway at the centre, and a small doorway on either side. No sculpture occupied the pediments, but the acroteria, which consisted of curly foliage, seem absurdly large; the branched mass above the peak of the roof was almost as tall as the pediment beneath it. A sculptured frieze was placed beneath the dentils, but the height accounted for less than half the entablature. The surviving slabs (most of which are in the Louvre) are poorly carved, and the design is hackneyed. Attic influence seems to be indicated by the presence of a frieze, while the bases of the columns are of the Attic type, which Hermogenes may actually have introduced to Asia Minor; he also used it in the temple of Dionysus at Teos. But in general his design shows an overpowering influence of the temple at Priene, which seems to have been his native town.

Hermogenes was also responsible for an altar at Priene. As at Pergamon, it was a long structure in a court enclosed on three sides and approached by steps in front; an Ionic colonnade faced the exterior and interior of the wings, and immediately behind ran a continuous pedestal for statues, one of which stood in each

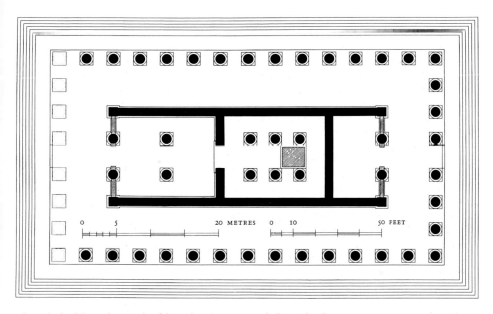

260 and 261. Magnesia, temple of Artemis, *c.* 150, restored plan and order

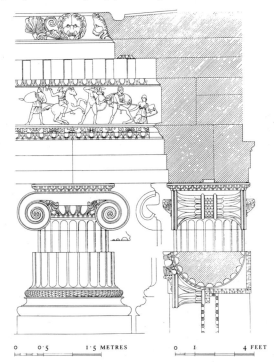

intercolumniation. The most likely date is about 150. The temple at Magnesia is probably to be placed at about the same date, in the reign of Attalus II of Pergamon, on the evidence of the form of swags and other details in the relief decoration of the opisthodomus,[25] together with its altar. The closest parallel to it is a smaller temple of Hecate at Lagina, the sculptured frieze of which can barely be older than the end of the century. This temple likewise was pseudodipteral, apparently with eight by eleven Corinthian columns; it contained only a porch, with two Ionic columns *in antis*, and an almost square cella.

A little monument of Mithradates VI, built at Delos in 102–101, resembled a porch [262]. The length barely exceeded 16 feet (4·96 m.). Two Ionic columns stood *in antis* and supported an entablature in which a plain frieze came beneath dentils. A medallion-framed bust occupied the pediment, and other medallioned busts were placed on the inward side of the walls. In a roughly contemporary sanctuary of some 'hero' at Calydon [263], medallions decorated the walls of a hall furnished for ritual meals. It is placed between the north side of the court and the projecting cult-room, which overlies the burial-chamber (vaulted, and accessible only through a vaulted stair-tunnel). The porch, which projects near by, was carried by a row of four pillars, with another row behind on either side. The choice of pillars instead of columns, as in the inner portico of many houses, may have been intended to convey a notion of domesticity, and the whole sanctuary was planned more like an enormous house than the precinct of a deity. That may also explain the use of a particularly elaborate form of support, two half-Doric capitals engaged to front and back of a pier. Similar columns are found in the palace (prob-

262. Delos, monument of Mithradates, 102-101, restoration of front

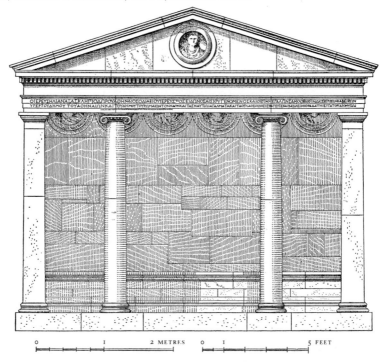

| 0 | | 1 | | 2 METRES | 0 | | 1 | | | 5 FEET |

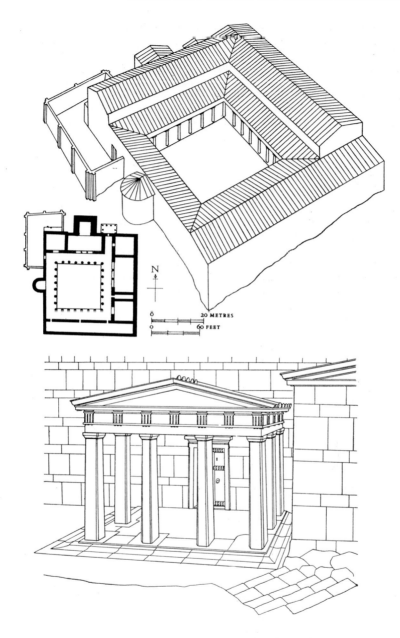

263. Calydon, heroum, second century, restored view, plan, and porch

ably of Antigonus Gonatas) at Vergina (below, p. 320). A very similar layout had been adopted a hundred years earlier for the cult of the divinized kings of Pergamon [353]: a court surrounded by a colonnade, behind which lay rooms on two sides while one end was occupied by an open-fronted antechamber, backed by a narrower shrine-room. Such obvious adaptations of the contemporary type of mansion or palace may well have seemed appropriate for a heroum, the sanctuary of a mortal who had acquired the status of 'hero' or demi-god. It must be emphasized that by this late period this status was acquired by wealth, and de facto from the construction of the heroum, rather than for official reasons, as in the case of Kineas at Ai Khanum.

No temples of any consequence remain from the first century. The weight of Roman taxation must have discouraged building in both Greece and Asia Minor; Syria retained its independence only till 64; the Ptolemies lasted another generation, but their surviving buildings are Egyptian in style.[26] A small Doric temple of Apollo Bresaeus, in Lesbos, deserves mention only because of the sculptured frieze on the architrave, a feature inspired no doubt by the early temple at Assos, on the neighbouring coast of Asia Minor.

At Delos building virtually ceased in 88, when Mithradates sacked the island. The work of the preceding years included an agreeable, though conventional, propylon of four Doric columns prostyle [264]; the frieze contained an

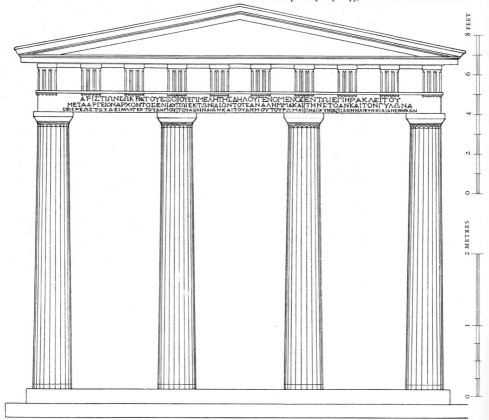

264. Mount Cynthium, Delos, propylon, 95–94, restoration

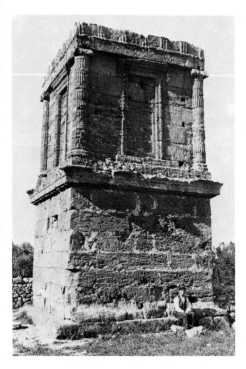

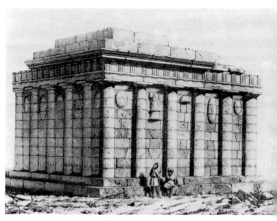

265 (*left*). Agrigento, tomb of 'Theron', early first century

266 (*below*). Suweida, tomb of Hamrath, early first century

additional triglyph in each intercolumniation. This marble structure of 95–94 replaced a limestone porch as the entrance to a sanctuary, which had gradually expanded over Mount Cynthium till the whole uneven mass of rock was dotted with little buildings.

A few surviving tombs of the early or mid first century are ultimately derived from such precedents as the Mausoleum. At Agrigento two were built in Greek style, although Sicily was fast becoming romanized. The larger (29 by 40¾ feet; 8·85 by 12·40 m.) is known as the Oratory of Phalaris; it consisted of a podium and a superimposed building with a prostyle porch, in which four Ionic columns carried a Doric entablature. The so-called Tomb of Theron [265] is a strongly tapered mass 16 feet square (4·81 m.); the plain podium rises from a wider base and ends at a cornice; in the upper storey the walls too are plain, except for a false door, but an Ionic column is engaged at each corner, and the entablature again is Doric, with seven little triglyphs on each side. The tomb of a Syrian named Hamrath, at Suweida [266], has only one storey; in each side, six Doric columns are engaged. The roof was pyramidal.

CHAPTER 20

MASONRY, VAULTING, AND PUBLIC WORKS

The Greek art of masonry reached its finest expression in secular buildings; temples invariably consisted, from the platform upwards, of uniformly smooth surfaces which gave less opportunity for a treatment interesting in itself, and in any case the treatment of masonry in a temple was of far less importance than the design of the building. But in secular work a rough surface and the jointing of the blocks often composed the greater part of the design. In this chapter, therefore, the masonry of temples is ignored, except in so far as the methods happen to be identical.

The Greeks were really megalithic builders. They used no mortar until the latest period, and in their best work, including that of temples, the blocks were fitted with extraordinary precision. Usually, however, contact between the ends of the blocks was not obtained over the whole of the two surfaces, but only along a narrow border round the edges; the centre was made concave and left rough. This labour-saving device, called anathyrosis, originated in Egypt and had already been adopted by the Myceneans. The Greeks made greater use of it, sometimes hollowing every concealed surface of the block, though when funds permitted they preferred to restrict the anathyrosis to upright joints, at which alone it did not add appreciably to the risk of breakage. To prevent lateral movement, blocks were secured by means of horizontal clamps and vertical dowels, both of metal [143]. These precautions were almost indispensable because of the frequency of earthquakes, but gave cause for much destruction in medieval times, when the very high value of metals repaid the cost of demolition and extraction. The clamps and dowels alike, though more often made of iron than of bronze, were fixed into place with a generous quantity of lead. Again the technique was of oriental origin.

The use of metal ties was, of course, expensive even in antiquity and was therefore restricted to the most esteemed buildings. The walls of others depended for security upon the mere weight of the individual blocks – which accounts for the megalithic character of almost every pretentious structure – or upon an interlocking of the blocks themselves. This method appears in an extreme form in the oldest Greek attempts at good masonry. Unless rectangular blocks were essential (for a purpose such as building a temple), the primitive mason imitated the appearance of traditional walling, which was composed of irregular pieces of stone roughly packed together, in the manner of the field-walls of the north of England or the terrace revetments in Mediterranean countries. In the style which seems to be the oldest of all [267], the blocks were cut with curved outlines and fitted together like a jig-saw puzzle.

This curvilinear masonry has been called Lesbian, from its prevalence in the fortifications

267. Old Smyrna, curvilinear masonry of temple platform, late seventh century

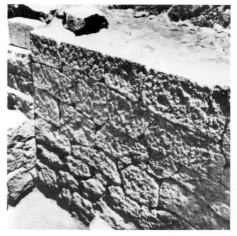

of Lesbos, but actually was widespread during the seventh century, though more common on the eastern side of the Aegean than in Greece itself. It was ousted fairly early[1] in the sixth century by a system of building with polygonal blocks of straight facets, or as nearly straight as might happen to be convenient. The retaining wall of the temple terrace at Delphi, at the back of the Athenian stoa [268], contains polygonal work mingled with curvilinear, as though it had been built during the transition. At Athens

excited prejudice against the disorder of old-fashioned polygonal. However the impulse arose, the approximation to courses became obvious in the polygonal of the early fifth century.

In the later part of the fifth century there appears another style of masonry, a compromise between rectangular and polygonal. The blocks are all flat at top and bottom, and equal in height throughout each course, but every now and then an end is cut on a slant, causing an overlap at the joint [273]. Usually overlaps occur towards left

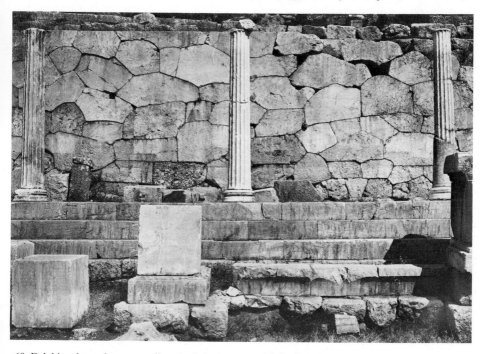

268. Delphi, polygonal terrace-wall, early sixth century, and Athenian stoa, c. 470

polygonal masonry is known to have reached its highest development around the middle of the sixth century. About 500 the blocks began to be laid in more or less horizontal rows. Even in the least regular walls the top and bottom had inevitably formed courses, and perhaps the new tendency grew up merely for the builders' convenience. But the seemliness which was then being attained in rectangular masonry may have

and right alternately, but seldom in immediate sequence; several rectangular blocks may intervene between one trapezium and the next. Masonry of this kind looked civilized and was easy to build, yet interlocked enough for the builders to feel safe in using comparatively small blocks. Consequently the style was much used, especially during the hundred years following its introduction, but as a rule for purposes which allowed a somewhat rough treatment of the surface.

Polygonal, because of its superior powers of cohesion, was never superseded for such purposes as fortification, where large blocks could be found on the spot in shapes easily trimmed to interlock; the projections, however, are less pointed than in early work. A revival of decorative polygonal also occurred in the Hellenistic period [269]. The style differs fun-

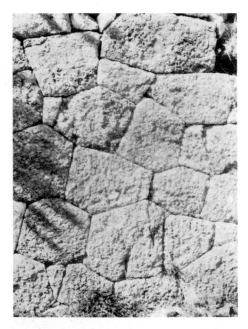

269. Cnidus, polygonal terrace-wall, third or second century

damentally from its predecessor of the sixth century; instead of selecting pieces of rock and altering their shape just enough to effect joins, the builders deliberately cut blocks into the most fantastic geometric figures. Of course this statement applies only to masonry intended for display; utilitarian polygonal continued as before, distinguishable from sixth-century work chiefly by the preponderance of projections at right angles or nearly right angles. Polygonal masonry looked at its best with an almost plane

surface, but the style was too quaint to profit from an absolutely smooth face. Except in the earliest work, therefore, the treatment tended to vary from a rough plane to genuine roughness in the case of fortifications.

Rectangular masonry took various forms, apart from the refined work used in temples and similar buildings. In the foundations of such buildings, and over the face of many free-standing walls, all the blocks are much longer than they are tall, but the length may vary along the course [270]. In other walls, whether or not the blocks were cut to a uniform length, some may run inwards as headers and by the shortness of the exposed face greatly diversify the appearance (as in the upper terrace of illustration 271); when the wall was thin enough the headers ran through from one face to the other. This type can rarely be older than the fifth century. Isodomic masonry, in which the courses are uniform in height and the blocks visibly uniform in length, was a fifth-century development; the joints are often placed perpendicularly to one another in alternate courses. Extreme regularity was monotonous, except in small surfaces, and in many walls alternate courses consist of long and short blocks [289].

The general practice was to place one or more taller courses at the foot of a wall, below the isodomic work, and if the difference in height was very considerable, to ease the transition by intervening courses of intermediate height. In many walls the treatment of the surface also differs according to the level, the upper courses being comparatively smooth and the base rough. This contrast could be seen at practically every temple of which the foundation showed above ground [187], but in free-standing walls is usually a sign of fourth century or later date.

Pseudisodomic masonry consists of alternate courses of two markedly different heights [281]. This style evolved very early [302]. But the best known example, the pedestal afterwards utilized for a Monument of Agrippa, just outside the Propylaea, is now known to date from about 175, and a great vogue for pseudisodomic prevailed about that time, especially in Asia

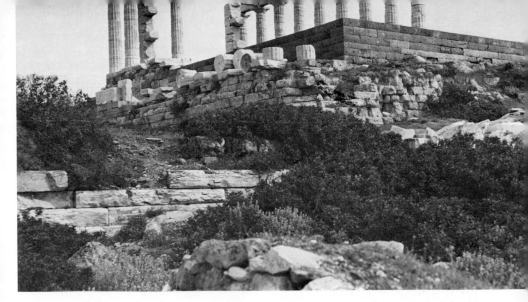

270. Sunium, platform of temple of Poseidon, mid fifth century, and predecessor of *c.* 500; fortification of 412 in foreground

271. Priene, fountain at corner of avenue and stepped street, below the supporting wall of the temple of Athena Polias, fourth century

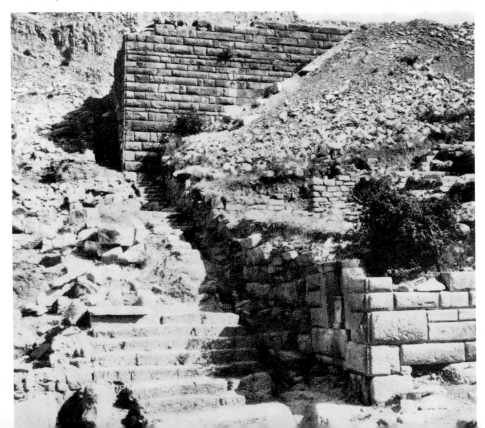

Minor; comparatively few earlier examples are known, and these tend to be less distinctively coursed [277]. To display the contrasting height, a plane or approximately plane surface was requisite, and the joints looked best if alternated in each course by being placed above one another only in courses of the same height. In the Hellenistic work in Asia Minor, promoted particularly by Pergamene architects, the blocks of the taller courses are frequently cut very thin, requiring separate face and rear blocks, and

a punch, the marks of which frequently remain as straight channels in the stone [274, 294]. The block might then be trimmed to whatever degree of smoothness was required, by means of coarse and also fine chisels. The subsequent process of polishing was naturally applicable only to decorative work; a surface was prepared with chisels and a punch (which leaves a distinctive stippled effect in unfinished work). It was then finally smoothed with rub stones and sand. Marble could be given a higher polish by a final

272. 'Eleutherae', Attic frontier fort, fourth century, wall-walk and tower

273. Messene, city wall and tower, mid fourth century

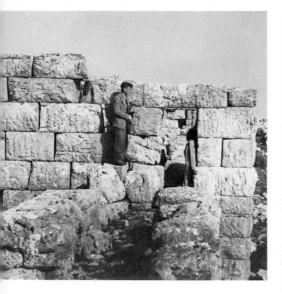

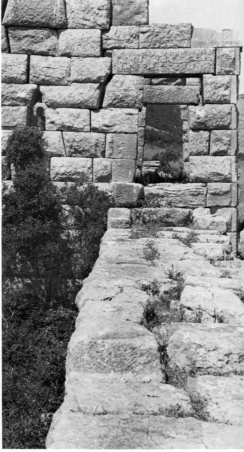

even then leaving a space between which would be filled with rubble, an obvious economy in construction costs.

A mason began the dressing of a block by using a pointed hammer to shape it roughly as desired, leaving several superfluous inches in each face except along the edges, where a strip was chiselled to the proper depth [272, 273]. This system of drafted margins was often retained, particularly during the later period, in finished work, for decorative effect. At the next stage the larger projections were removed with

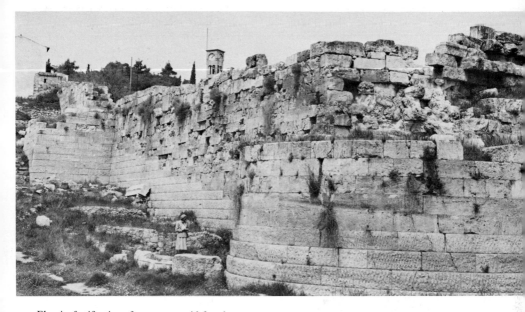

274. Eleusis, fortification of sanctuary, mid fourth century

rubbing with a soft material, such as leather.

The majority of walls were left with a fairly uneven surface. The bulge resulting from the preliminary hammering was often allowed to remain in all its roughness, or was only slightly trimmed, especially on the exterior of the wall; the interior was dressed [295]. The bulge might even be emphasized to a varying degree, usually at a rather late date, by smoothing into a regular curve, which was sharply separated from the level strip along the edges [271]. This type of surface is typical at Priene in the Hellenistic age. Walls composed of bulging blocks were necessarily rebated at the corners, from top to bottom, to a width of several inches [273, 275], if the builders wished to lay the courses perpendicular or at an even inclination. This smooth upright strip not only served a practical need, but also contributed to the design. Such reference lines were invariably cut in the construction of fine masonry, but disappeared when the adjacent surfaces received their final polish.

The finer examples of Greek walling rank high as works of art. The scale is not colossal as in Egyptian masonry, but the compositions are more elaborate, and the range of styles incomparably richer. Only at one other period in the world's history has masonry ever approached the same standards – in Peru under the Inca dynasty. The Peruvian styles were as numerous, and most of them correspond fairly closely with the Greek, as regards both the shapes of the blocks and the composition, though a smooth surface was habitual. Technically Peruvian work is superior because of the absence of anathyrosis (so far as my own observation goes), and the blocks in many buildings are enormously larger. Aesthetically the finest Greek masonry seems to me definitely preferable, although the Peruvian fits better into its environment; the one justifiable criticism of the Greek is that it tended to over-elaboration, and the cleverness of the composition thus became obtrusive. But this fault was rare except in late work.

The rapid development of masonry to this

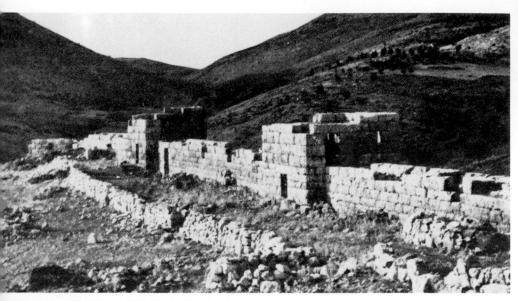

275. 'Eleutherae', Attic frontier fort, fourth century, interior

excellence was not accompanied by structural progress; the Greeks were slow to realize the advantages of the arch, remaining timid in application of the principle till the Christian era; only small spaces were covered by vaulting. This backwardness cannot be explained as due to mere ignorance. Although the peoples of the Bronze Age had built no arches, contact with the Orient ought soon to have taught the Greeks that wedge-shaped blocks could sustain themselves across a gap. The principle of the arch had been known both in Egypt and in Western Asia a couple of thousand years before Greek travellers began to frequent those countries, and vaulted buildings of impressive dimensions could be seen there. These, however, consisted of burnt brick, a material which the Greeks scarcely ever adopted, while the megalithic work, which they did admire, relied on flat lintels, like their own. The lintel, till the second century, was the only reputable means of spanning a gap, even though iron bars might need to be inserted as a precaution against cracking. The Greeks seem to have been wary of the out-

ward thrust exercised by vaults and arches; consequently, when these came to be used it was only in structures where such thrusts were amply counteracted, that is over openings in fortifications, where the adjacent masses of the continuous wall prevented movement, or in underground structures such as tombs, where the sides of the pit kept the structure in place. Arches were frequently used, however, provided they were unseen. Underground tombs, for instance, were commonly barrel-vaulted. The sixth-century example on Cyprus [276] is older than any yet found in Greece, a fact which may be significant in view of the oriental connexions of the island. An example of about 600 survives in Asia Minor inside the tumulus of Alyattes, but may be irrelevant, since there is no certainty that the Lydian king employed Greek masons to build his tomb. The first regular use of vaults in Greek architecture is to be attributed to the Macedonian kings in their series of chamber tombs (above, p. 270), beginning apparently about the middle of the fourth century. Slightly later than this (but still

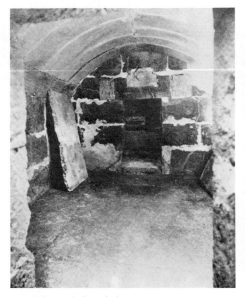

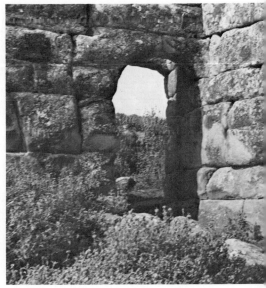

276. Pyla, tomb, late sixth century

277. Stratus, river gate of city, fourth century

before the end of the century) the arch and vault were used to cover gateways in fortification; there are examples at Corinth and Samos, though here the Greek architects were still most wary of the technique, clamping the voussoirs together quite unnecessarily, the usual manner of assuring that blocks will remain in place. By the third century, Greek architects could construct with confidence oblique and inclined vaults (the Ptolemaic propylon at Samothrace (above), the entrance passages at Didyma, and, probably later, the vaulted dromos to the Macedonian tomb at Pydna [249], both inclined and narrowing as it descends).

Some, if not all, of the oldest rounded gateways, which can plausibly be ascribed to the fifth century, are not genuine arches, but merely corbelled to a curve at the top. At Stratus [277], in masonry of such an advanced type that an early date is improbable, two immense blocks rest against each other to cover a postern, and the curvature of their lower surfaces gave no benefit except a higher clearance in the gateway (actually amounting to $11\frac{1}{2}$ feet). At

Palaiomanina, some miles lower down the river Achelous, the main gateway [278, 279] is spanned by a flat lintel resting on two such blocks, which do not meet. At Oeniadae, in the same area, a city known[2] to have been strongly fortified as early as 454, most of the numerous posterns contract towards the top; the sides either slant or curve as they rise, methods practised in the Bronze Age and continued into Hellenistic times [280]. A pointed arch, presumably of similar structure, is shown on a frieze which represents a siege; it belonged to a Lycian heroum of the early fourth century and is now in Vienna. (The site is known as Gjölbashi or Trysa.)

A few of the posterns at Oeniadae are genuinely arched, by means of voussoirs (wedge-shaped blocks), but the fact alone would not justify doubt of their contemporaneity with the others. The walls of Assos contain gates with the same variety of forms, all apparently built in the fourth century or even at the beginning of the third, and are backed by true vaulting over the space where the doors turned, that being too

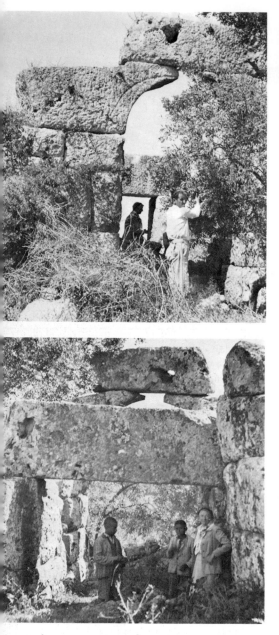

278 and 279. Palaiomanina, city gate, fifth century, exterior and interior

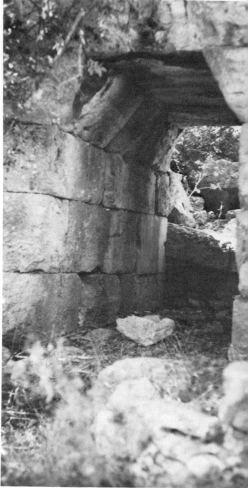

280. Ephesus, doorway of tower, c. 290

wide to be spanned by corbelling. On the other hand, the principal gateway has a corbelled rather than a true arch – while a guard chamber near by has a corbelled roof whose under surface is cut to resemble a true vault, demonstrating that these were known, but mistrusted, at least by architects who were not used to them. Much later, a lintel was thought preferable over an outer gateway to accompany an arch over the inner [281, 282].

During the second century any aesthetic prejudice disappeared, and a round arch even appears as a purely ornamental feature [334], spanning the entrance to the market-place at Priene. The weaker segmental arch (the curve of which is less than a semicircle) was often used, mainly over cisterns, at regular intervals which were bridged by slabs. Vaulting became more common, but was still restricted to spans too wide for corbelling; the form it took might be either semicircular or slightly pointed. Examples of two different heights covered a sloping tunnel at Pergamon and met where it changed direction, the lower vault abutting against the side of the higher, without intersecting. In the case of a stoa built at Delphi by King Attalus of Pergamon, the substructures turned at right angles on level ground, and the springs of arches can be seen in the walls in either direction. But apparently these are not the remains of continuous vaulting, but of a series of separate arches which give support to the floor above, like the segmental arches which ribbed the tops of cisterns. Cross-vaulting [283], formed by the intersection of barrel-vaults at the same level, occurs at Pergamon in a tomb of uncertain date but probably Hellenistic; the blocks at the junction are cut to fit both vaults. But probably cross-vaulting was invented by the Romans, whose habitual use of bricks encouraged the development of vaulting.

The dome is unquestionably a Roman invention (or perhaps, rather, of the Roman period, for it may well have developed in the eastern area, the former Hellenistic kingdoms); the nearest Greek equivalents were the conical roof and the corbelled vault, both inherited from the Bronze Age. Circular buildings above ground were generally made with conical roofs, while corbelled vaulting was restricted to subterranean tombs, well-houses, or cisterns, and in these the resemblance to the Mycenean tholos

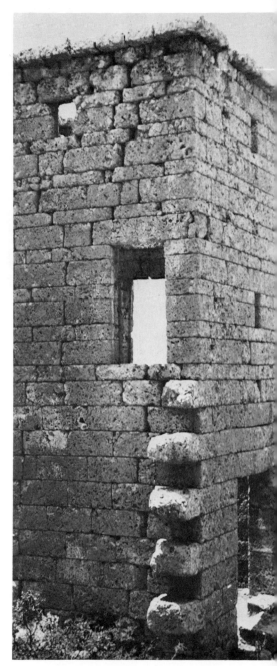

281. Sillyum, gatehouse tower, probably second century

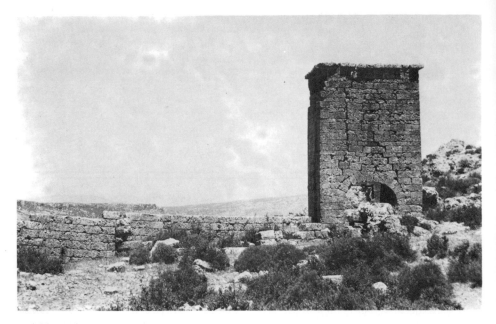

282. Sillyum, gatehouse tower,
probably second century

283. Pergamon, tomb, probably Hellenistic,
intersecting vaulting

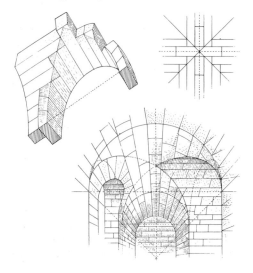

tomb is such as to have sometimes caused confusion in dating. Hellenistic architects also built tombs in this manner for foreign patrons, particularly in south Russia. A group of Galatian royal tombs, at Karalar in Asia Minor, includes one which contained an inscription of Deiotares II, who died in 43. Another (Tomb 'C') deserves attention for its two blind 'lantern-roofs', in which stone slabs are arranged in superimposed layers of concentric and ever-narrowing polygons [284]; the effect is suggestive of Islamic work. This type of roof is usually restricted to tombs in non-Greek areas – in Bulgaria, going back to the fourth century – and has been assumed to imitate a criss-cross of logs piled over the wooden burial-chamber of a native tumulus. But there are remnants of a 'lantern-roof' in the Argolid; the lowest slabs lie athwart two corners of a cistern, and are integrated with the Hellenistic enceinte of Katzingri fort.[3]

Considering the handicap of their technical incapacity, it is surprising how much and how well the Greeks managed to build. The master-

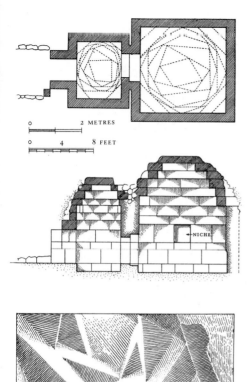

284. Karalar, tomb 'C', mid first century, plan, section, and ceiling

pieces of their best period are based on structural principles little more advanced than those of Stonehenge. They lifted heavy blocks with all the skill and ingenuity a nation of seamen could muster, but inefficient transport from the quarry over unmade roads inflated costs, and the labour involved was prodigious.

It should also be remembered that the temples and civic buildings, although they existed in such numbers, required less effort to erect

and to maintain than another class of building scarcely mentioned in books, the city-walls, citadels, and outlying forts.[4] There are substantial remains of these, usually in remote places where no subsequent builder felt tempted to reuse the material. Complete cities in Ionia were already surrounded by walls in the seventh century, or even earlier. Old Smyrna is an example of successive fortifications, dating back originally to a period no later than the second half of the ninth century, and eventually overwhelmed by the siegecraft of Alyattes, King of Lydia, at the end of the seventh century; these walls show a competence in masonry techniques (though their superstructures were substantially built of unbaked brick) long before they were employed in temple architecture.

Alyattes' methods of siegecraft originated in the Near East. The rise of the Persian Empire in the second part of the sixth century stimulated development of Greek fortification. Extensive walls built at Samos [285][5] combined with a substantial fleet enabled Polycrates to maintain for a while the independence of that island. It is doubtful whether any fortification system built by the Greeks could have withstood the Persians, once they had succeeded in investing it, and the walls of the Acropolis at Athens, substantially a survival from the Late Bronze Age, soon fell to Xerxes' assault. After Xerxes' invasion the Spartans wanted no fortifications to be built, a sensible enough proposal since, while none of those existing in 479 could keep out the Persians, once occupied by the Persians walled cities would provide bases which the more limited Greek techniques of siege warfare could not subdue; unlike the Persians, the free Greek communities, of whatever political form, could not afford the heavy loss of life inherent in siege attack. The Athenians, however, refortified, urged on by Themistocles who, it would seem, having understood the lesson of Polycrates, combined a fortified base (the Piraeus) with a powerful fleet. Later, the system was developed still further; Athens, four miles inland from Piraeus, was linked to the harbour by continuous long walls, and so

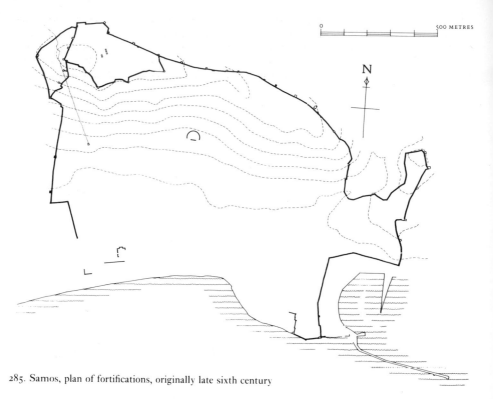

285. Samos, plan of fortifications, originally late sixth century

became immune to direct assault by the army of her great rival, Sparta.

To the end of the fifth century Greek fortifications remained relatively simple, since direct assault by infantry ill-equipped for specialized siegecraft, the normal condition of the Greek citizen soldier, was unlikely to succeed. A mere wall was in itself impregnable and the attackers preferred, if possible, to bring their enemies to surrender through starvation. The introduction of the ram mantlet, which supposedly took place in 441, eventually led to new methods of construction for gateways, with composite jambs rather than the monoliths which were preferred before. At the end of the fifth century, the Peloponnesian war between Athens and Sparta saw further developments, particularly of the fortified base in enemy territory, a device used by the Spartans in ravaging the Athenian countryside, but the city and the long walls were

immune until the Spartans were able to destroy the Athenian fleet. Even then the city fell to starvation rather than assault; the fortifications were dismantled.

Most surviving Greek fortifications belong to the subsequent fourth century and the Hellenistic age, their construction and form stimulated by developments in siege warfare, particularly catapults and assault weapons, mobile towers and landing bridges, first used by Syracuse in 398. In Hellenistic times it was most unusual for a city to remain unwalled. Although systems of walling became more elaborate, equipped with towers for torsion artillery and often provided with additional outworks, and although in general the walls themselves were more substantially built, it is unlikely that they were ever capable of withstanding a determined assault. Demetrius Poliorcetes' failure to capture Rhodes in 305 is exceptional.

Nevertheless, they offered some protection, certainly from casual or inadequately prepared assault. Even more, they were an embellishment to the city, and in architectural terms provided a distinct and important visual definition to the city limits. Methods of construction varied considerably, from region to region, as well as at different periods. Extensive fortification could be expensive, and there was obvious scope for economy both in material and the extent to

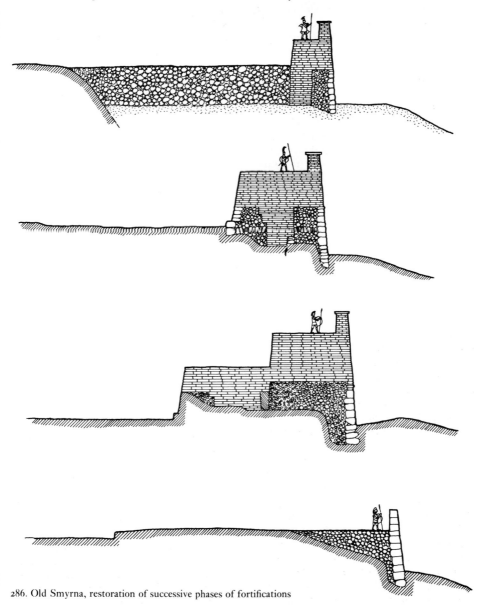

286. Old Smyrna, restoration of successive phases of fortifications

which skilled or time-consuming labour was required. In the earlier walls, unbaked mud brick was frequently employed over a stone plinth or footing. Provided the footing was solidly based on the bedrock it was difficult to undermine. Such walls could withstand the early methods of assault, and required protection from the weather rather than enemies. The faces were whitewashed over a coating of clay to protect them from rain; this would also have given them a unified and attractive appearance (Demosthenes bewails the negligence of mid-fourth-century Athens, which had failed to keep the walls properly whitewashed). The early walls of Old Smyrna [286] were of mud brick set on tall stonework with an inclined face, set back slightly from the footing; later walls (for example, those at Eleusis of the mid sixth century [287]) have brick faces flush with those of the underlying stone. A substantial section of the

it difficult to bring siege equipment too close. In fact, it appears that unbaked brick had a certain resilience to missiles.

Elsewhere in the fourth century masonry replaced brick. This might consist of random rubble, broken stones collected in their natural condition, but this could not provide the strength and size of wall now required. Stone specially quarried, trimmed, and fitted was essential. Such stonework rarely composed an entire wall; usually it was restricted to an outer and inner face, the space between being filled with inferior material, broken stone, clay, and such-like. Unbaked brick might be used, since it was stable and self-supporting. Rubble, being unstable, might exert pressure on the faces and various means, such as coursed stonework extending from the face into or even through the wall (in some structures dividing it into a series of boxlike compartments), were used; these had

287. Eleusis, Pisistratid sanctuary, *c.* 500, restoration

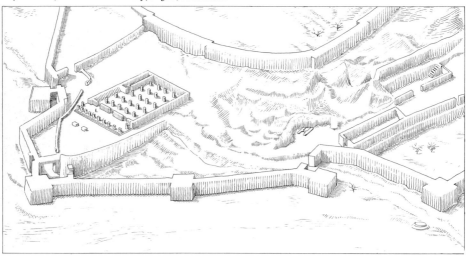

mud-brick superstructure of the city walls of Athens was found during the excavations in the Kerameikos area; even at the end of the fourth century Athens' walls still had a superstructure largely of mud brick, though they were further protected by an outwork (*proteichisma*), making

the additional advantage of preventing the collapse of long sections of wall should the face be breached by the enemy.

The potential of the stonework faces for decoration was exploited. Stones were carefully shaped and fitted, whether in level courses, of equal or varying height, or employing blocks of unequal height, in the various systems already described. It is difficult to assign even approximate dates to fortification solely on the basis of masonry style. The size of blocks employed varies, polygonal masonry tending to consist of larger stones than coursed masonry, but not approaching the colossal sizes employed in the Cyclopean masonry of the Late Bronze Age. The larger the blocks the more stable the wall would be, but reasonable, rather than overlarge, size meant greater ease of handling, still combined with stability, and in general the blocks are comparable in dimension with those employed in the more substantial buildings. In contrast to these, however, the surfaces were given the unsmoothed finishes described above, often emphasizing the individual blocks (while walls in buildings tried to render the joints as invisible as possible). Even in coursed masonry, the blocks are not usually regular in size. Defects in individual blocks may be made good by trimming and inserting smaller pieces of stone. Despite this contrast to the walls of buildings, fortifications, except in the cheapest or hastily constructed systems, provide not only the appearance of strength, but a balance and coherence which gave them an attractiveness and aesthetic quality rarely achieved in utilitarian masonry.

The appearance of the walls depends on much more than their method of construction. The height of the wall increased with the development of siegecraft, and parapets were a necessary protection against missiles, emphasizing height still further. More important are the towers and gates. In earlier fortifications (as far as we can tell, since many were subsequently replaced by more up-to-date systems) towers were infrequent, their principal function being to provide shelter for the guards. Later, towers were needed to house catapults, and became even more substantial as these weapons became heavier. In plan, at least ninety per cent of known towers are rectangular. Towers of semicircular plan [288] were possibly stronger, but more difficult to construct. When towers

were surmounted by rooms for the torsion artillery roofs were necessary to keep the machines dry; the tall towers at Aegosthena, perhaps the earliest to survive which were built for artillery, had gabled roofs, the forms of which are clearly discernible in the stonework [289] (cf. Perga [290]). Timber elements, in the roof, shelters for artillery openings in towers and for the parapets, even roofs over the parapet walks, have long since disappeared.

The last great developments of siegecraft, those made by the successors of Alexander, were tested in the sieges of Cypriot Salamis in 307 and Rhodes in 305–304. These in turn lead to new characteristics in the fortifications built subsequently. Towers become even larger, and are placed to cover all approaches with artillery fire from at least two of them. Walls are thicker and so stronger, battlements are frequently

288. Smyrna (Izmir), acropolis, corner tower, third century

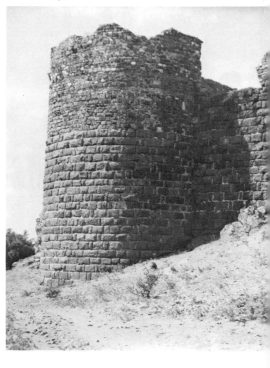

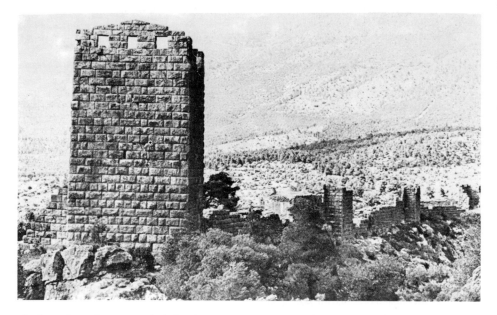

289. Aegosthena, fortress near Attic frontier,
probably third century

closed, with windows or slit openings only.
Ample provision is made for postern gates,
through which the defender might make sorties
to destroy the siege engines brought against
them.

Gates provided both problems (since they
constitute an obvious weakness in any fortification system) and opportunities for embellishment. The curtain wall had to be modified to
allow the opening to be defended, normally by
exposing any enemy actually assaulting the door
to attack from the flanks. Gates are therefore
normally set at the end of a forecourt (e.g.
Miletus, Sacred Gate [291]); systems were
developed with double gateways separated by

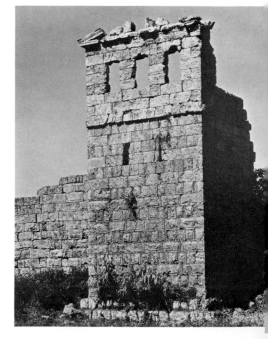

290. Perga, tower of city wall,
probably third century

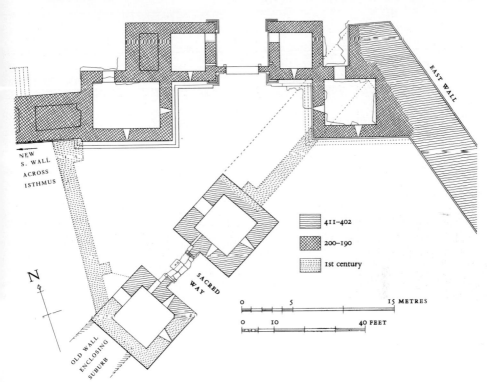

411–402

200–190

1st century

0   5   15 METRES

0   10   40 FEET

291. Miletus, Sacred Gate, restored plan

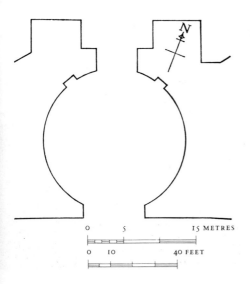

0   5   15 METRES

0   10   40 FEET

292. Messene, Arcadian Gate,
mid fourth century, plan

enclosed courts in which an enemy who had penetrated would be trapped, as at Messene for example [292–5]. Such systems are often strengthened further by flanking towers. The earlier gates are usually of simple type with overlapping walls, much in the manner of Mycenean fortifications (of which, of course, examples still survived in use down to the classical period). Gates of this type survive in the early fortification of Miletus on the Kalabak Tepe [296]. A more elaborate example of a gateway with a forecourt is the Dipylon (Double Gate) at Athens of the fifth-fourth centuries [297, 298]. Most elaborate of all are some gates of the Hellenistic age – the main entrance to

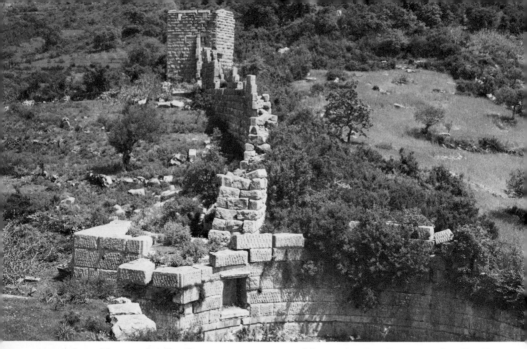

293 and 294. Messene, Arcadian Gate,
north wall with tower (*above*), and niche in gate
(*below, left*), mid fourth century

295. Messene, interior of tower near Arcadian Gate,
mid fourth century

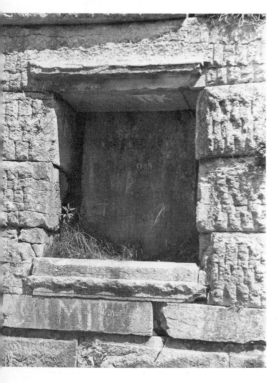

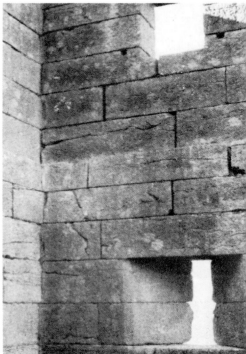

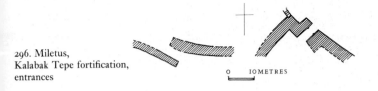

296. Miletus,
Kalabak Tepe fortification,
entrances

0   10 METRES

297. Athens, Dipylon, *Pompeion*, and Sacred Gate, fifth-fourth centuries, plan

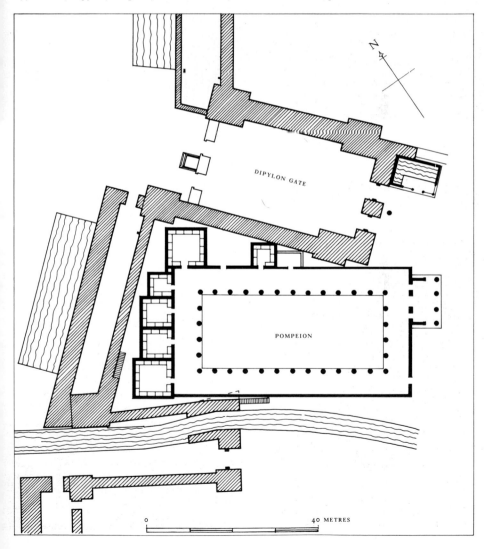

DIPYLON GATE

POMPEION

0   40 METRES

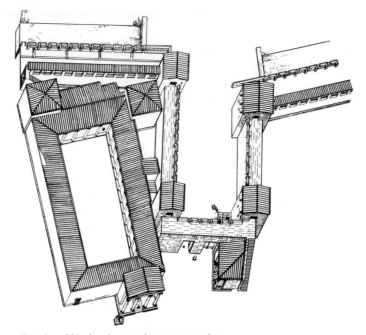

298. Athens, Dipylon, fifth–fourth centuries, reconstruction

Pergamon [299], or that at Side in Pamphylia [300]. Not all Hellenistic gateways are as elaborate or spectacular as these, and it is easier to see here the combination of strict military function with the desire for some embellishment. Gateways which were not at the main

299. Pergamon, main gate, early second century, plan

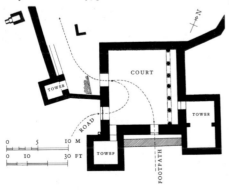

entrances to the cities might well remain simple in form, and this, of course, also applied to the posterns.

Expenditure upon defence restricted most of the Greek states in other forms of public works, and the consequent lack of experience impeded advance in engineering – except, of course, so far as it related to warfare. The tyrants of the late sixth century began the improvement of harbours, an activity essential for defence; wherever possible, fortified moles linked up with walls on land, enclosing the entire harbour except for a narrow entrance across which a chain could be stretched. The tyrants also improved the water supplies, at Samos by piercing a tunnel 1,100 feet long through a hill. Few later undertakings on so large a scale are recorded, and a Greek rival to the poorest Roman aqueduct has yet to be found. An archaic fountain-house at Megara contains forty octagonal pillars, which supported the roof, and there are traces of a porch. Such fountain-

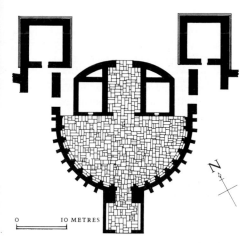

300. Side, main gate, Hellenistic, plan

columns might be disposed either prostyle or *in antis*. On the Olive-tree Pediment [302], from some tiny building on the Acropolis, a fountain-house is shown in profile, and the interior is

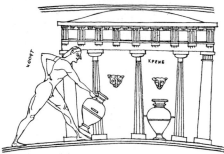

301. Drawing of a fountain on the François vase

houses, which established the type to which their successors almost invariably adhered, are represented on vases and other works of art [301]. The water was made to flow from ornamental spouts; most often it came out of the mouths of bronze lions' heads. The roof was sometimes corbelled, but more often gabled, and supported in front by columns, in which case the building resembled a temple porch; the

represented by an opening painted black; the figures of women originally carried water-pots on their heads.

At many places water was stored underground, in a spring-chamber or a cistern.[6] The Triglyph Wall at Corinth [303] was built about 500, above a spring-chamber, to which a flight of steps leads through an opening in the wall. The triglyphs were painted blue and the

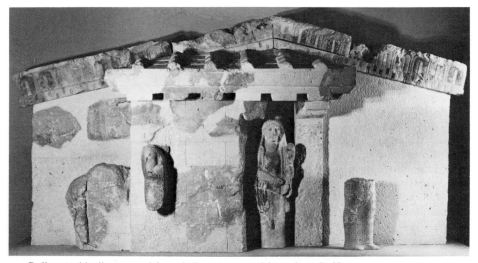

302. Pediment with olive-tree and fountain-house, *c.* 550. *Athens, Acropolis Museum*

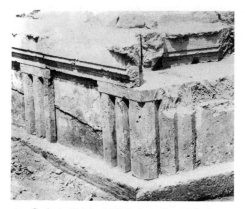

303. Corinth, Triglyph Wall above Sacred Spring, *c.* 500

metopes white, but topped with a blue band.[7] The simplified hawk's-beak moulding above the narrow fascia was decorated with broad tongues, alternately red and blue, with blue and red centres respectively; the borders were yellow. On the broad band above was a 'key' pattern in yellow and red on a blue ground, and from this projected a crowning member to preserve the colours from the weather.

In the Hellenistic period fountains and well-houses existed in great numbers.[8] They ranged from simple niches [271, 323] to quite large buildings with half a dozen columns or pillars along the front, and sometimes others on the sides or in the centre. A large fountain was placed, wherever feasible, in the market area of each city. A unique arrangement can be seen at Corinth in the approach to the torrential spring called Peirene [304]. The water had long since been penned up by a parapet wall behind the face of the rock, at the back of six compartments, separated by partitions which terminated externally in antae; at some late date (after rather than before 200) a pair of Ionic half-columns was placed on the parapet in each compartment, and linked by an entablature, above which the remaining space was filled in.

Roads and even the streets of cities were normally allowed to remain with a natural surface of trodden earth or rock; in fact the propor-

tion of paved streets must have been less in classical Greece than in Minoan Crete. Only one causeway and bridge survives [305].[9] This viaduct, in the neighbourhood of Cnidus, probably dates from within a generation or so of 300; the width is approximately 25 feet. The top of the bridge has fallen; the opening narrows upwards, the side walls being corbelled at such an angle that the slabs were probably laid flat across the gap. If so, the system was identical with that of some possibly Mycenean bridges. Nothing is known of the method of bridging employed in the famous viaduct at Alexandria, which crossed nearly a mile of lagoon to the Pharos island, and incorporated an aqueduct.

The Pharos, the tallest of Greek buildings and prototype of the world's lighthouses, has been utterly destroyed, but descriptions exist, notably one written in A.D. 1166 by an Andalusian Moor, who had taken measurements himself; the appearance, moreover, is more or less accurately imitated in later monuments and illustrated in works of art. It rose to its height of over 440 feet in three stages, each of which stood inwards of that below and itself tapered; the base was square (of about 100 feet), the middle portion octagonal and the top cylindrical.[10] Sostratus of Cnidus was the architect. The date, about 270, is too early for him to have made any considerable use of vaulting in order to lighten the structure; instead, he contrived that the colossal weight of almost solid masonry should press inwards from top to bottom. His skill is attested by the fact that the Pharos stood virtually intact for a thousand years, in spite of earthquakes, and retained much of the original shape through several more centuries, till a Sultan re-used the material to build a fort.

The Tower of the Winds at Athens is the only surviving horologium or clock tower [306–9]. It was built at or soon after the middle of the first century, not later than the year 37, at the cost of Andronicus of Cyrrhus (a town near the Euphrates). The building is octagonal ($25\frac{1}{2}$ feet in diameter), and bears at the top of each side a relief of the personified Wind which blew from

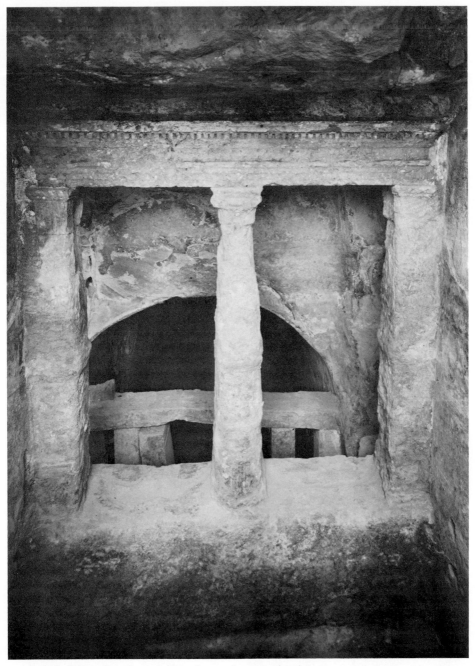

304. Corinth, Peirene fountain, probably early second century, interior

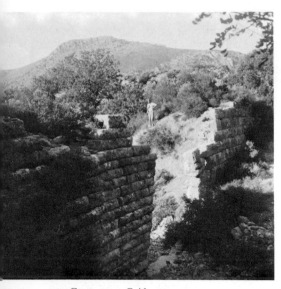

305. Çesme, near Cnidus,
viaduct with bridge, c. 300

306. Athens, 'Tower of the Winds', c. 40

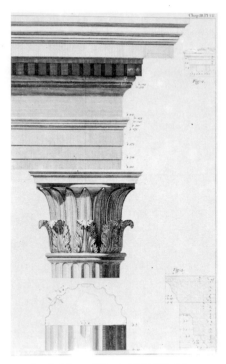

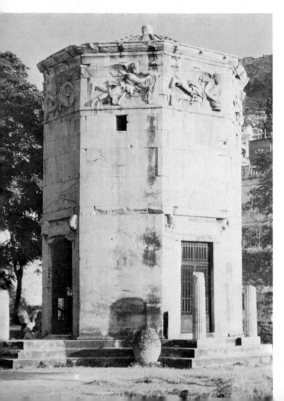

307 and 308. Athens, 'Tower of the Winds', c. 40,
porch Order (*above*)
and internal Doric Order (*opposite*)

that direction. Sundials were attached to the
sides, and a projecting turret held the tank that
supplied a water-clock. There were also two
porches, each with two Corinthian columns
prostyle carrying a pedimented entablature, the
back of which was engaged in a face of the tower.
In these columns the fluting is stopped just
above the foot of the shaft [307]. The capitals
belong to a late variant form, decorated only
with a single row of acanthus leaves beneath a
row of tall, narrow leaves, and the abacus is
square. From the summit of the tower rises an
octagonal Corinthian capital, upon which, 47
feet above ground, was pivoted a bronze statue
of a Triton holding a rod that acted as a wind-
vane. The roof consists of 24 triangular slabs,
which radiate downwards from a hole plugged
by the base of the capital; externally the roof is

octagonal, and carved to simulate tiles; the internal face is conical. A circular architrave masks the conjunction with the octagonal wall, and beneath it at each corner stands a little Doric column upon a circular cornice, which, of course, projects comparatively little from the centre of each side. To compensate for the diminutive scale of these columns, which are less than 4 feet high [308], the shafts are extremely rich; the upper part is fluted, the lower cannelated, in either case between fillets in the Ionic manner, which join at the transition. Two

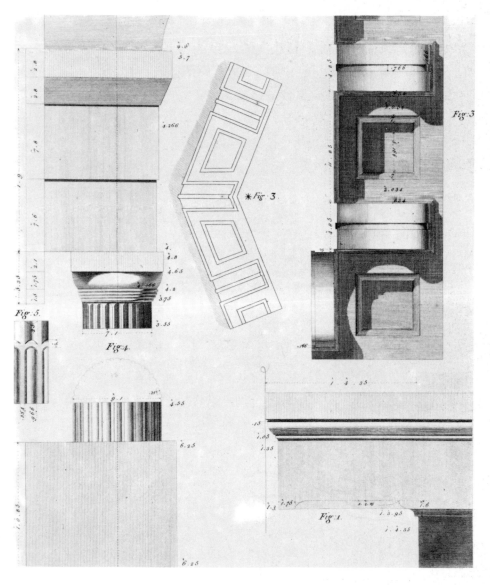

purely ornamental octagonal cornices interrupt the otherwise plain walls below [309]. The upper of these cornices rests upon consoles, and is topped by a row of dentils.

The originality of this building is exceptional, and of a character out of keeping with Hellenistic architecture as we know it. That may be explicable on the ground that all prototypes, among which the Pharos must be included, have been destroyed. In fact, the design is obviously Greek, both in the severity of decorative treatment and in the antiquated method of roofing. The contrast with work of the Roman Empire is extraordinary, considering the date.

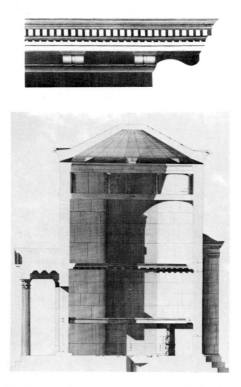

309. Athens, 'Tower of the Winds', *c.* 40, internal cornice and sectional elevation

CHAPTER 21

RESIDENTIAL BUILDINGS

With the collapse of the Bronze Age civilization the standard of living (on the archaeological evidence) dropped to a lower average level than had prevailed for the previous thousand years, and recovery was very slow. The ensuing five or six centuries are represented by too few remains of habitations, other than cottages or hovels, to allow of safe generalizations; only at Old Smyrna has a long sequence of houses been discovered, and their relevance to development in Greece is uncertain.[1] In an eighth-century town at Zagora on Andros, and in one not much later than 700 at Emporio on Chios, the larger houses follow Mycenean precedent by consisting of a hall alone or a hall entered through a porch; wooden posts, resting on stone discs or cylinders, stood inside, sometimes also in antis at the front of the porch. In preference to this pseudo-megaron, a more wealthy or business household at Zagora might occupy a number of smaller rooms along three sides of a courtyard, part of which was covered to form a veranda. No early instance is known of a hall preceded by a courtyard lined with rooms, over which it dominated; however, this apparent compromise may really have been just another item in the Mycenean heritage [cf. 75]. The two basic types of plan both persisted into the third century or even later, but the system of dispersing small and medium-sized rooms around the court was manifestly preferred in classical Greece; examples from the archaic period have been found at the Greek colonies in Sicily.[2] Much improved in the Hellenistic age, it became the accepted norm wherever Greeks had settled. It was, in fact, ideally suited to towns in which streets of more or less equal consequence crossed at right angles, forming blocks best divided into approximately square plots for houses. A hall, on the other hand, fitted readily on a long plot with a narrow frontage; hence, no doubt, its late

survival at Priene, where major streets necessarily followed the contours and were connected only by stepped alleys. The cramped area of a promontory had caused a primitive version of the same scheme to be adopted at Vrulia on Rhodes, a little settlement founded (seemingly for military purposes) about 650. It was laid out with a continuous line of houses along either side of the single street; they are almost uniform in plan, with the main room at the back approached through two smaller spaces, one of which may have been left open as a court.

Many vase-paintings depict homes of deities or legendary characters, and the earliest instances go back to the sixth century. At all periods the buildings are habitually shown in the semblance of a temple porch; it may therefore be surmised that the contemporary type of palace resembled a temple, at any rate as far as the entrance was concerned, and was distinguished by a pair of columns (usually in antis) joined by an architrave, under a frieze of tryglyphs and metopes and a cornice. In the earliest representations, such as the Attic 'François Vase' [87], the roof is drawn curving up from either side, either as a result of faulty perspective, or in an attempt to reproduce the gentle pitch of a thick mud roofing.

At an Aeolic city, identified (perhaps wrongly[3]) as Larisa, changes in palace accommodation can be followed over a period of two hundred years. The oldest palace [310], dating to the early part of the sixth century, consisted of a square chamber (c. 30 by 30 feet; 10 by 10 m.). A porch to the north was formed by columns between antae. These columns may have been surmounted by the Aeolic capitals previously attributed to the next palace. This, dating to 550, is like its predecessor to be related to Aegean architectural tradition, without the oriental influence previously suggested on the basis of an erroneous and unfounded reconstruction of its plan and elevation. Both buildings are the residences of tyrants on the acropolis of a Greek city.

About fifty years later another megaron was built at Larisa. It comprised a porch with two columns *in antis*, a square hall, and two square rooms at the back, each occupying half the width of the building (27 feet; 18·13 m.).

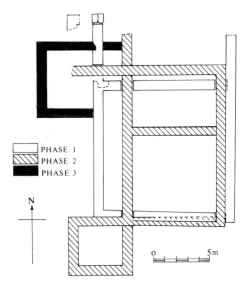

PHASE 1	
PHASE 2	
PHASE 3	

N

310. Larisa, early palace, early sixth century

Some fifty years later a court was enclosed outside the megaron. The open space was square, bounded by the porch columns and by pairs of lower columns on the other three sides, each of which was occupied by a room-like recess. Fully enclosed rooms were provided off three corners of the colonnade. An external stair rose to the fourth corner, up the side wall of the megaron. A smaller room, added soon afterwards, held a latrine.

A much larger palace in Cyprus, at Vouni, was at first planned in complete accordance with Syrian architectural conventions. The more public part was axially planned, from the entrance in one wall to the state apartments against the opposite wall. It was entered through a passage, which contained two successive gateways in its course, as had been the system in the gates of Troy, 2,000 years earlier. At the inner end of the passage a flight of steps led down into a court, on the other three sides of which ran a colonnade, and behind the colonnade lay a number of rooms of more or less equal size. This oriental layout, which dates from about 500, was greatly changed towards the middle and close of the fifth century under Greek influence. The most significant alteration was the conversion of the back of the palace into the front. The new entrance led sideways with three abrupt turns into a room at what had been the far corner of the court. One now had to pass through the court and climb the steps into the former entrance passage, which was transformed into a megaron by blocking the outer end. The two gateways were preserved, with the result that behind the steps lay successively a porch, a long hall, and a very short room terminating at the new outer wall.

This Greek reconstruction of Vouni exemplifies the differences and similarities between their domestic architecture and that of the Asiatic peoples. The typical Greek house, from this time onwards, is secluded from the public view by a bent entrance, and one of its rooms is far larger than the rest. The court at Vouni, with the cistern underneath it, the surrounding colonnade and the recessed spaces that opened off it, could all remain unchanged because such features were thought requisite by Greeks and Asiatics alike. Among other innovations at the palace the most striking was the provision of a hot bath (p. 349); that was a Greek luxury, but beyond the means of a private household. The Greeks made no alteration to the cemented rooms for cold bathing, or to the stone latrine shafts, which are in fact superior to any known to have existed in purely Greek lands during the next three centuries.

From authors of the latter part of the fifth century it is possible to obtain a fairly clear picture of Athenian housing at that time. Walls normally consisted of stone at the base, but otherwise of unbaked brick, and wood was used for the frames of doors and windows. The roofs of the better houses were tiled, but the poor still relied on mud-roofing, of which one example lasted till the time of Christ, when it was regarded as a venerable curiosity. The heart of the city was crowded with blocks of mean little houses, separated by tortuous alleys; spacious houses were rare except in the suburbs outside the town walls. Visitors to a fairly wealthy household stood in the porch and knocked or called to the porter, who sat close behind the door. The porch led to a courtyard bounded by verandas on one or more sides, and there were rooms behind for use in very hot or cold weather. The chief of these rooms was the dining-room, *andron*, so called because men who did not belong to the household were admitted to it. Women could use the court when no strange men were present, and also had their own quarters, shut off by a strong door not so much to keep them safe from drunken guests as to segregate the male and female slaves at night. A steep wooden stair led to the upper floor if there was one, or to the roof if that was flat. A speech by a litigant explains the arrangement of his family: 'My little house is divided into a ground and an upper floor, partitioned in the

same places; the lower rooms are for men's use and the upper for women's use. But after our child was born, his mother nursed him, and to save her the dangerous descent of the stairs whenever he had to be washed, I installed myself on the upper floor and the women on the ground' (Lysias I, 9).

Demosthenes asserts that luxurious houses were not built at Athens before his own lifetime, towards the middle of the fourth century, but this is an oratorical exaggeration. There are earlier references to luxurious houses (for example in Aristophanes' 'Clouds'), and archaeology has revealed the remains of houses of the fifth century which enjoyed a fair standard of comfort. An example, built about 420, was found underlying a later fortification (the Dema wall) between Athens and Eleusis [311]. Another example of the fourth century near Vari on the south-eastern slopes of Mount Hymettus seems to have included a tower, an indication of less settled conditions. These are rural houses.[4] They have their main range of rooms (of two storeys) along one side of the courtyard, other sides being occupied by less important rooms, or even a blank wall. The Dema house had a room recognized as an andron by the eccentric position of the door occasioned (as in the Pinakotheke of the Athenian Propylaea) by the

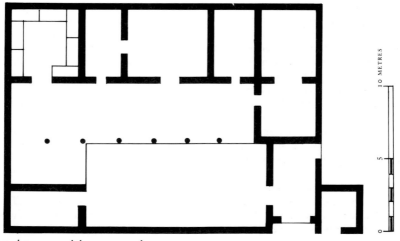

10 METRES

311. Dema house, near Athens, *c.* 420, plan

need to accommodate the couches round the wall. There are several examples of courtyard houses from Athens which show no consistency of plan, other than the existence of the courtyard.[5]

The type of house then favoured at Athens and many other places is best known from Olynthus, where a new suburb was laid out about 430 and completely built up long before the destruction of the city in 348 [312].[6] Each block of houses measures roughly a hundred yards by forty, in which each house occupies an area about twenty yards square. Building plots of regular size were evidently marked off, but within them plans vary considerably. In the individual plans the rooms invariably differ in size, but were almost always rectangular, and their arrangement also differs, though to less marked degree; there is no axial symmetry. A single roof seems to have run continuously over the northern half of each block of houses; separate roofs allowed for differences in the courts, which are all somewhat south of centre. The court is normally the largest unit in the house. The door on the street frontage led to it either directly or through a passage, to one side of which is a little porter's room. The court is usually cobbled, though sometimes cement or even bare earth was used for economy's sake. On one or more, or occasionally on all sides of the court was a veranda with a tiled roof, carried more often by wooden posts than stone pillars; in some houses stone capitals rested on the wooden posts. The wood was raised above the damp by means of stone bases, one of which incorporates some burnt bricks – the earliest Greek instance of the use of this material. A veranda is found on the north side of practically every court, and this was commonly taller than any on the other sides; the occupants could thereby enjoy the winter sunshine, sheltered from the terrible winds of Macedonia. The largest of the half-dozen rooms is the dining-room, the andron or *oecus*, which extends from the court to the external wall, and was situated at a corner, whenever possible, where it could be lit by windows on two sides. Because the Greeks ate reclining on couches and threw the refuse of the meal (preferably fish) on the floor, the couches were placed beside the walls on a raised platform, interrupted only at the doorway, and from the centre of the floor a drain communicated with the street to make cleaning easier. The platform is usually cemented, but in some houses the rest of the floor is covered with mosaic instead of cement; only rarely was mosaic used in rooms other than the andron, or an anteroom which led to it; indeed, floors of hardened earth are even more common than cement. The mosaics are executed in uncut pebbles of two or more colours; some mythological scenes are framed in elaborate patterns. The best, in a two-storeyed house just outside the town [313], shows Dionysus driving a pair of leopards [314], and incorporates some 50,000 pebbles; a small panel, of two Pans at the wine-pot, fills the gap in the platform by the doorway. A house at Eretria, dated to the early part of the fourth century, has mosaics of even better quality, particularly those in the dining room and its antechamber (the usual place, it seems, for mosaics, certainly at Olynthus). These are among the earliest mosaics found in Greece, but they are so accomplished that they must have had countless predecessors; in fact scraps have been excavated at the Phrygian site of Pazarlı in association with semi-Greek objects of the sixth century. Far more splendid are the mosaics found at Pella, in sumptuous houses of the late fourth century. These houses have much larger rooms, and their courts have peristyles of stone columns. They reflect the great wealth acquired by the Macedonians as a result of the conquests of Philip II and Alexander: but their arrangement is essentially the same as that in the houses of Olynthus.

The bathroom in these houses is provided with a cemented or (in rare instances) tiled floor and a short terracotta tub, almost of the Minoan shape apart from a depression for the feet. Terracotta basins are found in other parts of the houses; these were fixed on to the wall, through which pipes ran to carry the waste. Scarcely any indications of latrines have been found. Drains

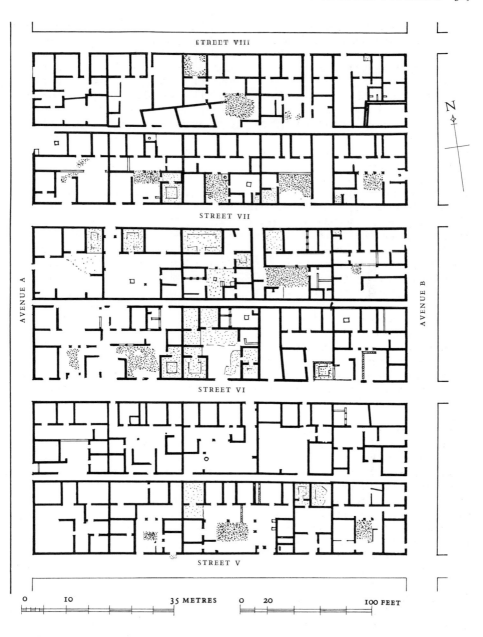

312. Olynthus, blocks of houses, begun *c.* 430, plan

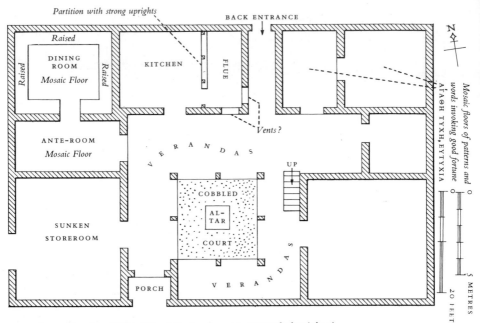

313 and 314. Olynthus, 'Villa of Good Fortune', *c.* 400, restored plan (*above*) and mosaic floors of dining room and doorway (*opposite*)

from the bathroom and the andron floors ran into the street or into a blocked alley which divided the backs of the houses. Occasionally rain-water was conserved in a cistern, but generally it was conducted by a drain to the exterior of the house (Pella had regular drains concealed under the streets). In a good many courts stands an altar for household worship. Scarcely any other fittings remain except round tables and basins of marble or terracotta, mounted on a central columnar support which spreads at the foot. Bronze or terracotta braziers served for heating.

At Olynthus, the walls consisted of sun-dried brick upon rubble foundations; consequently the arrangement on the upper floors is unknown. But enough is left of some walls to prove that they were stuccoed and painted, not with figure compositions, but in bands of colour. In one andron the lowest part of the walls was yellow, divided by vertical bands, and above this came a projecting band, moulded at the edges

and 6 inches wide, which was painted blue with a palmetted floral pattern; an area of red followed immediately above the projection. The ceilings must have been of unplastered wood. Roofs normally were tiled. The windows are likely to have been oblong, like those represented in contemporary vase-painting; actual examples at Ammotopos, where the length considerably exceeds the height, seem to belong to the late fourth or even the third century.

A few remains at other sites, notably in south Italy and Libya as well as those at Pella, indicate that the type of house we know from Olynthus was widespread in the fourth century. Even larger is a courtyard building at Vergina in Macedon [315],[7] placed above the city; from it, the great tumulus covering the royal chamber tombs is plainly visible. It is certainly the royal palace of the Hellenistic kings of Macedon, the Antigonids. Though this owes something to ordinary domestic architecture, it is not simply an enlarged house. The rooms are arranged

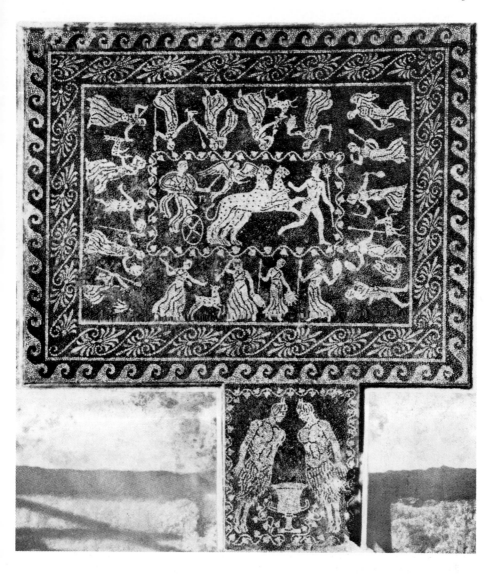

around a large central courtyard, with sixteen Doric columns along each side. There is a wide splendid entrance with a triple doorway centrally placed in the east side (the doorways to Greek houses are always placed to one side, often giving indirect access to the court, for greater privacy). The rooms round the court (the arrangements on the poorly preserved north side are not clear) seem to have been predominantly formal dining rooms. The most splendid are along the south. On this side a centrally placed vestibule, open to the court through a row of piers with engaged Ionic half-columns front and rear, gives access at either

315. Vergina, palace,
Hellenistic, plan

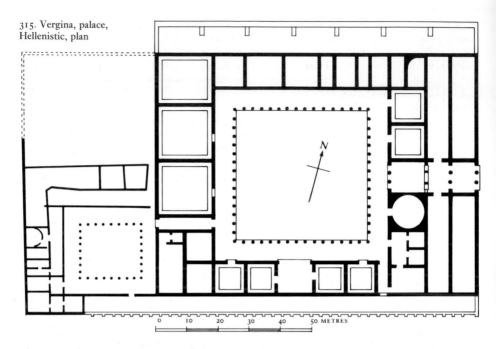

side through eccentrically placed doors with massive marble thresholds to rooms each capable of holding eleven large dining couches. These rooms, and a further room beyond each of them, entered from the court, had floors decorated with excellent pebble mosaics. A circular room to the side of the main entrance has been variously interpreted as a throne room, a bath, or a special room for playing the game of Kottabos, a favourite pastime of revellers at Greek dining parties, where wine was flicked from a cup by a reclining diner at a centrally placed objective, the reason for a circular room being that it gives no player an unfair advantage. Architecturally more important are three rooms on the west side. These have provision for a larger number of couches, and have an apparently unsupported span of over 50 feet (16 m.) – appreciably larger than that which can normally be covered by the limited techniques of Greek roof construction, and implying some more sophisticated method. Despite this, and the splendour of much of its fittings, the walls

of the palace are constructed, above the stone footings, of unbaked brick. There is another, smaller courtyard to the west, approached through a passage, which is probably the service quarters. The total ensemble is much more clearly arranged for banqueting than domesticity, and this presumably is its main function; it reflects architecturally the grades and different ranks of membership found in the courts of Hellenistic monarchs.

Other courtyard buildings provide accommodation for visitors, presumably those of some distinction, to the international religious sanctuary. The Theocoleum, in which the priests at Olympia resided [153, 154], consisted, apart from Roman additions, of a square court at the centre, a room on each side, and a room in each corner. No solid walls faced the court; an architrave supported by two columns *in antis* ran almost the whole length of each room. (Incidentally the combination here of Doric columns and an Ionic architrave is among the earliest instances of the mixture of Orders.) A larger precedent for this type of plan is known from the description by Thucydides (II 69) of an inn built at Plataea in 427, a two-storeyed building 200 feet square. The fourth-century inn at Epidauros,[8] called the *Katagogion*, measured 250 feet square, but was divided into four equal parts, each with its own central court. A portico with ten Doric columns on each side separated the rooms from the court, and must have been flat-roofed in order to provide access to the rooms on the upper storey. An oblong building of approximately the same size, at Olympia, was put up by one Leonidas of Naxos late in the fourth century, probably to serve as a hostel for distinguished visitors [153]. The square court was surrounded by a Doric portico, and the whole exterior was enclosed by a lower portico with 138 Ionic columns; obviously the rooms on the upper floor were entered from the flat roof of this outer colonnade. The small South-east Building at Olympia (immediately to the south of the Echo Stoa) also seems to have been provided with a flat-roofed colonnade, which ran only along the front and both ends. As a rule, however, hostels probably were given plain façades and a colonnade to separate the

court from the rooms, as in a probably fourth-century example at Cassope. Here the Doric columns were octagonal. It was a two-storey building; the upper courses of the walls consisted alternately of burnt brick and tile-faced timbers.

The survival of Mycenean plans in Asia Minor, as shown in the latest palace at Larisa, can be traced into the Hellenistic Age, especially at Priene. There the houses [316],[9] if they date from the late fourth or the third century, contained, as a distinct feature, a porch (if wide, with two columns *in antis*) and the main room behind it. One or two rooms might be placed beside this pseudo-megaron, as in the latest palace at Larisa, but apparently neither these nor any other rooms in the house were given comparable height, and it may be assumed that the porch, which might be as high as 20 feet, was often gabled independently. The outer walls of the houses, and even some of the inner walls, consist of stone, so far as they are preserved, but any upper rooms must have been built of sun-dried bricks. On the street frontage handsome bossed masonry was used whenever the owner's means allowed.

316. Priene, plan of house in original (*left*) and later forms

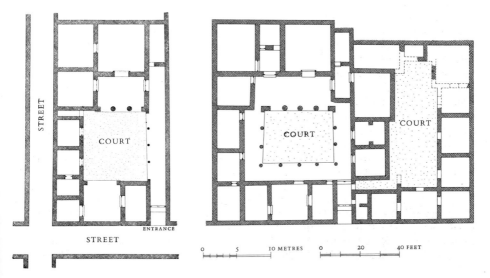

At a later date (probably within the second century) two adjoining houses at Priene were thrown into one, by cutting a series of doorways through the party-wall, and both courts were enlarged. (According to Vitruvius [VI. 7] the wealthier Greeks liked their houses to contain more than one court, but this is the only known example.) In what had been the larger house,[10] the old porch was demolished to make space for a colonnade built on all sides of the court. On the north side thicker and taller columns were used, to allow the winter sunshine to enter; this scheme, says Vitruvius, was called a Rhodian peristyle. It entailed additional expense and must have been regarded as a luxury; it occurs in some of the best houses at Delos, where examples have now been reconstructed [324].

Rock-cut tombs at Mustafa Pasha, Alexandria, very variable in their arrangement, may recall the courtyards of opulent Hellenistic houses,[11] but have been considerably modified for specifically funerary purposes; they should be compared with the heroum at Calydon (above, p. 284) [317]. The engaged Doric half-

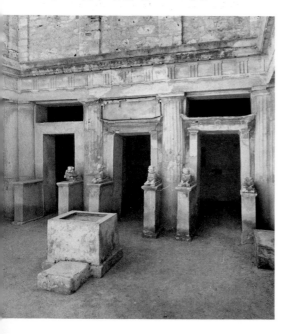

columns (or occasionally Corinthian pilasters) must in general correspond to the free-standing columns of actual buildings; a quarter-column stands on each side of the corners, with a plain strip between. The elaborate door-frames presumably represent wooden originals, but the proportions of the columns are evidently suitable only for stone or stuccoed brickwork. Traces of painted decoration remain on both lintels and walls, and include figure subjects as well as patterns. Two successive layers of painting remain in one chamber of another catacomb at Alexandria, in the suburb of Anfouchy. In the earlier scheme the walls had a greyish-yellow base and a tall dado veined to simulate marble or alabaster slabs; the upper part was divided into rectangles outlined with reddish-brown paint, as though in imitation of isodomic masonry. The later scheme also involved a tall dado painted like alabaster, above which the walls are chequered black and white except in every fourth course, which again simulates alabaster. The segmental barrel-vault has preserved the original decoration of yellow octagons, linked by black squares, while another ceiling appears to imitate in painted form the awning which covered a most famous example of ephemeral architecture, the dining pavilion of Ptolemy II.

The mural decoration of real buildings can seldom be restored with absolute certainty.[12] Fragments of stucco, coloured in imitation of various marbles, have been found in two royal palaces at Pergamon; the mosaic floors were the most sumptuous element in the decoration of these strangely small residences [353], in each of which by far the greater part was occupied by a court, colonnaded on every side. The restored section through a house at Delos [318], though unreliable in detail, must give a fair impression of late Hellenistic decoration. Here again the stucco was often modelled as well as painted, the better to simulate panelling with marble slabs –

317. Alexandria, Mustafa Pasha rock-cut tomb, probably second century

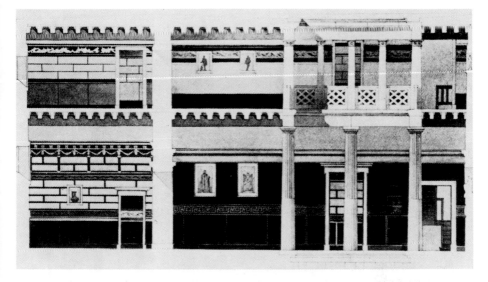

318. Delos, restored section through house, showing conjectural arrangement of mural decoration, probably second century

'incrustation', it is inaptly termed. Paintings with human figures were rare, and filled only a very restricted part of the wall; patterns too were on a small scale and treated with restraint. A timid use of architectural features in the paintings of Alexandrian tombs is interesting in view of the subsequent fashion for decoration of this kind at Pompeii.

The houses at Delos date in the main from the second half of the second century, though a few go back to the third century; the importance of the island as a commercial centre was enhanced in 136, when the Romans declared it a free port, and lasted only till 88. But comparable houses[13] have been found wherever Greeks lived, from Dura on the Euphrates to Olbia in south Russia and Saint-Rémy in France, and between them must cover a longer period of time. The type [319][14] was basically the same as that predominant in the fifth century (for instance, at Olynthus), but more and better accommodation was usually provided and the materials and workmanship are almost invariably superior. In the average house, floors of many rooms and of the court were composed of elaborate mosaics [320, 321], which were no longer made of natural pebbles, but of pieces of stone cut to shape. It was customary for the whole floor of the dining-room to be at one level, and the position of the couches was merely indicated in the mosaic. Often a marble curb edged the court and carried marble columns [322] with elegant capitals; the shafts, however, were sometimes left smooth or cut into a polygon [323], because fluting was so liable to injury. In congested towns few house-plots contained space to build a colonnade on every side of the court, but when this was possible the Rhodian type was favoured; in this, brackets projected from the taller columns to receive the architrave of the lower sides [324]. A two-storeyed colonnade [325] has been reconstructed at Delos in one of the larger houses which occupied an area of 120 by 60 feet (37 by 19 m.). The ground sloped up towards the back so steeply that five floors were required; the stairs were built of stone. Some quite creditable sculpture was placed around the court.

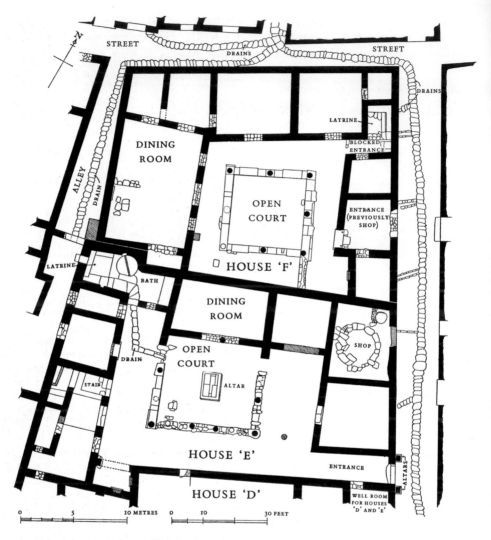

319. Delos, plan of two houses (II, F and E)
as reconstructed after 88

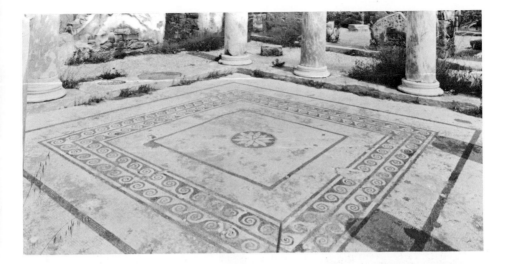

320. Delos, mosaic floor
of court in house,
probably second century

321. Delos,
'Maison des Masques',
mosaic floor,
probably second century

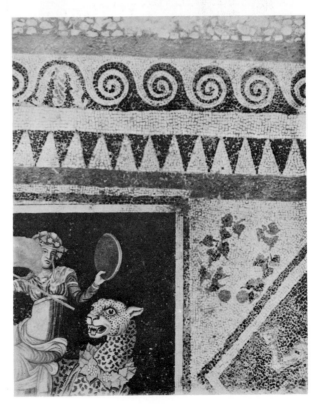

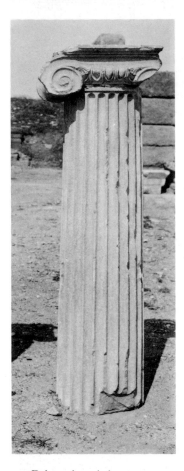

322. Delos, column in house,
probably second century

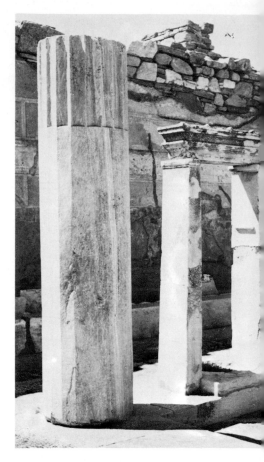

323. Delos, court with well and windlass-stand,
and mural decoration, in house,
probably second century

The roofs of these houses drained into the
court and so into a cistern beneath. No running
water is available on Delos, hence bathrooms
were rare. But as a rule a room off the entrance
passage contained a latrine, with a sunken border to the floor connected by a drain to the
street; at Olynthus very few latrines had existed,
but they had already become common when
Priene was built. From Hellenistic anecdotes
recorded by Vitruvius (x.16.7, 10) there is

reason to suppose that sewage was habitually
carried out of towns in its primary receptacles,
which could have stood arrayed below the
general floor-level of a domestic latrine.

Since the rock on Delos breaks readily into
rectangular blocks and mud for bricks could not
so easily be obtained, the frames of doors and
windows have often been preserved. Many of
the doorways are fairly ornate, and at some
houses a pair of columns stand outside the

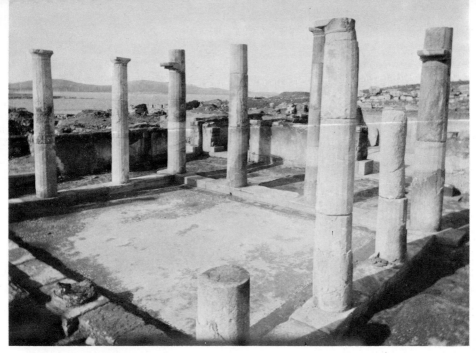

324. Delos, 'Maison des Masques', court with colonnade of two heights, probably second century

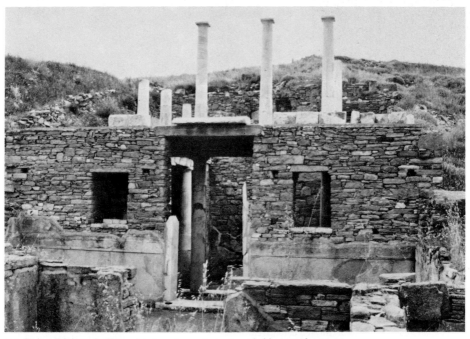

325. Delos, 'Maison de l'Hermès', two-storeyed court, probably second century

entrance. The windows were generally in plain frames, or might be bordered by pilasters with capitals like those of antae; such pilasters sometimes divided the window into several lights. On the ground floor the windows were placed high in the walls, which average about 13 feet in height. Upstairs the windows were lower and more numerous, and varied considerably in shape, and the rooms themselves were not so lofty. Sometimes the whole upper floor appears to have formed a separate flat.

The most remarkable window yet known was found at Piraeus, in the club-house or priests' quarters of the Dionysiasts' Guild, a building which contained inscriptions of the second century. This window had a long, rectangular frame ending in pilasters, but was divided into several lights by Ionic columns, and above the architrave ran a Doric entablature. Another large building of semi-domestic plan, the Hero's Sanctuary at Calydon (p. 284) [263], dates from about 100.

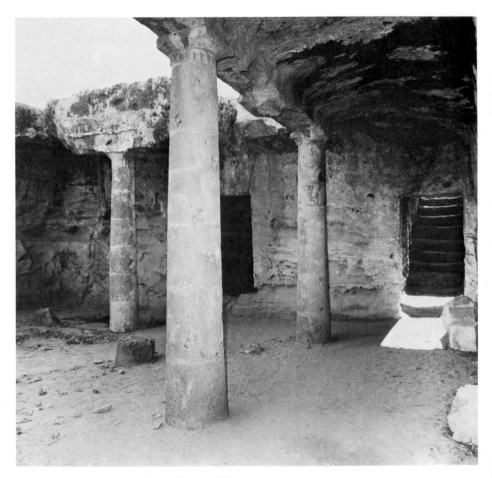

326. Paphos, court of rock-cut 'Royal Tomb', Hellenistic

The 'Royal Tombs' at Paphos, in Cyprus [326], are subterranean imitations of houses, cut in the rock, and appear to be somewhat later than most of the houses at Delos. Since Paphos was the centre of the Ptolemaic administration of Cyprus, they presumably reflect the same attitude to burial as the Mustafa Pasha tombs; they are not part of a Cypriot tradition.[15]

Few houses can be dated to the first century, but there can have been little further development; in fact, the Greek houses built early in the Christian era still adhered to the old type, except for the occasional intrusive example of a Roman plan. But the Roman house had already become transformed by the adoption of many elements of the Hellenistic type, and for this fusion the Italian community of rich businessmen at Delos may have been largely responsible.

CHAPTER 22

TOWN-PLANNING AND HALLS BEFORE 330

Very little is known about the layout of Greek cities before Hippodamus of Miletus introduced a system of orderly planning about 470 or 460. (A very early town at Zagora in the island of Andros which flourished from c. 900 until its total abandonment in the seventh century has rectangular rooms in groups, with a tendency (but nothing more) to straight alignment.) But it would be wrong to assume that earlier cities invariably presented an entirely haphazard appearance. In the seventh century the houses at Old Smyrna were laid out with a uniform orientation throughout at least several parts of the city, and the streets must therefore have run straight. And a small settlement – perhaps a military post – at Vrulia on Rhodes was laid out on an intelligible plan as early as 650. The site is long and narrow, and was entered at one end, where first an open sanctuary and next to it a public square occupied the whole width; the rest was divided longitudinally by a straight street lined with houses. A completely rectangular town plan at Olbia, a Milesian colony in south Russia, is also quite early; it seems to date from a reconstruction at the end of the sixth century, necessitated by a fire. Both these places, however, occupied unusually flat ground. A small city in Crete, Lato, should be more representative, the site being uneven and the layout old-fashioned. Its streets are narrow and tortuous. Its one open space occupied a steep-sided col between two hills [327]. Cramped though it is, this piece of ground was certainly the agora, the combined market-place and administrative centre of the State – *forum* is the Latin equivalent. It was probably laid out, in its entirety, in the second half of the fourth century, or even as late as the early third. A stoa closed it off from the main street, which winds (see arrows on the plan) from a gateway far below. In the middle was a large cistern and a shrine; at the

upper end, nine very wide steps rose against a terrace, on top of which was the prytaneum, which had a courtyard, probably with a central peristyle to the east, and, to the west, a room arranged as a *hestiatorium*, a dining room. Here the committee of the State met and the officials and public guests dined and, perhaps, slept. To the west of the steps were two small rooms. The steps would have provided standing-room for a couple of hundred people, or seats for about eighty-five; the treads are not wide enough to give room for the feet of persons sitting on the step above, as was the case with the theatral areas at Minoan palaces. Whether or not the Minoan tradition lived on, the steps were obviously meant to hold an audience, and two narrow flights with lower treads ran up through them in the manner seen in a normal Greek theatre. There were steps for the same purpose in an older Cretan town, Dreros, and, on monumental scale, enclosing part of an agora built after 317, at Morgantina in Sicily, where a speakers' platform was included.[1] At Athens too the Assembly of all the thousands of citizens met in the agora until about 500, when the Pnyx was constructed for the purpose, in a form afterwards universally adopted for theatres.

The Council (*Boule*) at Athens met in a special building, the Bouleuterion, on the west edge of the agora. It was originally built (over structures rather differently organized) some time after 508, when the Kleisthenic council, the 500, was instituted. It was square (78 by 76½ feet; 23·80 by 23·30 m.), with a partition some 20 feet inwards which cut off a lobby along one side. Apparently the speakers stood beside the middle of the partition, while the audience sat on benches parallel with the three outer walls; that can be deduced from the arrangement of the columns, of which there seem to have been five, three in a row facing the partition at two-

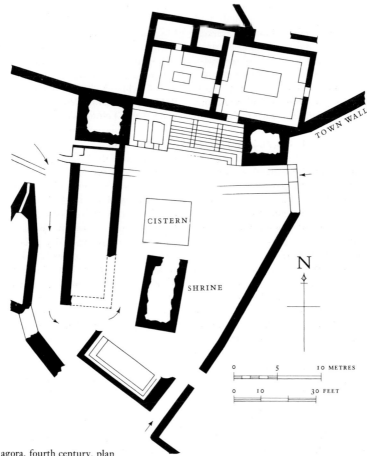

327. Lato, agora, fourth century, plan

thirds of the distance to the back wall, and one midway between each outer column of the row and the partition. The eminently practical scheme of this council-house may have set the ultimate pattern for buildings of its class, whereas all previous halls may have been long and narrow, exactly like non-peripteral temples. That type was still occasionally employed during the next two centuries, though only when a relatively small number of persons had to be accommodated. In some halls of this shape a row of columns was placed along the centre of the floor, to support the ridge of the roof.

An extraordinary, and to all appearances most unsuitable, variant at Olympia is best explained on the ground of the conservatism proper to a sanctuary of most venerable antiquity [153, 154]. A pair of round-ended halls, each twice as long as it was wide ($36\frac{1}{4}$ feet; 11·07 m.) and containing a row of columns along the centre to carry the ridge of the roof, were built parallel, one in the sixth and the other in the fifth century; in the Hellenistic period a square room was added to fill the gap between them, and then the whole façade was unified by a prostyle porch, with twenty-seven Ionic columns on the front and four returning on each side. That this agglomeration should have served as a council-house appears scarcely credible, but the identification is almost certain. Perhaps the older hall followed, as sentiment might demand, the shape of a predecessor; the plan is typical of the larger houses in the Middle and Late Bronze Age, and foundations of such have been discovered in other parts of the sacred precinct.

A great many halls of all periods show some relationship to a stoa; indeed, the Greeks made no clear distinction in their speech between an enclosed room and the open-fronted shelter with a lean-to or pitched roof, to which the term stoa is now conventionally restricted. A building which exemplifies the fusion was the hall, of about 540, in which votive gifts were displayed in the sanctuary on Samothrace. In proportions it resembled a temple ($32\frac{3}{4}$ by 74 feet; 10·70 by 22·6 m.); the horizontal cornice of the sides continued upwards as the sloping cornice of each gable, while an independent moulding of slighter projection outlined the base of a pediment. One of the sides was left open, with a Doric colonnade of limestone stretching between wooden antae; stone, wood and terracotta were intermingled in the entablature and gutter. The somewhat larger Anaktoron at Samothrace, a hall for initiation into the lower grade of the Cabeiric Mysteries, was entirely closed except for a row of three doorways along one side.

Another hall of the last years of the sixth century, the Telesterium built at Eleusis by the Pisistratids for the Mystery Play [287, 328], had more in common with the Council House of Athens. But instead of a lobby there was a prostyle porch with a colonnade along the east and one more column returning at either side, and the room itself was square, 83 feet internally. The south-west corner was occupied by a representation of the palace which formed the scene of the Play, but otherwise the outer walls were lined with nine continuous steps, too narrow for seats, on which the audience must have stood. The room would have contained no less than five rows of five columns each but for the intrusion of the 'palace', the front of which took the place of the last three columns of the row along the south wall. This was apparently the first Greek building roofed upon cross-rows of columns, an idea which could have been derived from Egypt.

Not long after its destruction by the Persians in 480, the Telesterium was rebuilt without a porch [328, bottom left]. The east wall stood on the foundations of the old porch, and a new west end elongated the hall to such an extent that the 'palace' became central in the south side. Three rows of seven columns, almost certainly Ionic, were placed closer to one another than to the walls, in order to give a better view to the spectators on the steps (of which there were seven, stretching continuously except on the east end, and where the 'palace' projected past them).

The new city of Miletus, the planning of which Hippodamus began some time after 479, most likely in 466, occupied a low peninsula stretching northwards into the sea.[2] It was divided by streets which cross at right angles but are spaced differently in the northern and southern parts of the town. In all they form roughly four hundred blocks, each a quarter longer than it is wide. In the northern portion, where the site is narrower, the longer side of each block measures about 96 feet and goes roughly north-west and south-east, across the peninsula; the streets are about 12 feet wide. In the more spacious southern portion the axis of the block is reversed, not precisely but almost so, with the result that again it accords with the shorter dimension of the built-up area. Here the blocks are nearly 140 feet long, the width of the streets is increased by a couple of feet, and two main avenues of some 25 feet wide run in either direction. They are not centrally placed among the minor streets, but conduct to widespread groups of public buildings and open spaces which together stretched in a belt across the peninsula. This civic area not only separated the northern and southern portions of the town, but also cut the northern in two by extending to

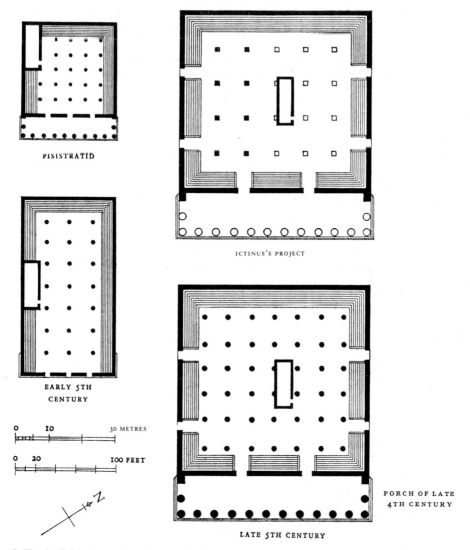

PISISTRATID

EARLY 5TH
CENTURY

ICTINUS'S PROJECT

PORCH OF LATE
4TH CENTURY

LATE 5TH CENTURY

328. Eleusis, Telesterium, plans of successive forms

what used to be a small harbour, an inlet behind the city wall, at which a chain could be raised across the mouth in times of danger.

In the civic area, so admirably central to every part of Miletus, all business, whether public or individual, was conducted; the rest of the city was purely residential. This division is characteristic of ancient Greek cities, and it has always been characteristic of Asiatic cities. At Miletus, as at many other places, the ground for

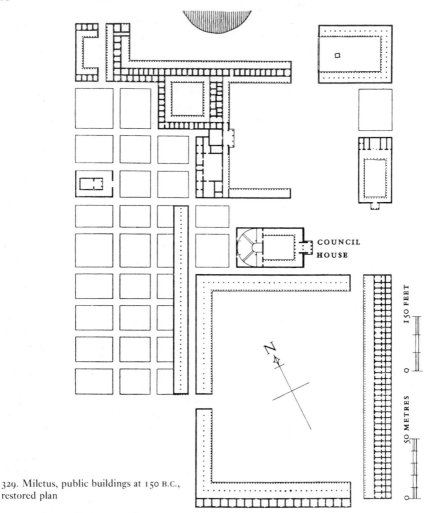

329. Miletus, public buildings at 150 B.C.,
restored plan

COUNCIL
HOUSE

150 FEET

50 METRES

the civic area must have been reserved from the start. Here lay the agora, and a number of buildings associated with it, mainly stoas, gradually arose upon and around it [329]. Although their size involved interruptions to the network of streets, a strictly rectangular layout on the same axis (mainly that of the northern section) was enforced upon them and gave them an evident relation to each other.

Hippodamus is often credited with the invention, for the Greeks, of the grid-plan system, and cities arranged in this way (which became more frequent with the development of new cities, or moving other ones to new sites, such as Priene about the middle of the fourth century) are often loosely referred to as Hippodamian. It is clear that the Greeks employed these plans, which are a natural convenience in dividing up newly allotted land, particularly when it is reasonably level (and even on hilly sites: Miletus is distinctly not level), at a much earlier date, as far back as the archaic colonizing period. Old Smyrna seems to have been arranged in a regular fashion already in the seventh century, and part of a very extensive grid plan has been revealed at Himera.

Another fifth-century scheme which originated before the influence of Hippodamus reached Greece, aroused the interest of Pausanias 600 years later; he remarks in his guidebook that Elis, which was founded in 471, was 'built in the older fashion, with the stoas standing unrelated to one another and separated by streets'. In fact the plan of Elis, so far as it has been excavated, resembles that of a sanctuary in its grouping of buildings far apart, each on its individual axis. Nor was it the latest example of the kind, although Hippodamus toured the Greek world laying out cities on his own principles and they became fairly generally accepted. Pericles fetched him to re-plan Piraeus, and here two main avenues crossed at right angles beside the agora, giving it access while keeping traffic aside. His influence, if not his own work, may be seen at Olynthus, in a residential suburb built late in the fifth century.[3] The site is a long plateau, which gradually contracts towards the north end. From side to side of it run streets uniformly some 16 feet wide, whereas those which run north and south are graduated, equally narrow if they follow the edge, but wider the nearer they are to the centre, where the avenue measures $22\frac{3}{4}$ feet. The spacing does not vary; the intervals between lengthwise streets measure $283\frac{1}{4}$ feet, and between cross-streets $116\frac{1}{2}$ feet, but half-way between these latter are alleys $4\frac{1}{2}$ feet wide, separating the backs of the houses [312]. The plan ceases to be wholly rectangular where the site contracts towards the point of the hill, but the irregularity is confined to the edges; the straight course of the western lengthwise street brings it to a stop against a re-entrant, and another opens from the last cross-street, behind the houses on the inward side, and runs in two successive slants to the north end. In mainland Greece the town of Halieis has streets which run in straight lines, though not forming a strictly rectangular grid. Within the blocks the house plans are extremely variable (though of courtyard type): they do not conform to the regular division of plot found at Olynthus.

From the fifth century onwards stoas were indispensable adjuncts of the agora. An early example (possibly of about 550) is the small Stoa Basileios (the office of the King Archon) at Athens (placed where the processional 'sacred way' enters the agora). It measures only 58 feet (17·75 m.) in length by 23 feet (7·18 m.) wide. The front rested on a Doric colonnade and could have seated nearly a hundred persons. The King Archon had religious and religiojudicial functions. The stoa was extensively rebuilt at the end of the fifth century. In general, the function of a stoa was primarily to offer shelter from the sun and rain, as in the case of those at sanctuaries, but they were also regularly used as meeting-places for business purposes; in a building of such length several groups of people could discuss their affairs in comparative privacy, even when there were no partitions across it. Eventually it became customary to divide the interior into a large number of market-stalls and shops and offices, by means of partitions, often of wood, which projected about halfway from the back wall towards the colonnade. Because of their greater depth, such stoas required a ridged roof with intermediate support. Sometimes the front wall of the compartments was utilized for the purpose, but often we find, instead or in addition, an internal colonnade, preferably Ionic in order to occupy as little space as possible; externally a Doric Order was the rule [cf. 336]. Actually the oldest instance of an internal colonnade in a stoa dates from the middle of the sixth century; the motive in this case was to enable visitors to the sanctuary of Hera at Samos to sleep under cover from driving rain [83]. Several stoas have compartments specially arranged as dining rooms: these are found in the original south stoa of the Athenian agora, and another at Brauron (like the south stoa to be dated to the end of the fifth century, or perhaps the early fourth) has rooms where the bronze-lined sockets to fix the feet of the dining couches are still preserved, along with solid tables of stone with marble slab tops.

This stoa was never completed.[4] The colonnade of the north side was finished, but wings to the west (with more rooms and an entrance, which were built) and the east, where there were no rooms, which would have completed the virtual enclosure of a small courtyard, with the temple to the south, were not extended beyond the first pair of columns. These two stoas seem to be the earliest with rooms at the back, a development of Athenian architecture which subsequently was widely copied.

Another variety of stoa broke the façade into a recessed centre and two projecting wings, along which the colonnade turned; in plan, at least, the scheme resembles a theatre's scene-building with paraskenia. A very fine example [330] was built at Athens in the late fifth century on the west side of the agora, and dedicated to Zeus Eleutherius, the Deliverer, a statue of whom must have stood on the large pedestal outside and constituted the focal point of the design. The external Doric colonnade comprised nine columns along the recess, spaced more widely than the others; including the angle columns in each case, there were four on either off-set and six on either wing, where the end

330. Athens, restored plan of agora in the second century

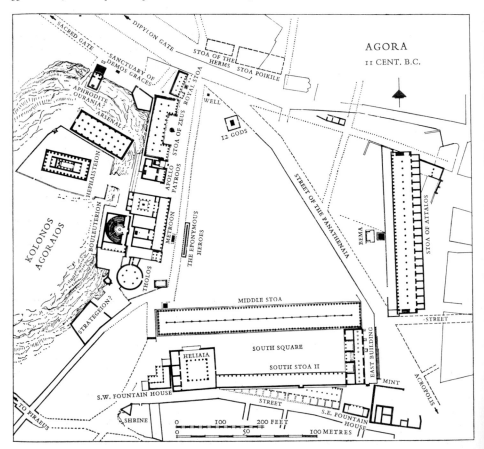

wall stopped short at an anta one intercolumniation inwards. At the wider spans of the centre two triglyphs were placed between each pair of columns instead of one elsewhere; in this respect, and to some extent as a whole, the design recalls the Propylaea. In the interior was a row of seven Ionic columns opposite every second column of the recessed portion and of the central intercolumniations of the wings, with another Ionic column interposed on each side in alignment with the recessed colonnade. Ridged roofs came forward over the wings, ending in pediments which contained no sculpture but supported acroteria; the main roof must also have been ridged, above the Ionic colonnade, so that valleys of the same depth were formed at its junctions with the wings. To this no parallel existed in the Propylaea.

A pyramidal roof covered the square concert-hall (Odeum) at Athens which Pericles commissioned, and may have been topped by a lantern with open sides, for light and ventilation; nine rows of nine columns gave support. Another large roof was designed by Ictinus for the Telesterium at Eleusis [328]. It has been suggested (but there is no archaeological evidence) that this too had arrangements for admitting light at the centre. Ictinus doubled the width of the building by extension westwards, with the result that the hall became square, about 170 feet each way internally; the 'palace' stood along the east side of the centre. He may have intended[5] to erect an oblong opening above the actual centre, and made preparations for columns to be placed unsymmetrically to support it; the arrangement involved five rows north to south but only four east to west, the direction parallel with the front of the 'palace'. The design, however, was abandoned, probably from fear of the enormous spans it entailed. Other architects completed the building, multiplying the number of columns and re-arranging them in seven rows of six. The centre, in the final design by Xenocles, was again oblong; he combined it with a ridged roof ending in pediments at east and west. Although Ictinus seems to have revived the Pisistratid

idea of a prostyle porch along the east, its construction may not have been seriously attempted till a hundred years later, when the architect Philo undertook it. His design involved twelve Doric columns on the façade and one more on either side between it and an anta; the total length was nearly 180 feet, making the pediment roughly equal to those of the Artemisium at Ephesus. Such final touches as the fluting were never completed.

A new Council House at Athens was likewise built shortly before 400 and a porch added about 300 [330]. It stood immediately behind its predecessor on rising ground, which was now hollowed out to form a sloping basis on three sides where tiers of benches were placed. In fact, the design of a theatre (or of the Pnyx) had been adapted to suit an enclosed hall. The shape is an oblong, and cuttings in the rock indicate the position of two pairs of columns, set respectively close to the front and back walls in order to cause as little obstruction as possible.

In 371 the Arcadian League founded Megalopolis for its capital, and within some thirty years of that date a hall called the Thersilium was built there for its Council, a body said to have numbered 10,000. The Thersilium could have seated 6,000 [331]. It was oblong; the

331. Megalopolis, Thersilium, mid fourth century, restored plan (later supports in outline)

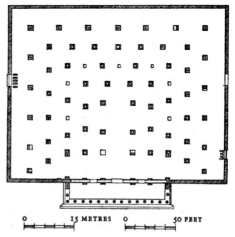

0   15 METRES   0   50 FEET

sides of 172 feet equalled the Telesterium in length, while the front and back measured 218½ feet (67·71 by 86·10 m.). The centre of the front consisted of a line of doorways; the two doorways in each of the other walls required steps, for the ground rose higher towards the back. Inside, the columns were placed to cause the minimum obstruction between the audience and the speaker, whose position was clearly at the centre of a square space delimited by four columns, which put him half-way between the side walls but nearer the front than the back. All other columns stood around these four, aligned in concentric and equidistant rectangles, but with the individual columns sited so that they radiated outwards from the speaker's position. Consequently their spacing varied in each row, and was especially wide in the third – too wide, as it proved, and at some later date intermediate, slighter, columns were inserted. The Order seems to have been Doric, with unfluted shafts. The roof they supported is known to have been tiled but its shape is uncertain. Proably there was a lantern carried by the columns of the speaker's square and the two between it and the front, the only others which are not radially placed. The prostyle porch outside the main entrance was a slightly later addition, and served also as the scene-building of the adjoining theatre. It comprised fourteen Doric columns along the façade – a record number beneath a pediment – in addition to one more and an anta on each return.

A building of the early fourth century, the *Pompeion* at Athens [297], should be mentioned here, because the Greeks presumably classed it as a hall. It served as the gallery and starting point for the Panathenaic procession, which advanced along the sacred way through the agora and on to the Acropolis at the opening of the festival of Athena. It consists of a courtyard measuring 57½ by 141 feet (17·50 by 43 m.) surrounded by a colonnade of simplified Ionic columns. The walls were of mud brick, except for a marble gateway in the east side, whose thresholds are rutted by the wheels of the chariots and other vehicles used in the procession. The building dates to the end of the fifth or the early fourth century, replacing a slightly earlier structure left uncompleted. Placed in an awkward angle between the city walls and the sacred gate, there was not space for a full line of rooms behind the colonnade. Instead it was given three pairs of rooms of different dimensions, which functioned as dining rooms for groups of seven, eleven, and fifteen couches respectively. There is also a fountain. A much smaller building of the mid fifth century (but afterwards reconstructed), the Lesche of the Cnidians at Delphi, served as a combined club and picture-gallery, possibly again as a dining room, and in it wooden pillars supported an overall roof.

In the fourth century the scale of stoas was increased, and it became customary to build stone partitions within; occasionally an upper floor was provided. An unusually large example, 525 feet long, is the so-called south stoa at Corinth,[6] with no less than seventy-one Doric columns along its straight façade. On the gutter was a row of water-spouts in the form of lions' heads separated by acanthus scrolls, and an antefix above each interval [332]; other antefixes stood on the roof-ridge, aligned with the lions' heads. Inside the stoa was an Ionic colonnade, and behind it a row of thirty-three shops, each with a doorway at the back, giving access to as many storerooms. Deep wells inside the shops tapped a supply of water from the spring of Peirene, which gushes out of the rock at the east end of the agora; perhaps the shopkeepers originally used them for cold storage, though in 146, when the Romans sacked Corinth and destroyed the stoa, one shop contained such goods as paint, clay, and lime, and another a variety of fancy pottery. In all, this stoa would appear to have fulfilled every business requirement of the time. It was probably built in 338. Stoas of the old simple kind were still in demand. One, which cannot be more than a few years earlier, served as a hostel at the Amphiaraeum, a medical centre in Boeotia; the front rested on Doric columns, and there was an Ionic colonnade inside.

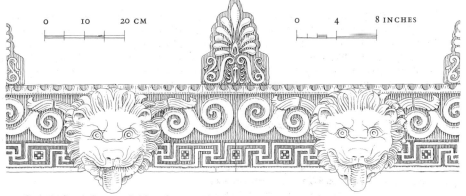

0   10   20 CM   0   4   8 INCHES

332. Corinth, South Stoa, probably 338, restored gutter

Very enterprising buildings of hall character were constructed at Piraeus for the Athenian navy. At several parts of the shore, a whole group of ships was housed together in one connected series of sheds extending far along the water-front and inland; the floor sloped down into the sea. The roof formed a series of ridges and valleys, supported by columns. Each gable may have covered two ships abreast, separated by a row of columns, because tall and low columns seem to have been placed in alternate rows.[7] There was also an arsenal at Piraeus to contain the movable equipment of the fleet. This was a gigantic hall under a single ridged roof [333].[8] The building is known only from an inscription which recorded the specifications in

333. Piraeus, arsenal, 340-330, restoration

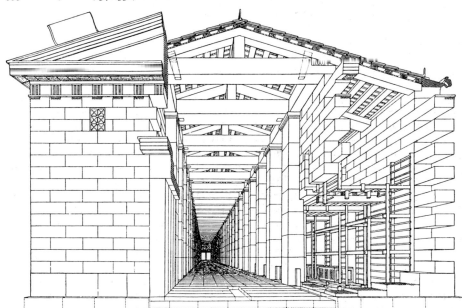

detail for the sake of establishing a check upon the contractors. They built it between 340 and 330, to the design of Philo, the architect who added the porch to the Telesterium. The dimensions are stated in feet 14 per cent longer than our measure, but I quote them unaltered, because conversion would obscure the simplicity of the proportions. The height was 27 feet to the top of a Doric frieze which surrounded the walls just below the cornice. The length, 405 feet, equalled fifteen times this height; the width, 55, was practically double it. There was a pediment at each end. Beneath its centre stood a marble pillar which separated a pair of doorways, 9 feet wide by 15½ feet high. The interior measured 50 by 400 feet. It was divided by two rows of thirty-five stone pillars or columns, 30 feet high, into a 20-foot nave and narrower aisles. Wooden architraves on these supports served as purlins of the roof, and other beams spanned the nave from column to column; upon the centre of each of these stood an upright block of timber which supported the ridge beam. A series of rafters was carried from the ridge beam over the architraves to the side walls, and supported smaller battens, on which in turn was fixed a continuous boarding; the terracotta tiles were laid on this in a bed of mud. The lighting must have been very poor; there were three windows at each end, and in the side walls only one opposite each intercolumniation and that quite small, 3 feet high and 2 feet wide.

Windows were probably much more frequent in secular buildings than can be proved by the majority of excavations. Dining-halls in the sanctuary of Delos were lit by windows even in the sixth century, and the numbers and the size of the windows are the most striking features in two unusually large dining-halls at Labranda, built about 350 by Mausolus and his successor Idrieus. In plan these resemble temples in antis, but for a rectangular niche at the back. The other walls were presumably lined with wooden couches arranged, like the stone couches in a dining-hall at Perachora,[9] for the guests to recline head to head in pairs. A table must have been placed beside each couple, as represented in vase-paintings of secular banquets.

Perachora belonged to Corinth, where details of the south stoa, believed to date from 338, are in one case more but in another less developed than the corresponding parts of a stoa at the outlying sanctuary (thereby demonstrating the fallibility of dating on stylistic analogies). Most of the colour-scheme of the Perachora stoa has been recovered. In the Doric colonnade of the lower storey, the stone was covered with white stucco, and small areas were then painted. Above regulae with red guttae and a red taenia came red triglyphs with blue grooves. The lowest band of the cornice bore a 'key' pattern, white against a black ground with touches of red; on the wave-moulding above was leaf and dart ornament, in red, white, and blue. The mutules were red underneath and the dripgroove was red. The wave-moulding at the top of the cornice bore a leaf-pattern in blue, red, white, and black. The Ionic columns of the upper storey were doubtless mainly white, but the base and capital were picked out with some red and blue. The colouring of the upper entablature, which was wooden, is unknown; the terracotta gutter was elaborately patterned on both face and soffit, with pale areas predominating over the necessarily dull red and black.

The Altar Court at Samothrace has been considered already (p. 278) because of its relevance to the Altar at Pergamon. Another sacrificial enclosure in the same sanctuary was entered through a propylon thought, from its style, to date from about 340. The broad but thin central portion and the two projecting wings were fronted with an Ionic colonnade, which turned the corners. Above the architrave (of three fascias) came a frieze, to which metal decoration was attached, and then dentils.

CHAPTER 23

HELLENISTIC TOWN-PLANNING AND HALLS

Alexander's conquest of the Persian Empire, completed in the year 330, gave new life to the Greek cities of Asia Minor, and the diffusion of Hellenism among the oriental peoples was stimulated by the foundation of Alexandria and countless other cities after the Greek model. A general increase of wealth during the Hellenistic Age is reflected in larger agora space and a more generous allowance of stoas, but in other respects no appreciable change can be seen in town-planning. Several Hellenistic cities have been excavated over a large proportion of their area. The oldest, Priene,[1] was refounded probably in 334, and in the main its buildings date from the third century. It occupied the sloping ground beneath an almost inaccessible acropolis, 1,000 feet high; the walls enclose the whole area with a very irregular line but the built-up portion (at the south) is divided on a

rectangular plan. The streets that run east and west, in which direction the ground is almost level, vary in width between $12\frac{1}{2}$ and $14\frac{1}{2}$ feet, apart from two larger avenues between which lay the agora; a stoa along its southern edge compelled a short diversion of one avenue, the other separated the open space from a stoa on the north. Eventually [334] this upper avenue entered the agora under a gateway, probably added in 156, which may be the earliest Greek instance of an ornamental arch. From south to north the ground rises steeply, and in that direction the streets are mostly narrower and include only one more avenue, likewise narrower. The blocks are longer from south to north, 155 feet compared with 116 feet in width.

An example of the treatment of flat ground may be seen at Dura-Europus, a Greek colony built on a plateau overlooking the Euphrates. It

334. Priene, agora, third century, gateway probably 156, restoration

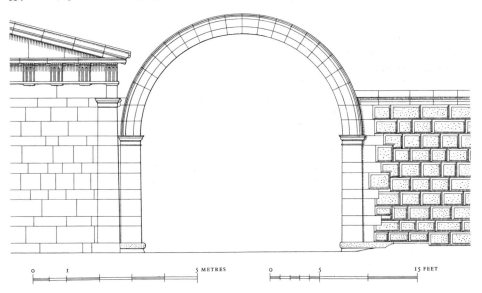

| 0 | 1 | | | | 5 METRES | | 0 | | | | 5 | | | | 15 FEET |

was founded within a few years of 300. Here the blocks have an average frontage to the larger streets of 123 feet and a length of as much as 325 feet along the narrow cross-streets. The route from Syria to Mesopotamia entered the town under a tall arch and formed the main avenue, which is 30 feet wide; the other streets in the same direction are about half as wide. Here again the rectangular plan is enclosed by less regular walls; a street ran along their inward side, presumably to enable their defenders to move rapidly to points where danger threatened. None of the larger cities of the Hellenized East has been excavated, but they seem to have all been built on rather similar plans; at a few of them the main avenue was lined with colonnades, an amenity which became general under the Roman Empire in these hot countries.

The remnants of a civic building at Sicyon can be dated only vaguely to the late fourth or early third century. It was square or nearly so, probably measuring about 130 feet a side, and contained Ionic columns arranged in four rows of four, equally spaced in relation to one another and to the walls. A piece of floor between the central square of columns and one of the walls was banked up with earth, against retaining walls, to form tiers of straight benches on three sides; these were stuccoed to make them keep their shape. In front of them were two curved benches of the same material. Some 250 persons could have been seated, and probably the Council met in this portion of the building. In various other small cities a stoa was built or utilized for a council-house, and if, as is conceivable, the building at Sicyon had been open along one or more sides, it would have combined all that the Greeks desired for that purpose. The value they attached to open-air accommodation is illustrated by the additions made around 300 to the Council House (Bouleuterium) at Athens [330]. This building stood behind, and so was reached from the agora through a passage which met it at a corner of the front; a deep porch was now constructed along the end of the hall with a return to its front, so that the passage led

directly to the colonnade. A propylon was also built across the mouth of the passage. This, like the porch, was Ionic; it faced the agora with four columns prostyle, while the inner end was given two in antis.

At Delos a hall,[2] the Neorium of the inscriptions, was especially built to hold a warship, probably that used by Demetrius Poliorcetes at the naval battle of Cypriot Salamis in 306 B.C., and dedicated to Apollo as a thankoffering for victory [335]. The main hall, which contained the ship, would in any case have been unduly long, but the length of the building was exaggerated to eight times the width by the inclusion of a deep prostyle porch at the front, and of an inner room behind the main hall. The cella appears to have had a pitched ceiling. The division between the main hall and the inner room took an unparalleled form. A Doric half-column was engaged in each wall, and two more stood between, facing outwards, each engaged in a pier which was ornamented on the flat inward side by a sculptured capital representing the forepart of a kneeling bull, perhaps the result of the influence of Achaemenid architecture. Over the inner room (which contained an altar) rose a tower-like lantern, the sloping roof of which consisted of slabs that were carved externally with sham tiles and internally with coffers.

The agora in Hellenistic cities was usually bordered on three sides by stoas,[3] and frequently that was effected by building a single stoa which turned the corners without change of design. More rarely all four sides of the space were lined with stoas separated by streets; a solitary L-shaped stoa was equally admissible. At a great commercial town a whole series of subordinate agoras and markets might have to be added, each with its stoas, of which a few might be devoted to particular trades but most seem to have been indiscriminately used. At Miletus especially [329] they covered a considerable proportion of the town, in a variety of shapes (all rectangular, in accordance with the general plan) and still more of sizes. The simple one-aisled type seldom provided enough space, and the majority contained an inner colonnade

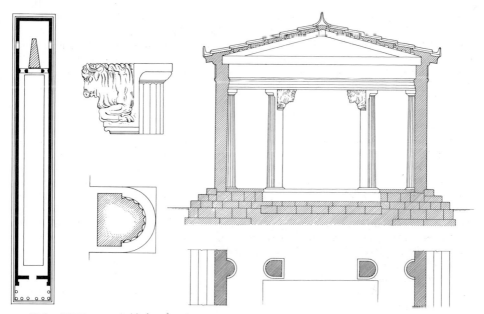

335. Delos, Neorium, probably late fourth century, restored section, details, and plan

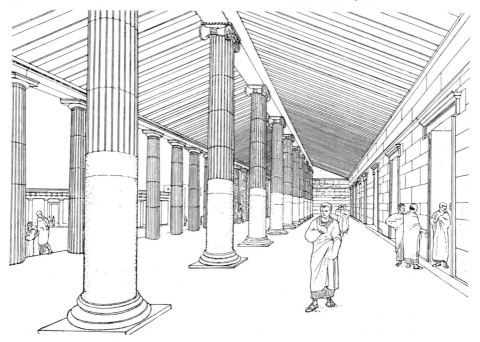

336. Priene, stoa, second century, restoration

[336] and shops or offices behind it, sometimes two or three rows deep. Occasionally the back was made directly accessible, either by doorways into the individual rooms or through another colonnade. Pergamene architects devised a type where the stoa is built over a terrace wall which provides level ground for the open space in front of it – often an agora. Under the stoa, against the terrace wall, runs a storeroom, lit with windows, and, below that, a row of shops opening from the lower ground level outside. Illustration 337 shows an example at

337. Assos, agora, possibly second century, restored view and plan

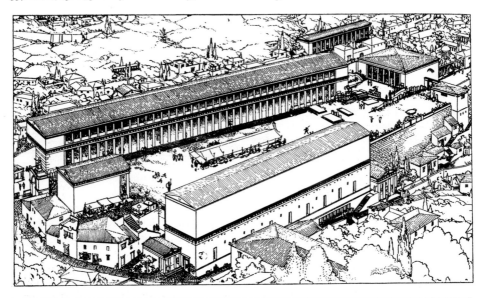

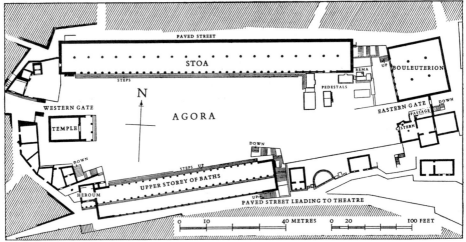

Assos, where the stoa on the south of the agora perhaps should have two storeys,[4] and a blank wall on the outside. A stoa with an upper floor was often built at congested places; as a rule an Ionic colonnade was superimposed on the Doric of the ground floor. Most façades were straight,

every other triglyph was carved with a bull's head, so placed as to give apparent support to the cornice [338]. Only one intermediate triglyph occurred over each intercolumniation, although the columns were spaced so widely that adherence to this old-fashioned convention

338. Delos, Stoa of Antigonus, c. 254, restoration of front

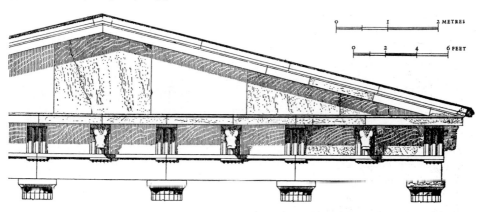

though a few Hellenistic designs recessed the centre behind pedimented wings, following the precedent set by the Stoa of Zeus at Athens. That method was adopted in two exceptionally fine stoas, the gifts of kings, which deserve a few lines of description. Neither had rooms behind. In the two-aisled Stoa of Antigonus at Delos, built about 254, additional columns were placed to support the valleys in the roof. Moreover

involved elongating the metopes. The Stoa of Philip at Megalopolis (more likely to be the gift of Philip II, and so dated 340–330, rather than Philip V, though there are parts of the superstructure in the style of that time, which would then have to be regarded as repairs) contained two internal Ionic colonnades, aligned with every third column of the Doric façade [339]. Its wings projected $13\frac{1}{2}$ feet and out of a total front-

339. Megalopolis, Stoa of Philip, c. 340–330 (?), restored half-plan

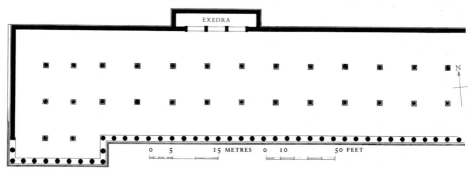

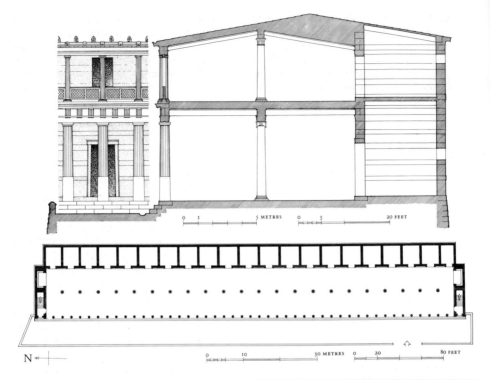

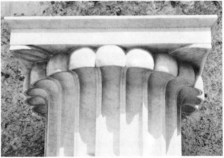

340 and 341. Athens, Stoa of Attalus,
mid second century, restored elevation,
section, and plan (*above*) and restored capital (*right*)

age of 510 feet each accounted for 55½ feet. The
normal width was little more, but two shallow
recesses (*exedras*) opened through the back wall;
each occupied one tenth of the total length. A
straight stoa, with which Attalus II of Pergamon
filled the east side of the agora at Athens, was
two-storeyed, as the site demanded, and backed
by shops [340]. It dates from about 140, by
which time an older stoa on the north side was
balanced by one across the south side; this was
open along the back as well as the front, and
formed the north side of an area now shut off
from the main agora, which seems to have been
used for legal business, rather than as a commercial agora.[5] This was bounded by other
stoas on east and south [330]. In his stoa Attalus

built the walls as well as the columns of marble,
an unusual luxury in stoas, though some, which
were intended for use as markets, were lined
with marble for cleanliness' sake. While his
upper Order was Ionic, the inner columns bore
palm-capitals of bell shape [341], in accordance
with contemporary Pergamene custom; the
nearest prototypes, in the Massalian Treasury at

Delphi, are 400 years older. (The stoa has now been entirely reconstructed as a museum, in which are displayed the finds of the American excavations in the agora.)

The Library at Pergamon, of the early second century, was accommodated at the back of a stoa, and consisted of several rooms and a hall for lectures. The books were stored in cabinets which rested upon stone pedestals close to the wall, into which the wood was bracketed. The older and vastly larger Library at Alexandria seems to have been taken as the model for the whole scheme at Pergamon. Public documents of Hellenistic Athens were kept in the Metroum [330], a building which resembled a house though actually it was a temple to the Mother.

Gymnasia and associated buildings may conveniently be treated here, regardless of date, because it seems that the types were established late in the fourth century and scarcely changed thereafter, except for the addition of more elaborate baths. The gymnasium proper formed a large open space, preferably lined with one or more stoas, and one of the annexes, the xystus, might be externally indistinguishable from a stoa, being simply a covered running-track. On the other hand the palaestra (wrestling school) was often a fairly elaborate building, planned like a very large house or hostel [153, 154].[6] Most of the space was invariably occupied by a central court, surrounded by a colonnade on all sides, and behind lay a single row of rooms (or occasionally a double row in some parts only). The larger rooms were usually fronted by a pair of columns *in antis*, while one side of the court might be lined with a second colonnade, in order, as Vitruvius says (V. 11), to provide a dry place in stormy weather. The rooms were devoted to specific purposes, including bathing. Troughs for washing in cold water are usually found; a cold plunge and a set of showers (supplied by a piped brook) can be seen at Delphi in the gymnasium built, at the latest, by about 330, and in some instances hot water and 'Turkish' vapour baths were added, though usually at a late date. The gymnasium at Delos has a series of rooms, of variable size, arranged round a peristyle court; its equipment is listed in an inscription of the second century B.C.

From casual allusions in literature it is known that sweat-baths were already common by the middle of the fifth century, and a private establishment of that period can be seen in the palace at Vouni, in Cyprus. Here rooms with cemented walls and floors, which slope to an outlet, were used for washing in hot and cold water respectively; the bathers splashed themselves from basins placed on stands. Provision was made for heating water in an adjacent room, and another was lined with fireplaces, above which flues rose to heat a sweat-room on top. At several Hellenistic public baths in Greece, dressing-rooms, latrines, furnace-rooms, etc., surrounded a couple of circular halls ringed with tubs to be filled with hot and cold water, and a third, much smaller, which was the sweat-room. The scheme at Oeniadae is simpler [342]. A rectangular room contained a tank of cold water, and two circular rooms were supplied with cauldrons of hot water surrounded by basin-like depressions in the floor, in which the

342. Oeniadae, bath, Hellenistic, plan

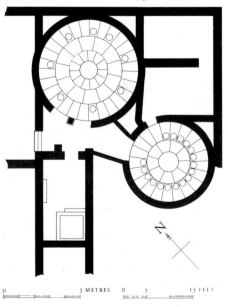

0   5 METRES   0   5   15 FEET

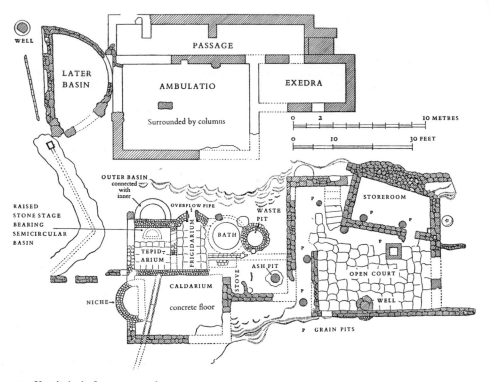

343. Kerch, bath, first century, plan

bathers could stand. If the water in one room was kept very hot it might have produced quite an effective steam bath, but at Gortys hot air circulated in brick channels beneath the floor. The roofs of these circular rooms may be restored, on the analogy of early Roman baths at Pompeii, in the shape of a cone with a hole at the top, which was covered by a removable hatch. A bath at Panticapaeum (Kerch in the Crimea), which is ascribed to the first century, seems to be a provincial version of the type Pausanias describes (VI. 23) as existing in the 'ancient' gymnasium at Elis. Three apsidal rooms [343] were provided for different temperatures and corresponded to the Roman frigidarium, tepidarium, and caldarium; a warm plunge-tank filled the apse of the tepidarium, from which it was separated by a raised platform bearing a smaller tank, while a circular cold plunge occupied a special room of its own. An adjacent building provided lounging accommodation.

The unusual Hypostyle Hall at Delos, a mercantile exchange, is securely dated about 210 by inscriptions which call it the Stoa of Poseidon (the term Hypostyle Hall is modern, and correctly applied to the multi-columned rooms of Egyptian architecture. There is not necessarily any deliberate copying of Egyptian concepts in the Delian building). It was, in fact, open along almost the whole of one side [344]; the walls returned only a short distance from the corners, and fifteen columns stood in the interval. Although Doric, these columns were fluted in the Ionic manner, at any rate for most of their height; the lower portion seems to have been left smooth, as was now becoming customary in secular buildings, where the flutes were particularly liable to suffer injury. The Doric

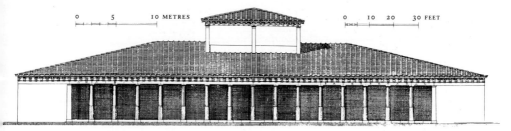

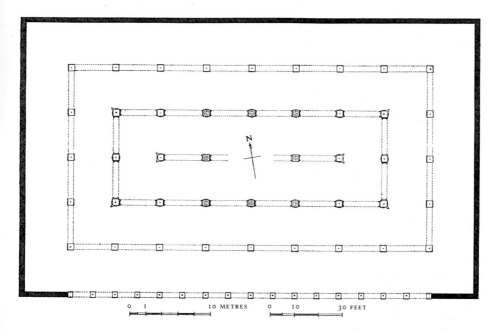

344 and 345. Delos, Hypostyle Hall, *c.* 210, restoration of front (*above*) and restored plan (*below*)

entablature continued along the walls all round the building; it contained three intermediate triglyphs over each intercolumniation. The plan [345] is oblong, 185 by 112½ feet (56·44 by 34·28 m.) and the internal columns stood in five ranks along the length, evenly spaced opposite every alternate column of the façade (at 18 feet, compared with 9 feet; 5·51 m. with 2·755 m.); there was, however, no column at the centre, so that the total number came to forty-four. They really formed two concentric rectangles, each with a continuous wooden architrave, plus two pairs of columns along the middle line, one on each side of the central gap. The outer rectangle [346] was composed of Doric columns, higher than those on the façade, but the inner rectangle and the middle pairs of still higher Ionic columns, extraordinarily simple in design [347]. The roof must therefore have been hipped, with a timber framework sloping up from the walls across the various columns. The eight columns which stood in a square around the central space carried square pillars which formed the open sides of a lantern above the main roof; these

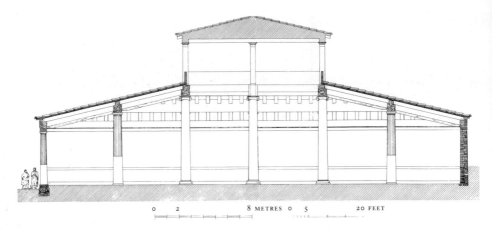

346 and 347. Delos, Hypostyle Hall, *c.* 210, restored section (*above*) and Ionic column (*below*)

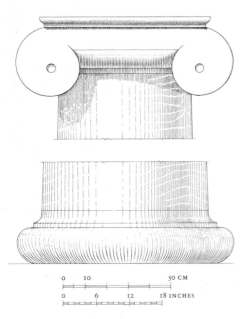

is, however, obvious from the manner in which the capitals are differentiated. Those at the corners of the inner rectangle were shaped like a normal angle-capital, having one pair of volutes bent towards the corner of the building, concave sides beneath the architraves, and consequently a division between the volutes of the inward corner. The capitals at either end of the middle row were given a pair of bent volutes at both the outward corners.

A number of Council Houses of the third or second century have been excavated. Two are square halls with internal columns arranged in a square; at Thasos a porch projected from the centre of one side, and at Assos [337] most of one side consisted of a line of six doorways separated by monolithic piers, the inward faces of which are shaped into unfluted half-columns. Another type is found in oblong shape at Heraclea and Notium; one of the longer walls formed the front, and inside, fairly close to the other three walls, stood a row of columns, inward from which ran tiers of straight stone benches facing an open piece of floor centred on the front wall. A more elaborate building of the same character [348, 349][7] at Priene, datable around 200, is practically square (64 feet wide by 66½ feet long; 20·25 by 21·06 m.). It is sunk

were braced by slabs which joined them at the base like a parapet. This is the only case in which the system of clerestory lighting can be investigated, though its details remain obscure because of the destruction of all the wooden elements. The scheme of the Ionic architraves

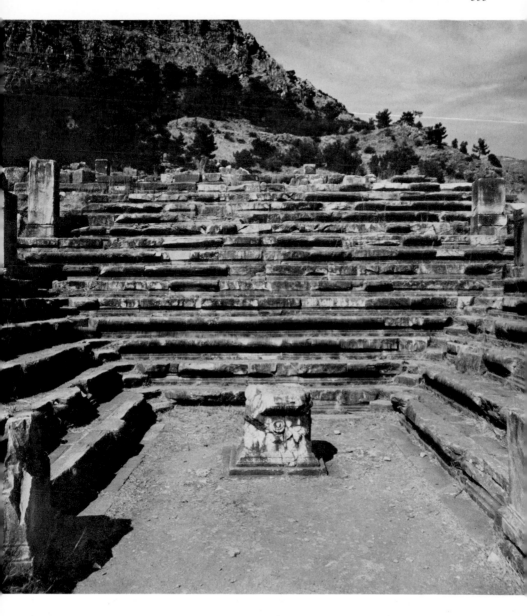

348. Priene, *Ekklesiasterion, c.* 200 view of interior

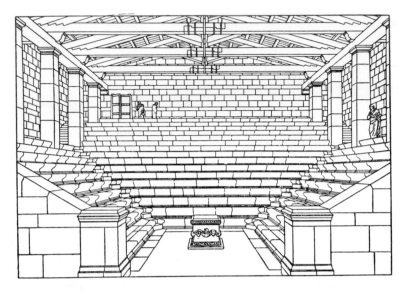

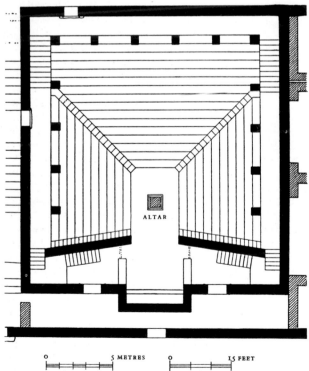

ALTAR

0   5 METRES   0   15 FEET

349 and 350. Priene, *Ekklesiasterion*, *c.* 200, restored interior and plan (*opposite*), and restoration of south wall (*below*)

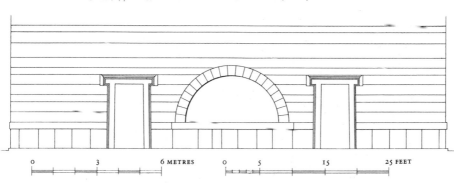

into a slope, after the manner of a theatre, and similarly equipped with stairs leading upwards through the benches and with retaining walls at their lower extremities; these walls, moreover, slant so that the tiers approach closer to the front wall the farther they recede from the speaker's area, following the precedent of a theatre's more than semicircular auditorium. But the middle block of benches rises higher than those at the sides, to the extent of six additional tiers. There was seating for 600 or 700 people, an astonishing number for the Council of a town like Priene, where the theatre could hold only 6,000 and there was housing within the fortifications for little more than 4,000. The hall is therefore more likely to have been the *Ekklesiasterion* where the Assembly of citizens met; probably all of them could have been crowded in. The hall was abnormally free from obstruction, as first built. Fourteen square pillars interrupted only the top row of benches and two more rose from the retaining walls, leaving a clear span of over 47 feet (*c.* 14·50 m.), the roofing of which must have given trouble; for it was afterwards thought necessary to reduce the span by rebuilding the supports among the lower benches and eventually to buttress them also. Passages between the original pillars and the walls are reached from the speaker's area by steps beside the retaining walls, and communicate with a street above and

with a stepped alley at the side of the building. The speaker's area contains an altar, centrally placed between the benches. It is strangely provided too with an open-air bench, occupying the whole of a light-well which projects outwards from the front wall behind a semicircular window of the same width, 14½ feet [350]. The officials who sat on the bench had their feet within the room but their heads outside. The arch of the window sprang from a dado course and must have risen 11 feet above floor level. Its lintel is carved externally with two fascias, like an Ionic architrave, below elaborate mouldings.

Yet another type of civic hall reproduces the curvature of a theatre's auditorium. An extraordinarily ornate example is the Council House[8] at Miletus, built to some extent at the cost of King Antiochus IV (175–164), as an inscription acknowledges. The plan [329] is oblong, 114½ by 79½ feet (34·84 by 24·28 m.). The stone benches could have seated well over 1,200; they curved slightly more than a semicircle but terminated against retaining walls parallel with the front wall, from which they were separated by a corridor (afterwards converted into a stage). Staircases fitted into the waste space of the corners above the auditorium. The roof seems to have originally been supported by two pairs of Ionic columns, set on equalizing pedestals beside the retaining walls and near the back wall, but as eventually reconstructed it rested on

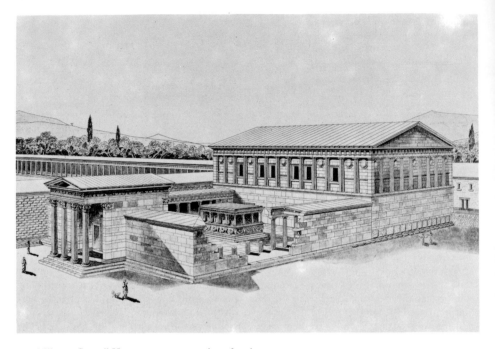

351. Miletus, Council House, *c.* 170, restoration of enclosure

a larger number of wooden posts. Above the level of the top benches, which rose to only about half the total height, the walls were divided by pilasters into panels, some of which contained large windows (except on the back wall). Externally the effect was that of a temple upon a tall base, reminiscent of the 'Nereid Monument' and the Mausoleum. The ends were pedimented, and an engaged Doric Order surrounded the building, standing on a ledge at half the height of the horizontal cornice; below this the walls consisted purely of decorative pseudisodomic masonry. The Order was composed of half-columns except at the corners, where pilasters took their place; they were backed by the pilasters on the inner side of the wall. A window occupied a considerable part of the intercolumniation in the case of six out of the thirteen on the front and four out of the nine on each end. A shield was carved near the top of every blank intercolumniation, at any rate on

the front and the south end. The echinus of the capitals was ornamented with an egg-and-dart pattern, such as regularly occurs on Ionic capitals, and its functional insignificance – it is nothing more than a quarter-circle moulding – also indicates a fusion of the Orders. That tendency is also shown by the intrusion of a row of dentils below the cornice. The frieze contained an additional triglyph over each intercolumniation, in accordance with Hellenistic custom; traces of red and blue paint remain.

This Council House at Miletus formed the chief feature in one of the most elaborate schemes of Greek planning [351]. Its front stretched across a court enclosed by continuing its end walls at rather less than half their height. A taller propylon at the opposite end was exactly centred on the hall, and so was a low tomb-shrine or altar inside the court; the Order in both was Corinthian. A Doric colonnade of intermediate height began at each corner of the

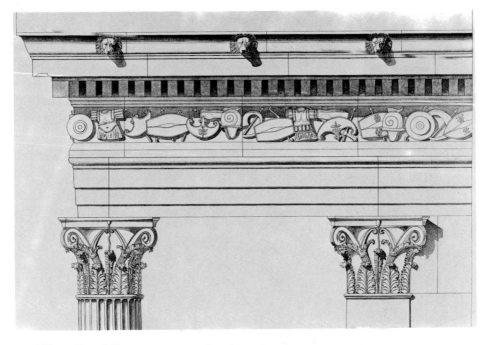

352. Miletus, Council House, *c.* 170, restoration of propylon

propylon, a trifle back from its inward façade, and made a deep border to the court northward and southward for a distance equal to the width of the entrance, whereupon it turned to meet the front of the hall, keeping the depth the same. The capitals of the propylon [352] are excessively intricate of detail, and its frieze was carved with weapons. Sculptured panels stood between the little columns of the shrine, above a continuous band carved with garlands, bulls' skulls, and lions' masks.

The choice of Pergamon as a capital enabled its kings to group a series of large buildings dramatically[9] upon the summit and sides of its acropolis [353]. Most of these are roughly contemporary with the Council House of Miletus, and very few can be appreciably older than 200; on the other hand some improvements and additions were made under the Roman Empire. The city spread over the southern slopes of a hill which contracts as it rises, ending in a ridge a

few hundred feet wide, which formed the acropolis and royal quarter. All the upper part was terraced into a great variety of levels, and the shapes of the terraces were necessarily somewhat irregular, while the angles they present are most diverse. At the approach lay an agora, with stoas on two and a half sides; at its west end stood a small temple. Immediately below lay the beginning of a stoa some 700 feet long, occupying a shelf which projects from the side of the acropolis with the aid of a retaining wall; the temple at its north end was Hellenistic but rebuilt by the emperor Caracalla, and the enormous theatre, scooped into the slope behind the stoa, is likewise a mixture of Hellenistic and Roman work [354]. The irregularity of the agora is due to the intrusion across one corner of a higher terrace on which the great Altar of Zeus stood, on quite a different axis [255]. Other terraces and buildings placed to its north and east must have been

353. Pergamon, plan of upper city

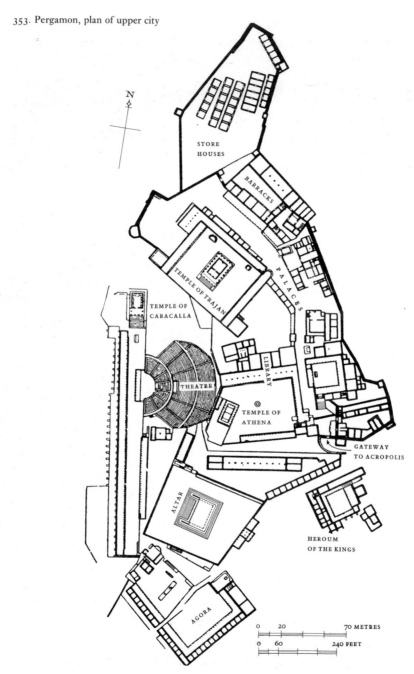

STORE
HOUSES

BARRACKS

PALACES

TEMPLE OF TRAJAN

TEMPLE OF
CARACALLA

LIBRARY

THEATRE

TEMPLE OF
ATHENA

GATEWAY
TO ACROPOLIS

ALTAR

HEROUM
OF THE KINGS

AGORA

0   20   70 METRES

0   60   240 FEET

354. Pergamon, theatre, mainly second century

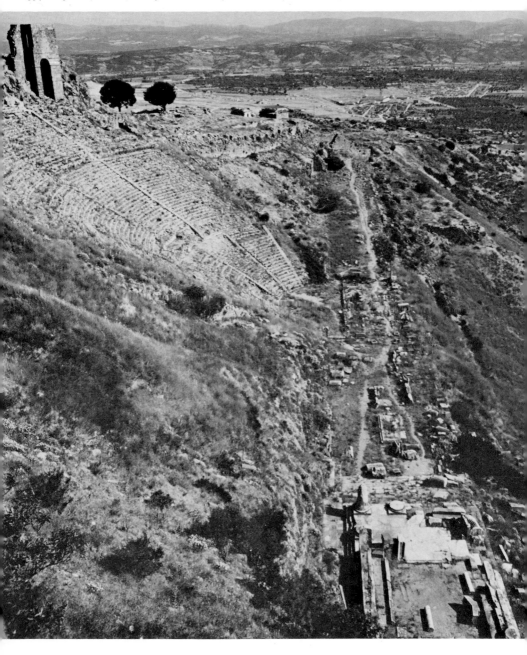

comparatively inconspicuous against their background of the acropolis wall and towers. The wall supported the terrace of the third-century temple dedicated to Athena and the stoas which faced it; rooms at the back of one of these contained the Library. Along the eastern edge of the acropolis stretched the palace buildings, with their barracks and storerooms towards the north end. The west side of the summit was widened under the Roman Empire, when the arches of a retaining wall were built along the top of the theatre and a huge terrace to the north supported a temple of Trajan which dominated the whole scene. Even before the more spectacular Roman additions the array of great buildings stepped upon the ridge must have been a splendid sight, confused though it was, and vulgar at close range. Nothing else the Greeks attempted came so near to rivalling the Acropolis of Athens.

The kingdom of Pergamon was annexed by Rome in 133, thirteen years after Greece itself. In the hundred years that followed, until Augustus founded the Empire, scarcely any public buildings seem to have been undertaken in Greek lands. The most notable exceptions are, significantly, due to foreign enterprise. The largest, the Agora of the Italians at Delos, was built at the close of the second century by Roman and other Italian merchants who frequented the port; they used it as their club and business headquarters. It consisted of a court, averaging about 200 feet a side, with a two-storeyed colonnade on all four sides, formed by Doric columns below and Ionic pillars above. An assortment of rooms and exedras which projected from the external wall must

have been added gradually, in accordance with the means and wishes of individual benefactors; there were also shops along the street, at the back of one wing. The Syrian merchants and ship-owners at Delos were likewise organized into a Guild – they called themselves the Poseidoniasts of Berytus (the modern Beirut) – and put up a large building during the last quarter of the second century. Both the Italians and the Poseidoniasts were content with masons' work of poor quality, and the designs are equally undistinguished. The same may be said of the Jewish synagogue at Delos. In the case of the Poseidoniasts the plan is mixed Greek and Syrian. A vestibule led to a court with a colonnade on the west side and a row of four chapels behind. On the north this court adjoined another, which was reserved for cult meetings; it was paved with mosaic. A much larger space on the east, adjoining the other two courts, was mainly occupied by a Doric colonnade, and the court which this enclosed on all four sides was itself smaller than either of the others; the mosaic paving is an addition of the first century. Along the south side were reception rooms behind the colonnade, and shops on the basement frontage to the street.

The best secular building of the first century, the 'Tower of the Winds' at Athens, has already been described (p. 310). A small agora, close to it, was built partly at the cost of Julius Caesar and Augustus, as an inscription on the entrance gateway records [355]. The style of the gateway is purely Greek, though the date must be later than 12 B.C. when Augustus adopted his nephew, Lucius, of whom a statue was placed on top; the boy died in A.D. 2.

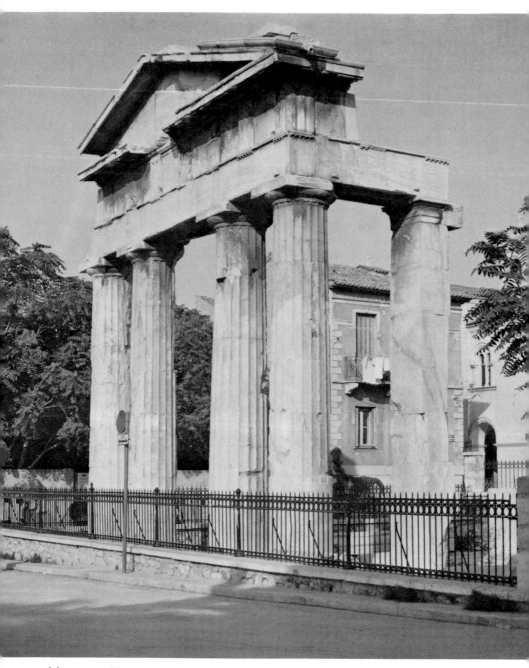

355. Athens, gate of Roman agora, *c.* 10

CHAPTER 24

OPEN STRUCTURES, ESPECIALLY THEATRES

The Greeks held most of their dramatic and athletic shows in the open air, for preference in some hollow overlooked by steep slopes on which the spectators stood or sat, often on wooden stands. Since nearly all cities lay on or near hills, nature had usually provided a spot which needed only a little terracing and excavating to meet the purpose; where nothing of the sort already existed, banks of earth were piled up into the required form. The hippodrome, the course where horses raced, was in most cases only cleared of obstructions but otherwise left without artificial improvements, and invariably without masonry. The stadium, in which athletic meetings took place, needed to have the race-track levelled and the sides embanked, though the height was not always equal on both sides; masonry was normally limited to one or more retaining-walls, and stone seating was a rare and always late feature.[1] The track was straight, averaging slightly over 600 feet in length, and double-width; in long races (the *dolichos*) the runners appear to have turned round off-centre posts, an example of which has been found at the closed end of the stadium at Nemea, placed short of the starting line. Such posts enabled runners to turn easily and to avoid stumbling over the starting blocks, which were elevated slightly above the ground level of the stadium. Single-turn races (*diaulos* and *hoplitodromos*) probably required separate posts for each competitor. There was a particularly ingenious starting gate in the old stadium at Isthmia (which was in the vicinity of the temple). Normally the starting lines were formed from blocks of stone with grooves in their upper surface. In many stadiums, of the Hellenistic age and later, the closed end would normally be curved. Examples of the Greek period are found at Nemea[2] and Isthmia. Some stadia, including earlier examples, have both ends straight (for

example, Olympia). In the former type the seating too curved around the turn and continued along the whole length of the track but did not extend along the straight end. Where stone seats were supplied they took the same form as the benches of theatres, from which they were unquestionably imitated; a long stone barrier is a late feature.

Horse racing (with chariots) was the most prestigious of the contests in the athletic festivals and took place in the hippodrome, which assumed truly monumental form in Roman times. The Greek hippodrome was not so developed, though it might have small buildings from which important spectators might view the races, and altars (there was one to Taraxippos, the panicker of horses, at Olympia). Another possible hippodrome has been identified at Isthmia.

The oldest known auditorium resembling the developed type of theatre, and in all likelihood the prototype for such, was the Pnyx at Athens, where the whole body of citizens met in Assembly and decided the affairs of the State. The site was a hill-side of rock in which was cut a platform for the speakers; a wall behind it deflected the voice, and the audience sat at higher levels on the slope, which curved around in front of the platform. This mainly natural hollow was used from about 500 to 404, when the arrangement was absolutely reversed; a tall semicircular retaining-wall was built lower down the slope and a filling of earth dumped between it and the platform to raise the seating gradually to the top. This construction may have followed soon after the first serious attempt to improve the theatre, which had begun as a natural hollow on the south slope of the Acropolis.

The architectural history of the Greek theatre was dictated by changes in dramatic technique, primarily at Athens, which was the home of legitimate drama and set the pattern for theatres. Unfortunately, the successive transformations of the theatre at Athens [356][3] are extremely difficult either to trace or to date. It would seem that tragedies and comedies of the great period, the middle and late fifth century, still required no raised stage, but involved the novel feature of a background of scenery, in most cases in the form of a building. The chorus and the actors performed alternately on the circular piece of ground called an orchestra, a word which literally means a dancing place. (That indeed had originally been its sole function, at a time when the dancing and singing of a chorus formed the entire proceedings.) The majority of the spectators sat on the rock slope overlooking the orchestra, and a few on wooden benches erected for the festival. There can, in fact, have been no need for any building except the adjoining temple of Dionysus, the god to whom the play was offered; the scenery, whether painted or solid, consisted of wood. The actors apparently made their entrances and exits by ramps leading to either side of the orchestra from the lower terrace where the temple stood; these were called *parodoi* ('side roads').

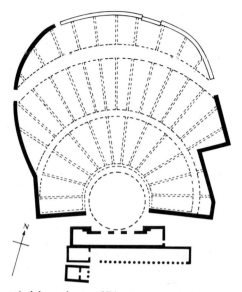

356. Athens, theatre of Dionysus, general plan

A small theatre at the Attic town of Thoricus retains a primitive scheme which had become immutable during the fifth century[4] [357]. A

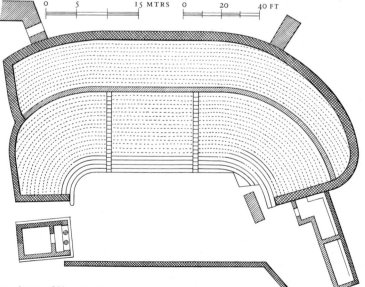

357. Thoricus, theatre, fifth century, restored plan

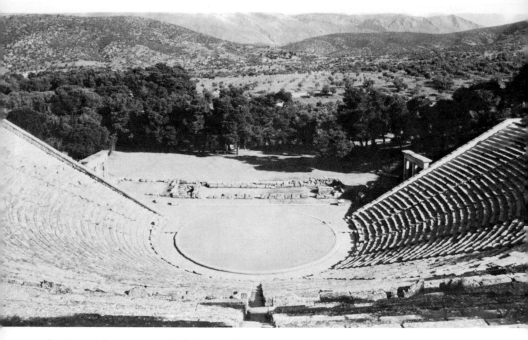

358 and 359 (*above and opposite*). Epidaurus, theatre

support wall for the first orchestra is dated by pottery of the period 525–480 which is associated with it. About the middle of the fifth century the orchestra was enlarged and a new support wall, further out, was constructed for it. The first stone seats were added (wooden seats had been used previously), an altar was placed in the east side of the orchestra, and a temple by the western end of the seats. The straight plan for the central part of the seating is most noticeable; similar plans have been found elsewhere (for example, at Rhamnus in Attica, and in an early theatre at Argos). The upper part of the seating at Thoricus is a later addition.

Late in the fifth century the Athenians built a new temple of Dionysus, a few yards lower down the slope [356]. Either at the same time or earlier they inserted a long, thin building between the temple and the theatre; it was, or became, a stoa with a colonnade facing the temple, but the back wall was utilized for holding scenery, as is clear from the presence of slits into

which beams could be socketed. The stoa provided a foyer, an amenity copied at many later theatres of all periods.

A subsequent development, which some would ascribe to the fifth century and others to the late fourth, added a special scene-building along the back of the stoa. It was 24 feet thick and so encroached upon the orchestra, which now therefore itself encroached upon the auditorium; the hollow was cut farther back into the slope, and the lower benches given a regular curve around the new orchestra. The curve was prolonged beyond a semicircle, flattening as it neared the new retaining-walls, which were built slanting outwards to either side from the orchestra. Projections (*paraskenia*) of the scene-building came out towards them, leaving a parodos between; the recessed centre extended slightly beyond the width of the orchestra. The interior contained dressing-rooms and no doubt also served as a store for scenery.

Similar plans, more or less obscured by later

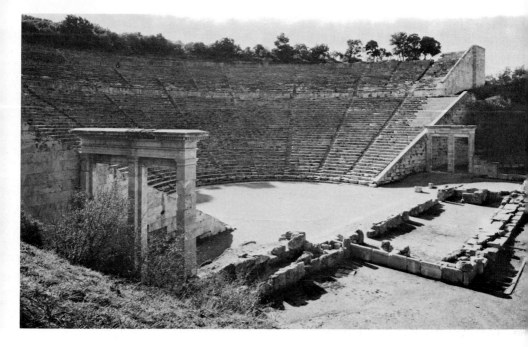

alterations, have been taken as proof that many theatres date from the late fifth or fourth centuries. The best preserved of them, Epidaurus, on epigraphic evidence belongs to the second half of the fourth century [358–62];[5] Pausanias, who considered this theatre the finest in Greece, ascribes it and the tholos in the same sanctuary to one architect, Polycleitus, thereby making the design go back to near 350. Even though this may be the result of confusion, chronologically it is not impossible. The auditorium, 387 feet in diameter, is sunk into a hill-side which allowed it to be symmetrically shaped all the way up, as could not be done with the theatre at Athens because of adjacent buildings and a cliff at the top. The wedge-shaped blocks of stone benches are separated by staircases, which are doubled in number above the horizontal dividing gangway. The slope is steeper above it, and the seats taller, 17 inches instead of 13 (a height which requires cushions). All are 2½ feet wide and hollowed beneath the edge to economize foot room. The benches cover more than a semicircle, owing to the slant of the retaining-walls above the parodoi, and the occupants of the seats near the edge could not see the scene well. But every seat had an excellent view of the orchestra, which is distinguished by a circle of white stone, 67 feet in diameter (conceivably a Hellenistic embellishment); the stone at its centre is presumably the base of an altar. This circle represents five-sixths of the curve of the lowest benches (the seats of honour) as far as five-sixths of a semicircle, after which the benches were laid out from a new centre on either side with a longer radius, so that more space is left at the inner ends of the parodoi to enable the audience – which could have numbered over 12,000 – to disperse quickly. Elegant doorways across each outer end caused little obstruction [362]. The original scene building, which must have been fairly tall, was placed with its nearest point over 45 feet distant from the centre of the

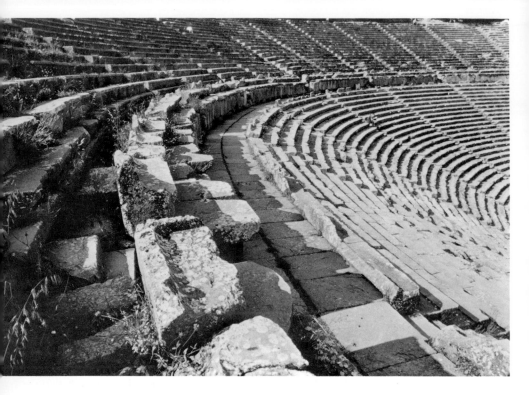

360-2. Epidaurus, upper division of seats
in theatre (*above*), plan (*opposite, above*),
and entrance to theatre (*opposite, below*)

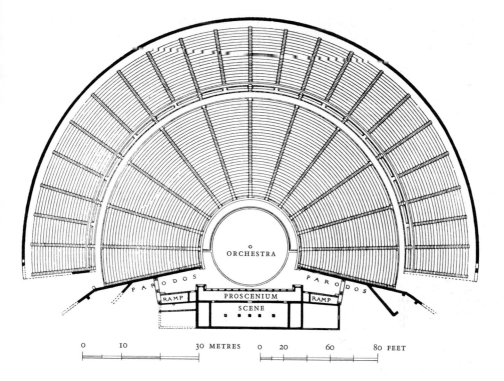

PARODOS

ORCHESTRA

PARODOS

RAMP

PROSCENIUM

SCENE

RAMP

0   10   30 METRES   0   20   60   80 FEET

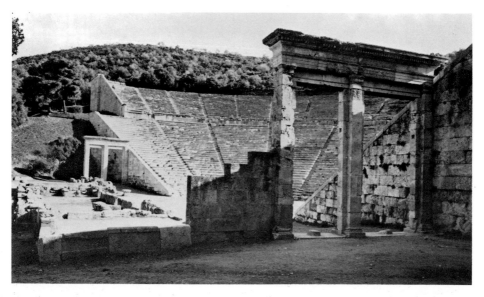

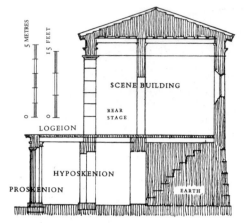

363. Oropus, theatre, restored section through stage

of individual character, but originated in farce of the Phlyax type, as is known from burlesque scenes on fourth-century vases showing actors on a stage supported by Doric or Ionic columns. Perhaps the oldest example of the Hellenistic theatre is at Priene [364, 365]. The auditorium dates from about 300 – the time when New Comedy started – but the raised stage may be a century later, although Athens had set a precedent for it at least as early as 292. The scene-building at Priene[6] was two-storeyed, and ten feet in advance of its straight front stood a one-storeyed row of pillars from which cross-beams ran back to the wall, supporting a flat wooden roof. Against the front of each pillar stood a half-column, carrying the architrave and a Doric frieze, so that a permanent background

orchestra. But in later Hellenistic times a raised stage was added along the façade.

This innovation [363] which brought the actors more clearly into view met a need that did not exist in legitimate drama till the development of New Comedy, with its portrayal

364 and 365. Priene,
theatre, restoration at late second century (*below*)
and restored original plan (*opposite*)

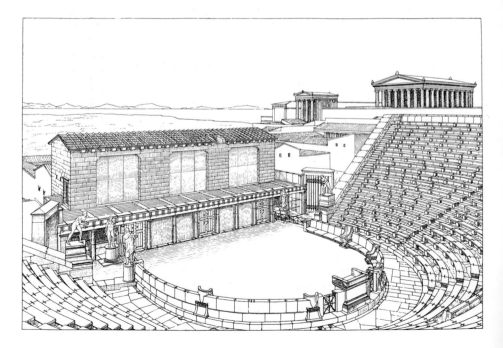

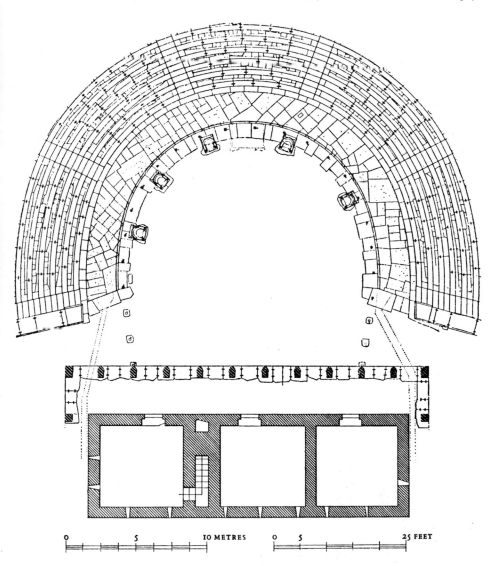

0   5   10 METRES   0   5   25 FEET

of architectural scenery existed at ground level, but there are also holes for bolting wooden panels of painted scenery between the pillars. The name given to this façade, proscenium, implies only that it stood advanced from the scene-building, the front of which must have continued to discharge its function of holding temporary scenery, though only in the upper storey. Later, the upper façade at Priene was opened for practically its entire length, in three great gaps [364], and similar arrangements existed in the late Hellenistic period at other theatres.[7] The tendency probably was to make increasing use of the raised stage, except for old-

366. Delos, theatre, restored plan

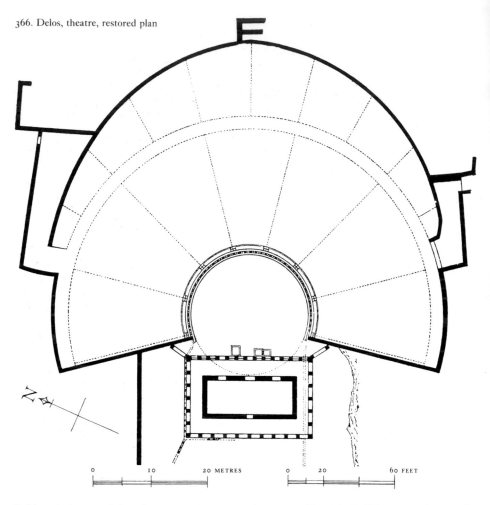

fashioned plays, and therefore to require more openings in the upper scene-front, both for the actors' use and to hold painted scenery.

The proscenium seems an adaptation of a one-storeyed flat-roofed type of portico which sometimes was provided along the exterior of a large two-storeyed building, in order to give direct access from the stairs to every portion of the upper floor. The earliest certain example, the Leonidaeum hostel (p. 323), belongs to the fourth century. One may suppose that this treatment was applied to a good many of the

larger residential buildings, such as the prytaneum in an important city, and so had come to be thought fitting to represent a legendary palace – as, in point of fact, may have been more or less correct historically. The derivation may account for the fact that at Priene and a few other places the proscenium was longer than the taller scene-building to which it is attached, while at Delos [366] the tall building was entirely surrounded by the proscenium and similar porticoes on the other three sides; the back portico corresponds, of

367. Ephesus, theatre, Hellenistic, restored plan

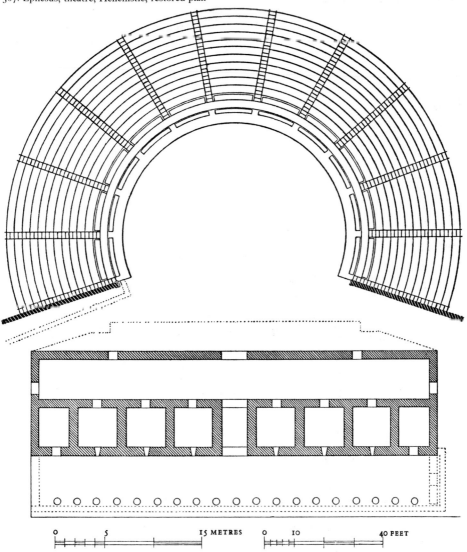

course, to the habitual stoa-foyer, so that the innovation was restricted to the sides. But the theatre at Ephesus [367] was built with a proscenium of the same length as the scene, and this strictly rectangular type became prevalent in Greece as well as Asia Minor. Its adoption naturally aroused distaste for the early plan of recessing the centre of the scene front behind solid projections (paraskenia); the last new theatre built on that plan dates from the middle of the second century, and at roughly the same time began the practice of demolishing the projections in old theatres. A proscenium was added to almost every old theatre[8] in the Hellenistic period, and the upper part of the scene-building was usually remodelled, simultaneously or afterwards, in order to secure more and wider openings.

A rather late development, scarcely to be traced before 150, was the practice of giving the proscenium an open front resting on free-standing columns which show no sign of devices theatre; examples at Segesta and Tyndaris in Sicily are plausibly dated early in the first century, when the island belonged to Rome, and seem from their resemblance to theatres at Pompeii to be semi-Roman.[9] At Segesta, the scene-building was twice as high as usual, and its front was decorated with two Orders, one above the other – in the recessed centre engaged, but in the wings free-standing so as to let the rooms within be seen. The wings projected aslant from the centre, thereby giving people seated at the sides of the auditorium a

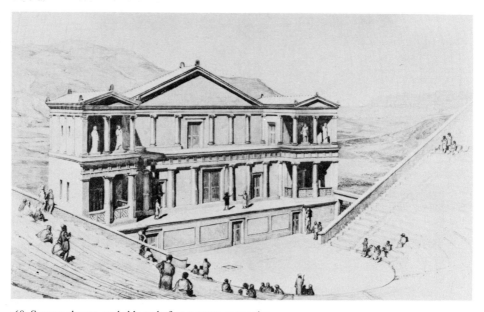

368. Segesta, theatre, probably early first century, restoration

to affix scenery, so that the portico behind them seems to have been left exposed to view during performances. One might imagine that it served as permanent scenery whenever the action of the play demanded two storeys, but the principal motive was probably a wish to conform with the florid architectural taste of the age. A comparable device was the application to the scene building of architectural decoration as a permanent background to the raised stage [368]. That first became habitual in the Roman type of better chance to follow the action of the play. There are no identifiable remains of the gables and pediments shown in illustration 368, and the roof should probably be restored more like that in illustration 364, perhaps with an attic.[10]

In all Hellenistic theatres the plan seems extraordinarily inept. Much of the raised stage must have been out of sight from a number of seats and only visible at awkward angles from others at the sides. This drawback was somewhat mitigated at another Sicilian town,

Morgantina, by making the seats curve to the extent of a semicircle but continue straight beyond it, as they would have done in a stadium. The eventual solution was to stop short the auditorium instead of extending it beyond a semicircle. This was done in Roman theatres. It may originate with the temporary wooden structures that the Romans used until Pompey built the first permanent theatre at Rome in 55 B.C.; but that was supposed to have been copied from the Greek theatre at Mytilene on the island of Lesbos, and if so, the development to the semicircular form may belong to the Late Hellenistic period. There is a splendid sequence of theatres, several of them Hellenistic in origin, in Asia Minor. The Hellenistic theatre at Miletus from the first seems to have had an auditorium which was very little more than a semicircle in plan, while that at Alinda is in fact straight: but even in Late Hellenistic times the form is still most variable. Four phases have been found from the Hellenistic stage-building of the theatre at Miletus, quite apart from continued development in the Roman period.

CHAPTER 25

EPILOGUE

In many ways a strenuous intellectual effort is required to form an appreciative judgement of Greek architecture. For one thing, every building is to some extent ruined. The wooden portions have invariably perished, any metal accessories have been looted, the sculptural decoration is never complete, the paint has vanished. Almost every roof has fallen, bringing light where there ought to be shade, and causing surfaces that were originally polished to weather like the rest. The demolition of walls, in order to obtain material for re-use, has often left columns standing clear which were intended to be seen against a background of masonry. The effect of many buildings has been transformed too by a rise or fall in the level of the surrounding ground, while in practically every case the character of the setting has changed beyond recognition; modern buildings stand around, or a town has lapsed into waste land, or a sanctuary is overgrown with trees and bushes.

The very fact of disuse effects a transformation of its own, making an academic exercise in design out of what used to be a place of worship or of living. With the aid of ancient literature and illustrations the expert may be able to restore in his mind's eye the activities in house or market, the visitors who entered the temple with their offerings, the long processions which led to it at the festivals, and the varied disarray that filled now empty spaces. But the best-trained imagination has its limitations. Take, for instance, that altar-stone outside the temple – it rises grey and worn, with flowers in the crevices and round about, amid grass and aromatic bushes gay with butterflies and bees: here the Greeks heard the bellowing of frantic cattle, watched the flies blacken the widening carpet of blood, and smelled a reek that was fouler than in any slaughter-house.

The spiritual gulf between the ancient and the modern worlds is broader than is generally realized. The Greeks, when their architecture reached its height, had only lately ceased to be a semi-primitive people. At Athens there was still legal provision whereby an animal or an implement could be tried for murder. Laws, of course, usually express the opinion of a past age even at the time of their enactment, but the most cultivated citizens were liable to think in a surprisingly old-fashioned manner. Sophocles, in his treatment of the Oedipus legend, accepts without question that national disasters will follow a son's unwitting breaking of the ancient tabus on patricide (although the father deserved nothing better) and on incest.

To the end of the period covered by this book the Greeks retained some relics of the primitive habit of mind. That is true not only of the smaller or more remote states, and of the poor, but also of the educated and wealthy, as is obvious from minor antiquities and from much of the literature. Even in the writings of thinkers to whom we feel akin, an occasional passage discloses an outlook we cannot grasp. (What proportion of readers understands the grounds for Socrates' condemnation or sees the point of his last words, 'We owe a cock to Asclepius'?) With intensive study the divergence seems ever deeper and of wider extent, so that I have heard one of the greatest living authorities on the literature (and on the architecture) startle an audience of classicists by affirming, without qualification, that the Greek mind is very alien to us. With my comparatively shallow knowledge of ancient literature, but after some years' personal experience of a society which is now emerging from a primitive culture, I picture the Greeks as more alien than I used to think them, and far more vividly.

The world in which these people lived was filled with unseen dangers, against which there were recognized safeguards, while omens and oracles supplied guidance for protected actions. Every natural object worthy of remark was the body or home of a spirit, who partook in some measure of divinity. The gods themselves, though greater, were only somewhat less localized manifestations of divinity, for each state had its patron among them – and built him a home which was finer than an ordinary house. Animism, pantheism, and unitary deism were facets of one and the same belief; each individual might adhere to whichever suited his intellectual capacity, and could, without the least inconsistency, switch his mode of thinking between one and another. The favour of the god or spirit and communion with him were obtainable by the sacrifice of animals, most of the flesh being eaten by the worshippers, or by less costly offerings of food or drink; advanced thought disapproved of human sacrifice, which was rumoured, however, to persist in obscure places. The ghosts of ancestors required frequent sustenance and propitiation by means of libations and, occasionally, food. The entire social structure depended on the ancestors; the state itself was a structure of clans and families. Social practice, together with artistic conventions, was indissolubly bound to religion, and equally governed by tradition; modifications could be introduced within the sacred framework but any change which would evidently break with tradition must be impious, and therefore dangerous to the state. A state might contain only a few square miles with a population no larger than an English village, but whatever its size and consequence the patriotism of its citizens was as fervid, constant, and irrationally exclusive as the feeling of a schoolboy for his still smaller group. Emulation between the states gave the commonest motive for undertaking public works, of a grandeur often out of all proportion to the revenue.

The paragraph above was actually written to describe present-day mentality in the West African bush, but has required no modification except a change in tense to make it applicable to the average Greek of the fifth century, when an educated minority was already emancipated. It should apply in an intensified form to the preceding two or three centuries, during which the shape of Hellenic civilization was decided, but the literature (apart from Hesiod) is less informative as regards that epoch. Legends which survive from still earlier times depict a genuinely primitive society, roughly comparable with that of the Vikings before their conversion to Christianity.

This picture may appear inconsistent with the archaeological information about the Myceneans of the Late Bronze Age, to whom all the legends avowedly refer – in reality some must be yet older traditions. Allowance must, of course, be made for accidental gaps in the oral transmission of a long-past manner of life, but upon investigation the omitted, forgotten topics are found to be significantly alike. Whereas, for instance, obsolete methods of warfare are fully described, Homer gives no hint that the Myceneans possessed a system of writing. And where the architecture is concerned, barbaric or flashy elements are mentioned but none of the features of greater refinement. As it happens, these, and the system of writing, had been adopted by the Myceneans from Minoan Crete, together with practically everything else which looks civilized in their apparatus of living. Accordingly the question is whether, in the Dark Age which followed on the collapse of their power, such details were forgotten merely because civilized things no longer pleased or because they had never been so thoroughly naturalized on the mainland as to take root there. Excavation suggests, though as yet it has not proved, that the latter answer is correct; direct Minoan influence seems to have been virtually confined to the wealthier capitals, the destruction of which should therefore have sufficed to obliterate even the memory of it. And so far as there was continuity in architecture through the Dark Age, the Mycenean elements which persisted owed comparatively little to Crete; actually the inheritance from the Middle Bronze Age outweighs the Minoan legacy.

Some of those architectural features of Minoan derivation which did survive into the Dark Age were abandoned at its close, when the Hellenic style took shape. The enduring results from the astonishing creative inventiveness of the Minoans, and from the transformation which it had inspired of the mainland peasant's hut into the Mycenean palace, were confined in normal Hellenic architecture to such details as the fluting of columns and the design of capitals. In Crete, however, a local type of temple kept the wide proportions which had been characteristic of Minoan rooms.

Actually Minoan architecture was so different in spirit that it would have seemed abhorrent to the Greeks of the Hellenic civilization, and perhaps it had appealed to very few in Mycenean times. It strikes, in fact, a discordantly modern note compared with any other of the world's past. Seen externally, each large building must have formed an unsymmetrical composition in which rectangular masses of various dimensions were piled together. The façade is likely to have been broken not only by windows but also by columned openings at different levels; seen from a distance, however, it may yet have achieved something of the solid grandeur of a casbah in the Atlas or a Tibetan lamasery. The interior was confusedly planned around a series of self-contained suites, interlocked one with another and intercommunicating but each also accessible directly though tortuously from the general entrance. A suite formed an unsymmetrical group of such basic elements as one or two rooms divisible by a row of double doors, a light-well behind, and a veranda at front or side or both. The decoration, often over-lavish, employed the strongest colours and complex yet determinedly obtrusive patterns; dim lighting, however, may sometimes have reduced garishness to sombre opulence. In the earlier palaces, at any rate, decorative schemes were favoured such as could nowadays be thought appropriate only to a cocktail bar or to an inferior but pretentious restaurant. But it must always be remembered that Minoan development was not allowed to run its natural course; the sudden, violent end came when a tendency towards orderly planning and restrained decoration had become evident.

The extraordinary divergence in spirit between the Minoan and any other variety of architecture in the Aegean area may perhaps be explicable on racial grounds. Such scraps of evidence as are already available indicate that the Minoans spoke a language which did not belong to the Indo-European family. The same may have been true of the founders of the Mycenean dynasties, but not of their subjects. Now that the palace archives can be deciphered, their language has proved to be a primitive form of Greek, and the scribes presumably were not members of the ruling caste but came from a lower stratum of society, descended from the older population of the mainland. Racially this population must, on archaeological grounds, have remained unchanged ever since the beginning of the Middle Bronze Age, when an invasion can be postulated. From the architectural point of view it does not matter whether those invaders introduced the Greek language or learnt it from their predecessors in the country, because the two peoples eventually merged, with the result that a continuous architectural inheritance can be traced right back through the Early Bronze Age and even into the Stone Age.

The peoples of the Stone and Early Bronze Ages have left nothing of architectural distinction, except at Troy, and even there the outstanding group of buildings is comparable in plan with an Ashanti fetish-house; backward tribes of equatorial Africa build today in the various forms characteristic of the other cultures. No excavation, however, has found relics of decoration equal to any that graces these modern parallels. In the case of a book concerned with architecture as an art, the only pre-Hellenic buildings which could deserve attention are the Minoan and Mycenean palaces and a couple of tholos tombs, were it not for the continuity of heritage which gives historical significance to the most primitive hovels.

One of the earliest types of building, the circular hut with a conical roof, can be seen to have evolved into the tholos tomb of the Myceneans and subsequently into the Hellenic tholos, nor did this course of three thousand years terminate its history; improved by the Roman addition of the dome, the same form can be recognized as continuing in the Byzantine church and in the mosque. The Hellenic sanctuary and its humbler counterpart, the rich man's house, are patently derived from the Mycenean palace compound, for which a precedent existed at Troy in the Early Bronze Age; nothing comparable is known during the intervening thousand years, but the resemblance seems too precise for mere coincidence. More surprising, because the hiatus may amount to two thousand years, is the parallel between the type of hall then in vogue at Troy, with a projection behind like a smaller edition of the porch in front, and the Hellenic temple with its opisthodomus balancing the porch. Except, however, for this one feature, we can watch the development of halls on the mainland of Greece from the same remote epoch, through successive innovations due to the invaders of the Middle Bronze Age and to Minoan influence upon the Myceneans, till the emergence of the temple.

Whereas Egyptian and Asiatic influences had been profound during the Bronze Age, the effects upon Hellenic architecture were comparatively trivial. Greeks constantly visited the pyramids and temples of Egypt, and a few went to Babylonia and saw ziggurats, but among their own structures the old-fashioned tumulus alone shows appreciation of the grandeur of a simple mass, though here and there a detail in a temple or the shape of a hall might be directly imitated from Egypt or Asia.

Basically, then, Hellenic architecture is a synthesis of the pre-Hellenic styles. Every one of the past cultures had made its contribution, thanks probably to a diversity of racial and social factors as well as to differences in the physical environment. (Even the Early Bronze Age inhabitants of the Cyclades had bequeathed something, by showing how to construct a corbelled vault with the rock fragments that littered their barren islands.) The accumulated stock of architectural heritage reached its maximum at the close of the Bronze Age and became impoverished in the ensuing dismal centuries of transition, but the several types of building persisted; the loss was not in essentials but in technical and aesthetic standards, in decency of workmanship, and in elegance and ornament.

When ease and wealth returned, and the Greeks learnt afresh how to build in stone, their first preoccupation was naturally to master the new technique, which they applied to reproducing the forms they were already accustomed to use in sun-dried brick and timber. As their skill increased, the whole scheme of proportions was improved, till the ideal arose of attaining perfection in that respect. Other considerations were sacrificed to achieve it, especially in the Doric temple. That supreme creation of Periclean Athens is really abstract sculpture. Regarded from the standpoint of utility as a building, the temple is ridiculous – all that magnificent and outrageously expensive casing to a cramped and ill-lit room which held nothing but an image or two and was never put to any mortal use. The exterior is infinitely the more important part. It was designed to look equally satisfactory from every angle, while the lines or surfaces that led in some particular direction were invariably countered by others, so that the eye could neither be conveyed away from the building nor come to rest on any point of it, but travelled unceasingly from one to another. The present impression of frigidity was mitigated near the top by the bright colours disposed here and there among the ornament and by the carved and painted figures; these supplied the only decorative element that was not rigidly geometrical. All the rest beats out a harmony and counterpoint which yet succeeds in being fluid, not frozen, and seems as uncontrived and inevitable as a Bach fugue. So the building pulsates with movement, up and down and from side to side of its taut anatomy, and nowhere escapes from control; ardour and exultation might be expressed only in the sculptural decoration.

The Athenians of that time lived in a glory of achievement and promise, unequalled in history, and they demanded of their every art that it be sublime. The disheartened generations that followed abandoned austerity for prettiness in every art, and evolved a comparatively luscious architecture. Ionic gained the preference over Doric because of the less forbidding character and greater abundance of its decoration. The invention of the Corinthian capital provided still more opportunity to avoid geometry, but a lingering sense of propriety restricted its use to interiors till a whole century had passed.

Then, in the Hellenistic Age when architects built as much for foreigners as for Greeks, opulence reigned and frivolity too might be introduced. The Orders were subject to all manner of variations and to fusion one with another, but still acted as a check on really novel development. The most striking change resulted from the acceleration of a long-established tendency to slighter proportions. These now became so attenuated as to make the temple light and airy. The slenderness of the columns exaggerated their height, causing an impression of upward movement. The top of the building shrank relatively to them; instead of expressing enough horizontal movement to counteract their effect, it appeared not much more than a lid imposed across them. In an attempt to restore the balance of horizontal and vertical masses the number of steps at the base was sometimes increased, but the expedient can scarcely have proved adequate; too wide a spread of steps would have constituted them into a truncated pyramid on which the temple itself could only perch as a separate and worse-balanced composition.

A drastic change of temple design was needed, and that the Greeks failed to accomplish because of their inability to break with the past when making their own experiments. Instead, their type of temple was superseded by the Roman, examples of which were built in Greek lands from the beginning of the Christian era. The Roman practice (actually inherited from the Etruscans) was to set the temple on a much higher platform bounded by a sheer drop all round except at the front, where steps cut their way through to the porch. Here alone were columns thought essential, and although for additional splendour their number might be increased to surround the whole building, the porch always stood well forward. Accordingly a clear focal point was given at the centre of the front – a notion entirely contrary to Greek principles. The architect's endeavour was now to make the full-on view of the front as imposing as he could, while, in compensation, he enriched the remainder of the exterior with bold repetitive decoration, to an extent which the Greeks had applied only to buildings so large that a part might otherwise seem to detach itself from the whole. The insoluble Hellenistic problem of trying to balance unequal horizontal and vertical zones did not arise with the tall platform; considering that the Roman system was already fully developed before the Hellenistic Age, and that a great many Greeks must have observed its characteristics, the prolonged struggle to adapt Hellenic traditional forms to suit Hellenistic proportions is evidence of the most devout conservatism.

The history of the theatre affords another instance of both the brilliance and the failings of Greek inventiveness. The theatre, by origin a purely Greek creation, has been accepted by the modern world as a logically inevitable architectural concept, but in a form developed by the Romans. And again, as in the case of the temple, the Greeks themselves accepted the Roman version at the beginning of the Christian era. Primarily the advantage lay in greater efficiency; the relation of seats to stage gave the audience a better view. The Roman method of construction, too, was immensely superior, and, with the seats raised on vaulting instead of sunk into a hill-side, the choice of site ceased to be restricted by nature. An incidental result of this change was to benefit design. The exterior in the Greek theatre had been mainly invisible or, at most, of insignificant aspect, but now it stood up conspicuously and offered immense scope to the architect.

The case of the theatre, therefore, illustrates the practical genius of the Romans in contrast with another instance of Greek adherence to a traditional form that no longer suited its purpose, and in contrast too with the Greek inadequacy at engineering. Or, one might rather say, inadequacy in practical matters – not less a characteristic of the Greeks than their brilliance at theorizing; habitual inventors of constitutions, they always failed abysmally at government.

However, engineering incompetence does not altogether account for the fact that the Greeks knew but did not exploit the principle of the vault. It is true that they took several centuries to discover the superiority of the round arch over other forms, and that when they did use it they normally made the vault unnecessarily heavy, thereby reducing the benefits obtainable. Lack of practice is the obvious explanation of such bungling, but why should they have lacked practice? For one thing, the rarity of arches in past times would have been enough to discourage their use, so traditionally-minded was the race. But there can be no doubt that arches were considered an aesthetically reprehensible substitute for the flat lintel, with which was associated everything of recognized beauty in architecture.

Here, then, we see clearly the motives for those qualities which distinguish Hellenic architecture. Because the high degree of civilization attained had not eradicated primitive beliefs, the Greeks venerated tradition regardless of its merits. They allowed improvements to be introduced into architectural practice, but abhorred revolutionary change – 'Nothing to excess' was the golden rule for human behaviour – and the improvements generally retained as conservative an aspect as possible. Practical advantage mattered little, economy not at all; the greater the cost and the less the utility, so much the more did the work enhance the repute of its owner, the city-state. Most potent of all means of emulation was the creation of a work of beauty.

Beauty, however, implied also something analogous to what we call the right thing; a building could not be beautiful unless it conformed with the long-established and universally admitted dogmas of the art, as well as having – and this ranked above all other qualities – correct proportions to the smallest detail. In actual fact, the greatest masterpiece of ancient Greece, the Parthenon, is the one building in the world which may be assessed as absolutely right.

LIST OF THE PRINCIPAL ABBREVIATIONS

A.A.A.	Ἀρχαιολογικὰ Ἀνάλεκτα ἐξ Ἀθηνῶν, *Athens Annals of Archaeology*
A.J.A.	*American Journal of Archaeology*
Arch. Anz.	*Archäologischer Anzeiger* (with *Jahrbuch des Deutschen Archäologischen Instituts*)
Ἀρχ. Δελτ.	Ἀρχαιολογικὸν Δελτίον
Arch. Rep.	*Archaeological Reports, Hellenic Society and British School at Athens*
Ath. Mitt.	*Athenische Mitteilungen, Deutsches Archäologisches Institut*
B.C.H.	*Bulletin de Correspondance Hellénique*
B.S.A.	*Annual of the British School at Athens*
Ἐφ. Ἀρχ.	Ἐφημερὶς Ἀρχαιολογική
Ist. Mitt.	*Istanbuler Mitteilungen*
J.D.I.	*Jahrbuch des Deutschen Archäologischen Instituts*
J.Ö.A.I.	*Jahreshefte des Oesterreichischen Archäologischen Instituts*
J.H.S.	*Journal of Hellenic Studies*
Πραχ.	Πρακτικὰ τῆς ἐν Ἀθήναις Ἀρχαιολογικῆς Ἑταιρείας
S.I.M.A.	*Studies in Mediterranean Archaeology*

NOTES

Bold numbers indicate page references.

CHAPTER 1

17.1. The chronology of the Bronze Age is based on the study of artefact sequences (especially pottery), scientific methods (radio-carbon, dendrochronology), and cross links with literate societies (mainly Egypt). It is subject to constant revision as study proceeds. Dates are approximate only, with a greater range of approximation in the earlier periods. It is unlikely that the inhabitants of Greece in the Early Bronze Age (EH) were Greek-speaking, but they probably were from the Middle Bronze Age (MH) onwards: Middle and Late Bronze Age Crete was not Greek-speaking until MMII (though the pre-Greek language was still spoken in some parts of Crete in historical times). Chronological terminology refers to the Bronze Age of mainland Greece as Helladic (Early, Middle, Late, abbreviated to EH, MH, LH, and further subdivided), to that of Crete as Minoan (EM, MM, LM, etc.), and of the Cyclades, generally, as Cycladic. These terms are conventional only, and have no implications for the nature of the population.

CHAPTER 2

20. 1. It is, however, possible to restore the Trojan buildings, and less plausibly the Mycenaean megaron and other pre-Hellenic types of building, as having had pitched roofs (Baldwin Smith, *A.J.A.*, XLVI (1942), 99, with many plans, by no means limited to the pre-Hellenic era). Such theories rest on no convincing evidence. All that is definitely known points to the conclusion that early roofs were generally flat throughout Asia Minor as well as in the Greek lands, and the probable exceptions seem to have been of very light construction. Direct evidence as regards the Trojan culture of the Early Bronze Age is obtainable from the outlying site of Thermi, where blocks of undetached houses, including some of irregular shape, could scarcely have been covered by ridged roofs (W. Lamb, *Excavations at Thermi*). The megaron at Pylos, for example, must have had a flat roof (C. W. Blegen and M. Rawson, *The Palace of Nestor at Pylos* (Princeton, 1966), 34).
21. 2. Extremely early buildings in the interior of Asia Minor were composed of pisé; in Greece, evidence for its use is mainly inferential, but continuity of practice should probably be assumed in order to explain its occurrence at the very end of the Bronze Age at a place so rich as Mycenae (Taylour and Papadimitriou, Αρχ. Δελτ., XVIII (1963), B.1, p. 82). In the parts of England where stone does not abound, the decay of old cottages and enclosure walls often reveals a similar type of construction, of clay stiffened with vegetable matter.

3. Curved walls were also built in the Trojan culture, but rarely. The backs of some houses at Thermi are irregularly rounded, either because the site was cramped or to avoid the additional work that would have been involved by corners (Lamb, *Excavations at Thermi*). The apsidal end of a house of Troy Ia is built thinner (averaging 18 inches; 45 cm.) than the rest of the external wall (of 20–24 inches; 50–60 cm.) or even the cross-wall, and with smaller stones; it is very questionable whether a brick wall on such a narrow plinth could have supported a flat roof, though it might have enclosed an open court, as seems to have been the function of a wall of the same width in Troy IIf. Another possibility is that the upper part of the wall and the roof both consisted of wattle-and-daub (Blegen, *Troy*, I, 1, 83, 304; cf. 103, 110; I, 2, figures 425, 460).
23. 4. The nomenclature may confuse. The phases distinguished by early excavators, especially phase II, have the required subdivisions indicated by the addition of lower case letters in sequence IIa, IIb ... etc. Individual buildings of the original phases are distinguished by the addition of a capital letter (Building IIA, IIB, etc.)
25. 5. The propylon has almost the same axis but is off-centred to the building IIA; this overlies a narrower predecessor, attributed to IIb, and the alignment of the propylon is directed approximately on the centre of the earlier porch. Perhaps the enclosing wall and propylon were laid out with the intention of retaining the earlier building in use; the dates of both its construction and its destruction have been only vaguely ascertained. In the succeeding phase, IId, the court was enlarged by rebuilding the enclosing wall a few paces outwards from its old line, and new spur-walls were built in slightly different positions in order to reconstruct the veranda; its plan at this date, however, is not altogether clear.

26. 6. Poliochni was apparently founded by immigrants from Asia Minor, who lived in thatched cottages, mostly of oval plan, during what is called the 'Black' period of the site. The oldest parts of the fortifications go back to the succeeding 'Blue' period; the next, the 'Green', overlapped with the foundation of Troy, and was followed by the 'Red', which probably began rather late in Troy I and lasted to Troy IIc. The fifth, or 'Yellow', period corresponds with Troy IId–g and ended in disaster. After a hiatus, the site was re-occupied for one more, 'Brown', period at the time of Troy V, supposedly the twentieth century.

7. See J. D. Evans and C. Renfrew, *Excavations at Saliagos* (1968), noting similarity in small finds to Bronze Age products.

8. A radio-carbon analysis of charcoal found at Khalandriani dated it within 80 years of 2580; presumably this does not apply to any late stage of occupation: that is, it belongs to the Cycladic cultural phase termed Keros-Syros.

29. 9. H. D. Hansen, *Early Civilization in Thessaly*, figure 19, illustrates a modern example of a circular hut.

10. Dinsmoor, *Architecture of Ancient Greece*, figure 2.

11. For Syrian domed houses see Copeland, *Antiquity*, XXIX (1955), 21.

12. Only preliminary accounts of the House of the Tiles have appeared so far. The most recent is in *Lerna in the Argolid: a short guide*, by J. L. Caskey and E. T. Blackburn (Athens, ASCS, 1977).

13. A double wall, containing chambers, delimited the south portion of an enclosure around the 'House of the Tiles' (Caskey, *Hesperia*, XXVII (1958), 132, figure 1). The excavator is likely to have been right in his first opinion that this wall was too flimsy to be a fortification; the short-lived 'towers' found subsequently, at a corner that probably overlooked a swamp, can more appropriately be identified as granaries, especially since the later floors were raised above ground level. Caskey and Blackburn (*op. cit.*), the latest account, consider that they were fortifications: the bastion makes this likely. There are possible other EH fortifications at Lake Vouliagmeni, near Perachora, but it has been suggested that these may have been terrace walls made necessary by the rising of the water level in the adjacent lake.

32. 14. Evans, *Anatolian Studies*, XXII (1972), 115.

15. Two pottery models of round huts, constructed apparently of thatch, have been found in Crete, but are probably Late Minoan (Evans, *Palace of Minos*, II, 1, figures 63 and 65). A circular well-house at Arkhanes, in which Late Minoan Ia pottery was found, was so slightly built that the roof must have been thatched (*ibid.*, figure 30).

34. 16. W. Cavanagh and R. R. Laxton, *B.S.A..*, LXXVI (1981).

CHAPTER 3

35. 1. Such practices as the sending of hostages or diplomatic missions to foreign courts, and inter-marriage between royal families, are obviously likely to have resulted in some common features in the designs of palaces. At Beycesultan, in the interior of Asia Minor, a palace anticipated Minoan conventions in that blocks of buildings lined all sides of a rectangular court and that many of the inner rooms opened on to light-wells; the period of occupation can be estimated only roughly as from 1900–1750 (Seton Lloyd and Mellaart, *Beycesultan*, II, 62, plan facing p. 8, restoration on p. 30, and III, 1, British Institute of Archaeology at Ankara, 1972). The divergences between Minoan and Asiatic palaces have been emphasized by Graham (*Mycenean Studies, Colloquium at 'Wingspread' 1961*, edited by E. L. Bennett (1964), 195); his criticisms as regards Beycesultan apply to preliminary statements which the excavators had subsequently modified.

2. For the proto-palatial remains at Phaestus, D. Levi, *Festòs e la civiltà minoica*, I. The façade was diversified into sections alternately recessed and advanced, as described on p. 36.

36. 3. The rounded north-east corner of the throne room may be part of an originally separate building.

4. A deep rock-cutting, called the 'hypogeum', seems to have been an adjunct to the first palace at Cnossus (Evans, *Palace of Minos*, I, 104, figure 74). It was probably a granary; the walls have not the impervious lining used in cisterns. The date can only be presumed from the circumstance that the top was removed and the pit filled to make a solid foundation for the south porch of Middle Minoan II, and from the great preponderance of Middle Minoan I compared with older sherds in the earth filling, a fact which suggests that little use had been made of the site till that period. The hypogeum was circular in plan and ovoid in elevation; the width is greatest at a height of 20–30 feet – probably half-way up to the original roof – and is narrower by several feet at floor-level, where the diameter is still nearly 24 feet. A staircase winds down a couple of feet behind the face of the vault, to which window-like openings were pierced at every few steps. Practically no light can have penetrated down the stair from the upper exit, and the rock roof of the vault is as likely to have extended across its entire area as to have included a man-hole with a removable cover. The function of the openings, which are about 3 feet wide, may have been, in the first instance, to allow the workmen when constructing the vault to extract the

rock fragments, and thereafter to provide access to the grain stored within at times when the accumulation choked the doorway at the foot of the stair. A second doorway at floor level was blocked in antiquity; it might have been the mouth of a passage by which the workmen could remove excavated material more easily than by the stair. But the entire hypogeum has been absurdly explained as a more or less secret entrance to the palace, on the supposition that the blocked doorway communicated with ground outside the enclosure.

37. 5. The supposed block-houses or police-posts in the countryside might, for all one can tell, have been inns, or served some equally innocuous purpose. A doubtful exception has been made for a building of Middle Minoan I at Khamaizi (Pendlebury, *Archaeology of Crete*, 100, figure 14; Robertson, *Greek and Roman Architecture*, figure 1), but wrongly according to subsequent investigation (Davaras, *A.A.A.*, V (1972), 283, revised plan on p. 287). The exterior is straight in one part but otherwise oval, 73 by 48 feet maximum. The shape was obviously adopted to utilize earlier curved walls as foundations, on a site restricted by nature, and the customary rectangular planning was modified as little as possible; most of the partitions are set at right angles, making the rooms rectangular except where they meet a stretch of the outer wall. An empty space in the centre presumably formed a diminutive court; it contains a rock-cut pit that served as a cistern. At the entrance, one wall radiates towards it, converging upon the other, which runs at right angles to the exterior, so forming a porch; on the opposite side of the building is a simple doorway which may have been used by another family, or by animals in such numbers as a shepherd might own or travellers bring to an inn.

6. Graham's discussion: *A.J.A.*, LXXXIII (1979), 64; Cnossus: Evans, *Palace of Minos*, I, 328.

38. 7. At Phaestus the west court was raised and extended for the new palace, burying the west façade of the earlier palace.

8. The model at Cnossus: Evans, *Palace of Minos*, I, 221; Mallia: Poursot, *B.C.H.*, XCV (1966), 514.

41. 9. Angeliki Lembessis, Ἐφ. Ἀρχ. (1976), 12 f.

CHAPTER 4

42. 1. For the importance of western Crete, and Khania, in Late Minoan III after the destruction of Cnossus, see now H. W. Catling, J. F. Cherry, R. E. Jones, J. T. Killen, 'The Linear B Inscribed Stirrup Jars and West Crete', *B.S.A.*, LXXV (1980), 49 f.

43. 2. Robertson, *Greek and Roman Architecture*, figure 7; Dinsmoor, *Architecture of Ancient Greece*, plate VII.

44. 3. Twisted shafts probably originated in or near Mesopotamia; the earliest example is an engaged half-column of brick at Tell er Rimah. Sight of Mycenean ivories may have inspired the Athenian dedications on the Acropolis, before 480, of large twisted shafts that probably supported votive offerings. In Roman times panels in relief were often framed between engaged twisted shafts, for their decorative value.

4. The restorations of miniature frescoes are even more disputable than those of large-scale paintings.

5. Dinsmoor, *op cit.*, plate VII.

47. 6. Dinsmoor, *op cit.*, plate V; Robertson, *op. cit.*, figure 3.

50. 7. J. Walter Graham discusses this controversy in 'Bathrooms and Lustral Chambers', in *Greece and the Eastern Mediterranean in Ancient History and Prehistory* (Studies presented to Fritz Schachermeyr on the occasion of his 80th birthday), 110 (with earlier bibliography). He feels that while many basins were for bathing, some definitely had a ritual purpose, and argues that the tendency of gypsum to dissolve should not be over-emphasized.

52. 8. Blocks of the parapet contained hollows in which the shafts had stood. The excavation obtained no evidence whatever for the shape of the columns and did not ascertain their precise height. They have since been rebuilt by guess, copying the representations of columns in frescoes and other contemporary works of art (Robertson, *op. cit.*, figure 4; Dinsmoor, *op. cit.*, plate VIII). An extraordinarily similar staircase, considering its small scale, has been found in a two-storeyed 'villa' at Pyrgos, in south-eastern Crete (Cadogan, *Palaces of Minoan Crete*, 149).

9. The reconstruction of the Hall of the Double Axes has been completed by attaching shields of painted zinc to the fresco. The shape chosen for the concrete columns is again purely hypothetical; if indeed the original columns tapered at all, they surely would not have done so to such an exaggerated degree as in the reconstruction. The spacing of the external colonnade restored along the east part of the south side is also questionable.

57. 10. *A.J.A.*, LXXXIII (1979), 67. For the dimensions and an earlier version of the restoration of the Minoan foot, *2nd International Congress of Cretology*, I (Athens, 1967), 157.

61. 11. *Arch. Rep.* (1972–3), 50.

CHAPTER 5

71. 1. Admirable preliminary reports were produced by the excavator, S. Marinatos, before his untimely death (*Excavations at Thera*). The West House, or House of the Admiral, is described in vol. VI (for the fresco, see especially colour plate 9).

73. 2. J. L. Caskey, *Hesperia*, XL (1971), 359. A more recent plan of the excavations: *Arch. Rep.* (1977–8), 52, figure 89. For Hagios Andreas (previously thought to be Middle Cycladic, and another example of double fortification) see now B. Philippaki, *A.A.A.*, VI, 93.

74. 3. The sides of most roofs may have curved convexly, but triangular gables are represented in a few rock-cut tombs (e.g. Frödin and Persson, *Asine*, figure 139).

75. 4. Dinsmoor, *op. cit.*, figure 14; Robertson, *op. cit.*, figure 20.

76. 5. Dinsmoor, *op. cit.*, figure 12.

CHAPTER 6

77. 1. *Arch. Rep.* (1977–8), 20.

78. 2. The engineering principles and method of design for the tholos tombs is discussed by W. G. Cavanagh and R. R. Laxton, *B.S.A.*, LXXVI (1981).

80. 3. For the latest, brief, discussion of the chronology, R. Hope Simpson and O. T. P. K. Dickinson, *Gazetteer of Aegean Civilization*, I (Göteborg, 1979), 36.

4. Dinsmoor, *op. cit.*, plate XV.

5. Dinsmoor, *op. cit.*, plate XIII; Robertson, *op. cit.*, plate. Ia.

82. 6. Dinsmoor, *op. cit.*, plate XVI.

7. The red stone, and probably the green also, came from the east coast of the Maina peninsula, the most southerly projection from the Peloponnese (*B.S.A.*, LXIII (1968), 331).

84. 8. These slabs are in the British Museum (*Catalogue of Sculpture*, I, 1, 27, nos. A 56–7), and can be identified as the 'marble' reliefs said to have been found by Elgin's men in the 'Treasury of Atreus'.

9. Dinsmoor, *op. cit.*, plate XIV.

85. 10. Dinsmoor, *op. cit.*, plate XIII.

CHAPTER 7

87. 1. An up-to-date brief account of all Mycenaean sites and the chronology, with full references: R. Hope-Simpson and O. T. P. K. Dickinson, *A Gazetteer of Aegean Civilization*.

89. 2. At Pylos, columns in the first palace bore 44 flutes, those in various parts of the second 32, 60, and 64 (C. W. Blegen and M. Rawson, *The Palace of Nestor*, I, 39–40). A large collection of architectural models in ivory, found inside a thirteenth-century house at Mycenae, includes over sixty miniature columns (*B.S.A.*, XLIX (1954), plate 40; L (1955), plate 30). These mostly taper downwards and are unfluted; zigzag decoration occurs, as in the 'Treasury of

Atreus'. A few shafts are fluted, perpendicularly or in spirals. Some of the capitals consist merely of an abacus and an echinus; in others a collar is added beneath, the echinus is concave, and the abacus face slants inwards both from above and from below. Exceptionally elaborate capitals are carved with tongue mouldings on the collar and the upper part of the echinus, the lower part being surrounded by leaves pointing upwards; this decoration must be derived from the Egyptian palm capitals.

3. Tiles reported from Malthi are probably Byzantine: R. Hope Simpson and O. T. P. K. Dickinson, *op. cit.*, 174.

4. J. Shaw, *B.S.A.*, LXXIII (1978), 225.

90. 5. Normally the porch is only slightly raised above the court, but the porch of a small megaron at Eleusis was approached up a pair of staircases, divided by a central platform (Dinsmoor, *op. cit.*, figure 10; Kardara, *A.A.A.*, V (1972), 123, figure 10).

6. A parallel to the megaron in the Early Bronze Age has also been found far inland in Asia Minor, at Kültepe – a hall, 40 feet wide, containing a hearth surrounded by four columns; it is datable about 2300 (Lloyd, *Proceedings of British Academy*, XLIX (1963), 153).

91. 7. The wall-circuit of Troy VI–VIIa must have had a total length of some 1771 feet (540 m.), of which about three-quarters can be traced, including four gates, two posterns, and three towers. The gates were about 10 feet (3 m.) wide, to take chariots. The south and north-west gates opened straight through the wall, the left side of which projected several metres. The right side projected at both the south-west gate, which was blocked before the close of Troy VI, and the east gate; these were bent entrances, with the doorway set behind in a special wall, which ran at a pronounced angle to the circuit. Another case of a bent entrance outflanked on the right is the narrow postern (blocked in VIIa) which led by means of steps into the south side of the north-east tower; Khalandriani supplies a precedent of a gateway that pierced the cheek of a tower, rounded, however. The circuit of Troy was built (with a considerable batter) in straight stretches, mostly $16\frac{1}{2}$–33 feet (5–10 m.) long, which met in jags a few centimetres deep, of no defensive value; compare the serrated face at Hagios Andreas (p. 73), but the jags at Troy are carved into the face of the blocks. Above the stone-work, which rose to a height of some 30 feet, stood a vertical wall of unbaked bricks.

93. 8. Reports of the latest excavations and plan: K. Kilian, *Arch. Anz.* (1978), 449 (Ausgrabungen in Tiryns 1976); *Arch. Anz.* (1979), 380 (Ausgrabungen in Tiryns 1977; for the cult room).

9. Dinsmoor, *op. cit.*, plate XIV.

97. 10. Dinsmoor, *op. cit.*, plates XI and XII.

98. 11. A theory that the missing parts composed the heads and wings of griffins (*'Εφ. 'Αρχ.* (1965), 7) is not easily reconciled with a physique too ponderous for flying.

100. 12. *Arch. Rep.* (1968–9), 11–12.

102. 13. Dinsmoor, *op. cit.* figure 8.

104. 14. The passage at the south corner led only to a shelf overlooking the precipice, as though intended for the disposal of refuse. For a large-scale plan of this eastern end of the citadel see *Πρακ.* (1966), 104.

15. Plans and sections of the spring-tunnels at Tiryns were published in *'Αρχ. Δελτ*, XIX (1964), B. 1, 112–15.

16. Graham (*A.J.A.*, LXI (1967), 353) has argued that the apparently oldest building at Pylos was intended from the first to contain a banquet hall and ancillary quarters.

106. 17. Plan: *Arch. Rep.* (1977–8), 53.

108. 18. This account is based on a brief note in R. Hope-Simpson and O. T. P. K. Dickinson, *op. cit.*, 239. Reports of recent excavations: *Πρακ.* (1955–61) (1979), 7.

19. K. A. Wardle, *B.S.A.*, LXXV (1980), 229.

20. Desborough, *The Greek Dark Ages* (London, 1972) 19 f.; Snodgrass, *The Dark Age of Greece* (Edinburgh, 1971), especially 360 f.

109. 21. J. Shaw, *B.S.A.*, LXXIII (1978), 235 f.

CHAPTER 8

110. 1. For detailed accounts of the Dark Age: Desborough, *The Greek Dark Ages* (London, 1972); Snodgrass, *The Dark Age of Greece* (Edinburgh, 1971); and the new edition of the *Cambridge Ancient History*, III, pt 1 (Cambridge, 1982).

111. 2. V. Karageorghis, *Kition* (London, 1976) (a general account, in advance of the full publication). For Mycenaean (Achaean) building, 58 f.; for the Phoenicians, 95 f. See also Dr Karageorghis' account in *Cambridge Ancient History*, III, pt 1, 511–33.

113. 3. J. J. Coulton, *The Architectural Development of the Greek Stoa* (Oxford, 1976), 18–19.

CHAPTER 9

116. 1. The great megaron at Tiryns was rebuilt on a narrower plan, using only one of the original side walls. The original floor level was retained, a fact which might suggest a reconstruction soon after the destruction of the palace and for the same purpose (the question of date must await the publication of the stratified pottery from this area). But a very early Doric capital was found on the site, and large numbers of votive statuettes in terracotta prove the existence in the sixth century of a cult of Hera, so that the building is at least as likely to have originated as her temple. The megaron at Eleusis (Note 5 to Chapter 7) is dubiously interpreted as the pre-Hellenic temple of Demeter.

The Bronze Age shrine on Keos (above, p. 73) continued in use, perhaps without interruption; but the later cult may have resulted from the accidental discovery of the head of a terracotta figure, and its recognition as a venerable object of cult. (Its sex was not recognized; originally female, it was subsequently worshipped as the god Dionysus.)

2. Previously it had been thought that the interior roof supports of the seventh-century temple went with the early wall, and belonged to the Protogeometric period. The most recent work at Lefkandi suggests that the colonnade extended round and behind the apse. A plan of the building, identified as a heroum, has been published in *Arch. Rep.* (1981–2), figure 32, p. 17, with a description.

118. 3. Dinsmoor, *op. cit.*, figure 15; Robertson, *op. cit.*, plate 1, b and c.

120. 4. Dinsmoor, *op. cit.*, figure 14; Robertson, *op. cit.*, figure 20.

5. Robertson, *op. cit.*, plate IIa.

CHAPTER 10

126. 1. A very striking instance of accidental fluting, which resulted from the use of a rounded stone adze, can be seen in a wooden statue of a bear, from a North American totem-pole, in the Museum of Archaeology and Ethnology at Cambridge, England.

130. 2. While the literal meaning of the word 'triglyph' is unquestionably 'carved in three', the derivation of 'metope' is somewhat obscure. Vitruvius (IV. 2.4) explained it on the ground that the Greek word for the hollow mortices in which they bedded beams or rafters was *opae*, literally 'holes' or 'eyes', hence the spaces between the mortices were called metopes, literally 'between *opae*'. This interpretation seems confirmed by an alternative use of 'metope' to describe the 'face' of a crab, i.e. the space between its eyes. An etymologically sound connexion with *metopon*, the word for a human 'forehead', is probably irrelevant but 'metope' has also been explained on that basis as meaning a 'facing'.

3. For hypothetical reconstructions, with triglyphs representing the ends of beams, see Dinsmoor, *op. cit.*, figure 20; *J.D.I.*, LXIII–LXIV (1948), 11, figure 7.

131. 4. The 'angle triglyph' problem is considered at

length by Robertson, *op. cit.*, 106–12. Difficulties arose also when a Doric frieze turned, less conspicuously, in a re-entrant [cf. 317]; various solutions were tried, none with outstanding success (Coulton, *B.S.A.*, LXI (1966), 132).

5. In Sicily, triglyphs appear to have occasionally been placed slightly behind the face of the architrave. It is worth noting that angle triglyphs, if set flush with the architrave, cannot be centred above the column and yet meet at the corner unless the width of each triglyph face equals the front-to-back thickness of the architrave. That is because the architrave lies with its centre over the centre of the columns; if the triglyph likewise is so centred, the distance from its centre to the corner of the architrave must equal half the thickness of the architrave. If the triglyph is narrower than the thickness of the architrave, it will fail to reach the corner by half the difference between the two dimensions.

132. 6. Two intermediate triglyphs were placed in the intercolumniations of a small Sicilian temple attributed to about 320–310 (G. Vallet and F. Villard, *Megara Hyblaea*, IV, *Le Temple du IVe siècle*); actually, however, a dating to the third century would be quite as plausible.

133. 7. This tomb at Politiko, the ancient Tamassus, is entered through a porch in which stand pilasters with Aeolic capitals, closer to the Syrian prototypes than any Greek examples. In other respects there seems little justification for classing the tomb as Syrian rather than Greek work, and in any case there is no resemblance to the Mycenean-Syrian tombs at Ras Shamra. The fanlight over the doorway to the sarcophagus-chamber was originally smooth, and the markings upon its surface are due to modern visitors. The strip of carving beneath represents water-lily flowers and buds. The width of the doorway is 3 feet 7 inches. Egyptian influence may account for the presence of a false door [98]; the fastenings of the bolt are indicated but the bolt itself has been broken short.

8. Delphi: J. P. Michaud, *Fouilles de Delphes*, II, *Le Temple en calcaire*. Vergina: full understanding must await the publication of the palace by M. Andronikos; for a plan of the palace, see our illustration 315.

137. 9. At Petsas' Tomb, Lefkadia (Ph. M. Petsas, *'O τάφος τῶν Λευκάδιων, πίναξ ί*) and the tomb of Philip at Vergina (personal observation).

138. 10. Coulton, *Greek Architects at Work* (London, 1977), 51 f.; *B.S.A.*, LXIX (1974), 61f.

CHAPTER 11

139. 1. The temple of Apollo at Cyrene is likely to have been a little earlier – the objects found beneath it belong to the end of the seventh century – but the pteron may not have been completed till later. The plan of the interior is unusual and obviously primitive; it might have been derived from the Ionic area. There was no porch, the cella contained two rows of five columns, and behind it was a shallow adytum with two more columns in continuation of each row. The upper part of the walls seems to have consisted of sun-dried brick. The pteron comprised six columns on the ends and eleven on the sides. They were spaced 9½ feet (2·90 m.) apart, axis to axis, and the diameter at the base is 3½ feet (1·10 m.); in the adytum the columns had a diameter of 30 inches (75 cm.) and the interaxial spacing was 7½ feet (2·30 m.). The columns were set into hollows in the pavement, a method suitable for wooden shafts.

2. Robertson, *op. cit.*, figure 26.

140. 3. For the argument that there was no predecessor: Mallwitz, 'Das Heraion von Olympia und seine Vorgänger', *J.D.I.*, LXXXI (1966), 310 f.

146. 4. The chronology and succession of temples on this site is a vexed issue. The inner foundations are of different size and working to the outer, suggesting the addition at some stage of a pteron. For the argument that this was already done in the seventh century (made more plausible by the excavation of the temple at Isthmia) see I. Beyer, *Arch. Anz.* (1977), 44 f.

5. Dinsmoor, *op. cit.*, figure 102 for plan.

147. 6. Small non-peripteral temples on the islands of Chios (at Emporio), Andros (at Zagora), and Tenos consisted only of a cella and an anteroom or 'closed porch' (A. Cambitoglou, *Zagora*, I, 20, plan V).

7. R. Martin, 'Bathycles de Magnésie et le "Trône" d'Apollo à Amyklae', *Revue archéologique* (1976), 205.

148. 8. Robertson, *op. cit.*, figure 36 for entablature.

149. 9. The imperfect inscription on the front of the temple may have recorded the names of both the architect (?Epicles) and the dedicator (Cleo … es) – the former as 'maker of the columns and other fine works' (Guarducci, *Archeologia Classica*, I (1949), 4). A metope from a totally lost temple (Y, Selinus) seems from its sculpture to be older than Apollo at Syracuse.

150. 10. Dinsmoor, *op. cit.*, figure 26 for plan. Riemann, *Röm. Mitt.*, LXXI (1964), 229, for dimensions.

151. 11. Dinsmoor, *op. cit.*, figure 29; or Robertson, *op. cit.*, figure 28.

12. Dinsmoor, *op. cit.*, plate XXI.

13. To judge from fragments of the terracotta sheathings, the slanting cornices of Temple 'C', of an early temple at Calydon, and of a Phrygian temple at Gordium, might all have begun well inwards from the corner, leaving a horizontal stretch between the end of the pediment and the eaves (Dyggve, *Das Laphrion*, 307, for general discussion and figures 177–81, 221;

for Temple 'C' see Gabrici, *Monumenti Antichi della Reale Accademia dei Lincei*, xxxv, plates xviii, xxv). A complete example in stone has been excavated at Paestum (J. Boardman, *The Greeks Overseas*, 193, figure 54, *A.J.A.*, lix (1955), 305, plate 85, figure 2). A shrine was built with only the roof projecting above ground, and the sloping cornice of each gable bends as it nears the corner, though the tiled roof maintains the same angle from ridge to eaves and so rises high above the bend. Offerings found in the shrine date late in the sixth century and include a significant dedication to a nymph (U. Kron, *J.D.I.*, lxxxvi (1971), 117, 'Zum Hypogäum von Paestum').

152. 14. The columns of temple 'F' were fluted all round from top to bottom, and the screens were fluted in mirror image where they met the columns – an ineffectual method of securing stability; a repair to one column was covered by the junction of a screen (Hodge, *A.J.A.*, lxviii (1964), 179, plate 61).

155. 15. Dinsmoor, *op. cit.*, figure 32.

158. 16. Robertson, *op. cit.*, figure 33.

17. An old restoration by Koldewey, often republished (e.g. Robertson, *op. cit.*, figure 32, or Dinsmoor, *op. cit.*, figure 38), incorrectly makes the cornice project along the end and side at different inclinations, causing an awkward junction at the corners; there may possibly have been such corners in other buildings (Note 13 to this chapter). For an apparently reliable restoration see illustration 124.

CHAPTER 12

160. 1. The two blocks of presumably a single capital were re-used as building material for seventh-century tombs in Crete, at Phrati (or Afrati); the abacus is carved with running spirals in the Bronze Age tradition, and the echinus with leaves, also probably imitated from some Bronze Age object although ultimately derived from Egyptian palm-ornament (Levi, *Annuario della Scuola di Atene*, x–xii (1927–9), 450, figure 586).

2. A very large 'Aeolic' capital from Larisa is known to have crowned a votive column, and probably the leaves shown in old illustrations did not belong to it (e.g. Robertson, *op. cit.*, plate ii, Dinsmoor, *op. cit.*, plate xviii). More capitals have been found at Mytilene (Hatzi, *A.A.A.*, v (1972), 43, figures 5, 6).

3. Yigal Shiloh, *The Proto-Aeolic Capital and Israelite Ashlar Masonry* (*Qedem, Monographs of the Institute of Archaeology*, xi) (The Hebrew University of Jerusalem, 1979). Ivory examples: Barnett, *The Nimrud Ivories in the BM*, plate iv.

161. 4. P. P. Betancourt, *The Aeolic Style in Architecture* (Princeton, 1977).

5. Dinsmoor, *op. cit.*, figure 53. Akurgal argues for a transition from Aeolic to Ionic (*Anatolia*, v (1960), 1, plates i–vi).

162. 6. Robertson, *op. cit.*, figure 39 for Ephesus.

163. 7. Robertson, *op. cit.*, figure 42; Dinsmoor, *op. cit.*, figure 48.

165. 8. G. Gruben, 'Das Archäische Didymaion', *J.D.I.*, lxxviii (1963), 153 f.

9. Robertson, *op. cit.*, figures 40 and 41; Dinsmoor, *op. cit.*, plate xxx.

166. 10. From Duwer in Phrygia, a non-Greek settlement: N. Thomas, *Arch. Rep.* (1964–5); W. W. Cummer, *Anadolu* (1970), 29.

11. Gruben, *op. cit.* (Note 8). A shorter restoration (Tuchelt, *Ist. Mitt.*, Beiheft 9) gives only seventeen columns along the side.

12. Robertson, *op. cit.*, figure 45 and Dinsmoor, *op. cit.*, figure 47 for Naucratis. Dinsmoor also illustrates (*op. cit.*, plate xxxi) a triple-scroll pilaster capital from Didyma; this, and another which is almost a duplicate, probably came from an altar built late in the sixth century, destroyed by the Persians, and replaced in the fifth century by a copy (Hahland, *J.D.I.*, lxxix (1964), 176). A similar capital, found in the sanctuary of Hera on Samos, is believed to come from an anta of the small building 'A', which has been identified as a temple of Aphrodite contemporary with the third Heraeum (Ziegenaus, *Ath. Mitt.*, lxxii (1957), 93, Beilage 100 and 101, plate xii). Capitals with a palmette carved in a central nick, on top of the echinus, have been found especially on Paros (*A.A.A.*, i (1968), 178 and – in English – 180). Other small, poorly preserved archaic temples have been found at Coressia and Carthaea on Keos (Lauter, *Arch. Anz.* (1979), 6).

13. The fourth temple is often called the Heraeum of Polycrates. Work may have been commenced in his reign, and at his command, but cannot have progressed far before his death in 523.

167. 14. Accidental as well as deliberate variations can be recognized in the spacing of the archaic columns; Gruben, *op. cit.* (Note 8).

15. The Lycians, a non-Greek people who inhabited the south-west corner of Asia Minor, have left illustrations of a comparable method in rock-cut tombs, a few of which may be as early as the sixth century. The simpler tombs are flat-roofed, with eaves which project along the front and are carved on the under side to simulate a contiguous series of thin round branches; the ends of thick, squared beams are shown protruding from the side walls, and these must have carried the branches which formed the bedding of the clay roof. Some tombs are gabled, presumably to conform with a Hellenizing fashion, and in these façades round logs are represented under the

horizontal cornice. Later tombs are entirely Greek in design. (Dinsmoor, *op. cit.*, plate XIX.)
168. 16. Dinsmoor, *op. cit.*, figure 50 for outline restoration of three treasuries.
17. Dinsmoor, *op. cit.*, plate XXXIII.
18. An apsidal temple, probably about 20 feet (6 m.) wide, entered through a porch with four Ionic prostyle columns, was built at Emporio not long before 450 (J. Boardman, *Chios: Greek Emporio*, 68).
171. 19. The decorated column stood at the front of the fourth Heraeum of Samos but cannot have belonged to the original set; on stylistic grounds it is ascribed to about 480. For Gruben's restoration, drawn on the evidence of a few fragments, see *'Αρχ Δελτ.*, XVIII (1963), B.2, 288 and figure 2, or H. Berve and G. Gruben, *Griechische Tempel und Heiligtümer*, figure 116. Compare also the decoration at Naucratis (Dinsmoor, *op. cit.*, figure 47); this type of decoration was used in the fifth century, in the Erechtheum at Athens, and is restored on analogy in the temple of Athena at Miletus (*Milet*, 1.8; but see for the date A. Mallwitz, *Ist. Mitt.*, XXVI (1976), 67).
172. 20. J. Travlos, *Pictorial Dictionary of Ancient Athens* (London, 1971), 112. It has been suggested by C. A. Picon ('The Ilissos Temple Reconsidered', *A.J.A.*, LXXXII (1978), 47), on the evidence of both sculptural and architectural style, that the temple was in fact built in the 420s, about the same time as the Nike Temple it so closely resembles (the frieze sculptures had been identified by F. Studniczka, *J.D.I.*, XXXI (1916), 169).
173. 21. A. A. Barrett and M. J. Vickers, *B.S.A.*, LXX (1975), 11 f.

CHAPTER 13

174. 1. Dinsmoor is the protagonist for the early dating; he suggests the year 507. The Treasury was built alongside a pedestal upon which the Athenians dedicated Persian weapons after the battle of Marathon in 490, and Pausanias's statement that the Treasury itself formed part of the dedication could be a mistake due to the ambiguous inscription on the pedestal. But a careful scrutiny of the pedestal led de la Coste-Messelière to believe that the inscription must refer to the Treasury (*Revue Archéologique*, New Series, XIX (1942–3), 15; cf. *Fouilles de Delphes*, IV, 259). The sculpture certainly gives an impression of being later than that of the temple at Delphi, which was carved between 513 and 505. The patterns on the walls, however, agree better with those on sixth-century vases (Dinsmoor, *A.J.A.*, L (1946), 86).
2. The treasury was rebuilt towards the beginning of this century, with insufficient care, and the unsightly modern jointing is misleading.

3. W. W. Würster, *Alt Ägina*, I.1, *Der Apollon Tempel* (Mainz, 1974).
4. Dinsmoor, *op. cit.*, plate XXIV. Much rebuilding has increased the height of the ruins to include part of the frieze.
178. 5. Würster, *op. cit.*, 115.
6. Dinsmoor, *op. cit.*, figure 28. Temple 'E' has been largely re-erected, in parts up to the horizontal cornice.
7. Dinsmoor, *op. cit.*, figure 43.
179. 8. There is some uncertainty as to the precise measurements, and their implications for the design, which affect the restoration. Compare illustration 148 with de Waele's Abb. 12.
184. 9. Arguments for dating after 440, on the ground of an alleged influence of the Parthenon, seem inconclusive (Gottlieb, *A.J.A.*, LVII (1953), 95).
10. Dinsmoor, *op. cit.*, figure 55.
11. Robertson, *op. cit.*, figure 17.
12. Dinsmoor, *op. cit.*, plate XXXIV.

CHAPTER 14

186. 1. For Lindos, see Dyggve, *Lindos, Fouilles de l'Acropole*, III. *Le Sanctuaire* (1960).
2. A complete plan of the existing remains: *Fouilles de Delphes*, II, *Atlas* (1975).
190. 3. For a discussion of the date etc. W. B. Dinsmoor Jr, *The Propylaia to the Athenian Akropolis*, I, *The Predecessors* (Princeton, N.J., 1980), especially 52–4.
194. 4. The inscriptions are so fragmentary as to prevent any accurate accounting of the building costs. A very low estimate (Stanier, *J.H.S.*, LXXXIII (1953), 68) gives a total of 469 talents.
5. Contrary to the fixed belief in some countries, Elgin did not steal the sculptures. He acted by authorization of the lawful government and the owner of the property, the Turkish Empire; moreover, he took every care to avoid causing damage, and eventually allowed the British Museum to buy the sculptures for a sum much less than he had expended. He can scarcely be blamed for failure to realize that Greece would gain its independence in time to prevent the complete destruction of the remains, an end which then seemed almost inevitable but for his work.
195. 6. Dinsmoor, *op. cit.*, figure 57; Robertson, *op. cit.*, figure 49.
204. 7. By J. Boardman, *Festschrift für Frank Brommer* (Mainz, 1977), 39 f. (Sculpture on temples never depicts contemporary scenes.)
205. 8. Robertson, *op. cit.*, figure 50 and Dinsmoor, *op. cit.*, figure 75 for project plans; Dinsmoor, *op. cit.*, plate L for section, and figure 76 for elevation.

9. An outer gateway to the Acropolis, at the foot of the slope, was an addition of the Roman period. The modern zigzag path eases the gradient for tourists, and attempts to reproduce what was once thought to be the ancient form of the approach.

208. 10. Robertson, *op. cit.*, figure 51.

11. Dinsmoor, *op. cit.*, figure 66.

12. By J. Travlos, *Pictorial Dictionary*, 482.

210. 13. Dinsmoor, *op. cit.*, figure 68 for plan, figure 69 for angle capital.

213. 14. Dinsmoor, *op. cit.*, plates XLV–XLIX; Robertson, *op. cit.*, plates IIIb and Va, and figures 16 and 56.

220. 15. Dinsmoor, *op. cit.*, figures 70 and 71 for project plans, largely hypothetical.

221. 16. Some dimensions of the Erechtheum may be useful. The central block, including the steps: 42¾ by 79 feet (13·004 by 24·073 m.). The east colonnade is 38¼ feet long (11·633 m.); that of the north porch 35 feet (10·717 m.) The columns of the east front 2¼ feet (0.692 m.) in lower diameter, 21½ feet (6·586 m.) high, or 9·52 times the diameter; intercolumniations of 7 feet (2·113 m.); entablature 5½ feet (1·678 m.) high. The columns of the north porch 2½ feet in normal lower diameter but 2¾ feet at the corners (0.817 and 0·824 m.), 25 feet (7·635 m.) high or 9·35 times the diameter; intercolumniations of 10¼ feet (3·097 m.) on the front, *c.* 10½ (3·149 m.) at the corners, 10 feet (3·067 m.) on the sides; entablature 5 feet (1·535 m.) high.

CHAPTER 15

222. 1. This is not to imply that these rules were applied in the fourth, let alone the fifth century B.C. (for the procedures of classical design, see J. J. Coulton, *Greek Architects at Work* (London, 1977), 'Towards Understanding Doric Design: The Stylobate and Intercolumniation', *B.S.A.*, LXIX (1974), 61, and 'General Considerations', *B.S.A.*, LXX (1975), 59. As to Vitruvius, a couple of sections, chosen almost at random, will illustrate the thoroughness of his rules. First, the height of the architrave. With columns 12–15 feet high, this should equal their lower diameter. With taller columns it should be related to their height, in the proportion of 1:13 for columns of 15–20 feet, 1:12½ for 20–25 feet, 1:12 for 25–30 feet (III. 5, 8). Secondly, the larger measurements of the doorway. 'Divide the height from pavement to metopes into three parts and a half, of which two constitute the height of the doors. The height thus obtained is to be divided into twelve parts, of which five and a half are given to the width of the bottom part of the door. This is diminished towards the top by the equivalent of one-third of the frame, if the height be not more than 16 feet. From 16 feet to 25 the upper part of the opening is contracted one-fourth part of the frame. From 25 to 30 feet the upper part is contracted one-eighth of the frame. Those that are higher should have their sides vertical. The thickness of the frame in front is to be equal to one-twelfth of the height of the door, and is to diminish towards the top a fourteenth part of its width. The height of the architrave is to be equal to the upper part of the frame' (IV. 6, 1).

223. 2. Dinsmoor, *op. cit.*, figure 60 for diagram.

3. The columns at corners were therefore often made thicker than the rest.

4. The Greeks worked to prevent this as busily as Gothic builders to encourage it.

227. 5. *Stones of Venice*, II, V.

CHAPTER 16

228. 1. Callimachus of Athens is said to have invented the capital at Corinth, inspired by the sight of an acanthus plant growing up through a basket. The innovation really consisted of applying leaves and shoots, imitated from the plant, to a bell shape such as had been used a hundred years earlier for the capitals of treasuries at Delphi, and carving the square abacus concave in plan on all four sides. The capital offered this structural advantage over Ionic, that it needed no modification at the corner of a colonnade. This was also achieved in a Peloponnesian version of Ionic which has capitals with volutes on all four sides, over columns with only twenty flutes (see below, p. 259).

2. The identification of this temple has been denied by E. B. Harrison on grounds of the identification of the cult statues by Alkamenes and their base (*A.J.A.*, LXXXI (1977), 137 f., 265 f., 411 f.).

3. Shortly before the time of Christ, a temple of Ares of the fifth century was moved from its original site at Acharnae and rebuilt in the agora without alteration to the design [330]. Parts of the temple of Poseidon at Sunium (by the same architect) were incorporated into it when the Romans moved it.

230. 4. Dinsmoor, *op. cit.*, figure 67, and *Hesperia*, XXXVII (1968), 159. The number of internal columns is not certain.

231. 5. Dinsmoor, *op. cit.*, plate XXXV. See R. Martin, 'L'Atelier Ictinos-Callicrates au temple de Bassae', *B.C.H.*, C (1976), 427 for an assessment of Athenian influence in the building. A fourth-century date proposed by Roux has found a measure of acceptance. Date about 415 for the frieze: C. Hofkes-Brukker and A. Mallwitz, *Der Bassai Fries* (completed before the cella, and so had to be altered to fit). (Reviser's note: Opinions about this temple seem often a matter of

personal preference. Professor Lawrence clearly accepts the attribution to Ictinus: I prefer to see in this temple local influences predominating – certainly in the plan and general arrangement (see my *Greek Sanctuaries* (London, 1976), 119), but Athenian influence on the second phase of construction is generally admitted.)

234. 6. Dinsmoor, *op. cit.*, plates XXXVI–XXXVII.
7. See Note 1 to this chapter.
8. See Note 3 to this chapter.

235. 9. Plommer has aptly cited Vitruvius' statement that internal columns can be made to look thicker than those outside by increasing the number of flutes, but he suggests that the poor quality of the marble induced the architect to order the small number of exceptionally wide flutes (*B.S.A.*, LV (1960), 218, with comparative drawings of fluting, figure 3 on p. 223). The exposed position of the temple, and the consequent weathering to be expected, may also have led to the reduction in the number of flutes.

10. The name 'Concord' has no authority. The temple (55½ by 129 feet; 16·925 by 39·42 m.) has a pteron of six by thirteen columns, 22 feet (6·70 m.) high. The date must be between 450 and 420, probably about 420. Dinsmoor, *op. cit.*, plate XXVI for exterior.

236. 11. A restoration which assumes the pitched roof to be Greek (Jeffery, *Archaeologia* (1928), figures 12 and 13) follows the precedent of the Cypriot tomb of my illustration 98.

12. Dinsmoor, *op. cit.*, plate XLIII for a restoration which assumes too many figures over the gable. Here, it is suggested, the pitched ceiling was necessary because the temple had to house an existing statue of Apollo, too tall to be fitted under a normal horizontal ceiling (P. Bruneau, *Guide de Délos*, 83).

13. Dinsmoor, *op. cit.*, plate XXVII. For the discovery of foundations for projected walls, see *Römische Mitteilungen*, LXXV (1968), 168; for curvature of base, D. Mertens, *ibid.*, LXXXI (1974), 107 f.; approaching mainland proportions for capital: Coulton, *B.S.A.*, LXXIV (1979), 101.

CHAPTER 17

239. 1. Dinsmoor, *op. cit.*, plate XXIX for restoration.
240. 2. Dinsmoor, *op. cit.*, plate LIX for external Order.
241. 3. Robertson, *op. cit.*, plate vb.
4. Pausanias also attributes the theatre to Polycleitus; the two buildings were under construction at no great distance in time from each other (see below, p. 365). For the dates, Burford, *Temple Builders at Epidauros*. The inscription calls the tholos the *Thymele*, a word of uncertain meaning and presumably obsolete before Pausanias's visit. He does not allude to the function of

the tholos. This has been the subject of much speculation; a theory that the building represented the tomb of Asclepius offers a valid explanation for the crypt, which must relate to the underworld.

243. 5. Restored from a (probably late) replica found outside. Robertson, *op. cit.*, plate vc; Dinsmoor, *op. cit.*, plate LVIII.

244. 6. The crypt formed a maze of concentric circles, the dividing walls being really the foundations for the tholos. The Greeks apparently built crypts solely to meet peculiar religious requirements. One of modest architectural pretensions, under the oracular temple at Claros, consisted of two rooms, one containing the spring from which the prophet drank to receive divine inspiration (Bean, *Aegean Turkey*, 194, plates 46–8). The approach involved a wilfully large number of abrupt turns. The time of construction is provisionally put early in the Hellenistic age. Late in the third century, a deliberately labyrinthine plan was adopted for the Oracle of the Dead at Ephyra; here, too, there is a crypt (Dakaris, *Antike Kunst, Erstes Beiheft, Neue Ausgrabungen in Griechenland* (1963), 51).

7. Mallwitz, *Olympia und seine Bauten*, 129; for details and restoration, H. Schleif, *Olympische Forschungen*, I, 1.

8. Robertson, *op. cit.*, figure 62 for capital.

245. 9. The shafts are carved with only twenty flutes, as in 'Peloponnesian' Ionic (see Note 1 to Chapter 16 and p. 259).

10. Dinsmoor, *op. cit.*, plate LIX.
11. Dinsmoor, *op. cit.*, plate LX.

246. 12. J. McCredie, *Hesperia*, XLVIII (1979), 35. The round building near the sanctuary of Hera at Perachora, mentioned by Xenophon in his *Hellenica* (book IV, chapter V) in connexion with the capture of the sanctuary by the Spartan king Agesilaus in 390 B.C., was excavated by R. A. Tomlinson in the summer of 1982. It was *c*. 28 m. in diameter, and consisted of a wall 2.50 m. high, of three courses of ashlars, surmounted by a coping. It had a cement and pebble floor. It probably served as a collecting tank for rain water, which was then channelled to a storage cistern which has yet to be discovered. There were no openings in the wall, and it was unroofed. Agesilaus used it as a temporary prison cage, so it must have been empty of water when he was there. It was probably built in the fifth century, and destroyed by Agesilaus on his departure.

CHAPTER 18

247. 1. P. Coupel and P. Demargne, *Fouilles de Xanthos*, III, *Le Monument des Néréides* (Paris, 1969).
248. 2. The Temple of Hippolytus(?) at Troezen is

similar: H. Knell, 'Tempel des Hippolytos(?)', *Arch. Anz.* (1978), 397. The colour in the temple of Asclepius was unusually well-preserved when excavated. The triglyphs were blue, the metopes white with red decoration, the mutules white with blue knobs, and between them were painted blue palmettes. On the upper part of the cornice ran a 'key' pattern in red on a blue ground, and blue leaves ornamented the wave-moulding above.

3. There is no clear evidence for the date. The previous temple is recorded to have been burnt in 394, and the present inadequate knowledge of the architectural and sculptural history of the fourth century indicates only the limits of 370–330. The building and the sculpture may together have required a large number of years for completion. A tablet was dedicated at Tegea after 350 by an artisan who had worked on the Mausoleum, and this fact has been interpreted to mean that Scopas re-engaged the man for work at the temple, when work on the Mausoleum came to an end – a plausible supposition but not the only possible explanation. Acroteria of the temple have been recognized in the 'Atalanta' formerly attributed to a pediment, and a similar but winged statue (*Arch. Rep.* (1960–1), 8, figure 10). There are important references to Tegea in Roux, *L'Architecture de l'Argolide*.

4 As a matter of fact two others were larger; it measured 63 by 56 feet.

249. 5. Robertson, *op. cit.*, figure 61.

6. It has usually been assumed that the temple was already complete and merely dedicated when Alexander marched through Ionia in 334. Recently D. Van Berchem has suggested that Priene was refounded only at that date, and that completion (and dedication) of the temple could have occurred at any subsequent point during Alexander's lifetime (*Alexandre et la restauration de Priene* (Mus. Helv., 1970), 198).

250. 7. A belief that the tiles consisted of marble was disproved by investigations reported in *Bonner Jahrbücher*, CLXIX (1969), 117.

251. 8. Dinsmoor, *op. cit.*, plate LV.

253. 9. Dinsmoor, *op. cit.*, plate LV.

254. 10. G. Waywell, *The Freestanding Sculpture of the Mausoleum at Halicarnassus* (London, 1979), 54.

11. So vague is present knowledge of third-century developments in both architecture and sculpture (even of human figures) that there is no firm basis for stylistic comparison of the Lion Tomb with early Hellenistic monuments; Krischen's ascription to the second century is perhaps out of keeping with the statue, though the different restoration he arbitrarily proposed makes the architecture conform with that dating. Newton's description of the tomb disagrees with the accompanying plan by stating that one of the

chambers led to a doorway. Outside this (or, according to the British Museum inventory, inside the tomb) was found a pot, a *guttus*. Though the shape is found as early as 348 (destruction of Olynthus) it persists through the third century. P. Callaghan is of the opinion that *gutti* with angular bodics (as this one is) are late, possibly as late as the second century: an example found at the Ptolemaic camp at Corone in Attica (*Hesperia*, XXXI (1962), plate 21, no. 39) of the Chremonidean war just before the middle of the third century still has the earlier rounded body. A date for the tomb in the second century is not precluded. The details of the Doric order (height of architrave to height of frieze, form of capital) seem later rather than earlier, cf. the Portico of Philip in Delos, and the stoa on Paros (W. Koenigs, 'Dorische Hallenlagen auf Paros', *Arch Anz.* (1978), 375). Corbelled false domes of similar type are known in Thracian tumuli attributed to the early or mid fourth century (Filow, *Bull. Inst. Bulgare*, XI (1937), 1). Rectangular chambers had received true burial vaults from the fourth-century Macedonian examples. It is unlikely that the principle was adopted to form stone domes over circular rooms until later. The unfinished Doric columns suggest a Hellenistic date.

12. In the case of another great tomb or cenotaph the lion was seated on a pedestal above the steps, and the square base bore Doric half columns to its full height; most details are unknown (Broneer, *The Lion Monument of Amphipolis*, 1941; Roger, *B.C.H.*, LXIII, 1939). More blocks from this monument, once re-used in a causeway over the river Strymon, were studied by Stella and Stephen Miller (*Ἀρχ. Δελτ.*, XXVIIA, 1972, 140 f.). They restore four engaged Doric half-columns on each façade of the base, with shields between, columns fluted only at the top. They warn that there is no proof that the Amphipolis lion belonged to this base, and that more discoveries are needed to elucidate the problems.

13. Dinsmoor, *op. cit.*, figure 81 shows the stepped base divided into two flights by a wide landing. Bammer prefers a simpler single flight of steps.

14. Dinsmoor, *op. cit.*, plate LIV for an unreliable restoration; Robertson, *op. cit.*, figure 63 for capital. Even Bammer's restoration has been challenged by B. F. Cook (*B.M. Quarterly*, XXXVII, 137, plates LXV–LXVI), who restores the angle of elevation of the roof from Bammer's 14 degrees to the 17 degrees originally suggested by J. T. Wood.

15. Dinsmoor, *op. cit.*, plate LVI.

256. 16. Throughout practically all the fourth century, Athens and the other leading cities of Greece were too impoverished to undertake grandiose new buildings; Nemea was an international sanctuary, normally controlled by Argos. The rebuilding may well have been supported by Philip of Macedon after

Chaeronea in 338. The Macedonian royal family claimed to be of Argive descent, and Argos supported the Macedonians against Sparta. Epidaurus, though also an international sanctuary, suffered from financial difficulties, to judge from the delay in completing the tholos. The temple in the Isthmian Sanctuary (international but controlled by Corinth) seems to have been left ruinous for decades after a fire in 390 (O. Broneer, *Isthmia*, I, *Temple of Poseidon*, 1971).

257. 17. By Stella G. Miller in a review of J. J. Coulton's *Architectural Development of the Greek Stoa* in *A.J.A.*, LXXXIII (1979), 114.

259. 18. This has been published by P. Hellström and T. Thieme in *Labraunda, The Swedish Excavations and Researches*, I, 3, *The Temple of Zeus* (Stockholm, 1982). It now seems certain that the mid-fourth-century peripteral temple encased an earlier, non-peripteral cella.

19. A coin found underneath the cella is one of an issue believed to have been struck, at earliest, in 306, but the consensus of other evidence suggests that the temple is likely to have been built about 330.

CHAPTER 19

261. 1. Mallwitz, *Olympia und seine Bauten*, 160.

2. Roux, *L'Architecture de l'Argolide*, 51.

264. 3. Berve, Gruben, Hirmer, *Greek Temples, Theatres and Shrines*, plate 169.

4. Berve, Gruben, Hirmer, *op. cit.*, plate 165.

5. Dinsmoor, *op. cit.*, plate LV (not very clear).

6. Robertson, *op. cit.*, plate VI.

265. 7. Dinsmoor, *op. cit.*, figure 84.

8. Dinsmoor, *op. cit.*, plate LVIII.

9. Roux, *op. cit.*, 213; (Temple L) 223.

10. A small temple of Demeter at Pergamon, and its altar, are known from inscriptions to date from roughly 270; tiers of long, straight seating were placed upon a slope outside, presumably for spectators of Mysteries (Bohtz and Albert, *Arch. Anz.* (1970), 391; model illustrated on p. 411, figures 37, 38).

267. 11. Antae, of course, had occasionally ended in half-columns ever since the sixth century, and Hellenistic instances are known. Columns (or part-columns) engaged against piers or wall ends are not uncommon. They occur in a temple of Artemis Agrotera on the hill of Mavrovouni above Siphai in Boeotia (Tomlinson and Fossey, *B.S.A.*, LXV (1970), 245); abundantly at Cyrene, especially in the tombs (Cassels, *British School at Rome*, XXIII (1955), 1 f.; Tomlinson, *B.S.A.*, LXII (1967), 241). The use of half-columns on the lateral faces of piers became common

practice in stoas (Coulton, *B.S.A.*, LXI (1966), 132 f.).

12. S. Reinach, *Bibliothèque des monuments figurés*, I (1888), reproduces the engravings of Kourno details and restorations by P. Le Bas, 'Architecture', 138, plates II, 1–11. An extraordinary plan, of uncertain but probably later date, may well be mentioned here. The temple of Artemis at Lusi, in Arcadia, began by consisting of a porch and opisthodomus, each with four Doric columns *in antis*, and a cella, into which piers or buttresses projected after the manner of Bassae. On the outer side of the wall a row of half-columns seems to have corresponded to the buttresses; each of the spans probably required an additional triglyph, whereas the free-standing columns were placed so close together that the traditional number sufficed. Afterwards a narrow hall was added against each of the cella walls to the full length of the building, almost doubling the width. A chapel on Thera has wrongly been assumed to have originated as a Ptolemaic temple of Hera Basileia; it was really a tomb, built under the late Roman empire though incorporating older material (*A.J.A.*, LXXIII (1969), 413, n. 70).

268. 13. Dodona, being situated in a remote and backward region, does not perhaps offer a type case, but the chronology of changes there would otherwise suggest that the Serapeum set the fashion for colonnaded courts. In 219, Aetolian invaders of Dodona pulled down the Sacred House of Zeus, a mere chapel (dated about 400) at the back of an empty enclosure, the wall of which had been built early in the third century. In the reconstruction, which was undertaken without perceptible delay, colonnades lined three sides of the court, including one interrupted by the protruding front of the new temple. This, like its tiny predecessor, contained an adytum as well as a cella, but the deep prostyle porch was an innovation. A similar porch was put at the entrance to the enclosure. (Dakaris, *Antike Kunst, Erstes Beiheft, Neue Ausgrabungen in Griechenland* (1963), 35. Cf. Ἐφ. Ἀρχ. (1959), plates 6–9.)

14. Dinsmoor, *op. cit.*, figure 93.

270. 15. P. Bernard, *Fouilles d'Aï Khanoum*, I, 85 f. For the temple, Bernard in *Comptes rendus de l'Académie des Inscriptions et Belles Lettres* (1969), 327.

16. Catalogue of tombs (not including M. Andronikos' subsequent exciting discoveries at Vergina): I. D. Pantermalis, Μακεδονικά, XII (1972), 147; Petsas' tomb at Lefkadia: P. M. Petsas, Ὁ Μακεδονικὸς τάφος τῶν Λευκαδιῶν; another large Ionic tomb at Lefkadia, brilliantly decorated, with a superb floral painting on the ceiling of the antechamber: C. Rhomiopoulou, *A.A.A.*, VI (1973), 87 f. Preliminary report on Vergina by M. Andronikos, *A.A.A.*, X (1977), 1 f.

275. 17. Dinsmoor, *op. cit.*, figure 102.

18. Dinsmoor, *op. cit.*, figure 101; Robertson, *op. cit.*, figure 69.

277. 19. For this dating C. Williams, *A.J.A.*, LXXVIII, 405 f., C. Börker, *Arch. Anz.*, LXXXVI (1971), 37 f.

278. 20. Dinsmoor, *op. cit.*, figure 51.

21. From stylistic analogies, the Altar Court has been dated between 340 and 330 with a dogmatic assurance that most scholars would not care to emulate. If a broken inscription along the architrave was really a dedication by Alexander's half-brother and heir, Arrhidaeus, completion not later than 321 would be an established fact. But this is far from certain.

22. Dinsmoor, *op. cit.*, plate LXVII.

282. 23. Inside the agora – Dinsmoor, *op. cit.*, figure 124 for plan.

24. Dinsmoor, *op. cit.*, plate LXV for capital.

284. 25. A discussion of this is to be published by P. Callaghan in *B.S.A.* I am grateful to him for this information. Abdullah Yaylali dates the temple frieze to 130–129 ('Der Fries des Artemision von Magnesia am Mäander', *Ist. Mitt.*, Beiheft XV, 1976).

286. 26. Some highly ornate Corinthian capitals at Alexandria may, however, antedate the time of Christ; Margaret Lyttleton, *Baroque Architecture in Classical Antiquity*, 47.

CHAPTER 20

289. 1. 'Lesbian' was a technical term in the fourth century for some other type of masonry, in which the blocks must have been cut into irregular shapes since Aristotle mentions that it was done with the aid of templates.

295. 2. In spite of Pericles' failure to capture Oeniadae in 454, the fact that the acropolis alone was held against attack in 219 has been interpreted to imply that the town was then still unfortified (Pauly-Wissowa, *Real-Encyclopädie*, VII. 34, column 2226). The wall now existing is of a type so obsolete for 219 that it must be early work, and any attempt to defend its three-mile perimeter would have been suicidal.

298. 3. The cistern at Katzingri has not been adequately published. Winter's photograph (in his *Greek Fortifications*, figure 39) shows less of the remaining vaulting than my unpublished negative in the Courtauld Institute (No. A70/124). For the fort see *Ath. Mitt.*, XL (1915), 106.

299. 4. This section is based on A. W. Lawrence, *Greek Aims in Fortification* (Oxford, 1980).

5. See *Samos*, XV: *Die Stadtmauer von Samos*, by Hermann J. Kienast (Bonn, 1978). This important study was published after A. W. Lawrence completed his *Greek Aims*.

309. 6. Specimens of waterproofing mortar contain an average of 36 per cent lime and 25 per cent sand, corresponding to proportions of 2:1 for unslaked lime and sand (Fowler, *Journal of Chemical Education*, XI (1934), 223). For Hellenistic cisterns, see F. E. Winter, *Greek Fortifications*, 52, figures 39, 40, 43; R. Vallois, *Les constructions antiques de Délos*, especially plate 31; Tomlinson, *B.S.A.*, LXIV (1969), 157, plates 45–7, for the huge example at Perachora, which is apsidal at both ends and was roofed, over stone beams, laid flat; he ascribes it to about 300. In houses at Delos rain-water was conducted from the roof to a cistern under the court, covered by slabs laid flat across segmental arches and then with mosaic.

310. 7. The colours were more brilliant at the time of excavation than in the restoration (*A.J.A.*, VI (1902), plate IX), which wrongly shows the metopes red because the original white had become stained, as was proved when more blocks were discovered. The frieze is not in its original arrangement, owing to changes made to the approach to the spring, probably early in the fourth century.

8. For typical Hellenistic fountain-houses see Orlandos, *Ἐφ. Ἀρχ.* (1937), II, 608 (at Tenos); Tomlinson, *B.S.A.*, LXIV (1969), 209 (at Perachora); Pietrogrande, *Africa Italiana*, VII (1940), 112 (at Cyrene).

9. Little streams in flat ground are covered, at Brauron and Thasos, by slab paving. The town wall of Messene crossed a fast-running brook, liable to spate, between the tall piers (now fallen) shown in an engraving of 1831 (*Expédition de la Morée*, I, plate 38. II).

10. Dinsmoor, *op. cit.*, plate LXVIII.

CHAPTER 21

315. 1. At Old Smyrna, a port which served the non-Greek interior of Asia Minor, an alternation of types of plan suggests changes in the city's resources and in its cultural allegiance, if not also its racial make-up. Oval huts were succeeded during the ninth century by rectangular houses of one large room; oval plans again predominated between about 750 and 650, and then a long type became prevalent, constructed at the base in good polygonal masonry, below the unbaked brick. This long type belongs to the late seventh and sixth centuries, when a house might contain a series of three fair-sized rooms giving an arrangement like a megaron, though the doorways were more often placed on the side than on the end walls; one room may have been a court. Many of these houses contained bathrooms equipped with a pottery tub; for a rich household the bathroom might even be sunk into the ground till a smooth rock floor could be provided. Quite small houses of the sixth century sometimes contained a court paved with flagstones. See *B.S.A.*, LIII–LIV (1958–9).

2. See especially Allegro and others, *Himera*, II.

3. The topographical grounds for J. M. Cook's doubt whether the site at Buruncuk can be that of Larisa are assessed by G. E. Bean, *Aegean Turkey*, 99.

317. 4. J. E. Jones, L. H. Sackett, and A. J. Graham, 'The Dema House in Attica', *B.S.A.*, LVII (1962), 75, and the same authors' 'An Attic Country House below the Cave of Pan at Vari', *B.S.A.*, LXVIII (1973), 355.

318. 5. Travlos, *Pictorial Dictionary*, 392 f.

6. Dinsmoor, *op. cit.*, figure 92 for two plans.

320. 7. M. Andronikos, *Vergina* (*S.I.M.A.*, XIII). The circular room: *A.J.A.*, LXXVI (1972), 78.

323. 8. Dinsmoor, *op. cit.*, figure 91 for plan. A long building (280 feet; 86 m.) at Nemea has been identified as a xenon. It was built as part of the general reconstruction of the sanctuary, towards the end of the fourth century. There was a row of oikoi between it and the temple (detailed plan: S. G. Miller, *Hesperia*, XLVII (1978), 66).

9. Dinsmoor, *op. cit.*, figure 117 for three plans.

324. 10. Robertson, *op. cit.*, figure 125 for restoration.

11. The 'palace' at Nippur in Iraq has been claimed as Greek in design, but the plan (*A.J.A.*, VIII (1904), plate XV) is, I believe, Babylonian in the main, though it includes also such definitely Greek features as a colonnade round the court and a doorway with two columns *in antis* outside the main room. The latter feature suggests a date in the third century, but the Parthians, who conquered this part of the Seleucid kingdom in 140, may have continued to build on that plan long after the Greeks had abandoned it. The columns consist of brick in accordance with local practice.

12. Coloured stucco, fallen off the internal wall surfaces of the Hieron at Samothrace, could be of any period or several periods from about 320, when the hall itself was erected, into the Christian era, but the scheme is likely to have originated not later than the addition of a sumptuous porch in the mid second century; red, white, and black panels, in simulation of stone blocks, were surmounted by projecting mouldings, and pilasters created an illusion of structure (P. W. Lehmann, *Samothrace Excavations*, 3, plates CIV–CVI). In a Ptolemaic house at Benghazi, mouldings over a doorway were painted sky-blue, red, yellow, and orange (*Society for Libyan Studies*, III, 9).

325. 13. A Hellenistic residential quarter at Phaestus was of poor quality (*'Αρχ. Δελτ.*, 19.B3 (1964), 448). A large group of Jewish rock-cut tombs in the Sanhedria suburb of Jerusalem includes two of architectural interest, which are ascribed to the middle of the second century (Jotham-Rothschild, *Palestine Exploration Quarterly* (1952), 23, plates VI–VII). In each case the courtyard was surrounded on three sides by benches, upon which the congregation sat during the performance of the last rites, and there are other Jewish peculiarities inside, but the general form is Hellenistic. The porch of Tomb VIII contains two unfluted Doric columns, with crude capitals standing between antae, the capitals of which consist of a series of mouldings; the architrave is overhung by a plain frieze. Tomb XIV (popularly called the Tomb of the Judges) was entered through a wide porch, which was completely open in front, but is framed by fascias, above which is a pediment richly carved with foliage.

14. Dinsmoor, *op. cit.*, figure 118 for five plans, plate LXX for photograph of a court; Robertson, *op. cit.*, plate XXIIa for plan showing mosaics.

331. 15. Recent excavations by S. Hadjisavvas at the Royal Tombs of Paphos for the Cyprus Department of Antiquities have revealed a splendid and lavishly decorated new tomb, unconventionally arranged since it does not have a central courtyard (it seems rather to have had its plan determined by a pre-existing quarry). In a paper presented to the Second International Congress of Cypriot Studies in April 1982, R. A. Tomlinson argued for a second-century date for these tombs.

CHAPTER 22

332. 1. Three contiguous flights of steps are arranged as though to form nearly half of a polygon; the excavators thought that a similar flight on a fourth side had been projected, though never begun.

334. 2. Dinsmoor, *op. cit.*, figure 123 for plan.

337. 3. Dinsmoor, *op. cit.*, figure 78 for plan.

338. 4. The stoa in the Attic sanctuary of Brauron is also the earliest that encloses three sides of a rectangular court, but only on two was there space for it to be backed by rooms (each 6.10 metres, or 20 feet, square). The Doric colonnade was completed on the inward side but left with only one column on each of the others. A hall for offerings extended behind all the rooms on the inward side. The original building and its reconstruction in 1961–2 are described, with a resumé in French, by Ch. Bouras, *'Η 'Αναστήλωσις τῆς Στοάς τῆς βραυρῶνος* (Athens, 1967).

339. 5. Robertson, *op. cit.*, figure 76 for sectional restorations.

340. 6. It used to be thought that this was situated in the agora of ancient Corinth. Charles K. Williams has demonstrated that the agora was not here: it was an area for athletic activity, until the destruction of

Corinth by the Romans in 146 B.C. With the foundation of the Roman colony at Corinth the area became an agora or forum.

341. 7. But in some Hellenistic sheds at Oeniadae each gable apparently covered only a single line of ships.

8. Discussion: K. Jeppesen, *Paradeigmata*, LXIX (with plans).

342. 9. R. A. Tomlinson, *B.S.A.*, LXIV (1969), 164 f.

CHAPTER 23

343. 1. Robertson, *op. cit.*, figures 83 and 84; Dinsmoor, *op. cit.*, figure 96 for plans. For the date, D. van Berchem, *Alexandre et la restauration de Priene* (Mus. Helv., 1970), 198.

344. 2. Date: J. Marcadé, *B.C.H.*, LXXV (1951), 55 f. Brief general account: P. Bruneau, *Guide de Délos*, 91. See also G. Roux, 'Problèmes déliens', *B.C.H.*, CV (1981), 61, who suggests that though Demetrius built the Neorion in 306, he never put a warship in it. The warship housed there by Antigonus Gonatas was bigger than the ship for which the building was originally intended, so that the prow had to project into the adytum, where extra foundations were added to support it.

3. The apparent rarity of stoas in small towns is no argument against their prevalence; if they had normally been built of wood, only careful excavation would reveal traces.

347. 4. According to J. J. Coulton – a pity, because the open colonnade on the south of this building would have afforded a spectacular view over the sea towards Lesbos.

348. 5. H. A. Thompson and R. E. Wycherley, *The Athenian Agora*, XIV, *The Agora of Athens*, 65 f.

349. 6. Dinsmoor, *op. cit.*, figure 116 for plan of supposed palaestra at Epidaurus, explained by Tomlinson as a dining-place for visitors to the sanctuary (*J.H.S.*, LXXXIX (1969), 106).

352. 7. Robertson, *op. cit.*, plate VII for photograph.

355. 8. Robertson, *op. cit.*, figures 79, 80, and 70 for plan, section, and capital.

357. 9. Dinsmoor, *op. cit.*, plate LXXI for model.

CHAPTER 24

362. 1. The stadium at Olympia has now been restored to the form it took in the fourth century. Both ends of it were straight. The retaining wall of the Delphi stadium was built during the fourth century.

2. The stadium at Nemea, of about 325, has a curved end and a barrel-vaulted entrance passage, possibly an indication of Macedonian interest in the reconstruc-tion of the sanctuary, which took place at this time. See S. Miller, *Hesperia*, XLVIII (1979), 96 f. for the tunnel and date.

363. 3. Although theatres must have been designed primarily for drama, public meetings were held in them; Livy (XXIV. 39. 1) reports an instance in Hellenistic Sicily, and the practice must have been widespread under the Roman empire (cf. Apuleius, *Golden Ass*, III.12).

4. T. Hackens, *Le Théâtre, Thorikos*, 1965, III (1967), 75 f.

365. 5. A. Burford, *B.S.A.*, LXI (1966), 296, Inscr. XIV (not known to von Gerkan when he dated the theatre to 300 B.C.). Blocks that had formed part of some building, datable by their style to the fourth century, were re-used in the foundations of both the lower part of the auditorium and the ramps that led to the original scene-front. Why and when this material came to be available is not known; the unidentified building cannot have perished from natural decay in the short time of its existence but must have suffered some disaster (if indeed it was ever completed). Inconclusive evidence, following this discovery, led von Gerkan to date the first stonework of the theatre to the beginning of the third century. Excavation beneath the upper seats failed to produce any pointer to their age, but he believed that they were added contemporaneously with the widening of the stage, probably early in the second century; the seats for important spectators would then have been trans-ferred from the edge of the orchestra to just above the gangway.

Taken literally, this theory conflicts with the apparent aesthetic unity of the entire auditorium; moreover, the lower seats alone would surely have made an ill-proportioned theatre, wasteful of natural advantages. I think, too, that the building of so many rows of stone seats might have required several lifetimes, considering how small were the resources of Epidaurus. No such programme of work could have been fulfilled in a single operation without an exceptionally large donation from some king, in which case the customary acknowledgements would have been made in the form of a statue and inscriptions, of which there are neither traces nor records. If the procedure followed in the case of the tholos is any guide, the administrators of the sanctuary would have arranged contracts for one section of the project after another, with intervals of inaction while contributions slowly accumulated, and this seems borne out by the noticeably variable batches of stone, of markedly different colouring, used in different parts of the auditorium.

Another theatre, built apparently simultaneously at Epidaurus town (on the coast some distance from the sanctuary of Asclepius), has inscriptions on the seats, recording the names of donors, of the fourth and third century, indicating piecemeal construction.

368. 6. Dinsmoor, *op. cit.*, plate LXIX for photograph. De Bernardi Ferrero (chronological table, vol. IV, 241) prefers a date 250–225 for the auditorium and original stage at Priene though the grounds for this are not clear. Details (the mouldings) have been dated to the first half of the third century (L. T. Shoe, *Profiles of Greek Mouldings*). De Bernardi Ferrero believes the three openings of the stage building to belong to this original phase. *Milet* IV.1, Taf. 37, shows the Hellenistic parodos wall and adaptations made in Roman times, when it was straightened very slightly near the stage building.

369. 7. Dinsmoor, *op. cit.*, figure 112 for restoration of theatre at Oropus.

372. 8. Dinsmoor, *op. cit.*, figure 110 for sectional restoration of theatre at Eretria.

9. The discovery, under the seats, of material datable about 300 induced Bernabò Brea to think that the theatre at Tyndaris assumed its shape at that time, two centuries before the earliest Roman stone theatres (*Rivista dell'Istituto Nazionale d'Archeologia e Storia del Arte*, N.S. XIII–XIV (1964–5), 99).

10. Bulle drew his restoration [368] before Marconi's excavation of the stage-building (*Notizie degli Scavi*, 6 V (1929), 295, plates XIII and XIV). The central portion was found to contain a long room between two shorter, and a row of pillars (60 cm. square) along the entire centre; these must have been floor-supports and are not reconcilable with Bulle's crosswise pitched roof. For further criticisms see von Gerkan in *Festschrift für A. Rumpf* (1950), 82.

BIBLIOGRAPHY

The present, highly selective bibliography is designed to provide the most valuable (or, in some cases, most easily accessible) references for every building or subject mentioned, and it also cites publications too recent to have been included by Dinsmoor or Robertson.

GENERAL WORKS

DINSMOOR, W. B. *The Architecture of Ancient Greece*. London and New York, 1950.
ROBERTSON, D. S. *A Handbook of Greek and Roman Architecture*. 2nd ed. Cambridge, 1943, and reprints.
These two general books are essential to students. Each contains a very long, comprehensive bibliography, and either or both should be consulted if full references are required.
BERVE, H. GRUBEN, G., and HIRMER, M., *Greek Temples, Theaters and Shrines*. New York, n.d.
BOARDMAN, J., DORIG, J., FUCHS, W., and HIRMER, M. *The Art and Architecture of Ancient Greece*. London, 1967.
Section on Architecture by J. Boardman.
COOK, R. M. *Greek Art*, London, 1972.
'Architecture' pages 173–246; 'Interior Decoration' pages 247–54.
COULTON. J. J. *Greek Architects at Work*. London, 1977.
MARTIN, R. *Manuel d'architecture grecque*, I. *Matériaux et techniques*. Paris, 1965.
MATZ, F. *Crete and Early Greece*. London, 1962.
In this book and Vermeule's (below) buildings are discussed in relation to Bronze Age culture in general. Inevitably, both are now outdated by recent discoveries.
MIRÉ, G. and V. DE, and VILLARD, F. *Sicile grecque*. Paris, 1955.
A book of photographs including many clear views of buildings.
ORLANDOS, A. K. *Les Matériaux de construction et la téchnique architecturale des anciens grecs*. 2 vols. Paris, 1966 and 1968.
PLOMMER, (W.) H. *Ancient and Classical Architecture*. London and New York, 1956.
STILWELL, R., ed. *Princeton Encyclopedia of Classical Sites*. Princeton, 1976.
A comprehensive (though variable) reference book.
VERMEULE, E. *Greece in the Bronze Age*. Chicago, 1964.

CHAPTER 2

ATKINSON, T. D., and others. *Excavations at Phylakopi in Melos (Suppl. Papers Soc. Prom. Hellenic Studies*, IV). London, 1904.
For Early Cycladic houses: see page 35.
BLEGEN, C. W. *Korakou, a Prehistoric Settlement near Corinth*. Boston and New York, 1921.
BLEGEN, C. W. *Zygouries, a Prehistoric Settlement in the Valley of Cleonae*. Cambridge, Mass., 1928.
BLEGEN, C. W. *Troy and the Trojans*. London, 1963.
BLEGEN, C. W., CASKEY, J. L., and RAWSON, M. *Troy, Excavations conducted by the University of Cincinnati, 1932–38*, I. 1950.
BRANIGAN, K. *The Tombs of Mesara*. London, 1970.
BRANIGAN, K. *The Foundations of Palatial Crete*. London, 1971.
BREA, L. BERNABO. *Poliochni*. Rome, 1964. Vol. II. Rome, 1976.
BULLE, H. *Orchomenos*, I. *Die älteren Siedelungsschichten (Abhandlungen der Bayerischen Akademie der Wissenschaften*, XXIV, 2). Munich, 1907.
CASKEY, J. L. 'Excavations at Lerna', *Hesperia*, XXIII, 1954; XXIV, 1955; XXV, 1956, plan on p. 166.
CASKEY, J. L. 'Chalandriani in Syros', *Essays in Memory of Karl Lehmann*. New York, 1964.
CHILDE, V. G. *The Dawn of European Civilization*. 5th ed. London, 1950.
For Early Cycladic tombs: see page 52.
DÖRPFELD, W., and others. *Troja und Ilion*. 2 vols. Athens, 1902.
DRAGENDORFF, H. 'Tiryns', *Ath. Mitt.*, XXXVIII (1913).
For Round Building, Tiryns: see page 334.
EVANS, Sir A. J. *The Palace of Minos at Knossos*. 4 vols. and index in 7. London, 1921–36.
EVANS, J. D. 'Excavations in the Neolithic Settlement at Knossos', *B.S.A.*, LIX (1964).
EVANS, J. D. 'Neolithic Cnossus', *Proceedings of the Prehistoric Society*, XXXVII (1971).
FIMMEN, D. *Die kretisch-mykenische Kultur*. 2nd ed. Leipzig, 1924.

GOLDMAN, H. *Excavations at Eutresis in Boeotia.* Cambridge, Mass., 1931.

GUEST-PAPAMANOLI, A. 'L'Emploi de la brique crue dans la domaine égéen à l'époque néolithique et à l'âge du bronze', *B.C.H.*, CII (1978), 3.

HOPE SIMPSON, R., and DICKINSON, O.T.P.K. *A Gazetteer of Aegean Civilization in the Bronze Age*, I. *The Mainland and Islands* (*S.I.M.A.*, LII). Göteborg, 1979.

LAMB, W. *Excavations at Thermi in Lesbos.* Cambridge, 1936.

MELLAART, J. 'Notes on the Architectural Remains of Troy I and II', *Anatolian Studies*, IX (1959).
Includes Poliochni: see pages 155 and 159.

MÜLLER, V. 'Development of the Megaron in Prehistoric Greece', *A.J.A.*, XLVIII (1944).

PENDLEBURY, J.D.S. *The Archaeology of Crete.* London, 1939.

PINI, I. *Beiträge zur minoischen Gräberkunde.* Wiesbaden, 1968.

PLASSART, A. *Exploration archéologique de Délos*, XI, *Les Sanctuaires et les cultes du Mont Cynthe.* Paris, 1928.
For Early Cycladic houses: see page 11.

RENFREW, C. *The Emergence of Civilisation: The Cyclades and the Aegean in the Third Millennium B.C.* London, 1972.

RODENWALDT, G. *Tiryns: Die Ergebnisse der Ausgrabungen*, II. Athens, 1912.

RUBENSOHN, O. 'Die prähistorischen und vorgeschichtlichen Bauten auf dem Burghügel von Paros', *Ath. Mitt.*, XLII (1917).
For Early Cycladic houses: see page I, plate 2.

SEAGER, R.B. *Excavations in the Island of Pseira.* Philadelphia, 1910.

SINOS, S. 'Eine Untersuchung der sogennanten Palastanlage von Vasiliki', *Arch. Anz.* (1970).

STEPHANOS, K. Ἀνασκαφαὶ ἐν Νάξῳ, Πρακ. (1906).
For Early Cycladic tombs: see page 86.

STEPHANOS, K. Ἀνασκαφαὶ ἐν Νάξῳ, Πρακ. (1908).
For Early Cycladic tombs: see page 116.

Transactions of Pennsylvania University Museum, I (1906) (for Vasiliki: see page 207) and II (1907) (for Vasiliki: see page 118).

TSOUNTAS, C. Κυκλαδικά, Ἐφ. Ἀρχ. (1898).
For Early Cycladic houses: see col. 169.

TSOUNTAS, C. Κυκλαδικά, Εφ. Ἀρχ. (1899).
For Early Cycladic tombs: see col. 80; for Khalandriani: see col. 118; for Early Cycladic houses: see col. 115.

TSOUNTAS, C. Αἱ προϊστορικαὶ Ἀκροπόλεις Διμηνιοῦ και Σέσκλου. Athens, 1908.

WARNER, J. 'The Megaron and Apsidal House in Early Bronze Age Western Anatolia', *A.J.A.*, LXXXIII (1979), 133.

XANTHOUDIDIS, S.A. *The Vaulted Tombs of Mesará.* London, 1924.

CHAPTER 3

EVANS, Sir A.J. *The Palace of Minos at Knossos.* 4 vols. and index in 7. London, 1921–36.

HUTCHINSON, R.W. 'Prehistoric Town Planning in Crete', *The Town Planning Review*, XXI, 3 (1950).

LEVI, D. *Festòs e la civiltà minoica.* Rome, 1976.

MATZ, F., ed. *Forschungen aus Kreta.* Berlin, 1951.
For Apesokari: see page 13, plates 16–18.

PENDLEBURY, J.D.S. *The Archaeology of Crete.* London, 1939.

PERNIER, L. *Il Palazzo minoico di Festos*, I and II. Rome, 1935, 1951.

PLATON, N. *Zakros.* New York and London, 1971.

SCHACHERMEYR, F. *Die minoische Kultur des alten Kreta.* Stuttgart, 1964.

CHAPTER 4

BOSANQUET, R.C. and DAWKINS, R.M. 'Excavations at Palaikastro', *B.S.A.*, VIII–XII (1901–2, 1905–6).

BOSSERT, H. T. *Alt-Kreta.* 2nd ed. Berlin, 1923.

CADOGAN, G. *Palaces of Minoan Crete.* London, 1976.

CADOGAN, G. *Arch. Rep.* (1977–8).
For Pyrgos.

CHAPOUTHIER, F., CHARBONNEAUX, J., and JOLY, R. *Fouilles exécutées à Mallia*, I–III. Paris, 1928–42.

CHAPOUTHIER, F., and DEMARGNE, P. *Fouilles exécutées à Mallia*, IV. Paris, 1962.

COLDSTREAM, J.N., and HUXLEY, G., eds. *Kythera Excavations and Studies.* London, 1972.

DUSSAUD, R. *Les Découvertes de Ras Shamra (Ugarit) et l'Ancien Testament.* 2nd ed. Paris, 1941.

ÉCOLE FRANÇAISE D'ATHÈNES. *Mallia: Plan du site, Plan du palais, Indices.* Paris, 1974.

EVANS, Sir A.J. 'The Prehistoric Tombs of Knossos', *Archaeologia*, LIX (1905).

EVANS, Sir A.J. 'The Tomb of the Double Axes', *Archaeologia*, LXV (1914).

EVANS, Sir A.J. *The Palace of Minos at Knossos.* 4 vols. and index in 7. London, 1921–36.

GRAHAM, J.W. *The Palaces of Crete.* 2nd ed. Princeton, 1969.

HATZIDAKIS, J. *Tylissos à l'époque minoenne.* Paris, 1921.

HAWES, H.B., and others. *Gournia, Vasiliki and other Prehistoric Sites on the Isthmus of Hierapetra, Crete*. Philadelphia, 1908.

HOGARTH, D.G. 'Excavations at Zakro, Crete', *B.S.A.*, VII (1900–1).
For Late Minoan III houses at Zakro: see pages 131, 138.

HOOD, S. *The Minoans*. London, New York, and Washington, 1971.

HUTCHINSON, R.W. *Prehistoric Crete*. London, 1968.

MARINATOS, S. Μεσομινωικὴ οἰκία ἐν κάτω Μεσαρᾶ, Ἀρχ. Δελτ., IX (1924–5).
For Middle Minoan houses in Messara: see page 53.

MARINATOS, S. Τὸ Μινωϊκὸν μέγαρον Σκλαβο-κάμπου, Ἐφ. Ἀρχ. (1939–41).
See page 81.

Memorie del Reale Istituto Lombardo di Scienze e Lettere, XXI (1899–1907).
For Hagia Triada: see page 235.

PELON, O. *Mallia, Maisons*, III, *Le quartier E*. Paris, 1970.

PELON, O. *Tholoi, tumuli et cercles funéraires*. Paris, 1976.

PENDLEBURY, J.D.S. *A Handbook to the Palace of Minos at Knossos*. London, 1933; 2nd ed. 1955.

PENDLEBURY, J.D.S. *The Archaeology of Crete*. London, 1939.

PERNIER, L. *Il Palazzo minoico di Festos*, I and II. Rome, 1935, 1951.

PERNIER, L., and BANTI, L. *Guida degli scavi italiani in Creta*. Rome, 1947.
For Hagia Triada.

PINI, I. *Beiträge zur minoischen Gräberkunde*. Wiesbaden, 1968.

SACKETT, L.H., POPHAM, M.R., and WARREN, P.M. 'Excavations at Palaikastro, VI', *B.S.A.*, LX (1965).

SAKELLARAKIS, K. *Ergon* (1977), 166.
For cemetery at Acharnes.

SCHACHERMEYR, F. *Die minoische Kultur des alten Kreta*. Stuttgart, 1964.

SCHAEFER, C.F.A. 'Die Stellung Ras Shamra-Ugarits zur kretischen und mykenischen Kultur', *J.D.I.*, LII (1937).

SHAW, J.W. 'Minoan Architecture: Materials and Techniques', *Annuario della Scuola Archeologica di Athene*, XLIX (1971) (1973).

SHAW, J.W. 'New Evidence for Minoan Roof Construction', *A.J.A.*, LXXXI (1977), 229.

SHAW, J.W. 'Evidence for the Minoan Tripartite Shrine', *A.J.A.*, LXXXII (1978), 429.

TIRÉ, C., and VAN EFFENTERRE, H. *Guide des fouilles françaises en Crète*. Paris, 1966.

VAN EFFENTERRE, H. and M. *Fouilles exécutées à Mallia; Le Centre politique*, I, *L'Agora*. Paris, 1969.

VAN EFFENTERRE, H. and M. *Mallia: Maisons*, IV, *Le Quartier* Θ.

XANTHOUDIDIS, S.A. Μινωικόν μέγαρον Νιροῦ, Ἐφ. Ἀρχ. (1922).

CHAPTER 5

ATKINSON, T.D., and others. *Excavations at Phylakopi in Melos* (*Suppl. Papers Soc. Prom. Hellenic Studies*, IV). London, 1904.

BLEGEN, C.W. *Korakou, a Prehistoric Settlement near Corinth*. Boston and New York, 1921.

DÖRPFELD, W. *Alt-Olympia*, I. Berlin, 1935.

FIMMEN, D. *Die kretisch-mykenische Kultur*. 2nd ed. Leipzig, 1924.

HARLAND, J.P. *Prehistoric Aigina*. Paris, 1925.

HOOD, M.S.F. 'Archaeology in Greece, 1954', *B.S.A.*, XLIX (1955).
For burial mound: see page 35, figure 7.

HOPE SIMPSON, R., and DICKINSON, O.T.P.K. *A Gazetteer of Aegean Civilization in the Bronze Age*, I, *the Mainland and Islands* (*S.I.M.A.*, LII). Göteborg, 1979.

MARINATOS, S. *Excavations at Thera*, I–VII. Athens, 1968–76.

MÜLLER, V. 'Development of the Megaron In Prehistoric Greece', *A.J.A.*, XLVIII (1944).

RHOMAIOS, K.A. Ἐκ τοῦ προϊστορικοῦ Θερμοῦ, Ἀρχ. Δελτ., I (1915).

TSOUNTAS, C. Κυκλαδικά, Ἐφ. Ἀρχ. (1899).
For Hagios Andreas: see col. 30.

VALMIN, M.N. *The Swedish Messenia Expedition*. Lund, 1938.
For Malthi.

CHAPTER 6

CAVANAGH, W.G., and LAXTON, R.R. 'The Structural Mechanics of the Mycenean Tholos Tomb', *B.S.A.*, LXXVI (1981).

DUSSARD, R. *Les Découvertes de Ras Shamra (Ugarit) et l'Ancien Testament*. 2nd ed. Paris, 1941.

ELLIS, S.E., HIGGINS, R.A. and HOPE SIMPSON, R. 'The Façade of the Treasury of Atreus at Mycenae', *B.S.A.*, LXIII (1968).

HAMMOND, N.G.L. 'Tumulus Burial in Albania, The Grave Circles of Mycenae and the Indo-Europeans', *B.S.A.*, LXII (1967), 77.

HOOD, M.F.S. 'Tholos Tombs of the Aegean', *Antiquity*, XXXIV (1960).

LOLLING, H., and BOHN, R. *Das Kuppelgrab bei Menidi*. Athens, 1880.

PELON, O. *Tholoi, tumuli et cercles funéraires*. Paris, 1976.

PERSSON, A.W. *Royal Tombs at Dendra near Midea*. Lund, 1931.

SCHAEFFER, C.F.A. 'Die Stellung Ras Shamra-Ugarits zur kretischen und mykenischen Kultur', *J.D.I.*, LII (1937).

SCHLIEMANN, H. *Orchomenos*. Leipzig, 1881.

WACE, A.J.B., and others. *Mycenae*. Princeton, 1949.

WACE, A.J.B., and HOOD, M.S.F. 'The Epano Phournos Tholos Tomb', *B.S.A.*, XLVIII (1953), 69.

CHAPTER 7

ATKINSON, T.D., and others. *Excavations at Phylakopi in Melos (Suppl. Papers Soc. Prom. Hellenic Studies*, IV). London, 1904.

BITTEL, K. *Die Ruinen von Boğazköy*. Berlin, 1937. For Hittite styles.

BITTEL, K. *Hattusha: the Capital of the Hittites*. New York and London, 1970.

BLEGEN, C.W., and RAWSON, M. *The Palace of Nestor at Pylos*, I. Princeton, 1966.

FIMMEN, D. *Die kretisch-mykenische Kultur*. 2nd ed. Leipzig, 1924.

FRANKFORT, H. *The Art and Architecture of the Ancient Orient*. London, 1954.

HOPE-SIMPSON, R., and DICKINSON, O.T.P.K. *A Gazetteer of Aegean Civilisation in the Bronze Age*, I, *The Mainland and Islands (S.I.M.A.*, LII). Göteborg, 1979.

IAKOVIDES, S. Ἡ Μυκηναϊκὴ Ἀκρόπολις τῶν Ἀθηνῶν. Athens, 1963.

JANNORAY, J., and VAN EFFENTERRE, H. 'Fouilles de Krisa', *B.C.H.*, LXI (1937). For megaron at Crisa: see page 316.

JANTZEN, U. *Tiryns IX; Grabungen in der Unterburg 1971*. Mainz, 1980.

KARO, G. *Führer durch Tiryns*. 2nd ed. Athens, 1934.

KERAMOPOULLOS, A.D. Αἱ βιομηχάνιαι καὶ τὸ ἐμπόριον τοῦ Κάδμου, Ἐφ. Ἀρχ. (1930). For Thebes: see page 31.

MÜLLER, V. 'Development of the Megaron in Prehistoric Greece', *A.J.A.*, XLVIII (1944).

MYLONAS, G.E. *Ancient Mycenae*. Princeton, 1957.

MYLONAS, G.E. 'The Walls and Gates of Mycenae', Ἐφ Ἀρχ. 1962 (1966); with English summary, page 187.

NOACK, F. 'Arne', *Ath. Mitt.*, XIX (1894). For Gla fortifications: see page 420.

PALMER, L.R. 'The Homeric and the Indo-European House', *Transactions of the Philological Society* (1948).

RAPP, G., and ASCHENBRENNER, S.E., eds. *Excavations at Nichoria in South West Messenia*, I. Minneapolis, 1978.

RIDDER, A. DE. 'Fouilles de Gha', *B.C.H.*, XVIII (1894). For Gla palace: see page 275.

RIDER, B.C. *The Greek House*. London, 1916. For Homeric evidence.

RODENWALDT, G. *Tiryns: Die Ergebnisse der Ausgrabungen*, II. Athens, 1912.

TAYLOUR, Lord William. *The Mycenaeans*. London, 1964.

THREPSIADES, I. Reports on Gla in Τὸ Ἔργον and Πραχ. For gates: see Πραχ. (1955), 121, figure 2, plate 40; (1957), 48, figures 2 and 4, plates 13–16, 27, and 28a. For palace: see Πραχ. (1960), 23. Air photograph of island: Πραχ. (1959), plate 26.

VALMIN, M.N. *The Swedish Messenia Expedition*. Lund, 1938.

WACE, A.J.B., and others. *Mycenae*. Princeton, 1949.

WACE, A.J.B. 'Notes on the Homeric House', *J.H.S.*, LXXI (1959). For Homeric evidence: see page 203.

WACE, H. *Mycenae Guide*. 1963.

CHAPTER 9

ARVANITOPOULLOS, A.S. Ἀνασκαφαὶ καὶ ἔρευναι ἐν Θεσσαλίᾳ, Πραχ. (1910–11). For Gonnus and Homolium.

AUBERSON, P. 'La Reconstitution du Daphnéphoreion d' Érétrie', *Antike Kunst*, XVII (1974), 60.

BOARDMAN, J. *B.S.A.*, LVIII (1963), 7, n. 24. For date of temple of Artemis Orthia. *B.S.A.*, XLIII (1948). For model of temple from Ithaca: see plate 45.

BUSCHOR, E. 'Heraion von Samos, frühe Bauten', *Ath. Mitt.*, LV (1930).

COLDSTREAM, J.N. *Geometric Greece*. London, 1977.

COURBIN, P. *L'Oikos des Naxiens (Délos*, fasc. XXXIII). Paris, 1980.

DAWKINS, R.M., and others. *The Sanctuary of Artemis Orthia at Sparta (Suppl. Papers Soc. Prom. Hellenic Studies*, V). London, 1929.

DESBOROUGH, V. *The Greek Dark Ages*. London, 1972.

DRERUP, H. 'Griechische Architektur zur Zeit Homers', *Arch. Anz.* (1964), col. 180.

GERKAN, A. VON. 'Die Herkunft des Dorischen Gebälks', *J.D.I.*, LXIII–LXIV (1948–9).

For 'Megaron B', Thermum: see page 6; for dating bronze statuettes cf. F. Matz, *Geschichte der griechischen Kunst*, I (1950).

KAWERAU, G., and SOTERIADIS, G. 'Der Apollotempel zu Thermos', *Antike Denkmäler*, II (1902–8).

KJELLBERG, L., and BOEHLAU, J. *Larisa am Hermos, die Ergebnisse der Ausgrabungen*, I. Stockholm and Berlin, 1940.

For wide temples: see page 78, figure 13.

MARINATOS, S. 'Le Temple géometrique de Dréros', *B.C.H.*, LX (1936).

MYLONAS, G.E., ed. *Studies presented to D.M. Robinson*, I. St Louis, Mo., 1951.

For models of temples: see page 259, plates 11, 12.

PAYNE, H. 'On the Thermon Metopes', *B.S.A.*, XXVII (1925–6).

PAYNE, H. *Perachora, the Sanctuaries of Hera Akraia and Limenia*, I. Oxford, 1940.

PENDLEBURY, J.D.S. 'Excavations in the Plain of Lasithi, III', *B.S.A.*, XXXVIII (1937–8).

For Karphi: see page 75.

PENDLEBURY, J.D.S. *The Archaeology of Crete.* London, 1939.

PERNIER, L. 'Tempii arcaici sulla Patela di Prinias', *Annuario della Scuola Italiana di Atene*, I (1914).

PERNIER, L. 'New Elements for the Study of the Archaic Temple of Prinias', *A.J.A.*, XXXVIII (1934).

POPHAM, M.R., SACKETT, L.H., and THEMELIS, P.G. *Lefkandi*, I. *The Settlement.* London, 1980.

RIZZA, G., and SCRINARI, V. ST M. *Il Santuario sull'acropoli di Gortina.* Rome, 1968.

For restoration see figure 76.

SAVIGNONI, L. 'Il Pythion di Gortyna', *Monumenti Antichi della R. Accademia Nazionale dei Lincei*, XVIII (1907).

SCHMALTZ, B. 'Bemerkung zu Thermos B', *Arch. Anz.* (1980), 318.

SNODGRASS, A.M. *The Dark Age of Greece.* Edinburgh, 1971.

SOTERIADIS, G. Ἀνασκαφαὶ ἐν Θερμῳ, Ἐφ. Ἀρχ., (1900, 1903).

For 'Megaron B', Thermum.

VALLOIS, R. *Architecture hellénique et hellénistique à Délos*, I. Paris, 1944.

For predecessor of Oikos of the Naxians, Delos: see pages 18, 115.

VAN BUREN, E.D. *Archaic Fictile Revetments in Sicily and Magna Graecia.* London, 1923.

VAN BUREN, E.D. *Greek Fictile Revetments in the Archaic Period.* London, 1926.

CHAPTER 10

ASHMOLE, B. *Architect and Sculptor in Classical Greece.* London, 1972.

BEYER, I. 'Der Triglyphenfries von Thermos C', *Arch. Anz.* (1972), 197 f.

BOWEN, M.L. 'Some Observations on the Origin of Triglyphs', *B.S.A.*, XLV (1950).

BRONEER, O. *Isthmia*, I, *The Temple of Poseidon.* Princeton, 1971.

CALI, F. *L'Ordre grecque.* Paris, 1958.

Photographs of Doric, largely details.

COOK, R.M. 'A Note on the Origin of the Triglyph', *B.S.A.*, XLVI (1951).

COOK, R.M. 'The Archetypal Doric Temple', *B.S.A.*, LXV (1970).

DYGGVE, E. *Das Laphrion, der Tempelbezirk von Calydon.* Copenhagen, 1949.

For unfluted columns: see page 122.

HODGE, A.T. *The Woodwork of Greek Roofs.* Cambridge, 1960.

KAHLER, H. *Das griechische Metopenbild.* Munich, 1949.

KALPAXIS, T.E. 'Zum aussergewohnlichen Triglyphenfries von Apollontempel C in Thermos', *Arch. Anz.* (1974), 105.

LAPALUS, E. *Le Fronton sculpté en Grèce, des origines à la fin du IV siècle.* Paris, 1947.

LAWRENCE, A.W. *Greek and Roman Sculpture.* London, 1972.

MONTUORO, P.Z., and ZANOTTI-BIANCO, U. *Heraion alla Foce del Sele.* Rome, 1951.

PICARD, C., and COURBY, F. *Recherches archéologiques à Stratos.* Paris, 1924.

For unfluted columns: see figure 19.

RICHTER, G.M.A. *The Sculpture and Sculptors of the Greeks.* 4th ed. New Haven, 1970.

ROBINSON, D.M. *Excavations at Olynthus*, II. Baltimore, 1930.

For coloured stucco mouldings, ? fifth century: see plates 2, 3.

SHOE, L.T. *Profiles of Greek Mouldings.* 2 vols. Cambridge, Mass., 1936.

SHOE, L.T. *Profiles of Western Greek Mouldings.* Rome, 1952.

SOLON, L.T. *Polychromy, Architectural and Structural.* New York, 1924.

VAN BUREN, E.D. *Archaic Fictile Revetments in Sicily and Magna Graecia.* London, 1923.

VAN BUREN, E.D. *Greek Fictile Revetments in the Archaic Period.* London, 1926.

WESENBERG, B. *Kapitelle und Basen (Beiheft der Bonner Jahrbücher, Bd 32).* 1971.

WIEGAND, T. *Die archäische Poros-Architektur der Akropolis zu Athen.* Text and atlas. Kassel and Leipzig, 1904.

CHAPTER 11

AUBERSON, P. *Eretria*, I. *Temple d'Apollon Daphnéphoros*. Bern, 1968.

BACON, F.H., CLARKE, J.T., and KOLDEWEY, R. *Investigations at Assos*. Cambridge, Mass., 1902–21.

CULTRERA, G. 'L'Apollonion-Artemision di Ortigia in Siracusa', *Monumenti Antichi della R. Accademia dei Lincei*, XLI (1951).
For Temple of Apollo, Syracuse: see page 813.

DE WAELE, J. 'Der Entwurf der dorischen Tempel von Akragas', *Arch. Anz.* (1980), 180

DE WAELE, J. 'Der Entwurf der dorischen Tempel von Paestum', *Arch. Anz.* (1980), 267.

DINSMOOR, W.B. 'The Greek Temples at Paestum', *Memoirs of the American Academy at Rome*, XX (1950).

DYGGVE, E. *Das Laphrion, der Tempelbezirk von Calydon*. Copenhagen, 1948.
For apsidal buildings: see page 274.

FURTWANGLER, A., and others. *Aegina: Das Heiligtum der Aphaia*. 2 vols. Munich, 1906.

GABRICI, E. 'Il Santuario della Malophoros a Selinunte', *Monumenti Antichi della R. Accademia Nazionale dei Lincei*, XXXII (1927–8).
For Gaggera.

GABRICI, E. 'Acropoli di Selinunte', *Monumenti Antichi della R. Accademia Nazionale dei Lincei*, XXXIII (1929).

GABRICI, E. 'Studi archeologici selinuntine', *Monumenti Antichi della R. Accademia dei Lincei*, XLIII (1956).

GALLET DE SANTERRE, H. *Exploration archéologique de Délos*, XXIV, *La Terrasse des Lions, le Letöon et le monument de granite*. Paris, 1959.

HERMANN, K. 'Die Griebel Rekonstruktion des Schatzhauses von Megara', *Ath. Mitt.*, LXXXIX (1974), 75.

HODGE, A.T. *The Woodwork of Greek Roofs*. Cambridge, 1960.

KJELLBERG, L., and BOEHLAU, J. *Larisa am Hermos, die Ergebnisse der Ausgrabungen*, I. Stockholm and Berlin, 1940.
For apsidal buildings: see page 75.

KLEIN, W. 'Zum Thron des Apollon von Amyklae', *Ath. Mitt.*, XXXVIII (1922).

KOLDEWEY, R., and PUCHSTEIN, O. *Die griechischen Tempel in Unteritalien und Sicilien*. Berlin, 1899.

KRAUSS, F. *Paestum, die griechischen Tempel*. 3rd ed. Berlin, 1976.

KRAUSS, F. *Die Tempel von Paestum*, I.I, *Der Athenatempel*. Berlin, 1959.

KRAUSS, F. 'Paestum, Basilika', *Festschrift für C. Weickert*. Berlin, 1955.

KUNZE, E., and SCHLEIF, H. *Olympische Forschungen*, I. Berlin, 1944.
For Treasury of Gela: see page 83.

LAPALUS, E. *Le Fronton sculpté en Grèce, des origines à la fin du IVe siècle*. Paris, 1947.

LEHMANN, K. and P.W. *Samothrace. Excavations*, 4.1, *The Hall of Votive Gifts*. New York, 1962.

MALLWITZ, A. *Olympia und seine Bauten*. Munich, 1972.

MARCONI, P. *Himera, lo scavo del tempio della Vittoria e del temenos*. Rome, 1931.
Also in *Atti e Memorie della Società Magna Grecia* (1930).

MONTUORO, P.Z., and ZANOTTI-BIANCO, U. *Heraion alla Foce del Sele*. Rome, 1951.

ORSI, P. 'L'Olympieion di Siracusa', *Monumenti Antichi della R. Accademia Nazionale dei Lincei*, XIII (1903).

ORSI, P. 'Templum Apollonis Alaei ad Crimisa-Promontorium', *Atti e Memorie della Società Magna Grecia* (1932).

PERNIER, L. 'L'Artémision di Cirene', *Africa Italiana*, IV (1931).

PLOMMER, W.H. 'The Archaic Acropolis: Some Problems', *J.H.S.*, LXXX (1960), 127.

RHOMAIOS, K.A. Ἀρχαῖον ἱερὸν παρὰ τὸν Ταξιάρχην τῆς Αἰτωλιάς, Ἀρχ. Δελτ., X (1926).

RIEMANN, H. 'Zum Artemistempel von Korkyra', *J.D.I.*, LVIII (1943).

RIEMANN, H. 'Der Peisistratidische Athenatempel', *Mitteilungen des Deutschen Archäologischen Instituts*, III (1950).
For new restoration: see page 7.

RIEMANN, H. 'Zur Grundrissinterpretation des Enneastylos von Poseidonia', *Römische Mitteilungen*, LXXII (1965).
On mathematics of layout of 'Basilica'.

RODENWALDT, G., and others. *Korkyra, Archäische Bauten und Bildwerke*, I and II. Berlin, 1939–40.

SHOE, L.T. *Profiles of Greek Mouldings*. 2 vols. Cambridge, Mass., 1936.

SHOE, L.T. *Profiles of Western Greek Mouldings*. Rome, 1952.

STILLWELL, R. *Corinth*, I, ii, *Architecture*. Cambridge, Mass., 1941.

TRAVLOS, J. *Pictorial Dictionary of Ancient Athens*. London/New York, 1971.

VAN BUREN, E.D. *Archaic Fictile Revetments in Sicily and Magna Graecia*. London, 1923.

VAN BUREN, E.D. *Greek Fictile Revetments in the Archaic Period*. London, 1926.

YALOURIS, N. 'Das Akroter des Heraions in Olympia', *Ath. Mitt.*, LXXXVII (1972), 85.

CHAPTER 12

ALZINGER, W. 'Von der Archaik zur Klassik', *J.O.A.I.*, L (1972–5), 169.

BETANCOURT, P. P. *The Aeolic Style in Architecture*. Princeton, 1977.

BOARDMAN, J. 'Chian and Early Ionic Architecture', *Antiquaries Journal*, XXXIX (1959). For chronology of capitals, etc.: see page 197. Cf. also a capital from Halicarnassus dated *c.* 500 by Martin, *Revue des Études anciennes*, LXI (1959), page 65, plates I and II.

BÜSING-KOLBE, A. 'Frühe griechische Türen', *J.D.I.*, XCIII (1978), 66. Chapters 12, 13, 14, 16, 19 (esp. Macedonian tombs).

DAUX, G. *Fouilles de Delphes*, II, *Les deux trésors*. Paris, 1923.

DEMANGEL, R. *Fouilles de Delphes*, II, *Les temples de tuf*. Paris, 1923.

DEMANGEL, R. *La Frise ionique*. Paris, 1933.

DINSMOOR, W.B. 'Studies of the Delphian Treasuries', *B.C.H.*, XXXVI and XXXVII (1912 and 1913).

GRUBEN, G. 'Das archäische Didymaion', *J.D.I.*, LXXVIII (1963).

GRUBEN, G. 'Naxos and Paros', *Arch. Anz.* (1972), 317

GRUBEN, G. and KOENIGS, W. 'Der Hekatompedos von Naxos und der Burgtempel von Paros', *Arch. Anz.* (1970).

HAHLAND, W. 'Didyma im 5. Jahrhundert v. Chr.', *J.D.I.*, LXXIX (1964).

HOGARTH, D.G. *British Museum: Excavations at Ephesus, the Archaic Artemisia*. Text and atlas. London, 1908.

HUMANN, C., and others. *Magnesia am Maeander: Bericht uber die Ergebnisse der Ausgrabungen der Jahre 1891–93*. Berlin, 1904.

JACOBSTHAL, P. 'The Date of the Ephesian Foundation-Deposit', *J.H.S.*, LXXI (1951). For date of foundation of temple, Ephesus: see page 85. *J.H.S.*, LXXII (1952). For water-lily capital, Old Smyrna: see plate VI, 3.

KJELLBERG, L., and BOEHLAU, J. *Larisa am Hermos, die Ergebnisse der Ausgrabungen*, I. Stockholm and Berlin, 1940.

KOLDEWEY, R. *Die antiken Baureste der Insel Lesbos*. Berlin, 1890.

KOLDEWEY, R. *Neandria*. Berlin, 1891.

PETERSEN, E., and LUSCHAN, F.V. *Reisen in Lykien, Milyas und Kibyratis*. Vienna, 1889.

POULSEN, F. *Delphi*. London, 1920.

PUCHSTEIN, O. *Das Ionische Capitell*. Berlin, 1887.

REUTHER, O. *Der Heratempel von Samos, Der Bau seit der Zeit Polykrates*. Berlin, 1957.

RUBENSOHN, O. 'Der ionische Burgtempel auf Paros', *Arch. Anz.*, XXVIII–XXIX (1923–4). For doorways: see figures in columns 287–90.

STUART, J., and REVETT, N. *The Antiquities of Athens*, I. London, 1762; 2nd ed. (ed. W. Kinnaird), 1825. For Temple on the Ilissus: see Chapter 11.

TUCHELT, K. *Vorarbeiten zu einer Topographie von Didyma* (with references for the earliest temples there) (*Ist. Mitt.*, Beiheft 9). Tübingen, 1973.

WEICKERT, C. *Das lesbische Kymation*. Leipzig, 1913.

WELTER, G. 'Altionische Tempel', *Ath. Mitt.*, XLIX (1924).

WESENBERG, B. *Kapitelle und Basen* (*Beiheft der Bonner Jahrbücher*, Bd 32). 1971.

CHAPTER 13

ASHMOLE, B. *Architect and Sculptor in Classical Greece*. London, 1972.

AUDIAT, J. *Fouilles de Delphes*, II, *Le Trésor des Athéniens*. Paris, 1933.

BANKEL, H. 'Aegina, Aphaia-Tempel III', *Arch. Anz.* (1980), 171.

BELL, M. 'Stylobate and Roof in the Olympieion at Akragas', *A.J.A.*, LXXXIV (1980), 359.

CURTIUS, E., ADLER, F., and others. *Olympia: Die Ergebnisse der vom Deutschen Reich veranstalteten Ausgrabungen*, text II and atlas I. Berlin, 1892.

DE WAELE, J. 'Der Entwurf des dorischen Tempel von Akragas', *Arch. Anz.* (1980), 180.

DE WAELE, J. 'Der Entwurf der dorischen Tempel von Paestum', *Arch. Anz.* (1980), 267.

DINSMOOR, W.B. 'The Olympieum at Acragas', *Memoirs of the American Academy at Rome*, XX (1950).

DINSMOOR, W.B. 'The Greek Temples at Paestum', *Memoirs of the American Academy at Rome*, XX (1950).

FURTWÄNGLER, A., and others. *Aegina: Das Heiligtum der Aphaia*. 2 vols. Munich, 1906.

HERMANN, H.–V. *Olympia*. Munich, 1972.

KOLDEWEY, R., and PUCHSTEIN, O. *Die griechischen Tempel in Unteritalien und Sicilien*. Berlin, 1899.

KRAUSS, F. *Paestum, die griechischen Tempel*. Berlin, 1943.

MALLWITZ, A. *Olympia und seine Bauten*. Munich, 1972.

MÖBIUS, H. *Die Ornamente der griechischen Grabstelen*. Berlin, 1929.

OHLY, D., and SCHWANDNER, E–L. 'Aegina, Aphaia Tempel I', *Arch. Anz.*, LXXXV (1970), 49.
OHLY, D., and SCHWANDNER, E–L. 'Aegina, Aphaia Tempel II', *Arch. Anz.*, LXXXVI (1971), 505.
WÜRSTER, W.W. *Alt Ägina*, I.I, *Der Apollon Tempel*. Mainz, 1974.

CHAPTER 14

AMANDRY, P. 'Observations sur les monuments de l'Héraion d'Argos', *Hesperia*, XXI (1952).
AMANDRY, P. *Fouilles de Delphes*, II, *La Colonne des Naxiens et la Portique des Athéniens*. Paris, 1953.
BALANOS, N.M. *Les Monuments de l'Acropole*. 2 vols. Paris, 1938.
BOERSMA, J.S. *Athenian Building Policy from 561–404*. Groningen, 1970.
BRUNEAU, P., and DUCAT, J. *Guide de Délos*. Paris, 1965.
    For plan of Hieron: see facing page 75.
BUNDGAARD, J.A. *Mnesicles*. Copenhagen, 1957.
    In English, for Propylaea.
BUNDGAARD, J.A. *The Excavation of the Athenian Acropolis*. Copenhagen, 1974.
BUNDGAARD, J.A. *Parthenon and the Mycenaean City on the Heights*. Copenhagen, 1976.
BURFORD, A. 'The Builders of the Parthenon', *Greece and Rome*, Supplement to vol. X, Parthenos and Parthenon, 1963.
    For translation of inscriptions and timetable of work: see page 23.
CARPENTER, R. *The Architects of the Parthenon*. Harmondsworth, 1970.
COURBY, F. 'Le Sanctuaire d'Apollon Délien', *B.C.H.*, XLV (1921).
    For plan of Delos (west part of sanctuary): see page 211, figure 2.
DINSMOOR, W.B., Jr. *The Propylaia to the Athenian Acropolis*, I. Princeton, 1980.
DOXIADES, C. *Architectural Space in Ancient Greece*. Cambridge, Mass., 1972.
ÉCOLE FRANÇAISE D'ATHÈNES. *Fouilles de Delphes*, II, *Atlas*. Paris, 1975.
FURTWÄNGLER, A., and others. *Aegina: Das Heiligtum der Aphaia*. 2 vols. Munich, 1906.
GABRICI, E. 'Il Santuario della Malophoros a Selinunte', *Monumenti Antichi della R. Accademia Nazionale dei Lincei*, XXXII (1927–8).
    For Gaggera.
GABRICI, E. 'Acropoli di Selinunte', *Monumenti Antichi della R. Accademia Nazionale dei Lincei*, XXXIII (1929).
GARDINER, E.N. *Olympia, its History and Remains*. Oxford, 1925.

GRAHAM, J.W. 'A New Model of the Athenian Acropolis in the Royal Ontario Museum', *The Phoenix*, XIV (1960).
GROPENGIESSER, H. *Die pflanzlichen Akrotere klassischer Tempel*. Mainz, 1961.
    For acroteria of Parthenon.
GRUBEN, G. 'Die Südhalle', *Ath. Mitt.*, LXXII (1957).
    For stoa at Samos Heraeum: see page 52, and restoration, plate VII. Cf. a small stoa at Didyma, *Arch. Rep.* (1964–5), page 52.
Guides bleus. La Grèce.
    For plan of Delos.
HERMANN, H.-V. *Olympia*. Munich, 1972.
HILL, I.T. *The Ancient City of Athens*. London, 1953.
HOPPER, R.J. *The Acropolis*. London, 1971.
KNELL, H. *Perikleische Baukunst*. Darmstadt, 1979.
KONTES, I.Τὸ Ἱερὸν τῆς Ὀλυμπίας κατὰ τὸν Δ'. π.Χ. αἰῶνα. Athens, 1958.
    For period plans of Olympia: see plates 1–6. For plans of other sanctuaries: see plates 7–17.
LAUTER, H. 'Zur frühclassischen Neuplanung des Heraions von Argos', *Ath. Mitt.*, LXXXVIII (1973), 175.
LAWRENCE, A.W. 'The Acropolis and Persepolis', *J.H.S.*, LXXI (1951).
MALLWITZ, A. *Olympia und seine Bauten*. Munich, 1972.
MARTIENSSEN, R.D. *The Idea of Space in Greek Architecture*. Johannesburg, 1956.
ORLANDOS, A.K. Ἡ Ἀρχιτεκτονική τοῦ Παρθενῶνος. Athens, 1977.
PATON, J.M., and STEVENS, G.P. *The Erechtheum*. Text and Atlas. Cambridge, Mass., 1927.
PENROSE, F.C. *An Investigation of the Principles of Athenian Architecture*. 2nd ed. London, 1888 (reprinted).
PICARD, C., and BOISSONAS, F. *L'Acropole d'Athènes, l'enceinte, l'entrée, le bastion d'Athéna Niké, les Propylées*. Paris, 1930.
PICARD, C., and BOISSONAS, F. *L'Acropole d'Athènes, le plateau supérieur, l'Erechtheion, les annexes sud*. Paris, 1930.
POULSEN, F. *Delphi*. London, 1920.
PRASCHNIKER, C. 'Die Akroterien des Parthenon', *J.Ö.A.I.*, XII (1910).
SCHLEIF, H. 'Der grosse Altar der Hera von Samos', *Ath. Mitt.*, LVIII (1933).
SCRANTON, R. 'Group Design in Greek Architecture', *Art Bulletin*, XXXI, no. 4 (1949).
STEVENS, G.P. *The Periclean Entrance Court of the Acropolis of Athens*. Cambridge, Mass., 1940.
STEVENS, G.P. *Restorations of Classical Buildings*. Princeton, 1955.

TIBERI, C. *Mnesicle l'architetto dei Propilei*. [Rome, 1964].

TOMLINSON, R.A. *Greek Sanctuaries*. London, 1976.

TRAVLOS, J. *Pictorial Dictionary of Ancient Athens*. London/New York, 1971.

TSCHIRA, A. 'Untersuchungen in Süden des Parthenon', *J.D.I.*, LXXXVII (1972), 158.

VALLOIS, R. *Constructions antiques de Délos, Documents*. Paris, 1953.
For plan of Delos: see plate I.

WALDSTEIN, Sir C., and others. *The Argive Heraeum*. 2 vols. Boston and New York, 1902–5.

WELLER, C.H. 'The Pre-Periclean Propylon of the Acropolis at Athens', *A.J.A.*, VIII (1904).

ZIEGENAUS, O. 'Der Südbau', and 'Die Tempelgruppe im Norden des Altarplatzes', *Ath. Mitt.*, LXXII (1957).
For minor temples in the Heraeum Sanctuary, Samos, identified by Buschor, *ibid.*, page 77.

CHAPTER 15

BALANOS, N.M. *Les Monuments de l'Acropole*. 2 vols. Paris, 1938.

GOODYEAR, W.H. *Greek Refinements: Studies in Temperamental Architecture*. New Haven, 1912.

ORLANDOS, A.K. Ἡ Ἀρχιτεκτονικὴ τοῦ Παρθενῶνος. Athens, 1977.

PENROSE, F.C. *An Investigation of the Principles of Athenian Architecture*. 2nd ed. London, 1888 (reprinted).

STEVENS, G.P. 'Concerning the Curvature of the Steps of the Parthenon', *A.J.A.*, XXXVIII (1934).

STEVENS, G.P 'The Curves of the North Stylobate of the Parthenon', *Hesperia*, XII (1943).

CHAPTER 16

ADAM, J-P. 'Le Temple de Héra II à Paestum', *Revue Archéologique* (1973), 219.

BESCHI, L. 'Disiecta membra del Tempio di Poseidon a Capo Sounio', *Annuario*, XXXI–XXXII (1969–70), 417.

BESCHI, L. 'Disiecta membra del Tempio di Poseidon II', *Ἐφ. Ἀρχ.* (1972), 173.

COURBY, F. *Exploration archéologique de Délos* XII, *Les Temples d'Apollon*. Paris, 1931.

DELIVORRIAS, A. *Attische Giebelskulpturen und Akrotere des fünften Jahrhunderts (Tübingen Studien zur Archäologie und Kunstgeschichte*, Bd 1). Tübingen, 1974.

DINSMOOR, W.B. 'The Temple of Apollo at Bassae', *Metropolitan Museum Studies*, IV (1933).

DINSMOOR, W.B. 'A Further Note on Bassai', *A.J.A.*, XLIII (1939).
Cf. Hahland, *J.D.I.*, LXIII–LXIV (1948–9), 14.

DINSMOOR, W.B., Jr. 'The Roof of the Hephaisteion', *A.J.A.*, LXXX (1976), 223.

HOFKES-BRUKKER, C., and MALLWITZ, A. *Der Bassai Fries*. Munich, 1975.

KNELL, H. 'Vier attische Tempel klassicher Zeit', *Arch. Anz.*, LXXXVIII (1973), 94.

KNELL, H. *Perikleische Baukunst*. Darmstadt, 1979.

KOCH, H. *Studien zum Theseustempel in Athen*. Berlin, 1955.

KOLDEWEY, R., and PUCHSTEIN, O. *Die griechischen Tempel in Unteritalien und Sicilien*. Berlin, 1899.

MCALLISTER, M.H. 'The Temple of Ares at Athens', *Hesperia*, XXVIII (1959), I.

MARCONI, P. *Agrigento, topografia ed arte*. Florence, 1929.

MARTIN, R. 'L'Atelier Ictinos-Callicrates au temple de Bassai', *B.C.H.*, C (1976).

PLOMMER, W.H. 'Three Attic Temples', *B.S.A.*, XLV (1950).
For restorations of temple of Hephaestus and temples at Sunium and Rhamnus: see page 66, plates 7–9.

PLOMMER, W.H. 'The Temple of Poseidon on Cape Sunium', *B.S.A.*, LV (1960).

ROUX, G. *L'Architecture de l'Argolide aux IVe et IIIe siècles*. Paris, 1961.
For Bassae.

SCRANTON, R. 'Interior Design of Greek Temples', *A.J.A.*, L (1946).
For design of cellas: see page 39.

THOMPSON, H.A. 'Itinerant Temples of Attica', *A.J.A.*, LXVI (1926), 206.

TRAVLOS, J. *Pictorial Dictionary of Ancient Athens*. London/New York, 1971.

WOTSCHITZKY, A. 'Zum korinthischen Kapitell im Apollontempel zu Bassae', *J.Ö.A.I.*, XXXVII (1948).

CHAPTER 17

A.J.A., XLIX (1945).
For Hellenistic tholos tomb, Kazanlik: see page 402.

BAUER, H. 'Lysikratesdenkmal, Bauabstand und Rekonstruktion', *Ath. Mitt.*, XCII (1977), 197.

BEAN, G.E. *Aegean Turkey*. London, 1966.
For Tomb of Tantalus: see page 60, figures 5 and 6, and plate 5.

BURFORD, A. *The Greek Temple-Builders at Epidauros*. Liverpool, 1969.
For inscriptions.

CHARBONNEAUX, J. *Fouilles de Delphes*, II, *La Tholos*. Paris, 1925.

CONZE, A., and others. *Archäologische Untersuchungen auf Samothrake*, I. Vienna, 1875.

DEFRASSE, A., and LECHAT, H. *Épidaure, restauration et description des principaux monuments du sanctuaire d'Asclépios*. Paris, 1895.

EBERT, M. *Reallexikon der Vorgeschichte*, XIV. Berlin, 1929.
For 'Tomb of Tantalus': see page 308, plate 61X.

FASTJE, J. 'Der Rundbau von Paros', *Arch. Anz.* (1972), 421.

KJELLBERG, L., and BOEHLAU, J. *Larisa am Hermos, die Ergebnisse der Ausgrabungen*, I. Stockholm and Berlin, 1940.
For tumulus tombs: see figure 20, plate 31.

MCCREDIE, J.R. 'Samothrace Supplementary Investigations 1968–77', *Hesperia*, XLVIII (1979), 1.

MILLER, S.G. 'The Philippeion and Macedonian Hellenistic Architecture', *Ath. Mitt.*, LXXXVIII (1973), 189.

MILLER, S.G. *The Prytaneion*. Berkeley and Los Angeles, 1978.
For the Tholos at Athens.

MILTNER, F. and H. 'Bericht über eine Voruntersuchung in Alt-Smyrna', *J.O.A.I.*, XXVII, Beiblatt.
For tumulus tombs: see page 152.

ROBERT, F. *Thymélè: Recherches sur la signification et la destination des monuments circulaires dans l'architecture religieuse de la Grèce*. Paris, 1939.

ROUX, G. *L'Architecture de l'Argolide aux IVe et IIIe siècles*. Paris, 1961.

SCHLEIF, H., and KUNZE, E. *Olympische Forschungen*, I. Berlin, 1945.
For Philippeum.

STUART, J., and REVETT, N. *The Antiquities of Athens*, I. London, 1762; 2nd ed. (ed. W. Kinnaird), 1825.
For Monument of Lysicrates: see chapter IV.

TRAVLOS, J. *Pictorial Dictionary of Ancient Athens*. London/New York, 1971.
For Tholos at Athens.

CHAPTER 18

ALTZINGER, W. 'Ionische Kapitelle aus Ephesos', *J.O.A.I.*, XLVI (1961–3).

BAMMER, A. *Die Architektur des jüngeren Artemision von Ephesos*. Wiesbaden, 1972.

BAUER, H. 'Korinthische Kapitelle des 4 und 3 Jahrhunderts v. Chr.', *Ath. Mitt.*, Beiheft 3 (1973).

BEAN, G.E., and COOK, J.M. 'The Cnidia', *B.S.A.*, XLVII (1952).
For Lion Tomb, Cnidus: see page 181, n. 44.

BOUSQUET, J. *Fouilles de Delphes*, II, *Le Trésor de Cyrène*. Paris, 1952.

BRITISH MUSEUM. *Catalogue of Sculpture*, number 1350.
For Lion Tomb, Cnidus.

BURFORD, A. *The Greek Temple-Builders at Epidauros*. Liverpool, 1969.
For inscriptions.

COOK, J.M., and PLOMMER, W.H. *The Sanctuary of Hemithea at Kastabos*. Cambridge, 1966.

COUPEL, P., and DEMARGNE, P. *Fouilles de Xanthos*, III, *Le Monument des Néreides*. Paris, 1969.

COURBY, F. 'Le Sanctuaire d'Apollon Délien', *B.C.H.*, XLV (1921).
For Temple 'A' (Keraton) Delos: see page 210, plates V–VII.

DEFRASSE, A., and LECHAT, H. *Épidaure, restauration et description des principaux monuments du sanctuaire d'Asclépios*. Paris, 1895.

DUGAS, C., BERCHMANS, J., and CLEMMENSEN, M. *Le Sanctuaire d'Aléa Athéna a Tégée au IVe siècle*. Paris, 1924.

DYGGVE, E. *Das Laphrion, der Tempelbezirk von Calydon*. Copenhagen, 1948.

GABELMANN, H. 'Zur Chronologie der Königsnekropole von Sidon', *Arch. Anz.* (1979), 163.

GUILLON, P. 'Mesures de longueur à Akraiphia' and 'Terres-cuites du Ptoion', *B.C.H.*, LX (1936).
For Temple of Ge-Demeter, Acraephia: see pages 9, 416.

HAMDY-BEY, O., and REINACH, T. *Une Nécropole royale à Sidon*. 2 vols. Paris, 1892–6.

HELLSTRÖM, P., and THIEME, T. 'The Temple of Zeus at Labraunda. A Preliminary Note', *Svenska Forskningsinstitutet i Istanbul, Meddelanden*, IV (1979), 5.

HILL, B.H. *The Temple of Zeus at Nemea*. Princeton, 1966.

JEPPESEN, K. *Paradeigmata*. Aarhus, 1958.
For Mausoleum.

JEPPESEN, K. 'Neue Ergebnisse zur Wiederherstellung des Maussolleions von Halikarnassos', *Ist. Mitt.*, XXVI (1976), 47.

KERAMOPOULLOS, A.D. Θηβαϊκά, Ἀρχ. Δελτ., III (1917).
For Temple of Apollo, Thebes: see page 33.

KJELLBERG, L., and BOEHLAU, J. *Larisa am Hermos, die Ergebnisse der Ausgrabungen*, I. Stockholm and Berlin, 1940.
For Temple of Ge-Demeter, Acraephia: see page 68.

KNELL, H. 'Der Artemis Tempel in Kalydon und der Poseidon Tempel in Molykreia', *Arch. Anz.* (1973), 448.

KNELL, H. 'Der Demetertempel in Lepreon', *A.A.A.*, XII (1979), 53.

KRISCHEN, F. 'Löwenmonument und Mausolleion', *Römische Mitteilungen, Deutsches Archäologisches Institut*, LIX (1944).

MATZ, F. 'Hellenistische und römische Grabbauten', *Die Antike*, IV (1928).
For types of tombs: see page 266.

NEWTON, Sir C.T. *History of Discoveries at Halicarnassus, Cnidus, and Branchidae.* Text and Atlas. London 1861–3.

ORLANDOS, A.K. Ὁ ναὸς τοῦ Ἀπόλλωνος Πτῴου, Ἀρχ. Δελτ., I (1915).

PLOMMER, W.H. Review of Bammer, *Die Architektur des jüngeren Artemision von Ephesos*, in *J.H.S.*, XCIV (1974), 249.

RIEMANN, H. 'Pytheos', in Pauly-Wissowa, *Real-Encyclopädie*, XLVII (1963), cols. 371–513.

ROUX, G. *L'Architecture de l'Argolide aux IVe et IIIe siècles.* Paris, 1961.

RUMPF, A. 'Classical and Post-Classical Greek Painting', *J.H.S.*, LXVII (1947).
For metopes from tomb at Cyrene: see page 12, plates I–III.

SCHEDE, M. *Die Ruinen von Priene, kurze Beschreibung.* Berlin, 1964.

VALLOIS, R. *Architecture hellénique et hellénistique à Délos*, I. Paris, 1944.
For Temple 'A' (Keraton), Delos: see pages 30, 131.

WAYWELL, G. *The Free-standing Sculpture of the Mausoleum at Halicarnassus.* London, 1979.

WEICKERT, C. *Das lesbische Kymation.* Leipzig, 1913.

WIEGAND, T., and SCHRADER, H. *Priene: Ergebnisse der Ausgrabungen und Untersuchungen in den Jahren 1895–98.* Berlin, 1904.

CHAPTER 19

ADRIANI, A. *La Nécropole de Moustafa Pacha.* Alexandria, 1936.
A.J.A., LXXI (1967).
For Travlos' model of Eleusis sanctuary, plate 69.

Alterthümer von Pergamon. Berlin, 1885–.
For temple of Athena: see vol. 2; for temple of Hera: see vol. 6; for Heroum of the Kings: see vol. 12.

ANDRONIKOS, M. Βεργίνα. Οἱ Βασίλικοι Τάφοι, *A.A.A.*, X (1977), 1.

AURES, A. 'Étude des dimensions du temple ... sur le cap Zéphyrium ...', *Revue Archéologique*, XX (1869).
Cf. *Arch. Zeitung* (1866), plate CCX.

B.C.H., XLIX (1925).
For Temple of the Bastion, Delos: see page 466.

B.C.H., L (1926).
For Temple of the Bastion, Delos: see page 568.

B.C.H., LXII (1938).
For temple, Olus: see plate XLIII.

BEQUIGNON, Y., and LAUMONIER, A. 'Fouilles de Téos', *B.C.H.*, XLIX (1925).

BÖRKER, C. 'Die Datierung des Zeus-Tempels von Olba ...', *Arch. Anz.* (1971).

BUNDGAARD, J. 'The Building Contract from Lebadeia', *Classica et Mediaevalia*, VIII (1946).

BÜSING, H.H. *Die griechische Halbsäule.* Wiesbaden, 1970.

CHAPOUTHIER, F. *Exploration archéologique de Délos*, XVI, *Le Sanctuaire des dieux de Samothrace.* Paris, 1935.
For Monument of Mithradates and Sanctuary of Cabeiri.

COURBY, F. 'Le Sanctuaire d'Apollon Délien', *B.C.H.*, XLV (1921).
For Temple of Artemis 'D', Delos: see page 215, plates V–VI.

COURBY, M.F. *Fouilles de Delphes*, II, *La Terrasse du Temple.* Paris, 1927.
For Monument of Aristaeneta: see page 257; for Pedestal of Prusias: see page 262; for Pedestal of Aemilius Paulus: see page 302.

DYGGVE, E., POULSEN, F., and RHOMAIOS, K.A. 'Das Heroon von Kalydon', *Kongelige Danske Videnskabernes Selskab, Skrifter, Historisk og Filosofisk Afdeling*, 7 Raekke IV, 4 (1934).

GARBA, S. *Illustrated London News*, CLXXXIV (21 April 1934); CLXXXVI (8 June 1935).
For Hermopolis.

GERKAN, A. VON. *Der Altar des Artemistempels in Magnesia am Mäander.* Berlin, 1929.

GERKAN, A. VON. 'Das Säulenproblem des Naiskos von Didyma', *Ist. Mitt.*, XI (1961).

HERZOG, R., and others. *Kos, Ergebnisse der deutschen Ausgrabungen und Forschungen.* Berlin, 1932.

HEUZEY, L., and DAUMET, H. *Mission archéologique de Macédoine.* 2 vols. Paris, 1867–76.

HILLER VON GAERTRINGEN, F. *Thera*, I. Berlin, 1899.
For 'chapel': see page 306.

HOOD, M.S.F. 'Archaeology in Greece, 1954', *B.S.A.*, XLIX (1955).
For Macedonian tombs: see p. 38, figures 8 and 9.

HÖRMANN, H. *Die inneren Propyläen von Eleusis.* Berlin, 1932.

HUMANN, C., and others. *Magnesia am Maeander: Bericht über die Ergebnisse der Ausgrabungen der Jahre 1891–93.* Berlin, 1904.

KÄHLER, H. *Der grosse Fries von Pergamon.* Berlin, 1948.
For Altar, Pergamon.

KEIL, J. 'Vorläufiger Bericht', *J.O.A.I.*, XXVII–XXX (1933–7), Beiblatt.
For Belevi. Cf. *Anz. Wien* (1949), page 51.

KEIL, J. *Führer durch Ephesos.* Vienna, 1959.
Includes Belevi at end.

KEIL, J., and WILHELM, A. *Denkmäler aus dem rauhen Kilikien, Monumenta Asiae Minoris Antiqua*, III. Manchester, 1931.
For Uzunçaburç.

KINCH, K.F. 'Le Tombeau de Niausta', *Kongelige Danske Videnskabernes Selskab, Skrifter, Historisk og Filosofisk Afdeling*, 7 Raekke IV, 3 (1920).
For the same Doric tomb see Ἀρχ. Ἐφ. (1971), 146.

KLEINER, G. 'Diadochengräber', *Sitzungsberichte Frankfurt*, I (1962).
For Belevi.

KOLDEWEY, R. *Die antiken Baureste der Insel Lesbos.* Berlin, 1890.

KRAUSS, F. 'Die Höhe der Säulen des Naiskos im Tempel von Didyma', *Ist. Mitt.*, XI (1961).

LEHMANN, K., and SPITTLE, D. *Samothrace. Excavations*, 4, II, *The Altar Court.* New York, 1964.

LEONARDOS, U. Ἀνασκαφαὶ τοῦ ἐν Λυκοσούρᾳ ἱεροῦ τῆς Δεσποίνης, Πραχ (1896).

MACRIDY-BEY, T. 'Un Tumulus macédonien à Langaza', *J.D.I.*, XXVI (1911).

MÜLLER, W. *Der Pergamon-altar.* Leipzig, 1973.

NOSHY, I. *The Arts in Ptolemaic Egypt.* London, 1937.

ORLANDOS, A.K. Ὁ ἐν Στράτῳ τῆς Ἀκαρνανίας ναὸς τοῦ Δίος, Ἀρχ. Δελτ., VIII (1923).

PANTERMALIS, D. Ὁ νέος Μακεδονικός τάφος τῆς Βεργίνας, Μακεδονικά, XII (1972), 147.

PETSAS, PH. Ὁ Τάφος τῶν Λευκάδιων. Athens, 1966.
A Macedonian tomb with painted figures.

PICARD, C., and COURBY, F. *Recherches archéologiques à Stratos d'Acarnanie.* Paris, 1924.

PLASSART, A. *Exploration archéologique de Délos*, XI, *Les Sanctuaires et les cultes du Mont Cynthe.* Paris, 1928.
For Mt Cynthium and Temple of Agatha Tyche.

PRICE, M., and TRELL, B. *Coins and their Cities.* London, 1977.
Especially the coin evidence for the Great Altar of Pergamon.

REICHEL, W., and WILHELM, A. 'Das Heiligtum der Artemis zu Lusoi', *J.Ö.A.I.*, IV (1901).

RHOMAIOS, K.A. Ὁ Μακεδονικός τάφος τῆς Βεργίνας. Athens, 1951.

ROBERT, F. *Exploration archéologique de Délos*, XX, *Trois sanctuaires sur le rivage occidental.* Paris, 1953.
For Sanctuary of Asclepius.

ROUX, G. *L'Architecture de l'Argolide aux IVe et IIIe siècles.* Paris, 1961.

ROWE, A., and DRIOTON, E. 'Discovery of the Famous Temple and Enclosure of Serapis at Alexandria', *Annales du Service des Antiquités*, Suppl. 2. Cairo, 1946.

SAVIGNONI, L. 'Il Python di Gortyna', *Monumenti Antichi della R. Accademia Nazionale dei Lincei*, XVIII (1907).

SCHEDE, M. *Die Ruinen von Priene, kurze Beschreibung.* Berlin, 1964.

SCHOBER, A. *Der Fries des Hekateions von Lagina.* Baden-Vienna, 1933.

TRAVLOS, J. *Pictorial Dictionary of Ancient Athens.* London, 1971.

VALLOIS, R. 'Topographie Délienne, II', *B.C.H.*, LIII (1929).
For Dodekatheon.

VOIGTLÄNDER, W. *Der Jüngste Apollon Tempel von Didyma (Ist. Mitt.*, Beiheft 14). Tübingen, 1975.

WACE, A.J.B., MEGAW, A.H.S., and SKEAT, T.C. *Hermopolis Magna, Ashmunein.* Alexandria, 1959.
The authors were unable, for political reasons, to study the material after their excavation or to oversee the publication of their report. For capitals: see page 8 and coloured plate I.

WELTER, G. 'Das Olympieion in Athen', *Ath. Mitt.*, XLVIII (1923).

WIEGAND, T. *Didyma*, I. Berlin, 1941.

WIEGAND, T., and SHRADER, H. *Priene: Ergebnisse der Ausgrabungen und Untersuchungen in den Jahren 1895–98.* Berlin, 1904.

WILL, E. 'Le Sanctuaire syrien de Délos', *Annales arch. de Syrie*, I (1951), 59.

WILLIAMS, C. 'The Corinthian Temple of Zeus Olbius', *A.J.A.*, LXXVIII (1974), 405.

YAVIS, C.G. *Greek Altars.* St Louis, Mo., 1949.

YAYLALI, A. *Der Fries des Artemisions von Magnesia am Mäander (Ist. Mitt.*, Beiheft 15). Tübingen, 1976.

ZSCHIETZSCHMANN, W. 'Die inneren Propyläen von Eleusis', *Arch. Anz.*, XLVIII (1933).

CHAPTER 20

Arch. Anz. (1916), col. 215.
For early arches.

ASIN PALACIOS, M., and OTERO, M.L. 'The Pharos of Alexandria', *Proc. Brit. Acad.*, XIX (1933).

BEAN, G.E., and COOK, J.M. 'The Cnidia', *B.S.A.*, XLVII (1952).
For viaduct, Çesme: see page 180.

BOYD, T.D. 'The Arch and Vault in Greek Architecture', *A.J.A.*, LXXXII (1978), 83.

BUSCHOR, E. 'Der Ölbaumgiebel', *Ath. Mitt.*, XLVII (1922).
For Olive-tree Pediment: see page 81.

CARPENTER, R. *Ancient Corinth, A Guide to the Excavations and Museum*. Athens, 1960.

CHAMONARD, J. *Exploration archéologique de Délos*, VIII, *Le Quartier du Théâtre*. Paris, 1924.
For cisterns.

CHILDS, W.A.P. 'Prolegomena to a Lycian Chronology, II. The Heroon from Trysa', *Revue Archéologique* (1976), 281.

COUPRY, J. 'Les Tumuli de Karalar et la Sepulture du roi Déiotares II', *Revue Archéologique* (1935).

DINSMOOR, W.B. 'Structural Iron in Greek Architecture', *A.J.A.*, XXVI (1922).

DUNKLEY, B. 'Greek Fountain-Buildings before 300 B.C.', *B.S.A.*, XXXVI (1935–6).

DURM, J. 'Die Kuppelgräber von Pantikapaion', *J.Ö.A.I.*, X (1907).

EICHLER, F. *Die Reliefs des Heroon von Gjölbaschi-Trysa*. Vienna, 1950.

GRUBEN, G. 'Das Quellhaus von Megara', Ἀρχ. Δελτ. XIX (1964).

HILL, B.H. *Corinth*, I, VI, I, *The Springs*. Princeton, 1964.
Cf. *Hesperia*, XXXIX (1969), 36.

JOHNS, C.N. 'The Citadel, Jerusalem', *Quarterly of Department of Antiquities in Palestine*, XIV.
For 'Tower of David', Jerusalem: see page 121.

KEIL, J., and WILHELM, A. *Monumenta Asiae Minoris Antiqua*, III, *Denkmäler aus dem rauhen Kilikier*. Manchester, 1931.
For Uzunçaburç.

KRISCHEN, F. *Die Stadtmauern von Pompeji und griechische Festungsbaukunst in Unteritalien und Sizilien*. Berlin, 1941.

LAWRENCE, A.W. *Greek Aims in Fortification*. Oxford, 1980.

LORENZEN, E. *The Arsenal at Piraeus*. Copenhagen, 1964.

MARTIN, R. *Manuel d'architecture grecque*, I. *Matériaux et techniques*. Paris, 1965.
For methods of handling blocks: see page 201, with restorations of tackle.

PICARD, C., and COURBY, F. *Recherches archéologiques à Stratos d'Acarnanie*. Paris, 1924.

PLASSART, A. *Exploration archéologique de Délos*,

XI, *Les Sanctuaires et les cultes du Mont Cynthe*. Paris, 1928.
For the Cave, Delos: see page 240, plate VI.

POWELL, B., and SEARS, J.M. 'Oeniadae', *A.J.A.*, VIII (1904).

ROBINSON, H. 'The Tower of the Winds and the Roman Market-place', *A.J.A.*, XLVII (1943).

SCRANTON, R.L. *Greek Walls*. Cambridge, Mass., 1941.

STÄHLIN, F., and others. *Pagasai und Demetrias*. Berlin and Leipzig, 1934.
For fortification.

STAMELMAN, A. 'Reflections on the Roof of the Tower of the Winds in Athens', *Arch. Eph.* (1974), 221.

STUART, J., and REVETT, N. *The Antiquities of Athens*, I. London, 1762; 2nd ed. (ed. W. Kinnaird), 1825.
For 'Tower of the Winds': see Chapter III.

TOMLINSON, R.A. 'Vaulting Techniques in the Macedonian Tombs', *Archaia Makedonia*, II. Thessaloniki, 1977.

TRAVLOS, J. *Pictorial Dictionary of Ancient Athens*. London/New York, 1971.

UGUZ, R. 'Karalar Hafriyati', *Türk Tarih*, II (1934).
For Tombs, Karalar. For analogous roofing, cf. *Turkish Bellaten*, X (1946), plates I–XI; R.S. Young, *A.J.A.*, LX (1956), 250, plate 81.

WINTER, F.E. 'The Chronology of the Euryalos Fortress at Syracuse', *A.J.A.*, LXVII (1963).

WINTER, F.E. *Greek Fortifications*. London, 1971.

WREDE, W. *Attische Mauern*. Athens, 1933.

CHAPTER 21

ADRIANI, A., and others. *Himera*, I. Rome, 1970.

ALLEGRO, N., and others. *Himera*, II. Rome, 1976.

BOARDMAN, J. *Excavations in Chios 1952–5. Greek Emporio*. London, 1967.

BOYD, T.D., and RUDOLPH, W.W. 'The Lower Town of Halieis 1970–77', *Hesperia*, XLVII (1978), 333.

BRUNEAU, P., and DUCAT, J. *Guide de Délos*. Paris, 1965. 2nd ed. 1966.

BRUNEAU, P., and VATIN, C. *Exploration archéologique de Délos*, XXVII, *L'îlot de la Maison des Comédiens*. Paris, 1970.

CAMBITOGLOU, A. *Zagora*, I. Sydney, 1971.

CHAMONARD, J. *Exploration archéologique de Délos*, VIII, *Le Quartier du Théâtre*. 2 vols. Paris, 1924.
For houses.

CHAPOUTHIER, F. *Exploration archéologique de Délos*, XVI, *Le Sanctuaire des dieux de Samothrace*. Paris, 1935. For dining-halls: see page 79.

COOK, J.M. 'Old Smyrna, 1948–1951', *B.S.A.*, LIII–LIV (1958–9).

COOK, J.M. *The Greeks in the East*. London, 1962.

CURTIUS, E., ADLER, F., and others. *Olympia: Die Ergebnisse der vom Deutschen Reich veranstalteten Ausgrabungen*, text II and atlas I. Berlin, 1892.

DELORME, J. 'La Maison dite de l'Hermés, à Délos', *B.C.H.*, LXXVII (1953), 444.

DUCREY, P., and METZGER, I.R. 'La Maison aux mosaïques à Érétrie', *Antike Kunst*, XXII (1979), 3.

FARDINER, E.N. *Olympia, its History and Remains*. Oxford, 1925.

GJERSTAD, E. 'The Palace at Vouni', *Skrifter utgivna av Svenska Institutet i Rom*, II (1932).

GRAHAM, J.W. 'Origins and Interrelations of the Greek House and the Roman House', *The Phoenix*, XX (1966).

For many schematic plans see pages 24–9.

GRAHAM, J.W. 'Notes on Houses and Housing-districts at Abdera and Himera', *A.J.A.*, LXXIV (1970).

HAMMOND, N.G.L. 'Hellenic Houses at Ammotopos in Epirus', *B.S.A.*, XLVIII (1953).

See page 135, plates 33, 34.

HERMANN, H.-V. *Olympia*. Munich, 1972.

HOOD, M.S.F. 'Archaeology in Greece, 1954', *B.S.A.*, XLIX (1955).

For Cassope: see page 13.

KINCH, K.F. and H. *Fouilles de Vroulia*. Berlin, 1914.

KJELLBERG, L., and BOEHLAU, J. *Larisa am Hermos, die Ergebnisse der Ausgrabungen*, I, *1902*. Stockholm and Berlin, 1940.

KOSAY, H.Z. *Pazarlı Hafriyati Raporu: Les Fouilles de Pazarlı*. Ankara, 1941.

KRAUSE, I. 'Grundformen des griechischen Pastashaus', *Arch. Anz.* (1977), 164.

LAIDLAW, W.A. *A History of Delos*. Oxford, 1933.

LAUTER, H. 'Die beiden älteren Tyrannenpaläste in Larisa am Hermos', *Bonner Jahrbuch*, CLXXV (1975), 33.

LAUTER-BUFE, H., and LAUTER, H. 'Wohnhäuser und Stadtviertel des klassischen Athens', *Ath. Mitt.*, LXXXVI (1971), 109.

MARTIENSSEN, R.D. *The Idea of Space in Greek Architecture*. Johannesburg, 1956.

MINNS, E.H. *Scythians and Greeks*. Cambridge, 1913.

For Olbia: see pages 345, 394.

PAGENSTECHER, R. *Nekropolis: Untersuchungen über Gestalt und Entwicklung der alexandrinischen Grabanlagen und ihrer Malereien*. Leipzig, 1919.

PICARD, C. *Exploration archéologique de Délos*, VI, *L'Établissement des Poseidoniastes de Bérytos*. Paris, 1921.

For dining-halls: see figure 111.

POTTIER, E. 'Les Hypogées doriques de Nea Paphos', *B.C.H.*, IV (1880).

Cf. Pauly-Wissowa, *Real-Encyclopädie*, XVIII. 3, p. 945.

ROBERTSON, C.M. 'Greek Mosaics', *J.H.S.*, LXXXV (1965).

ROBINSON, D.M., and others. *Excavations at Olynthus*, VIII and XII. Baltimore, 1938 and 1946.

ROLLAND, H. *Fouilles de Glanum*. 2 vols. Paris, 1946 and 1958.

For Saint-Rémy.

SCHEDE, M. *Die Ruinen von Priene, kurze Beschreibung*. Berlin, 1964.

TRAVLOS, J. *Pictorial Dictionary of Ancient Athens*. London/New York, 1971.

For houses see p. 392, figures 505–15.

WIEGAND, T. 'Dystos', *Ath. Mitt.*, XXVI (1899).

WIEGAND, T., and SCHRADER, H. *Priene: Ergebnisse der Ausgrabungen und Untersuchungen in den Jahren 1895–8*. Berlin, 1904.

CHAPTER 22

ADRIANI, A., and others. *Himera*, I. Rome, 1970.

ALLEGRO, N., and others. *Himera*, II. Rome, 1976.

AMANDRY, P. *Fouilles de Delphes*, II, *La Colonne des Naxiens et la Portique des Athéniens*. Paris, 1953.

Athenian Agora, The. A guide to the excavations. Athens, 1962.

BOYD, T.D., and RUDOLPH, W.W. 'The Lower Town of Halieis 1970–77', *Hesperia*, XLVII (1978), 333.

BRONEER, O. *Corinth*, I, IV, *The South Stoa*. Princeton, 1955.

BRÜCKNER, A. 'Mitteilungen aus dem Kerameikos V', *Ath. Mitt.*, LVI (1931).

For Pompeion: see page 12.

CAMBITOGLOU, A. 'Excavations at Zagora, Andros', Πραχ. (1972), 251.

CARPENTER, R. *Ancient Corinth, A Guide to the Excavations and Museum*. Athens, 1960.

COULTON, J.J. 'The Stoa by the Harbour at Perachora', *B.S.A.*, LIX (1964).

For coloured plates: see facing page 100 and plate 18.

COULTON, J.J. 'The Stoa at the Amphiaraion, Oropos', *B.S.A.*, LXIII (1968).

COULTON, J.J. *The Architectural Development of the Greek Stoa*. Oxford, 1976.

COURBY, F. 'Le Sanctuaire d'Apollon Délien', *B.C.H.*, XLV (1921).

For stoa of the Naxians, Delos: see page 238, plate VII: for Oikos of the Naxians, Delos: see page 233, plate VII.

DUCREY, P., and PICARD, O. 'Recherches à Lato, V. Le Prytanée', *B.C.H.*, XCVI (1972), 567.

FABRICIUS, E., and LEHMANN-HARTLEBEN, K. 'Städtebau', Pauly-Wissowa, *Real-Encyclopädie*, IIIA, col. 1982. 1929.

GARDNER, E.A., SCHULTZ, R.W., and others. *Excavations at Megalopolis, 1890–1 (Suppl. Papers Soc. Prom. Hellenic Studies*, I). London, 1892.

GERKAN, A. VON. *Griechische Städteanlagen.* Berlin and Leipzig, 1924.

KASTRIOTIS, P. Περίκλειον ᾠδεῖον, Ἐφ. Ἀρχ. (1922).

KINCH, K.F. and H. *Fouilles de Vroulia.* Berlin, 1914.

KRIESIS, A. *Greek Town Building.* Athens, 1965.

KRISCHEN, F. *Die griechische Stadt, Wiederherstellungen.* Berlin, 1938.

LEHMANN, K. *Samothrace.* 3rd ed. Locust Valley, 1966.

LLINAS, C. 'Le portique coudé de Perachora', *B.C.H.*, LXXXIX (1965).

MARSTRAND, V. *Arsenalet i Piraeus og Oldtidens Byggeregler.* Copenhagen, 1922.

MARTIN, R. *Recherches sur l'agora grecque.* Paris, 1951.

MARTIN, R. *L'Urbanisme dans la Grèce antique.* Paris, 1956.

MCDONALD, W.A. *The Political Meeting Places of the Greeks.* Baltimore, 1943.

MILLER, S.G. *The Prytaneion.* Berkeley and Los Angeles, 1978.

NOACK, F. *Eleusis, die baugeschichtliche Entwicklung des Heiligtums.* 2 vols. Berlin and Leipzig, 1927.

PLOMMER, H. 'Vitruvian Studies', *B.S.A.*, LXV (1971).
For Oikos of the Naxians: see page 186 and restorations figures 3 and 4.

POUILLOUX, J. *Fouilles de Delphes, II. Topographie et architecture: La Région nord du sanctuaire.* Paris, 1960.
For Lesche of the Cnidians.

STILLWELL, R., and SJÖQVIST, E. 'Excavations at Serra Orlando', *A.J.A.*, LXI (1957).
For steps at Morgantina: see page 152, plates 53–7. Cf. *Illustrated London News*, 9 November 1957, page 788.

THOMPSON, H.A. 'The Buildings on the West Side of the Agora', *Hesperia*, VI (1937).

THOMPSON, H.A., and WYCHERLEY, R.E. *The Athenian Agora* XVI: *The Agora of Athens, the history, shape and uses of an ancient city center.* Princeton, 1972.

TOMLINSON, R.A. *B.S.A.*, LXIV (1969), 164.
For Perachora dining-hall.

TRAVLOS, J. Τὸ Ἀνάκτορον τῆς Ἐλευσῖνος, Ἐφ. Ἀρχ. (1950–1).
For 'palace': see page 1.

TRAVLOS, J. *Pictorial Dictionary of Ancient Athens.* London/New York, 1971.

VALLOIS, R. *Architecture hellénique et hellénistique à Délos*, I. Paris, 1944.
For Oikos of the Naxians: see pages 16, 23, 126; for lantern roofs: see pages 165, 255.

WESTHOLM, A. *Labraunda*, I. 2, *The Architecture of the Hieron.* Lund, 1963.

WYCHERLEY, R.E. *How the Greeks Built Cities.* 2nd ed. London and New York, 1962.

CHAPTER 23

Athenian Agora, The. A guide to the excavations. Athens, 1962.

AUDIAT, J. *Exploration archéologique de Délos*, XXVIII, *Le Gymnase.* Paris, 1970.

CALLMER, C. 'Antike Bibliotheken', *Skrifter utgivna av Svenska Institutet i Rom*, X (1944).

COOK, J.M. 'Bath-tubs in ancient Greece', *Greece and Rome*, VI (1959).

COOK, J.M., and BOARDMAN, J. 'Archaeology in Greece, 1953', *J.H.S.*, LXXIV (1954).
For model of Stoa of Attalus: see page 28, figure 4.

COULTON, J.J. *The Architectural Development of the Greek Stoa.* Oxford, 1976.

COURBY, F. *Exploration archéologique de Délos*, V, *Le Portique d'Antigone ou du nord-est.* Paris, 1912.

DELORME, J. 'Recherches au gymnase d'Épidaure', *B.C.H.*, LXX (1946).

DELORME, J. *Gymnasion.* Paris, 1960.

FABRICIUS, E., and LEHMANN-HARTLEBEN, K. 'Städtebau', Pauly-Wissowa, *Real-Encyclopädie*, IIIA, col. 1982. 1929.

GARDNER, E.A., SCHULTZ, R.W., and others. *Excavations at Megalopolis, 1890–91 (Suppl. Papers Soc. Prom. Hellenic Studies*, I). London, 1892.

GERKAN, A. VON. *Griechische Städteanlagen.* Berlin and Leipzig, 1924.

GINOUVES, R. 'Gortys d'Arcadie, l'Établissement thermal', *B.C.H.*, LXXIX (1955).

GINOUVES, R. *Balaneutike.* Paris, 1962.
For baths; cf. *Notizie degli Scavi* (1960), 181.

HARRIS, H.A. *Greek Athletes and Athletics.* London, 1964.

HUMANN, C., and others. *Magnesia am Maeander: Bericht über die Ergebnisse der Ausgrabungen der Jahre 1891–93.* Berlin, 1904.

JANNORAY, J., and DUCOUX, H. *Fouilles de Delphes*, II, *La Gymnase.* Paris, 1953.

KRIESIS, A. *Greek Town Building.* Athens, 1965.

KRISCHEN, F. *Die griechische Stadt, Wiederherstellungen.* Berlin, 1938.

KUNZE, E., SCHLEIF, H., and EILMANN, R. *III*

Bericht über die Ausgrabungen in Olympia. Berlin, 1941.

LAPALUS, E. *Exploration archéologique de Délos*, XIX, *L'Agora des Italiens*. Paris, 1939.

LEROUX, G. *Exploration archéologique de Délos*, III, *La Salle Hypostyle*. Paris, 1909.

MARCONI, P. *Agrigento, topografia ed arte*. Florence, 1929.

MARTIENSSEN, R.D. *The Idea of Space in Greek Architecture*. Johannesburg, 1956.

MARTIN, R. *Recherches sur l'agora grecque*. Paris, 1951.

MARTIN, R. *L'Urbanisme dans la Grèce antique*. Paris, 1956.

MCDONALD, W.A. *The Political Meeting Places of the Greeks*. Baltimore, 1943.

MILLER, S.G. *The Prytaneion*. Berkeley and Los Angeles, 1978.

MINNS, E.H. *Scythians and Greeks*. Cambridge, 1913.

For baths, Panticapaeum: see page 565.

ROBINSON, H. 'The Tower of the Winds and the Roman Market-Place', *A.J.A.*, XLVII (1943).

ROSTOVTZEFF, M.I. *Dura-Europos and its Art*. Oxford, 1938.

ROUX, G. 'À propos des gymnases de Delphes et de Délos', *B.C.H.*, CIV (1980), 127.

SCHEDE, M. *Die Ruinen von Priene, kurze Beschreibung*. Berlin, 1964.

SCHLEIF, H. 'Der grosse Altar der Hera von Samos', *Ath. Mitt.*, LVIII (1933).

SCRANTON, R.L. *Greek Architecture*. London and New York, 1962.

For Stoa of Attalus, model and rebuilding.

THOMPSON, H.A. 'The Buildings on the West Side of the Agora', *Hesperia*, VI (1937).

THOMPSON, H.A. *The Stoa of Attalus II in Athens* (Picture Book no. 2, American School at Athens). Princeton, 1959.

THOMPSON, H.A., and WYCHERLEY, R.E. *The Athenian Agora*, XIV: *The Agora of Athens, the history, shape and uses of an ancient city center*. Princeton, 1972.

TRAVLOS, J. *Pictorial Dictionary of Ancient Athens*. London/New York, 1971.

TUCHELT, K. 'Buleuterion und Ara Augusta', *Ist. Mitt.*, XXV (1975), 91.

Bouleuterion at Miletus and related monuments.

VALLOIS, R. *Architecture hellénique et hellénistique à Délos*, I. Paris, 1944.

For Pythium (i.e. Neorium) Delos: see pages 33, 131, 153, 244, 278, figure 3; for Gymnasium, Delos: see page 176.

VALLOIS, R. *Constructions antiques de Délos, Documents*. Paris, 1953.

For Pythium (i.e. Neorium), Delos: see plates V, VI; for Gymnasium, Delos: see plate 1.

VALLOIS, R., and POULSEN, G. *Exploration archéologique de Délos*, II, *Complement, Nouvelles recherches sur la Salle Hypostyle*. Paris, 1914.

WIEGAND, T., and others. *Milet: Ergebnisse der Ausgrabungen und Untersuchungen seit dem Jahre 1899*. Berlin, 1906.

For Council-House: see vol. I, 2.

WIEGAND, T., and SCHRADER, H. *Priene: Ergebnisse der Ausgrabungen und Untersuchungen in den Jahren 1895–98*. Berlin, 1904.

WYCHERLEY, R.E. *How the Greeks Built Cities*. 2nd ed. London and New York, 1962.

CHAPTER 24

BIEBER, M. *The History of the Greek and Roman Theater*. Princeton, 1961.

BOUSQUET, J. 'Harmonie au théâtre d'Épidaure', *Revue Archéologique*, XLI (1953).

For mathematical relations.

BRONEER, O. *Isthmia*, II, *Topography and Architecture*. Princeton, 1973.

For the stadia page 46 f.; for the hippodrome page 117.

BULLE, H. 'Untersuchungen an griechischen Theatern', *Abhandlungen der Münchner Akademie*, XXXIII (1928).

BURFORD, A. *The Greek Temple-Builders at Epidauros*. Liverpool, 1969.

For inscriptions.

DE BERNARDI-FERRERO, D. *Teatri classici in Asia Minore*. Rome, 1966–74.

DILKE, O.A.W. 'The Greek Theatre Cavea', *B.S.A.*, XLIII (1948).

GEBHARD, E. *The Theatre at Isthmia*. Chicago/London, 1973.

GERKAN, A. VON. 'Nochmals die Skene des Theaters von Priene', *Ist. Mitt.*, XIII–XIV (1963–4).

GERKAN, A. VON, and MÜLLER-WIENER, W. *Das Theater von Epidauros*. Stuttgart, 1961.

With detailed plans.

GINOUVES, R. *Le Théâtron à gradins droits et l'Odéion d'Argos*. Paris, 1972.

HARRIS, H.A. *Greek Athletes and Athletics*. London, 1964.

For stadium.

KRAUSS, F. 'Die hellenistischen Buhnen des Theaters von Milet', *Römische Mitteilungen*, LXXI (1964).

For restorations: see plates 31 and 32.

KRAUSS, F., and ALTENHOFER, E. *Das Theater von Milet (Milet IV.1)*. Berlin, 1973.

MALLWITZ, A. *Olympia und seine Bauten*. Munich, 1972.

For stadium at Olympia: see pages 180–6.

MILLER, S.G. 'Excavations at Nemea', *Hesperia*, XLVI (1977), 26.

MILLER, S.G. 'Turns and Lanes in the Ancient Stadium', *A.J.A.*, LXXXIV (1980), 159.

MUSSCHE, H.F. *Monumenta Graeca et Romana*, II, *Greek Architecture, 2, Civil and Military Architecture*. Leiden, 1964.
For photographs of theatres: see plates 74–90.

PICKARD-CAMBRIDGE, A.W. *The Theatre of Dionysus in Athens*. Oxford, 1946.

STILLWELL, R. 'The Theater of Morgantina', Κώκαλος, X–XI (1964–5).
For plan: see plate LI.

TRAVLOS, J. *Pictorial Dictionary of Ancient Athens*. London/New York, 1971.
For Pnyx and Theatre of Dionysus at Athens.

WEBSTER, T.B.L. *Griechische Bühnenaltertümer*. Göttingen, 1963.

WEBSTER, T.B.L. *Greek Theatre Production*. 2nd ed. London and New York, 1970.

LIST OF ILLUSTRATIONS

All dates are B.C.

124 and 125. Paestum, temple of 'Ceres', late sixth century, entablature and restoration of gable (Koldewey and Puchstein, *op. cit.*, figure 17) and view (Anderson, Rome)

126. Neandria, temple, restored capital (P.P. Betancourt, *The Aeolic Style*, figure 32)

127. Samos, third Heraeum, begun *c.* 570 (?), column bases (the two parts of each may not belong together) (*Ath. Mitt.*, LV (1930), figure 38)

128 and 129. Ephesus, temple of Artemis, *c.* 560, restoration of columns (Hogarth, *Excavations at Ephesus*, Atlas, plate XV) and restored capital. London, British Museum (British Museum)

130. Samos, fourth Heraeum, begun *c.* 525, restored plan (*Ath. Mitt.*, LV (1930), Beilage XXVII)

131. Magnesia, early temple of Artemis, Ionic base (Humann, *Magnesia am Maeander*, figure 33)

132. Delphi, Treasury of Siphnos, *c.* 525. Restoration. *Paris, Louvre, and Delphi Museum* (École française d'Athènes)

133. Ornament from an Ionic treasury, late sixth century. *Delphi Museum* (École française d'Athènes)

134-6. Delphi, Treasury of Massalia, late sixth century, base (École française d'Athènes), detailed restorations (front, column base seen from above, capitals and entablature seen from below) (*Fouilles de Delphes* II, plate XXVII), and restored elevation (École française d'Athènes)

137. Delos, Thesmophorium, early fifth century, plan (*B.C.H.*, LIII (1929), plate IX)

138. Locri, Maraza temple, mid fifth century, columns (Dinsmoor, *Architecture of Ancient Greece*, figure 49)

139 and 140. Athens, temple on the Ilissus, *c.* 450, restored elevation, capital, and plan of angle capital (Stuart and Revett)

141. Delphi, Athenian Stoa, and Athens, Temple on the Ilissus, column bases (Puchstein, *Die Ionische Säule*, figure 57)

142 (A) and (B). Delphi, Athenian Treasury, *c.* 500-485, front (J. Allan Cash Ltd) and patterns incised on inner cornice (*A.J.A.*, L (1946), figure 3)

143-6. Aegina, temple of Aphaia, early fifth century, sectional restoration (Furtwängler), interior columns (restored) (Sheridan Photo Library), east end (Sheridan Photo Library), and plan (Dinsmoor, *Architecture of Ancient Greece*, figure 42)

147 and 148. Agrigento, Olympieum, begun *c.* 500,

plan (partly restored) (Dinsmoor, *Architecture of Ancient Greece*, figure 40) and restoration (Koldewey and Puchstein, *Die Griechischen Tempel in Unteritalien*, figure 143)

149-51. Paestum, temple of 'Neptune', early or mid fifth century, east end (Leonard von Matt), restored plan (Dinsmoor, *Architecture of Ancient Greece*, figure 36, and De Waele, *Arch. Anz.* (1980), 367, Abb. 13), and interior (Anderson, Rome)

152 (A) and (B). Olympia, temple of Zeus, *c.* 460, restored elevation of east front and section through porch (Curtius)

153 and 154. Olympia, sanctuary, plan (*Neue Deutsche Ausgrabungen*, p.264, Beilage 1, and Mallwitz, *Olympia und seine Bauten*) and restoration (Durm, and Mallwitz, *op. cit.*)

155. Athens, Old Propylon, 480s, restoration of exterior (W.B. Dinsmoor Jr, *The Propylaia to the Athenian Acropolis*, 1)

156. Restored plan of the Acropolis of Athens at 400 B.C. (*Hesperia*, V, figure 6, and W.B. Dinsmoor Jr, *op. cit.*)

157. Model of the Acropolis of Athens under the early Roman empire. *Athens, Agora Museum* (Agora Excavations)

158 and 159. Athens, Parthenon, 447-432, from behind east front of Propylaea and west end (D. Harissiadis)

160. Athens, Parthenon, 447-432, south side and east end (Sonia Halliday)

161. Athens, Parthenon, 447-432, curvature in steps (D. Harissiadis)

162 and 163. Athens, Parthenon, 447-432, south-east corner (Walter Hege) and restoration of north-west corner with painted decoration (Penrose)

164. Athens, Parthenon, 447-432, section through outer colonnade and porch at west end (Stuart and Revett)

165 and 166. Athens, Parthenon, 447-432, east pediment, metopes and frieze (D. Harissiadis), and frieze on the west end (German Archaeological Institute, Athens)

167 and 168. Athens, Parthenon, 447-432, ornament painted along top of architrave and on anta capital (Penrose)

169 and 170. Athens, Parthenon, 447-432, paving on side and front (Marquand, *Handbook of Greek Architecture*, figure 307) and sectional view of front (British Museum, *Guide to Sculpture of the Parthenon*)

227. Cnidus, Lion Tomb, probably Hellenistic, restored elevation (height 63 feet overall) (*Die
Antike*, IV (1928), figure 2)
228. (A) and (B). Sarcophagus of mourners from
Sidon, mid fourth century. *Istanbul Museum*
229-31. Nemea, temple of Zeus, late fourth century,
section through adytum and cella (Hill, *Temple
of Zeus at Nemea*, plate VIII), order at front
(Society of Dilettanti), and columns (D.
Harissiadis)
232 and 233. Didyma, temple of Apollo, fourth century and later, front and north side (German
Archaeological Institute, Istanbul), and decorated column base from front (Sonia Halliday)
234. Didyma, temple of Apollo, fourth century
and later, interior of cella with entrances and
inner staircase (Sonia Halliday)
235-7. Didyma, temple of Apollo, fourth century
and later, restored section through porch and
part of court with side of shrine (Wiegand,
Didyma I, Zeichnungen 10), restored plan
(Dinsmoor, *Architecture of Ancient Greece*, figure
83), and restored elevation of front of shrine
(Wiegand, Zeichnungen 67)
238. Didyma, temple of Apollo, fourth century
and later, pilaster capital and griffin frieze
(Wiegand, *Didyma* I, Zeichnungen 33)
239. Cos, temple 'B', early third century, restoration
(Scharmann)
240. Samothrace, Ptolemaeum, mid third century,
restoration of side (Conze, *Neue Archäologische
Unterschungen auf Samothrake*, plate XLVI)
241. Pergamon, stoa of Athena, first half of the
second century, restored elevation (*Altertümer
von Pergamon* II, plate XXI)
242. Delphi, monument of Aristaeneta, *c.* 270, restoration (*Fouilles de Delphes* II, figure 202)
243. Delphi, capital of two-columned monument,
third century (D. Harissiadis)
244. Delphi, reconstructed shaft of acanthus column,
probably third century. *Delphi Museum* (Courtauld Institute)
245. Pydna, façade of tomb inside tumulus, late
third-early second century (Heuzey)
246 and 247. Vergina, Ionic tomb, mid third century,
interior and façade (Sheridan Photo Library)
248. Vergina, tomb of Philip, probably 336 (M. Andronikos)
249. Pydna, Macedonian vaulted tomb, late third or
early second century, axonometric view (R.A.
Tomlinson)

250. Langaza, marble door of tomb, third century.
Istanbul Museum
251 and 252. Athens, temple of Olympian Zeus,
c. 170 (D. Harissiadis)
253. Uzunçaburc, temple of Zeus Olbius, second
century (*Monumenta Asiae Minoris Antiqua*, III,
plate XXIV)
254. Cos, sanctuary of Asclepius, second century,
restoration (Scharmann)
255 and 256. Pergamon, altar of Zeus, *c.* 165, restoration and restored plan (*J.D.I.*, XLIX (1934),
figure 3)
257. Delphi, pedestal of Prusias, *c.* 180 (*Fouilles de
Delphes* II, figure 206)
258. Delphi, pedestal of Aemilius Paulus, *c.* 168, restoration (*ibid.*, figure 250)
259. Delos, temple of Isis, second century (École
française d'Archéologie)
260 and 261. Magnesia, temple of Artemis, *c.* 150,
restored plan and order (Humann, *Magnesia am
Maeander*, figures 30 and 35)
262. Delos, monument of Mithradates, 102-101, restoration of front (*Exploration archéologique de
Délos* XVI, figure 56)
263. Calydon, heroum, second century, restored
view, plan, and porch (Dyggve, *Das Heroon von
Calydon*, figure 100)
264. Mount Cynthium, Delos, propylon, 95-94, restoration (*Exploration archéologique de Délos* XI,
figure 73)
265. Agrigento, tomb of 'Theron', early first century
(Alinari, Florence)
266. Suweida, tomb of Hamrath, early first century
(de Vogüé)
267. Old Smyrna, curvilinear masonry of temple
platform, late seventh century (J.M. Cook)
268. Delphi, polygonal terrace-wall, early sixth
century, and Athenian stoa, *c.* 470 (German
Archaeological Institute, Athens)
269. Cnidus, polygonal terrace-wall, third or second
century (J.M. Cook)
270. Sunium, platform of temple of Poseidon, mid
fifth century, and predecessor of *c.* 500; fortification of 412 in foreground (Courtauld Institute)
271. Priene, fountain at corner of avenue and stepped
street, below supporting wall of the temple of
Athena Polias, fourth century (Berlin Museum)
272. 'Eleutherae', Attic frontier fort, fourth century,
wall-walk and tower (Courtauld Institute)
273. Messene, city wall and tower, mid fourth century (Courtauld Institute)

323. Delos, court with well and windlass-stand, and mural decoration, in house, probably second century (Dimitri Papadimou)

324. Delos, 'Maison des Masques', court with colonnade of two heights, probably second century (École française d'Athènes)

325. Delos, 'Maison de l'Hermès', two-storeyed court, probably second century (Sheridan Photo Library)

326. Paphos, court of rock-cut 'Royal Tomb', Hellenistic (Sonia Halliday)

327. Lato, agora, fourth century, plan (Wycherley, *How the Greeks Built Cities*, figure 10)

328. Eleusis, Telesterium, plans of successive forms (*'Eφ. 'Aρχ.* (1950–1), figure 10)

329. Miletus, public buildings at 150 B.C., restored plan (*J.H.S.*, LXII (1942), figure 2)

330. Athens, restored plan of agora in the second century (Agora Excavations, Athens)

331. Megalopolis, Thersilium, mid fourth century, restored plan (*J.H.S.*, XIII (1892–3), plate XXI)

332. Corinth, South Stoa, probably 338, restored gutter (O. Broneer, *Corinth* I, IV, *The South Stoa*, figure 13)

333. Piraeus, arsenal, 340–330, restoration (Marstrand, *Arsenalet i Piraeus*, figure 88)

334. Priene, agora, third century, gateway probably 156, restoration (Robertson, *Greek and Roman Architecture*, figure 85)

335. Delos, Neorium, probably late fourth century, restored section, details (Dinsmoor, *Architecture of Ancient Greece*, figure 105), and plan (P. Bruneau and J. Ducat, *Guide de Délos*, figure 11)

336. Priene, stoa, second century, restoration (Schede, *Die Ruinen von Priene*, figure 63)

337. Assos, agora, possibly second century, restored view and plan (Clarke and Bacon, *Investigations at Assos*, figure 4)

338. Delos, Stoa of Antigonus, c. 254, restoration of front (*Exploration archéologique de Délos* V, plate III)

339. Megalopolis, Stoa of Philip, c. 340–330 (?), restored half-plan (E.A. Gardner, *Excavations at Megalopolis*, plate XV, with corrections)

340 and 341. Athens, Stoa of Attalus, mid second century, restored elevation, section, and plan and restored capital (Agora Excavations)

342. Oeniadae, bath, Hellenistic, plan (Marquand, *Handbook of Greek Architecture*, figure 364)

343. Kerch, bath, first century, plan (Minns, *Scythians and Greeks*, figure 345)

344-7. Delos, Hypostyle Hall, c. 210, restoration of front (*Exploration archéologique de Délos* II, plate II), restored plan (*ibid.* plate I), restored section (*ibid.* plate II), and Ionic column (*ibid.* I, figure 46)

348-50. Priene, *Ekklesiasterion*, c. 200, view of interior (Sonia Halliday), restored interior and plan (Wycherley, *How the Greeks built Cities*, figure 37, and Robertson, *Greek and Roman Architecture*, figure 78), and restoration of south wall (Wiegand, *Priene*, figure 223)

351 and 352. Miletus, Council House, c. 170, restoration of enclosure and of propylon (Wiegand)

353. Pergamon, plan of upper city (*J.H.S.*, LXII (1942), figure 6)

354. Pergamon, theatre, mainly second century (Sonia Halliday)

355. Athens, gate of Roman agora, c. 10 (D. Harissiadis)

356. Athens, theatre of Dionysus, general plan (Pickard-Cambridge, *Theatre of Dionysus in Athens*, plan 1)

357. Thoricus, theatre, fifth century, restored plan (Bieber, *History of Greek Theater*, figure 167)

358 and 359. Epidaurus, theatre (Sonia Halliday and D. Harissiadis)

360-2. Epidaurus, upper division of seats in theatre (Sheridan Photo Library), plan (Pickard-Cambridge, *Theatre of Dionysus in Athens*, figure 70), and entrance to theatre (D. Harissiadis)

363. Oropus, theatre, restored section through stage (Bieber, *History of Greek Theater*, figure 304)

364 and 365. Priene, theatre, restoration at late second century (Schede, *Die Ruinen von Priene*, figure 85) and restored original plan (Bieber, *History of Greek Theater*, figure 293)

366. Delos, theatre, restored plan (Pickard-Cambridge, *Theatre of Dionysus in Athens*, figure 74)

367. Ephesus, theatre, Hellenistic, restored plan (De Bernardi, *Teatri classici in Asia Minore*, IV, figure 142)

368. Segesta, theatre, probably early first century, restoration (H. Bulle)

INDEX

Entries and numbers in **bold type** may be used also as glossary definitions. References to the Notes are given only where they indicate matters of special interest or importance: such references are given to the page on which the note occurs, followed by the number of the chapter to which it belongs, and the number of the note. Thus 389(16)[3] indicates page 389, chapter 16, note 3.